The Speaking Tree

The Speaking Tree. Moghul. c. 1650.

The Speaking Tree

A Study of Indian Culture and Society

RICHARD LANNOY

1971

Oxford University Press

New York · Bombay · London

Contents

List of Illustrations

Frontispiece: The Speaking Tree which rebuked Alexander the Great for the futility of conquering India and foretold his doom. Moghul. *c.* 1650 A.D. By courtesy of the Islamisches Museum, Berlin.

Between pages 20 and 21 in Part One

1. Monster at entrance of cave. Rock. Ellorā. *c.* 7th. cent. A.D. Photo: author.

2. Rock painting, different periods, Ādamgad, Madhya Pradesh. The elephant ($1\frac{1}{2}$ metres long), possibly mesolithic, executed in red ochre, is about seven thousand years old. The buffalo (3 metres long) is probably neolithic, as are the smaller bovines. The giraffe and warriors on horseback are early medieval. The dark horsemen with spears and swords, and the foot-soldiers with shields and swords, were executed by nomadic tribal herdsmen in recent centuries. Copy by V. S. Wakankar. Photo: Musée de l'Homme.

3. Elephant, Benares. Contemporary folk mural. Photo: author.

4. Rock painting, different periods, Bhimbetka, Madhya Pradesh. The two dark animals (one an antelope) are probably early neolithic. A second artist added the black figures. The white paintings are probably late neolithic; they include elephant, buffalo, deer, cattle, and figures with spears. A fourth artist painted the horses and figures with bows, shields, and swords on the lower section of the rock. Copy by V. S. Wakankar. Photo: Musée de l'Homme.

5. Back view of a male torso, Harappā. Red sandstone. *c.* 2000 B.C. National Museum, New Delhi. Photo: Larkin Bros.

6. Stone head, Mundigak. Probably earliest Harappan phase, *c.* 2500 B.C. Kabul Museum. Photo: Casal/Musée Guimet.

7. Tree goddess encircled by pipal tree, figure with sacrificial beast, and row of attendant deities. Harappan seal. *c.* 2000 B.C. National Museum, New Delhi. Photo: Archaeological Survey of India.

8. Humped bull. Harappan seal. *c.* 2000 B.C. National Museum, New Delhi. Photo: Archaeological Survey of India.

9. Horned ithyphallic deity, perhaps the prototype of Shiva, seated in yogic posture. Harappan seal. *c.* 2000 B.C. National Museum, New Delhi. Photo: Archaeological Survey of India.

Between pages 116 and 117 in Part Two

10. Queen in palace scene. Painting, Cave I, Ajantā. End of 6th century A.D. Photo: Archaeological Survey of India.

Between pages 180 and 181 in Part Three

Acknowledgements

FOR permission to quote extracts I am indebted to the following: from *Conquest of Violence: the Gandhian Philosophy of Conflict* by Joan Bondurant, published by the University of California Press, to the Regents of the University of California; from *The Continent of Circe* by Nirad C. Chaudhuri to the author and to Chatto and Windus Ltd. and Oxford University Press, New York; from *Contributions to Indian Sociology* to Mr. Louis Dumont and Dr. D. F. Pocock and to Mouton Publishers; from *The Divided Self* by R. D. Laing to the author and to Tavistock Publications Ltd.; from *Focus and Diversions* by L. L. Whyte to the author and to the Cresset Press and George Braziller, Inc.; from *Gandhi's Truth* by Erik H. Erikson to the author and to Faber and Faber Ltd. and W. W. Norton & Company; from *Hinduism* by R. C. Zaehner to the author and to the Clarendon Press; from *The Intellectual History of Europe* by Friedrich Heer to the author and to George Weidenfeld & Nicolson Ltd.; from the *International Journal of Electroencephalography and Clinical Neurophysiology* to H. Gastaut and N. N. Das and to Masson & Cie; from *The King and the Corpse* by H. Zimmer to the author and to Princeton University Press; from *Purdah* by Frieda H. Das to the author and to Routledge & Kegan Paul Ltd.; from *Purity and Danger* by Mary Douglas to the author and to Routledge & Kegan Paul Ltd. and Frederick A. Praeger, Inc.; from an unpublished speech 'Quality of Life in India' by S. H. Vatsyayan to the speaker and to the International Association for Cultural Freedom, Indian Branch; from *Quest* to Professor A. S. Ayyub and to the International Association for Cultural Freedom, Indian Branch; from *Savitri* by Sri Aurobindo to the Mother and the Sri Aurobindo Ashram Press; from passages quoting Nirmal Kumar Bose, Pyarelal Nayar, and Glorney Bolton in *Talking of Gandhiji*, edited by Francis Watson and Maurice Brown, to the editors and to Longmans; from *The Thirteen Principal Upanishads*, translated by R. E. Hume, to the translator and to Oxford University Press; from essays by A. B. Shah and Dr. M. K. Haldar in *Tradition and Modernity in India*, edited by A. B. Shah and C. R. M. Rao, to the authors and editors and to the International Association for Cultural Freedom, Indian Branch, and Manaktalas, Bombay; and from *The Unconscious before Freud* by L. L. Whyte, published by Tavistock Publications Ltd., to David Higham Associates, Ltd.

For permission to reproduce photographs of works of art I am also indebted to the Staatliche Museen, Berlin, G.D.R.; the Musée de l'Homme, Paris; the Government of India Archaeological Survey of India, New Delhi; Sven Gahlin Esq., London; the Horniman Museum, London; the Musée Guimet, Paris; the Maharaja of Jaipur and the Jaipur Museum; the Trustees of the British Museum, London; the Chester Beatty Library, Dublin; Bharat Kala Bhavan, Benares; and the Metropolitan Museum of Art (Rogers Fund, 1927), New York.

My indebtedness to others is enormous. In every instance where a thought has been borrowed consciously from any one of them I have tried to give credit. In some cases I may have unconsciously used the thought of another as my own. If this has become part of my own thinking and I cannot name the sources, I am nevertheless grateful to them.

Thanks are due to numerous friends who offered generous hospitality during the five periods I have spent in India, and those who have consented to answer my persistent questions.

I would also like to thank for their help Shanti and Sadiq Ali, who first encouraged me to write this book; Maurice Auger for patient and perceptive comments; Warner Muensterberger, who gave the manuscript of Part Two a severe and complete examination; Robert Skelton of the Indian Section, Victoria and Albert Museum, for his help in locating rare illustrations; Deben Bhattacharya, Mr. and Mrs. José Vicente Dias, Bemvinda Dias, Joe Geraci, Abdul Wahid Khan, Mary Oppliger, the Śrī Ānandamayi Sangha, and Stella Snead for their kind assistance on many occasions. I would also like to thank a helper, who prefers anonymity, for frank criticism so generously given with respect to the Zero idea and the chapter on Gandhi.

My greatest debt is to my wife Violet, whose criticism, encouragement, and patience sustained me during the ten years when I was writing this book.

RICHARD LANNOY

Norfolk,
    October 1970.

Preface

This book is an analytical study of Indian culture and society, with the chief aim of identifying the origins of the nation's contemporary problems. Though generally manifested in urgent economic terms, these have their root causes in the historical development of India's system of values and thought, as reflected in its cultural and social organization. In other words, the present study will examine India's capacity for innovation and creativity, its receptivity to change in social and family relations, and the ability to utilize human, technical, and physical resources for social reconstruction. The complexity of India's task is on a scale unprecedented at any previous period in its history, and can be accomplished only if its people themselves have the capacity for change—and the will to take decisive action.

To assess this capacity for change we will have to reach deep into the motivational structure of India's society and its culture. This will include analysis of the organizational basis of social action and cohesion, and at the same time an assessment of the extent to which the traditional forces that strongly colour, if they do not indeed determine, the character of the human factor, are hostile to innovation.

Very little work has been done on the relationship between India's traditional value systems and social action in general. There is much debate, but little correlation of data, concerning the tensions created by the impact of modernity on tradition within the context of the need and desire for economic and social change, and the difficulties inherent in the process of continuous innovation and development to which India is now committed.

Virtually no sector of Indian society is entirely unaffected by the process of transformation, but there are many instances where, once the stimulus has been found, and at least a degree of creative ferment is generated, change proceeds according to patterns for which there is no parallel in Western history. Yet the fact remains that, while India is 'pulling itself up by its own bootstraps', it is doing so with methods largely foreign, or which did not emerge until less than a century ago.

In seeking to devise methods which will effectively ameliorate the tragic conditions under which the majority of the population are condemned to live, the national leadership cannot afford to neglect the long-term necessity to modernize the social structure. This is not to deny the compelling priority of food production. Gandhi neatly summed up the urgency of this problem when he said, 'If God were to appear in India, He would have to take the form of a loaf of bread.' But the influence of ideas alien to Indian culture on a sequence of major decisions and thus the deep rearrangements of inner structure could lead, besides destroying India's sense of identity, to decisions incompatible with one another and to the weakening of social cohesion and, consequently, of the capacity for concerted social action. Modernization, if it is to be capable of organic growth, has to emerge from a balance between structural continuity and structural change, or, in other words, from a synthesis between the old culture and the new demands of society.

There is much debate in India on the possible synthesis, though the tension is sufficiently acute to have prompted some extremists to proclaim such a synthesis impossible. For them the body of India's traditional attitudes and habits must be totally abandoned: India should start again with a clean slate. Other extremists would like to see the 'purity' of traditional culture and the Dharma—Moral Law—preserved at all costs; borrowing of alien ideas should be brought to an end and the old ideas of Indian spirituality revived. What is sometimes overlooked is precisely that inherent, but hidden, dialectical factor within the process of social reconstruction which can initiate creative interrelations between indigenous and alien value systems.

In the dialectic at the root of this transitional stage may be found, not the curse afflicting the nation's potential for change, as it is commonly taken to be, but the very seed from which growth and renewal arise. Without wholehearted acceptance of this fact, the formative power of imagination, its capacity for structure, may be seriously impaired. Synthesis does not result from merely juxtaposing two unalterably conflicting opposites, but each new departure, each new reintegration, involves breaking down *both* elements to form a new, though not alien, social configuration. In practice, however, the tendency in India has been to shirk true synthesis, particularly in the field of social relations. What happens is that hierarchical inequality is assumed between apparent incompatibles, their stability ensured by juxtaposition with each other through the ascendancy of one over the other. What we see, therefore, is a shifting of hierarchical positions, as India adopts the theoretical orientations of universal modern values and received ideas in the economic, social, or scientific spheres. The Indian instinct for borrowing and at the same time conserving, for clinging to everything and never rejecting what is outworn or outmoded, gives rise not only to a conservative attitude, but also to its elevation to the status of religious dogma and prime social duty. This piling up of traits was once compared by Nehru to a palimpsest, an ancient manuscript written upon over and over again without the preceding layer being completely obliterated. This pattern presents a strange timeless patchwork of traits, one spatially juxtaposed with the next, each remaining in the same position as when it was first introduced or borrowed.

What India requires is not a kind of static hierarchical equilibrium between tradition and modernity; growth arises from conflict, from the open, as distinct from the covert and apologetic, acceptance of incessant struggle. So long as social reconstruction is founded on the ideals of an open society, whatever is valuable in tradition will, in fact, survive and grow; what has ceased to be viable in a modern context will then be abandoned. In this way there is no danger of India losing its identity; on the contrary, it will become more itself. But this is no panacea, for a society remade will ever remain a society to be remade—in tireless experiment.

There is some justice in the claim that too much attention has been paid to the imagined difficulty of changing the attitudes of the conservative element in India's population, who, no less than the more flexible elements, long for the material rewards of 'progress'—in so desperately impoverished a country it could hardly be otherwise. For instance, given effective government support, even the tradition-directed peasant has proved his readiness to adopt improved means of production without at the same time submitting to a slow and costly form of re-education. In this sense, practical ability proves more flexible and receptive than any supposed educational backwardness. But there is another dimension to the problem: chronic instability frequently prevents either the Centre or the States from effectively implementing development programmes, and is responsible for the redeployment of limited resources upon projects intended to placate pressure groups rather than to further the national interest. Political instability in India may be traced to internal tension within the pluralistic society, and this pluralism is rooted in the traditional attitudes of its constituent elements towards each other. Any study concerned with social action and decision-making in India's transitional society will, therefore, have to include an analysis of that network of relationships.

Despite the predominantly Hindu nature of the society, it should be pointed out that other communities, though relegated to the status of 'minority' groups, have also made important contributions to the national culture. The distinction between the various communities on a purely religious basis is, however, less sharp in those sectors where the principle of secularism has already had some effect in breaking down religious barriers. While Hinduism does act as a unifying factor, the pluralistic structure is undoubtedly reinforced by differences within the Hindu community itself, arising from local practices, as well as by the various linguistic and sectarian groups or sub-groups. The pluralistic structure has been further accentuated in some sectors in recent decades by the unequal rate of economic and cultural development. This complex of differences, found sometimes within the same geographical sub-unit, gives the appearance of contradictions and anachronisms which dismay the outside observer, and often Indians themselves. Nevertheless, this too has a structure of its own.

But it should not be forgotten that for two thousand years of its history India really was *Hindustan*, almost completely Hindu; even Buddhist heterodoxy went through a long process of integration with the parent faith before it was finally assimilated. Today the majority of the Indian population is, of course, Hindu; the deepest foundations of India's Great Tradition are also largely Hindu.

Every author who analyses Indian culture and society as a whole can either ignore the existence of substantial minority groups and exclusively focus on Hindu society (even glossing over the divergences between numerous sub-cultures of the majority), or he can select data from Hindu society which can be related to, or contrasted with, the situation in minority communities. Hindu culture patterns have influenced virtually every minority group, including the Christians, Muslims, and Parsis. Further, no matter what group is the subject of study, all share in common the conditions of co-existence. By far the greater part of the present study is inevitably concerned with Hindu society. As N. C. Chaudhuri has put it:

> They [the Hindus] are the masters and rulers. They have regained political power after many centuries, and are fully aware of it, perhaps over-aware. They are also the only source of energy for the country considered as a human machine; and it is their desires and aspirations which are keeping it running. No other element counts. As the current jargon describes all the non-Hindus, they are only *minorities*.
>
> . . . At least, I have no hesitation in saying that if the history of India has taken a certain course in the last fifty years, or for that matter in the last thousand, that is due, above all, to the Hindu character. It has been the most decisive determining influence on the historical process. I feel equally certain that it will remain so and shape the form of everything that is being undertaken for and in the country.[1]

The solution adopted here is to focus for the most part on Hindu society, but to qualify generalizations regarding Indian society as a whole by reference, wherever possible, to the situation obtaining among minorities. To avoid the cumbersome apparatus of endless qualification, the attitude of the majority towards communities outside the holistic Hindu social order is analysed separately; it is hoped thereby to identify the means employed, both in the past and in the present, to secure a degree of cohesion among the population as a whole.

One-eighth of the world's entire population lives in India. The political system of this immense nation is the product of its heterogeneous ethnic and

[1] Nirad C. Chaudhuri, *The Continent of Circe*, Chatto and Windus, London, 1965, p. 86.

linguistic composition; some changes in the direction of universalization have been effected during the past century through the application of ideas stemming from foreign sources. The absence of a unified national culture has frequently created problems in the attempt to evolve an integrative framework for national solidarity. On the other hand, the sheer size of India places it in the category of continental nations, along with China, Russia, the United States, and Brazil; in none of these has it proved feasible to form a completely homogeneous, centralized political structure. Given the comparatively rudimentary means of political centralization at the disposal of India's rulers in the past, they were probably right in making no more than tentative and infrequent efforts to establish a monolithic state; tensions within the pluralistic state were not susceptible to control from above. On the contrary, the Indian temperament was more true to itself in seeking to contain tensions within a loose federalism.

Throughout its history India has been under unified national rule for not more than four relatively brief periods. It is doubtful if the essentially pluralistic structure of Indian society will be replaced in the foreseeable future by a monolithic uniformity. The recent history of India shows little evidence that this is either remotely feasible or desirable. India's pluralistic structure will surely continue to be modernized, whatever political ideology the nation espouses, and however much separatist movements in the States succeed in their aims; and *modern* pluralism is a *structure*—a multi-lingual, multi-cultural nation-state—not a mere sum of 'sectors' reacting upon one another, as heterogeneous India so long remained. The difficulty here is that an out-dated formula is being applied; the old fashioned brand of nineteenth-century nationalism which regards a nation as one people, with one culture and one language. True, India's pluralism now presents a structural weakness fraught with political danger; but that is no reason to foist on it a nostalgic uni-lingual, uni-cultural nationalism (which the supporters of Hindi believe they can do). What is needed to transform Indian pluralism into a cohesive structure is not cultural nostalgia but the sinews of a forward-looking creativity.

The idea of national identity—the self-awareness of the nation, its self-image, and its values—springs from a desire for fixed points of reference in the enlarged world of today. The self-image of India is tentative in character and has evolved from the way it perceives its history from ancient times through many centuries of decline and foreign domination to the decades of its recently achieved status as an independent sovereign state. The difficulties in forming a contemporary national self-image may be more clearly appreciated when it is realized that while India is now building a modern, secular state, its traditions are permeated by a sophisticated religious sensibility. One of the primary concerns of India's leaders is consequently to build up a cohesive, integrative, and secular nationalism from the sundry particularistic forces which are so strongly engrained. It is inevitable that the emotional needs of a newly independent nation have prompted influential persons to focus the national energies more on an idealized image than on one which emerges through a discriminating insight into history. However, until the contradictions and, what is less often appreciated, the affinities between India's pluralistic cultural tradition and the new elements of contemporary civilization are frankly faced, and until a clearer image of its identity is thereby obtained, it will be difficult for the nation to define its place and role in a fast-changing world. Because of these contradictions and affinities the individual also remains divided within himself. The search for clearer definition and constant redefinition has to be conducted within the continuous sequence of actions and choices in response to very grave economic and political problems. Yet if it is not undertaken with concerted objectivity, India is in danger of failing to set itself consistently and with determination to any major undertaking.

Methodology

It may be helpful to explain the basis on which some of the material has been selected, and the sequence in which it is arranged.

The present study differs in several ways, both in content and in presentation, from a chronicle of Indian cultural history. The five parts of the book conform to a mosaic pattern dictated by the interdisciplinary nature of the subject. Implicit in the idea of a mosaic is the relation between its components, which make up a unified field, so that the treatment of each must concern the relationship with the other components. This approach requires that each be examined in various contexts, though each examination is conducted from a different standpoint and, consequently, in a different perspective. Five aspects of Indian culture are examined—art, the family system, the social system, value systems, and religious institutions—each of which comprises a separate part of the book. For example, there will be occasion to refer more than once to such key historical periods as the Aryan invasions, or the Mauryan, Gupta, and Moghul empires; but in each case different elements will be the subject of analysis. The five parts are subdivided into chapters, each of which is devoted to the analysis of the respective theme from a different point of view. Continuity in political, economic, social, and cultural factors serves as a basis to trace the origin and nature of recent change. By this means it is possible to arrive at a study in depth of the multi-dimensional, total cultural pattern from different viewpoints, which may range over the same historical period.

The themes mentioned above are by no means exhaustive; the Hindu religion, to which one part of the book might be expected to be exclusively devoted, is so much an integral way of life that it permeates all aspects of this study. The themes of each part embrace many features of Indian civilization important to the understanding of its current problems—i.e., pluralistic, ethnic, and linguistic composition, Westernization and modernization, poverty, minority groups, the gap between the élite and the masses, education, food shortage, population pressure, social ferment. The extreme complexity of Indian society cannot be reduced to any simplified scheme of treatment without the risk of inaccurate generalization. Nevertheless, one cannot fail to be struck by the fact that the holistic social order is *structured* according to an intrinsic logic pertaining to itself, and it follows, therefore, that our legitimate task is to identify the links between the constituent elements. No single book can possibly take into account every regional variant, every historical quirk, or every modern innovation. What can be attempted, however, is to trace the ideological basis on which empirical fact is founded. For this reason, traditional cultural manifestations will be placed in the foreground of the analysis. While each of the themes treated in this study has, from necessity, to be reduced to a somewhat schematic order, inaccuracy or lack of specific data is partly checked by corresponding data drawn from other fields in subsequent parts of the book. Links are identified wherever possible, and the concluding section of the book is devoted to the drawing of certain conclusions from the assembled data. But no attempt has been made to accommodate the facts to a single principle or range of principles, or to the strait-jacket of a hypothesis. It is hoped that the mosaic treatment employed here will assist the reader to grasp some of the cardinal factors in the formation of a rich and exceedingly diverse culture, and thence to exercise his own judgement in assessing the complexities which confront him on closer acquaintance with the day-to-day features of life in any given region of India.

The first part of the book, a detailed analysis of Indian art history, which may seem unconventional in a study of this nature, may need some explanation. Its inclusion here arises from a personal conviction, though hardly an unusual one, that in a culture of aesthetic orientation like India's, it is the arts, particularly the plastic arts, which reveal the culture's organic development and patterns of continuity more clearly and more tangibly than any other cultural activity. A historical survey of Indian art reveals the values of the total cultural pattern in a most vivid way, and an understanding of these values is indispensable for the study of themes to be treated in later parts. Developments in art (and in other fields treated in the subsequent parts on the social structure, value systems, and attitudes) will serve as a useful context in which to explain certain key historical developments of a more general kind, without which the nature of the most intractable problems faced by India today cannot be properly understood. Visual art is the aspect of Indian culture which exhibits in its most intense form the natural creativity of India. The creative predicament in which India finds itself today is essentially what this book is about—creative, when understood in its broadest application, not exclusively to artistic activity only.

Art history *precedes* analysis of the family and social systems for two reasons. First, it establishes in the reader's mind the broader evolution of India from ancient times to the present day much more clearly than the more obscure historical evolution of social institutions, and more vividly than a dynastic chronicle. Secondly, of all Indian cultural manifestations it is the least abstract. Once the apparatus of datelines and dynasties has been set up in an easily visualized context, undivided attention can be given to the human and institutional complexities. But Indian art history will be viewed less for its intrinsic aesthetic value than for its capacity to give order to human feelings, and therefore to supply us with information which can be obtained from no other source. Subsequently, whether we are examining the family, the caste, or the social order as a whole, a background knowledge of how the Indian organizes the expression of his feelings helps to keep us in touch with the emotional substratum of his being.

The family system (Part Two) is treated separately from the social system (Part Three) in order to emphasize character-formation. In the context of a functional study devoted to the problems of continuity and change, attitudes towards the traditional social values, indeed towards tradition as a whole, are formed more by socialization within the kinship system than by formal education. It is therefore within the family that we can observe degrees of flexibility or resistance to change. Similarly, it is through the kinship system that the individual is related to his caste—the key institution of the social system. As is well known, the hierarchical gradation of the caste system is deficient in vertical mobility. By placing the family and caste systems adjacent to each other, it is possible to determine how mobility traditionally operates within the limits set by the social system, how the society responds to external agents of change, and how both systems interact on each other in modern times.

Parts Four and Five are devoted to aspects of Hindu thought, ethics, and religion, in an attempt to identify the motivational structure, attitudes, and patterns of decision-making among modern Indians, on whom traditional thought and religion still exert considerable influence. Both are necessarily selective, partly due to the vast amount of available material, but more because those aspects which concern us must be relevant to the contemporary theme of this study. For this reason, more attention is paid to neglected but much more urgent ethical problems than to either mysticism or

Hindu speculation on the nature of Ultimate Reality, on which a considerable body of research is already available. Similarly, there is an analysis of the *social context* in which mystical techniques have been developed through the centuries, in view of the significance of 'non-rational' or 'para-normal' modes of thinking to the Indian context. False assumptions regarding the cliché-ridden themes of 'Indian wisdom', 'Hindu spirituality', and 'Yoga' abound, both in India and outside; the whole topic is coloured by emotional primitivism and the subjectivity of the personal *quest*. For this study it is more important to attempt an objective assessment of the felt need for some form of indigenous Indian alternative to the purely secular and pragmatic desire for material betterment.

Part Five, for example, is devoted to the role of the Renouncer and the cult of authoritarian religious charisma; it includes analysis of a contemporary guru, not because such figures play a role of very profound historical significance, but rather because their lives reveal particularly vividly how the principle of sacred authority still operates. The institution itself also illustrates aspects of the Indian mentality which are of prime importance in the interpretation of Indian culture as a whole. The complex question of Mahātma Gandhi's role as holy man, social reformer, and nationalist is more comprehensible when related to these traditional institutions which he adapted to his own ends and politicized. While there is some danger in regarding a unique movement like Gandhism as *representative* of modern Indian attitudes towards social and political leadership, the case of Gandhi serves as a pretext to examine the issues involved in the slow transition from a religious to a secular society.

People interested in India fall into two distinct categories: those who seek information and those who believe its way of life has something to teach them personally. Some among the latter display credulity in their efforts to abstract the quintessence of wisdom from Indian culture while ignoring the fact that its creative thinking is the result of very distinctive conditions which at one time prevailed in its social matrix. For the 'mysticism' of India is the product of a way of seeing *all* things as interconnected; the Indian spiritual quest was not originally undertaken for personal emotional satisfaction by 'outsiders'—self-secluded, single individuals—or isolated groups. On the contrary, the responsibility of the contemplative originated in a cosmic view which included the whole of society. Further, the contemplative's role in relation to that society was sanctioned by rites of initiation. A private, personal quest of the individual would therefore be regarded as a sterile pursuit when detached from the social reality to which its pattern of spiritual discipline was inseparably tied. It seems to me very much an open question whether that integral way of life has survived into modern times; the evidence will be examined in the course of the present study.

Note on the Illustrations

The fifty-six illustrations have been selected to serve three purposes: to illustrate themes, styles, and individual works of art specifically referred to in Part One, to indicate how certain key concepts, social themes, and psychological trends referred to in the rest of the text are visualized by Indian artists, and to represent those more elusive feelings which express the quality of life that no words of mine can convey. Where an illustration amplifies a point in the text, the reader is referred to the Plate number. Some of the works included have not been reproduced before, or only in specialist journals. More attention has been given to stressing the remarkable continuity of the Indian artistic sensibility—the plates cover a span of no less than seven thousand years—than to including works from every major period or region. The twenty-four pages of plates are grouped in four- or eight-page folios. Each folio illustrates a theme.

The Moghul miniature of the Speaking Tree, reproduced as the frontispiece, illustrates a legend which provides this book with its title. When Alexander the Great reached 'the furthest forests of India' the inhabitants led him, in the dead of night, to an oracular tree which could answer questions in the language of any man who addressed it. The trunk was made of snakes, animal heads sprouted from the boughs, and it bore fruit like beautiful women, who sang the praises of the Sun and Moon. According to Pseudo-Callisthenes, the tree warned Alexander of the futility of invading India with intent to obtain dominion over it. Known as the Waqwaq Tree in Islamic tradition, it was often portrayed on Harappan seals four millennia ago as sprouting heads of a bovine unicorn, encircling a female divinity (see Plate 7), or even growing from her body. The association of India with oracular trees bearing strange fruit derives from tales of the tree-worship which has flourished there since remote antiquity. European maps of India Ultima from the twelfth century and later show the Speaking Tree.

The first folio of plates—works of art dating from prehistory, the second millennium B.C., and recent folk tradition—illustrates the striking continuity in the language of form employed by the Indian artist to give order to his experience. The second folio—selected from the classical and medieval periods—shows the profundity of the mythopoeic imagination; since the world of myth derives so much from early memories of childhood, this folio is placed in Part Two, on the Family System. The text of Part Three explains how the Indian body social was literally modelled on the image of the human body; the body as microcosm is the theme of the third folio of plates. The fourth groups together a number of images of a more abstract nature, signs rich in symbolism, most of them expressly created for contemplation, or as aids to the undertaking of an inner journey down the path to knowledge; hence it will be found in Part Four, adjacent to a chapter on the chief concepts of traditional Indian thought. In the fifth folio, consisting of miniature paintings, court artists glimpse the world of enchantment where the private and introspective confronts the world of nature, of man; these seven paintings are placed in Part Five—where traditional ideas on spiritual enlightenment are examined—because the goal which every pilgrim seeks is where he turns and sees the world with new eyes, illuminated.

In order to keep verbal statements from impinging more than is necessary on the illustrations themselves, fuller descriptions of the subjects of the plates and their sources are given in the List of Illustrations on pp. ix–xii.

A Note on the Transcription of Indian Words

For ease in reading, common words and names have been retained in their Anglicized forms: Shiva for Śiva, Krishna for Kṛṣtna, Benares for Varanasi, Brahman, Kshatrya, Vaishya for *brāhmana, kṣatrya, vaiśya*.

A bar over a vowel indicates that it is long, except in the case of *e* and *o* which are long if unmarked. An *a* is pronounced as the vowel in 'cut', *i* as in 'fit', *u* as in 'pull'; *ā, ī,* and *ū* as in 'psalm', 'magazine', and 'ruse'; *e* as in 'they'; *o* as in 'show'; *ai* as in 'light', *au* as in 'now'. An *ś* is pronounced as in 'shell', *č* as in 'chit'.

In Sanskrit the long penultimate is stressed, the antepenultimate when the penultimate is short: *Mahāyā́na, Mahābhā́rata, Rāmā́yana.*

Part One The Aesthetic Factor in
Indian History

Introduction

Any picture of Indian civilization obtained from an examination of works of art alone must be incomplete, and too favourable. An attempt to correct this is made in Parts Two and Three by a study of India's endeavours to create a holistic social order. The causes of stagnation, fragmentation, and recent change in Indian society, and the role played by psychological and economic factors in its development, will be analysed in the following order: in Part Two, the structure of the family system; genetic development and personality formation; and recent changes in the traditional family system. In Part Three attention shifts from the family to the social system of which it is a part. While reference to the social structure will inevitably be made in dealing with the family, explanation of such institutions as caste must be deferred till their detailed examination in Part Three.

No attempt will be made to trace origins diachronically, either in the family system or in the social matrix, because these are buried in the complex historical interaction of the two systems and can only be viewed synchronically. What is important is not whether child-care helps to explain aspects of social behaviour or vice versa—both are inextricably meshed together—but that the analysis refers to the roots of a situation here and now. Between the critical factors, familial and social, there is indeed a very close resemblance precisely because of their mutual influence. A large proportion of the data refers to the traditional pattern, but this does not mean necessarily the historical past, for the overwhelming majority of Indians (say 70 per cent at a *minimum* in a population of over 500 million) are still tradition-directed; moreover, changes cannot be understood in the crucial area of the minority who are subject to modernization without reference to that tradition. 'Tradition' in this study will perhaps be more applicable to pre-industrial India in a non-historical sense, i.e. the India which continues to be either unaffected or only marginally affected by industrialization. Even if we were to set a date for the earliest moment when pre-industrial India was affected by the global upheavals which have been the primary determinants of Western-type change in the last four centuries, we cannot place it farther back than the mid-nineteenth century; modern Western-type technology did not begin to effect structural changes in the society until the end of the nineteenth century. Prior to that date the Industrial Revolution, while it had a severely disruptive effect on the socio-economic condition

which strikes the visitor immediately. The basic modulor component—brick—remains the same size and shape. The invention of burnt-brick in the Near East, and its transmission to the peoples of the Indus Valley, were of decisive importance for the emergence of an empirical ordering capacity. The ability to sustain uniform and repetitive means of production is an indispensable precondition for the organization of cities and empires. Implicit in this uniform repeatability is a high level of technical co-ordination. Wherever such a level is reached it reveals a sense of relatedness, an orchestration of all measurable factors in the interdependent unity: God, nature, and man. Though our knowledge of the Indus Valley civilization is scanty, everything which has survived endorses this conclusion.

The Indus Valley civilization, with its more than seventy known sites, covered an enormous area of territory extending beyond the great tracts of alluvial land in the main Indus Valley, from the Arabian Sea to as far east as Delhi. That is to say, it covered most of what is now West Pakistan, including Sind, and a large part of Baluchistan, the whole of the Punjāb, north as far as the Himalayan foothills, and north-east to Alamgirpur between the Ganges and Jamuna rivers. Over this entire area of some half a million square miles the culture was so uniform as to suggest not a city-state but a unified empire, the largest before Roman times, and at least twice the size of Old Kingdom Egypt.

The people were dark-skinned, the features of the majority probably resembling those of the modern Dravidians in South India (who are believed by some to be the descendants of the Harappans), though three distinct ethnic types have been traced.

The two largest cities, Mohenjo-daro in the south, Harappā in the north, were big metropolises in an advanced stage of civilization, each with a population of not more than 35,000 (according to H. T. Lambrick). It was a utilitarian culture and though phases of its history have been revealed by excavation, no change in the people's way of life is discernible.[1]

At that early stage in agricultural technique, we must assume, on the

[1] The dating of this civilization is at present under revision, as a result of the discovery of important new sites. Considerable evidence now exists to prove that the earliest phase of settlement, known as the pre-Harappan, began around the opening of the third millennium B.C. Recent excavations provide repeated evidence, notably at Kalibangan, Mundigak, and Harappā itself, of continuity in material culture from pre-Harappan to Harappan times, suggesting that a large if not a major element in the Harappan civilization must derive from the pre-Harappan culture of the Indus Valley itself: B. and F. R. Allchin, *Birth of Indian Civilisation: India and Pakistan before 500 B.C.*, Penguin Books, Harmondsworth, 1968, p. 123. It has been found, for example, that the brick-sizes in the pre-Harappan level at Kalibangan had already been standardized, while many uniform Harappan pottery models have their pre-Harappan prototypes. Radiocarbon dating suggests 'a period of not more than four centuries for the Harappan civilization, between 2150 and 1750 B.C.': Allchin (1968), p. 140.

basis of available evidence, that only in the Indus Valley were conditions favourable to the development on Indian soil of an organized urban civilization. That is to say, a system of flood control was essential if large concentrations of population were to be both protected from seasonal inundation and supplied with adequate quantities of food. Elsewhere India was still clad in jungle, while swamp conditions prevailed to the east in the Gangetic valley, until intensive reclamation was carried out around the beginning of the first millennium B.C. Outside the Indus Valley the country could only support a thin population of tribal food-collectors, 'whose technology was based primarily upon stone, and whose principal tools were the bow and arrow, the trap, the snare and the digging stick'.[1] The Indus plain alone was dry enough and the land not so heavily forested as to defy felling with small, soft-metal blades. The cities of Mohenjo-daro and Harappā could obtain their food from soil light enough for the primitive toothed harrow (as D. D. Kosambi suggests), but with sufficient rainfall for irrigation by simple riverine inundation (as suggested by Lambrick, who has personally observed this method as it is employed for primitive irrigation in Sind today, involving 'an absolute minimum of skill, labour and aid of implements'[2]). One thing is clear: settlement on the Indus plain itself would have been impossible without the use of burnt-brick as a means of flood defence. Simple tools could produce a substantial food surplus, while the river served as a convenient trade-route.

Both cities possessed a well-fortified citadel raised on a platform defended by crenellated walls 40 feet wide at the base and 35 feet high. Within this enclosure were the public buildings, while the town proper extended around it for a square mile. This basic uniform layout displays the most amazing, indeed unprecedented, standardization in prehistory. The oriented street grid divided the workers' houses into blocks, within which were many narrow unplanned lanes. Shops and craft workshops reveal specialized occupational groups such as potters, brickmakers, dyers, metal-workers, shell-ornament-makers, bead-makers, seal-makers, carpenters, glaziers, stone-cutters, and goldsmiths. The existence of specialized groups such as scribes and priests, administrators, traders and caravan-leaders, farmers, and sweepers, is, as the Allchins point out, implicit. While no temple has been identified, it has been assumed that the most important structure in the citadel was a temple dedicated to a mother-goddess. The presence of large tanks and bathing-places, and the finest drainage system of any prior to Roman times, suggest that ritual ablutions figured as prominently in the lives of the people then as they do now. Each house had a spacious bathroom and ablutions were performed, as today, by pouring water from a pot. Quantities of shards of mass-produced clay cups for drinking have been

[1] Allchin (1968), p. 112.   [2] Quoted by Allchin (1968), p. 260.

found round the wells. Probably the pollution tabu on drinking twice from the same cup, so familiar in modern India, was already established, and the cups were deliberately discarded after use.

Two interrelated factors may account for the stable character of this civilization. First, there must have existed some means of class division and class suppression, with the food-producers subservient to an upper class, whether this division was maintained by force or by religious persuasion. Secondly, it may be inferred from comparative Mesopotamian data with regard to the quantity and quality of luxury articles, weapons, and temple treasuries, that there was a *relatively* low surplus, and by implication, therefore, little stimulus of hard competition or the corresponding need for innovation, which might thereby have endangered the social order through popular revolution. All archaeologists who have worked in the Indus Valley have commented on what the Allchins describe as the 'innate conservatism, which in many respects demands comparison with Indian conservatism of later times'.[1]

Class division and subservience were probably attained by religious persuasion rather than violent coercion. The weapons which have been unearthed are clearly inadequate as a means for ensuring subservience of a labour class by military force. As in all branches of standardized, uniform Harappan technology, it is possible to typify the limited range of weapons with a single set of examples drawn from one site alone.[2] By using better documented comparative data from the Middle East, we can infer with reasonable accuracy that the working-class population deferred to a trader class who had a monopoly of profits through the enforcement of religious sanctions, rather as was the case in medieval India. The changelessness of the undeciphered script (Plates 7, 8, and 9) on cult and trading seals (around 200 pictographic characters alone were used, for which B. B. Lal has offered certain proof that they were written from right to left) points to a wealthy class who felt absolutely secure in their monopoly. Thus it was in the interests of this class to maintain a static tradition, and what the cautious Allchins go so far as to describe as 'a degree of administrative control undreamt of elsewhere'.[3] This is of great interest to us today, in view of the subsequent history of India. It suggests that the sedentary, non-violent, conservative pattern of social life in India, with self-contained groups and hereditary specialists—to be incorporated into the caste system through religious sanctions (backed, it is true, in later years by an alliance of Brahman and Kshatrya, priest and soldier)—has existed since prehistory, its durability, in part at least, ensured by the relatively meagre means of

[1] Allchin (1968), p. 137.
[2] cf. Kosambi (1956), pp. 58–9, and Allchin (1968), pp. 132–3.
[3] Allchin (1968), p. 268.

production and small degree of capital formation. Given the technical proficiency and uniformity, only the above suggestions would explain, at least in part, why the Harappans failed to create a culture on an equivalent scale of magnificence to that of contemporaneous civilizations of the Near and Middle East.[1]

The few exquisite small-scale figurines which have survived (there being no monumental works), as distinct from a mass of wholly undistinguished and standardized utilitarian artefacts, present us with a curiously ambivalent picture of this technically highly organized people. These works of art are surprisingly lively, especially the small naturalistic terracotta animals and statuettes of nearly naked women with elaborate headdresses.

Indian art history opens with one rare and enigmatic masterpiece, the small male Harappā torso,[2] no more than three inches high, but already displaying the relaxed tropical naturalism which is the most characteristic stylistic feature associated with India. Greek geometrical harmony and concern for athletic perfection are quite alien to the plastic sensibility of India. A limestone head from Mundigak[3] likewise announces the more stylized, hieratic component in the Indian tradition, and could easily have been executed at any time in the four thousand years since it was actually carved.

Many important iconographic and formal elements which were to recur in subsequent epochs, are first found on the Harappan seals. The most striking example is a horned fertility god in an ithyphallic yogic posture, which may well be an early prototype of the Hindu Shiva (Plate 9). In several seals portraying an arch formed by the bough of a tree and sheltering a tree-goddess, we have a formal motif which became one of the commonest devices in all subsequent periods (Plate 7). The torso of a dancer from Harappā displays a characteristic twist and movement that

---

[1] Since a substantial amount of archaeological research of recent decades has confirmed the highly conservative pattern of prehistoric India, it would be as well to summarize the conclusions which archaeologists are now drawing, in the words of the most recent general survey: 'Many pieces of equipment, such as the bullock carts, provided prototypes for subsequent generations of Indian craftsmen, to spread through the whole subcontinent and survive into the twentieth century.' Allchin (1968), p. 323. The same applies to the neolithic–chalcolithic culture of the Deccan and peninsular India. 'There is an extraordinary continuity linking even the earliest settlements with the whole subsequent pattern of life. . . . We now know that for at least a millennium prior to the arrival of iron [around 1000 B.C.] there were established settlements in Karnataka, and probably also in other parts of the peninsula, and these settlements show evidence of a remarkable continuity of culture. Many modern cultural traits appear to derive from them, and a substantial part of the population shows physical affinities to the Neolithic people. In the light of all this it is difficult to believe that the Dravidian languages do not owe their origin to the same people who produced the Neolithic cultures there.' Ibid., pp. 325–7.

[2] National Museum, New Delhi—Plate 5.

[3] Kabul Museum—Plate 6.

became well-known in the poses of classical art and is similar to the stance in which numerous Chōḷa bronze images of the dancing Shiva Nataraj were portrayed during the late medieval period in the Dravidian South.

Another familiar motif is that of a nude man represented as a repeat-motif in rigidly upright posture, his legs slightly apart, arms held parallel with the sides of his body, which recurs later as the Jain Tīrthaṇkara, repeated row upon row (Plates 7 and 35). The hieratic style favoured by that religious community (strongest in those parts of India once included within the Indus Valley civilization, and always associated with urban trading classes), its rigid conformism, and its utilitarian outlook, so resemble the Harappan culture that it appears more than likely that the prehistoric traits were handed down over many centuries.

After this enigmatic beginning nothing of any artistic importance has been recovered for a period lasting for more than a thousand years, between the end of the Indus Valley civilization around 1750 B.C. and the beginning of the Mauryan empire in the third century B.C. In this crucial gap occurred the Aryan conquests, the composition of the Vedas, Upanishads, and Epics, the teaching of the Buddha, and the rise of Indo-Aryan culture. In a land of images, this supremely important period has so far failed to yield a single work of visual art of equivalent historical significance. Thus, though we regard India's as one of the most ancient civilizations in the world, its classical art is not even as old as Greek classicism. By far the greater part of classical Indian art which has survived precedes the flowering of Christian art by only a few centuries and ends at the time of the rise of Islam in the Near East.

It is claimed that since the artefacts of the Aryan period were made of perishable materials such as wood, nothing could have survived so long. But this in itself is revealing. The fact of a people who do not create works of art in durable materials, already says something about their culture. The Aryans were nomadic tribes of pastoral raiders, though militarily much more advanced than the Harappans; the idea of living in permanent settlements, urban or agricultural, was inimical to their way of life; they evidently possessed no script, were not notably interested in building, and were in most respects culturally inferior to the indigenes. Aryan energies were manifested in other ways; the plastic arts went into a millennial hibernation, to emerge in the Mauryan period, their Harappan motifs and forms still recognizable beneath an Iranian-influenced veneer.

It is widely assumed (but not yet proved) that the tribes of Indo-European-speaking horse- and chariot-riders (both were introduced into India by the Aryans) who called themselves *āryā*, were responsible for the conquest and partial destruction of the Indus Valley cities. These tribes, who spoke Sanskrit and were conscious of being Aryans in an

ethnic sense, can best be visualized, Kosambi suggests, as representatives
of a distinctive new way of life and speech—military conquerors with a
loose collective identity and predisposition to cultural borrowing somewhat similar to the Arab conquerors of two thousand years later. The
Aryans appear to have entered India from the Iranian plateau both to the
north and south of the Rājasthān desert in several distinct waves, the
earliest being *c.* 1750 B.C., and the last between *c.* 1300 and 1000 B.C.,
which penetrated as far as the peninsula, bringing bronze and eventually
iron. It used to be thought that the Aryans totally destroyed the Indus
Valley cities and pushed back the indigenes into the forests. Neither, we
now know, is strictly true. The Allchins summarize present archaeological
evidence thus: 'sites in Sind and in the country immediately to the east, in
South Rājasthān and Saurashtra, testify to no profound break in the record
of settled life. In the Punjāb at Harappā too, the Cemetery H culture
[post-Harappan] shows evidence of a remarkable fusion of Harappan
traits and new traits of Iranian origin.'[1] Likewise, careful sifting of evidence
in the Aryan Vedic literature has shown that many non-Aryan tribes were
Aryanized and that colonization, in particular the settlement of the Gangetic
basin in the late Aryan period (which coincided with the spread of rice
cultivation in sufficient quantities to support the increased population),
was conducted not by the original Aryan tribes, but the Aryanized indigenes and products of intermarriage.

This is a period of Indian history for which archaeological evidence is
even more sparse than for the Harappan; details can only be adduced from
the few material traces which have survived, corroborated by research in
Vedic literature. Thus we may infer that the sedentary Harappans were no
match against the mobile Aryans, and the cities were quickly overrun. The
same system which for so long had averted internal disorder and violence
(as may be deduced from the archaeological evidence, which differs in this
respect from that for the more turbulent Mesopotamians, for example)
could not defend itself. The evidence now presents us with a picture of
considerable cultural, technological, and social synthesis between Aryans
and indigenes, with the Aryans devising new methods of production in
conjunction with the conquered people, and uniting previously separated
people into new types of social organization, while gradually adapting their
nomadic way of life to that of settled agriculture through population
pressure and the need to meet the demands for higher, more efficient food
production. Only in the last phase, around 1000 B.C., was the settlement of
extensive new tracts of land to the east of the Punjāb in the Gangetic basin
made possible by more sophisticated technology, crop cultivation, and
co-ordination of the labour force.

[1] Allchin (1968), p. 323.

The gradual adoption of plough-cultivation to augment cattle-breeding led to regular food production and, in consequence, to increase in the population divided into increasingly differentiated social groups. The Aryan word for the indigenes was *dāsa*, which in classical Sanskrit means 'slave', 'bondsman', or 'helot'; in the later Aryan period the word was already acquiring that meaning. The *Ṛg Veda* refers to the *dāsa* as two-footed beasts, or *paśu*. Kosambi defines *dāsa* status as a specifically Indian form of helotry, not actual chattel slavery. This servile class was incorporated into the new Aryan social order under the name *śūdra*, labourer or cultivator, while Aryan, or Aryanized, tribal chiefs constituted an oligarchy with virtually absolute power over the labour force employed in the clearing and cultivation of virgin lands.

Intermarriage of the Aryan and the tribally reorganized non-Aryan was permitted early in the period. The new type of social organization, primarily evolved by the Aryan overlords and continuously modified by the Aryanized (for further details see pp. 141–5 and 177–9), was based on the four *varṇas* ('colours'), classes or estates: Brahman (priest), Kshatrya (warrior), Vaishya (trader), and Śūdra (cultivator). The ingenuous system of status, power, and accruing spiritual merit was as effective as had been the Harappan social system before the arrival of the Aryans. It would appear that among the indigenous cultural traits which were later incorporated into the Indo-Aryan synthesis was the non-violent element in the principle of religious subservience that prevailed throughout the Harappan period, and which is also implicit in, indeed a fundamental aspect of, the later, full-fledged caste system on its emergence around the beginning of our era. Further, the doctrine of *ahiṃsā* (non-violence) was first propounded by the Jains, whose religious iconography and aesthetic sensibility, almost certainly non-Aryan in origin as we have already noted, bore a close resemblance to those of the Harappans.[1] The principal Aryan cultural achievement was the composition of the Vedic hymns, memorized by generation after generation and not written down until much later. The Vedas and the social system are the nucleus of later Indian culture, but after the emergence of what we now call Hinduism in the last centuries before our era, the 'underground', non-Aryan culture increasingly came to the fore in all non-Brahman, non-Kshatrya communities and was eventually incorporated in the main tradition by the Brahman priesthood, acting in their role of cultural frontiersmen. All that need be said at this point about

[1] There is no documentary proof of the connection between Harappan and Jain culture, but, as Zimmer has demonstrated—see Zimmer (1951 and 1968)—there is a very marked affinity in the feeling-tone of these regionally related cultures, an intuitive judgement which has often been employed by orthodox historians to assess stylistic or religious origins.

the caste system is that elements in both the Harappan (faint as is the inferential evidence) and the Aryan social systems *foreshadow*, but do not account for, the highly complex and sophisticated form of hierarchical social organization which ultimately emerged from their interaction at a later period. Thus the Indian way of borrowing while conserving, of juxtaposing the new and the old in hierarchical relations, would seem to originate in this great racial interaction nearly four thousand years ago.

The universal empire

With the rise of Magadhan power in the Eastern Gangetic plain (fifth and sixth centuries B.C.) the heterogeneous population of northern India reached a stage of advancement and common language which permitted considerable trade and cultural exchange between one region and another. The combined forces of a new religion—Buddhism—and the Magadhan state, under the enlightened rule of King Bimbisāra, inspired a new form of flexibility that loosened social barriers and the hold of outmoded tribal customs, particularly in the resurgent urban areas of culture. The influence of this movement, initiated at Magadha, was to spread far and wide in the country.

Lay Buddhism, first practised among non-Brahman, Kshatrya classes, had a considerable appeal to influential merchant and trading classes engaged in the new productive forms—trade, commodity production, merchant capital. Its anti-caste bias also ensured the wide and speedy diffusion of its dynamic ethic through different classes and communities. But the Magadhan state was further unified by the establishment of a new type of army. Where formerly there were only armed tribes, Bimbisāra's army owed allegiance to him alone and was the main support of the King's absolute power. This was something entirely new in Indian history. The army also ensured protection of trade-routes and rights of private ownership among commercial entrepreneurs.

The ethic of Buddhism is based on certain hidden assumptions which reveal the stage now reached by society. The strict injunction against adultery[1] indicates the establishment of a rigid family identity and the decline of tribal group-marriage. Combined with the injunction against theft and encroachment upon the possessions of others—the concept of private, individual property was also new—these form the essential ethical basis for freer trade; since the injunction against killing includes the slaughter of animals, it could only have been initiated by an urban class who were not directly involved in agricultural production. For this doctrine of non-violence

[1] See p. 334.

would have been inconceivable in an economy like that of the old Aryan pastoralism, or in one incapable of producing a considerable surplus. Moreover the Vedic religion of the Aryan tribes was sacrificial, while the anti-sacrificial Buddhist teachings were not only a protest against Brahman ritualism and exclusiveness; they were also against sacrifice itself—a wasteful and burdensome practice in a society which had developed beyond food-collecting to the consolidation of a food-producing economy. The concept of sacrifice is basically a tribal phenomenon, a celebration of collective tribal unity by the communal owners of livestock (Plate 7). As soon as livestock was privately owned, the cost of sacrifices also became prohibitive. Finally, according to the new doctrine of *karma*, a man would be reborn in a caste appropriate to his moral progress in his former life, not into any special clan based on blood ancestry. These facts show quite clearly that Buddhism cut across narrow tribal, caste, and sectarian interests, and catered to the needs of the whole Magadhan society. Viewed in this context the Buddhist *nirvāṇa* and the Brahminical *moksha* are no longer states of pure negation but a kind of spiritual classlessness achieved through cumulative (and by analogy 'productive') effort in successive rebirth. *Nirvāṇa* is both a goal— a golden age of immortal, perfect innocence—and, as will be shown in later chapters, a nostalgic harking back to the classless, undifferentiated collective unity of an earlier period, when food was ample and could be collected without productive labour by men free from the anxiety of property management and competitive drives.

The Mauryan emperors Chandragupta and Ashoka achieved the first political unification of virtually the entire sub-continent in the third century B.C. They were also responsible for giving the state its absolute power, and for curbing the development of the trade guilds and private enterprise beyond certain limits. During the latter's rule, the whole machinery of the state was subjected to the moral principle of benevolent welfare—*Dhamma* —the primacy of social ethics and justice over violent coercion. Ever since the creation of the Mauryan empire, India has been haunted by the idea of a single pan-Indian *imperium*, ruled by the Divine Right of the Kshatrya *chakravartin*.[1] Mauryan Caesarism was both bolstered and moderated under

---

[1] See p. 219 and p. 290 below, and Plate 48. The *chakra*, literally 'wheel', has various meanings: the universal law, its reflection in the moral law of man; the universal power, and the focus of spiritual power in human consciousness; the universal sun, and the inner light of illumination. A *chakravartin* is the world-ruler of an empire; Buddhists believe that the Buddha was a *chakravartin* in a previous life. In the future a Bodhisattva will appear on earth to dispel the powers of darkness and unite the world as *chakravartin*. The Buddha's sovereignty embraces the whole universe in so far as he knows it, and therefore is free from it and can free others by his knowledge. The rim of the *chakra* symbolizes the world in its entirety, infinite movement, the unending cycle of life, death, and rebirth. The spokes represent the different paths which lead from the rim to

Ashoka by the ideology of Buddhism, which while he was in power virtually became the state religion.

The creative vitality prevailing in the Mauryan period also coincided with the development of new productive means introduced on a very large scale by the State. Through the genius of Ashoka, these methods were evolved in close harmony with the general needs of society. A century and a half after Ashoka's death (231 B.C.), notably at Sānchī (Plate 12), the artist's imaginative powers would soon achieve complete concordance with the ideal of all-embracing unity sought by all classes in common. But it should be understood that Sānchī was an artistic climax following a period of profound moral revolution and religious transformation which originated in the Magadhan period at the time of the Buddha, three centuries earlier. Mauryan statecraft and vigorous productive enterprises were more a reflection of this transformation than its instigators, while Ashoka himself saw his role as the servant of the people.

Although Ashoka never dispensed with his vast army of soldiers, bureaucrats, and spies, his moral prestige as a righteous ruler of his subjects paved the way for the permanent establishment of a hierarchically graded caste system among the peasantry, who were deprived of arms and forced to live more or less helpless under tolerably benevolent state protection. Their surplus wealth usually found its way into the state treasury, which in return supplied them with cattle, utensils, and tools. Irrigation was under state management in all crown villages. India's first universal empire, with its static principle of authority, existed without large-scale chattel slavery; the labourers (Śūdras) now had the status of helots, while the trade and artisan guilds of the larger towns were permitted to bear arms. The idea of the virtually self-sufficient, non-commodity-producing village was first realized in Magadha; it became the basic social and productive unit of the whole kingdom. Land settlement by this means was undertaken across the whole of India under direct state control during the great Mauryan expansion (321 to 185 B.C.). There was no place for guilds in the self-sufficient village Śūdra communities. In the early phase of Mauryan expansion the society had engaged in large-scale commodity production and trade, in which the state itself enjoyed a virtual monopoly. But the trend towards a more and more static village economy could not long support a top-heavy bureaucracy; state control was therefore gradually decentralized, for however much the king desired to retain his power, the trend towards a closed

the hub, from movement to peace, from sorrow to *nirvāṇa*, truth, Realization. Thus the wheel represents tolerance, law, sovereignty, the universal and the individual, stability and movement. It also stands for the spiritual faculties of man; there are seven inner *chakras* of psychic power (Plate 47). When these hidden forces of mind and body are released the individual becomes a *chakravartin*.

village economy no longer permitted it. The high productivity rate of state enterprises rapidly declined and never reappeared on anything like the same scale or under equally unified central control. Thus, paradoxically, India's perennial agrarian decentralization and chronic internal disorder originated in the most massively state-controlled economy it ever produced. The same error was repeated more than once: successive empires enjoyed no more than brief periods of prosperity before the closed economy of the village settlements they invariably patronized halted all further growth. It could not be otherwise, since commodity production (expropriated by the state to support an indispensable army and bureaucracy) always *declined* in inverse ratio to the *increase* in population in the village settlements. Nor could the patriarchal, extended-family system, an integral part of the social structure in the village settlements which had developed but a small step beyond the basic communal tribal unit, become a feudal manor household. In these factors which caused the stagnation and eventual dissolution of the Mauryan empire lies the key to many of India's subsequent social, political, and economic ills.

The first great period of Indian art was stimulated by the mood of hope which accompanied establishment of a unified state by Chandragupta and Ashoka. Imperial might is reflected in the grandiose style of the Ashoka pillars, the Sārnāth lion capital (based on *axis mundi* symbolism—Plate 48), and the life-size Rāmpūrvā bull, with their ponderous masses and highly polished surfaces. They chose a style currently in vogue across wide areas of the Middle East, noticeably Iranian in its derivation (as were many of the political ideas of the Mauryas), and appealing to the tastes of ruling art patrons.

Among the many Buddhist *stūpas*, or commemorative tumuli, which Ashoka constructed during his long reign, the most important were those of Bhārhut, Sārnāth, Sānchī, and Takshashilā. These *stūpas* have not survived in their original form, and their sculptural decoration was completed after Ashoka's death. Here for the first time since the destruction of the Indus Valley civilization, we see the archaic mythology of the deeply rooted folk culture emerging into the stream of the Great Tradition. The tree goddess, a familiar motif of Harappan seals, reappears on a monumental scale, along with figurative imagery intertwined with luxuriant tropical plant forms. These too were to become familiar in the Buddhist and Hindu art of many subsequent periods.

Chapter Two Art and Society

According to ancient Hindu tradition, the artist, or *śilpin*, is the intermediary who transmits the revelation of Viśvakarma, the divine artificer, to society. Art, or *śilpa*, includes the full spectrum of creative activity: ritual, skill, craft, the formative imagination. The act of creation is itself a rite, surrounded by esoteric lore and invested with the aura of magical powers. Until modern times the *śilpin* was assigned an organic role within the society through membership in a *group*; that is to say he was a member of an artisan caste, a guild, or a court, and these groups were an integral part of the larger social order. Each artist was endowed with individual landholdings which were cultivated by each *śilpin* family. There were no such persons as individual, self-sufficient artists in the Western sense.

The relations between the *śilpin*, his patron, or *yajamāna*, and society were sacrificial. The root of all Indian tradition concerning *śilpa* was the construction of the Vedic sacrificial altar, or *vēdi*, within a series of concentric magic circles inscribed on the consecrated ground. The building of the altar was a symbolic reconstitution of the dismembered Cosmic Man, from whose limbs the divisions of society sprang. The altar was a throne to be occupied by the invisible gods to whom the sacrifice was addressed. Thus the sacrifice was a rite of triple conjunction, uniting the human domain of the whole society with the divine inside the sacred dimension of a tabernacle. The patron commissioning a temple, shrine, palace, or city was the *sacrifier* who selected a priest as his *sacrificer*, who would act in the role of architect and overseer of the *śilpin* hierarchy: the maker of the building, the surveyor, the sculptor, and the plasterer-painter. Like the sacrificial offering (e.g. an animal or harvest produce), the work of art was invested with magical potency and merit by its makers and this was transferred to the patron as the society's elected representative, thereby leading to the acquisition of a spiritual value by the community. In this sense the artist's role was one of fundamental solidarity, ensuring the restoration to the society of its lost unity.

Other-mindedness

The materials from which images were carved reveal the functional role of the image in a materially restricted environment. The *permanence* of the material, the *form* man has fashioned from it, like the tools with which he domesticated his natural environment, were the only means available to give order to his experience—as though his life depended on it. Today, every village home still possesses its clay or metal images made to *last*, thus to neutralize the anguish of impermanence and change.

The task of India's earliest inhabitants was to fuse tool and purpose into effective action. The patterns and forms of tool, house, and cultivation have always been the meeting-points of actions dictated by necessity. The pattern of thought, religion, social organization, and custom was interdependently related to those effective actions. It mapped the relations man felt between nature and himself. Senses and reason created a landscape—albeit a primitive one—in which the agricultural community developed according to a purposefully structured sequence of feeling, thought, and action. That many of the gods in the domestic and community shrines are of grotesque and alarming aspect (Plates 29 and 30) reveals the immensity of the challenge which untamed and, to a large extent, still untameable nature, in all its sub-tropical violence, posed to the people who settled there. By ordering their sensory experiences, the early food-producers established a working, if provisional, harmony with their physical surroundings. In the course of time nature revealed some secrets of its form and structure, but never wholly lost its alien, dangerous aspect. The first image with which the inhabitants of India pictured nature was that of the great mother—prodigiously fecund and at the same time destructive. The grotesque terracotta figurines unearthed from pre-Harappan and Harappan settlements do not differ greatly from the violent images still favoured by most rural Indian communities today. Violent natural calamities still punctuate the rhythm of village life. Storms, floods, earthquakes, famines, and pestilence have left their savage imprint on the features of the local godlings. In the wake of natural, and perhaps human, catastrophes, old, outworn images and symbols have been revalorized, such as the figure of the black goddess Kālī. The demons and destructive elements of nature are still associated with the jungle (Plate 33); the peasants believe waste land and virgin forest to be peopled with infernal creatures more menacing even than the wild beasts.

While clearing the jungle in ancient times, and domesticating the elephant and buffalo roaming the primeval swamps, man was exploring his precarious environment with his senses and learning about its forms and textures. The cycle of the seasons, night following day, birth, procreation, and death, the solar, lunar, and planetary cycles, all revealed innate order. While they were barely susceptible to human organizing, they were the source of fecundity, prosperity, and health as well as of poverty, disease, and death. Sense experience brought intimacy with nature, awareness of its patterns, and an ebullient enjoyment of the natural world. Memories of this satisfying connection with natural process and with other human beings were soon given concrete form by the creative imagination in images of sensuous immediacy and rich plasticity. Just as we talk of a cash nexus to indicate some economic bonds between man and man, so can we also talk of a symbol nexus between man and nature, man and man.

In spite of increasing division of labour and the introduction of individual property rights, the Indian village has never lost its deep original connection with the unity of tribal organization. One of the most conspicuous traits of Indian culture is the survival, in the midst of both caste and urban society, of tribal pockets—small communities of food-gatherers eking out a livelihood on the fringes of society. It is one function of the caste system to absorb these elements into the pluralistic society without violence or intense conflict. On this principle of co-existence of social inequalities the rhythm and stability of the society have rested for more than two thousand years. Art in all its forms—story-telling, dance, chanting, image-making—is a social activity which counterbalances the tensions within the collective that have come about through the progressive division of labour, inter-caste rivalry, inequality in hierarchical status, and disputes over private property. These tensions are healed by the transfiguring, socially unifying function of art—which in the case of village India is at its most active during the various seasonal festivals.

Artistic expression in the Indian village festival is ecstatic in character. The Hindu festival, with its oracles who fall into a state of possession, its orgiastic trance dances and collective rapture (Plate 39), is in the deepest sense a restoration of collective unity. This survival of ceremonies and rites from the tribal phase is an almost universal feature throughout rural India.[1] During such a festival equilibrium between the discordant factions

[1] Evidence from two archaeologists for the antiquity and continuity of India's seasonal festivals may be cited here:

Throughout central and southern, and indeed all parts of India there are numerous seasonal or annual fairs and markets, frequently linked with religious festivals. These are often held at a temple, or sometimes far from any settlement beside some natural feature such as a hill or a spring. Many scholars have been impressed by their evident antiquity. Whole families will travel many miles in order to attend the largest fairs, and they form important social occasions. Moreover, they frequently serve as cattle markets at which breeders sell their young oxen to the agriculturalists. Such fairs would provide a suitable mechanism for the sort of economic relations between groups which we have postulated, and may well have continued with little change since Neolithic times. Their roots may in some instances be even more ancient.

B. Allchin and F. R. Allchin, *Birth of Indian Civilisation*, Penguin Books, Harmondsworth, 1968, pp. 267–8.

For a brilliant reconstruction of the prehistoric phases in the development of religious cults and festivals still practised in the Deccan, see Kosambi (1962 and 1967). Also see below, Part Three, Chapter Five, for an analysis of the social role of festivals.

of the collective is restored, as it is in all archaic communities, by manifestations of a seemingly disordered character, such as catatonic trance,
hysteria, fits of dissociation, and drug intoxication.

This state of possession, of being 'beside oneself', or what in Sanskrit is
called *anya-manas*—'other-mindedness'—precipitates the individual back
into the undifferentiated, tensionless, collective unity. It is through the
state of disequilibrium that equilibrium is once again achieved, and harmonious relation with the outside world regained. There are numerous
instances in history when the spiritual void induced by excessive social
differentiation has led to emotional outbreaks of collective demoniacal
possession intended to restore the lost unity. In our own time there have
been instances of this kind of collective frenzy or crowd hysteria which
has sporadically swept through societies in the process of asserting some
form of nationalist or group relation with the world. To an anthropologist
such manifestations are not merely bizarre or passive responses, but

creative attempts of the people to reform their own institutions, to meet *new*
demands or withstand *new* pressures. In the broadest sense their aims are to
secure a fuller life.[1]

In former times only certain charismatic individuals, virtuosos of *ekstasis*,
were trained to be tribal magicians, sorcerers who redressed the imbalance
in primitive society. Ecstatic ceremonial is at the root of some highly
developed art forms. Plato, for instance, was evidently referring to the
practice of socially valorized possession by the lyric artist in a passage from
the *Ion*:

For the epic poets, all the good ones, have their excellence, not from art, but
are inspired, possessed, and thus they utter all these admirable poems. So it is
also with the good lyric poets; as the worshipping Corybantes are not in their
senses when they dance, so the lyric poets are not in their senses when they make
these lovely lyric poems. No, when once they launch into harmony and rhythm,
they are seized with the Bacchic transport, and are possessed—as the Bacchantes,
when possessed, draw milk and honey from the rivers, but not when in their
senses.[2]

The utterances of the possessed are the voice of the collective manifest in
a violent manner. As we shall see, ancient Indian texts which contain specific
instructions for the artist's work, refer to controlled trance techniques
which bear a close resemblance to the possession to which Plato is referring.
It is in the village festival that we can still see how deeply the ecstatic
imagery of Indian visionary art was related to the social life of the people.
It may be objected that it is a contradiction to relate ecstasy to social life,

[1] Raymond Firth, 'Social change in the Western Pacific', *Journal of the Royal Society of
Arts*, 101, London, 1953, p. 815.
[2] Tr. Lane Cooper.

Plate 1. Monster at entrance of cave. Rock. Ellorā. *C.* seventh century A.D. *Author.*

above left 2. Rock painting, Ādamgad. Mesolithic, neolithic, and later. *Musée de l'Homme, Paris.*
left 3. Elephant, Benares. Contemporary folk mural. *Author.*
above 4. Rock painting, Bhimbetka. Mesolithic, neolithic, and later. *Musée de l'Homme, Paris.*

above left 5. Harappā torso. Red sandstone. *c.* 2000 B.C. *Larkin Bros., London.*

above right 6. Stone head, Mundigak. *c.* 2500 B.C. *Casal/Musée Guimet.*

right 7. Tree goddess and deities. Harappan seal. *c.* 2000 B.C. *Archaeological Survey of India.*

below left 8. Humped bull. Harappan seal. *c.* 2000 B.C. *Archaeological Survey of India.*

below right 9. Horned deity. Harappan seal. *c.* 2000 B.C. *Archaeological Survey of India.*

or that visionary art is social, not individual. Trance, possession, and heightened consciousness, as will be shown in Part Three, have an important social function in India; they are *structured*, integral aspects of collective life. When consciousness is modified by such techniques the oracle or participant experiences states which are totally private and incommunicable. But his acts—dance, incantation, image-making—executed during or after heightened awareness do effectively communicate certain aspects of his experiences. These expressive acts will be instrumental in effecting an equivalent response in others. The state of rapture induces a sense of collective solidarity and the interconnectedness of things; in conjunction with ritual it unites the society and brings it into harmonious union with all cosmic process.

Visionary art

The Indian aesthetic sense is based on an intuition of order which differs, for example, from the Euclidean harmony of Greek and Renaissance order. Hindu and Buddhist monuments achieve a strange fusion of architecture and sculpture (Plates 13, 15, 27, and 49) which is organic in origin rather than mathematical and structural. Elsewhere in the world artistic styles of a similar basic character—fantastic, dreamlike, richly sculptured—have also appeared, among them the South-East Asian styles (which owe their early inspiration to India) and the pre Columbian styles of Central America; but while these styles are visionary in character, their architectonic basis is quite different. I will tentatively suggest *oneiric* (from the Greek word for dream: *oneiros*) as the most appropriate term to describe Indian art as a whole. We do not 'see' dreams, but experience them as a simultaneity of multiple sensory impressions and memories. Indian art is generally synaesthetic—a mixture of media combined in a manner which resembles, but is not identical with, oneiric experience.

Though India invented the decimal system and the zero, its mathematical genius remained submerged in enigma and mystery when employed in the service of the plastic arts. Take, for example, the use of geometrically patterned *yantras* (Plate 40) which were used as cosmographical ground-plans for temple architecture: they give order and proportion of a non Euclidean character to the natural plastic exuberance of the Indian temperament. 'The plan [of a temple] is prescribed by the most elaborate geomantic rites. Every slightest measurement in the temple is determined by the most specific laws of proportion . . . to put structure in harmony with the mystical numerical basis of the universe and time itself.'[1]

[1] Rowland (1953).

The earliest and most striking example of this architectural cosmography is the Buddhist *stūpa* (third century B.C.–third century A.D.), a formal arrangement of gateways (*torana*) and stone railings enclosing the traditional tumulus, or burial shrine of Buddhist relics. The origin of the hemispherical *stūpa* dome, or *anda* (egg), is somewhat complex. It was a symbol of the dome of heaven, enclosing the world mountain, the mast crowning the top signifying the world-axis. In its symbolic function the *anda* was close to the idea of the Greek *omphalos*, the navel of the world; worshippers circumambulated the circular terrace within the high railing— a familiar rite of orientation within a sacred space. At several of the early Buddhist *stūpas* clay figurines of a mother goddess have been unearthed, and these have been linked with the surviving custom among certain Nepali tribes of building hemispherical tumuli as representations of the breast of a fertility goddess. The hemispherical shape of the Sānchī *stūpas* may thus be associated not only with funerary rites but with fertility rites as well. Figures of female tree guardians (*yakshas*) are given great prominence on the ends of the *torana* beams. The scenes from the life of the Buddha and the Jātakas (tales from the former lives of the Buddha) portrayed on *stūpa* reliefs are full of symbolic death and rebirth rites which originated in pre-Aryan fertility cults. The Sānchī reliefs are also the first example in art to treat the Buddhist theme of paradise, later a favourite subject in China and Japan, which made its first appearance in the Ashokan idea of *svarga*, heavenly salvation. There exist a number of early Buddhist texts which describe the techniques of concentration for inducing visions of *svarga*, one of the commonest exercises of the Mahāyāna Buddhist school. The Sānchī reliefs might be described as the product of a Buddhist Primitive School in which this theme is first portrayed (Plate 12). The ornamental *toranas*, a uniquely Indian contribution to Buddhist iconography, have the symbolic function of gateways to Paradise. They are an interesting example of the metamorphosis of a simple geometrical structure—in this case the wooden beams of a ceremonial gate—into an oneiric piece of sculpture.

Aldous Huxley, who related experiences under hallucinogenic drugs with oneiric works of art, has the following comment to make about their effect, which is particularly revealing in the present context:

The typical mescalin or lysergic acid experience begins with perceptions of coloured, moving, living geometrical forms. In time, pure geometry becomes concrete, and the visionary perceives, not patterns, but patterned things, such as carpets, carvings, mosaics. These give place to vast and complicated buildings, in the midst of landscapes.[1]

[1] Aldous Huxley, *Heaven and Hell*, Chatto and Windus, London, 1956, p. 80.

The similarity between the visionary experiences of mystics and those caused by hallucinogenic drugs is well known; in India the two have frequently been combined. But what appear to have been even more important in the formal invention of fantastic plastic structures are the Indian techniques of mental concentration and heightened consciousness which come under the inclusive term 'Yoga'. The techniques of visual and mental concentration devised by Indians are numerous; they are not necessarily associated with mystical or religious concentration, but are known to have a physical basis. By whatever means the Indian artist and architect arrived at the intricacy of their formal devices, we can clearly see that visionary techniques have profoundly influenced both the two main categories of forms, the geometrical and the organic.

On the Sānchī gateways (*c.* first century A.D.) one of the chief characteristics of mature Indian art is already manifest: all organic forms look as if they were derivatives of one primal substance, whether they represent vegetable, mineral, animal, or human shapes (Plate 12). Whole buildings seem to grow from the soil; their surfaces blossom with figures, beasts, and foliage (Plate 26), all of which are part of the same plantlike growth. Costumes, headdresses, and festoons of jewellery are metamorphosed into the same substance (Plates 16 and 18). This striking oneiric effect is obtained in very simple ways; surfaces are smooth and convex, figures cluster in sinuous stalk patterns, their bodies weaving in the poses of the dance (Plate 19), their arms like tendrils of creepers terminating in blossoming hands, fingers curled round the stems of lotus flowers. It is not just a matter of abundant detail carved in a single material—stone; there is a concerted attempt to express the unity of all life in formal terms.

There is an affinity between these formal devices and the ecstatic food philosophy of the Vedic Hymn of Food, with its idea of tribal consumption of sacrificial food in a rite of communal solidarity. According to this philosophy, all creatures are produced from food, live by food, and pass into food, revealing a particularly intense feeling of identity with nature. Similarly the cyclic conception of creation flowing from the One into the manifold and returning back to its source, appears to have had some influence on the flowing, sinuous, organic forms that swell to the surface in high relief without breaking away from the matrix and appear to melt back into it (Plate 14). This characteristic tactile flow of sculptural form expresses a response to life that may be discerned in all aspects of Indian culture. Its affinities with the continuous narrative of fresco painting, the structure of Indian modal music, and the cyclical structure of the Sanskrit poetic drama will be analysed later.

It is common to find the snaking roots of lianas adhering to the surface of rock. This smooth and sinuous form is as common to Indian nature as gnarled tree forms are to Europe. The sculptors spontaneously turned to these most typical natural analogies, as their Romanesque counterparts in Northern Europe studied the growth of oak and elm. One often in India sees the trunk of some huge tree locked in the embrace of a creeper, or one trunk coiled round another in a marriage as sensuous as the couplings (*maithuna*) of the Indian deities (Plate 17). The union of figure with matrix, adorer with adored, subject with object, functions on the same analogy at all levels, both abstract and plastic. Poet and dramatist also resorted to the image of the creeper for the same purposes as the sculptor.[1]

Already at Bhārhut and Sānchī the human figure is treated almost as a special kind of plant. In the art of Mathurā, Sārnāth, and various other centres of Gupta art, which thrived between the second and sixth centuries A.D., the human figure is separated from its mantle of plants, and assumes the formal qualities of stalks and creepers (Plates 16 and 20). Thus transformed, it becomes a creature of unearthly receptivity, a gentle and serene vehicle for the spiritual states to which Mahāyāna Buddhism and Hindu religious or contemplative schools aspire: the state of self-absorption. But we have only to compare a Wei Buddha from China with the great Sārnāth Buddha (Gupta period) to appreciate how deeply Indian art is permeated by the sensuous, even in its portrayal of contemplative spirituality.

All the stylistic characteristics so far mentioned are oneiric in character, and vividly express that dawning consciousness somewhere midway between the plateau of dream and full waking—a kind of recollection in tranquillity of the rapture of visionary experience, which reflects both psychological *and* physical well-being. But the early classical art of Mathurā, which directly continues the same sumptuous celebration of physical well-being as Bhārhut, was not concerned with psychological states at all; it made robust, virile statements of superabundant health. These extroverted Buddhist 'primitives' sit or stand in total immobility, but in the course of time a change comes over the stylistic treatment. The great dorsal expansion and progressively indrawn gaze of the Buddha betray a working knowledge of yogic physical training and mental concentration. With the Sārnāth school, coming a century later, a narcissistic inwardness first appears—a plastic representation of *yogic* inwardness, which is never regarded as taking place separately from the physiological processes which various kinds of acrobatic physical exercise are believed to induce. Both schools portray the Buddha's body as almost naked, with delicate lines of gauze drapery over one shoulder, or tied at the waist, an effective device to suggest stillness and a state of trance. Drapery has often been used to express the psychological state of the subject which it clothes; in

[1] The treatment of the banyan tree in Plate 50, though belonging to a different aspect of the aesthetic tradition, is an illustration of this convention.

this case the cloth becomes increasingly refined and subtle in its smooth modelling. The folds have the look of a kind of extra-sensitive skin rather than a garment, covering the flesh without obscuring the contours of the body underneath it. The jungle creeper has metamorphosed into drapery clinging to a body radiant with the sap of inward bliss.

The portrayals of physical well-being and inward states do not conflict; on the contrary, they are progressively unified until they achieve a vivid plastic equivalent of a single conception—the Indian attempt to resolve the body-mind dualism in a state of aesthetic rapture. As in classical yogic philosophy, inward states, mystical *ekstasis*, ineffable bliss, union of the soul with the absolute—all are achieved through mastery of body and mind; through their integration a state of unified consciousness is achieved. In mature Buddhist art, and in the Hindu images of the Gupta period, plastic representation of this harmonious balance is achieved with the simplest of formal means (Plate 10).

The link between the aesthetic sense and systems of thought was of great significance in the development of Indian unitary ideas. Sacred art is technically closer to pantheism than to pure mysticism, either monistic or theistic. When developed to a pitch of ecstatic contemplation, this unitive experience of aesthetic character is more accurately termed 'natural mysticism', a state of identification of the human soul with the whole of Nature (Plate 34). It would seem that this kind of inclusive experience has had a direct and profound influence on Indian art, which frequently conveys a feeling of exalted pantheistic emotion. But pure mysticism is an exercise in concentration on supra-sensuous, ultimate reality, to the complete exclusion of everything else (Plate 37). Art and mysticism are, in fact, *complementary*: two different modes of experience altogether. Though mysticism may influence the ideas of the artist, *art itself does not share the same goal*. Indeed, the goal of pure monistic mysticism is *isolation*, when the external world, the body, the unconscious and the conscious mind, will cease to 'exist'. At the most, Nature and the world are *māyā*, 'creative illusion'. Furthermore, this isolation is achieved by asceticism, and at no point in its history can Indian art be called ascetic.

The evolution of all Indian art from the second century B.C. onwards was closely linked to the idea of union with God through popular devotion, or *bhakti* (Plates 39 and 55)—a term, incidentally, which also means 'sexual desire'.[1] This religious movement flourished concurrently with classical mythology, the point of intersection between religion and art. In the words of Śukrachārya, who wrote one of the classic treatises on

---

[1] 'The word is also very frequently used for sexual love and sexual union, and this aspect of it tends to be emphasized in the later *bhakti* sects: in the Gītā, however, there is no faintest suggestion of this.' Zaehner (1962), p. 122.

Hindu aesthetics, 'the characteristics of images are determined by the relation that subsists between the adorer and the adored'.[1] It is in Hindu devotional literature that we find the clearest formulation of an oneiric art at the service of Indian religion. According to Coomaraswamy, who was one of the first scholars to interpret Indian aesthetic theory:

Now in theistic Hinduism, where the method of Yoga is employed, that is, focused attention leading to the realisation of identity of consciousness with the object considered, whether or not this object be God, these descriptions, now called . . . trance formulae . . . provide the germ from which the form of the deity is to be visualised. For example, 'I worship our gentle lady Bhuvaneśvari, like the risen sun, lovely, victorious, destroying defects in prayer, with a shining crown on her head, three-eyed and with swinging earrings adorned with diverse gems, as a lotus-lady, abounding in treasure, making the gestures of charity and giving assurance' . . . To the form thus conceived imagined flowers and other offerings are to be made.[2]

Coomaraswamy also quotes two key passages from Indian texts, the first from Śukrachārya:

One should set up in temples the images of angels who are the objects of his devotion, by mental vision of their attributes; it is for the full achievement of this yoga-vision that the proper lineaments of images are prescribed; therefore the mortal imager should resort to trance-vision, for thus and not otherwise, and surely not by direct perception, is the end to be attained.[3]

The most authoritative and complete definition of Indian aesthetic theory is contained in the following passage from the *Sahitya Darpana*, freely translated by Coomaraswamy:

Pure aesthetic experience is theirs in whom the knowledge of ideal beauty is innate; it is known intuitively, in intellectual ecstasy without accompaniment of ideation, at the highest level of conscious being; born of one mother with the vision of God, its life is as it were a flash of blinding light of transmundane origin, impossible to analyse, and yet in the image of our very being.[4]

The aesthetics of the *śilpins* were handed down by word of mouth to fellow guild members long before they were written down relatively late in Indian art history, mostly in the Middle Ages, certainly not before the end of the Gupta period. In the light of virtually all work surviving from the periods preceding these written textbooks, or *śilpa śāstras*, it would appear that during the classical era, or up till approximately the sixth century A.D., the plastic arts gave expression to sentiments which accord with the teaching of theistic salvation religions, as distinct from mystical thought, but

---

[1] Quoted in A. K. Coomaraswamy, *The Transformation of Nature in Art*, Constable, London, 1934.
[2] Ibid.   [3] Ibid.   [4] Ibid.

were not entirely unaffected by more esoteric and abstruse aesthetic and philosophical concepts. During the Gupta period the Puranic myths of the principal deities were compiled by the Brahmans, and Indian temple art moved in the direction of greater emphasis on cult images, either in the round or in relief, representing groups and single deities (Plates 18 and 19). This occurred simultaneously in both Hindu and Buddhist art between the second and seventh centuries of our era. With the rise of the cults of Shiva and Vishnu, Rāma and Krishna (the first images of the last-named deity were carved at Mathurā in the second century A.D.), the importance of idol worship became paramount. With it developed a complete iconography, codified in the *śilpa śāstras*.

In the period of medieval feudalism, preoccupation with the rules of iconography led to increasing creative aridity. That the rules laid down in the *śilpa śāstras* had this effect is not surprising, since they were heavily influenced, if not actually edited, by Brahman scholastics, and were not the work of creative artists, with whose more direct, unintellectual sensory awareness the mystical, ascetic bias was at cross-purposes. Unlike Greek mythology, which was the creation of artists, poets, and philosophers, the Hindu myths became the exclusive province of the priestly castes. In spite of the imaginative richness of the myths—nourished by the lore of numerous folk traditions—Indian religious pandits never recognized the primacy of the creative imagination but attempted to bring it under the control of static priestly authority, which discouraged innovation.

Both the Indian mystic and the Indian artist, it is true, strive to attain a condition of unity, of order; but then, order is of two kinds, exclusive and inclusive. Mystical concentration of will on a single object is the very antithesis of the artistic impulse, which is rather the diffusion of imagination over all objects. Aesthetic immersion and yogic *kaivalya*, isolation, are opposed to one another. It should be said, however, that the classical texts on aesthetics do not suggest that the artist was to master the techniques of yoga for their own sake, but to use the techniques of concentration and inward visualization as a practical aid. The texts refer to the meaninglessness of transient effects in Nature because these merely distract the artist with trivialities of appearance. The subjects of his art, though drawn from nature, are to be rendered by the artist as it were *sub specie aeternitatis*; or as Meister Eckhart expresses it from a Christian mystic's viewpoint, echoing Indian aesthetic theory, 'form is a revelation of essence'.

What is of great interest to us, then, is how the Indian artist utilized the techniques of the yogic schools. These schools of meditation evolved a psychology of perception which was the most advanced at that period of history. Indian oneiric artists evidently knew of such physiological phenomena as the scintillating, phantom-like geometries called phosphenes

(Plate 23), produced by pressure on the retina, the maṇḍalas of advanced yogic meditation (Plate 22), the *chakras* (literally 'wheels') of Kuṇḍalinī yoga (Plate 47), the hallucinations experienced when the body is subjected to forced contemplation in a restricted, darkened environment and deprived of sleep and food (Plate 37). The experiences induced by hallucinogenating drugs were regarded as cruder because they were unstructured and less subtle than fully mastered mental concentration. Psychedelic states have undoubtedly left their imprint on Indian classical art. But what is more interesting and more important, is the artist's understanding of the physiological laws on which our intuition of inner orderliness rests. They relate us to the underlying order of Nature and of society, irrespective of the artist's skill in embodying the religious ideals of Buddhism, Hinduism, or Jainism.

While the majority of Indian works of art are more or less realistic representations of deities, myths, and symbols, there are also signs, diagrams, charts, and memory-aids for use in solitary meditation (including *yantras*). Sometimes this kind of image incorporates words (Plate 36), *mantras* (magico-mystical phrases), and even whole poems into the design. Tantric and Jain images of this more abstract genre often employ a rigorous syntax of geomantic and colour symbolism: each geometrical figure is associated with a particular deity, each colour corresponds to a *rasa*, or emotional resonance. Paintings of this sort were included in handwritten mystical texts; they aimed at an illustrative precision analogous to hermetic language —*sandābāsā*, or 'twilight language'—thus amplifying the meaning of the poetry which they accompanied.

Tantra, derived from the Sanskrit root, *tan*, to expand, means a system of languages designed to achieve expansion of knowledge. Among these languages are erotic ritual, poetry, speculative texts, painting, and sculpture, which constitute a special semantic—verbal, pictorial, corporeal. The idea that the human body is a microcosm (Plates 34, 36, and 47) is essential to Tantric art, and it is expressed ritualistically in a number of ways. Both Tantric sexual rites and images related to this ritual are metaphors for the fire sacrifice, while the body of the woman is a homology of the Vedic altar. The ritual partner becomes a mystical terrain to be explored like the streets and sanctuaries of a holy city by a pilgrim. The Tantric poet Sahāra even discovers a sacred geography in his own body:

> I have walked with pilgrims, wandered round holy places.
> Nothing seems more sacred than my own body.
> Here flow the sacred Jamuna and the mother Ganges,
> Here are Prayaga and Benares, here the Sun and Moon.

Based on a magical physiology and an erotic alchemy, Tantra aims at the restoration of unity by the conjunction of opposites. The root conjunction is the primordial mystery of the androgyne—Puruśa, or cosmic archetype of the human species—before differentiation into male and female, pure and impure castes, good and evil. The Tantric anatomy of the human body is conceived on the analogy of the earth and sky, its members associated with sun and moon, stars and planets, in perpetually changing conjunctions. Thus, under the sign of the sun in this magical physiology, the right axial vein symbolizes the masculine aspect and is associated with the tongue, subtle breath (*prāna*, analogous to the Greek *pneuma*), the consonants of the alphabet, and the river Jamuna. The left vein, under the sign of the moon, which symbolizes the feminine aspect, is associated with exhalation, the vowels, and the river Ganges. The central vein, which unites the right and left veins in a kind of double helix, marks the point of intersection and metamorphosis of masculine and feminine (Plates 37 and 47).

Tantric art is, perhaps, not so much an illustration as a *translation* of a reality, a presence situated beyond the domain of what can be expressed in form. It is one of several Indian attempts to plumb the mystery of formlessness (Plate 35). For example, sacred temple images, or cult images, reputed to possess the most potent magical qualities, are frequently aniconic, vermilion, white, or black stones of extremely rudimentary shape (Plates 30 and 31). Sometimes they are not even carved, but are curiously shaped natural forms that caught someone's eye as possessing *numen*—sacred potency. A shrine would be built over such a stone *in situ*, and in the course of time (possibly several thousand years) great sanctity or healing powers came to be associated with it. Crude as these *mūrti* ('images') often are, they exert a compelling fascination on the minds of pilgrims. This is based, I believe, on an intuitive knowledge of how certain very striking shapes can —violently or subtly—modify the worshipper's state of mind. Modern abstract sculpture has begun to rediscover this knowledge. That some images release powerful emotions (usually a sense of the imminence of danger), but that others do not, is well known to the seasoned pilgrim. The reputed degree of sanctity attributed to famous *mūrti* does seem to correspond to the degree of their amorphousness and lack of resemblance to anything but themselves, their mysterious *otherness*—a startling aura of bathos and the utterly new. While the use of aniconic *mūrti* is certainly very ancient, the more recent and sophisticated Tantric theory is to assert that if certain non-figurative colours and shapes are arranged in special combinations, they will vibrate on the eye of the adept so that he enters a psycho-physiological state of enhanced receptivity.

As with the crude and inartistic hewn log kept in a sacred and reserved precinct of Greek temples, a Hindu cult image is not an artistic sculpture or bronze displayed in a public portion of the temple, but a crude lump of carved or uncarved stone, the remains of a sacred tree, or a simple stone *linga*, or phallic symbol (Plate 45), capped with a mask of gold, silver, or bronze. In such instances, the psychologist would probably assume that a connection exists between the sacred and the dangerous, the dangerous with the expression of tabued erotic-aggressive impulses and repressed pregenital wishes—in other words, with the most basic of forbidden impulses. Certainly the imagery of the Hindu *mūrti* supports such a theory. They permit elemental statements about that which is tabued—sacredness—for which the images of artistic beauty, products of accomplished technique, are an alibi.

To enjoy the sensuous immediacy of Indian art there is no need, however, to study abstruse theories, for this is an art which also expresses a vigorous, extraverted, physical imagination. Even works which embody more subtle metaphysical concepts are accompanied by charming details from ordinary life, born, it would seem, from sheer exuberance and fun. No art is more direct in its approach, more immediate in its appeal, than the minor, small-scale, and intimate work which embellishes the tops, sides, bases, lintels, pillars, doors, and arches of Indian monuments. It is sensuous, vigorous, impetuous, humorous, innocent, bawdy, lyrical, tender; above all it celebrates a state of physical well-being and abundance. Though usually rural in theme, it is not peasant art. Traditions of great refinement penetrated the world of the artisan and craftsman to be fertilized anew by ebullient folklore, legend, and cult-imagery, recalling the countless small-scale masterpieces which adorn the chapter houses, cloisters, and choir-stalls of medieval churches all over Europe. Work continued in this vein right into the nineteenth century.

Chapter Three The Art of the Cave Sanctuaries

The social background

As we have seen in the case of the Bhārhut and Sānchī *stūpas*, Buddhist art of the post-Mauryan period, like the new Buddhist *religion*, incorporated the 'old gods' within a new system. The art of Sānchī is representative of a great *public* monument; but there is a second category of monumental art of quite a different kind, namely that which served the needs of Buddhist *monasticism*. This second type is mostly confined to the excavation of rock sanctuaries and monasteries (Plate 13).

For a thousand years almost all the most important sculptural monuments were *caves*. This is the most singular fact about Indian art, and distinguishes it from that of other civilizations. It is true that a great deal of important work in materials less durable than rock has been destroyed, but there is nothing to suggest, from the surviving masterpieces, that they ever attained the same degree of aesthetic integration, which is an ideal of Indian art, and the one most completely realized in the art of the cave sanctuaries. It is also true that there exist notable examples of rock carving elsewhere in the world, such as Abu Simbel, Petra, and the cliffs of the Shansi. The custom of cutting rock-hewn chambers apparently originated in Egypt, spread to Persia, and reached India during the Mauryan period. Chinese cave art of the Six Dynasties (AD 220–589) and T'ang dynasty (618–906) was derived from Indian models. Cave 19 at Ajantā was probably one of the actual prototypes.[1] But nothing in the extensive remains of this great Chinese offshoot can be compared with that of India for its profound sense of organic unity. In India it was essentially an art of mass, whereas in China the primeval mystique was refined into a more linear treatment. It is this 'primevalness' of the Indian cave which is so arresting, and for this reason we must search for the motive which could have sustained such prodigious labours over a period of 1,300 years.

The man-made caves of India, more than 1,200 in all, were excavated between the third century B.C. and the tenth century A.D. One of the earliest

---

[1] An Indian monk, Tan-yao, persuaded the Emperor Wen Ch'eng of the Northern Wei dynasty to have five colossal Buddhas carved in the Yung-kang cliff. According to an inscription of the T'ang dynasty, another Indian monk, Lo Ts'un, was in charge of excavating the Cave of Unequalled Height at Tun-huang in A.D. 366.

of all the caves bears an inscription stating that it was constructed on behalf of the Ājīvika ascetic monks (followers of Gośāla, a disciple of the Jain Mahāvīra), who enjoyed the protection and support of Ashoka. The most important sites are: Beḍsā (Plate 13), Bhājā, Kārlī, Udayagiri, Ajantā (Plate 20), Ellorā (Plates 19, 21, and 26), Aurangābād, Bādāmi (Plates 16 and 17), Elephanta (Plate 18). The group of temples and boulders at Mahābalipuram was also carved from rock, but although they share the same aesthetic, they cannot really be classed as caves (Plates 14 and 15).

The sanctuaries, cells, and assembly halls were cut from nearly perpendicular cliffs to a depth of a hundred feet, or more in some cases. They were excavated with a chisel about $\frac{3}{4}''$ wide, and included complete halls, temples with elaborately decorated columns, galleries, and shrines. The two largest structures, at Kārlī and Ellorā, are staggering in their dimensions.

The Kailāsh temple at Ellorā, a complete *sunken* Brahmanical temple carved out in the late seventh and eighth centuries A.D., is over 100 feet high, the largest structure in India to survive from ancient times, larger than the Parthenon. This representation of Shiva's mountain home, Mount Kailāsh in the Himalaya, took more than a century to carve, and three million cubic feet of stone were removed before it was completed. An inscription records the exclamation of the last architect on looking at his work: 'Wonderful! O how could I ever have done it?'

Kārlī, an earlier work, is 135 feet long by 50 feet wide. It is located in a precipitous, jungle-clad area close to a number of food-collecting aboriginal tribal settlements that have probably been in occupation longer than the sanctuary itself. At the site of the caves there is a shrine to a mother goddess, Ekavīrā (also known to the villagers as Yamāī, a death-goddess, cf. Kosambi, 1956, Plate 45, for a similar image at Beḍsā), which was built and is still financed by the Koḷī fishermen's tribe from Bombay island, and to it an annual pilgrimage is made. The caves were begun about 150 B.C. and completed by A.D. 150. They are situated near the junction of several trade-routes to the coast, and the main trade-route on the Deccan plateau. Ajantā, Beḍsā, Koṇḍāṇe, and Bhājā also mark the junctions of ancient trade-routes. Similarly, the Nāsik caves are close to the river-crossing of several important stone-age trade-routes, and a neolithic village has been excavated at the top of the Ellorā cave-hill.

At Kārlī, some of the donors were Greeks, who probably travelled up to the site from Greek trade settlements at Dhenukākaṭa and Sopārā, the latter an important port referred to in well-known ancient texts such as Ptolemy and the *Periplus of the Erythrean Sea*. We know from the latter that the region was still thickly covered with jungle in the period of excavation, wild beasts of prey roamed the forest, and little or none of it was yet brought under cultivation. Numerous donors have left their names on various portions of the Kārlī caves—the richest of all the groups of caves for inscriptions. The son-in-law of a Sātavāhana king boasts of cash donations to Brahmans and the gift of a village to the monks. A perfume-vendor and a carpenter also gave cash, as did numerous merchants, physicians, officials, blacksmiths, flower-vendors, braziers, ploughmen, and householders to other caves, such as those at Nāsik, Kuḍā, and Kaṇherī. An inscription at Nāsik makes it quite clear that the craftsmen-donors were organized into rich and powerful guilds. There is also evidence that even at this early date the Buddhist monks were slack in their observance of strict rules, for they handled silver directly and received lavish gifts of property and land. Individual property-holdings were not unknown either, and a nun called Asāḍhamitā was affluent enough to donate the cash for the stone band at the base of the Kārlī arch.

In the early period, therefore, caves with a unified plan were the product of close co-operation between different sections of a new, flexible, and developing society that was not yet settled into a closed village economy, but had, on the contrary, recently evolved a commodity-producing economy under the thriving, expansionist Sātavāhana dynasty. It was certainly an economy prosperous enough to allow artisans the ready cash to make substantial donations. This is a marked contrast to the last period of cave excavation, such as the later caves at Ellorā, and at Elephanta. By this time the open Sātavāhana economy had disappeared; donorship was wholly anonymous (there is not a single inscription at Elephanta), because once the artisans were settled in the, by then, almost universal closed village system, cash donations were out of the question. In the late period only royal dynasties could afford to finance these colossal undertakings and their style betrays the need of the artist to express the interests of his patrons in a courtly, aristocratic manner, absent from the early work.

In order to understand the function of these caves in society at the time, the meaning of the word 'monastic' should be made clear. Though Indian monasticism does resemble similar Christian institutions, the two arose under quite different historical conditions and were organized on lines that are as dissimilar as the doctrines of Christianity and Indian religion themselves. The imagery of the Buddhist caves, and even the mode in which financial support was accepted by the monks, represent a departure from the tenets of the Vinaya. But the cave sanctuaries *were not exclusively monastic*: they actually served two purposes, and unless this fact is appreciated, their role in the cultural development of India will be misunderstood.

First, the caves were a retreat (*layanam*) for monks, whose goal was always, and above everything, to achieve *nirvāṇa*,[1] union with the absolute, or the ultimate mystery. Secondly, the sites selected for excavation of sanctuaries were ideal retreats possessing all the characteristics of sacred *mana* or numen—and it is more than probable that these sites were already regarded as holy places by the local people—and were places to which the laity could make pilgrimages at the time of seasonal festivals. In other words, the retreat to the forest was not the privilege of the monastic orders, but something in which the entire society could, at least to some extent, participate from time to time. Kārlī provides us with valuable evidence of this, as it is one of the major sites still recognized as a holy place.

We might profitably compare these sanctuaries to a centre of pilgrimage more familiar to the Western reader, such as the holy isle of Delos from the eighth to the first century B.C. Like the Indian cave sites, all the most important of which were situated near a major trade-route, the tiny island of Delos, as yachtsmen who know the Greek islands will confirm, is located at a crucial intersection of several major sea routes. Here, every four years, a great festival was held, and ships loaded with officials and worshippers converged on it from the Greek city-states to participate in rites which had been continued since the days of prehistory, when human sacrifice had probably been practised on the island hilltop. The Indian cave sanctuaries, in spite of their relative inaccessibility up precipitous ledges and through jungle infested with wild beasts, were well-known centres of pilgrimage in which numerous members of the society had at least a spiritual, if not a financial, interest. For this very reason they are the very opposite of forbiddingly austere retreats for ascetic monks, and their art reflects the interests of the entire society, from king to commoner. Human beings generally wish to be free of labour, to be beautiful and sexually satisfied in the most luxurious and varied way they can imagine. This motive, however, like every other basic human impulse, was originally contained within an all-inclusive religious system and completely at one with it. It was the kind of movement instigated by the Buddha and other 'protestant' reformers which sought to 'purify' religion of these aspects. In this respect the Buddha's own views were not observed for long, and the later cave sanctuaries are the product of a return to a more permissive outlook.

One final point should be made clear in order to describe the focal role of the cave sanctuaries in the life of the people as a whole. The Buddhist *vihāra*, or monastery, as it still is in Buddhist countries, was an important

---

[1] The term *nirvāṇa* is not exclusive to Buddhist tradition. 'The metaphor is derived from the image of the flame. *Nir-va* means "to blow out; to cease to draw breath". *Nirvāṇa* is "blown out": the fire of desire, for want of fuel, is quenched and pacified.' Zimmer (1951), fn. p. 183.

centre of social life in the villages, a kind of 'clubroom' or 'village hall', the venue of the secular as well as the sacred, even though the monks and nuns were themselves celibate and took their vows seriously.

The retreat to the forest

> In a clean, level spot, free from pebbles, fire, and gravel,
> By the sound of water and other propinquities
> Favourable to thought, not offensive to the eye,
> In a hidden retreat protected from the wind, one should practise Yoga.
>
> Fog, smoke, sun, fire, wind,
> Fire-flies, lightning, a crystal, a moon—
> These are the preliminary appearances,
> Which produce the manifestation of Brahmā in Yoga.[1]

To understand the motivation for the creation of this most important Indian monumental art   the cave sanctuaries—we must briefly retrace our steps to that watershed in history, the period between the sixth and third centuries B.C. During that time, when society became increasingly differentiated, the intellectual climate of India was characterized not only by early Buddhism, but by the rise of sophism, the schools of metaphysics, and the ascetic sects. The new urban man felt increasingly alienated from nature; social discipline called for by new productive techniques created a sense of anxiety among the more individualistic non-conformists. At all such periods of inner crisis and difficulty, man retreated into the forest to test his own strength and recover the sense of identity with his surroundings. At this moment of spiritual crisis in India, the Upanishads (from which the above quotation is taken) and 'forest books' were composed by mystics who retreated to the solitude of the forest, to wrestle with their inner selves and seek union through Nature with the All. 'These high-minded men,' writes the dramatist Bhāsa in *The Vision of Vasavadatta*, 'make their home in the forest to escape from the brutalities of a town.' Similarly, the Buddhist monks were enjoined to pass a period of time each year (the monsoon months) residing in a place of permanent shelter, preferably in forest caves.

This idea of the retreat to the solitude of nature became one of the most persistent and important traits in the development of Indian culture, owing to the prestige which renunciation conferred; the practice evolved in accordance with the pattern of priestly education of the Brahmans. The novice withdrew to the forest retreat of his chosen teacher for a period of twelve years or more. The most significant feature of this life, and the one

[1] Transl. R. E. Hume, *The Thirteen Principal Upanishads*, Oxford University Press, Madras, 1949, p. 398.

which should be emphasized if the ethos of the forest retreat is to be fully grasped, is that the novice gathered, though *never produced*, food for his guru. The ideal of a carefree, simpler pattern of life in which there was no need to engage in hard productive labour for survival, had in itself a profound emotional appeal (even among kings, a legendary example of which is illustrated in Plate 54). Though this needs no further explanation, as it still remains the dream of urban man even in the most industrially advanced societies, it should be remembered that the co-existence of food-collecting tribes alongside industrious food-producing communities gave to the archaic Indian ideal of the forest retreat a very concrete and specific connotation. The surviving tribal life, with its sense of collective unity, abundantly evident, aroused in the city-dwellers ancestral memories of times in the not too distant past when society was not split into antagonistic classes and castes, nor condemned to unremitting labour. The pattern continues to the present day. As many observers have noted, there is a very marked contrast between the Hindu, caste-ridden Indian village society, with its poverty, its careworn ethos of hard labour on exhausted soil, its tabu-ridden family relationships, on the one hand, and on the other, a carefree, colourful, joyous, extraverted tribal way of life in the refreshing environment of the forest. But envy for these communities by social misfits in the caste system takes a much stronger form too, as it has since very ancient times: a hankering for the less organized, the less rationalized, even the relatively lawless state. Just as the Dantes, Rousseaus, and Thoreaus of India developed their inner orientation in the forest retreat, so too have its Robin Hoods found shelter and strength there. The romanticism of the *dacoit*, or bandit, and other forms of anarchic social protest, also figure among the components of forest nostalgia. In recent times these types of idealized banditry, 'robbing the rich to pay the poor', have been linked with the cult of 'old gods' and the revalorization of primitive customs. The *thaggi*, a celebrated sect of bandits finally suppressed in the nineteenth century, were worshippers of the aboriginal black goddess of destruction, Kālī. In the ancient period we are dealing with, the contemplative sects who retreated to the forest turned once more to the 'old gods', the mother goddesses (Plate 21), the tree and snake deities (Plates 16 and 20) of the forest tribes.

In the myth of Uttarakuru, the Hindu paradise, we possess valuable documentary evidence for this relation between the ideal of a forest retreat and nostalgia for the collective unity of the tribe. The Uttara-kurus were a northern branch of the Kurus, a tribe who, along with the Pāṇḍavas, are the protagonists of the *Mahābhārata*, and their kingdom flourished during the lifetime of the Buddha. The Uttara-kurus had a legendary reputation: they were believed to inhabit an inaccessible region of the Himalaya, where they lived a pure life. Their land had never been brought under the plough and they lived on wild rice from untilled soil. In the *Aitareya Brāhmaṇa*, a late Vedic text on sacrificial lore, the land of the Uttara-kurus is described as a place of the gods, a kind of Olympus, while the Buddhist texts written several centuries later, speak of it as the Golden Land, which shines day and night; its land is level, there is absolute calm, and its trees bear no thorns. 'The distance from legend or myth to reality, never very great in India, was small at the period and for the sources. When compared with other paradisaic legends the grain of fact seems to be the tradition of a free, happy, peaceful, tribal life with neither agriculture nor aggression.'[1]

If the ideal surroundings for the Buddhist sanctuaries were indeed the kind of thickly forested ravine generally selected, why did they not *build*, instead of resorting to the exceedingly slow technique of excavating from the living rock.

Why *caves*?

Curiously enough, no writer has attempted more than a hesitant and partial answer to the question, which is fundamental to a full understanding of Indian art. For it is here that India makes its most original contribution to the language of form, and here too that the Indian artist succeeded in projecting the totality of a people's ideals, a community of feeling shared by the entire society. There is nothing in the history of Indian culture which attains the same grandeur of vision; other examples, whatever the medium of expression, seem fragmentary in comparison, mere facets of the unitary whole. Certainly so consistent a preference for mining permanent structures directly from the earth deserves some attempt at an explanation.

Permanence, aesthetic unity, shelter which would be cool in summer, security, and refuge are all obvious needs of the monastic communities which the caves served. A peasant cave-builder in Lin Ling village, northern Shansi, where many homes are excavated from the hillside for practical convenience, told Jan Myrdal that a cave 'is a good dwelling and one that is easy to keep warm in winter, while it is always cool in summer. And you never need to think about maintenance.'[2] But these practical issues are not sufficient to explain excavation on such an ostentatious scale, over so long a period. The lavishness of the caves excavated in the Deccan, for instance, is due to the generosity of the Āndhras (Sātavāhanas), which lasted five hundred years—unusually long for India. After the invasions of the Kushānas and Huns the thickly forested Deccan beyond the natural barrier of the Vindhya range became a natural refuge for many northerners. Here the guilds, with their opportunity for patronage, were particularly active. But

[1] Kosambi (1956), p. 118.
[2] *Report from a Chinese Village*, M. Michael (trans.), Penguin Books, Harmondsworth, 1967, p. 54.

this still does not answer the question: why *caves*? I would suggest that the answer has a number of facets, each of which will be analysed in turn.

One of the chief traits of monumental cave excavation between the third century B.C. and the seventh century A.D. is that it shows a marked tendency to incorporate archaic, rustic, and even tribal features, which serve no functional purpose whatsoever. For example, wooden beam construction and forms derived from wooden architecture are imitated in stone down to the last detail (Plate 13), as they were by the Greeks when they replaced wooden temples with permanent stone structures. It will shortly be shown that this kind of archaism, involving extremely patient and skilled craftsmanship, extends to iconography, layout, symbolism, and mythology as well. It would therefore seem fair to say that a deeply nostalgic element runs throughout all Indian monumental art designed for the forest contemplatives during the classical period. This is only one example in the history of architecture of a very common desire to conserve an old form long associated with a specific sacred rite.

Art does not so much create new experience, but deepens and purifies the old. Treasures of knowing and feeling which were no more than potentialities diffused through the old order, are brought together in new patterns. It is a process of *reculer pour mieux sauter*. The psychological habit of conservation of traditional forms was used by the Buddhists to develop *new* forms. The retreat to the primeval dark woods meant retreat to the hidden depths of the mind as well. These inner wanderings are projected by the creative imagination in analogous convolutions of line. The intricate plant motifs, both painted and carved (Plates 22 and 26), but especially the great relief carvings, sweep in lateral rhythms of sinuous undulation across the monastic cave sanctuaries. Such labyrinthine plasticity, which attains an unusual monumentality in the caves, is man's most natural artistic mode of expressing inner richness and a yearning for self-realization in a severely inhibiting setting. The cave sanctuaries impose precisely these very restricted limitations.

I would tentatively suggest that the detailing of the cave architecture may reflect not only nostalgia for wooden construction, but a conscious recreation of a primitive ethos, integrally part of the fertility theme. The sheer difficulty of detailed execution suggests a more compulsive motivation than adaptation of an available vernacular style. Furthermore, the incorporation of this symbolism, along with rites of death and rebirth which originally belonged to the cult of a mother goddess, lies at the root of the transformation of early Buddhist doctrine into a devotional religion. Numerous examples of this 'prestige of beginnings' will be cited. To some extent, the continuity of every civilization is assured by nostalgia for old ways; in

India this nostalgia is an integral part of a system, of which one cardinal feature is *rites* which restore to the society its sense of primal innocence and unity. The *rites* performed in the cave sanctuaries were based on the symbolism of the Eternal Return.

The earliest excavations were Buddhist, and the most impressive type of structure evolved was the *caitya*, a vaulted nave into which the monks introduced a spherical *dāgoba*, derived from the hemispherical *stūpa* (Plate 13), the origin of which was similarly associated with death and fertility symbolism—an earthen tumulus of neolithic funerary cults. In the pre-Buddhist period the ashes of chiefs were buried in tumuli, usually in a sacred grove. It also may be remembered that figurines of the goddess have been unearthed from several *stūpas*, and that the Nepali Terai tribes still worship and circumambulate tumuli which are breast-shaped. A *caitya* (marked by a simple wooden structure) is a sacred spot, held by the village folk to be the abode of female earth-spirits, or *yakshas*, such as figure on the 'beams' of the Sānchī *stūpa* gateways. The Buddhists took over the tumulus symbol and placed it inside the rock *caitya*. They not only put the *stūpa*, now a *dāgoba*, or sphere on a cylindrical base, within the rock, but they also went to immense pains to imitate the structure of the older wooden *caitya*, even down to the beam joints, as if there were some *magic of resemblance* (mimesis) in the act of making the stone version as close a replica as possible of the wooden original. There was no *functional* purpose in executing this laborious task any more than there is a functional motive in decorating a Madison Avenue duplex suite with Louis Quatorze furniture. The difference in the consistency of nostalgia here is that the cave decoration formed an integral part of a ritualistic restoration of the Beginnings.[1] Though the details of the design were to change, the basic structure retained its original rustic character for a thousand years. Instead of the ashes of Aryan heroes and chiefs, the *dāgoba* marked the Buddha's 'death', his translation into *nirvāna*; in other words, his death and rebirth into another mode of being. The *dāgoba* rose from the rock in the centre of the rounded end of the apse-shaped nave; rows of columns on either side acted as a substitute for the trees of the sacred grove (some of which can still be seen in the Deccan near cave sites), and these formed a gallery for the monks' use during their circumambulations of the *dāgoba*. Like the hemispherical dome of the *stūpa*, the round top of the *dāgoba* was also called the *anda*, or egg of rebirth, and it was situated in the place normally reserved for the deity. In the earliest *caityas* the *dāgoba* was severe and unadorned, but in the late sixth century A.D., eight hundred years after the construction of the first cave

[1] The same procedure was followed by the carvers of Christian cave sanctuaries in Ethiopia, and from what we know of these latter sects it is possible that their motivation was similar.

caitya, the figure of the standing Buddha emerges from the round shell of the egg, the 'death-in-life womb of final peace' (Zimmer).

As time went by and the resources of the monastic orders increased, the decoration became more lavish. In the early caves the ribs, beams, and vaulting remain plain and undecorated statements of a wooden armature, but serve no structural function. In several of the large caves, including the Kārlī *caitya*, actual wooden beams were inserted, and portions of these have survived. The armature was steadily overlaid with sumptuous decoration, doorways were encrusted with *yakshas* and snake gods twined among the boughs of trees in both the Buddhist and the Hindu shrines carved in imitation of them. The iconography of these ubiquitous gateways—the 'narrow gate'—is very ancient. One can still see in remote rural districts entrances to primitive shrines on which the local earth and tree goddesses are carved. These also represent deities which have survived since pre-Aryan times, the same ones, in fact, which figure at the entrances of the caves. They also appear on the gateways of all the main *stūpas*, from Bhārhut to Amarāvatī. Amorous couples are later woven into the design, as at Ajantā, and these in turn were to become the erotic *maithuna* couples of medieval temple imagery. In the Hindu caves the door guardians are silent colossi—the *dvarapalas* (Plate 18, centre)—while the late Buddhist caves have Bodhisattvas as door guardians, some carved and some painted. In the continuous evolution and reciprocal influence of Buddhist, Jain, and Hindu iconography from crude fertility to the highest personification of divine love and compassion, we can observe the Indian fondness for expressing abstract concepts of an increasingly refined nature in concrete terms understandable to all. This is particularly evident in the imagery and symbolism of the Hindu sanctuaries which represent the 'World Mountain', and it is here that we will come nearer to answering the question: why caves? For the Brahmanism of the later cave period deliberately set out to revalorize the mythology most deeply rooted in the popular imagination of the non-Buddhist masses. Its primitivism is therefore more explicit than that of the Buddhist sanctuaries.

In these Hindu caves the shrine enclosing the *liṅgā*, the cosmic phallus, replaces the Buddhist *dāgoba*, and is located in the centre, like the *axis mundi* of European classical antiquity. The world is oriented round this cosmic axis; hence it is located 'in the middle', or in 'the navel of the earth'. The shrine is called the *garbha-griha*, 'womb-house'. The supreme *axis mundi* symbol of India is the mythical Mount Meru at the centre of the Himalaya, with which Mount Kailāsh is assimilated in the Shaivite texts. There exists an abundance of comparative material from which Professor Éliade has deduced that all sanctuaries are 'doors of the gods', and hence places of passage between heaven and earth; any penetration downwards usually signifies a break-through to the underworld, the world of the dead. Subterranean shrines are the umbilici linking historic to primeval times and the mythical 'beginnings'. For all Asian religions, temples mark the intersection of the three cosmic levels, earth, heaven, and the underworld. The assimilation of temples with cosmic mountains is not unique to India. The names given to Babylonian sanctuaries are an example: 'Mountain of the House', 'House of the Mountain of all Lands', 'Link between Heaven and Earth'. The mountain home of Shiva and his marriage (the Greek *hieros gamos*) to Pārvatī, 'Daughter of the Mountain', are portrayed in the relief sculptures of Ellorā and Elephanta. The carving of this mountain palace by man in imitation of the cosmic construction originally performed by the gods, in the form of a sunken temple hewn from the side of a cliff, was an unprecedented act of patience in the ritual efforts of man to achieve communication with the gods. There are several other examples of the Kailāsh temple-symbol still in existence, though that of Ellorā is carved on the most magnificent scale. The ideal nature of the symbol is echoed in a medieval text: 'Our scriptures teach that the architecture of our temples is all Kailāśabhāvana, that is of forms prevailing in Kailāsh.' This is an example of what was called the principle of *pratibimba*, 'the reconstruction in architecture or sculpture of the imagined structure of supernatural things or regions, in order that men may have access to them or power over them through an immanent symbol'.[1] The routine of everyday life was rejected because something else was possible, another mode of being. This *sacred* mode could only transcend the human condition after a complete rupture and 'death'. The caves would provide the simplest and best setting in which to achieve rebirth to an enhanced and more lucid state of consciousness —a complete unification of the spirit.

The conjunction of monasticism and fertility cults is significant. We are dealing with a mode of living integrally linked with the symbolism of initiatory rites of death and rebirth, where *mortification* of the flesh precedes initiation into an enhanced mode of life. Such rites are accompanied by the enactment of body-destruction and self-annihilation fantasies. The conjunction of death and fertility cults figures in a number of ancient societies; the cult of Yamāī, the mother and death goddess of Kārlī, already referred to, is but one example. There are certain Indus Valley figurines which represent a 'grim embodiment of the mother-goddess who is also guardian of the dead—an underworld deity concerned alike with the corpse and the seed corn buried beneath the earth'.[2] In Mediterranean antiquity the myth of the maiden goddess carried off to the bridal chamber of the underworld deity is widespread, notably in Orphism.

[1] Rowland (1953).
[2] S. Piggott, *Prehistoric India*, Penguin Books, Harmondsworth, 1950, p. 127.

Erotic art came to be associated with fertility cults and death and re-generation rites, in both ancient India and Greece. The symbol of the sepulchral phallus was common in classical antiquity. In the Hindu cave shrines the sanctum contains no sculptural decoration or imagery except the stone *liṇgā* (ancient symbol of cosmic energy as a conceptualized phallus). In view of the great prominence of erotic imagery in the cave sanctuaries it is worth remembering that, as Professor Siegfried Giedion puts it, 'in pre-history it was the concept of fertility rather than the sexual act which gave birth to their symbols'. Indian art preserves in unbroken sequence the evolution of fertility symbols from the pre-Harappan to the erotic imagery of later periods. This was accomplished during a period of two or three thousand years, but even then the original traits of the pre-Aryan fertility cults were never entirely lost, although the emphasis in devotional religion and in the cults of divine love was remote from tribal orgiasticism (Plates 7, 9, 17, 21, and 45).

The subjects portrayed in cave art were never meant to be a clinical description of reality. On the contrary, their purpose was to sharpen perception of a transcendent mode of being superior to that of ordinary life, magically suggestive of parapsychological 'states of consciousness' attained through meditation, trance, or ecstatic vision. The choice of an oneiric style was a logical necessity, or rather an organic response to the deepest intuitions of the Indian mind. Such a style would not be exclusively con-cerned with a literal transcription of dreams, as attempted by the Surrealists in our own day. It would have to be as close an aesthetic *equivalent* as possible to the yogic penetration into all modalities of consciousness. The yogin is said to maintain a completely detached 'witnessing consciousness' while exploring the waking state, sleep with dreams, dreamless sleep, and cataleptic consciousness. This simultaneous wakefulness and somnolence is reflected in the cave imagery, as in the great 'open' eyes of the Mahesha-mūrti at Elephanta, which have no pupils (Plate 18). The same simul-taneity of consciousness is represented in innumerable dancing gods and fighting titans; they drift through fluid dream-stuff or well from the rock to fight with rhythmical somnambulist movements.

The substance of the rock itself exerted a compelling fascination upon the men who mined the caves. Its very permanence invested the rock with the significance of something absolute, eternal, that could be achieved by no other technical means quite so effectively. This primal substance, assimilated to *māyā*, or *prakṛti*, Mother Nature, was also the material of the world mountain, and was conceptualized as the female earth which gives birth to the wild play of mirage-like forms. For the Buddhists this flux of forms could be both material and psychic; for the Hindus the flux was dreamed by Brahmā or born from the goddess Mahā-Māyā. For both religions life as we know it is no more and no less than the stupendous oneiric fantasy of the Supreme Imagination. The mystic uncovers the presence of this super-reality within himself. But the artist, working with physical matter, sees in the amorphous rock a substance which can be wrought in microcosmic imitation of the forms born of the macrocosmic dream. The art of the cave sanctuaries is a luminous representation of *māyā* as creative illusion in all its depths of multiple meaning (Plate 21).

At Bhājā and Khandagiri there are several fine reliefs of the early cave period which illustrate this idea of shimmering rock as the primal substance. The two beautiful reliefs of the second century B.C. at Bhājā are executed, as Zimmer says,

in a distinctly 'visionary' style. . . . The figures emerge from the rock and cover its surface in thin, rippling layers, like subtle waves of cloudlike substance; so that, though carved from solid rock, they suggest a kind of mirage. The substance of the stone seems to have assumed the contours of lightly fleeting emanations. Formless, undifferentiated, anonymous rock is in the very process, as it were, of transforming itself into individualised and animate forms. Thus the basic conception of *māyā* is inflected in this style. It represents the apparition of living forms, out of the formless primal substance; it illustrates the phenomenal, mirage-like character of all existence, earthly and divine.[1]

The structure and ornamentation of the caves were deliberately designed to induce total participation during ritual circumambulation. The acoustics of one Ajantā *vihāra*, or assembly hall (Cave VI), are such that any sound long continues to echo round the walls. The whole structure seems to have been tuned like a drum. One can imagine what an overpowering effect these waves of sound vibrations had on the Buddhist monks as they processed round and round the gallery of this sombre echo-chamber, filtered sunlight projecting on its walls glimmering patterns, their prayers booming and reverberating among ponderous colonnades.[2] But it was not merely the dramatic blend of media which encircled the worshipper. A hollowed-out space in living rock is a totally different environment from a building constructed of quarried stone. The human organism responds in each case with a different kind of empathy. *Buildings* are fashioned in sequence by a series of uniformly repeatable elements, segment by segment, from a foundation *upwards* to the conjunction of walls and roof; the occupant empathizes with a *visible* tension between gravity and soaring tensile strength. Entering a great building is to experience an almost imperceptible

[1] H. Zimmer, *Myths and Symbols in Indian Art and Civilisation*, ed. Joseph Campbell, Bollingen Series VI, Pantheon Books, New York, 1946, p. 120.

[2] Cave VI is unique in that a sizeable area of the ceiling fell away during excavation, leaving a seam of shimmering, crystalline rock which, it would seem reasonable to assume, so struck the anchorites with its mysterious beauty that it was left untouched—a great swirling mass of stone protruding from the roof.

tensing in the skeletal muscles in response to constructional tension. *Caves,* on the other hand, are scooped out by a *downward* plunge of the chisel from ceiling to floor in the direction of gravity; the occupant empathizes with an *invisible* but sensed resistance, an unrelenting pressure in the rock enveloping him; sculpted images and glowing pigments on the skin of the rock well forth from the deeps. To enter an Indian cave sanctuary is to experience a relaxation of physical tension in response to the implacable weight and density of the solid rock (Plate 13). If the body were, so to speak, left to its own devices, the appropriate movement in such an environment would be a serpentine undulation of the whole body, a giving in, a surrender. The resonating echo-chamber unifies sensory awareness—an indispensable feature of the Buddhist contemplative discipline—more effectively than could the construction techniques of the builder.

E. M. Forster's symbol of the Marabar Caves has acquired a popular significance quite independent of its legitimate and intended role within the fictional scheme of *A Passage to India*. This is probably because the modern world is fascinated by the inclusive field of echoing resonance which the Indian cave world conjures up in the imagination. The technological environment in which we now live creates a highly complex field of interconnectedness, and in this vortex we seek the reassurance of far simpler types of wrap-around environment. I doubt if Forster's young readers today have the slightest sympathy with Mrs. Moore's total disorientation subsequent to hearing the echo in the Marabar Caves. From what I have seen of their rapturous response to the perfect echoing acoustics of Cave VI at Ajantā, they regard the Indian cave world, the psychedelic lights-show, and total theatre as kindred media. As Mrs. Moore's train meanders through the countryside, taking her away from the hated Marabar, she is filled with loathing when the same minaret looms up outside the train window again and again, each time viewed from a different angle, depending on the twists and turns of the railway line. This multiple perspective on a single object is seen through the eyes of Mrs. Moore as yet another irritating feature of a country which consistently upsets the Western equilibrium. Both the echoing cave and the multiple minaret are vivid examples of the aesthetic dysphoria which the non-sequential, intuitive, tactile culture of India often induces in Europeans of an older generation conditioned by rationalism and Euclidean space (e.g. see p. 108).

The Ajantā frescoes

To adapt the famous phrase of Le Corbusier, a cave is not just a machine to live in, but a machine for acquiring knowledge of various modalities of consciousness. Within this deliberately limited horizon the anchorites spent their lives cultivating an enhanced mode of consciousness, enclosed by sumptuous vistas of form and colour vibrating continuously with changes in the pattern of filtered sunlight. Descriptions of Uttarakuru, that legendary Hindu paradise in the Himalaya already referred to, recall the unearthly vision depicted on the walls.

The land is watered by lakes with golden lotuses. There are rivers by thousands, full of leaves of the colour of sapphire and lapis lazuli; and the lakes, resplendent like the morning sun, are adorned by golden beds of red lotus. The country all around is covered by jewels and precious stones, with gay beds of blue lotus, golden-petalled. Instead of sand, pearls, gems, and gold form the banks of the rivers, which are overhung with trees of fire-bright gold. These trees perpetually bear flowers and fruit, give forth a sweet fragrance and abound with birds. (*Rāmāyana*.)

The asceticism of anchorites has, as Huxley pointed out, 'a double motivation. If men and women torment their bodies, it is because they hope in this way to atone for past sins and avoid future punishments; it is also because they long to visit the mind's antipodes and do some visionary sightseeing.'[1] No doubt St. John of the Cross would have taken a dim view of Huxley's breezy 'double motivation', but for our purposes the 'mind's antipodes' is a useful term to describe one aspect of visionary experience which interested the cave artists. Under the conditions of the anchorites' restricted environment

all colours are intensified to a pitch far beyond anything seen in the normal state, and at the same time the mind's capacity for recognising fine distinctions of tone and hue is notably heightened. . . . Praeternatural light and colour are common to all visionary experiences. And along with light and colour there goes, in every case, a recognition of heightened significance. The self-luminous objects which we see in the mind's antipodes possess a meaning, and this meaning is, in some sort, as intense as their colour. Significance here is identical with being; for, at the mind's antipodes, objects do not stand for anything but themselves. . . . And their meaning consists in this, that they are intensely themselves and, being intensely themselves, are manifestations of the essential givenness, the non-human otherness of the universe.[2]

For this reason, the profusion of luxuriant panels representing flowers and foliage on the walls and ceilings at Ajantā (Plate 22) are not there to serve only a decorative function. Like every other device at the command of the cave artists, they are used to enhance visionary experience. The cave artist has a natural impulse to take pleasure in ornament, and rhythmic repetition of certain simple shapes. However, if the caves so decorated were only filled with ornamentation, their point as sanctuaries would have been lost.

[1] Huxley (1956), p. 74.   [2] Ibid., p. 80.

Ajantā should be seen in the early days of the monsoon when the trees are in flower. Only then can one appreciate the tremendous emotional release when colour and fertility are restored to the dry soil after the long hot season. With the first rains, a furry grass-like green mist carpets the soil of Ajantā. From the cracks between the rocks on the cliff face where the caves are excavated, burst tufts of grass, foliage, and creepers. For barely more than a couple of weeks the surface of the earth is luminous with this exquisitely soft bloom. The whole landscape becomes a rug, and the sheer precipices seem to swell and press into the field of vision like a painting, two-dimensional, flat and without perspective. It is one enormous close-up, a sudden projection of growing, sprouting vegetation thrust upwards and outwards. Only in childhood does the earth seem so *close*. In this brief spell nature conspires to bring together mystery and beauty in harmony with the universal laws governing life and matter.

The caves of Ajantā offer the sole remaining opportunity to visualize the way a combination of colour and form was originally fused in a wrap-around synaesthesia. The Ajantā style is unique in the history of Asian fresco[1] painting; this is not commonly acknowledged because there are too many related styles which at first sight resemble it. I would compare the current absence of critical recognition of its unique characteristics to the reputation of Vermeer in the past, at the time when he was barely distinguished from the school of little Dutch masters. The richness and splendour of Ajantā are indeed well-known, but the unusual qualities of style which distinguish it from Central Asian, Chinese, Japanese, and Ceylonese frescoes are rarely noticed. Yet these qualities yield much valuable information.

At first sight it is the genial 'Buddhist humanism' which strikes the visitor. Yet these reassuringly human scenes are not quite what they seem to be. For one thing, even the best preserved are exceedingly elusive to 'read'; one must make an appreciable effort to slow down one's reading of their visual language in order to perceive the spatial and tactile relations established between the figures. There is no *recession*—all *advance* towards the eye, looming from a strange undifferentiated source to wrap around the viewer. This is not an optical illusion of cave-light; on close examination it will be found to result from a controlled use of almost equal *tones* in the variation of local colour. A patch of green, say, juxtaposed to a patch of red, is of very nearly the same tonality when photographed in monochrome (as in the

[1] A word here on the use of the term *fresco*: the cave paintings are not technically what is known, since the Italian Renaissance, as fresco painting, the medium of which was an egg-tempera. At Ajantā the surface of the rock was spread with a layer of clay, cowdung, and rice husks; over this was laid a coat of white lime-plaster the thickness of an egg-shell. This surface was kept moist while the colour was applied, and afterwards burnished.

relation of the queen to the other figures in Plate 10). Because of this tonal equality one is constantly discovering new figures which were unseen through the deliberately unaccented or 'suppressed' tonality of detail, and the tempo of this slow discovery is very precisely calculated. Every figure has a counter-figure, every body an anti-body. This effect is not the result of deciphering damaged paintings in poor light; it is most pronounced in the best preserved paintings. Each figure is inseparable from its environment. The optical basis of this technique is very simple and is frequently used by Bonnard, Vuillard, and Matisse to obtain a hallucinating, visionary effect; the later, psychedelic poster artists made a trick of it. One can assume that the Ajantā painters discovered the effect under similar lighting conditions. There is one vital difference, however: at Ajantā there is no source of light in the frescoes, a fact which says much about the metaphysic of the cave sanctuaries. Objects are their own light when experienced by *all* the senses in harmony, and such harmony was the goal of the cave ritual.[1]

In the subtle *in*equality of emphasis between an accented figure and an unaccented one in juxtaposition with it (the latter at first unnoticed) lies the chromatic basis of this style and the key to the value it so reticently asserts. For the act of discovery whereby we only very gradually absorb the components of a given fresco is *not*, as in more familiar narrative styles, primarily based on gestures, actions, the direction of a glance, but on the evoked sensation of touch through colour and tone. When viewed by flickering light, as was intended, only fragmentary glimpses of the colours and lines of the objects depicted can be obtained. A body undulates towards the eye from an indistinguishable blur; moments (perhaps minutes) later, a second body wells out of the blur and is seen to be intertwined with the first. The viewer is so involved in this optical assimilation that his relation to the other figure only proceeds gradually from the tactile to the emotional recognition of its significance. It cannot be reduced to verbal interpretation, as it is pure tactile sensation.

Once this relation is established, the eye is skilfully led in a circular movement round the newly identified detail. Of a human figure it will be noticed that it is neither wholly subject to the laws of gravity, nor does it float. This weightless buoyancy is achieved by making the solar plexus or hip-joint the axial point of equilibrium and by drawing the limbs from different viewpoints. The most graphic example of this technique occurs a number of times (Plate 10): a seated female figure supports herself by placing the full weight of her leaning body on one arm, the hand at the

---

[1] This tonal technique was probably employed elsewhere in India, although the only extensive evidence of this is the most neglected major school of fresco painting in India —that of eighteenth-century Cochin, a fine example of synaesthesia, very closely associated with the Kathakali dance drama.

level of the viewer's eye, the navel from about ten inches higher, her breasts viewed midway between these levels and to the side, her foot from above. The cushion on which she is seated is seen in bird's-eye view. To accent this gliding viewpoint, the hand on which she is firmly leaning *does not even touch the ground*, but floats at least a dozen inches above it. Indeed the 'ground' does not exist as a firm plane at all, but dissolves into a flower-sprinkled area without density. There is no question of poor workmanship here. The skill with which the drawing is executed—the sculptured body richly swelling from a background blur of unaccented figures—leaves no doubt that the pose has been precisely calculated. That other figures in slightly *different* poses share in common the tensed arm and floating hand indicates complete conscious control. Examples of this pose are featured in some of the most often reproduced details from the frescoes—but no critic has commented on the singularity. Why?

Possibly because the eye does not *see* any anomaly. The Ajantā style approaches as near as it is likely for an artist to get to a felicitous rendering of tactile sensations normally experienced subconsciously. These are *felt* rather than *seen* when the eye is subordinate to a *total* receptivity of *all* the senses. Here the eye functions quite differently from its linear reading of a flat image. It explores the non-visual properties of spatial forms, creating a sign language or optical braille for the tactually-educated. The seated queen with the floating hand is drawn so that we obtain information which cannot be had by looking at her from a single, fixed viewpoint to which we are conditioned by the artifice of optical perspective.[1]

This kind of tactile, unified-field awareness is not a mere quirk, but the product of an integral outlook common to societies which have not been deeply conditioned by reading print. Such was the situation when the Ajantā frescoes were executed. It has been proved by optical experiments that people conditioned to tactile modes of perception tend to use scanning eye movements.[2] In such cases, images are not taken in by a glance through focusing the retina on a point slightly in front of the picture plane, as a print-reading eye does. Rather, the viewer scans it piecemeal—not in perspective but empathically. This is confirmed by the indifference of the tactile artist to the single pyramidal tableau contained within a border, which is the commonest structure for the Western-type image. The multiple-perspective, shifting viewpoint employed in the portrayal of figures, animals, and objects at Ajantā is one of the most graphic demonstrations of this scanning vision.

[1] See McLuhan, *The Gutenberg Galaxy* (1964) for an erudite explanation of fixed-viewpoint vision.
[2] Cf. John Wilson, 'Film Literacy in Africa', in *Canadian Communications*, I, 4, Summer 1961, pp. 7–14.

Before drawing conclusions about the metaphysic of the frescoes from this vital, though seemingly insignificant, detail, the effect of this perceptual mode on the Ajantā style will be noted. Firstly, the scanning vision imposes its own non-lineal, atemporal, or non-sequential scheme on narrative technique. The closest to this method which Western art approaches is the medieval 'continuous narrative', in which the same figure is portrayed within a single organized 'frame' several times, to represent different moments in the narrative sequence. These multiple images compress the time-scheme into a simultaneous description of various actions which we then break up into its logical time-sequence. The painter leads the eye by clear linear steps from left to right, up or down, from the first event in the story to its conclusion. The convention looks archaic to a modern eye, but we accept it for what it is—an artifice. At Ajantā, on the other hand, while a figure will be represented in successive events of the story, their sequence is not read by the eye in linear time. This form of narrative multiple representation operates much like Mrs. Moore's view of the minaret from the train window. Past and future are simultaneously apprehended and the eye moves in a circular direction round the events without coming to rest at the still point of the turning world—because to the Indian concept of cyclical time, there is no such point (nor is there what we call the *vanishing point* of Renaissance perspective). It could be said that the Ajantā artist is concerned with the *order of sensuousness*, as distinct from the *order of reason*, to use Schiller's terms. What saves the viewer from vertigo is a continuous, sensed apprehension of a still plenitude *behind* the figures. There are no planes, empty spaces, or mists (as in Chinese landscape painting) and no background, strictly speaking, from which the figures are to loom—only other figures, plants, rocks, flowers, and ambiguously constructed architectural boxes, all pressing outwards. The logic of this style demands that movements and gestures can only be described in terms of the area or space in which they occur; we cannot identify a figure except by comparing its position with others around it. Every outline is an inline, as Professor Alan Watts puts it in another context, a spontaneous rather than a calculated reflection of the Buddhist world-view, the *dharmadhatu*, translated by Watts as 'the field of related functions'.[1] Everything is foreground, everything is simultaneous, existing in the Eternal Present. That the eye is prevented from immediately assimilating this simultaneity by deliberate 'suppression' of detail is a subtle artifice. For the discovery that these hidden details were there all the time originates in, and records, the tactile mode of perception whereby simultaneity—the flash of truth which sees the apparently unrelated as ultimately interconnected—is finally known, not by the mind alone, but by a co-ordination of mind and body. There is nothing intellec-

[1] Cf. Watts (1961).

tual about the Ajantā frescoes. Everything of importance is perceived by direct apprehension. Nor is there anything in the imagery of these frescoes which refers to mystical union with the ultimate; the idealized figures maintain imperturbable poise and physical equilibrium between the disturbances of action on the surface of life and the stillness of the visionary deeps; this poise is formal and aesthetic. That the figures are advancing towards the viewer from somewhere which is never defined has been remarked on by several writers, and this undifferentiated continuum has been appropriately linked with the Buddhist concept of *Śūnya*—the Void (for an explanation of this term—which does not mean negation but inexhaustible potentiality—see Part Five, Introduction).

The cave art forms part of a synaesthesia appealing to all the senses simultaneously, by chanting of Pāli and Sanskrit verses in a magical, resonating echo-chamber embellished with frescoes and sculpture. This environment 'demands participation and involvement in depth of the whole being, as does the sense of touch'.[1] We must imagine the overpowering effect of scanning the frescoes in the flickering light of oil-lamps, conditions under which the 'reading' is slow, and the delayed-action effect of 'suppressed' details far more pronounced and subtle than under the modern arc-lights which have been installed. One is reminded of a passage in Yeats where he describes a film projector as playing 'a spume upon the ghostly paradigm of things'. The Ajantā artists used a brush instead—modelling form with a very faint highlight which, combined with filtered sunlight and flickering lamps, envelopes the figures in a pearly sheen.

To use a currently much-abused term where it seems fully warranted, the Ajantā style surpasses the oneiric and reaches an authentic psychedelic intensity. This was assisted, one would suspect, through both yogic techniques of concentration (which, as we have seen, does not have the same goal as artistic creation), and heterodox techniques for attaining *ekstasis* (which do, partly, share a common goal), which may or may not have included experience of hallucinogenic drugs.[2] The slowing of the

---

[1] McLuhan, *Understanding Media* (1964), p. 357.

[2] It would be as well to point out here precisely what is the position held in classical Indian texts with regard to ritual intoxication by hallucinogenic drugs by quoting the following brief but authoritative remarks by Professor Mircéa Éliade:

We know that Patañjali himself puts simples (*auṣadhi*), together with *samādhi*, among the means of obtaining the *siddhis* [magico-ecstatic powers]. 'Simples' can mean either ecstasy-inducing narcotics or the 'herbs' from which the elixir of longevity was extracted. In any case, hemp and similar drugs produce *ecstasy* and not the yogic *samādhi* [unconditioned mental concentration—enstasis]; these mystical means properly belong to the phenomenology of ecstasy . . . and they were only reluctantly admitted into the sphere of classic Yoga. Yet the fact that Patañjali himself refers to the magico-ecstatic virtues of simples is both significant and pregnant with consequences; it proves the pressure exercised by the ecstatics, their will to substitute their methods

time-scale, the tactile relations of the figures, the ebb and flow of emerging detail, the erotic evocation of released muscular tension attained at the end of the orgasmic phase of sexual intercourse, and the almost uncannily vivid suggestion, through tonal modelling, of the fine sheen of perspiration accompanying the latter—these are characteristically heightened effects of chemically-induced hallucinosis. Such a conclusion may irritate puritans; in qualification it must be accepted that the artists could never have achieved these effects without advancing beyond induced visionary experience. As every ancient text instructed, the *śilpin* was to develop sufficient powers of enhanced consciousness to apprehend the mysterious plenitude from which their visions are so felicitously portrayed as emerging.

To impose received Western ideas about organized religion and asceticism on an interpretation of the cave ethos is a dangerous procedure. I would go so far as to say that wherever civilization has borrowed from, or attempted to restore, the ethos of the folk—be it tribal or peasant in nature—a prime component of the resulting cultural manifestations will not be religious nor even mythological in nature, but that rare and special flower of the creative imagination best described as the 'Faërie', in the full archaic sense of the word, or 'beauty that is an enchantment' (J. R. R. Tolkien). It is the Faërie which, ultimately, lingers in memory after a visit to the Ajantā caves, and not only because the explicit portrayal of tribal and humble

---

for the disciplines of classic Yoga. And in fact a certain number of Śāktas and members of other ecstatic and orgiastic movements used, and still use, opium and hashish. The majority of these ecstatics are in more or less direct dependence upon Śiva—in other words, belong to an aboriginal cultural substratum.

M. Éliade, *Yoga: Immortality and Freedom*, W. B. Trask (trans.), Routledge and Kegan Paul, London, 1958, p. 338.

We do not know whether the Buddhist artists of Ajantā used drugs. Tantric Buddhism, which, like its Hindu counterpart (to which Professor Éliade alludes in the penultimate sentence above), had already made its appearance by the time the main Ajantā frescoes were painted, would have tolerated ritual drug intoxication. Although the Ajantā caves have no known connection with Tantrism, the fresco imagery is, according to W. G. Archer, heterodox in relation to Indian Mahāyāna Buddhism. In so far as it therefore pertains to the phenomenology of ecstasy more than to that of *samādhi*, and as the *śilpin* was of relatively low status in the social hierarchy, we may assume that the Ajantā artists were either in contact with, or belonged to, the cultural stratum where ritual drug intoxication was not uncommon. The psychological outlook which can be adduced from the sensuous imagery at Ajantā certainly has affinities with the Tantric strain in Indian art (cf. Zimmer (1951), Part III, Chapter 5). In my view, the Ajantā style shows traces of having been influenced both by yogic types of concentration and by the culture of the ecstatics; I include ecstasy-inducing drugs in the latter after having compared the Ajantā style with that of artists *known* to have had experience of ritual drug-intoxication in various parts of the world. But at Ajantā, this kind of intoxication was probably only one among a variety of ecstasy-inducing techniques employed, and not the most important.

folk in cave art is relatively diminutive, a characteristic of Faërie imagery. It is primarily due to the fact that, alienated from society, the anchorites could best satisfy certain primordial desires through the making or glimpsing of Faërie.

This is not to imply that the Ajantā frescoes depict some impalpable fairyland. On the contrary, they are replete with robust, vigorously naturalistic detail which proves that the artists had by no means lost contact with reality (see the detail of the miserly Brahman Jūjaka in Plate 11). Indeed, there is an inscription of the fifth century A.D. in Cave XXVI which declares, 'A man continues to enjoy himself in paradise as long as his memory is green in the world.' If we concentrate for another moment on the stylistic device which ensures a very slow deciphering of the scenes, the precise quality of this contact with reality will become apparent. By tonal *equality*, but contrast in local colour between one figure and another, an *unequal* interdependence is established, one figure acquiring a more brilliant accent than others. The relation between the figures is fundamentally *hierarchical*, the normal mode whereby relations in the society of that period were perceived, namely a multi-dimensional structure of hierarchical interdependence. There is nothing unusual in the fact that hierarchy figures in the style of an art; that of the most hierarchic society, Byzantium, is clearly reflected in the Byzantine style. What is unique here is the technical means which India employed to this end. Just as in the rapture of the festival the society recovers the unity lost through social division, so does the fresco artist of Ajantā unite the social hierarchy in tonal resonance.

The loveliest details at Ajantā explicitly refer to tactility—the hands—which blossom, entwine, lie limp, and uncurl. In the best portrayal of a *maithuna* couple, admired in reproduction by D. H. Lawrence for the delicacy with which the touching hands are shown, close inspection reveals that the the girl is *not* touching the man, while he, at the most, is touching her lightly with the tips of two fingers. The delicacy with which numerous Ajantā figures are brought into tactile contact is a striking endorsement of the primacy Indian culture gave to the tactile sense. Yet this same tactile sensitivity accounts for one of the most depressing customs which man has ever imposed on man—untouchability. Rules of touch and touch-me-not are not only imposed on the outcaste, but as we shall see in Part Three, feature in all intercaste relations. The poetic delicacy of art transmutes a restraint originating in pollution phobias into a celebration of tenderness. This fact emphasizes the caution which should be exercised in interpreting society through its art. In this case there is no contradiction, only a vivid example of art's capacity to invest the raw material of the life which nurtures it with a transfiguring grace. It should not, however, blind us to the facts of empirical reality. The will to good is frustrated in every human society because each society is itself less than perfect and, in consequence, its members are mutilated. The challenge this poses for the observer is to trace to their sources the causes of the kind of mutilations which Indian society inflicts.

Sanskrit drama and the art of fresco

In this section a comparison will be drawn between two media—fresco painting and Sanskrit drama—which flourished concurrently. The golden age of Sanskrit drama spans a period from roughly the second to the ninth centuries A.D.[1] While its origins are different from the art of the cave sanctuaries, both went into decline at the same time and for what appear to be the same reasons. Politically, India's ruling élite was going through a period of severe stress; it never recovered either the confidence or the cultural sophistication it had enjoyed in former times. But there were other forces at work too, and one of them was a resurgence of Hindu religiosity and Brahman assertiveness. The urbane wit and elegance which had provided the holistic sacred culture with its essential leaven during the classical period was stifled in the wholly different spiritual atmosphere of provincial feudalism and rusticity. Similarly, scholasticism, the punditry of the ever more firmly entrenched Brahman literati, dealt a blow to the old oral culture. Two sure signs of this were the appreciable coarsening of the plastic arts, and the dimming resonance of that synaesthesia which had pervaded the arts in the classical period.

Sanskrit drama was a literary refinement of the waning oral culture which had long invested the arts of ancient India with magisterial power. It amplified with words what was suggested in the visual imagery of the cave frescoes, in a period when courtly culture freely mixed together Hindu and Buddhist mythology. While less representative of Indian culture than, say, Ajantā, designed as it was for a specialist minority audience of urbane sophistication, the poetic drama shared certain traits in common with the art of fresco painting because both were refined products of a sensibility deriving from magico-orgiastic rites. Sanskrit plays, for example, were dedicated (in a wholly non-sectarian sense) to the orgiastic deity of rapture, Shiva, Lord of the Dance, god of creation and destruction; Shiva too was the principal deity to whom the Hindu caves were dedicated. The extreme importance given to the stylized trance and swoon in numerous Sanskrit plays (the swoon also figured in the themes of the Ajantā frescoes) indicates its ancient links with the rapture and possession of the seasonal

[1] Roughly five hundred plays have survived, of which no more than twenty or thirty are works of undisputed excellence; cf. Wells (1963), p. 82.

festival. In both cases total participation of the viewer was ensured by a skilful combination of sensory experience. The 'wrap-around' effect already noted in connection with the caves was conveyed on the stage by adapting the technically brilliant virtuosity of Vedic incantation and phonetic science to the needs of the world's most richly textured style of poetic drama. The affinities between the two media can be made more specific.

First, affinity in narrative structure: as we have seen, the 'continuous narrative' of the Ajantā frescoes is cyclical and non-sequential. Similarly, the dramatic structure of a Sanskrit play is cyclical—based on the themes of separation and reunion—it ends as it begins; various devices are used, such as the dream, the trance, the premonition, the flashback, to disrupt the linearity of time and make the action recoil upon itself. Both media rely on the theory of modal music and aesthetic rapture—*rasa*—to devise a sequence of movements, scenes, or acts which is cyclical, each one emphasizing a single aesthetic *mood* on the analogy of the musical *rāga*.

Secondly, affinity in spiritual outlook: it has been shown that the figures in the Ajantā frescoes appear to emerge from a mysterious, undifferentiated continuum and that their weightless buoyancy derives from a tension or poise between an unseen stillness and the *perpetuum mobile* of the action in which they participate. 'The basic theme', writes Henry Wells in his lively study of Sanskrit drama, to which I am much indebted, 'of all Indian drama is spiritual equilibrium, poise between opposites, rest and fulfilment at the centre of violent motion.'[1] Wells also points out that whereas Greek drama in its conclusion presents a 'dénouement', or untying of the knot, Sanskrit drama ends with a tying together of diverse threads[2] a consequence of the pervasive awareness of a harmony subsisting beneath contradictions. Such ethical conflict as there is (conflict between the sexes is never introduced) may be compared to the stylized symmetry of the tournament, the game, or ritualized gambling.[3]

Wells summarizes the cyclical and spiritual aspects of the Sanskrit play as follows:

The lost are found, the generations bound together; the stories echo the seasonal and cyclical myths. The contrasts resemble those in the procession of the year, a circular dance of months and days. The play is not a river ending in the sea, either in mystical union with God or in fulfilment of human ambition. Rather, it is a celebration of cosmic poise, a highly formal and unmistakably aesthetic projection of life idealistically conceived.[4]

[1] Wells, op. cit., p. 30.
[2] Ibid., p. 147.
[3] This is an important point which will become clearer in those sections of Parts Three and Four where the play principle is analysed.
[4] Ibid., p. 43.

Thirdly, affinity in vision-inducing technique: words and images are used to draw the viewer into a vortex of multiple perspective. Sanskrit drama is distinguished from the Greek, Chinese, Japanese, and Elizabethan by the almost excessive action-stopping employment of lyrically descriptive passages in which off-stage events, landscapes, dreams, visionary journeys, and flight are evoked solely by poetic incantation (the technique is not in any way comparable with that of the Greek Chorus). These passages, in which the resources of highly inflected Sanskrit are fully utilized, may be compared to the deliberate slowing down of the time-sense in the Ajantā frescoes. While these devices make the greatest demands on the viewer, they are effective because they do assure depth participation.

The vision-inducing technique is used most successfully in a way peculiar to Sanskrit drama by making the characters themselves comment on the action while it is actually happening. Sometimes a special commentator is employed to interpret imagined sights and stage journeys by words alone, and not by dramatic representation on stage. This running commentary, which rakes the action, or the imagined action, like a panning movie-camera, is fundamental to the conception of the drama. Among the most interesting examples of the technique are word-pictures to evoke the transporting qualities of *frescoes*, which are invisible to the audience, in a famous scene from *Rama's Later History* by Bhavabhūti. Elsewhere the favourite themes are storms, aerial views of India, battles, and, most extraordinary of all, a trance-like wandering through the halls of a sumptuous —but wholly invisible—palace, in Act Four of *The Little Clay Cart*. By poetic artifice and resonating sound the dramatist builds in the mind's eye a gliding, multiple-perspective vision of fantastic architectural structures. The technique recalls the riveting scene of Gloucester's attempted suicide from the imagined cliffs of Dover in *King Lear*.

But there is one vital difference from *King Lear*, however, and in contrasting Shakespeare's method with that of Sanskrit drama fresh insight into the Indian outlook on life is obtained. As Professor McLuhan has shown, Edgar's dizzyingly precise description of the imagined shore far below Dover Cliffs is the first piece of verbal three-dimensional perspective in any literature. This significant detail is an integral part of the dramatic structure of *King Lear*, where, McLuhan points out, 'Shakespeare explains minutely that the very principle of *action* is the splitting up of social operations and of the private sense of life into specialised segments'.[1] We may compare the riveting of the attention by one sense only, the eye, in the Dover cliffs scene—a form of hypnosis in linear sequence—with the multiple-perspective, zoom-lens sensation of being enveloped by imagined architecture in the palace scene from *The Little Clay Cart*. Here an appeal

[1] McLuhan (1964), p. 17.

is made to all the senses simultaneously. Again, this dramatic device may be seen as the verbal equivalent of the technique of the Ajantā frescoes.

Now, a multi-dimensional interplay of all the senses in a unified field, and human relations conceived as hierarchically interdependent parts of a unified whole, are linked phenomena. The Sanskrit dramatist and the Ajantā artist restore to specialized, hierarchical social segments the lost sense of unity. In *Lear* action splits; in Sanskrit drama and cave painting action unites. Actually, the dramatist scans life like a fresco as the action proceeds, commented upon by the protagonists themselves in the whispered tones of an inner, detached, witnessing consciousness. 'The entire text', Wells remarks of the climax in Act Four to Kālidāsa's *Shakuntalā*, 'is a reflection of itself, like an image mirrored in still water.'

It will become more apparent in Part Three how revealing this aesthetic faculty to express the social order is, for there it will be shown how the cohesion of a society hierarchically graded into interdependent castes is, in part, assured by its artists. The linguistic conventions of Sanskrit drama, complex almost to the point of excess, endorse the sociological context as well as the creative role of the artist as unifier: characters of exalted rank alone speak Sanskrit, the rest in the Prakrit, or vernacular appropriate to their status and occupation, and this 'reflects on the stage the caste system in society and even italicises it'.[1] Linguistic and social diversity is welded into an orchestrated pattern which, Wells believes, is rooted in choreographic and musical tradition.[2] In the Ajantā frescoes the hierarchical society is very minutely observed through gradations of scale, costume, and features. But the technical means employed to evoke the interdependence of castes is equally complex and is based on a form of rich chromaticism stressing inequality through contrasts in local colour and solidarity through equality of tone. In conclusion, it may be pointed out that an equivalent technique was used by the cave sculptors. 'The sculpture', says Élie Faure, mirroring the remark of Wells on *Shakuntalā*, 'remains drowned in its atmosphere of stone.' The cave sanctuary and the poetic drama were the most natural and organic media with which to express the simultaneous sensory awareness of an inward-looking, hierarchically interdependent, closed society.

[1] Wells, op. cit., p. 116.
[2] See pp. 276–7 for an analysis of structural similarities in Indian modal music, pp. 190–93 in the popular arts, and Part Four, Chapter One, in traditional systems of thought.

Chapter Four The Hindu Temple

The Brahman ascendancy

The use of the term 'medieval' in an Indian context is a controversial problem among historians.

> The term 'Mediaeval' to designate the historical periods after the fall of the Gupta Empire, is an extremely unfortunate one: first, because it invites comparison with the Mediaeval Period in the West, and secondly, because the word, in its European usages a synonym for the Middle Ages, implies an interregnum —between two moments of supreme cultural achievement, the Classical and the Renaissance. . . . It is rather the final and inevitable development out of the maturity of Gupta art. Perhaps the word 'Baroque' is more appropriate.[1]

While I partly agree with Professor Rowland's warning, I feel he has not taken into account the less visible, but none the less significant, links between the development of India during this period, and the overall historical trend which affected the entire intercontinental land-mass of Asia and its extreme western peninsula—Europe. Many aspects of Indian society in this period went through a process of natural evolution not so very dissimilar from that of the Middle East and Europe; natural, because these trends originated in ancient times, or arose out of the conditions then prevailing, when both continents shared many things in common, particularly the primary techniques of production. In religion also, medieval India, Byzantium, Islam, and medieval Europe shared much more in common than is often acknowledged. India was never entirely cut off from these cross-currents of history; even during periods of reduced contact, common human needs still led it in directions closely akin to those of Europe in more respects than that of 'feudalism'. Furthermore, with the advent of Islam, whose followers were to be found in both worlds, and who acted as culture-bearers between them, India was influenced by events and by ideas that touched Europe, or even originated in Europe, at a number of points.

In the period more generally termed 'medieval' in India, cave art reached its final peak with the excavation of Elephanta in the eighth century; by the ninth it was a spent force. In the last caves at Ellorā, a group of ninth-century Jain sanctuaries, the forms are already stiff and the life has gone out of them. Tactile plasticity was replaced by hieratic linearity. Except in

[1] Rowland, op. cit.

eastern India, Buddhism was on the wane and the mass devotional cults of the Hindu revival were sweeping across the sub-continent, to affect the whole course of India's artistic development. Shaṅkara's philosophy of 'illusionism' and 'non-action', and Rāmānuja's major role in the rise of the *bhakti* movement, encouraged an even greater sense of dependence on the supernatural than before. Following the Gupta era, during which the cave monasteries had received lavish patronage, the political framework disintegrated, notwithstanding the efforts of a remarkable monarch, Harsha, to reinforce it; there followed a social reorganization bearing close affinities with feudalism, in which the Brahmans, who dominated Indian educational institutions, played a cardinal role. Popular religious movements were fatalistic, while prestigious ascetic orders, influenced by Shaṅkara's interpretation of the *Bhagavad Gītā*, discouraged any concerted effort to launch a new economic and political drive for unity. Social organization became increasingly rigid, and the guilds, almost exclusively confined to the urban centres, bolstered their own power by using the caste system for their own ends, enforcing localization of all industries. The lure of a non-commodity-producing agrarian economy brought north India's period of buoyant expansion to a close. A disrupted political structure and indifference to the outside world made the north-west vulnerable to outside attack. The first determined wave of aggression came in the eleventh century from the Muslims, followed by wave after wave of well-organized bands of plunderers, against whose mobility Indian troops were no match. However, the conservative atmosphere of a closed feudal world did not extinguish the fires of creative energy, but redirected them to new fields of expression, originating in the then dynamic and more liberal cultural climate of peninsular India.

We will now examine several significant aspects of Hindu temple art, particularly changes in the treatment of space resulting from the different needs of the structural temple, the reflection of social rigidity in the temple imagery, and the stylistic evolution in increasingly elaborate surface ornamentation.

The caves had served the needs of monks and laymen in search of an ideal environment in which to practise meditation; but *bhakti* called for a wholly different kind of religious sanctuary. So there arose a new kind of public building: constructed temples, built not of wood, as they had been hitherto, but of stone, or of brick. This development of a temple architecture more appropriate to the religious sentiments and ceremonial needs of the time proceeded concurrently with the later phase of cave monasticism. Brahmanical religion had never died out during the Buddhist ascendancy, and when, finally, Hindu revivalism asserted itself, it did not come as a sudden uprush of popular sentiment, but was more an efflorescence which had been preparing for centuries. For example, the Epics, the Gītā, and the Purāṇas accomplished a synthesis of Brahmanism and popular non-Aryan cults in the same period as the flowering of Indian Buddhist art, while in places such as Bādāmi and Ellorā, Hindus excavated caves adjoining those of the Buddhists.

The earliest temple construction to have survived belongs to the Gupta period; the principal transitional work was a group of temples at Mahā-balipuram, for this stands halfway between pure rock-carved cave art and the free-standing medieval temple (Plates 15 and 27). Mahābalipuram, one of India's supreme sculptural masterpieces, and of exceptional stylistic purity, also represents the last phase in the nostalgia for origins. For the temples carved from the living rock are free-standing replicas of contemporary structures built of more rustic materials, in exactly the same way as were the *toranas* and *caityas* of early Buddhist art.

The most striking feature of the group is the telling and harmonious relation which a series of small temples and reliefs carved from boulders establish with their physical surroundings. Mahābalipuram was the capital of the Pallava kingdom, and its seaport. It is situated in flat, dun-coloured terrain relieved only by the green of rice-fields and sparse vegetation. The temples hug the ground because they were carved directly from a cluster of boulders. Their towers do not rise over the plain to assert their verticality. Their intimacy with the earth is further enhanced by their colour—the same as the sandy soil. Approaching the five *rathas*, stone pavilions or 'chariots', through the trees, it is easy to mistake them for one of the numerous small mud villages passed on the way. The forms of their carved roofs are derived from rustic vernacular architecture, and though much refined and ornamented, their humble 'toy-town' appearance is at first so palpable that one may be led to mistake them for the work of the local villagers. Here, at the moment in history when the closed village system was about to become universal throughout India, the earth-bound agrarian civilization of India is finally celebrated in a single unique monument. We are once more in the world of asymmetrical, intimate, fondled shapes of the Indian village, but this time the sleekly moulded forms are the product of the master *śilpin*'s chisel; the rustic prototype has been transformed by a sophisticated and refined sensibility.

The Mahābalipuram temples were carved for royal patrons, the Pallava court, and proved to be of seminal importance to the subsequent develop-ment of temple architecture in the new feudal society which developed in the twilight of the Gupta era. The elegant and attenuated figures with their tall crowns and cool, aristocratic aloofness stand within the firm boundaries of the rectangular frames of the niches they adorn. The lateral rhythms of the crowded Sānchī reliefs are held in check; the proportions of the divine figures, and their positioning within the structure, already show signs of being conceived on the lines of the mathematical formulae of iconography written down in the *śilpa śāstras*. A linear structure was born from the old matrix of enveloping volumes. There is buoyancy in the Pallava imagery, but the rich, ponderous fecundity of the Deccan cave figures and the sensuous pliancy of the northern Gupta figures have been pared down to a new refinement and angularity. It is this linear flattening and attenuation which heralds the beginning of a quite different historical phase, to become more and more decorative, accomplished, and finally even frenzied.

The cave sanctuary was an enclosed space to which all the monks had free access, and in which they could stand face to face with the cult symbol, whether a *dāgoba* or *liṅgā*. The organization of space was an integral aspect of monastic ceremonial. The spiritual relation of the brethren with the Buddha or deity is spatially expressed in the accessible central shrine. In the Buddhist *ćaityas* the worshippers are not isolated from the *dāgoba*, and only in the last caves, when Buddhism had become almost indistinguishable from Hindu devotional religion, is the image of the Buddha placed apart in a separate cell.

But in the case of the Brahmanical temples, the imagery gradually came to express a new religious concept—the remoteness of God: direct access to the deity was generally reserved for the officiating priest. It was considered necessary that the laity and the lower castes be kept at a distance from the most hallowed images. Since Hindu worship was not congregational, architects did not build open structures. Not until the enormous temple complex was evolved in south India in the later medieval phase was any large space made available for the laity in outer halls. These huge buildings were, in any case, more an agglomeration of individual shrines enclosed within a wall than integrated structures. There exists no plastic relation between the towers situated at the four points of the wall and the pavilions constructed piecemeal within this space to house a plurality of deities associated with their respective castes. The lack of unity reflects the caste divisions of society, not the communal solidarity linking its components, as in the cave sanctuaries. Although the unity of hierarchical interdependence between castes is brilliantly dramatized by the unified mass of an architecture based on the tower, or cluster of towers, in the nucleus from which every temple complex grew, their sprawling outgrowths bear witness to the fact that social solidarity was subject to increasing pluralistic stress. Agglomerations of cult shrines both in temple enclosures and in pilgrim cities provide us with precise diagrams of the indefinite extension of caste gradation to which the society was subject (Plate 42).

The devaluation of interior space was also the natural result of a mounting rigidity of the hierarchical social structure, dramatizing the ascendancy of the Brahmans. The interior of the structural temple was designed round a single focal point, usually a stele on which the cult deity was carved in high relief. There was no attempt to pierce the walls and introduce light into the shrine; on the contrary, every effort was made to keep the lighting as subdued as possible, so that the image of the deity could be artfully illuminated with lamps by the priest and his acolytes during the climax of the daily ceremony. When large halls were required, as a setting for sacred dance recitals, for example, they were filled with forests of intricately carved pillars.

From the eighth century onwards the arts became more hieratic, but at the same time manifested a continuing urge to break out into passionate and ecstatic affirmation. Worked in a less obdurate material than living rock, the sculptures became more polished and elegant, while the more malleable stone block permitted greater ease in handling, resulting in a coarsening of tactile values.

Now that the temple was constructed of slabs of stone, sculpture itself had to be modified to fit the new scheme. The imagery was split into numerous small units; rolling lateral rhythms disappeared, replaced by horizontal bands of figures arranged in a didactic sequence, which could be 'read' like the palm-leaf strips of a sacred text. An extremely rare document—a copy of the original plan and elevation of the Sun Temple at Konārak (thirteenth century A.D.), which was made from the architect's drawing about a century after its construction—reveals the connection with reading a palm-leaf text. The drawing is spread over about a dozen palm-leaf strips which must be laid out like the slats of a Venetian blind to 'read' the whole design. The horizontal bands of sculpture are accommodated to the depth of the palm leaves. This is a graphic example of the commanding influence which manuscript linearity had over the form and content of visual media. It is also an indication of the increasing ascendancy of the Brahman *pandit*, who, from now on, supervises the work of the *śilpin*.

Religious devotion, as distinct from monastic meditation, demanded imposing structures focusing the attention of the worshipper on a complicated mythology. Narrative reliefs were rarely carved in the medieval temples. Rhythms were built up from single units, usually hieratic deities interspersed with celestial figures and *maithuna* couples, assembled in dense friezes and ornamental borders. It was soon discovered that the more the sculptural decoration could be built up, and the more densely packed the figures, the more could the surface achieve a flowing or soaring ecstatic rhythm. The tower was the principal feature of the temple. By accumulating rows of figures endlessly repeated in stereotyped units piled one on top of the other, an extraordinary oneiric effect could be obtained (Plate 27). These towers were the combined expression of both religious and temporal power. Like the ziggurat and the pyramid, the temple tower became the emblem of a dominant ruling power or king, as well as the symbol of contact with the divine established by the king.

The temples often appear to be enormous chariots, either in a metaphorical sense or, as in the case of Konārak and Hampi, symbolic representations of them, contrived to proclaim the message of the popular salvation religions, but like the caste system into which society was by then strictly organized, the basic scheme is already internally fragmented. It is a supremely theatrical art, an immense *machine* put at the disposal of the gods for their intervention in the drama of a decadent play—where the *deus ex machina* is no more than a cumbersome, artificial device to conceal an incapacity for structural transformation of the society from within.[1] The mysteries are hallowed by all the devices of ecstasy. Efforts to maintain a state of exaltation among the worshippers lead to the glorification of the temple dance as the principal theme of the sculptural decoration. It is significant that one of the most important of the medieval artists' textbooks, the *Vishnudharmottaram*, refers to the need for knowledge of dancing. Rows of images are portrayed in the poses of the classical dance (in the course of time, becoming highly mannered and artificial in their portrayal of violent movement); the geometry of motion animates all surface decoration with pulsating rhythm. The ecstatic dance of religious possession gives formal shape to the law of internal and unarrested circulation, the life urge, irrepressible as the beating heart, the pounding blood.

Society was jointly controlled by an alliance of Brahman and Kshatrya, priest and king. Temple imagery often quite clearly reflects the tastes of the ruling military dynasties who financed their construction. In fact, the heavenly city of the gods which forms the overall theme of the temple imagery is modelled on life in the medieval court, with the deity dressed in royal regalia, surrounded by celestial attendants, musicians, and dancers,

---

[1] The association of the temple and the chariot is an interesting example of the interaction of classical and village India. The Vedic Aryan mythology of chariot-riding gods became a common feature of Hindu iconography (Vedic hymns ascribe symbolic significance to various parts of the chariot—e.g., time with the wheel). It was a custom, probably Neolithic in origin, to carry sacred village images in bullock carts during religious processions. Later, decorated processional carts, reserved for this purpose, came into use, and the connection between the cart and the chariot of the gods was made explicit. In a large number of temple cities and towns these carts were replaced by elaborately carved wooden chariots (many of which have been preserved and are still in use), often of colossal size, like the famous chariot of Jagannath at Puri (which gave us the word 'juggernaut'), in which the cult image of that name was taken out from the Jagannath temple in procession during festivals. It is also common to construct lightweight chariots for use during seasonal festivals, much as they were in medieval and Renaissance Europe, as mobile platforms on which people posed in the costume of sacred figures. The stone *rathas* of Mahābalipuram should also be included in this constellation of chariot iconography.

like the earthly patrons and their courtiers who endowed the Brahmans with land and funds.

A streak of irrepressible, anarchic naturalism was always breaking through Hindu temple art. The themes of the artisan sculptors arose from their closer daily relation with nature, while the master sculptors specialized in portraying the more abstract ideas of the priesthood. The professional and economic interests of the artisans coincided with the more extraverted physical activities sponsored by their royal patrons in their leisure hours: hunting, horsemanship, trials of physical prowess, erotic pastimes. In their decorative friezes, these artisans of low social status served their royal masters well, celebrating with unforced naturalism the sports and pastimes, processions and feasts they had observed from life.

The Temple of the Sun at Konārak is a magnificent example of the harmonious co-operation of sculptor, architect, and patron to conceive and execute a building which fused their several interests into a remarkable plastic unity. This work is really a single piece of sculpture fashioned on a gigantic scale, a monolithic mass enriched with a myriad sculptural details. As in all cases where artistic, social, and religious life are integral parts of a ritualistic culture, temple art reflects the desire to escape from the anguish of life in time. Though art and mysticism are complementary modes of expression, yoga and Indian temple sculptors shared a common obsession: acquisition of certain godlike qualities, the attributes of the demiurge— the ferocity, the inhuman ruthlessness of Shiva, for example. The yogi *masters* the body, the sculptor *masters* his materials by the use of yogic techniques of muscular co-ordination in order to portray the ideal yogic body. 'Time is vanquished,' as Malraux says, 'by the images that human hands created to defy it.'

Erotic art

Temple eroticism had a long evolution, which has been referred to in preceding sections, where it was shown to have derived from fertility cults. It was not a uniform phenomenon, but its innumerable variants share certain common features. It is virtually impossible to advance any claims of a theoretical nature which will make sense to those who have not actually visited the temples and seen how the *totality* of their imagery accords with a religious affirmation of life. We are more or less bound by the changes which have conditioned our ideas on society, religion, and sexuality, to assume a moralistic approach. We tend, however unconsciously, to judge this erotic art as *morally* good, or *morally* bad. But we can at least make a conscious effort to accept that there was once, a thousand years or more ago, an ecstatic *religion* in which the erotic occupied a central role, and was regarded as a valid means to attain religious salvation. Medieval Indian temple art asserts, in different terms, exactly what Nietzsche called the 'transvaluation of all values', the necessity of getting beyond good and evil, which in the last analysis is the transposition of monism into the language of form. That this attempt to transcend good and evil eventually leads, more often than not, to gross vulgarity or barbarism is a reflection on the society, not on its art.

The greater proportion of medieval temple sculpture is of an explicitly erotic character, and this is not limited only to the celebrated *maithuna* couples, but pervades most figurative imagery. The literary equivalent of this eroticism is not so much the Tantric texts as the *Gīta Govinda*—a passionate celebration of the love between Krishna and Rādhā—the celebrated erotic poem by Jayadeva, poet laureate of King Lakshamana Sena of Bengal in the late twelfth century.

The aim of all mystical eroticism is to create unity from duality. Krishna, like Dionysus, is a god of transgression, and his divinity is all the more numinous and potent because he rejects the rule of reason. His scandalous behaviour and folly as the trickster hero, his delirious dance with the *gopīs* (which comprise what is called Krishna-Līlā, Plate 39), which seem to the puritan mind to be no more than licentiousness disguised under a cloak of religiosity, actually deepened the power of his sacred charisma. Krishna is divine in proportion to his superiority as a great lover. Though religion has become associated with law, reason, and so-called moral propriety, this was not always so, nor, as we have seen, is it always the case in modern Hinduism, especially of the villages. In ancient times, worshippers were encouraged to commit excesses during festivals as the surest way to achieve *catharsis*, ecstasy, the purging climax of the orgiastic feast, the surmounting of duality.

According to the prevailing ideas of the ecstatic cults of the Indian Middle Ages a pure act of disinterested love could not be attained with the married partner, since this form of sexual union was associated with the birth of children. Transfiguring ecstasy was believed more easily attainable through adulterous, abnormal, or incestuous intercourse, an *'acte gratuit'* in which the least concern with utility is finally obliterated, time suspended, death overcome. For this reason it is not surprising to find what some would call 'unnatural acts' frequently portrayed on the erotic temple friezes.

The artistic quality of this Hindu erotic sculpture varies considerably; most of it is of the same level of artistic excellence as the minor decorative panels, and appears to have been executed by artisans of no more than average skill, relative to other work of the period. There are few pieces that achieve the same degree of excellence as we find in the finest works of monumental sculpture (Plate 17). The success with which images of explicit sexual delight serve the overall aesthetic mood of any given temple, depends on the degree to which the artists have brought erotic interest into harmony with other themes, such as the sacred dance and scenes from the Epics or the life of Krishna, and these, in turn, were also imbued with erotic overtones in performance.

What first strikes one at the temples of Khajurāho and Orissā is the suggestion of the reproductive process which is conveyed by the whole temple mass; towers loom from the forest thickets like the sporangia of some colossal organism. Sexual imagery in the details is only incidental to this more forceful overall impression. Even temples without *maithuna* couples give the same powerfully erotic impression. The insistent portrayal of genital activity is certainly not out of keeping with the general effect of ease and unforced gaiety.

The erotic imagery of Khajurāho is aristocratic, courtly, more tense than the relaxed style of Konārak. There is a certain aggressiveness in the waspy little Khajurāho nymphets; their highly stylized bodies conform to the mannered idiom of the whole, and are flexed like taut bows. The elongated slits of their half lowered eyes give a sting to their pert and darting glances. They fling themselves on their men with the quivering metallic ardour of insects. While some embrace their partners with hesitant eagerness, thrusting their triple-curved bodies from the deep niches into the sunlight, others shyly retreat into the shadows, faces tilted with *knowing* smiles. Theirs is a less than innocent appeal to our complicity, while they watch the scenes of passionate abandonment. They are all permanently arrested at the age between girlhood and maturity. In that period the age of consummation in marriage was very young. The medieval institution of child-marriage restored an adolescent conception of love to the very heart of the erotic life, as it did in medieval Europe. Nevertheless, Hindu eroticism supplies further evidence of popular preference for the biological and immediate, against the metaphysical and other-worldly, in a somewhat similar way to medieval Christianity, which replaced the abstract Holy Trinity with the biological warmth of the Holy Family in response to the emotional needs of the people; that the Brahmans were still more permissive to erotic life is a measure of the greater degree to which the physical always permeated Hindu religion.

In order to claim for Hindu erotic art a seriousness worthy of the pedant's attention, to justify its didactic respectability as part of a promotion campaign to advance the ideas of high philosophy, all kinds of pretentious claims have been made. In most cases, however, the significance of this imagery is no more weighty than the orgiastic scenes portrayed on Greek wine cups. Erotic art is also confused with erotology, and is treated as a kind of documentary manual of Indian sexual habits. But the lyrical or bawdy sensuality of these works should not be mistaken for a kind of medieval Masters-Johnson documentary on the human sexual response. The *maithuna* couples are *ideal* beings—in other words, projections of sexual fantasy. We should recall the Freudian theory that such art is an expression of *unsuccessful* fantasies. Freud thought that the artist is basically a man who cannot act out his fantasies and therefore falls back on fantasy projection.

The great orgiastic Hindu festivals (which still continue in modified form) and the medieval carnival of Europe, reflected a state of constant erotic tension. The difference was in the degree of clandestine concealment of erotica which resulted from this situation, more so in Europe than in India. The production of erotic art on a monumental scale was probably no greater in India than it had been in classical European antiquity. The real difference between the two medieval cultures here is that in Europe the 'Underground' aspect has left comparatively fewer traces of its existence; whereas in certain Indian kingdoms 'idealistic' cultures were more tolerant towards 'Underground' culture, which flourished at a high and conspicuous level, leaving substantial evidence of its vigorous life.

There is a well-known saying which reveals why the medieval Church took strenuous steps to see that this did not happen in Europe: '*Amor spiritualis facile labitur in nudum carnalem amorem*' (literally, 'spiritual love easily falls into sheer carnal love')—an indication of Christian hostility towards any orgiastic religiosity or 'passive' mysticism similar to the ecstatic cults of *bhakti* (Plates 39 and 55) which were actively encouraged in India on a mass scale. Christianity was always suspicious of any sign of 'passive' submission to the divine will in mystic union, since the soul's intoxication might blur the distinctions between good and evil. In India, ritualized eroticism and mystical union are two aspects of a single phenomenon—the attempt to transcend antinomies.

If *māyā*—'reality'—is taken literally as meaning 'illusion', all actions viewed in this light become morally ambiguous—'All is God' (see footnote on p. 368). No sharp distinction can then exist between the exalted detachment of the sage and the sensuality of the libertine. Hindu antinomianism is proclaimed by the *bhakti* saint Rāmprasād: 'Do as you wish. Who wants Nirvana!'[1]

[1] A number of writers on the subject of erotic art have tried to link it with the sixteenth-century Vaishnava-Sahajiyā cult and related Tantric heterodoxies. But according to Chaṇḍīdās, a Vaishnava poet affiliated to the Sahajiyā movement, ideal love between a man and a woman is the most difficult of all goals: 'To attain salvation through the love of woman, make your body like a dry stick—for he that pervades the universe seen of none, can only be found by one who knows the secret of love.' Whatever Chaṇḍīdās's secret was, and this he does not divulge, it is obvious that temple erotica have nothing to do with making the body like a dry stick (see pp. 389–90 and 405–07).

Nor was Hindu eroticism a private gesture in the manner of Romantic individualism. In fact it was the exact opposite: a blurring of self in the sexual embrace. This is remote from the Western ideal of 'romantic love' in personal relationships. The Western conception of romantic love could never have arisen without the Western conception of personality, which ultimately leads to the equally un-Indian concept of democratic equality of the sexes. The Eastern view of the Western love-relationship is neatly phrased by Malraux in the fictional dialogue of *The Temptation of the West*: 'To lose myself in [romantic love of] a woman it would be first necessary for me to believe in myself.'

From one point of view the weakness of medieval erotic art is its mystical quietism (if that term may be used here in a non-technical sense), and not its explicit portrayal of the sexual act. This lack of what Dr. Alex Comfort calls a 'hard core' is accompanied by a deep sense of *play*—a quality which is undoubtedly pleasing to contemporary taste and to be found, happily, in the best erotic imagery of Picasso and Miró. Dr. Comfort rightly insists, however, on the modern need

to accept unpleasant emotion as the final test of earnest. . . . I do not think . . . that a post-scientific culture, even if it is no longer compulsively activist, will ever be able to return to quietism, either mystical or hedonist, though it may accommodate some of the insights about organic form, non-meddling in observation and the like—Western biology already does so, but with an added dimension of objective intellect which has come to stay. Nor are we likely to be any less aware in the future of the Romantic conviction of struggle, even when it ceases completely to be a mere product of unconscious resentments. . . . Faced with Gautama's choice between suffering with experience and withdrawal without, we have chosen the first. Quietism offends our sense of human solidarity, and I will be surprised if that sense ever becomes less necessary with time.[1]

The sad (or is it only the patina of age which makes them look so?), tender figures on the walls of the Ajantā caves and Konārak temple belong to a world as remote from India's sexual puritanism today as the Greek gods from the modern West. One could well imagine an Ajantā princess speaking the very same words which Burckhardt made the Vatican Hermes say: 'You are astonished that I am so sad, I, one of the Olympians living in perpetual bliss and immortal joy? Indeed we possessed everything: glory, heavenly beauty, eternal youth, everlasting pleasure, and yet we were not happy. . . . We lived only for ourselves and inflicted suffering on all others. . . . We were not good, and hence we had to perish.'[2]

[1] Alex Comfort, *Darwin and the Naked Lady*, Routledge & Kegan Paul, London, 1961, p. 162.
[2] Trans. in Erich Heller, *The Disinherited Mind*, Penguin Books, Harmondsworth, 1961, p. 77.

Chapter Five Twilight of the Gods

India's aesthetic problem in the late Middle Ages may be reduced to a single issue. Once the artist no longer served the compact and relatively small religious fraternities, he had to embody in formal language the values of a more complex society with multiple relationships and ethical contradictions (during the medieval period the society had absorbed waves of northern immigration from the Kushāṇas and Hūṇas to the Gurjaras). The pluralistic society of India could no longer be represented in terms of a homogeneous Hindu myth, and its religious rapture gradually lost its primary function of a socially cohesive force. To break through the forms of archaicism, the society would have had to make a massive and concerted effort on a scale comparable to that which galvanized Europe in the days of Dante, Petrarch, and the rise of capitalism in the Italian city-states. The fostering of popular magico-ecstatic cults by the Hindus, which gave the medieval efflorescence its unique character, could hardly have resulted in the kind of socio-economic change and intellectual ferment that took place in the late European Middle Ages.

Though the early Muslims borrowed many valuable ideas from Hindu mathematics, once the momentum had gone out of Indian science, the westward flow of ideas from India came to an end. The first intellectual and political drive of Islam—Arab and Persian—had also petered out by the time waves of military adventurers poured into India in the eleventh century (the first Arab military action occurred in Sind in A.D. 712, the same year as they landed in Spain, but its effects were confined to a small area). The Islamic catalyst, fruitful though it briefly proved in Europe, and then only to a limited extent, failed for a number of reasons as an agent of radical renewal and change on Indian soil until a new level of stability was reached in the Moghul period. In this section we will briefly examine the new phase of Indian history which was to have important effects on the evolution of the country towards a modern state; the partial cultural synthesis it achieved and its failure to transform the traditional socio-economic system will be assessed.

The Muslim period

The brunt of the Muslim invasions was borne by the north-western Indian kingdoms, ruled by Rājputs, feudal dynasties of Kshatrya clans who were themselves descended from the Hūṇas and other Central Asian tribes. They were a haughty and aristocratic class, brought up from boyhood to enjoy the arts of war, hunting, and hawking; they were extremely brave and evolved a code of chivalry similar to that of the European knights. 'The Rājput chieftains were imbued with all the kindred virtues of the Western cavalier, but were far superior in mental attainments' (Tod). For all their valour, they wasted their energies on endless internecine quarrels instead of forming some sort of confederacy against the common enemy. Their rule was basically unstable, primarily because Hindu social organization isolated them from the rest of the community. Only Kshatryas were trained in arms; the other castes consequently did not develop a strong nationalistic solidarity. Further, the Hindu indifference to history, and belief in the innate superiority of their God-given social order, blinded them to the reality of the great power which had grown up on their western flank.

The closed society of India did not foster an adventurous military outlook. While the Rājputs were second to none in sheer courage, their military tactics were outmoded. They did not breed their own horses, but were content to import them from Arabia and Persia; their infantry was an undisciplined rabble, and like the armies who had engaged in battle with the forces of Alexander, they placed too much faith in the invincibility of their war elephants, which proved worse than useless against the mobile, well-trained Muslim cavalry. The same pattern had been repeated every time more predatory and mobile invaders swept into India from the West; it was the case in Aryan times, and it continued until the arrival of the European colonialists, a striking example of the consequences to which a civilization deficient in a sense of history is subject. The sedentary indigenes, for all their bravery, proved no match against a quicker, more ruthless foe, although the Rājputs proved, by sheer obstinacy and extreme valour, to be the toughest in resistance. Babur, Moghul conqueror of Hindustan, said they 'knew how to die but did not know how to fight'. Throughout Muslim rule the Rājputs continued to rebel, but northern India never presented a united front against the invader and this was the undoing of the Hindu kingdoms from the tenth century to the eighteenth.

The Muslims, on the other hand, belonged to a vast power system which occupied the entire Near and Middle East, north Africa, parts of southern Europe, and later virtually the whole of southern Asia. Their horizons were broader, expansionist, and supranational; inspired by the ideal of a universal state, they were prepared to take practical steps and specific military action to advance their ends. The political organization of Islam was infinitely superior to anything seen on Indian soil for many centuries, and when stable rule was eventually established by the Moghuls, the Indians themselves took pride in safeguarding their affiliations with the larger Islamic parent society.

Many of the Muslim rulers were soldiers of fortune who had risen from the ranks; they were quixotic, ruthless, often psychotic, extraordinarily learned, highly cultivated in their tastes—in fact they had the outlook of the *conquistador* or *condottiere*. They did not mingle with the conquered until late in their domination of India; close contact with the Hindu way of life was mostly confined to the sexual plane. They remained apart, aspiring to direct the subject people, their obstinate proselytism maintaining between them and in themselves an atmosphere of combat that forbade them to rest. Everything they created on Indian soil, in comparison with Hindu culture, was melancholic, evanescent, arrogant, romantic; it was too often exquisitely, magnificently, sumptuously useless. For all that, and in this lies the strength and weakness of their creations, they *beautified* India.

Babur—the 'Tiger'—founder of the Moghul dynasty, was born in 1494, a Barlas Turk descended from both Genghiz Khan and Timur (Tamburlaine). The word *Moghul* has the same meaning as *Mongol*, and was originally used to denote the pagan hordes of Genghiz Khan, but it was applied loosely in India to all Muslims from Central Asia. The Moghul dynasty was also known as the House of Timur—the Timurids. The greatest of the emperors was Akbar (1556–1605), a man of immense appeal; melancholic, fearless, of intensely inquiring mind, he was ruthless in war, and though illiterate, deeply interested in religion, philosophy, and the mechanical sciences, had a great love of beauty and a wider vision of welding India into a new pluralistic unity. He set up the greatest administrative structure since Ashoka, from which all subsequent political unity in India ultimately derives. He made the people of the country aware that a central administration had become an indispensable condition of social existence. 'Although I am master of so vast a kingdom,' Akbar wrote in his memoirs, 'yet, since true greatness consists in doing the will of God, my mind is not at ease in this diversity of sects and creeds, and apart from the outward pomp of circumstance, with what satisfaction in my despondency can I undertake the sway of Empire?' According to Akbar's devoted biographer and historian, Abu'l Fazl,

From early childhood he had passed through the most diverse phases of religious practices and beliefs and had collected with a peculiar talent in selection all books that can teach, and thus there gradually grew in his mind the conviction that there were sensible men in all religions, and austere thinkers and men with miraculous gifts in all nations. If some truth were thus found everywhere, why should Truth be restricted to one religion or to a comparatively new creed like Islam, scarcely a thousand years old?[1]

One cannot but conclude that this foreigner, Akbar, surrounded by that 'diversity of sects and creeds', was one of many who succumbed to the theosophical religious dilettantism which has since become so much a feature of the Indian religious scene to which foreigners have access.

Akbar was prone to strange spiritual crises. After one of these he decided to create a new eclectic religion, the Din-i-Illahi, which would synthesize the best elements in the Islamic, Hindu, and Christian faiths: to

prescribe for the whole empire gods, ceremonies, sacrifices, mysteries, rules, solemnities, and whatever was required to constitute one perfect religion. . . . We ought therefore to bring them all into one, but in such a fashion that they should be both 'one and all'; with the great advantage of not losing what is good in one religion, while gaining what is even better in another. In this way honour would be rendered to God, peace would be given to the peoples, and security to the empire.[2]

The principal creative achievement of the Muslim period did, without conscious intent, further these aims; it took the form of co-operation, in an impressive quantity of Muslim building, between two highly dissimilar schools of architecture: the indigenous and the Islamic. In the pattern of all Islamic cultural expansion, the Turco-Afghans brought with them ideas they had learnt elsewhere—in this case the arch, the dome, and the minaret—but heavily relied on the indigenous skills of the subject peoples; hence the style of the Hindu master-builders is plainly visible in all the local variants of Islamic architecture. This was bound to happen when an architecture of structure confronted an architecture of mass. Compared to the great periods of Persian architecture, Muslim work in India is provincial and lacks crystalline purity of line. The refined geometry is replaced by something more ponderous, somnolent. In the early centuries, much of the work bears the imprint of grim and forbidding tyrant conquerors. The forts, mausoleums, and towers of victory testify to ruthless military prowess.

Two factors are of cardinal importance in the creation of this Indo-Muslim architecture: first, the Muslim conquerors did not *like* India; as a result, their conception of architecture did not wholly suit Indian conditions. Secondly, these highly mobile cavalrymen and idol-smashers came from dry mountainous or desert uplands to plunder the riches of the idolatrous and sedentary heathen in the humid, steaming jungles.

[1] Abul Fazl, *Ain-i-Akbari*, Blochmann and Jarrett, Calcutta, 1875–91.
[2] Ibid.

But while the confrontation between two virtually incompatible religious systems led to implacable mutual hatred between their respective followers, on the other hand the dictates of a craft, wrestling with recalcitrant materials, brought the two systems together on more organic terms. The Muslim interdiction upon the expression of the living form, the human image, was partly circumvented in the torrid imagistic climate of India by allowing calligraphic and geometrical decoration to fill out with the sap of tropical creepers and cover the walls of mosques with jungles of luxuriant decoration. The arabesque was tropicalized; through the added technical repertoire of the Muslims the web of oneiric Hindu geometry became a new visionary celebration. The result was something unique, very Indian, and impressive in a grave, melancholic, romantic way. How very different are the results of the transplantation to European soil of Islamic architecture—the structurally graceful Moorish tower of Seville and the great mosque at Cordoba, for example—in comparison with the structurally ponderous Kutb Minar and the Muwwat-ul-Islam built in the earliest Indo-Islamic period. These already seem to have assimilated India's tropical sensuousness and love of monolithic sculpted mass. And what else does the Gol Gumbāz, a vast tomb at Bijāpūr with one of the largest domes in the world, suggest but the great bulb of Sānchī *stūpa* hollowed out and raised on a huge masonry cube! Even the Taj Mahal, the purest expression of Islamic architecture in India, rises from the mist of the Jamuna like a pearly mirage. Are we not urged to view it by moonlight—when its profile is softened and veiled? The interior of the Taj is a denial of the airy Islamic space and purity of line which we associate with the great mosques of the desert countries; it evokes the numinous half-light of a cave sumptuously fretted with patterned marble foliage.

The most subtle achievement of the Indo-Muslim period, Akbar's own creation, the city of Fatehpur Sikri, is an excellent illustration of this assimilative power. As capital of the Moghul Empire, it was the administrative hub of a vast state. And this its plan dramatized in a manner which must have had an unforgettable impact on all who visited it when Akbar was in residence. At the very centre was located an original variation of the *axis mundi* symbol—the huge pillar of the Emperor's Hall of Private Audience, on top of which Akbar himself sat enthroned (Plate 49). Here one catches echoes of the ancient Indo-Iranian concept of an *imperium* and its effective symbolic propagation by the edict-writing Mauryan, Ashoka. But this is the only occasion where axial symmetry is employed. Surrounding this axis were some of the most structurally elegant, airy, open courts and pavilions ever built by Indians (Plate 28). Mass is replaced by space, closed forms by open forms, an interesting case of traditional modalities being employed to different effect to suit a new scale of values.

The special merit of these buildings is to create a mood of relaxation like that induced by the cave sanctuaries, though not derived from the same order of plasticity. The source of this feeling is perceptively analysed by Jacqueline Tyrwhitt:

Most of the buildings . . . are themselves symmetrical in their design, but their *spatial setting* is never axial. While it is clear at first glance that this is an ordered composition, one looks in vain for the key to it in terms of Western academic art . . . nowhere is there a fixed centre: nowhere a point from which the observer can dominate the whole. . . . From the moment he steps within this urban core he becomes an intimate part of the scene, which does not impose itself upon him, but discloses itself gradually to him, at his own pace and according to his own pleasure. (Italics mine.)[1]

The tyranny of the single viewpoint, vanishing point, and 'vista' are replaced by space frames which establish a panoramic field of vision moving slowly through some 60 or 90 degrees. This is the conceptual antithesis of a static and closed universe. The 'zoom-lens' effect, mentioned earlier, is no longer the mode of probing inner space but an outward exploration. Miss Tyrwhitt also describes a seemingly solid background wall of stone which is later perceived as a *transparent* screen. This use of the pierced *jali* wall is an ingenious adoption of the traditional oneiric surface decoration to serve a wholly different end (Plate 23).

This was the city built by the most enlightened ruler of India since ancient times; it perfectly expressed the open society Akbar longed to create—though he never achieved this dream—and for which he sought concrete visual demonstration. Fatehpur Sikri was a tragic political failure, but its failure has nothing to do with its architecture, which remains the most perfect plastic expression of the liberal society which every great Indian ruler has vainly striven to realize.

Rājput culture, and that of other independent Hindu kingdoms elsewhere in India, benefited from the new Islamic influence. The Rājputs were great builders of palaces, irrigation works, bathing-places, reservoirs, and hunting lodges. Their genius was particularly well displayed in the construction of vast and impregnable fortresses crowning rocky hilltops of their arid region. The forts of Man Singh at Gwalior, Chitor, Ranthambor, and the palaces of Amber, Jaisalmer, Jodhpur, and Udaipur, are some of the most magnificent of their kind in the world.

The most revealing case-history of a Rājput king caught between the two

---

[1] J. Tyrwhitt, 'The Moving Eye', in *Explorations in Communication*, ed. E. Carpenter and M. McLuhan, Beacon Press, Boston, 1960, p. 90. There is no contradiction between the axial symbolism within the Hall of Private Audience and its absence from the spatial planning of the various buildings. For the Hall is indeed *private*—an enclosed space bounded by its own walls, which confine the axial plan to the interior.

worlds, old and new, was that of Jai Singh, the eighteenth-century ruler of Jaipur and an ally of the Moghul emperor. Jai Singh abandoned the outmoded fortress of Amber to build the pink city of Jaipur from scratch. He collected Sanskrit pandits from different parts of India and set up institutions expressly to restore classical Hindu learning to its original purity (some of these institutions still exist). His pandits also scoured the ancient texts for lore relating to town planning. Jai Singh then proceeded to build his new city on a rectangular grid, rigidly laid out, with broad avenues dividing the different parts into cosmographical sections as the Mauryans did, and the Harappans too. In addition he had obtained, probably from Jesuits, some idea of the plans of Versailles, conceived by a European Sun King, for whom it appears that he, a 'descendant of the Sun', felt a certain kindred feeling. Not content merely to restore the ancient unity which had never quite faded from the Hindu memory, Jai Singh had five magnificent observatories constructed to his own specifications in order to *rectify* the errors in the old Sanskrit tables. He himself personally supervised the design of these graceful instruments in the same way that, two centuries earlier, Tycho Brahe had designed the Uraniberg on the island of Hveen in the Danish Sund. Jai Singh likewise became a meticulous and conscientious astronomer, measuring the movement of the stars and planets with remarkable accuracy. Yet Jai Singh was not, as has been maintained, the first modern scientist in India, nor a forward-looking astronomer like Kepler or Galileo. Born after the invention of the optical telescope, his were the last of the 'stone age' observatories, beautiful as works of art though they were, astonishing in the inventiveness of their strange design, and even more accurate in basic measurement than their fifteenth-century predecessors at Samarkand. Like Akbar, who was insatiably curious about mechanical devices and who played polo in the dark with an ignited ball of his own invention, Jai Singh was a typical example of the traditional Indian empiricist—inventor for his immediate needs, but incapable of a consistent sequential rationality transcending the necessities of the moment.

The Rājput courts were also great centres of literature, drama, poetry, and art, and the strength of this culture lay in the constant nurture of its roots by the folklore of the region. It is no accident that Rājput, Moghul, Persian, and medieval Christian painting all favoured the miniature (Plates 34, 39, 46, 47, and 50–56), the illuminated manuscript, and the ideal representation of the *hortus occlusus*, the enclosed paradise garden. Muslim artists had a considerable influence on the development of this exquisite minor art in Europe through contact with Spain and southern France. The *hortus occlusus*, with its flowers and idyllically costumed, legendary occupants rendered in bright, clear colours, shows harmony with a small part of nature, a serene refuge isolated and detached from the larger menacing background of untamed and dangerous forests (Frontispiece). Another minor art form, the Rāgamāla paintings, symbolized and illustrated the modal music of the classical court singers and instrumentalists. This was a serial art, exquisite forerunner of the strip-cartoon, each picture serving to represent a single aesthetic emotion, or *rasa*, in response to the changes in seasons, the infinite quest of love, and different moods of day and night (Plate 55).

Synaesthesia in the modern world

A price had to be paid in India for many centuries for the artificial prolonging, under the Muslims, of the entrancing pleasures of visionary delight. It is a tragic fact that the debts, both financial and psychological, of the Moghul empire in its declining years of wasteful extravagance, were incurred at compound interest, and have never been paid. The life of prodigal luxury enjoyed by autocratic rulers and the conspicuous consumption of aristocratic élites at the expense of the productive classes are with us still in the India of the mid-twentieth century. The form has changed but the attitude endures.[1]

Indian society not only failed to generate fresh energy in any corporate sense, but it also hindered the emergence of a personal quest which could have thrown up leaders to challenge and stimulate. The sense of community, which had been India's greatest strength, did not preserve the inner well-being which sustains and renews vitality. Though unchecked individualism has been the cause of some of Europe's deepest troubles particularly since the Renaissance, its absence has equally been responsible for Asia's dormancy during centuries of Western achievement. As Malraux has pointed

---

[1] The artificiality of the Muslim courtly life-style may be said to be one of degree. It was the scale of the luxurious way of life and the degree to which this was conducted apart from the people which were artificial, taken in combination with the ruinous fiscal policies of the post-Akbar period. Such conspicuous consumption is not without precedent among the feudal courts of the Hindu kingdoms, but with one vital difference —an integral part of the caste society's cultural life had always been the participation in, and enjoyment of, ecstatic religious festivals by the productive classes at village level. From the descriptions written by European travellers who visited the Moghul courts, it appears that the mass of the north Indian population suffered a great deal from the expropriation of their production to defray the expenses of the courts and their costly internecine wars. The institutional checks of the Hindu system, such as were built into the *jajmānī* system (to be examined in Part Three), did not prevent exploitation, but they certainly ensured a broad-based cultural celebration among the masses, which the Muslim courts, foreign as they were in origin, were less in a position to achieve. India has not been alone in displaying, from time to time, indifference to poverty, but the socio-political system of the Indo-Muslim period revealed the dangers of severing cultural life from the masses.

out, 'for three hundred years, the world has not produced a single work of art comparable with the supreme works of the West. What is challenged in our culture is challenged by the *past* of other cultures.'

The art of India had something vital to say as long as its purpose was to restore lost unity to men, to guide the individual with his sense of insecurity and anguish in time, within an enhanced collective life. In a restricted environment, or within the protective shell of caste, this restoration was effective (see above, pp. 19–21). But the problems of a disintegrating political structure, and the divisive tendencies inherent in the caste system, afflicted India for many centuries. A highly complex and multi-racial society had for too long sought to maintain unity on a substructure of myth. An all-embracing consciousness could not develop so long as the mythic substructure was not replaced by a firm sense of history.

We have seen how India's consistent, sometimes fearless, ascetic-orgiastic exploration of the non-rational realms of consciousness led to the creation of a profound sense of organic order in the field of plastic form and structure; this order was quite different from the Euclidean harmony of the West. We have also seen how this frequently led to the artificial inducement of ecstasy when the stability or health of the society was seriously threatened. Beyond a certain point such techniques are incapable of further development, and lead only to confusion, morbidity, or madness. Yet while India remained in a state of equilibrium and health, the intuitive, aesthetic sense of order nurtured a subtle and life-fulfilling culture.

At the moment when the West has reached the apogee of the individualist experiment in creative modes of expression, and seems to have embarked on a re-discovery of social, collective organization, not only has the non-individualistic art of the East aroused new and widespread occidental respect, but Western individualism is being seriously re-examined; this is reflected in the Western art of our time. The aesthetic philosophy of the modern West has, in fact, brought us closer to the cultures of Asia.

The modern Indian artist, antithesis of the *śilpin* by reason of the individual stance he has adopted as an integral consequence of westernization and modernization (which will be analysed in Parts Three and Four), watches this process with dismay from the sidelines to which the historical situation has relegated him. For him individualism is an incompleted development which he had embarked on with reluctance; already he shows signs of abandoning it. From his angle of vision as a forward-looking individual, the radical re-orientation of Western culture towards simultaneous sensory awareness and synaesthesia, which is happening almost without the participants' awareness of the direction in which it is leading, has an uncanny element of *déjà vu*, of something which is infinitely fascinating, but which—*in the Indian context*—is fraught with reactionary associations. What for a Western artist is a progressive movement forward is, to an Indian artist, a retrogressive movement backwards. But as a *social* being who feels alienated by his tentative, and in origin *Western*, individualism from the web of a traditional order, he is tempted to take the plunge and follow his Western peers. It is still too soon for him to realize that, like every Western artist, he too is a *primitive* confronting a situation without precedent and that no one knows exactly what the role of the individual in an electronic age will be. The technological culture-lag of a developing nation like India places it in communication with global trends, subjects its artists to the psychological pressures which are the consequence of those trends, but does not yet allow the technological environment which sustains the new type of creativity emerging in the West.

Once the modern artist made art its own absolute, the act of creation constituting its own value, it ceased to serve religion, but became a faith. The logical end of such an attitude is to turn creativity into something very close to a mystical activity. This is what has happened in the work of a surprisingly large number of modern artists; for example Monet, Redon, Bonnard, Rouault, Kandinsky, Brancusi, Chagall, Miró, Klee, Ernst, Matta, Tobey, the Surrealists, the abstract expressionists, and Minimal Art. A certain kind of art has *numen* without being *sacred*; it is emotive without being 'true'. It transports the viewer to the mind's antipodes, and it does this in ways which, in some respects, recall the visionary techniques and the oneiric patterned structures of Indian and other Asian art. We have already referred to the autonomy of the cave world as an expression of the autonomy of certain spiritual states (see above, pp. 41–2). Modern art affirms the autonomy of painting, often borrowing from the terminology of yoga and Zen Buddhism for a supporting theory. Modern expressionism has eliminated man, except for the projection of inward states through gesture and tactile values. Everywhere in the best new painting, films, plays, and music, we see the artist trying to break out of the strait-jacket of rationalism, to unite the media in new forms of synaesthesia, to break down the sequential time-scheme and create a new wrap-around environment.

Cézanne once wrote: 'We are a shimmering chaos. I come in front of my theme, I lose myself in it. Nature speaks to everyone. Alas, Landscape has never been painted. Man ought not to be present, but completely absorbed into the landscape. The great Buddhist invention, Nirvana, solace without passion, without anecdotes, colours!' (see the descriptive passage on the shimmering rock surface of caves, p. 43 and n.). D. H. Lawrence, propounding a more extreme form of aesthetic vitalism, made Paul Morel say: 'Only this shimmeriness is the real living. The shape is a dead crust.' This has always been the Eastern approach. In his Indian tale, *The Transposed Heads*, Thomas Mann described the paintings and sculptures in a Hindu temple as like an 'all-encompassing labyrinthine flux of the animal, human and divine'. Carved out of rock were

visions of life in the flesh, all jumbled together, just as life is, out of skin and bones, marrow and sinews, sperm and sweat and tears and ropy rheum, filth and urine and gall; thick with passions, anger, lust, envy, and despair; lovers' partings and bonds unloved; with hunger and thirst, old age, sorrow and death; all this for ever fed by the sweet, hot streaming blood-stream, suffering and enjoying in a thousand shapes, teeming, devouring, turning into one another.[1]

As Yeats says, the peculiar heroism of modern artists is chiefly manifested in their unflinching attentiveness to the world's and the self's chaos as revealed to them by the contents of their own minds. The first man to show this kind of attentiveness was Leonardo da Vinci, and the gap of centuries does not alter the fact that he has a profound affinity with the visionary artists of our own time. A man of profound, almost morbid pessimism and deep insight into man's yearning for self-annihilation in nature, he would have understood the dilemma of the modern artist. His own confidence in the Renaissance idea of the rationality of nature was dissolved by the urge to self-destruction which he found at the heart of nature. 'The hope and desire,' he wrote, 'of returning to the first state of chaos is like [that of] the moth to the light.'

The Indian artists of today have unconsciously absorbed from their own traditions a similar aesthetic preoccupation with the dark and obscure reaches of the mind. But because the traditional culture no longer sustains and supports them, they have fallen into the romantic error of the modern occidental artist—they yearn for absorption in the forms of nature, a yearning to lose identity arising from a hesitant sense of individual identity at a stage of transition to a modern culture pattern. In the almost insuperably difficult task of creating a new art form, the modern Indian artists too, like their forebears, have a compulsion to seek inspiration in the state of induced ecstasy, of being 'beside oneself' in the 'other mind', the *anya manas*, as if the act of creation were a violent reaction to the detested rationality.

They lack a vocabulary of change. That power of aesthetic enthusiasm to disclose universal truth, born within a unitary culture now vanished, leads, in the individual artist of today, to little more than vaporous abstractions and picturesque romanticism. It survives with vigour only in India's classical music, and to a lesser extent in the rhythm of the classical dance. Nowhere does one find the unmistakably authentic Indian spirit as truthfully expressed as in modern India's most *distinctive* artistic achievement—music—because, of all the arts, it is most completely itself, irreduceably symbolic; and, because it has nothing to do with literal description of 'reality', it is classical

[1] Thomas Mann, *Stories of a Lifetime*, Martin Secker and Warburg, London, 1961, Vol. 2, p. 240.

music alone which can remain traditional, and live on its past, without at the same time being subject to the decadence of the rest of the cultural pattern.

Indian pop music, on the other hand, has not yet reached the stage of mass *participation* as it has done in Europe and America. On the contrary, while it pervades the lives of the Indian masses as does no other form of entertainment, it remains a dreamy music which summons them into a far-away world of unreal passions and substitute gratification. Here is a people sick at heart and full of music, but distracted from the human predicament by the highly organized mass media. The pop arts of India merely block individuation, alienate people from personal experience, and intensify their moral isolation from each other, from reality, and from themselves. The ground for the diffusion of the mass media had been effectively prepared through centuries of assiduously cultivated voluptuousness in the arts of public entertainment. There is no escape from the raucous noise blaring from loudspeakers, cafés, cinemas, wedding shamianas, radios, in a desperate attempt to drown the insistent sound of despair, frustration, misery, to dissolve in the shimmering, reverberating waves of the all-embracing flux.

The Indian aesthetic sensibility was once the primary means to create a civilization. Some of the most advanced Western thinking of our day is devoted to the problem of reconciling the aesthetic with the scientific, while overcoming the disastrous effects of having allowed bourgeois aesthetic culture to have become implicated in modern fascism. There is every hope that India may play a positive role in this reconciliation.

The message of the partial Indo-Muslim synthesis is a stern challenge: nostalgia is inadequate if unaccompanied by rigorous, far-reaching reassessment which alone can provide an organic creative renewal. India's is a sensuous culture, and the new configurations mapped out through the plastic arts have always had a powerful, formative influence on the quality of life. Order, balance, and rhythmic sequence have a much more direct and important role to play in the creation of a culture than is generally supposed. They are the tools, to be precise, with which to *make* order, reveal connections. Here the Indian aesthetic sensibility can meet on common ground with Western science to bring logic out of the complex, illogical, and contradictory living process. Powerful, immediate sensory images supply that model of relatedness which India most urgently needs.

As a source of inspiration and of psychic or cultural renewal today, the art of India's past plays a peculiarly maternal role. The very violence with which young Indians repudiate the stifling embrace of the past indicates the true nature of the tension. Indian mythology, symbolism, and art are replete with tales of heroes slaying the demon-witch or wrestling with the spectre in the flying corpse (cf. Zimmer, 1968). Much of that heritage was devoted to the representation of the unconscious, of night, darkness, death, and rebirth; to come to terms with it today demands exceptional heroism. Yet young India will have to grapple with it, or the present fixation will continue to sap the will and haunt the timorous like a feared and unappeasable Medusa. It was in the mirror of his shield that Perseus faced his destiny.

Part Two The Family System

Introduction

Any picture of Indian civilization obtained from an examination of works of art alone must be incomplete, and too favourable. An attempt to correct this is made in Parts Two and Three by a study of India's endeavours to create a holistic social order. The causes of stagnation, fragmentation, and recent change in Indian society, and the role played by psychological and economic factors in its development, will be analysed in the following order: in Part Two, the structure of the family system; genetic development and personality formation; and recent changes in the traditional family system. In Part Three attention shifts from the family to the social system of which it is a part. While reference to the social structure will inevitably be made in dealing with the family, explanation of such institutions as caste must be deferred till their detailed examination in Part Three.

No attempt will be made to trace origins diachronically, either in the family system or in the social matrix, because these are buried in the complex historical interaction of the two systems and can only be viewed synchronically. What is important is not whether child-care helps to explain aspects of social behaviour or vice versa—both are inextricably meshed together—but that the analysis refers to the roots of a situation here and now. Between the critical factors, familial and social, there is indeed a very close resemblance precisely because of their mutual influence. A large proportion of the data refers to the traditional pattern, but this does not mean necessarily the historical past, for the overwhelming majority of Indians (say 70 per cent at a *minimum* in a population of over 500 million) are still tradition-directed; moreover, changes cannot be understood in the crucial area of the minority who are subject to modernization without reference to that tradition. 'Tradition' in this study will perhaps be more applicable to pre-industrial India in a non-historical sense, i.e. the India which continues to be either unaffected or only marginally affected by industrialization. Even if we were to set a date for the earliest moment when pre-industrial India was affected by the global upheavals which have been the primary determinants of Western-type change in the last four centuries, we cannot place it farther back than the mid-nineteenth century; modern Western-type technology did not begin to effect structural changes in the society until the end of the nineteenth century. Prior to that date the Industrial Revolution, while it had a severely disruptive effect on the socio-economic condition of large regional belts, made no impression on the structure and value systems of the traditional Indian society. Roughly 400 million people are still living under pre-industrial conditions. More precise analysis of the covert change in attitudes of these masses, too early yet to have wrought structural change in familial, social, and political organization, will be given at the end of Part Three. No attempt is made here to demarcate the frontiers between tradition and modernity.

It is not my intention to treat such hypothetical constructions as 'modal personality'. Social, cultural, and psychological 'inconsistencies' are too frequent in a pluralistic society consisting of 500 million people to attempt so ambitious—and probably misguided—a project. The analysis of the family system will therefore be exploratory, incomplete, and open. We still lack scientific confirmation, quantification, and experimental verification in this field, while the attribution of specific causality to child-rearing practices has proved unreliable. But these practices can provide valuable 'clues' to adult character, though only to its adaptive features and promoted reactions rather than to its 'causes'. These child-rearing modes which I believe to be most commonly practised, in both urban and rural India (a distinction which has far less sociological significance in India than it has in Euro-America—as will be seen in Part Three), will be viewed as but one part of the cultural totality. This is, however, a significant part because child-rearing is a natural means to transmit the configuration from one generation to the next. There is not a single conclusion to be drawn from the material of Part Two which has validity if considered in isolation from the social totality—it being my view that the idea of a fundamental psyche as First Cause, or even pivot, of society is an abstraction. My observations are an attempt—crude and unscientific, perhaps—to convey to the reader some impression of *ethos* and *behaviour*, as experienced while living with Indian families of different classes in the rural Deccan, Uttar Pradesh, Bengal, Rājasthān, the Punjāb, and in cities like Delhi, Bombay, Calcutta, and Benares. While there were obvious differences between one family and another, and particularly between Hindus and Muslims, their similarities were more striking and more significant. To identify divergencies from the norm would require an entire book at the very least. For this kind of data the reader is referred to works cited in footnotes and the Bibliography.

Chapter One The Child

It is not easy to make an imaginative adjustment to the tiny, expanding world of the Indian child. But it is important to swing round and confront the restricted, changing, bewildering scene through his eyes, since it is the way a child is brought up in the first years of its life which will influence the child's future perceptions. There is an unbroken link between the family world around him, the society in which he will grow up, and its outlook towards the *force majeure* of Nature. In the setting of the joint-family system (a complex adaptation to the productivity pattern of an agricultural community), we will see how the elasticity of social forms is a response to mutability, the specially Indian flavour of insistence upon relative values, ambivalent polarities with no immutable ethics of human arbitration and choice. The Indian child learns about his environment more by observation than through explicit parental instruction. This is thought to be the only really adequate way for him to find his way in the world, superior even to formal education.

Child is more independent of family

From birth the Indian child is precipitated into an environment which may be characterized, perhaps like every family system, by patterned ambivalence. It begins with brief, but intense indulgence, alternating with casual attention and discipline; it continues with strict authoritarian discipline interspersed with adulation, pampering, and conflicting instruction from a plurality of parent-surrogates. It is this 'inconsistency' of training which is so marked; yet we should be on our guard against applying this word indiscriminately to the relaxed flexibility of child-care, which reflects the vagaries of life in a none too congenial environment.

This ambivalence is misunderstood by many observers, who would prefer a more cut-and-dried pattern as the determining situation. A psychiatrist, for example, comments on the Hindu doctrine 'that denies to no single human impulse its right to exist. . . . Thus they are always worthy of the highest reverence, love and attention. This realisation summons every person truly to integrate his entire being, to assimilate knowingly, to unfold and to apply in action all talents given to him.'[1] As far as it goes this is true, but it is only half the truth. Almost in the same breath, but without seeking to explain the apparent contradiction, Dr. Boss goes on to record the remark of a young Hindu: 'At home everything sexual has always been

[1] Boss (1965), p. 60.

banned as evil, unnatural and dirty.'[1] These two polar extremes may be said to typify the ambivalence in the Indian family value-system. The attitude to which the young man refers is an example of ascetic, punitive, authoritarian paternalism, while the inclusive, indulgent, permissive, and tolerant maternal attitude identified by Dr. Boss represents the opposite trend. Dr. Boss is only partly correct, in my view, when he claims that widespread neurotic conflict arises because 'children have abruptly imposed on them a very brusque withdrawal by their parents, a vehement insistence on the most meticulous cleanliness, and extreme prudery in the erotic sphere; all this follows an initial pre-genital period in which the child is pampered and indulged to the utmost'.[2] It is his assumption that discipline is imposed 'abruptly' which leaves Dr. Boss's conclusions open to criticism. It is now admitted by some observers that the transition from indulgence to disciplined training is gradual in India—in fact, much less abrupt than in many other societies. While the child is not expected to look after itself until comparatively late in its development, I would suggest that punitive discipline actually begins (in a haphazard, irregular pattern) much *earlier* than is generally realized. The joint-family system, it should be emphasized, does not invariably provide the nest-warmth, perfect security, and clearly prescribed rights and duties usually attributed to it.

In studying the Indian family, we should bear in mind the following points: 1. The relation of man to an overpowering natural environment subject to violent change and swift dissolution. 2. The importance placed by tradition on the primacy of learning by *observation* in a setting both hostile and bounteous. 3. The patterned ambivalence of the family system reflecting the human dilemma caused by the environment.

The joint family

The Indian family was, until recent times, based on an extended or joint-family system, which originated in Vedic times. It was patriarchal: the oldest male member was absolute head, under whose roof his younger brothers and their families, his sons, their wives and children, and his grandchildren all lived. They ate food cooked at one hearth, held property in common, participated in common family worship, and were related to each other according to one of the several kinship systems prevailing in India. Rights and duties, sentiments and authority constituted its unity. Members were related by an interlocking pattern of mutual dependence, individuality was subordinate to collective solidarity, and the younger generation strictly, but not systematically, controlled by the elders.

[1] Boss (1965), p. 75.   [2] Ibid., p. 74.

In north India the more widely known patrilineal system is followed so there is no need to go into its precise structure. But the kinship system of south India needs a brief explanation. Here, traces of a matrilineal system remain, and although the once common practices of cross-cousin marriage, and especially uncle–niece marriage, are now looked on as archaic, affective relations between children and the maternal uncle are more intense than in the north. The most important difference is that the young bride does not enter a completely strange household, as she does in the north. On the contrary, she usually has known her husband and mother-in-law from childhood, since daughters frequently marry their father's nephews and especially the youngest son of his eldest sister. The mother-in-law would be the bride's aunt, and relations between her own family and her in-laws will be less distant than in the strictly patrilineal north. For this reason— and not only because Muslim influence was far less strong in the south (no segregation in purdah was practised in the south)—the relationship between husband and wife is less constrained and women are less secluded. It is significant that the popular emotional religiosity of the *bhakti* cults originated as a southern movement and peninsular Indian religion includes a more extensive and popular form of ethical teaching, exemplified by the genial *Tirukural*. On the other hand, the more closed-in kinship pattern— predetermined from the moment of birth—accentuated the conservative outlook of the southern family system, linking decision-making and marriage choice close to the collective interest. For in this region existing kinship bonds are strengthened, whereas the marriage ties of a northern family link it with a number of villages in a looser affinity. Therefore, a woman's character is formed by an imperative adaptation to a new set of customs and people in the north, while a southern woman develops in a relaxed atmosphere of family relations within an inward-looking system.

In modern times the urban middle-class joint family is splitting up, its various sections living under separate roofs. But the basic structural relations have persisted and many of these families reunite on important occasions, such as festivals and marriages. This pattern is not necessarily broken by modern urbanism, for the ancestral home remains not merely a symbol, but the heart of a family's sense of identity. Ultimate authority is still vested in the oldest male member, and family discussions and disputes are generally still referred to him. His sisters and married daughters, though living with their husbands' families, also return home on special occasions, and sometimes when they are widowed, though these generally continue to reside in their husbands' homes. Today young couples tend to live independently.

The joint family belongs to a larger *gotra*, or clan, within which inter-marriage is forbidden (this is not universal). The clan, in turn, is part of the subcaste, which determines hereditary occupation. Marriage must be within the subcaste, and it is only an exceedingly small minority who break this rule, although the trend in attitudes is towards a gradual liberalization. Selection of marriage partners on caste lines is not confined to Hindus, but is also observed, though less overtly, by Indian Christians and Muslims.

The joint family is a microcosm of the profoundly pluralistic nature of Indian culture in all its manifestations. Under one roof are gathered several branches of an extended family, living together, pooling their resources, sharing their property and their incomes, a pattern which expands in response to a centrifugal momentum, as basic to Indian civilization as the splitting of a single cell into two parts and the repetition of this original division *ad infinitum*. Thus the 'cells' of father, mother, sons, and daughters spread outwards in ever less clearly defined fissions within the family, tribe, and caste. The diffuse pattern of numerous parent-surrogates (common to the majority of joint families) makes it very difficult for a child to mould his developing personality on a well-defined model. Unrelated personal traits function with an unusual degree of autonomy, externalized in contiguous, plural projections. Indian dilettantism and the frequency among the highly educated of polymath intellectuals and multiple personalities such as Tagore and Nehru may well be a reaction to this pluralistic pattern. A Hindu may work in an office, dress in Western work clothes, adopt a competitive outlook in business, and freely mix with other castes during working hours; at the end of the day he will return home, dress in Hindu clothes, worship a plurality of deities in the temple, but invite to his dinner-table only the members of his own caste (under modern conditions of freer commensality guests will probably be members of the same 'faction' or club of a more or less exclusive character). One of the most obvious signs of psychological plurality (as distinct from the normal human inconsistencies and contradictions) is the principle of polytheism itself, which acknowledged some thirty-three gods in Vedic times and has since multiplied them to several thousand; the godhead is not conceived as a personalized, patriarchal father-figure, but as an abstract, supreme spirit.

The emotionally constrained interpersonal relationships which we still find in the typical rural joint family have had decisive consequences for every aspect of life in India. The emotional control essential to this collective life—in other words the celebrated 'serenity' and 'impassive calm'— can be traced to the conditions under which the vast majority of the population have lived since ancient times (Plate 51). In spite of this there are frequent outbursts, and this sudden way of letting off steam is also reflected in the pattern of child-care. In such close quarters there is a minimum of privacy. On the tamped-earth stage of the walled courtyard—ringed by an

auditorium of roof terraces—are enacted all the major dramas in the family
life-cycle; few events escape the eye of everyone else. Moreover, a high
percentage of Indian women are rigidly confined to this courtyard throughout their lives, either by higher caste rules of seclusion, or by the sheer
drudgery which is the lot of the poorer classes, and the absence of a community social centre. Life revolves round a common hearth, the children
play with their siblings and first cousins in an atmosphere charged with
jealousies among a group of women who came together originally as
strangers, or rent by quarrels between them and their authoritarian menfolk. The Indian mother cannot but acquiesce in aggression directed towards herself by her children too, for these soon learn that the status of a
woman is subservient to that of men.

The worst aspect of the system lay in the crushing imposition of conformity,
the killing of all initiative and incentive to individual effort during the critical
formative period of youth, the utter lack of training to responsibility; in the
premium it put on idleness, in the disheartening exploitation of able and earning
members by the parasitic weak, and more than all in the unrestricted property
power consigned to one single hand which not infrequently encourages crass
mismanagement.[1]

The waste of human resources and the fact that all members of the family
were exposed to each other's capricious, often narrow, and untrained minds,
had a debasing effect on the mental and spiritual vitality of society as a
whole, even though the elders of village society may have possessed outstanding shrewdness of human judgement.

This is not to say that the extended-family system is devoid of good
features; on the contrary, it has contributed enormously to the stability
and psychological health of the society for millennia. But while it is well-
known that the Indian family system has provided a very high measure of
security and ensured the continuity of rich traditional values and culture,
this should not blind us to the fact that, under certain conditions, some of
its members' needs are frustrated or they are subject to tension.

Infancy

The description of the genetic development of the child and the principal
family relationships within the joint system which follows cannot possibly
take into account all the regional and caste variants which exist. But it is
my experience that a great many points are common to the majority of the
population; some significant exceptions will be mentioned briefly.

[1] F. H. Das, *Purdah: the status of Indian women*, Kegan Paul, Trench, Trubner, London, 1932.

A Hindu child grows up within the security of the extended kinship system and has few contacts with other groups until he goes to school. The nucleus of the new personality which forms out of the interaction of mother and baby is very different in India from that in the Euro-American pattern. Although the mother is chiefly responsible for the care of the child, the close contact between the child and the mother, other females, mother-surrogates, and, among the affluent, *ayahs* (nannies), continues for much longer than in many other cultures.[1] During the first few days after birth mother and child remain secluded in an inner room in a state of ritual impurity. No contact with other members of the family is permitted until ritual ablutions have been performed. At this time the child's horoscope is prepared and a name selected for it. Then the house is purified, but the mother does not resume her full activities for another thirty-four days, a custom which is on the decline; this period of impurity affords her the essential rest after confinement. The child will be fed at the breast for at least two years, if not more; a period of four years is not unknown. By the time this period ends the child is accustomed to a fairly generous diet, and though weaning is gradual it is still a wrench and may lead to anger. Ideally, it will be fed any time that it cries, and every effort is made to stop its crying, which is considered weakening.

The infant has close contact with the mother's body for several years. It is the custom for a mother to carry her baby astride her hip a great deal of the time, one arm supporting its back, and so she is free to move about and work with her other arm. In this position it is easy to feed the baby, whose head is level with her breast. Relatives, and particularly elder sisters, carry the baby the same way. It is also worth noting that most babies in villages are completely naked, or wear no more than a single cotton upper garment. In certain rural districts, especially in the south, the mother wears no blouse, but carries the baby under the upper part of her sari. In former times many women wore no upper garment. Here the child's physical closeness to the mother was complete. I have often seen women, in all parts of India, carrying their babies while working in the immense labour gangs recruited for the construction of the great dams of India's national development projects, and suckling them from time to time. In any case most infants are virtually never left alone (indeed they cannot be in those homes where women are segregated and live in cramped quarters); even if a baby is put in a cradle (Plate 51) or laid on the ground, as far as the mother's work permits it will be picked up and suckled as soon as it cries. This is how parents would *like* to care for their baby. Here is the source of the

---

[1] An Indian psychoanalyst, with whom I discussed this point, considers it a key factor in Indian character formation, and one which has, unfortunately, been almost totally neglected by field workers.

indulgence-theory on which a number of observers have based their conclusions. In practice, the pattern of indulgence is *irregular*, depending on
the work routine, the family's economic resources, and the regional
ecology.

In theory, the Hindu ideal is a very high degree of infant indulgence. In
practice, it is generally the higher castes which can afford to do this, for the
pampering of children is more feasible among the affluent. In a comparative
study of six cultures conducted in different parts of the world under the
direction of Professor John Whiting, the Indian sample—a Rājput
(Kshatrya) village in north India—shows that the warmth and intensity of
mother–child relations came relatively low in the scale.[1] This may be due to
the more rugged upbringing considered appropriate to a former military
caste. A Brahman caste might have revealed a situation closer to the ideal of
consistent indulgence.[2]

If we look closer at the pattern of child-care a somewhat different picture
emerges. First, in joint-family life, since there are many young children
under one roof, and one in every ten children born will probably die in
infancy, babies are not the extraordinary, somewhat mysterious creatures
which they may seem if the mother is more isolated. Except for the firstborn son, they tend to be taken for granted, and no child is considered
unique. Furthermore, these ideas are reinforced by the belief in rebirth;
the individual is not born once and once only, therefore he cannot be
regarded as a unique event.

The mother has probably witnessed the birth of several babies, watched
them being nursed, watched them grow up, and perhaps taken an active
part in looking after them since her own childhood. She may have seen
them die too. When her own child cries, or falls sick, or burns its fingers if
it crawls too near the hearth, she is not beset by feelings of intense anxiety
or guilt. Thus the baby receives attention from its mother, or mother-
surrogates, only when it cries or fusses. Comforting ceases when its crying
ceases. Rather than stimulating the child's response by creative play, the
adult tries to reduce it. Such indulgence as this implies would tend to foster
'a sense of the mutability of all things' and a pattern of irregular effusiveness, such as Professor Francis L. Hsu has suggested.

Secondly, a mother's housework is exceedingly onerous; due to the
primitive level of technological development, cooking and cleaning are
lengthy and arduous. A woman may also have to work a good deal in the
fields, or gather fuel. Moreover, the fields and the well may be at some

[1] Cf. Minturn and Hitchcock (1966). The author wishes to acknowledge his debt to
this study for valuable data in the preparation of the present chapter.

[2] The question of narcissistic personality traits accentuated by infant oral indulgence
will be examined in Part Five.

distance from the home. Under such circumstances, even if there are plenty of mother-surrogates, the mother cannot give her child her undivided attention unless she lives in an exceptionally sheltered home. Thirdly, living at such close quarters as members of a joint family almost invariably do, much time and energy is taken up in domestic bickering between sisters-in-law and mothers-in-law. Frustration, bitterness, and frayed nerves are hardly the ideal atmosphere in which to lavish attention upon a screaming infant. Nor does the principle of parent-surrogates always work out well in practice, owing to the rampant jealousies existing between the pent-in womenfolk.

But there are also other factors which diminish indulgence, which, apart from occasional reference in field studies, have not received enough attention. For it is here that unintentionally punitive conditioning enters the idealized picture of unfailingly solicitous nest-warmth. The first of these is malnutrition itself: women who may desire to breast-feed their babies for two years or more may be physically unable to do so, or may become pregnant again only a few months after the baby's birth; at the same time they will be too poor to buy a regular and adequate supply of supplementary milk. Secondly, perhaps due to concepts of pollution, probably unconsciously Indian mothers tend to be rough while bathing their children. They rarely use soap, and apply a good deal of friction to skins which may be particularly sensitive because of prickly heat and the other skin troubles caused by the climate. The daily bath may therefore be a distressing experience for the child to face.[1]

In the average Indian home, infants suffer considerably from the extremes of the climate. Skin breaks out in sores very easily, prickly heat can cause a severe rash, and the only remedies are oils and powders. The monsoon can be a terrible ordeal for a baby, especially since inadequate housing cannot protect it completely from damp. Muddy floors are often awash, clothing rots, insects and flies torment it; bandicoots and rodents terrify, often injure, and sometimes kill babies. Dust chafes the skin and inflames the eyes, and when it is wrapped in cottons during the full heat of summer, or the damp and darkness of the monsoon, the child grows restive. Sleep in excessive heat is difficult enough; in addition, adult Indians are in the habit of talking and quarrelling loudly at night or during the hot noonday siesta, disturbing the child's quiet and sleep. Winter in north India can be piercingly cold, especially since few people have adequate footwear and woollens; windows are unglazed, floors are of tamped earth, concrete, or stone. In this region the hot desert winds of high summer are acutely uncomfortable and even adults sometimes die at that time if their health is run down. Infants may also be terrified by jackals crying in the night, by the

[1] Cf. Minturn and Hitchcock, op. cit., p. 110.

proximity of wild beasts, and by the crows which swoop down with noisy cawing to snatch food from their hands. Sudden changes in routine which have their origin in nature are not going to reinforce the child's sense of security. It is in such conditions that the individual grows up to regard all change as painful, to believe that he can do nothing to reduce his vulnerability to it and that any state or condition, pleasure or pain, will soon pass —and recur again. The child 'spends his first two years as a passive observer of the busy courtyard life. He is never alone, never the centre of attention.' [1] If he is, in a sense, lucky enough to receive the indulgence of the social ideal, his retreat to a narcissistic position will be tempered by the impersonal, formalized aloofness and emotional control which accompany life at close quarters; he will also experience a sense of cocoon-like autonomy, swathed, when cradled, from head to toe, with few toys, few *objects* to handle; he concentrates either on looking, or on himself, on his own body. However fatalistic the Indian peasant may be about misfortune, the ravages of dysentery, malaria, smallpox, and more virulent tropical diseases, none to my knowledge is indifferent to the acute discomforts of the climate. The infant, whose experience will determine so much of his future outlook, is not in any position to distinguish these impersonal frustrations and irritations from the rewards and punishments he receives in total dependence at his mother's breast. To the infant, not only the good but also the bad things come from the (omnipotent) mother; and this is reflected in the ambivalent character of the goddess Kālī.

It is my opinion that deprivation and frustration form a crucial aspect of the infantile situation, that the first, or oral, phase, is one of prolonged unilateral dependence which is not without a high degree of painful conditioning which leads to early development of aggressive demands. These may or may not be counteracted by passive longings, depending on the success with which the model of intense indulgence is achieved. This may sound technical, but is the clearest way we have to render a considerable proportion of data on character formation explicable.

The pre-school child

The next phase of development starts with the introduction of positive and negative training. During its first years the child is cared for in the women's quarters, which are generally set apart as far as economic conditions permit. Though it is said that a child thus cared for has a greater sense of security, the plurality of mother-surrogates may lead to feelings of ambiguity regarding the mother and the whole feminine world. During

[1] Ibid., p. 112.

this period the father has much less to do with the child than the womenfolk.

Parents do not show signs of over-anxious concern for babies to be clean
and dry. In this sphere genial tolerance and permissiveness prevail; toilet
training is extremely easy-going and no fuss attends the process; babies
and young children are never scolded if they make a mess. Up till the
age of two or more the child performs its toilet function when and where it
pleases, without any scolding from the mother, who wipes up after it.
After about two and a half the child is taught to go out in the yard and only
at about the age of five is it expected to start using the lavatory or visit the
fields with a pot of water. Up till that age the mother or some other woman
washes it herself with water. There are very strict rules of faecal pollution
in the Hindu system; these are only gradually instilled into the growing
child, and not until it is between two and three years old. It is significant
that these instructions go hand in hand with warnings about the pollution
which the touch of the low castes causes, although this tabu is on the decline
in cities. At the same time the child learns that for three days of the month,
during menstruation, his mother mysteriously withdraws into seclusion
and becomes an agent of pollution herself. If faecal pollution occurs, or the
pollution of contact with a member of the Untouchable castes, or with a
woman in menstruation (who may be the mother), the grandmother or
mother-surrogate, who also teaches the child what is shameful or indecent,
will tell him to bath and change his clothes. The degree to which these
tabus are observed today varies a great deal from class to class, but their
enforcement is extremely widespread and pollution rules have left an indelible impression on every adult. In spite of a national campaign to eliminate Untouchability it is very hard to change deeply instilled attitudes
regarding pollution which from infancy have been second nature to the
majority of the population. Conversely, the teaching of the Untouchable
child to avoid all contact with the high castes is equally, if not even more,
strict.

Mary Douglas, in a recent study on pollution, has some perceptive
comments to make on the Indian situation.

That the sociological approach to caste pollution is much more convincing
than a psychoanalytic approach is clear when we consider what the Indian's
private attitudes to defecation are. In the ritual we know that to touch excrement
is to be defiled and that the latrine cleaners stand in the lowest grade of the
caste hierarchy. If this pollution rule expressed individual anxieties we would
expect Hindus to be controlled and secretive about the act of defecation.[1]

As is well known, this is definitely not the case; Indians are extremely
casual in this respect.

[1] Mary Douglas, *Purity and Danger*, Routledge and Kegan Paul, London, 1966, p. 124.

As we know it, dirt is essentially disorder. There is no such thing as absolute dirt: it exists in the eye of the beholder. If we shun dirt, it is not because of craven fear, still less dread or holy terror. Nor do our ideas about disease account for the range of our behaviour in cleaning or avoiding dirt. Dirt offends against order. Eliminating it is not a negative movement, but a positive effort to organise the environment.[1]

Dirt in nature may be said to be relative too; but in comparison with, say, Swiss or Scandinavian nature, tropical Indian nature is comparatively dirty; there is very little a man can do to change this situation. In the dry season dust penetrates almost everything except a hermetically sealed container; in the monsoon most villages, towns, and cities become clogged with mud and water. Extreme humidity brings mould to articles which a European would assume to be impermeable: shoes, camera cases and lenses, clothes stowed in closets, paper, books. No wall surface in India can be tropicalized: bricks sweat, mud crumbles, plaster blackens and grows a green mould. In villages, the profusion of cattle, and their proximity to the domestic courtyard and hearth, add to the dirt. Inadequate technology has, over many centuries, inured the Indian to the idea that to wage an incessant war against the natural sources of dirt is a losing game. On the other hand, everyone in India is made acutely aware of the link between bowel movement and health—almost to the point of obsession—the consequence of which is hypersensitivity regarding personal hygiene and the Hindu washing mania.[2]

Indian tradition orders society according to an organismic theory; the various limbs and orifices are identified with specialized occupations. There is not only a caste hierarchy for the body of society, but also a hierarchical system for the organs and substances of the physical body, and a hierarchical system of food, of the senses, of the mental faculties (Plate 36). We will have more to say about the key question of pollution in Part Three; the subject has wider implications than may at first be apparent. Experience teaches the Indian that his state of mind and spiritual vitality are subject to the state of his body; he cannot draw a line of division between physical and spiritual health. Traditional Hindu thought places exactly equal value on Matter and Spirit—*both* are eternal and *divine* principles. *Buddhi*—Man's intellect—is an emanation of primal Matter. Such an inclusive attitude which brings the body into the domain of religion is a legacy which can be traced to the universal Indian experience in early childhood, when the infant is forced to concentrate on himself, on his own

[1] Ibid., p. 2.
[2] For a comprehensive and balanced assessment of the influence of the Indian climate, cf. Appendix 10, 'Climate and Its Economic Consequences in South Asia', in Gunnar Myrdal, *Asian Drama*, London, 1968.

body. The child thus explores all the erotic potentialities of his own body, and these early experiences are recalled by fantasy reparation in the erotically charged content of religion, art, and yoga.

The traditional Indian system of child training has evolved from the belief in the primacy of observation rather than direct instruction, and rewards are as infrequent as is purposeful encouragement. Concrete rewards are usually given, in the form of food, rather than non-material rewards such as expression of love, or praise for tasks well done. Rewards for specific acts of good behaviour are extremely rare, whereas negative training, control by punishment, is the preferred method, with strong emphasis on respect for adults and superiors. Scolding, curses, and slaps are administered not only by the mother and father but by older children and all relatives resident under the one roof. More often than not, punishment reflects the hierarchical status and not a personal threat of love withheld. Thus reprimands imply conduct demeaning to caste status and a common scolding is to call the child an Untouchable or to threaten outcasting. Bogeys, such as ghosts, demons, witches (Plates 32 and 33), and the black goddess of destruction, Kālī, are invoked as dark and threatening, unclean, or frightening fantasies; pollution by Untouchables falls into the same class of threats. In the last resort a mother who cannot control her child will lock it in a dark room. Since older women like to relate ghost stories to each other within earshot of the children, such punishment may be a terrifying experience for the child. This common form of control calls to mind Róheim's celebrated remark that men huddle into hordes as a substitute for parents, to save themselves from independence, from 'being left alone in the dark'.[1] It is significant, too, that one of the techniques used by Indian holy men, prolonged meditation in a dark room, is regarded as a severe 'ordeal'.

In noticing the rarity with which children are complimented for specific good behaviour, it should be pointed out that in Indian ethics good and evil are always *relative*; precise definition of intrinsically good or bad deeds is avoided; the fruit of all action (*karma*) is, in a sense, deferred and diffused, a gradual accumulation to be garnered in the *next* life rather than rendered to account in the here and now. There is no eternal damnation, only the endless round of rebirth, the wheel of sorrow.

There is very little emphasis on self-reliance. Transition from infancy to independence is prolonged. A child will continue to sleep with its mother, perhaps with one or two brothers and sisters, for anything up to five years. Similarly, it will be bathed till it is five or six, fed by hand till it is five, and dressed up to the same age. It learns to walk on its own, and learns to talk more by imitation than by precept; children are considered too young for

[1] G. Róheim, *The Origin and Function of Culture*, New York, 1943.

much verbal instruction before the age of five and no attempt is made to build up a model of desired behaviour through long 'talks'.

There is consistency here, for the child is left to observe a diversity of interdependent role-playing among people of both sexes and all ages. It could hardly be otherwise; this passivity in training is a consequence of the joint-family situation, where the child's conduct varies according to the hierarchical status of any particular relative. Obedience and respect go with the principle of authoritarian control, with a variety of formal terms of greeting, use of kinship terms, politeness, and deference. It is not until the male child comes under the direct discipline of the father after the age of five (only then is he permitted to remain with the menfolk for any long periods of time) that he learns to exert dominance, often of a hectoring nature, over persons of lower age or caste status. The son learns that women are lower in status than men very early in life, and this he soon exploits to his own advantage. The position of any woman (or for that matter any adult man as well) in a hierarchical system is such that they must constantly be making demands, or pleading to superiors, for one thing or another. The son (and to a lesser extent, daughter too) soon picks up this habit and develops a persistently demanding outlook. This can put the mother, who is subject to the control of the men, the mother-in-law and senior sisters-in-law, at a great disadvantage in controlling boys. One frequently notices that children between the ages of three and seven, some-times until puberty, go through a trying stage of almost constant whining, in the hope of regaining the precariously indulgent attention they were accustomed to in infancy. In a sense too, the son is more socially mobile than his mother, and can escape beyond areas where women are permitted to move. Whoever the female disciplinarian may be, her authority can seldom be absolute, except it may be for the senior grandmother who sometimes inherits an unchallengeable position. A child finds out that anger may be effective. This is important for adult life; violent outbursts of anger, if directed against anyone of uncertain status, are often effective and hence exploited.

Parents prefer their children to play in groups rather than alone; games are unstructured, but the sexes, as in adult life, are not mixed. Generally the economy necessitates the teaching of work skills (again through ob-servation) at an early age, but since this kind of activity is required to ensure an adequate livelihood, it is devoid of the play element, and the model of performance placed before the child is that of the adult. Thus the child's performance is not appreciated and praised, as it falls short of the standard to which it is forced to aspire. In these circumstances learning cannot be viewed as of value for its own sake, whether it is agricultural, or that of a craft, or actual schooling in class. The relatively few and fortunate whose parents take an active interest in their studies, are, again by force of economic necessity (or because of the pressure of competition), made aware more of the need to get good grades and pass exams than of learning as an ethical ideal.

We may also repeat here that nature in India is full of threats to the child's safety, such as wild beasts, snakes, swamps, quicksands, and the like. The child also has few toys or tools with which to develop a confident relationship with its environment; he cautiously explores a restricted field with eyes and hands, his skin sensitized by the climate. He learns by involvement in an audile-tactile continuum, where all man-made objects are visibly, palpably, the products of plastic manipulation. It is hard for the Western observer to appreciate the sensory immediacy of this world, since it lacks the tempero-spatial perspective, the projection of distant goals, the drawing up of character models, and the lure of exploration which are intrinsic parts of character-formation in the Western world.

Modern conditions present the individual Indian with a much greater challenge: a wider variety of tools which he must learn to master, at least in adult life, if not in childhood. Individual Indians make excellent mechanics, but the fundamental problem generally in training young people in the use of machines is to inculcate a responsible attitude towards tool and machine maintenance. This is a serious problem, as I know from first-hand knowledge of newly set-up mechanized farms, community projects, and engineering training colleges. Town and country are littered with rusting machinery—abandoned as useless, not because of wear (it may have been used only once), but because it broke down through faulty maintenance. There are two causes, as I see it: lack of curiosity, based on early upbringing, to find out how a machine works—no passion to take things apart and reassemble them—and passivity in the attitude towards tools, either due to caste specialization or child training. This should be qualified, for it is clear that India's craftsmen have long possessed exceptional manual dexterity. Craft traditions are handed down by hereditary castes for many generations, and the training of their children begins at a very young age indeed. Occupational specialization does permit the acquisition of expert manual skills. Erik Erikson makes the following observation on inferiority feelings which are particularly relevant in the context of Indian rewards and punishments:

The more confusing specialization becomes . . . the more indistinct are the eventual goals of initiative; and the more complicated social reality, the vaguer are the father's and mother's role in it. . . .
The child's danger . . . lies in a sense of inadequacy and inferiority. If he despairs of his tools and skills or of his status among his tool partners, he may be discouraged from identification with them and with a section of the tool

world. To lose hope of such 'industrial' association may pull him back to the more isolated, less tool-conscious familial rivalry of the oedipal time. The child despairs of his equipment in the tool world and in anatomy, and considers himself doomed to mediocrity or inadequacy.[1]

To conclude these observations on child training we may summarize as follows. The greatest emphasis is placed on passivity of observation with scarcely any goal-orientation save consolidation of status. Neither self-reliance nor instruction in sustained, disciplined effort to achieve distant goals is taught. Giving help to others depends on the status of those involved, not on spontaneous charity. Punishment, which can be severe, is favoured more than a consistent system of rewards for specific good behaviour. Models of conduct are relative, impersonal, and formed through imitation rather than through any 'perspective' shaped by the parents' 'talks'.

Father and son

In our country the father is still not a family friend, but a dictator . . . culturally we expect the father to be a sort of authority, and every member of the family must try to keep him happy. The family is ready to accept this type of dictatorship. . . . We still feel that we are not able to speak frankly or discuss all our desires with our fathers. Whenever children want to ask something they speak with their mothers. This is because of fear of the dictatorship, and not fear of the father as a person. The father is the head of the family. Sometimes he is used as a policeman over all the activities of the children, and I think that is the reason for the relationship I have observed in many families. The children are never free in activities and speech in the company of their fathers. But though the child is always in its mother's company it still likes to follow the father's mannerisms. . . . The father thinks that to look after the child's training is not his field and so he should not waste his time with the child. Many fathers do not even know what their children are learning in school. . . .[2]

While it is true that the joint-family father is a seemingly remote, aloof, and much feared figure among several disciplinary male figures (among which, but not in all kinship systems, the principal one would often be the maternal uncle), there is a special bond which unites father and son. This is not only because the son will inherit his father's authority and will also be the family's main breadwinner. As Professor Dumont puts it:

Economic aspects certainly play an important rôle in the joint family, but at the same time its core from the point of view of kinship is likely to lie in the

[1] Erik H. Erikson, *Childhood and Society* (rev. ed.), Hogarth Press, London, 1964, p. 251.
[2] An Indian woman psychologist, quoted by Margaret Cormack in *The Hindu Woman*, Asia Publishing House, London, 1961, pp. 16–17.

extreme solidarity between father and son (in relation to ancestors), which makes of this pair, and of the family group around it, the real subject of the institution and resists an enquiry made in terms of individual agents.[1]

Families almost invariably hope for a son; producing a male heir is enjoined on the father as a religious and economic necessity. There is always great rejoicing when the first child is a male. A son guarantees the continuation of the generations and he will perform the last rites after the father's death to ensure a peaceable departure to the world of the ancestors. The word *putra*, son, means 'he who protects from going to hell'. Having a son not only assures a man social dignity and status, but through their functional solidarity father and son are jointly and successively responsible for the maintenance of all other members of the family. In fact, the relationship is one of *mutual dependence*. The son must obey his father unquestioningly, pay him formal respect, for example, touching his father's feet on parting or reunion, and offer him the completest support in every need, both in life and after death. Likewise, the father owes his son support, a good education, the best possible marital arrangement, sound caste and kinship relations, and inheritance of property. Much of the interaction between father and son takes place in the context of caste and kin dispute, factionalism, and distrust for out-groups. The principal aspect of paternal socialization is the transmission of information to sons on the various feuds, alliances, and friendships in which the family has been involved from generation to generation, thus reflecting its status image within the community.

We may assume that the rigid, formal system of obligations with its culturally prescribed alienation (on a personal level) between father and son acts as a control on the son's unconscious oedipal wishes. Probably because of sexual connotations, fathers in many parts of India were only supposed to hold, play, or interact with their nephews, never their sons. Disciplining might also, for the same reason, be permitted the father in the privacy of the home and not among his adult male peers. Similarly, even the general welfare of sons used frequently to be the responsibility of the grandfather or uncles. At the same time the aloofness of the father would suggest unconscious resentment of the son. The duty of the son to perform his father's last rites accentuates the father's dependence on the son. The manifold restrictions placed on intimacy between father and son control their feelings of ambivalence to each other. An external, disciplined paternal training and an internal, oral-aggressive mechanism help to circumvent, or altogether avoid, conflict. The strong overt hostility to the father by rebellious sons which is so much a feature of Western patriarchal societies, is

[1] Louis Dumont, *Contributions to Indian Sociology*, VIII, Mouton & Co., The Hague, p. 94.

checked in the Indian joint family not only by plural discipline and the code of formal respect, but also by the narcissistic streak which gives the father a strong sense of identification with his son, preventing excessive authoritarian rule of the kind we associate with, for example, ancient Roman families. It is not without interest that, as the philologists point out, the word used in connection with the joint family in all ancient lawbooks of the Hindus is not 'jointness' but *'unseparatedness'*. Formal, punitive as paternal authority may be, it should be seen as part of the patterned ambivalence already referred to—here a matter of etiquette within a nevertheless somewhat loosely regulated group. The result, as observers have noted, can often be a state of suppressed hostility, overt quarrels, and restlessness which is rarely carried to the point of total rupture. We will notice this state of perpetually unresolved conflict later, in analysing the caste system.

A proverb summarizes the father–son relationship thus: A son should be treated as a prince for five years; as a slave for ten years; but from his sixteenth birthday, as a friend.

Chapter Two   Family Relationships

Assessing ties of affection and sentiment in the Indian family is no easier than elsewhere. In a perceptive and comprehensive study of the urban Hindu family, Dr. Aileen Ross provides an interesting glimpse into this sensitive domain in her tabulation of the degrees with which affective intensity is felt. In a mixed sample of 157 she found that emotional attitudes of family members towards each other were rated as follows: mother–son 115, brother–sister 90, brother–brother 75, father–son 74, father–children 24, husband–wife 16, sister–sister 5. While mother–son relationships would be expected to yield the greatest emotional intensity in India, the low rating ascribed to husband–wife relationships must give those who would assume it would come second on the list cause to revise their assumptions. While this sample can only be a pointer, the relatively low warmth of husband–wife relations indicates how dangerous it is to project a Western scale of values on modern India. The sample was taken in urban, middle class, Westernized Bangalore.[1]

It should be remembered that however important *psychologically* the husband–wife relationship is, it cannot be regarded as of primary *structural* importance in the Hindu joint family. 'For the ancient sages declare that a bride is given to the family of her husband, and not to the husband alone' (Āpastamba, *c.* fourth century B.C.). It is easy to see, in this context, how the most important ceremony in Indian social life remains the wedding, which marks the intersection of the family and caste systems. The largest number of family, caste, and kin assemble for this celebration. The marriage feast serves as the reaffirmation of a network of caste alliances and hierarchical gradations to which both families are committed. It also involves the most costly expenditure in the family budget and has been the major cause of chronic debt among the peasantry.

The status of women

Pre-Manu India accorded women equality with men in the Vedic sacrifice. At that time women could become priests; there was no immolation of the widow on her husband's funeral pyre (*satī*), and widows were allowed to

[1] Ross (1961), p.137.

remarry. The Vedic age was more liberal in its attitude towards women than the long period following the composition of the *Laws of Manu*, which became the canon law of Hinduism. 'Though destitute of virtue, or seeking pleasure elsewhere, or devoid of good qualities, yet a husband must be constantly worshipped as a god by a faithful wife.'[1] The husband cannot be displaced even though he 'be devoid of good qualities, addicted to evil passion, fond of spirituous liquors or diseased'. 'To *Śūdras* [menial castes], women and servants' the Vedas are now sealed. 'No sacrifice, no vow, no fast must be performed by women apart from their husbands; if a wife obeys her husband, she will, for that reason alone, be exalted in heaven.'[1]

Manu draws a distinction between the woman as sexual partner and the woman as mother; the latter is accorded very high status: 'A spiritual teacher exceeds a world teacher ten times, a father exceeds a spiritual teacher one hundred times, but a mother exceeds a thousand times a father's claim to honour on the part of a child and as its educator.'[1] Thus the dual status of the woman figures very early in Indian history, and although her position in society has varied to some extent at different periods and in different regions, the ambivalence and duality of her role has continued to be an important feature of Indian society. As a wife she seduces her husband away from his work and his spiritual duties, but as a *mother* she is revered.

Satī, child marriage, female infanticide, the low status of widows, and *purdah*, all had serious consequences for Indian society. There were several causes for child marriage. There was the need to ensure the early birth of a son in an era of short life-expectancy—for only the son could perform the funeral rites essential to the welfare of a man's departed soul during its sojourn in purgatory. Further, a boy's upbringing made his first sexual relations with his bride less of a challenge to his virility if the bride had already been known to him for some years during her early adolescence, when he and his family had been accustomed to giving her orders. In modern times, for example, many Hindus have confessed that their upbringing in a joint family made them too nervous to enjoy the company of a woman freely while studying abroad, unless she were a prostitute. Consummation in child marriage came very early after the attainment of puberty, when the young bride was perhaps no more than twelve, more often fourteen or fifteen.[2] At this age she was shy, obedient, and unformed,

---

[1] Bühler (tr.) (1886).

[2] According to Frederick Osborn, 'The average age of brides at first marriage in France in the late eighteenth century was about twenty-five years, and this average has remained fairly constant up to the last few years. Even around 1930, 38 per cent of all women aged twenty-five to twenty-nine years old were still unmarried in the Netherlands, 41 per cent in England, 48 per cent in Switzerland, and 52 per cent in Norway—in contrast to 1 per cent in Korea, 2 per cent in India, 4 per cent in Formosa, and 8·5 per cent in Japan.' Osborn (1962), p. 97.

and the man had no fear that he would have to contend with a mature personality on a basis of sexual equality.) Early marriage has also been conducive to high fertility, which the necessity for giving birth to sons directly encourages.

Girls who were betrothed when quite young children returned to live with their parents for some years. (As a result of child marriage there used to be an enormous number of women who became widows while still children, and they were expected to remain so for the rest of their lives.) However, it has been estimated that only 30 per cent of Indian widows never remarried in former times. Lower castes, Muslims, and Sikhs were permitted re-marriage. Child marriage became a crushing burden for poor families, who could not afford to provide the necessary dowries. Fearful of not being able to scrape together enough money and find their daughters husbands while still very young, families in certain regions resorted to the practice of female infanticide on a scale that was by no means negligible. Infanticide was a fairly widespread method of population control in primitive societies and was practised in many parts of Asia, especially in Japan. Many Hindu widows escaped from a life of servitude, frequent fasts, shaven hair, and absence of legal protection, by becoming prostitutes. Only rarely did widows have a chance to gain fulfilment as matriarchs in the joint family, though in some cases they actually became its head.

With the advent of Islam, the higher-caste Hindus adopted the Muslim custom of *purdah* seclusion.[1] Some Hindus have said this was to protect their women from being carried off by Muslims, but the adoption of *purdah* by the higher classes was more a part of the acculturation which occurred with the establishment of Muslim rule over wide areas of the country. It should also be clear from the foregoing account that *purdah* coincided to a great extent with the increasing tendency of the Hindu family and caste systems to seclude their women. In ancient times virtue itself was considered the real *purdah*, to which was now added the complete assurance of psychological and physical seclusion for the genteel. While *purdah*, as practised by Muslims, was Islamic in origin, seclusion of women is already implicit in the *Laws of Manu*. G. S. Ghurye has pointed out that the Sanskrit words for ancient Indian garments worn by women include *avaguṇthana*, 'wrapper', and *nirangī*, 'extinguisher'.

The disappearance of head-dress [in the Gupta period] was accompanied by the strengthening of the sentiment for the practice of drawing one portion of the scarf, which has been almost an invariable constituent of the sartorial ensemble

---

[1] Islamic *purdah* customs include living in strictly segregated quarters, the wearing of the *burka* (a garment covering the whole body, with screened eye-holes), travelling in closed vehicles, and concealment of the whole body from anyone but the woman's husband or close kin.

of females from the Vedic times onwards, over the head. The purpose of this practice and the social sanction of this sentiment . . . lay in the idea that it was improper for married *élite* ladies to expose their faces to the gaze of strangers in daily intercourse.[1]

The word *purdah* is therefore used here in a general sense, to include not only the borrowed Islamic custom, but also the more deeply instilled Indian ideal of feminine modesty and seclusion. Special instances of Hindu *purdah*, such as the extreme seclusion of Nambudiri women in Kerala, are beyond the scope of this study. *Purdah* remained, for instance, long after the danger of Muslim aggression had vanished. But never more than around 15 per cent of adult women were kept in full Islamic-style *purdah*, and only in the higher castes, where it became a symbol of prestige, even if it was not so originally. The Islamic custom was not introduced in south India, where Muslim influence and military domination were much weaker. Although Islamic-style *purdah* was thus far from universal, its social and psychological effects on the status of women in general were incalculable, for not only was it the practice of the most influential classes, but it was adopted in those very regions which took the lead culturally during the Indo-Muslim period. The Hindu woman was not so fortunate in *purdah* as her Muslim sister. Property protection and social privilege were granted to women by the Koran, though not by Hindu law at that period. Widow remarriage, divorce, and remarriage for Muslim wives partly compensated for polygamy and veiling. Although Islamic-style *purdah* has now almost disappeared among the Hindus in India, its psychological effects and its customs, which had existed for many hundreds of years, are too deeply rooted in, or connected with, the India-wide concept of feminine modesty and seclusion, not to have left a very deep imprint on the personalities of the Hindu woman and her children.

Generally speaking, the lower down the caste and economic hierarchy, the more equal are the relations between the sexes: especially where men and women work together in fields, factories, and labour gangs. In south India, where the pre-Aryan cult of the mother-goddess occupies a special position in relation to the matrilineal kinship system, social intercourse between the sexes is more informal.

The daughter-in-law newly arrived in a large and unknown joint family is subject to every form of humiliation until she becomes pregnant. But this, in the case of a child bride, did not happen for several years, during which she was unceasingly reminded by every form of innuendo that her sole duty was to conceive a son by her husband 'when the time comes'. The bride has little fresh air and sunshine. One notices, in northern Indian homes

[1] G. S. Ghurye, *Indian Costume*, Popular Book Depot, Bombay, 1951, p. 124.

where Islamic-style *purdah* is still observed, the unhealthy pallor and sickly looks of the girls assembled during wedding feasts. They are unsure of themselves, socially immature, emotionally undisciplined, and inclined to be hysterical.

The new bride is an object of prying and pawing curiosity, every detail of her costume, ornaments, and behaviour loudly commented on, the colour of her skin the source of discussion among the men. She has to be completely obedient to her husband and elders throughout days of arduous ceremonies. Husband and wife sit on the new marriage-bed in front of the assembled guests, and endure the teasing and bawdy humour of their relatives and friends, the women tittering behind their veils. At one temple ceremony at which I was present, the bride was ignored while the heads of the two families sat in ceremonial attire with their accountants and their bulky ledgers to discuss the financial transactions associated with the marriage. Heaps of banknotes were piled in front of them on the marble floor at the feet of the deity. In such circumstances a bride would feel her prestige and status in economic terms, but have little sense of being regarded as a woman with a personality of her own.

Mother and son

No affective relationship in the Indian family is warmer or more intense than that between mother and son. It has been so since the establishment of the joint-family system in late Vedic times, and it continues to be so, even in the urban middle-class nuclear family. There is one important qualification, however: extreme intensity in this relationship is generally focused on only *one* son, often but not invariably the firstborn. While the father is supreme in his authority, the mother is the centre of domestic life; this is ensured, in fact, by the segregation of women and the aloofness of the father. Prolonged unilateral dependence from infancy up to the age of three or more, and the inculcation of passivity, docility, obedience, and respect, especially when reinforced by excessive (though irregular) indulgence, all tend to encourage a son's very deep attachment to his mother. That it is current psychological theory to link indulgence with aggressive feelings towards the mother and fantasies of a frightening 'terrible mother' (Plate 32) of the Kālī-type, does not lessen the validity of this statement; on the contrary, it is reinforced. Hindu myth is replete with imagery relating to fantasies of both omnipotence and dependence, which can be traced to their common origin in pleasure of receptivity and privileged freedom during earliest years.

In a report on the character-formation of the southern Chinese in

America, Dr. Warner Muensterberger has observed a somewhat similar situation:

In her rivalry with her brothers and other male contemporaries, the woman finds her chief, socially acceptable gratification in becoming the mother of a son. So that, in addition to its biological function, childbearing, to a woman, serves the cause of self-assertion. The woman then is characterised by her ambivalent strivings to become, on the one hand, an overprotective mother and, on the other hand, a demanding and prohibiting one—wish-fulfilling and vindictive. . . . The early deprivation and submissiveness which, as a young girl and a young daughter-in-law, a woman has to observe, can be gradually given up after she has borne a son. The woman's deep need to overcome her frustrating position is largely met by her becoming the mother of a boy child. This changes her strategic position. Her narcissistic desire for reparation and her ego ideal demand that this son be virile, but she uses him at the same time as her instrument. Here her unconscious ambivalence towards the male breaks through. She has the need to establish her superiority. So with her feeling of maternal love, coexist feelings of envy and retaliation.[1]

The effects on Indian culture of the deep-seated maternal attachment are of profound importance to our study. But we should be careful not to use the familiar Western model of the mother-dominated son, for the Indian family and caste systems considerably mitigate the effeminacy we usually associate with that type. The commonest sublimation is intense mother-goddess worship and worship of womanhood in the abstract. But the total cultural pattern turns full circle once again, recoiling upon the individual members in the form of contempt, uncertainty, and distrust of the woman, her continued restriction in status, and a secret dependence upon her. The Indian woman in turn sums up her feelings about her firstborn son in the proverb: 'More exacting than the neck-husband is the belly husband.'

The Hindu male tends to seek in his wife not a mate but a mother. The network of available social contact in the kinship and caste systems facilitates a normal adjustment to life, but *outside* the social mechanism which these provide, the adolescent or adult male has a fear of emotional commitment (cf. G. M. Carstairs, 1957). There will be a number of occasions in the course of this study when the intense warmth of the mother–son relationship in an influential minority of high-caste families will be referred to. It will be recalled that the art of the cave sanctuaries is connected with the desire to recapture the state of privileged freedom associated with

[1] W. Muensterberger, 'Orality and Dependence, Characteristics of Southern Chinese', *Psychoanalysis and the Social Sciences*, Vol. 3, New York, p. 64. In a personal communication, Muensterberger endorses this comparison between aspects of Chinese and Indian child-rearing (identification of the woman with the baby and identification of self with ungiving mother). He points out that a girl brought up according to the above pattern, who may then become a possessive, narcissistic mother, gives her boy his distorted picture of womanhood.

childhood. One can deduce from the challenge placed on the individual living in an Indian urban environment, that it has not greatly changed since the fifth century B.C. The tendency to retreat in numbers to the 'forest grove' first appeared in response to stresses which the extended-kinship system was not designed, and which it has failed ever since, to meet. More will be said on the psychological traits which lie behind the elaborate culture of the Renouncer in Part Five.

Erik Erikson pursues a most interesting line of thought with regard to the mother–son relationship in India, which is worth quoting *in extenso*, as it has the authority of an internationally renowned psychoanalyst. Taking as his starting-point his own direct observation of Indian play-patterns, he notes that, in invented folk plays, the children create

. . . a play universe filled to the periphery with blocks, people, and animals but with little differentiation between outdoors and indoors, jungle and city, or, indeed, one scene from another. If one finally asks what (and, indeed, *where*) is *the* 'exciting scene', one finds it embedded somewhere where nobody could have discerned it as an individual event and certainly not as a central one. . . . Significant moments embedded in a moving sea of unfathomable multiformity: does not life on the street or at home anywhere offer such an over-all configurational impression? In fact, this is the way I have come to feel about India, often not without a trace of sensory and emotional seasickness. For one moves in a space-time so filled with visual and auditory occurrences that it is very difficult to lift an episode out of the flux of events, a fact out of the stream of feelings, a circumscribed relationship out of a fusion of multiple encounters. If, in all this, I should endow one word with a meaning which unites it all, the word is *fusion*.[1]

Erikson then proceeds to relate this effect of fusion to joint-family living, and to the genesis of a fundamental polarity:

There is, no doubt, a deep recurring need to escape the multitude, and there is a remarkable capacity for being alone in the middle of a crowd. . . . But aloneness, too, is often dominated by a deep nostalgia for fusing with another, and this in an exclusive and lasting fashion, be that 'Other' a mentor or a god, the Universe—or the innermost Self.[2]

The deep nostalgia for fusion is reborn, it seems, from generation to generation out of the diffusion of the mother in the joint-family, in which she must respond to each and, at the same time, to all, and thus can belong to the individual child only in fleeting moments and to nobody for good or for long. A tentative interpretation would suggest that the child feels guilty in a way largely unknown in the West. . . . For the child wants his mother to himself, while she must spread her love.[3]

[1] E. Erikson, *Gandhi's Truth: on the origins of militant non-violence*, Faber and Faber, London, 1970, p. 40. See p. 44 above on E. M. Forster and Mrs. Moore.
[2] Ibid., p. 41.   [3] Ibid., p. 42.

Erikson then notes the plurality of relatives and mother-substitutes in the joint family, explaining how such relationships are consequently free from oedipal rivalry.

The wider family, therefore, permits a closeness, often expressed physically and affectively in a true 'togetherness', deeply touching and yet somewhat disturbing to the Western observer. To hurt or to abandon the uncle or the aunt or the older brother or older sister, therefore, can provoke a peculiar and lifelong guilt; and to be hurt by them, forever gnawing resentment. Thus many live always dependent, expectant, demanding, sulking, despairing, and yet always seeking the fusion which affirms, confirms, fulfils. Such expectance of reunification by fate *can*, in turn, lead to an utterly passive sense of non-responsibility as an individual, and to a waiting for salvation by some form of re-immersion. . . . every Indian, be he never so well educated and pragmatic, lives also in a feminine space-time that is deep inside a HERE and in the very centre of a NOW, not so much an observer of a continuum of means but a participant in a flux marked by the intensity of confluence.[1]

Here, I think, Erikson prematurely abandons the polarity he observed earlier, for the Indian is indeed both a participant in a flux and also a detached observer of it; he can just as much yearn for fission as for fusion, and, as will be shown in Part Three, he has infused the social system with an unceasing rhythm of fission and fusion. Erikson concludes his interpretation:

Historically all this *may* be related to an ancient and stubborn trend to preserve the India of the mother goddesses against all the conquerors, their father gods, and their historical logic. The power of the mother goddesses probably has also given India that basic bisexuality which, at least to her British conquerors, appeared contemptible and yet also uncanny and irresistible in every sense of the word.[2]

To conclude, we should hear an Indian advance a characteristically favourable attitude towards the Hindu ideal of reverence for the mother and wife (compare Plate 52):

In the beginning, according to Indian mythology, was Shakti, and Shakti, which means energy, has in Sanskrit a feminine gender. The cosmos was her creation, her child. . . . And what could be nobler than to see the Creator as a Mother? It is the mother, not the father, who comes to mind first whenever the word 'creation' is mentioned. Woman's eternal energy, her natural ability to give and to feed life, to add cell to cell, make man look relatively unimportant to the scheme of things. . . . One can be sure of one's mother if not of one's father; and if this is true on earth, it may also be true of the cosmos. . . . All other loves, the loves of the betrothed, of married couples, of friends, of fathers for their sons, of brothers and sisters, are based on reciprocity, and are forms of friendship; mother love alone can be one-sided. . . . Consequently, it seems to me that if

[1] Erikson (1970), p. 43.   [2] Ibid., p. 44.

God is love, He should be conceived of as Mother and not Father. . . . There was a time in my youth when I made myself sick with love of God. . . . I . . . concentrated on the face of my mother, believing that if God was, He must be a supreme image of my mother's disinterested love. . . .[1]

Family and society

Before concluding this analysis of family relations a word should be said about the link between traditional family life and the basic social institution of caste. The caste system will be analysed at the beginning of Part Three; here a point in Professor Hsu's interesting study, *Clan, Caste and Club*, helps to elucidate the attitude of the joint family to the total social system. The all-inclusiveness of the extended family does not, says Hsu, encourage its members to develop an outgoing and relaxed sociability beyond its protective shelter. The vagueness of the kinship ties, a remote father, impersonal relations with elders, segregation of women in their quarters, leave the individual unsatisfied. The emotional insecurity characteristic of all *personal* relationships, as distinct from the safer and more regularized obligations of formal caste and family ties, can be seen to reflect the emotional pattern of child-care in the extended family. Dependence on supernatural powers does, nevertheless, attract the Hindu away from the family.

This supernatural orientation dovetails well with diluted human bonds and fosters perpetual searches for nonworldly anchorages. . . . The predominantly supernatural-centered Hindu family fosters in the individual a centrifugal outlook . . . tends to propel the Hindu individual away from his moorings in his family and forces him to venture into the unknown.[2]

Yet the Hindu, like all human beings, needs psychological ties with fellow human beings for sociability, security, and status. Caste and subcaste, with their cohesive and yet fissile traits, are at once the Indian solution to this contradiction and an expression of it.

The pattern of unilateral dependence encourages a feeling of individual helplessness as well as depersonalized group solidarity. The egoistic impulses which child-care encourages are later checked by a system of interdependent privileges and responsibilities. Hinduism eventually curbs and channels into norms of behaviour the emotional effusiveness natural to early childhood. But that early stage in the upbringing of the child continues long enough for those egoistic impulses to reappear if the social checks break down. Discipline is imposed through social and religious

[1] Krishnalal Shridharani, *My India, My America*, Duell, Sloan & Pearce, Inc., New York, 1941, p. 199.
[2] Hsu (1963), pp. 5 and 225.

institutions with greater authority than that of parents. The individual has no means to exercise choice in marriage, and the joint family lessens the possibility of any single member becoming the focus of spoiling. But this kind of discipline and conformity which the family itself imposes is incomplete; a remote father, and an indulgent mother, whose freedom of action is confined for the most part within her limited and segregated domain, leave the way open for their children to seek meaningful relationships within the caste and sect. Well-defined religious and caste duties compensate for the diffused nature of home discipline; priests and gurus supplement the authority of the father figure, but as with the plurality of father and mother figures in the joint family, so the same picture is revealed on the religious plane. Polytheism and tolerance of social pluralism (caste) are interrelated, while indifference to political unification of the heterogeneous society is endorsed by this plurality of paternal authority.

The importance of solidarity pervades all the mutually interdependent groups. Responsibility is shared in common rather than exercised with personal authority. The tasks of all family and caste members are precisely determined; a child first begins to observe these by watching the highly stylized etiquette of family assemblies. Duties are so arranged as to reduce the element of *individual* competition (as distinct from *group* competition); the ideal of the self-sufficient village economy with its exchange of specialized services between the inhabitants (and a minimum exchange of cash) ensures that every man performs his allotted task, but does not excel above others. Exceptional ability is rarely encouraged in rural caste society and among urban artisan castes, so that the standard of workmanship and efficiency is kept in balance.[1] The law of moral consequences, *karma*, helps to co-ordinate those egoistic impulses with the interests of society as a whole. Failure to do his duty, which before everything means caste duty, would spoil the individual's spiritual chances. Caste duty is by definition social duty and is recognized by all. In this way egoistic impulses are effectively harnessed to the interests of society and kept in harmony with religious goals.

Personal ambition, on the other hand, tends to overreach prescribed rules. Most of the important schools of Indian thought lay great emphasis on actions performed with complete detachment, and therefore ascribe the highest spiritual attainments to those accruing from deeds that are wholly impersonal. Making action the means of expression of personal desires and ambitions merely enchains one to the fetters of *karma*. Personal initiative cannot be beneficial to moral progress because the essence of escape from *karma* is to free oneself from one's desires. Good actions, as conceived by

---

[1] Ambivalence with regard to the encouragement of academic performance is examined in the Conclusion.

the ethical teaching of any given caste, are non-egoistic in everything but the desire to achieve salvation.

Family, caste, and religion acknowledge the helplessness of the individual and the power of the group. In all three spheres authority is addressed by means of abject pleas, but without any accompanying loss of self-respect. Confession of helplessness to parents, guru, caste, or gods is the most exquisite consolation—admitting one immediately to the enfolding embrace of the All. To cry for help does not cast one into a limbo of anxiety and lonely admission of personal inadequacy, but elicits a favourable response from the collective power of which the individual is an indissoluble part (Plate 54).

The sense of achievement is based on the success with which the individual fulfils his prescribed duties and not on his efforts to transcend them. In his social relations he acts with confidence so long as the relationship is on customary lines, formal, impersonal, an exchange of obligations. But if the relationship has no connection with the network of social obligations and is based solely on mutual regard and affection, he may feel uncertain and distrustful. This hesitancy in personal relations is probably the result of the ambivalent relations of love he experienced in the bosom of his own family. In such circumstances he is liable to bursts of emotional effusiveness in personal relationships, followed by periods of remoteness and apparent indifference. 'Personality' is less important than status; preoccupation with the latter still survives in the changing pattern of independent friendships, though it may no longer have specific caste connotations.

The caste-oriented individual finds little stimulus to develop consistent personal integrity and sincerity in accordance with his own conscience, for these belong to the sphere of personality, the sense of self, the ego—a shadowy, vaguely defined area of himself which he is conditioned to regard as either unreal or displeasing to God. Before authority, father-figures, and God he must be as nothing, desireless, without any will of his own. To escape the sense of helplessness, that is to say, to improve his situation either socially or spiritually, he devotes himself to the acquisition of power, fundamentally an act of self-punitive asceticism (cf. G. M. Carstairs, 1957). The ardent devotee who surrenders his manhood and becomes once again a helpless infant, grows accustomed to getting what he wants. Fits of optimism periodically seize the tradition-directed individual, during which all his difficulties seem to dissolve miraculously, particularly if he is insistent enough to exercise a tyrannical hold over his inferiors, tempted by the belief that he himself is omnipotent.

Chapter Three   Sexual Relationships

There is probably nothing in the life of foreign peoples more prone to misconception than the way they conduct their sexual life. India is no exception; the foreigner often forms a coloured, not to say lurid, picture compounded of erotic temple sculpture, the *Kāma Sūtra*, mystical orgiasticism, and Bombay's 'street of the cages'. At the same time, while he has probably heard about the cult of phallic deities, the foreigner also notices a counter-emphasis in religion on asceticism, a puritanical social life with a tabu on overt expression of tenderness between young people, and sentimental movie romances in which kissing is prohibited. All these things exist, of course, while the Indian cultural heritage projected by the tourist industry is pervaded by a distinctively Indian atmosphere of sensuality. The actual situation is also complex, but if we are to understand it we must penetrate the screen of romanticism to the lives of real men and women. It seems that every alternate generation in the West produces a small, but obtrusive, minority who are vaguely attracted by the fantasy of a heightened Indian sexuality; the cult of psychedelic Hindu eroticism in the 1960s was just such a case. This too we must circumvent if anything like an objective assessment is to be made.

In spite of the ban on the movie kiss, the Indian cinema and popular literature reveal an emphasis on the erotic. Again, the foreign observer is likely to be struck by the vulgarity with which some modern urban groups flaunt their sex appeal; he or she is also likely to be the recipient of somewhat lurid confidences about personal sex life couched in exclusively physical terms. The coarse behaviour of youths on city streets and, if the visitor is a linguist, his encounters with the bawdy humour of the peasant or the salacious jokes of the popular theatre, are also reminders that Indians, like all other people, enjoy discarding the polite fictions of a decorous façade. It is well-known that India is faced with the acute social problem of the abduction of women. All these facts are easily discerned and significant aspects of Indian sexual life. What are both more important and more difficult to discern are the value systems and quality of sexual relations between individuals. Segregation of the sexes, and a tabu code on serious open discussion among private groups (as distinct from trivial banter and innuendoes—common enough even at middle-class parties), make it all the more difficult to arrive at reliable conclusions, in addition to the obvious difficulty of investigating an inherently private domain.

There are a few points which should be examined briefly, as these will reveal the challenge to the relationship between man and woman now posed by changes in family organization.

Asceticism and orgiasticism

The Indian woman is looked upon in turn with idealization, desire, and alarm (Plates 10, 55, and 32). Though subservient to man, she nevertheless dominates a certain section of his life as a mother; as she grows older she often has an increasingly important say in family affairs. She is both raised to the level of a goddess in the home, and herself should revere her husband as a god, though this religious element has almost vanished from urban middle-class homes. Similarly, sexual love is raised to the level of mystical ecstasy, but is also looked upon as the most severe hindrance to the spiritual development of the husband. The woman is both a Sītā, the Hindu ideal of the selfless and devoted wife, and the terrible Kālī, a witch-like goddess who punishes and deprives her children of pleasure. Women whose sexual demands are refused are believed to become witches, and must therefore be appeased, lest they turn against men in reprisal. The pollution tabus associated with menstruation are also an important factor in domestic life. Since a woman must live in isolation for four days during menstruation, the entire household is aware of the fact, and the attention of every member of the household is drawn thus to the one domain left in which husband and wife might otherwise enjoy complete privacy. This has the effect of emphasizing the physical aspect of sexual life in the relationship of husband and wife and belittling everything else. It also reminds others of the wife's inferior status as an agent of pollution.

It is very widely believed in India that a woman's craving for sexual satisfaction constitutes a threat to a man's physical and psychological well-being. According to the ideas of popular Indian hygiene, a man should, as far as possible, practise seminal thrift, for the loss of semen is considered weakening. The traditional dietary system is based on food categories which are 'heating' and 'cooling', foods which either inflame the passions or cool them (see Part Three, Chapter Five). Eggs, milk, sugar, and honey are believed to build up 'good semen' for fertility, or 'recirculation' in the body. The schools of yoga and asceticism are much concerned with the problem of how to retain semen and to ensure its 'recirculation' in the psycho-physiological system, whereby it is believed that greater spiritual vitality is assured. By the same token, to satisfy the carnal needs of his wife a husband must sacrifice a portion of his spiritual vitality. The more Sanskritized the customs of a caste, the more are restrictions imposed on the frequency of intercourse. The scriptures are full of mythical incidents in which women are the decoys of the gods, distracting ascetics and deities from penance and meditation. This is all the more important in view of the widely held traditional Indian belief that a woman has greater need of sexual satisfaction than a man. Many restrictions on the woman are designed to prevent her from succumbing to the unbridled lust to which, according to this belief, her own physiology makes her prone. There is unusual emphasis in moral teaching on the need to achieve freedom from sexual desire. The pre-occupation with sexual continence (the prestige of *brahmāchārya*—chastity—and elaborate safeguards to ensure a chaste spiritual hygiene) amounts almost to an obsession in the higher castes, save the military. We know from the fieldwork of psychologists and doctors that a common cause of anxiety among men of all castes is due to fears about loss of semen (cf. Carstairs 1957).

This ambivalent adult image of women, which has been endorsed by India's religious teachers, is related to the experiences of infancy and childhood. The ambivalence-pattern—over-protectiveness, domineering fathers, punitive discipline, the segregation and low status of women, and sexual innuendoes in front of sons among the menfolk—leads to contradic-tory ideas about sexuality, which, though similar to Western confusion between idealization of chastity and the need to propagate the species, are based on a different determining childhood situation. This is reflected in religious ideas, which range from pure asceticism on the one hand, through introverted, narcissistic, yogic sublimation, to the ordinary sexual life of the householder, and on to orgiasticism, eroticized ecstasy, and idealized spiritual love, or *sahaja*, on the other. This range of religiously valorized sexual attitudes is coloured by a similar diversity of attitudes regarding purity and pollution, from the extreme compulsive fear of pollution on the one hand to morbid preoccupation or perverse eroticism on the other. This latter hierarchy is of some importance to the understanding of Indian sexuality since the genitals, and all bodily discharges, are regarded as polluting. Thus the more typical response is to impose some restriction on sexuality, linked with the washing mania, while the atypical response, invested as it is with the excitement of transgression, and therefore with holiness and power, may be summed up in the aphorism used by mystics, yogic ascetics, and sadhus alike: 'filth and sandalpaste are *one*'.[1] In a word, the general climate may be said to be antinomian, which accords with the monistic pattern of the Great Tradition, while the individual temperament

[1] A paste made from powdered and fragrant-smelling sandalwood for use in ritual as body- or image-adornment.

is afforded the widest latitude, from highly idealistic morality, through genial toleration, to compulsive extremes (Plates 37, 55, and 46).

The complexity of sexual attitudes is apparent even from the Vedic age, which is normally associated with a frank acceptance of the flesh in sensual pleasures—for example, in the coarse, uncomplicated, and bucolic descriptions of sexual activity among deities. At the same time, however, we find the first references there to the forced continence and guilt feelings for which Indian religion and literature are well known. There is an element of asceticism in the Vedic sacrifice. Mauss regards the 'sacrifice' of the priest and the patron in the ritual preparation for the ceremony as the original source of the ascetic mysticism of later Hinduism.

But there is, in addition, one significant feature of Vedic sacrifice which has an important bearing on Indian attitudes to sexuality. This is the decidedly grotesque conclusion to the greatest of all Vedic sacrifices—the Royal Aśvamedha, or Horse Sacrifice. Performed on behalf of chieftains or kings, the Horse Sacrifice (which lingered on in feudal India, notably in Rājasthān, where the last known sacrifice was performed in the eighteenth century at Jaipur and a marble horse installed in a commemorative shrine) required a vast number of Brahmans of four specialist castes. On the sacrifice the well-being of the Vedic tribe rested, ensuring fertility and supreme royal power over other kings. A stallion was allowed to roam at will for a year; wherever it went, the king of that territory would either have to fight or cede sovereignty. Meanwhile, the chief sacrificer submitted to lengthy self-punitive asceticism and purification rites. On return to the sacrificial enclosure, the stallion was worshipped by the king's wives and later suffocated. Here begins the macabre rite in which the senior queen lies down and 'cohabits' with the dead horse to the accompaniment of ritualistic invocations of bucolic crudity delivered by the chief sacrificer:

Come, lay thy seed well in the channel of the one who has opened her thighs. O thou, potent of manhood, set in motion the organ that is to women the nourisher of life. It darts into the sheath, their hidden lover, darkly buffeting, back and forth.

Finally, the queen sits beside the carcass while the Brahmans dismember it, remove the marrow, cook it, and offer the steaming potion to the king, who thereby imbibes the 'soul-stuff' on behalf of his people, as the queen had symbolically absorbed into herself the consecrated male potency.[1] This is the first recorded evidence of a constellation of psychological factors which

[1] For the relevant material cf. *Śatapatha Brāhmaṇa*, tr. J. Eggeling, Sacred Books of the East, 12, 26, 41, 43, 44, Clarendon Press, Oxford, 1882–1900; *Taittirīya Saṃhitā*, tr. A. B. Keith, *Veda of the Black Yajus School Entitled Taittirīya Saṃhitā*, Harvard Oriental Series, XVIII-XIX, Harvard University Press, Cambridge, Mass., 1914; and the works of Professor J. J. Meyer.

10. Queen in palace scene. Fresco. Ajantā. Sixth century A.D. *Archaeological Survey of India.*

11. Brahman receiving ransom money from king. Fresco. Ajantā. Fifth century A.D. *Archaeological Survey of India.*

above 12. Village scene. Sānchī gateway. First century A.D. *André Martin, Paris.*
below 13. Rock-carved Buddhist *ćaitya* with *dāgoba*. Bedsā. *c.* 175 B.C. *Stella Snead.*

above right 14. Descent of Ganges. Rock. Mahābalipuram. Seventh century A.D. *Author.*
below right 15. Group of *rathas*. Rock. Mahābalipuram. Seventh century A.D. *Author.*

left 16. Nāga king. Rock. Bādāmi. Sixth century A.D. *Author.*

right 17. Maithuna. Rock. Bādāmi. A.D. 587. *Author.*

below 18. Ardhanārīśvara, Maheshamūrti. Rock. Elephanta. Eighth century A.D. *Author.*

opposite, above left 19. Shiva dancing. Rock. Ellorā. Seventh century A.D. *Author.*

opposite, above right 20. Nāga king and queen. Rock. Ajantā. Sixth century A.D. *Author.*

opposite, below 21. Seven mother goddesses. Rock. Ellorā. Seventh century A.D. *Author.*

above 22. Ceiling. Detail. Fresco. Ajantā. Fifth century A.D. *De Harcourt/UNESCO.*

opposite, above 23. Marble screen. Fatehpur Sikri. A.D. 1580. *Author.*
opposite, left centre 24. Mirror inlay. Rājasthān. Eighteenth century. A.D. *Author.*
opposite, right centre 25. Painted arch. Agra. A.D. 1648. *Author.*
opposite, below 26. Lotus leaves. Rock. Ellorā. Seventh century A.D. *Author.*

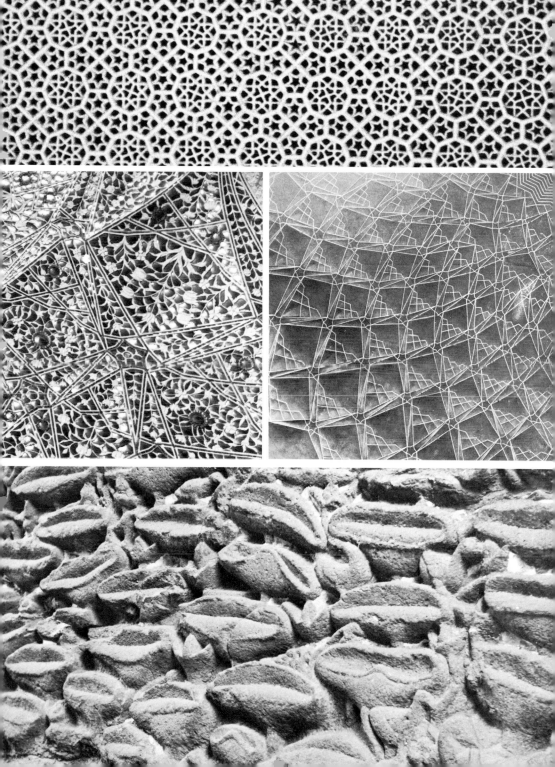

Plate 27 *above*. Kaṇḍāriya Mahādeva and Devī Jagadambā temples, Khajurāho. Eleventh century A.D. *André Martin, Paris.*

Plate 28 *below*. Women's apartments and baths. Fatehpur Sikri. Sixteenth century A.D. *Louis Frédérick/Rapho.*

recur throughout the history of Indian sexuality, giving rise to customs, the principal characteristics of which are the ritual retention of semen, avoidance of orgasm, symbolic *coitus interruptus*, and the attribution of magico-religious potency to semen when it is conserved within the body. The corpus of yogic tradition includes such related ideas as the 'permanently' chaste ithyphallus, 'storing of semen in the head', and, in its Tantric form, ritualistic *coitus reservatus* with a consecrated sexual partner. The main principle of these archaic practices (which are still resorted to) is that the performance of the sexual act without emission is a means of obtaining spiritual power. These rites are no longer of interest to any but a small minority of Indians, but they are manifestations of widespread beliefs in the need to minimize loss of semen. Day-to-day male preoccupation with inadvertent loss of semen, pollution rules, and strict regulation in the frequency of intercourse according to the customs of one's caste, dietary habits designed to check loss of semen but increase its supply and 'recirculation' in the physical system, and the universal ideal of 'renunciation', or at least continence, in the latter half of life, all indicate widespread concern with the need for self-torture in physical sexuality for the sake of spiritual salvation.

While this introverted, often morbid, sexuality which made its first recorded appearance in symbolic coitus with the dead sacrificial horse, continued to exert a powerful influence on the development of religious orgiasticism, a more vigorous, extraverted sexuality can be seen to have played a prominent role in more secular classical culture. N. C. Chaudhuri, who tends to over-emphasize the devastating climatic conditions of India with a characteristic loathing, believes that the Hindus turned unconsciously to a programme of sexual rehabilitation as a form of climatic adaptation. This, he claims, resulted in 'a high and even intangible value [which] the Hindu set on a purely physical satisfaction'.[1] With the flowering of classical culture the upper classes revealed a hyperaesthetic interest in sexuality, obvious in their poetry, drama, and fresco painting. Chaudhuri thinks that this acted as a kind of 'counterthesis' to the cruder, but also more religious, literary culture of the Vedas and Epics. The romanticization of sex in the classical age (and its modish emulation in our own day by the exquisites of the urban upper classes) had, he says with justice, 'an irresistible fervour, graciousness, and *douceur*. The Hindus succeeded in creating a *courtoisie*, as it were, of the sex act, and, if I might coin the word, also a troubadourism, with pretty conceits, and gestures, and symbols. Incapable of transcending the flesh, they showed their ingenuity in etherealising it.'[2]

Chaudhuri mentions, only in passing, that the mass of Hindus shared none of this idealization of sex. True, but he makes no reference to the

[1] N. C. Chaudhuri, *The Continent of Circe*, Chatto and Windus, London, 1965, p. 189.
[2] Ibid., p. 200.

strong undercurrent of lurid, frequently morbid sexuality that originated in the folklore of the masses, but which mingled in the streams of Puranic, Tantric, and *bhakti* Hinduism to be carried along into the Great Tradition throughout the classical period. Much of the sorcery, witchcraft, sacrificial cults, magico-religious formulae, and drug techniques was only made 'respectable' through Sanskritization in the feudal Middle Ages, but these are evidently of ancient origin in the regional folk traditions—and all are pervaded by the kind of sexual morbidity and catharism which Chaudhuri wrongly places later in his historical scheme. But what he deduces from these aspects of Hindu sexuality appears to be sound enough:

> The Hindus, on the other hand, were frightened by the idea of naked lust in women, and even when they knew that it existed up to a point, they tried desperately to turn a blind eye to it. Furthermore, they actually looked up to the woman to rescue their lust from its creeping paralysis. Therefore they would beg the woman's desire as a favour, with grace and humility. There was in this Hindu begging something of the gallantry of the knight kneeling at the feet of his lady-love. . . .
>
> But it should be obvious that the Hindu man's clinging dependence on the woman imposed too great a burden on her, and in the end it proved too heavy. In Sanskrit literature the fatigue of coitus is an ever-present accompaniment to the feminine existence. . . . Nevertheless, in the earlier ages . . . the burden was not as crushing as it finally became.[1]
>
> In his revulsion from sexual enjoyment he was capable of some very tortured psychological and physiological acrobatics, but to have complete freedom was the last thing he cared for, because to give up lust was for him to turn his back on life itself. So, even when he abandoned the world, his abnegation did not exclude an insidious and disguised lust. A peeping, pricking, tormenting naughty little thing had to keep up even the sadhu's faith in spirituality.[2]

The *Kāma Sūtra*

The acrobatics with which the Hindus spurred on their declining potency are the subject of an overrated text, Vātsyāyana's *Kāma Sūtra*, the product of an effete, enervating, courtly culture in decline. The *Kāma Sūtra* became a standard manual on the art of love, but its appeal was restricted to court circles and the upper classes. Censorship, suppression, and the depredations of time have had their way, and consequently, for lack of other, and probably earlier, texts surviving, the *Kāma Sūtra* has become a historical landmark in erotology. It was written between the first and fourth centuries A.D. and belongs to a tradition of courtly love which still has the traces of

[1] Chaudhuri (1965i), pp. 204–5.
[2] Ibid., p. 203.

magic tribal lore. The *Kāma Sūtra* is wholly devoid of the sexual mysticism represented by Khajurāho and Orissan temples, the Mahāyāna, Shaiva, and Vaishnava cults. Sexual passion is not identified with divine passion and the union of opposites. All that Vātsyāyana is concerned with is imparting instruction for the pursuit of pleasure.

The *Kāma Sūtra* has probably come down to us in a slightly bowdlerized version which suffered at the hands of Brahman censors. It is a manual for erotic specialists, in the same sense that the *Arthashāstra* is a manual for power specialists, and it drily lists the techniques of sex. For Vātsyāyana each type of lover has a separate point of view, and he asserts the usual Indian principle of an ethic for each according to his own nature. He then proceeds to number and classify in hierarchical order each type with systematic pedantry and thoroughness, to the delight of German erotologists. But his broad-minded advice to each type that they should practise what is uniquely appropriate to their situation is more enlightened than the theories of some more modern erotologists. Vātsyāyana, then, is an interesting example of the intellectual who adopted a liberal outlook within the pluralist frame of the Indian social hierarchy. It is important to remember this because, even though he probably lived in an age when caste stratification was not yet afflicted with the dogmatic rigidity of later centuries, it is easy to assume that liberal views like Vātsyāyana's would be inconceivable in a caste society.

The prevailing sententiousness is occasionally relieved by humorous advice on, for instance, the ways to overcome the resistance of married women, or how the senior wife can foment trouble among her younger colleagues. K. M. Panikkar, in his Introduction to the Burton–Arbuthnot translation, denies Vātsyāyana's moral inconsistency. The author's object, he says, is 'a thoroughly moral one—that of instructing men and women in the legitimate pleasures of the senses'. But this hardly accords with Vātsyāyana's advice to eunuch shampooers, or on the acquisition of village women by 'a mere word to the headman', the rape of women made drunk, and the use of corrupt harem go-betweens.

K. M. Panikkar is only partly right in claiming that the *Kāma Sūtra* reflects a condition of high civilization. It is true that women then enjoyed a higher status than they did later in Indian history. He lists the education of women, freedom of social intercourse, remarriage of widows, as evidence of this. But Vātsyāyana's class-conscious picture of life in the royal harems, the treatment of slaves, abduction of peasant women, and the like, leaves Panikkar's claim in need of qualification. As we have already said, the class for whom the *Kāma Sūtra* was written would have been rather more 'decadent' than 'high'. To be fair, Vātsyāyana, for all his nonsense about dead vultures and camel bones for aphrodisiacs, and for all his pedantry and urban frivolity, is not guilty of emotional falsification; he is not an inveterate fantasist like de Sade, he is witty and amusing; usually, and this is the most important of his virtues, he is humane. 'Of all the lovers of a girl,' he says, 'he only is her true husband who possesses the qualities that are liked by her, and such a husband only enjoys real superiority over her because he is the husband of love.'

Marital relations

There is a widespread notion among foreigners that every literate Indian reads the *Kāma Sūtra*. This is not so, although copies do circulate in the colleges. Attempts by parents to give their children sound advice and preparation for marriage are uncommon. Older women wait until just before marriage to inform them about its physical aspect. When a girl marries and moves into her husband's household she suffers homesickness, and often domestic hardship. She only gradually becomes acquainted with her husband, whom she has never seen, in most cases, before her wedding day. She meets him at the end of an exhausting day, and not until everyone has gone to bed. This is probably the only time when she is either permitted, or has the time, to talk to him. Submissive, confused with fear and sleepiness, she comes face to face with a virtual stranger. For most young couples, unaffected by the more liberal trends of the cities, this is the reality behind the romantic Western picture of India's sophisticated cult of the *Kāma Sūtra*.

Frieda Das, a European woman who lived for many years in India, describes the relationship of a young Hindu bride to her husband:

... in her loneliness and intimidation, the comfort and relaxation of sheer physical proximity to this one being in her strange surroundings brought it about that she began to cleave to her husband more than anyone in the new household. Though she did not realise it, her husband came to take the place of a father in the little bride's feelings. As the insurmountable barrier of exaggerated respect and obedience had, in the past, put an unnatural distance between herself and her father, she was apt to find this substitute-father more comforting, or at least more approachable, than her own parent had been. ...

In the first instance two things were bound to happen. The greater a girl's innate but undeveloped capacity for individual choice, volition, and action—all tendencies sharply deprecated from her earliest days by those who surround her —the deeper the sublimation of these qualities and the more intensely did she finally throw herself into forms of expression of exactly opposite characteristics: unquestioning obedience, total abnegation of self-will, tireless service, lack of initiative. The greater her frustrated urge to outer freedom and independence, the fuller her escape into spiritual submission.[1]

[1] Frieda H. Das, *Purdah: the status of Indian women*, Kegan Paul, Trench, Trubner, London, 1932, pp. 106–7.

Pursuit of this theme in literary sources is a far from satisfactory procedure because there are few sincere and open statements. Chaudhuri is perhaps one of the very few who does write with frankness on sexual problems.
His emotional style is somewhat obtrusive, but his comments are valuable
for what they reveal about the modern Indian attitude to sexuality. His is
the point of view of a highly individualistic, Westernized writer looking
with pained detachment at, and at some remove from, a way of life which
appals him: 'the strain on the woman became worse. . . . The pain and
fatigue became a constant smart, and the para-erotic langour was transformed into para-erotic smouldering . . . as married life advanced, sensibility declined and violence increased. This personal trend was recapitu-
lated in collective life.'[1] Through successive attempts to assuage her desire,
the man killed the woman's response, but

also killed the woman's mercy, and his sexual life took a new turn . . . he turned
into an impossible egotist. . . . It would be a mistake to think that all Hindu
women acquiesced in the torture inflicted on them. . . . Some took their revenge.
. . . I am not sure where I read it, to my recollection it is in Tulsīdās, but the
saying at all events is there, and it is a terrifying saying: 'The charmer of the
night is the tigress of the day, and yet every home has its pet tigress.'

'The moralists,' he continues, 'must already have seen something like
what I have been observing in Hindu married life since my boyhood. It
would be grossly unfair to the women as well as to Hindu society to say
that this state of affairs was or is general, but still it was and is widespread
enough to constitute a serious moral situation.' He then makes two further
points about the inability of women in this predicament to protect themselves. They assert their power in a different way—firstly:

Even as a boy I could detect in ageing women, who had not been released
from the mood by widowhood, not only indifference to the life's partner, but almost passive hatred. The women threw about taunts, slighting remarks, and even
darker innuendoes not fully understood by us, when speaking of their husbands.
Had we not been quite used to this kind of talk we should have been shocked.
Yet in their nightly bed the two, who felt almost a loathing for each other,
would oblige the respective bodies from the prickings of the most desiccated
lust, and hate each other all the more for it. Throughout married life the drying
up of the lust without its atrophy, and the growth of the repulsion marched
step in step.

Secondly, no overseer in a galley could be more ruthless in making the wretched
slaves row than these women in prodding their husbands to earn money.[2]

There is undoubtedly a brighter side to the picture of traditional Hindu
marriage, with its well-known emphasis on feminine devotion and religiosity (as in Plate 52). This is especially true of millions of marriages among

[1] Chaudhuri (1965), p. 205.   [2] Ibid., pp. 206–8.

castes who followed the *bhakti* cults. An example of this equally characteristic feature of well-adjusted harmony is the marriage of the famous Hindu social reformer Ranade and his wife Rāmābai. Although Rāmābai never had enough sleep after all her domestic toils, she used to share with her husband a period of hymn-reading before dawn every morning. She treasured the memory of these hours when she listened to her husband reading the verses of Tukaram:

> At such moments, in that lovely light of the earliest dawn, when I saw his countenance filled with worship, my own heart overflowed with tenderness, and my love for him and my worship of him increased involuntarily. When I was alone my mind would be filled with thoughts of him in our human relations. But in those morning hours I was conscious, though for a moment at a time only, of a kind of spiritual power in him, and I saw him as an almost super-human being.[1]

While it would be quite incorrect to assume that the pious traditional family invariably stultified emotional maturity, there is surely a connection to be drawn between the mechanistic and sterile sexual relationship to which numerous (but by no means all) Indian couples are reduced and the impersonal pattern of joint-family life, with its emphasis on the subordination of emotional ties to the solidarity of the group. While the joint-family system undoubtedly saved Indian society from the excesses of internal conflict, and the spirit of rebelliousness and discontent among the youth to which the West is prone, it has not saved the individual from a desperate hollowness in his sex life and the atrophy of his spirit of adventure.[2]

---

[1] Rāmābai Ranade, *Himself, the Autobiography of a Hindu Lady*, tr. Katherine Gates, Longmans, Green & Co., Inc., New York, 1938, pp. 93–4.

[2] In a personal communication, Muensterberger considers that the most striking feature about Indian character-formation is 'the obvious lack or limits of true object relationship', and cites the lack of toys ('transitional objects') as one example of the lack of aids in the transition from a primary narcissistic position to an object cathexis. He also sees a connection between the mechanical attitude towards sexual relationships in the *Kāma Sūtra* and abstaining from or avoiding genuine object love. Āpastamba's reference, cited above, to 'a bride given to the family' implies the ideal of a relatively desexualized husband–wife relationship. 'The husband,' Muensterberger continues, 'makes love not for his own pleasure but to please the family, while the woman is regarded as a commodity. Because of the fear of passivity one becomes seemingly active, holds back and controls orgasm. The husband refuses to give *her*. Sexual intercourse is not a matter of gratification but of burden.' It is true that in the religious culture and literature of India, avoidance of object-relationship is frequently cited as the essential condition for a spiritual quest, but the normal, complex pattern of joint-family interaction does not support such a reduction to a single determining situation. I wish to avoid the suggestion that the psyche is prior to societal determinations, or to construct a single overall theory based on the lack of 'true object cathexes'. Though I am greatly indebted to Muensterberger for drawing my attention to an important point, I have refrained from developing the idea further as it would exceed the exploratory, open-ended scheme of the analysis. Object cathexis, it seems to me, is a culture-conditioned

Of the greatest importance to India's future, therefore, will be the effects of the worldwide sexual revolution of modern times. Especially in India, the consequences of contraceptive facilities are, sooner or later, bound to have a chain reaction of profound significance, not only on the rate of population increase, but also on the pattern of social life between the sexes. Hitherto the latter has been circumscribed by tabus on pollution and sexual contact between castes, and concerning the status of women. Decline in the appeal and effectiveness of religious curbs on mixed socialization under modern conditions, the pattern of co-education, and the use of reliable contraception, are already weakening the purist's case for retaining the strict rules which have been so much a feature of life in India during recent centuries. Nuclear family life leads to an equalization of the marital relationship and this is already visible among the Indian professional classes. More important still, the pattern of liberalization in sexual mores with which the West is now familiar, has already reached India, and with freer association between young men and women a new kind of emotional reciprocity is bound to develop. The negative effects of liberalization—coarseness, molestation, vulgarity in manners—are not likely to be permanent, even if they continue for many decades to be obtrusive. Until recently, the Western source of this trend was partially concealed by the atmosphere of emotional religiosity, as in the case of the Ranades, where there was an undoubted, but unobtrusive, nineteenth-century Western influence. Today, when such religiosity is far less intense, emotional reciprocity has appreciably changed the social atmosphere among the middle classes, though without actually dissolving their Indian cultural identity.

---

concept based on certain Western assumptions, and can only be applied in an Indian context with considerable caution, supported by detailed case-work. The influence of ascetic thought on Indian culture and society is a matter which will be examined in Part Three, Chapter Five, and Part Five, Chapter One.

Chapter Four   Change in the Family System

Wherever there has recently been a radical betterment of the economic conditions of sectors of the Indian population, correspondingly great changes have been found in the pattern of family life. Structurally, there is a change from the joint to the nuclear system; culturally, the change usually includes Westernization. The most affected groups are the middle classes and the industrial proletariat. Geographically, the process is unevenly distributed and is confined almost wholly to urban areas, or districts which have been subject to intensive industrial development or resettlement. Thus certain tribal areas rich in mineral wealth have undergone radical change, and agricultural communities living on the periphery of urban areas have been affected. Today, the urban Indian scene is socially complex, with a mixture of communities of all classes living in loosely structured agglomerations. Vestiges of tribal culture, peasant villages, traders living in joint families, middle-class nuclear families, large aristocratic joint families, and rich, highly Westernized élites are all concentrated in or around the urban areas, reflecting a wide diversity of occupations from factory workers to entire colonies of bureaucrats and clerks, from traditional artisans and craftsmen to middle-class professional people and a managerial élite.

The impact of urbanism

Generally, the urban middle class, especially the highly Westernized, have changed from the joint-family system to the nuclear system. But these nucleated families often maintain close kinship ties with the original joint family (usually located at some distance from the city in the ancestral village), though the links with the traditional value system are not easily discerned by the outside observer. Furthermore, a high proportion of adults in nuclear families over the age of forty have lived in a joint family, passed through a transitional phase where they set up separate households on marriage, taking their parents with them, and after the latter's deaths, now live in a fully 'nuclear' state. But the general trend towards nuclear families is by no means uniform. Recent surveys show that in some cities there is a swing back to the joint system. This may be due to severe economic pressures on the middle class and general retrenchment caused by acute financial difficulties in the industrial sector. There are signs, too, that many nuclear families suffer from a sense of alienation.

Urbanization, wealth, and geographical mobility (which usually takes the form either of moving to a city distant from home to take up a new post, or the transfer system of bureaucracy or the private firm), Western-style education or overseas education in the West, and even the industrial environment, do not erode the foundations of the joint-family system in every case. Striking examples of the retention of traditional kinship, preserved for centuries after geographical dispersal, are the Marwari business community, and to a lesser extent the Saraswat Brahmans. Both communities are scattered throughout the country, but have not severed their connections with the ancestral joint-family system and ancestral homeland.

The joint-family system is efficient to the degree that well-defined duties are learnt by emulation of elders living in close proximity. The younger generation gradually fill these positions in the corporate function of the family unit without anxiety, resentment, or revolt. But once the chain of occupational uniformity is broken and a young man learns a new job through training outside the home and caste, stress is felt and the system loses both its *raison d'être* and its efficiency. Where individuals from a joint-family background have had the chance of higher education and increased occupational mobility, these have given the initial psychological impetus: a sense of individuality with a desire for greater independence. In turn this greater degree of individual liberty fosters the desire for a higher standard of living. Among more sophisticated young couples the initiative for leaving the joint family often comes from the wife, whereas psychological conditioning sometimes prevents the husband from himself contemplating such a move. Even then, he may prefer the excuse of a post offered him at some distance to save open conflict with his family.

In castes with less sense of corporate identity, the greater the opportunity for economic profit, the weaker the ties of extended kinship become. A family organization which served the economic and psychological needs of the feudal agricultural communities becomes increasingly cumbersome and restrictive after several generations of industrial modernization. But it is unlikely to disappear completely until the three generations involved in any given family unit have equally undergone full psychological adjustment to the nuclear system. This is especially important in the sphere of attitudes, values, and interpersonal relations. Many factors are involved in what social historians, accustomed to Western models, regard as the inevitable destruction of the extended-kinship system by economic change. Among these we may list the impact of developing mercantilism, industrialization, the emergence of the unified nation state, and a capitalist bourgeoisie. While all these now affect the Indian situation, there are, however, a number of imponderable factors, due to the lack of precedents: 'accelerated development' through a technology infinitely more sophisticated than anything known in the West at the time of the latter's comparable surge forward, an excessive, unparalleled population pressure, greater extremes of poverty—and, above all, the caste system. Not since the Middle Ages has Europe had a social organization in any way like the pervasive web of the traditional Hindu way of life—the seamless universe of hierarchical interdependence. Nor has India ever had centralizing institutions of Church or State rooted in the social system. While scope for individual initiative and mobility undoubtedly exists now in India, there is no precedent for the overall change in depth with which it is faced, save in China. Perhaps nowhere else in the non-Western, developing world, is there a comparable example of a great nation with such complex traditional institutions, the flaunting and open defiance of which constitutes such a high element of risk on the part of the individual, the family, or the collective.

The nuclear family

In human terms we can say that such changes as are actually occurring in Indian family life take two basic forms: emancipation of the son from the dominance of his parents, and the woman's desire to overcome her subordinate position. As we have seen, in former times women stayed at home and men went out into the world. Now the pattern is changing and many women, after obtaining better education, either earn their living because of a need to augment family resources, or take up professional jobs because they want to enlarge their horizons and become responsible citizens who can contribute to the national effort. The result is that men must help more with domestic work. Furthermore, a very sizeable proportion of the male population (Rājputs, ex-landlords, and Brahmans particularly) have had to take up work with a lower traditional status. Since women are taking professional jobs, once exclusively a male preserve, and gaining thereby a higher social status, severe problems of adjustment may arise, particularly in the relations between the sexes. While couples marry later nowadays, the age difference between husband and wife has scarcely changed, with the exception of the wealthier middle class (cf. Ross, 1961). This suggests that men still fear loss of authority, and instinctively prefer a marital relationship which accords with the old pattern of unequal dependence. Sociologists have found that even among the urban middle class a significant proportion of male adults still admit that they feel 'completely dependent' on their parents, while about the same proportion of women feel 'completely independent' of them. Let us therefore examine what the most fundamental and widespread changes are for men and women who have broken away from the joint-family system.

Removed from his kinsmen, the father of a nuclear family has to make decisions on his own, or after consultation with his wife—the latter being a new feature which many men would consider a threat to their own authority. In India's present state of economic instability the father's financial burdens will be acutely difficult to bear, especially if he lives in a big city, where the cost of living has been going up very quickly for some years and the race for higher standards of living has become almost as competitive as in any Western city. Improved global communications tend to make Western models the standards of aspiration—far higher than the financial resources in India permit. A father in this situation will have to seek good accommodation and not only pay for his sons' education (there is a 'degree spiral' as there is a price spiral), but for his daughters' too, and later provide their dowries. Longer years of schooling for his children are generally followed by several years' wait before they find themselves jobs. The latter are so scarce that it is now rarer for the educated to be employed in work commensurate with their training and abilities. On the positive side, relations between husband and wife are more equal than they were, and a new sense of companionship and love will gradually replace the ideals of dependence and traditional loyalty to kin. Since the small urban family does not provide a satisfactory social life in virtual isolation, socialization will be enlarged beyond family and neighbours to include a variety of friendships formed outside the traditional social network. Socialization will also include a larger number of impersonal relationships through associations at work or in clubs.

Change for the women in a nuclear family is no less marked. Increased aspirations deriving from education and employment have suddenly thrust the women into a much larger and more complex world. Their skill at co-ordinating a diversity of family activities is also brought into full play. Without the help of her kinswomen, the mother now assumes a role in family affairs which is almost equivalent in responsibility to that of the father in the patriarchal joint family, while her husband has become more like the 'harassed breadwinner' of the West. One of the most significant effects of this reversal of roles is that the mother–son relationship, intensified by the absence of other mother-surrogates, may create greater tensions for the boy when he leaves home and enters the competitive outside world.

For both men and women these changed circumstances have no clear trend, nor have new ways been devised to give a solid basis to their closer companionship. The interdependence and comparatively well-defined duties of traditional family life, following an immemorial pattern, once fostered the calm and unquestioning poise which results from a highly formalized, hierarchical socialization. As everywhere in the world where industrial urbanization occurs, the poise of those who are faced with the unfamiliar, impersonal relations of modern urban life quickly dissolves. In compensation, there is a tendency to project on individual charismatic figures the role of the authoritative and sheltering parent in a relationship of dependence; such an attachment cannot, under normal day-to-day conditions, be other than precarious. Under these circumstances, the traditional Indian serenity and patience in the face of the hardships of life breaks down, to be replaced by nervousness, restlessness, and a hard, desperate, sullen feeling of a world bereft of love. Such a state of accidia is frequently linked with deeper psychological frustration of the kind we have already examined when dealing with sexual problems.

The younger generation

The vast majority of adolescents know with certainty that their parents will arrange their marriages for them. This has an enormously important influence on their behaviour and upon their initiative in relationships. Girls, for instance, are seldom faced with the need to make difficult decisions on their own, either in their own families or in the families into which they marry, because important problems will be deliberated on by everyone. Where boys and girls have opportunities of mixing, at modern co-educational institutions, their relationships tend to remain very much in the category of nervous, titillating, and tentative skirmishes. Deeper attachments are still rare because they are socially disapproved of, and involve a greater element of hazard than they do in the West. More and more, however, boys and girls in the towns are getting to know their future marriage partners. The custom of the couples never being permitted to meet until the actual marriage ceremony, is gradually being relaxed. The boy and girl may meet in front of the families, or photographs are exchanged. Children exercise the right of 'veto' in progressive families, and they may have known each other at school. 'Love marriages' are still uncommon among either Hindus or Muslims, but they occur with more and more frequency in the towns. There are signs of a reaction, however, especially among those acquainted with previous cases of failure, which, from the absence of guiding precedents, are not uncommon in this kind of marriage at present.

Girls at college in the cities may have to put up with a considerable amount of vulgar molestation from boys; this has become a serious social problem in some of the larger cities. The atmosphere of sexual tension is very marked in many large educational institutions, and both boys and girls feel intensely frustrated by the restrictions imposed on their associating without a chaperone. In consequence the boys tend to be aggressive and coarse in the way they express their feelings towards the girls. This is inflamed by the recent trend among the smartest girls to introduce a touch of sex appeal into the traditionally chaste style of their costume.

For the son education means postponement of marriage; economic insecurity makes him reluctant to commit himself or become emotionally entangled before he is properly settled in life. Competitive pressure makes him extremely anxious about examinations, getting higher grades, and other tensions which are familiar all over the world. These pressures are exacerbated by the sense of insecurity within the family, where parents are likely to be unsure of their authority. Parents and children in a nuclear family are prone to feel resentment towards each other whenever the sense of isolation from kin, never felt in the joint family, most affects their individual psychological well-being. Moreover the collective system survived through the transmission of hereditary skills from father to son; working under his father, the son was not obliged to develop a sense of initiative, as he now must, in order to do well in his career.

A very large proportion of the young men who now congregate in the cities are quite new to this kind of freedom and it is likely to disorient them, give them feelings of inferiority; the lure of greater material incentives may put them off balance. But even more than their parents, they have a need to cultivate friendships; these are less likely to be formed within the carefully graded hierarchical groups, with their traditional loyalties already pre-established. Youth organizations and summer camps are comparatively rare—confined as they, for the most part, are to students in high schools and colleges—and only a privileged minority are trained to mix with different kinds of people, or to cultivate leadership skills.

Daughters, on the other hand, may experience less difficulty in tension with their parents. They too are likely to marry later, but this has the effect of strengthening their relationships with their mothers. To prepare themselves for marriage in a nuclear family, where the advice of older women is not so readily available, they turn more to their mothers than in the collective system. But their problems over socialization are more acute because of the conventional prudery about the opposite sex.

There are fewer signs of the turbulent forms of adolescent stress among Hindu girls than in the West because very few girls go to college, and even those do not lose their close ties with their families. At times of crisis, however, inner conflicts and resentment against her status may force a woman to rebel, as may be seen from the militancy of women during the Independence struggle, and in the vociferous objection to restrictive rules in the more expensive co-educational institutions. Where tradition is still very strong the conflicts of adolescent girls are turned inwards in various forms of passivity and resignation.

It would be wrong to think that the restricted life of a woman in so conservative an atmosphere prevents her from developing a strong sense of self-respect. On the contrary, her sense of identity with the family and her role as a wife and mother give her dignity and pride. Though artistically creative women may very often feel frustrated, most are content in the certainty that their ultimate role is to preserve unity and continuity in the chain of life. Indian society, whatever the religious background, seems to foster and develop in women rather than in men vitality and resilience under the circumstances of a life which might be judged extremely circumscribed by Western standards. Change from the joint to the nuclear system has not had any fundamental effect on this situation. Coomaraswamy, a Ceylonese who was apt to be sentimental in his views on Indian womanhood, has been proved substantially correct when he said, some forty years ago, that a

> Hindu woman is given the opportunity to realise rather than to express herself. She is given the opportunity to be a woman. . . . We do not identify freedom with self-assertion. . . . The oriental woman is what she is, only because our social and religious culture has permitted her to be and to remain essentially feminine.[1]

In spite of, or perhaps because of, the particular traits described above that are to be found in a high proportion of relationships between men and women, the latter have achieved positions of great influence in Indian society. In the first two post-Independence decades women attained positions of distinction in many walks of life. Some of the most independent-minded leaders and most competent professional people are women; their distinction in politics is well known. Besides the election of Mrs. Indira Gandhi as Prime Minister in 1966, ninety-five women were returned to the national Parliament and 195 to State legislatures.

In this century Indian women have undergone a social revolution rather more far-reaching and radical than that of men. In fact this quiet revolution (it also had its spectacular moments in the nationalist struggle) is the most important element in the social changes which have occurred in modern India. Women have proved themselves more than equal to their, as yet, only partially accomplished emancipation, and have not lost their essential femininity. Even when they become highly competent in professional life Indian women show no sign of acquiring those masculine traits of behaviour

[1] A. K. Coomaraswamy *The Dance of Shiva*, Simpkin Marshall, London, 1924.

which are familiar in their counterparts in Anglo-Saxon countries. Their sense of power is already sufficiently deeply rooted in, and identified with, the family, especially in those women who are over forty-five, for them to feel no need to resort to the kinds of aggressive assertion which intensely competitive, male-dominated Western societies demand. This is one more reason why mother-dependence does not automatically assume the character of a neurosis in the Indian male; the balance of masculinity and femininity is less distorted by the emancipated woman. The prudent woman takes care not to contravene society's most basic ideas of what a woman should do and be, but even then many have acted with courage to defy conventions they thought outmoded or unnecessarily restrictive.

Part Three The Social Structure

Introduction

We come now to the most complex and difficult aspect of this study: India's social structure, including its most intricate feature, the caste system. An enormous amount of data and descriptive literature on the subject has been published in recent decades, but less attention has been given to an examination of the underlying structure as a whole. For reasons of space, and in an attempt to reach the heart of the matter, this part will concentrate more on structure and less on descriptive examples.

Many otherwise reliable observers of India have been content to give a summary history of the 'original four castes' (there were no such entities) and their fission into innumerable sub-castes, then proceed to description of caste exclusivism, and end with an account of the lowering of caste barriers today. This is not only inaccurate but misleading; the result has been that the present social stratification is portrayed as confusing, inexplicable, and iniquitous, with effective reform hopefully on the way and the caste system in rapid decline. Studies inspired by the standards of Western egalitarianism led (however admirably motivated) to a distortion of such reform as has been attempted. Consequently misunderstanding among liberals and democrats of the actual process of social change in India has been altogether too partial. Put in its simplest terms, the politicians' and reformers' problem is essentially this: India's traditional social structure was based on institutionalized inequality, while today the government—and supposedly the nation too—is committed to social equality. The former is 'bad', the latter 'good'. However much one may sympathize with the liberal and progressive desire to see social inequalities abolished and caste barriers fall, we must be careful to distinguish between value judgements and ideology on the one hand, and the actual state of affairs on the other.

The policy of the country's leaders has long been to eradicate the evils of the old social system in order to attain more humane goals; that policy has met with some success, but also with some failures. Untouchability was declared illegal by the Constitution, but as has been said times without number, 'it cannot be eliminated by a mere stroke of the pen'. Exploitation, degradation, indignity, abuse of privilege, subjection—all are vaguely, and with some justice, associated with the institution of caste. But social change has made very slow progress in India, the caste system is not only almost as strong as it ever was but it has exacerbated division within society, while traditionalism has retarded the pace of development. Why is this so? Why have the diversified and brilliantly planned development projects not succeeded in weakening the outworn social structure in the way everyone once so optimistically predicted?

One reason why this question has not been satisfactorily answered is that we lack accurate knowledge of the traditional social structure. It was not until around the mid-1950s that more sophisticated sociological methods began to reveal from the mass of data anything like an adequate picture of the system. Only now, therefore, are we beginning to reap the benefit of detailed field studies conducted by dedicated scholars, Indian and foreign. However, no completely satisfactory explanations have yet been given of how the caste system originated, why it has persisted without fundamental change for so long, and what is the essential function it performs in the total social order. What can be done here is to outline a number of significant links, which may help towards answers, or at least a more comprehensive picture of the interrelated factors. I would like to record a special debt to the brilliant work of Professors Francis Hsu and Louis Dumont, and to the Chicago school, whose recent theoretical studies on caste have greatly contributed to our overall understanding of the system. In the present study, the existing body of information is supplemented by my own observation in the field.

Part Three will not, however, be confined to analysis of the caste system. It will also include description of the social order as a whole, and the relations between the social and the political systems. The later chapters will examine the degree of mobility which was attained within the social system in former times, and its capacity for change under modern conditions. Thus the same situation will be reviewed from different angles; its multi-dimensional structure will form a mosaic, the pattern of which is altered with each fresh perspective. So long as the theme is structural it will be viewed synchronically; but at the point when the evolution and capacity for change of traditional institutions is analysed, a diachronic scheme is adopted.

Chapter One The Caste System

Caste and common sense

'No one is allowed to marry outside his own caste or exercise any calling or art except his own.' This unexceptional and commonplace remark of an ambassador new to India is the kind of rough generalization innumerable visitors make on their first encounter with the operation of the caste system. The interesting point about it is that this comment was written roughly two thousand three hundred years ago by Megasthenes, envoy of Seleucus to the court of Chandragupta in the early days of the Mauryan empire. As far as it goes it is still true today of the majority of Hindus, particularly in rural areas.

Observing the complex division of society into *jātis*, or small groups, as distinct from classes, the Portuguese of the sixteenth century gave them the name of *castas* (derived from the Latin *castus*, 'pure'), from which the word 'caste' as applied to the Indian social structure originates. If the Indian caste system were to be compared with other forms of caste organization elsewhere in the world, one would still have to conclude that it is the most distinctive feature of Indian culture; it has remained the bedrock of the social structure from ancient times to the present day. Caste may variously be described as a system of institutionalized inequality, a social instrument of assimilation, an archaic form of 'trade unionism', and an extension of the joint-family system reflecting the pattern of kinship interdependence upon the total social structure. But inaccuracies are present in such generalizations. The following two descriptive definitions are more apt.

A caste system is one whereby a society is divided up into a number of self-contained and completely segregated units (castes), the mutual relations between which are ritually determined in a graded scale.[1]

We must conceive of a group, united, closed, and at least in theory hereditary, provided with a measure of organisation which is traditional and independent, with a headman, and with a council . . .; that is often combined in the keeping of certain festivals; that is bound together by a common occupation, and shares common customs in regard particularly to marriage, to the consumption of food and drink, and to various cases of pollution; finally, a group which has the power to maintain its authority by means of a jurisdiction which, though rather attenuated, is capable of making the authority of the community effectively felt by the

---

[1] J. H. Hutton, *Caste in India*, 4th ed., Oxford University Press, Bombay, 1963, p. 50.

imposition of various penalties, the most important being permanent or temporary expulsion from the group: such in epitome, as it seems to us, is a caste.[1]

We may add to these descriptions the following details: each caste is a social unit in itself while at the same time it is a group within the total system; it may (and often does) have customs which differ from those of other castes; the system is an organic product of the total religious world view—'Before everything else, without caste there is no Hindu' (Max Weber).

There are numerous 'common sense' theories on caste origins and most of the likely ones had all been proposed by the end of the nineteenth century: secular, racial, priestly exclusivism, extreme forms of aristocracy, totem and tabu, etc. None is true in either a realistic, 'no nonsense', or a scientific sense; all imply comparison with either Western or primitive institutions. Senart was the first to see that neither race nor occupation is by itself enough to cause this system to come into being, or to account for its restrictions on commensality and marriage. There is no ethnic distinction between castes, and the few occupations in any given region do not account for innumerable caste categories. Since approximately 70 per cent of the population is engaged in agriculture, the functional interpretation of the Hindu social system makes no sense. All these theories fail because they do not take into account hierarchic gradation and India's religious concepts. Nor is it enough to bundle all of them together in a composite explanation. Indian apologists occasionally prefer a purely secular theory which accords with their desire for social reform. Yet in order to arrive at a reasonably precise account of caste institutions we have to start somewhere in the domain of familiar human experience before embarking on a technical, if more precise, explanation.

Norman Douglas, reflecting on human nature in general, once said: 'Caste underlies every form of refinement; it is a man's best prophylactic against that mass feeling which would make a cypher of him.' Something of a Brahman himself, Douglas knew what he was talking about; 'caste' in this metaphorical sense merely refers to the sense of group identity and exclusiveness. At the same time his remark contains a human truth which should not be forgotten in the Indian context.

The Indian social system should be viewed first as a basic urge of our biological species to accord *hierarchic* value to differences, to affirm variety, and to arrange the constituent elements in a scale of mutual dependence. First and foremost, this system was a harmony unifying diversity. Like all human systems, it was tragically imperfect; the subservient outcastes, for most of ancient history comprising 5 per cent of the population (at a

[1] E. Senart, *Les Castes dans l'Inde*, Paris, 1927, p. 35. Translated in Hutton (1963), p. 50.

conservative estimate) and in modern times rising to roughly 14 per cent (over sixty million people), came to be the symbol of India's own brand of human injustice, victims of a system which kept people alive in squalor—as many as other civilizations might slaughter in war or offer as sacrifice to the gods in the course of a generation.

In the technical exposition of caste which follows, the Indian zeal for affirming variety and conserving differences should be kept in mind while the methods evolved for subjecting those differences to ordered gradation are observed. The intricacies of the caste structure should not allow us to forget essential human concerns—the quality of life, human feeling, and emotions—which must be temporarily kept in the background for reasons of clarity.

At this point I would like to quote the distinguished social anthropologist Edmund Leach:

> There is nothing peculiar to Indian caste. Internally, a caste presents itself to its members as a network of kin relationships, but this network is of no specific type. The kinship systems of caste-ordered societies vary, but all types are readily duplicated in other societies historically unconnected with the Indian world.[1]

We will shortly see that the three basic characteristics of Indian caste structure, opposition of pure and impure, hierarchy, and specialization, are all universal traits. Moreover hierarchy is not alien to professedly egalitarian societies, and the concepts of purity and pollution are never wholly absent even from 'rationally' and 'ethically' ordered modern societies. The Indian social order is certainly distinctive; caste may also appear to be a very peculiar institution with many irrationalities, contradictions, and ambiguities. But it provides a uniquely consistent and at the same time flexible framework large enough to embrace these contradictions without either endangering its stability or succumbing to long pressure from internal heterodoxy. Rather than adopt a negative approach to so formidable and sophisticated a system of collective representation, the method proposed here is to view the phenomenon of caste as a distinctive variant of the universal tendency to hierarchization. One problem has always bedevilled analysis of the caste system: finding an adequate terminology with which to translate a multi-dimensional structure into a verbal linear sequence. We will therefore divide the examination into three sections: hierarchy, status, and pollution.

[1] *Aspects of Caste in South India, Ceylon and North West Pakistan*, E. R. Leach (ed.), Cambridge, 1960, p. 7.

Hierarchy

The caste system was, and indeed still remains, as inseparable and as fundamental a part of the social order, indeed a *valued* part by the great majority of Hindus, as the principle of social equality is a valued ideal of modern democracy. Social hierarchies are universal: in no society, not even those which purport to be wholly egalitarian, are they completely absent. Indeed we are now at the beginning of a period when the principle of hierarchy is for the first time the subject of serious scholarly attention throughout the fields of the social and natural sciences, just as for a century or more preceding it the principle of egalitarianism was a matter of constant preoccupation. Originally the word 'hierarchy' was applied to religious gradation; since its adoption by scientists, biologists rather than sociologists were the first to apply it successfully to universal phenomena. 'The hierarchy of relations . . . will perhaps be the leading idea of the future' (Joseph Needham, 1932). The role of hierarchy is being reassessed in order to accord more closely with the facts, even though the principle of social equality has not been abandoned as an ideal.

Professor Dumont defines hierarchy, as applied to the caste system, as 'a principle of gradation of elements in a whole with reference to the whole, it being understood that in most societies it is religion which provides the view of the whole, and that the gradation will thus be intrinsically religious.'[1]

Considered as a biological species, man, using Dumont's terms, is either Homo Aequalis or Homo Hierarchicus. No doubt he has over-simplified the contrast, for neither exists in his pure aboriginal state—we are all a varying mixture of the two; but his point is a useful one. For our purposes it may be helpful to consider hierarchy on the same lines as Mr. Arthur Koestler, who treats it as a biological, universal law of life, which man unconsciously projects on his collective representation.

The individual, *qua* biological organism, constitutes a nicely integrated hierarchy of molecules, cells, organs, and organ systems. Looking inward into the space enclosed by the boundaries of his skin, he can rightly assert that he is something complete and unique, a whole. But facing outward, he is constantly—sometimes pleasantly, sometimes painfully—reminded that he is a part, an elementary unit in one or several social hierarchies.[2]

Dissatisfied with the terminology of 'whole' and 'part' (which do not exist anywhere in an absolute sense), Koestler has coined the useful word 'holon' from the Greek *holos*—whole—to designate the 'nodes on the

[1] L. Dumont, *Homo Hierarchicus*, Paris, 1967, p. 92. My translation.
[2] Arthur Koestler, *The Ghost in the Machine*, London, 1967, p. 50.

hierarchic tree'. 'The organism', he says, 'is to be regarded as a multi-levelled hierarchy of semi-autonomous sub-wholes, branching into sub-wholes of a lower order, and so on. Sub-wholes on any level of the hierarchy are referred to as *holons*.'[1] A part of an organism is a holon, a complete organism or an individual is a holon, and there are social holons—family, clan, tribe, caste, and so on. The term is particularly appropriate in dealing with Indian hierarchy. In the case of India we are, after all, dealing with what has sometimes been called holistic social organization, as distinct from individualistic social organization. The Durkheimian dichotomy of sacred and profane is particularly inappropriate when applied to the Indian context. The crucial disjunction between ritual status and power, priest and king, Brahman and Kshatrya, which is at the root of Indian hierarchy, does not strip the king's power of its sacred essence. The concept of the holon preserves the unitary nature of Indian hierarchy, while the image of a hierarchical tree reminds us that Indian gradation is non-linear, multi-dimensional, and interdependent. No single caste can be considered in isolation. For hierarchy is also an exchange of services, of mutually in-dispensable aid between holons. Two further quotations from Koestler will help us to see the *logic* of the caste hierarchy, rather than considering it as an anomaly; the fact that the caste hierarchy shares this logic with biological organization relates it, as it should be related, with universal human experience. For our purposes we will accept Koestler's equating caste with 'social holon':

> Biological holons are self-regulating open systems which display both the autonomous properties of wholes and the dependent properties of parts. This dichotomy is present on every level of every type of hierarchic organisation. . . .[2]
> Every holon has the dual tendency to preserve and assert its individuality as a quasi-autonomous whole; and to function as an integrated part of an (existing or evolving) larger whole. This polarity between the Self-Assertive and Integra-tive tendencies is inherent in the concept of hierarchic order; and a universal characteristic of life.[3]

Status and power

We now come to the most crucial point in the understanding of the caste system, the relationship of the *varṇa* and the *jāti* systems. The Vedic theory of *varṇa* is the first textual reference we have to the Indian *theory* of social organization which makes the distinction between status (usually associated with religious supremacy) and power (pertaining to the temporal). This

[1] Ibid., p. 341.   [2] Ibid., p. 341.   [3] Ibid., p. 343.

varṇa system is closely linked to the *jāti* system, i.e. castes and sub-castes, and often the two are confused and taken for the same thing. For instance, the *varṇa* system comprises the four categories, Brahman, Kshatrya, Vaishya, and Śūdra, which are not the 'four original castes', as is commonly believed, but *classes*, estates.

The distinction between status and power of the *varṇa* system probably occurred in the course of the cultural contact between the Aryan and Harappan civilizations. When the nomadic pastoral Aryans reached India their division of labour was rudimentary; the king was pivot of the system, and the tribe was divided into three social *classes*, the warriors or aristocracy, the priests, and the common people. Hereditary castes were unknown, intermarriage between classes was not forbidden, and the Brahman priest-hood—a distinctive Indian idea of sacerdotal function—was slow to develop. We must assume from evidence in the Vedic texts that the Aryan king originally possessed ritual power. In view of the eventual *ritual status* supremacy of the Brahman in the *varṇa* system, we can only speculate that this development may very well have resulted from the interaction of Aryan religious concepts (at first looser and more flexible than those of the highly urbanized sedentary Harappans called *dāsas* in the Vedas) with the indigenous religion. We cannot, in the present state of our knowledge, be certain that the Harappan priesthood occupied the pivotal status role in that society, but, as we have seen in Part One, it is highly likely. Thus it can only be a speculative assumption that the Aryan society in which the priest-hood enjoyed limited status, came face to face with another society in which the priests (who were literate, whereas the Aryans apparently were not) enjoyed a higher, if not supreme, status. By the time the *Brāhmaṇas* were composed in the late Vedic period, and the *varṇa* system had been incor-porated into the Rg *Veda*, the Brahman claim to supreme ritual status over the king had been at least partially accepted as a *fait accompli*. Here lies our crucial factor: *disjunction of power and status*.

As Dumont points out, hierarchic gradation of *status* became absolutely distinct from the gradation of power.

> Hierarchy culminates in the Brahman, or priest; it is the Brahman who consecrates the king's power, which otherwise depends on force (this results from the dichotomy). . . . While the Brahman is spiritually or absolutely supreme, he is materially dependent; whilst the king is materially the master, he is spiri-tually subordinate.[1]

Dumont links this form of dyarchy to the traditional relation of *dharma*, spiritual order, and *artha*, worldly pleasure and power, the latter legitimate only within the limits set by the former. The religious nature of all social

---

[1] L. Dumont, *Contributions to Sociology*, V, October 1961, p. 35.

activity is revealed in the *gift* to Brahmans: material goods in exchange for a spiritual good. Thus material goods are transformed into values. Since the Brahman represents the apex of religious status all exchange of services gravitates round his pivotal role. The king is guardian of all material wealth, or, if one likes, its agent. The *Brāhmaṇ* priest is the microcosm of the macrocosmic *Brahman*, or Divine substratum, the point where the sacred in man meets the universal sacred priest as repository of universal *Brahman*. Through the sacrifice the priest mediator transmits the sacred to the king, and through the king it flows into the body of society. The circle is completed by the substance of the sacrifice itself, the gift of sacrificial animals which the society itself offers. While we are still some distance from explaining caste gradation, we have arrived at the unitary hierarchical order which encircles it. The religious and economic unity of the society is inseparably linked with the cosmic order. 'Hierarchy integrates the society by reference to its values' (Dumont).

The *Puruśasūkta* hymn of the *Ṛg Veda* compares the society with a giant organism: the Brahmans are its head, the Kshatryas its arms, the Vaishyas its trunk, the Śūdras its feet. It is expressly stated in the text that no part of the whole may claim exclusive importance and superiority over the others; collaboration and exchange of services are the essence of this organismic theory, the various organs of the projected Puruśa body-image are related in structural consistency.[1] The fact that this *varṇa* system was originally conceived as an organism reminds us that we cannot regard it as a linear order. Dumézil was the first to point to its real structure as a series of successive dichotomies. The fourfold order is divided into the initiated and the excluded, the *twice-born* Āryās (the first three classes) and the *dāsas*, or intermarried *dāsa* Āryā, later called Śūdras. This division was of crucial importance because it preserved non-Aryan religions in quasi-isolation from Brahmanism, while this assortment of cults later developed in uneasy symbiosis with Brahmanism. The twice-born initiates were in their turn divided in two: the Vaishyas formed one group, the Brahmans and Kshatryas another. The latter pair opposed itself to all the rest, but were united with them by their interdependence.

Finally, the different specialist tasks among the Brahmans themselves became associated with degrees of ritualistic purity and impurity. For example, the priest who actually killed the sacrificial beast was lower in ritual status than the presiding priest. It was in the extension of this Vedic principle of graded ritual status to the entire range of social life that caste classification—division into *jāti*—originated. Not, be it noted, that the

[1] Vishnu as cosmic demiurge is a later variant of this symbolism; the hierarchical disposition of deities within the body of Vishnu echoes the organismic social system. See Plate 34.

acquisition of purity or impurity was the *cause* of caste distinctions but on the contrary, the *form* of them. Two Brahman castes in opposition to one another would *both* claim superiority over the other.[1] The pivotal role of the Brahman within the ritual status scheme, and the legitimization of the king's power within the limits set by that scheme, account for the determining role of ritual status in the *jāti* system according to the degree of purity and impurity. To repeat: the core of the *varṇa* system is the distinction between Brahman and Kshatrya, and the core of the *jāti* system is the distinction between pure and impure directly arising from Brahman ritual supremacy in the *varṇa* system. This conclusion, however, is still too abstract for our purposes and a number of points will have to be examined more closely.

The *varṇa* system is the classical theory of the Indian social order and figures in the ancient texts, whereas the *jāti* system is an empirical order, verifiable by direct observation of caste ranking and other familiar distinctions in the latter system as we know it today. The empirical importance of the *jāti* system is in no way lessened by the fact that it was never consistently expounded in such major classical texts as the *Laws of Manu*, which were composed before the caste system had fully crystallized. An element of confusion between the two results from widespread application of the *varṇa* scheme to the classification of castes. Nevertheless, the *varṇas* must always be viewed as *classes*, in the Indian sense, like the estates of medieval Europe, where the idea of an 'estate' is not at all limited to that of a 'class' in the modern sense.

The *varṇa* system is virtually uniform throughout India, although in the South there is scarcely any recognition of classes between Brahmans and Śūdras. The *jāti* system is by no means uniform, varying from region to region; nevertheless, in spite of different ranking, the system of pure-impure provides the sole common basis of the *jāti* system. Dumont regards these two systems as homologous and to have interacted on each other.

The relations between *jāti* are not explained systematically in the original texts on social organization. Is this because the institution of *jāti* was originally non-Aryan? I would like to suggest that this may well be so, although we cannot be certain. All early Indian textual references to *jātis*, or *jāti*-type groups, are confined to the enumeration of occupational specialists outside the pale of the *varṇa* system, i.e. non-Aryans, where emphasis is displaced from function to birth, or the origin of which is described as resulting from mixture of *varṇas*. Now, if we accept that the religions of the *dāsas* and their descendants—Śūdras, Untouchables, and some of the earliest groups referred to as distinct from the *varṇa* classes— were not, at least for a very long period, assimilated to Brahmanism, we

[1] Cf. Dumont (1966), p. 67.

may reasonably assume that they preserved such social grouping as prevailed among the Harappans (and perhaps other indigenes) before the Aryan invasions. While it can only be speculation, there appear to be two interacting movements here: the Brahman gradation of purity and impurity, eventually leading to classification in *jāti*, and a second gradation, residual or evolving, among groups excluded from Brahman rites. Theories of a racial origin for the caste system are not supported by the facts and are not proposed here. What may have occurred is a defensive reaction on the part of the Aryan rulers, massively outnumbered by the indigenes, in which elements of the non-Aryan system of social division were incorporated into the emergent pure–impure opposition; the trend would have been given added impetus by increasing occupational differentiation. While the determining principle remained the pure–impure opposition, and power was differentiated from status, changes in the means of production and association of occupations with purity and pollution demanded the extension of a social ranking which accorded with *both* criteria.

To summarize, we can do no better than quote an authoritative structural definition of the caste system by Professor Dumont, condensed from a paper in *Contributions to Indian Sociology*:[1]

The society is divided into a large number of permanent groups which are at once specialised, hierarchised and separated (in matter of marriage, food, physical contact) in relation to each other. The common basis of these three features is opposition of pure and impure, an opposition of its nature hierarchical which implies separation and, on the professional level, specialisation of the occupations relevant to the opposition. This basic opposition can segment itself without limit. The religious scale of hierarchy is related to the secular scale of power and wealth.

Purity and pollution

Before we can attempt to concretize the full structural complexity of the caste system as we now know it we must examine the conceptual meaning of purity and pollution. Because of the magico-religious ideas on which the theme of this section is based, the reader may find the subject obscure. In fact, the whole question of pollution is of the greatest importance, and obscure as are some ideas connected with it, it cannot be ignored if we are to elucidate the consequences of magical thought on the psychology of the caste Hindu. We will first observe the prevalence of pollution tabus in all civilizations, including the most advanced and modern; then we will determine the effect of pollution rules on Indian social organization. We

[1] No. V, 1961, pp. 34–5.

will also note the significance of food as a magical substance with the power to modify social relations. But food directly affects the body, so we will next find how the body image is projected on social organization. Finally we shall analyse a single, important rite, and from this draw a basic conclusion for the psychology of dependence implicit in the caste system.

It is a commonplace that Hindu society pays exceptional attention to purity and pollution. The very existence and frequent use of the English word 'untouchable' (*aspr̥çya* in Sanskrit) reflects this preoccupation. We have already noted attitudes regarding physical hygiene, bodily pollutions, and the compulsive washing habit. However, a distinction must be drawn between *customs*, widespread as these may be, and the less immediately visible *system* on which, as we shall see, they are based. The idea that opposition of pure and impure can be the form which social distinctions take may appear startling, but it is not unknown in societies besides India's, though less consistently applied.

Individual members of a given society, however highly organized, do not view their own social system in terms of consistent theory. In the ordinary course of events, our knowledge of our own social structure is acquired piecemeal. The high degree of consistency revealed by the Hindu theory and customs associated with concepts of purity and pollution is not a matter of day-to-day knowledge in India; it is none the less important for having been evolved and applied organically and, for the most part, unconsciously, as have most basic principles of social order.[1] We are not dealing with a systematic philosophy subscribed to voluntarily by individuals. Indian ideas of purity and pollution are extensively treated in the scriptures and the law books; other texts enumerate rules without any attempt at the exposition of consistent theory.

In her comparative study, *Purity and Danger*, Mrs. Mary Douglas defines the system implicit in pollution rules as follows:

> Defilement is never an isolated event. It cannot occur except in view of a systematic ordering of ideas. Hence any piecemeal interpretation of the pollution rules of another culture is bound to fail. For the only way in which pollution ideas make sense is in reference to a total structure of thought whose key-stone, boundaries, margins and internal lines are held in relation by rituals of separation.[2]

From the 'common-sense' point of view, eliminating dirt is, consciously or not, a positive attempt to introduce greater order into the environment; such is the universal human attitude to dirt, and it is implicit in the custom

[1] For reasons of space, analysis of inconsistencies, regional differences, and variants in custom cannot be included in this study. More important is the need for an approach flexible enough to take into account what Professor McKim Marriott has called 'evidences of accretion and of transmutation in form without replacement and without rationalisation of the accumulated and transformed elements'.

[2] Mary Douglas, *Purity and Danger*, Routledge & Kegan Paul, London, 1966, p. 41.

of 'spring cleaning' even if its ritualistic origin has been forgotten. But whereas Western society conceives the business of eliminating dirt to be a matter of aesthetics and hygiene, Indian society is primarily concerned with sacred contagion and dread of pollution by members of society who are specialists in the elimination of impurity. While impurity is associated with physical dirt, it does not mean that we can reduce Indian pollution concepts to a matter of mere hygiene. Mrs. Douglas drily makes the point: 'Even if some of Moses's dietary rules were hygienically beneficial it is a pity to treat him as an enlightened public health administrator, rather than as a spiritual leader.'[1] In India hygiene is a principle subordinate to an essentially religious system of pollution concepts closer to the Mosaic law than to Western hygienic notions. If we accept the more inclusive idea of eliminating dirt as a universal effort to create order, there is no reason why we should not apply it to Indian attitudes towards dirt, as long as we draw the important distinction between a secularized, common-sense approach, and a ritualistic system (in the latter sacred and secular are undifferentiated).

We have already noted the Indian sense of vulnerable, bodily exposure to nature and that the ever-present threat of the organic world is seen as coming either from outside, from the environment, in the form of dirt, or from within the body, in all forms of bodily discharge. The amorphous fear of some external substance getting into one and transforming one's personality or health is present in many peoples. Geoffrey Gorer refers to it in his Postscript to the 1964 edition of *The American People* as 'the fear of dangerous foreign matter getting into one without one's knowledge', and he cites atomic fall-out, chemical pesticides, and even ideological 'contamination' as specific examples of the tendency to ascribe this fear to the most surprising, tangible or intangible, agencies of pollution.

Now these threats, or in other words dangers, of pollution are handled and dealt with in the Indian system by *every* member of society. It is the degree of contact with polluting agents whereby the social status of each individual is gauged. In India proximity to the contaminating factor is thought to constitute a *permanent* pollution if it is of sufficient intensity. Not only is a person thus placed regarded as in a state of pollution throughout his life; he also transmits this indelible pollution to his children. Here pollution is both *collective* and *hereditary*. At the same time there are degrees of collective hereditary pollution, which are reflected in the graded status, for example, of specialized castes engaged in polluting work, such as leather-making, barbers, launderers, sweepers, and funeral attendants. Similarly, there are forms of *temporary* pollution which can be overcome by ritual purification, as by sprinkling of water, or a ritual bath, or a temple-rite, a penance, or ingestion of purifying substances. In the daily routine of

[1] Ibid., p. 29.

the individual, pollution is as minutely graded as it is on the collective, caste-occupational scale. Thus a man goes through a daily sequence of graded pollution in relation to his activities. He is impure on waking, becomes acutely vulnerable to pollution during excretion, eating, and sexual relations, is at a state of maximum purity after a bath (the time most propitious for performance of daily religious rites), is purer before eating than after, and must wash after eating, lest he pollute others; he will be vulnerable to pollution during work and social relations with others, and may be polluted by contact with certain objects, substances, or food vessels. Again, while every individual is subject to temporary states of relative purity and impurity, this in turn is related to the degree of pollution of everyone else, between one caste and another collectively, and between groups of castes in relation to the polar extremes on the pure–impure scale: Brahman and Untouchable. Thus both these extremes are at the same time subject to individual degrees of purity and impurity, and collectively opposed in an absolute sense. The network of purity and pollution is thorough, generally consistent in detail within its terms, and permeates every conceivable aspect of life. Nothing is impermeable to pollution: no person, no thing, no act.

Since a minimal degree of purification is a necessary condition for the individual in relation to society lest he pollute others, it follows that the state of purity *unites* him with others, while pollution *divides* him, as one caste is separated from another according to the intensity of its permanent pollution, or as the individual is isolated for a carefully prescribed period after contracting a particularly contagious pollution (e.g. after the death of a relative or birth of a child, or during menstruation). We shall see later that this oscillating movement between *union* and *division* is of cardinal importance in the stabilization of social order, or if one likes, it acts as a kind of thermostat which mechanically regulates social interrelationship. If there is no absolute purity there is no absolutely consistent observation of pollution rules either, for this would be humanly impossible. Nevertheless, though communities and individuals differ today in the degree to which they compromise with the rules, the majority of Hindus, Jains, and Sikhs, and to a much lesser extent Muslims, Parsis, and Christians, are still very considerably affected by them, even if they do not subscribe to the beliefs on which they are founded (though here again, the statistical majority among Hindus actually do believe).

The educated, Westernized, modern Indian no longer subscribes to this magico-religious way of thinking. But if pollution tabus are still seen to be operative in the societies of Europe and America, it is hardly likely that a society far more deeply permeated by concern with pollution will produce wholly emancipated individuals in a matter of a few generations.

The Hindu is more conscious of the gradation of social groups according to their degree of purity than of the precise division of castes into occupations. More important is the need here to identify in concrete terms the sources of pollution and how these have determined a specific structure. The details differ from region to region, but the underlying principles of the system are universal. Thus the basic assumption: pollution is so dangerous to social well-being that its elimination is an essential task which can only be performed by specialists. Without Untouchables to take upon themselves the society's impurity there can be no Brahmans, and therefore no purity. In one sense the Brahman and the Untouchable share a common task: the spiritual security and well-being of all. This principle of interdependence is symbolized, for example, by the ritual services of 'polluted' castes like drummers (because they use animal skins), which are indispensable for the performance of the community rites, by the role of barbers at marriages and deaths, of washermen at births. In fact ritual services are not exclusively in the hands of Brahman priests; each caste has its own priests, and in ritual terms each caste is priestly in its relations with other castes. We will return to this matter when dealing with the *jajmāni* system, which reveals the origins of this priestly function in the sacrificial system— disjunction between the agent who performs a ritual task and the patron on whose behalf it is undertaken. For example, clothes are 'purified' by the launderer, and vessels for the sacred domestic hearth are made by the potter (who is also assigned the task of making images of the gods for domestic worship). Yet again we see the impossibility of absolute distinctions between sacred and profane.

The sacredness of the cow is a crucial factor in the Hindu system of pollution concepts. There is some dispute over the origins of the cow's sacredness. The cult of the cow originated among the meat-eating Aryan pastoral nomads; it is common for cattle-breeding tribes to hold their cattle in some sort of veneration, and, like the Nuer of Sudan, to kill and eat them only on sacrificial occasions. The transition from the blood sacrifice of Vedic society to *ahiṃsā*, vegetarianism, and veneration of the cow, was a very slow process, during which the cow at all times retained its symbolic, quasi-divine significance. As the Brahman moved from a subordinate role to the apex of the social order, and the sacrificial pattern was transformed into a system of hierarchical castes, the cow assumed a special mediating role. Half-animal and half-divine, the cow, as perfect purity, is identified with the Brahman, whereas the Untouchable is charged with the disposal of the cow's cadaver. All intermediate caste gradations are situated along the axis of purity and impurity relative to the antitheses. The 'five products' of the cow become the purificatory agents for securing protection against pollution of the social antitheses, the pure and the impure. For the products of the cow are copious, both edible and inedible; essentially reducible to milk and faeces, these purificatory products may be described as a 'sacred congruence'—agents with the power to transcend opposites.[1]

By the third century A.D. certain specialized occupational groups were already listed in the *Laws of Manu*. It is evident that pollution rules had been linked with caste gradation for several centuries. But it was not until the consolidation of a quasi-feudal, agriculturally oriented society several centuries after the composition of the law books in their present form, that a fully fledged caste *system* may be said to have come into existence. However, in the law books purification rites in connection with birth and death form an important theme. A much wider range of rules was established, including the division of purity into three categories—the body, the family, and objects. Bodily impurities included secretions, notably those connected with the mouth and with excretion, and those deriving from the association of the left hand with these. Familial impurity was classified according to the proximity of relatives who came into contact either with the mother and child at the time of delivery, or with the corpse of a relative. Object pollution was graded according to the ease with which vessels and tools could be purified according to their utility and their material value. Thus earthenware can be replaced, brass cleaned; a brass cup is polluted after contact with the mouth, a leaf plate should be thrown away after eating; silk is purer than cotton, gold purer than brass, therefore silk and gold are appropriate materials for ritual purposes.

When it is a question of caste ranking, the simplest and most frequently applied criterion concerns who may receive food and water from whom without incurring pollution. To receive food from another is to share, to a degree, in that other's nature. Most societies regard food as belonging to magical health-giving categories of an 'irrational', non-scientific character. By the rules of such sympathetic magic the American male consumes steak 'because it provides red blood'. In India the most important quality of food is the degree to which it is pollution-prone. Water is believed to be especially pollution-prone, therefore the rules are carefully observed and constitute one of the clearest means by which the society represents its status gradations. An important distinction is drawn between cooked and uncooked food, and again between the relative purity of cooked foods. Thus uncooked food can be received from a lower caste, but not cooked food of certain pollution-prone categories. Again, commensality is restricted to castes ranked in alliances, while it is common to observe how caste groups who eat together at a village feast are separated from each other, and seated at graded distances. There are, in fact, two food systems of classification—the one mentioned above, and a triple gradation according to degrees of

[1] Cf. Mauss (1966), pp. 53–9.

nourishment and quality: *sattvas* (pertaining to light, spirituality, subtlety), *rajas* (pertaining to the passions, energy, physical vitality, and strength), *tamas* (pertaining to darkness, lethargy, stupidity, heaviness). The three categories are called *gunas*, a philosophical concept for the triple quality inherent in *all* matter, inorganic and organic, including the body, the temperament, and food. In fact, the three are traditionally associated with the *varnas*: Brahmans (*sattva*), Kshatryas and Vaishyas (*rajas*), Śūdras and Untouchables (*tamas*).

Sattva represents purity and spirituality, and needs no elaboration here. *Rajas* has a connotation which is easily understood, for it is a *raja* who typifies the *rajas* quality—fiery, passionate, virile, the sovereign master of all action. The high affect and dread of *tamas* has a peculiarly Indian connotation; to catch the unique meaning of the term I quote Nirad Chaudhuri:

> It was the perpetual sight of an oozing of uncleanliness into the consciousness, taken with the visible fact of the proneness of all things to decompose in a tropical country, that created the characteristic Hindu concept of *tamas*, as the lowest of the *gunas* or attributes. The word *tamas* literally means darkness, but in Hindu thought and feeling it stands really for a very comprehensive term for all kinds of squalor—material, biological, intellectual, moral, and spiritual. Suffering in *tamas* was the Hindu hubris.[1]

Food is cooked on the sacred hearth; any pollution it may have acquired from the donor or vendor is removed. But once it is cooked, and the family which has cooked it has already, so to speak, participated in it (some foods are relatively neutral and cooking alone is believed to transform them into *sattvas*, *rajas*, or *tamas* substances according to the corresponding temperament of the cook), the food is still highly pollution-prone. A stranger's shadow, the glance of a low-caste man are enough, in some cases, to pollute it. Ingested food is believed to transmit certain qualities in the nature of the donor and the cook, besides (in the case of meat) 'toxic' essences passed on from the psycho-physiological system of an animal violently done to death. I have heard it said that non-Hindus, and particularly Westerners, even when vegetarian, are regarded by the inmates of Brahman *ashrāms* as not only polluting because of their imperfect dietary system, but spiritually 'retarded', because they have absorbed 'toxic' substances through heredity, 'bad' *karma*, and accepting food from Untouchables. By orthodox Brahman standards a foreigner is polluting for these reasons alone and not because he has been brought up to hold different religious beliefs.

Additional factors in the pollution system are: gradation according to caste for sharing the tobacco pipe or hookah at smoking parties (the principal occasion for informal socialization in villages throughout the great

[1] N. C. Chaudhuri, *The Continent of Circe*, Chatto and Windus, London, 1965, p. 171.

majority of regions), use of the same wells, distance from the sanctuary of a temple, the right to wear certain kinds of garments and ornaments (until recently low castes in Kerala, southern India, were forbidden to wear clothes above the waist), use of umbrellas and shoes, language restrictions (vocabulary, terminology, modes of addressing superiors, cupping the hand over the mouth to limit pollution by breath), use of building materials (low castes, again in southern India, were forbidden to build homes of brick). It should also be remembered that since each caste has its own food rules and therefore a distinctive diet, and since intermarriage between castes is either forbidden or extremely rare (selection of brides is restricted in many cases to an extremely limited range of kin), physical traits of near-uniformity are hereditary in a great many castes, enabling one in a small rural community to recognize another's caste by his features alone, even if he may not have a distinctive mode of dress (which many castes do have). Thus hierarchic gradation is constantly borne in upon the mind of every individual.

Castes are also graded according to their marriage customs. The reason for this is that such practices as hypergamy (marriage to a woman of slightly lower subcaste), the age at which marriage is performed (pre-puberty, post-puberty), whether a caste permits divorce or not, whether a caste permits widow remarriage, the regulations on frequency of intercourse, rules regarding adultery, and in some cases whether a caste permits inter-subcaste marriage—all involve regulation of contact with the pollution agents of sexual physiology in varying degrees. It is evident from the above classification systems that personal and collective pollutions are based on a common denominator; for it should now be clear that the determining factor of pollution rules directly leads back to the experience of the self with the body. It remains for us to examine this unifying factor, and to relate experience of the body and the self's experience with society to the pattern of child care already analysed in Part Two.

To do so, let it be recalled that the *varṇa* system was first formulated as an organismic theory in the *Puruṣasūkta* hymn of the R̥g Veda, where the body social was literally modelled on the image of the human body. There also exists a related Hindu concept that the ideal of holiness and the wholeness of the body form parts of a single system. No strict division between physical and spiritual well-being is drawn; or, to be more precise, spiritual development cannot be achieved without physical well-being. The images of the healthy individual body and its metabolism are projected on social organization, so that status in society reflects the Hindu's image of his own body—how its parts are co-ordinated and function according to the hierarchy of anatomical purity. The ideal Hindu body-image (Puruṣa archetype) is hierarchically ordered, as are all Indian cosmologies (Plates 34 and 36) so that the human organism, and by analogy the social and cosmic organisms, exist in a state of equilibrium between 'upward' and 'downward' gravitation. Downward all things gravitate towards darkness, differentiation, decay, and dissolution (*tamas*). The body below the waist, bodily secretions, internal 'humours', are 'dark', polluting, nauseating, and potentially harmful. Upward, all things move in the direction of light, undifferentiation, unity, spirituality (*sattva*). In metaphysics these ideas correspond to the general cosmic rhythm, moving along the downward path, following the line of creation from unity to increasing physical differentiation, and along the return path, from the physical through the mental and back to unity, or oneness with the original divine substratum. The vital essence of the individual (microcosmic *puruśa*, not to be confused with the macrocosmic Puruśa archetype) was identified in the *Brihadāraṇyaka Upanishad* with semen, while, according to ancient Indian medicine, semen contains the vital energy which sustains a man's health. Semen, the Indian believes, should be expended only very rarely if a healthy body and a spiritual tone are to develop. According to this theory, which is very widely believed—probably by an overwhelming majority of Hindus—semen is made in the head from blood and so long as it is stored there through self-control it becomes a kind of nectar. But since man is a sensual animal, physically the nectar flows downwards, becomes semen, and is expended, with commensurate loss of vitality, through the promptings of sexuality. The association of the head with storage of semen accounts for the very high pollution intensity attributed to saliva and all discharges from inside the body, which are regarded as 'spoiled semen'. Excessive sexual gratification is believed to lead, as a result, to both physical and spiritual degeneration. These associations of bodily discharges with semen are wholly consistent with the dread of contact with any individual or group whose task it is to remove excreta, or whose work brings them into close proximity with these polluting *tamas* substances.

But the dread of contact with *tamas* substances is also due to the body's capacity to absorb or ingest pollution; this, if anything, is dreaded even more. The ingestion of food is, of course, heavily loaded with affect, due to the association with oral pleasure and infancy. Food is 'cooked' in the stomach, yielding *rasa*, and this in turn gives blood, and from blood forms semen. Any pollution reaching the inside of the body via the mouth will therefore contaminate the vital essence itself. At the same time, the individual is vulnerable to more generalized, more alarming—because elusive— threats: sudden *eruption* of internal defilement in the organism through the three bodily humours, phlegm, bile, and wind, or *invasion* by polluting substances from outside, including witches and evil spirits. We know from cults of possession practised by many castes throughout India that these mysterious assaults are generally regarded as manifestations of a terrible mother-goddess or nagging ancestral spirit who is, specifically, hypersensitive to the slightest infraction of intercaste pollution rules. It is interesting that Mary Douglas constructs a theory of Indian caste pollution around this idea of threat to the body, or more specifically 'how the symbolism of the body's boundaries is used in this kind of unfunny wit to express danger to the community boundaries'.[1]

According to Mrs. Douglas, the Coorgs may be taken as a typical case of corporate caste dread. 'They treat the body as if it were a beleaguered town, every ingress and exit guarded for spies and traitors. Anything issuing from the body is never to be re-admitted, but strictly avoided. The most dangerous pollution is for anything which has once emerged gaining re-entry.'[2] She cites the authority of Dumont that Coorg concepts of purity and pollution are typical of the total caste system. 'The whole system represents a body in which by the division of labour the head does the thinking and praying and the most despised parts carry away waste matter. . . . The sad wit of pollution as it comments on bodily functions symbolises descent in the caste structure by contact with faeces, blood and corpses.'[3] She then gives an interesting explanation for this:

> When rituals express anxiety about the body's orifices the sociological counterpart of this anxiety is a care to protect the political and cultural unity of a minority group. The Israelites were always in their history a hard-pressed minority. In their beliefs all the bodily issues were polluting, blood, pus, excreta, semen, etc. The threatened boundaries of their body politic would be well mirrored in their care for the integrity, unity and purity of the physical body.
>
> The Hindu caste system, while embracing all minorities, embraces them each as a distinctive, cultural sub-unit. In any given locality, any sub-caste is likely to be a minority. The purer and higher its caste status, the more of a minority it must be. Therefore the revulsion from touching corpses and excreta does not merely express the order of caste in the system as a whole. The anxiety about bodily margins expresses danger to group survival.[4]

I believe this is substantially correct, although the idea of minority anxiety does not fully accord with the few facts we have on early Indian attitudes to pollution. Plural, inter-minority anxiety did, however, contribute to the development of the caste system by the whole of society, through interaction rather than through imposition of rules by an élite group. The earliest reference we have to complete purification rites in India reveals *individual* 'anxiety about bodily margins'. This is the Vedic purification or *dīkshā*, whereby the sacrifier prepares himself for the great Soma sacrifice. In their classic analysis of sacrifice, Hubert and Mauss describe how the sacrifier (the man on whose behalf the sacrifice is performed) must first

---

[1] Douglas (1966), p. 122.   [2] Ibid., p. 123.   [3] Ibid., p. 123.   [4] Ibid., p. 124.

withdraw to a very small, specially constructed hut in a state of relative pollution—he is *separated* for purification. Dangerous polluting agents are removed by the shaving of hair and cutting of nails.

After taking a bath of purification he dons a brand-new linen garment, thereby indicating that a new existence is about to begin for him. Then, after various anointings, he is dressed in the skin of a black antelope. This is the solemn moment when the new creature stirs within him. He has become a foetus. His head is veiled and he is made to clench his fists, for the embryo in its bag has its fists clenched. He is made to walk around the hearth just as the foetus moves within the womb. He remains in this state until the great ceremony of the introduction of the soma. Then he unclenches his fists, he unveils himself, he is born into the divine existence, he is a god.

But once his divine nature has been proclaimed, it confers upon him the rights and imposes upon him the duties of a god, or at least those of a holy man. He must have no contact with men of impure caste, nor with women; he does not reply to those who question him; he must not be touched. Being a god, he is dispensed from all sacrifice. He consumes only milk, the food of fasting.[1]

The *Aitareya Brāhmaṇa* is explicit in its account of the symbolic nature of this purification: 'The bath signifies his conception, the hut is the womb, the garment the amnion, the skin of the black antelope the chorion.'[2]

There are several points to notice here. Firstly, the *imitation* of a god, or, as in the version in the *Taittirīya Saṃhitā*, *imitation* of a Brahman. All purification after pollution is, in a sense, imitation of Brahman purity, just as all etiquette observed in relation to members of inferior or superior castes is a dramatization, an imitation. The element of *mimesis* is a point we shall return to when dealing with play theory. Secondly, this rite, which we may regard as a paradigm of all subsequent purification rites, is performed by a *yajamāna*, or *sacrifier* (we may identify him as a king or chief; in other words, he is ritually inferior to the Brahman he employs as his *sacrificer*—there is an important distinction in words here which we owe to Mauss). As we shall soon see, the term *'jajmānī* system', retained till this day, on which division of labour among castes is based, originates from the Sanskrit word *yajamāna*. Obviously the sacrifier can only be considered in relation to the sacrificer, and that this *relation* is established by purification, by elimination of all physical impurities and the attainment of what amounts to the nearest a human being can approach to the absolute purity of an isolated monad (Plate 35), in a state of helpless *dependence* which alone ensures his biological survival. Hence the importance of this ancient rite to our understanding of all pollution rules today. It is the most complete model of how purity can be achieved.

[1] H. Hubert and M. Mauss, *Essay on the Nature and Function of Sacrifice*, Cohen and West, London, 1965, pp. 20-1.
[2] Ibid., p. 21.

With the third point we reach our conclusion, namely: this purification is an overt *imitation* (there is no reason to exceed our brief and call it 're-gression', though that is implicit in the quotation from the *Brāhmaṇas* cited above) of the infant's dependence on the mother. I would suggest a theory which has not, to my knowledge, been put forward in this context: that rites of purification, where one caste simultaneously establishes a relation of opposition and yet solidarity with another, express a fundamental *dependence* upon the body social; that this relation implies an ambivalence between inferiority and dread of domination, bearing the imprint of ideas concerning a threat to the boundaries of the body, its exits and entrances, or what is called in the *Atharva-Veda* 'the lotus of nine doors'; and that this image of vulnerability, dependence, and opposition is based on the learned and conditioned ability to dramatize an infantile attitude which the culture chooses to preserve and to put at the disposal of the individual, to be used by him and his fellow caste members in inter-caste relations.

We have now penetrated as deep into the origins and underlying principles of the caste system—caste ideology—as the facts permit. We must now take into account the external organization of the social order.

Chapter Two The Organization of Castes

The last chapter was concerned with structural relations between castes; it will now be shown in what ways the social order as a whole is organized into communities on a caste basis. There is no doubt that increasing complexity in the means of production, consequent occupational diversity, and the absorption into the social structure of indigenous tribes and foreign ethnic groups *contributed* to the differentiation; but to make division of labour the determining factor does not accord with the facts, any more than does racial prejudice. To get to the root of the organization of the occupational caste divisions we must turn our attention to the social contract, or *jajmānī* system, and the manner in which this was integrated with the degrees of pollution. This in turn will help to define the nature of economic and political relations between castes.

The *jajmānī* system

The term *jajmān* may be translated as 'patron', and hence the *jajmānī* system as that of patronage though not equivalent to the European meaning of that word. In the *jajmānī* system the village is the *locus* within which there exists an exchange of services and gifts between patron and client, and payment in kind is the general practice. But we should not lose sight of the term's etymological meaning, a procedure which is seldom followed consistently in accounts of this virtually all-India system; the specific connotation of this 'economy' then becomes clearer. As we have seen, the word *jajmānī* is derived from the Vedic term for a patron who employs a Brahman to perform a sacrifice for the community. In its original sense, therefore, *jajmānī* economic relations were an exchange of gifts, and collective reciprocity was implicit. To the present day this meaning has never essentially changed, although the unitary nature of the system is now subject to considerable stress through the introduction of money as the medium of exchange.

The first point to notice, therefore, is the specifically religious nature of *jajmān*. Secondly, the system is a substitute for the *sacrificial* pattern, in so far as it is a ritualistic relation between master and servant, the patron and the person he employs. One suspects that the *jajmānī* system first appeared in the period when Vedic sacrifice was abandoned as the primary religious rite of the Hindus—that it was a substitution for sacrifice on another, more functional level, rather in the same way as purification rites spread beyond the sacrificial domain to include the entire gamut of social regulation. *Jajmān* came to mean all the basic reciprocal relations of patronage, not merely that between Kshatrya and Brahman; it is a privilege and a responsibility for a family to patronize not only the domestic priest, but also all other specialists in the village. The system ensures the services of specialists and their subsistence; in exchange they receive annual gifts of products from the soil—a fixed portion of the crops—cloth and, though not invariably, money.

Rewards are given in accordance with hierarchical status and are not related to the 'economic' value of the services rendered, even if such a scale of values, or prices, is in some cases already established on the open market. While redistribution of goods, and gradation of means of production, are unequally divided among hierarchic castes according to their ritual status, the balance between those who give and those who receive does, in fact, mean an interdependence favourable to the latter. However, we should not regard the system as a one-way movement, for the rich patron is ritualistically or economically dependent upon his 'inferiors', be they Brahmans or barbers. The intrinsically religious nature of the system is dramatized during the occasions when it combines exchange of services and of gifts with family rites, festivals, and above all marriages. At such times the *jajmān* gives special gifts, and receives special services. The system is reciprocal to the extent that a man of comparatively low caste will serve a Brahman patron on certain occasions, while on others the same Brahman will serve him, in turn, in his role of priest at family rites. The relation between patron and client (which includes those of the rich man and his dependants, landowner and tenant, creditor and debtor, master and servant) is basically a personal one, even intimate, though conflict is also common. In some cases of ancestral, or particularly strong, dependence and intimacy, it is the patron's responsibility to find his servant a marriage partner. While these relationships accord with the familiar Western 'feudal' bond between master and servant, they also entail much more, in view of the fundamental religious interdependence of the *jajmānī* system.

The most important structural aspect of the social order is the role of the 'dominant caste'—a newly coined term for a virtually universal feature of Indian village social gradation. In almost all villages one caste, either through numbers, riches, or hereditary status, is dominant, no matter what its position may be in the regional unit comprising a full caste hierarchy. In fact it generally is Rājput, Kshatrya, or peasant proprietor, although in South India it is often a Brahman caste. This dominant caste (in some cases several castes) owns land, while others do not. It possesses economic and political power, although these are linked to the larger system of kingdom, state, or region. All other castes are dependent; their relations with the dominant caste are *personal*. Whatever the caste, its role as patron in relation to other castes of the village is the collective equivalent of a king. The history of *jajmān*, the evolution of power and government, reveal a fairly consistent, though complex, sequence in the delegation of authority, commencing with kings and gradually filtering down through vassals till it reaches the hereditary ruling family, or headman, or clan landlords of the villages. We have already seen in Part One how the archetype of king-and-court pervades the symbolism of temple iconography. Here we see a similar repeat-pattern running throughout social organization, so that successive hierarchic levels reproduce the king-and-court, each preserving the dual Kshatrya–Brahman *imperium*. *Jajmān* is such a 'court', although it can be, and often is, completely severed from its original monarchical nexus.

In his studies of Kishan Garhi, a village in Uttar Pradesh, McKim Marriott describes certain aspects of the *jajmānī* system which are revealing:

Hocart points out that many of the kinds of ritual relationships which exist among Indian village castes today may be regarded as results of a 'degradation of the royal style'. If the king has a royal chaplain or a royal barber in his retinue, then no peasant home can afford to be without one. Even a poor householder in Kishan Garhi today retains six or seven servants of different castes mainly to serve him in ceremonial ways demonstrative of his own caste rank. Householders and their servants formally address each other by courtly titles. Thus the Brahman priest is called 'Great King' (*Mahārāj*) or 'Learned Man' (*Panditji*), the Potter is called 'Ruler of the People' (*Prajāpat*), the Barber 'Lord Barber' (*Rāū Thākur*), the Carpenter 'Master Craftsman' (*Mistrī*), the Sweeper 'Headman' (*Mehtar*), or 'Sergeant' (*Jamādār*).[1]

The royal style is an agent in social evolution by *imitation* (Kshatrya-ization), and cultural patterns are similarly transmitted by the dominant caste by reason of its higher standard of living. Today the major influence in this respect is certainly education; other models for imitation include costume, entertainment, and styles in home living. The main types of imitation, Sanskritization and Westernization, will be dealt with later as they are not essential features of the *jajmānī* system.

The king was the traditional monitor of all major caste disputes; he administered justice, handing out awards of higher or lower status among castes and meting out punishment for infringement of rules. At his side the Brahman tendered advice based on the scriptures; his role in the dual

[1] McKim Marriott, *Village India: Studies in the Little Community*, Chicago U.P., 1955, p. 189.

imperium included the imposition of penance on wrongdoers, as distinct from punishment. Thus *artha*, secular law or power and punishment in this context, and *dharma*, sacred law, comprise the nucleus on which government is traditionally based; but *artha* has always been subsumed by *dharma*. The key to the authority of the *jajmānī* system is found here. Dr. D. F. Pocock summarizes the situation as follows:

The dominant caste itself maintains its own position and the relationship of service with other castes by the *fact* of its profane or secular politico-economic power. At the same time it is dependent upon other castes for economic needs and for that status which makes it superior to all except the Brahman. . . . On the one hand are religious specialists who, whether paid with cash or with produce, annually or on the spot, maintain usually, but not necessarily, an inherited relationship with their patrons (the dominant caste) *to whose status they are essential*. To the relationship between such castes and their patrons I would reserve the name of *jajmānī* relationships. In another category I have placed castes whose hereditary specialisation is not a direct result of the exigencies of the caste system, but is ascribed by an extension of the ideology of caste. The occupation of this category is both open and general and corresponds to what we should call mere economic activity.[1]

I question the words 'mere economic activity', since it is in the *jajmānī* system itself that we discover the specific characteristics of India's traditional attitude towards all economic and political activity. The three elements which comprise the *economic relations* within a village are: money—power—status. As we have already seen, the castes are economically rewarded according to their relative status in the hierarchy, and the power of the dominant caste is legitimized through that same status; in other words, hierarchy remains the determining factor in the *jajmānī* system, as it does in the larger caste system. It can also be seen that the economic relations between castes depend on the relation of each to the whole—a form of collective reciprocity diametrically opposed to the impersonal, individual, competitive, and merit-oriented open market of the modern type, aptly described by Knight: 'Economic relations are *impersonal*. . . . It is the market, the exchange opportunity, which is functionally real, not the other human beings; these are not even means to action. The relation is neither one of cooperation nor one of mutual exploitation. . . .'[2] We have also seen in Part One that the 'village communities' of India are not commodity-producing, cash economies; at the most, money is subsidiary to exchange of goods. We begin to see more clearly why money, and economic values in general, play a subordinate role in the traditional agricultural economy,

---

[1] D. F. Pocock, 'Notes on Jajmānī Relationships', in *Contributions to Indian Sociology*, VI, pp. 89, 91.
[2] F. H. Knight, *The Ethics of Competition*, New York, 1935, p. 282.

encircled as it is by a symbolic value system of commanding importance. The unity of this total universe within which all experience is ordered may best be described as a field of consistently symbolic action.

There is a symbol for the intimate relationship between the economic and religious elements of the *jajmānī* system which will help to express this situation more vividly. In certain regions the hierarchical distribution of power *within* the dominant caste is formulated on the analogy of the basic monetary unit, the rupee coin. This idea is very ancient, and although not universal, it typifies the Indian attitude to power. A rupee used to consist of sixteen annas; until the recent introduction of decimal coinage, the unit of weights and values had been a ratio of sixteen ever since the Indus Valley civilization. In the particular local *jajmānī* systems the members of the senior lineage in the dominant caste controlled, say, ten annas out of the rupee, the junior lineage six annas; and within each lineage power, prestige, and property were divided between several branches. At first glance this symbolism appears to reverse our order of precedence, with economic values determining both power and status. But this lineage gradation is no more than a part of the *jajmānī* system, it is determined by hereditary status, based like the entire hierarchy on relative purity, and legitimized through the alliance of the royal family, to whom the village patrons are related, with their Brahmans. The symbolic, as distinct from economic, significance of the rupee–anna scale, originates from the very meaning of money itself. The word *anna* means 'food'—the Hindu goddess of food is called Anna-purnā—and as Ruskin said: 'All *essential* production is for the mouth; and is finally measured by the mouth.' An anna was originally the token of a square meal. Food is the magic substance of communion or the means for paying religious debts in the sacrifice. The very idea of price is derived by Laum from ritual distribution of the sacred food. Even Marx invokes the alchemical mystery of money and the 'mystical', 'fetishistic' character of commodities, the value of which points to a 'world beyond', 'outside the real elements of social wealth'.

There is nothing particularly strange about the fact that in traditional India economic activity is submerged in non-economic relations of a ritual character. The consensus among ethnographers is that primitive economic systems all share this trait, however elaborate their systems of ownership, division of labour, and exchange. Karl Polanyi notes the following traits of a primitive economy: 'the absence of the motive of gain; the absence of the principle of labouring for remuneration; the absence of any separate and distinct institution based on economic motives'.[1] The only way to define the medium of exchange in the economy of a collective hierarchy such as the *jajmānī* system is by the idea of the *gift* as defined by Mauss.

[1] *The Great Transformation*, New York, 1944, p. 47.

This avoids the element of contradiction between the principle of collective reciprocity and the pure motive of gain. Mauss draws the incomplete conclusion, however, that the gift exchange is a primal act of social solidarity. The gift exchange of the *jajmān* is also, in fact, precisely what is implied in the very word *jajmān*: *sacrifice*. The three elements comprising this form of patronage are all subsumed by religion and may be more precisely termed status—power—sacrifice, than money—power—status. Money as such entered the mixed economy in its symbolic form as a mark of the sacred and as a token of gift exchange. The exercise of power was similarly subordinate to, and legitimized by, religion; the patron exercised political dominion by reason of dependents essential to his status. The system was not ruptured by the collapse of the monarchical hierarchy on whose superior authority the patron's power ultimately rested, for that power was already free to become increasingly secular by the very fact of its disjunction from and subordination to ritual status. In fact, the decadence of the *jajmānī* system in modern times originates precisely where we would expect it—in monetization. Only with the introduction of money could the idea of the individual competing on the open market develop. Once the profit motive was introduced into economic relations *between* villagers the ideals of sacrifice, service, and reciprocity were dealt a severe blow. The one element which change to a pure economic system has not completely destroyed is the ultimate pivot of *jajmān*: sacred status. Later we shall determine the extent to which this significant remnant can still exert an influence on the social system subjected to modernization (Part Five).

The little community

While the village community is internally organized on the model of the feudal court—and it is probable that, in South India at least, internal organization occasionally attained a remarkable degree of sophistication, even a 'republican' type of local autonomy—it is also part of a larger system. In former times the latter was either a kingdom or some form of clan organization. Today the village is part of an administrative system of local, district, and regional government of some complexity. But it is not so much administrative systems with which we are concerned, but the sociocultural dynamics of the relation between the little community and the outer community.

In the *Ṛg Veda* the Universe is conceived as expanding outward from a central point. All Indian spatial and communal schemata follow the same pattern of axial orientation. Srinivas states that the umbilical cord of a

Coorg's eldest son is buried in the central plot of the ancestral estate. This is a widespread custom in India; it is even observed by Roman Catholics in Goa. Many such references to a symbolic *centre* are to be found in the regional ideology of community orientation. But we should be on our guard against the conventional idea that Indian communities are always inward-looking. Certainly the traditional 'pre-economic' system, and the absence of easy communication in a tropical country with few roads, left many agricultural communities in relative isolation. The self-sufficient, non-commodity-producing village settlement is essentially the invention of the modern economist; it is only applicable when the agricultural economy is viewed retrospectively in relation to modern economic systems. In actual fact the Indian village was always part of a larger communal unit, linked by a network of exchange of services, of goods, of women. Useful as it is to define the comparative autonomy of a village in terms of monetary circulation and political administration, it should be seen more through the eyes of its inhabitants as the axis of their own Universe—expanding outwards from a central point to a network of kinship, caste, and linked services in a larger administrative district, from thence to the limits of its linguistic homogeneity, and finally to the perimeter of religious allegiance, in an ever-widening circle of decreasing loyalty.

The Vedic axial cosmology was tribal in origin; by the time Ashoka introduced the axial pillar surmounted by the wheel of *dharma* as the symbolic axis of the cosmos, India was governed by a centralized bureaucracy. After the collapse of universal empires, centralism was replaced by the feudal structure of numerous 'centres without margins', to use Henri Pirenne's phrase. The Mauryan–Vākāṭaka–Gupta pattern had fostered economic interplay between centre and margins, but with the spread of the *jajmānī* pattern, movable wealth no longer played an essential part in economic life.

If we turn to the administrative system whereby villages were grouped together under territorial control of feudal kings, we find a link between caste and territorial hierarchies. A caste is identified with a profession, while sub-castes are identified with a territory, region, or locality. Confronted with the hierarchy of unequal wealth and power in Kishan Garhi, Marriott decided that 'some formality and fixity of lands and offices through the devices of a greater state seems everywhere to underlie the order of caste ranking'. The *jajmānī* microcosm was part of a larger whole, measured rather vaguely in terms of land. Until the monetization of the rural economy, the principal criterion of power was indeed land-ownership; but property rights, a problem of extreme complexity and regional variation, need not detain us here, as they were not a fundamental part of the Indian social structure. What is important to remember, however, is that prior to monetization land was not regarded as a private commodity; it was owned by hereditary right, while its management entitled the proprietor to a share of the produce, the hierarchy of professional castes to their graded shares (traditionally, the king also received one-sixth according to the local *jajmāni* pattern). Property rights were normally conferred or annulled by the king, but holdings were frequently expropriated through violence. Today, when monetization has disrupted the *jajmāni* system, economics finally determines attitudes of tenants towards land-ownership. But land has not yet become firmly associated in the popular imagination either with private or collective ownership; it was never collectively owned so much as leased out, with share of the produce hierarchically distributed to all. There is no horizontal, holistic mysticism of the soil; vertical, hierarchical interdependence and *jajmāni* reciprocity have constituted the communal sensibility since time immemorial. Bureaucratic centralization and redistribution of hereditary land rights by force have never fundamentally affected this basic continuity. *Homo hierarchicus* does not become *homo economicus* without profound socio-political modifications.

It is largely due to the Chicago school of sociology that we know a great deal more about the relationship, in Robert Redfield's terms, between India's many Little Traditions and the Great Tradition than was known a generation ago. Marriott, in his studies of village life in Uttar Pradesh, has analysed the position of little communities of India, where villages are mostly clustered together. The South Indian kinship system, on the other hand, is confined to a small area surrounding any given village; the arteries of communication grow progressively weaker beyond these limits. In Marriott's village of Kishan Garhi there exist marital ties with more than three hundred other villages; fifty-seven marriages connect it with sixteen towns and cities. Half these alliances are located within a fourteen-mile radius, and some link with villages forty miles distant. Oscar Lewis, writing of a village near Delhi, identified more than two hundred such marriage ties. He also describes the system of inter-village relations as consisting of a four-village unit, a twenty-village unit regarded as descended from a common ancestor, culminating through successive groupings in a three-hundred-and-sixty village unit, all of whose ancestors were believed to have been related in the distant past. Similar types of inter-village hierarchies are to be found elsewhere in India; their origin is presumably linked with monarchy. As we might expect from these data, the economy of the village is also linked to the larger administrative system. In Kishan Garhi, for example, approximately a third of the village crops are sold every year outside the village. Three-quarters of the livestock were brought in from outside, a third of the credit for financing agriculture; forty-four outside specialists periodically supplied goods and services. Such figures give some indication of the extent to which a typical pre-industrial village formed part of a larger community.[1]

Like status and power, authority in the village used to be divided between Brahmans and the dominant caste—one arbitrating religious, the other judiciary disputes. When the occasion warranted it, a *panchāyat*, or council of elders from the dominant caste, was convened either to settle differences between castes or internal disputes within a caste. This *panchāyat* was not a permanent body, though it may have had the responsibility of general administration and tax collection, besides regulating internal affairs and relations with the administrative representatives of feudal chiefs and kings. If there were a serious dispute between the *varṇas* or the *jātis*, the king, advised by the priesthood, acted as the final arbiter. The *panchāyat* of the dominant caste acted like a court within the village. It had the equivalent function of the district magistrate's court in modern times and as far as possible it also played the role of local police. It is still common for village councils to avoid calling in the police, and to administer rough justice on the spot.

The internal affairs of each middle or low caste were governed by its own caste *panchāyat*, and by *sabhās*, a rather loose association found among high castes. Councils covering the affairs of a caste within a readily accessible region also existed, though some were rarely convened; in many cases, particularly among middle and low castes, these still survive. Generally speaking it is the lower castes which have possessed the strongest *panchāyat* organization, run by permanent officials with written records going back a century or more. But there is an enormously wide range of institutional practice under the heading of caste councils. Again, authority was either of a secular nature or vested in the symbolic head of the caste—the *guru*— who was usually but not always a Brahman. Offences brought to the notice of the caste *panchāyat*, perhaps later referred to the dominant caste or the Brahmans for final arbitration, are likely to concern breaches of rules of pollution, commensality, sex, marriage, remarriage, killing cows, addressing Brahmans without due respect to their status, and any practice which would prejudice the collective status of the caste.

No strict division can be drawn between India's rural and urban social organization, for the vast majority of city-dwellers maintain their ties with the original axis of their micro universe, the ancestral village. The urban Indian usually regards himself as a migrant to the city. It is a matter of common observation to find the modern Indian town or city divided into 'colonies' on caste lines (more recently on occupational lines). If these segregated urban social cells are investigated more closely, traces of the old residential units, or *pattis*, *panchāyats*, and inter-village units can still be

[1] Marriott (1955), pp. 154 and 174–5.

found. Common terms for a 'ward' or 'neighbourhood' are *mohalla* or
basti; these again may be subdivided, and each forms an exogamous unit.
Elders of the small subdivisions form *panchāyats* to govern a cluster of anything up to a hundred houses. This is not surprising since even the pattern
of Euro-American urbanization reveals the persistence of collectivities of
urban villagers. The rapid spread of urban agglomerations has also led to
the incorporation of villages on the periphery of the original urban nucleus
without their complete assimilation, so that many Indian cities consist of a
collection of villages. Mud huts of peasants survive—and are rebuilt in the
traditional materials—their original *pattis* remaining intact in the midst of
built-up areas.

We may summarize the government of castes within a territorial region
under two main headings: the Linguistic Regional societies, or Little
Traditions, specific, exclusive, and hierarchical; and the Great Tradition,
all-Indian in character, on which has been grafted the non-hierarchical,
democratic, secular liberalism of modern times. The relation between Little
Traditions and Great Tradition cannot be compared to individual buckets
of water poured into one reservoir; the relation is reciprocal. 'Both little
communities and greater communities are mutually necessary conditions
of each other's existence in their present form. One must consider both in
order to thoroughly understand either' (Marriott).

The reciprocal spongelike action of give-and-take between Little Tradition and Great Tradition was facilitated by two kinds of culture-bearers,
one from each domain. Marriott identifies the two streams as an upward
movement of *Universalization* and a downward movement of *Parochializ-
ation*. One nourished the Great Tradition with the emergent elements of the
village folk culture (which was often highly literate and sophisticated),
while the other transmitted the universal, generally urban culture of the
Brahmans.

We have now completed the analysis of the caste system and its organization. The reader may wonder whether this archaism is not, largely, irrelevant; whether the several vital interconnected parts survive under modern
conditions. The question of durability is a controversial one. True, change
in one small detail of the parts brings change to the whole, and it is
economic change which is the most powerful agency for mobility to have
affected the integrity of the old holistic system. Nevertheless, this kind of
change is slow precisely because of its interconnectedness. The psychology
of the vast majority of Hindus is still fundamentally a caste psychology,
whatever radical changes have affected their outward lives. In the caste
system, as in the family system, it is only when three generations have been
consistently emancipated from the older psychological outlook that an
appreciable change is apparent in personal relations. The educated élite

may be forward-looking; it may also be effective in implementing change. But an infinitely larger number of people, however much they may be groping for a better life, look nostalgically over their shoulders at what still seems to be a logically coherent, reassuringly familiar system superior to, and safer than, the apparently anarchic and threatening new order of the future. Mobility and change were not, as we shall soon see, impossible to accomplish within the caste system, although their results were circumscribed. These traditional processes also continue in the present transitional period, but we first need to identify them before we begin to assess the effects of new agencies for change.

Chapter Three The Antipodes

Another dimension to the organization of society may be discerned in the relations of the caste system to non-caste groups, i.e. tribal societies and semi-tribal communities which have been excluded from or remain outside the caste system. In its toleration of these groups as separate entities, Hindu society reveals its attitude towards change and advancement. For inherent in the caste system is the acceptance of opposites without social or philosophical conflict—unlike what would be or has been the case in Europe.

In India we are dealing with a civilization of the highest complexity, a social system of impressive, even astonishing endurance. At the same time this civilization has retained its profoundly archaic, not to say primitive, foundations; furthermore, the vast majority of its population live under conditions of backwardness. In short, the advanced Indian civilization nurses its most primitive elements. To identify the root cause of this conservation we must turn to evidence of the way in which these highly civilized people have co-existed for thousands of years with primitive tribes in what one may describe as a relationship of mutual need. In the next few pages I will attempt to explain the origins of this attitude towards social groups at the farthest remove from developed centres of civilization.

It is necessary to define our terms: by primitive we normally mean undifferentiated; by advanced and developed we mean differentiated. The socio-economic system 'advances' according to the degree to which it develops specialized economic and social institutions. Generally, differentiation in modes of thought is understood to proceed in accordance with differentiated social conditions, yet in India, as with the social development of humanity as a whole, we find that communities co-exist at every level of differentiation, and that highly differentiated *thought* systems are not always a direct reflection of the physical standard of living. The thought which went into the making, for example, of the Central Indian tribal *Ghotul*, or youth-dormitory, is far in advance of the sophistication with which adolescent institutions are conceived in detribalized, caste, or urban Indian society. The criterion of advancement is therefore not to be found exclusively in the degree of differentiation.

There is only one kind of differentiation in thought that is relevant, and that provides a criterion that we can apply equally to different cultures and to the history of our own scientific ideas. That criterion is based on the Kantian principle that thought can only advance by freeing itself from the shackles of its own subjective conditions.[1]

Conservation of primitive traits

The difference between the high culture of the Indian Great Tradition and the unassimilated primitive elements on or beyond the borders of the society, is in the comparative lack of self-awareness and objectivity of the latter elements. And if we compare Indian civilization as a whole with modern Western civilization, it is the former which has not been freed to the same degree as the latter from the subjective limitations of its own thought-processes. That the high civilization of India retains to a greater degree than modern Western civilization its primitive thought-systems is the cause and the effect of social co-existence of the tribes, the partially detribalized, and the completely detribalized, in physical proximity. The caste system itself reveals this preference for internal co-existence by establishing a framework for interaction among castes without minimizing the identity and distinctness of each caste. Again, the caste society as a whole should be viewed in spatial juxtaposition with non-caste societies. Thus we have internal juxtaposition of castes, and external juxtaposition of castes and self-contained tribes. These self-contained societies are interspersed among the castes according to their geographic location. Their physical proximity has led to another kind of relationship. Indian tribe and non-tribe have been defined sociologically as a *continuum*. Thus we are presented with formidable difficulties in analysis. Put in its simplest terms the situation is something like the following: the Hindu caste system has a built-in tendency to conserve, rather than to transform, primitive tribal elements which have been assimilated into it; at the same time, it has not assimilated into the caste structure a sizeable number of tribal peoples who are geographically encircled by it. Indian civilization demonstrates to a striking degree its emotional need for a primitive substratum, in spite of the fact that, save for rare occasions in the Classical period and earlier, it has emphatically disavowed any such need. Dominant peoples like those they hold in subjection to remain as they imagine them—lazy, feckless, libidinous —because it confirms their self-image as industrious, orderly, adult, and socially organized. The corollary is that the subject-people represent a *negative identity* in the unconscious of the dominant—what it has been warned *not* to become. Such a negative identity can acquire great psychic

[1] Mary Douglas, *Purity and Danger*, Routledge and Kegan Paul, London, 1966, p. 78.

potency among disaffected elements of the dominant people, a rejuvenating catalyst sufficient to spark revolution within its social system.

Advanced civilizations tend to assume that primitive peoples and tribes have remained in a state of childlike undifferentiation. The members of the higher castes in India project on lower castes, outcastes, and tribes, the dangers and temptations they associate with their own childhood—repressed 'lower instincts' and shameful innermost thoughts. But at the same time as these innermost thoughts are equated with those of low status, that is, with negative identity, they are also tied up with the higher castes' unconscious and ambivalent attitudes towards memories of their own early childhood. The despised represent both the state of lost innocence and those repressed contents which the more civilized have not been able to accept: negative identity could be called the secret self, not as civilized man is, but rather as he fears he may be. The outcastes, then, stand for the higher castes' fear of themselves. There exists an emotional need for the social scapegoat and a *terrain vague* where repressed instincts are permitted total freedom of expression. The existence of people who do not abide by the rules of 'civilized' caste society is not only tolerated, as they are a convenient receptacle for indulgence in projected fantasies; they are also actively prevented from joining the society.

There is no doubt that the civilized élite of India recognized it as in their interests to keep the excluded groups in a state of subjection, as part of the normal procedure for maintaining power and privilege. But this was not exclusively motivated by economic considerations or fear of economic rivalry. The excluded peoples could easily have been exploited for economic profit; however, this was rarely done until the late nineteenth century, and the tribes which did adopt settled agricultural production were assimilated into the caste system. Those others who were located in regions where assimilation was feasible, either showed no interest in changing their way of life, which was far more individualistic and unrepressed, less hemmed in by rules than that of the castes; or they were deprived of the means to advancement by the caste society itself because of a deeper psychological satisfaction to be obtained from the fact that the excluded peoples were (in the eyes of the more advanced) libidinous and unrepressed and did not engage in the *work* of settled production (Plate 53). Now, these are the psychological traits which caste society reactivates and harnesses to creative expression in the role-reversal of religious *ekstasis* at seasonal festivals.

There are many examples of the interplay between the repressive and libidinous elements in Hindu society. For instance, on the one hand the extremely strict rules imposed on the upper caste stratum reveal a high degree of psychological repression which accompanies the advance of civilization, while on the other hand the most characteristic feature of

Indian culture is the persistent vitality, not to say obtrusiveness, of its folk cultures amidst the classical refinements of the Great Tradition. But the most striking example is undoubtedly the relation between Tantric Hinduism (a revalorization of primitive magic and ritualized orgiasticism) and the more ascetic and puritanical Brahmanical orthodoxy. Tantrism is not so much a sect as a tendency, and while its primitive traits are still much in evidence, it has left its unmistakable imprint on modern Hinduism.[1] Tantric rites, however, are regarded by the orthodox as primitive, dangerous, and irrational. In a great number of cases the value-systems and the ethical tenets of such sub-cultures are in direct opposition to orthodoxy. This is a universal phenomenon of all pre-industrial civilizations; the history of medieval Europe, with its incessant campaigns to repress heresies originating in the cultural 'underground' of the folk, is perhaps the example which will come most readily to the reader's mind. 'It was from contact with the underground that spiritually creative thought received its secret, indefinable and yet determining character.'[2] The personal underground of the subconscious high-caste mind feeds consciousness from below (Plates 29–33). Every well-documented case of a great creative Indian personality abounds in evidence of such contacts with the non-rational culture of excluded peoples and classes. Indeed, a number of these men were born of low caste or emerged from beyond the caste system, like the Buddha from the Śākya tribe.

The repressed Eros (in India such deities and culture heroes as Shiva and Krishna, who originated in the folk cults, personify Eros (Plates 19, 39, 55, and 56)) provides the impulse in the quest for satisfaction denied by the regime of caste rules. This form of creative regression arising from the pressure of unacknowledged desires brings into prominence submerged elements of the mixed population. The association of these submerged or excluded elements with pollution accounts for the aura of extreme danger surrounding all Hindu cults of religious rapture, which have the character of mass contagion by irrationalism.[3] The high culture of Brahmanism devised a number of curbs to check mass hysteria, and to direct dangerous impulses along socially creative channels. But as the Brahman intellectuals withdrew farther into a world of their own, the popular mind was left increasingly

---

[1] 'Tantrism is pre-eminently the expression of the indigenous spirituality, the reaction of the not fully Hinduized popular strata.' M. Éliade, *Yoga: Immortality and Freedom*, Routledge and Kegan Paul, London, 1958, p. 105.

[2] Friedrich Heer, *The Intellectual History of Europe*, Weidenfeld & Nicolson, London, 1966, p. 50.

[3] This important aspect of rural culture is rarely treated in sociological studies on India. For the most vivid, accurate, and amusing description of rapture and role-reversal in a Hindu village festival the reader is referred to M. Marriott, 'The Feast of Love', in Singer (1965), pp. 200–12.

defenceless against eruptions of primitive irrationalism. Historians have established a connection between phases of mass hysteria, dance frenzies, or other psychic epidemics, and intolerable social conditions; it will be shown later that during corporate manifestations of irrationalism in India important roles are formally ascribed to persons originating from excluded social groups who specialize, not in subverting the system which brought about these social conditions, but in the performance of rites of protest to make them more tolerable.

In medieval Europe it was the powerful institutions of Church and State which exercised control over the threat, imagined or otherwise, of anarchy from below.

The most alert representatives of the higher culture, from the end of the period of antiquity until the nineteenth century, lived in a state of perpetual anxiety lest the world relapse into barbarism and fall away from culture and good manners. They were always afraid that knowledge, the arts and pure doctrine would be lost. In their fear, they forged chains with which they shackled those formative forces of life and kept them in a state of repression.[1]

Due to the incessant aggressive tension prevailing in Europe this repression elicited a positive response in the form of political revolutionary movements. 'The positive reaction took the form of an acceptance of the underground into the upper world, giving it a place in government, or in a proclamation of the sovereignty of the underground itself after the revolution.'[2]

In India it was the extreme flexibility of the caste ideology itself which posed a similar threat to the representatives of the higher culture. If one likes, this is the attitude of 'If you can't beat them, join them.' Perhaps we may best understand the psychological consequences of this Indian situation by drawing an analogy with that of late Roman civilization:

Every Roman was surrounded by slaves. The slave and his psychology flooded ancient Italy, and every Roman became inwardly, and of course unwittingly, a slave. Because living constantly in the atmosphere of slaves, he became infected through the unconscious with their psychology. No one can shield himself from such an influence.[3]

If we substitute 'Hindu' for 'Roman' and 'partially de-tribalized groups' for 'slave' we will have a picture of what happened in India. Of course the Hindu was not re-tribalized, any more than a Roman patrician 'became' a slave, and the degree to which primitive thought-processes have pervaded Hindu caste psychology has varied enormously. The surest indication of

---

[1] Heer (1966), p. 51.   [2] Ibid., p. 51.
[3] C. G. Jung, *Contributions to Analytical Psychology*, Kegan Paul, Trench, Trubner & Co., London, 1928.

the permeation of Indian higher culture by primitive thought-patterns is the durability of conceptual ambivalence in all traditional schools of thought from the Vedic age to the modern. As in Europe, linguistic research reveals numerous instances of this ambivalence in higher culture; it was not until the thirteenth century, when Christianity began its systematic onslaught on antinomianism and monism, that such ambivalence began to be purged from Western theology.

It is necessary to point out that no value-judgement is implied by these observations. The conservation and interpenetration of primitive cultural elements has had both its advantages and disadvantages for Indian society. Much of what was borrowed by the Aryan from the non-Aryan, by the caste from the tribe, has been greatly beneficial to the health and vitality of Indian civilization. At the same time, some, but not all, primitive attitudes conserved *within* the caste society have contributed to stagnation. The importance of the tendency to conserve, or to engage in personal relationship with, those peoples outside caste society but inside Indian territory, may best be understood by analysing relations with aboriginal tribes, and this will be done in the next section.

As world history shows, rejected classes have frequently played a role in transforming a social system. For a thousand years, the history of medieval Europe reveals a constant succession of revolts. The same period in India witnessed not one single recorded case of similar action; herein lies the significant difference in the role played by the 'underground' in Indian culture. There were socio-religious movements among the lower castes, but these did not challenge the political order. Just as pressure for change from within the caste society is accommodated so long as it does not interfere with the social order, so also is pressure for change from outside accommodated if it can be ringed around with certain rules. Replacement of the system has not been accomplished for three thousand years. The situation in modern times will engage our attention later.

Dual organization

Relations with excluded classes are an interesting variant of dual organization. One of the most pervasive Indian views is that the entire phenomenal world is a balance of opposing forces (binary opposition). This dual organization is as fundamental to the Indian outlook as cell and sex divisions are fundamental processes to the biologist. As we have seen, in the daily life of caste society the commonest manifestation of opposition is that of purity and impurity. In traditional Indian thought the basic complementaries are form and flux, or order and disorder. In social institutions we have already encountered the disjunction of power and status, ascribed to king and priest respectively; the disjunction of pure Brahman and Untouchable menial; and finally, the unequal relation between one caste and another, in superiority and inferiority (Plates 53 and 54). Everything in the complex social structure of India reflects this dual organization.

The earliest and most striking mythological complementaries whereby India defined form and flux were the Vedic brotherhood of *Devas*, gods, and *Āsuras*, anti-gods—the latter term is usually rendered by the misleading term 'demons'. The *Āsuras* are not demonic in the Christian sense of the word, they are antipodal, the polar opposite of gods, a complete reversal of everything which the gods represent. In the *Brāhmaṇas* they are associated with non-Aryan cults. We must employ the analogy of two sides of the same coin to formulate the Indian sense of interdependence between opposites, including this example of dual organization.

Castes were a device for coming to terms with the *other* in a holistic system. The otherness of a caste is its social function, its identity within an equilibrium of differences. Untouchables, tribes, Buddhists, Jains, Muslims, Sikhs, Parsis, Christians, Jews, were 'outside' the caste system and yet also a part of India. The major development in recent history has been the integration of these groups, who have played an important role in the total society without being assimilated into the Hindu system. Consciousness of that total society, divided as it was into numerous political entities, did not begin to dawn until Akbar's times. If we project ourselves within caste society we can see how the excluded communities fall into the vague category of phenomena called *para*. This Sanskrit word expresses the potency of the non-structured flux, chaos, disorder, the irrational substratum. *Para* may mean the unknown, the strange, the remote, the alien, the hostile, or simply the 'other'. But the implicitly unequal balance between the known and the unknown always reveals interdependence. *Para* does not imply dis*para*gement, as do most associations of the word 'other' in Western languages. One of the few instances when the English 'other' corresponds to the connotation of *para* is in 'other world', 'other-worldly'. The word 'paradise', which is cognate with the Sanskrit *para-deśa*, recalls exactly what we mean by this non-structured para-world, and the ambivalence associated with it. (We have already encountered the association of paradise in Indian religion with the legendary tribal food-gatherers of Uttarakuru.) I propose the word 'Antipodes' with which to describe the para-world. Relations between the society and its antipodes were not so much dialectical, which implies conflict and its resolution in synthesis, as cyclical. I would define the social Antipodes as para-communities, or groups, who either occupy an interstitial position within the society, or in a marginal terrain imprecisely located beyond the society's external boundaries.[1] One might characterize the culture of the Antipodes as the 'underground' component in the Little Tradition. It may be recalled that Huxley used the term 'mind's antipodes' with which to describe the domain of visionary experience; similarly, the image of the social Antipodes is formed in the deeps of the mind (as in the story of King Lavana, depicted in Plate 53), and while it may be outwardly manifested in ostracism of social groups, the paradox of creativity is that the form which aesthetic expression of that image takes will be of a heightened visionary character. The Mexicans in *Plumed Serpent*, most lurid of D. H. Lawrence's novels, are such projections. So too are the noble savages of Uttarakuru. The specific manner in which the energies generated by antipodal inter-action were utilized by the caste society will form the subject of Chapter Five. The point to make here is that it was in a festal cult that the com-munity and culture of the Antipodes was brought into contact with the higher culture of the Great Tradition. An analogy might, for example, be drawn from medieval German traditional law which, according to Pro-fessor Heer, 'required that the emperor . . . play with the illegitimate children of his lower class subjects on the first of May. . . .' Every move-ment generated by antipodal interaction proclaimed a *return* to the old order, or right, traditional, and sacred ways. Professor Heer also notes that

the most important element in this fundamental reality of custom was that of *répétition malgré les échecs*, the steady re-assumption and repetition of old forms of work, technique, thought and prayer despite innumerable crises, disillusionments and catastrophes. . . . The culture of [this closed society] was based upon a grasp of the earth and the world of things. . . . Constant repetition of the same work created the rhythm of life, a rhythm expressed in a perpetual repetition of the same ritual actions. The same songs, the same prayers (endlessly lengthy litanies, and prayers for the different hours of the day), sustained the spiritual and festal culture of the people.[2]

This does not necessarily lead to a reactionary stance. When the Bengali Brahman poet Chaṇḍīdās, a Vaishnava-Sahajin (and temple priest), openly declared his love for the washerwoman Rami—an untouchable—he aroused outraged opposition in orthodox quarters. The celebration, in great poetry, of a sacramental relationship true to the spirit of Krishna's *līlā* with a member of the social Antipodes constituted a radical challenge to the en-tire socio-religious hierarchy. But the psychodynamics of antipodal polarization are plain for all to see in this instance: secret sympathy for the famous lovers infused the Bengali Vaishnava movement with a reck-less fevour, the consequences of which have not yet entirely abated. For

---

[1] Cf. Douglas (1966), pp. 98–104, and V. W. Turner, *The Ritual Process*, Routledge and Kegan Paul, London, 1969.

[2] Heer (1966), p. 56.

besides inspiring a lively tradition of lyric poetry, the courage of Chaṇḍīdās has political undertones which are not lost in the charged atmosphere of modern Bengali society.

The Antipodes *remained* at a more primitive level of cultural differentiation. The age-long building up out of the deposit left by successive Indian religious movements, was a process similar to what Gilbert Murray called 'the Inherited Conglomerate'. A new belief-pattern rarely effaced the pattern that was there before; either the old lived on as an unconfessed and half-conscious element in the new—or else the new revalorized and refined one particular element which had previously been subordinated.

Anthropology seems to show that these Inherited Conglomerates have practically no chance of being true or even sensible; and, on the other hand, that no society can exist without them or even submit to any drastic correction of them without social danger.[1]

Rules have been imposed on every minority group of the Antipodes that it should exist at peace within the corporate, encircling social framework. But up to a point it never sought to impose any centralized dominion over the internal affairs of minorities. Recent exceptions, such as the Muslims, the Nāgas, the Goans, the Kashmīris, reveal the ambivalence of feelings for the Antipodes, compounded with the political exigences of modern nationalism. In the context of European absolute monarchy, imperialism, the militancy and fanaticism of the Church (wars of religion, proselytism, inquisitions, witch hunts), India has always appeared *laissez-faire* in the government of its pluralistic society.

In the sections which follow it will be seen that the social Antipodes have had an important influence on political and social organization. We may thus far summarize as follows: pluralism in Hindu society is the result of conserving antipodal minority groups; this pluralism did not allow for conflict or a dialectic which could have acted as a stimulus to advancement and eventual integration of various groups; on the contrary, it emerged from a basis of co-existence and acted as a curb on innovation in the means of production, technology, and social institutions, and thereby also prevented the establishment of unified states with resources commensurate to the task of mastering an acutely intractable physical environment. Such problems were beyond the limited powers of the ruling classes and the only solution available was adopted, though without conscious intent: the social order came to dominate the political system. We will proceed, after examining inter-ethnic relations between caste society and non-caste society, then to consider institutions, ideas, and values which have been subject to very gradual transformation in the course of history.

[1] Gilbert Murray, *Greek Studies*, p. 67.

Chapter Four Tribal Society

Historical background

We will begin this chapter by briefly noting the ethnic structure of the Indian peoples. The earliest human inhabitants of the Indian peninsula may have been the so-called pre-Dravidians, proto-Australoids, or Veddids, who entered from the north-west in two or more waves. The first wave appears to have consisted of food-gatherers and hunters without clans or clan-totemism, the second of localized clans. With population increase, migrations, and clan dispersal, they seem to have evolved group totemism in the Chota Nagpur district, where the only case of strongly formed Indian patrilineal totemism survives among the Birhor tribe. The Veddid element, which is allied to the aborigines of Australia, of the Indian archipelago, parts of the South-East Asian mainland, and Indonesia, is found in most tribes of southern and central India, among the lower castes and mixed with other elements in all levels of society, though to a lesser extent among the higher castes.

The next group to enter India were probably the Palaemongoloid Austroasiatics from the north-east, who are still concentrated in the Assam hills and the North-East Frontier Agency, though some penetrated to Bihār and Orissā. These are the Munda speaking tribal groups of today, who probably developed their relatively strong totemism on Indian soil from their earlier proto-totemic organization. The period of their entry may have coincided with the creation of the Indus Valley civilization by the so-called Harappans (a non-ethnic term), in which evidence of totemism is almost non-existent. The Harappans, who developed the city-states, were, as some believe, of the proto-Mediterranean race and equipped with a knowledge of metals; others claim that the urban population was composed of both proto-Mediterranean and Veddid peoples.

Opinions differ as to the sequence of Aryan and Dravidian invasions. Some scholars place the arrival of the latter, round-headed peoples from the north-west, prior to the Aryan conquest and around the third millennium B.C., when there was a wave of racial disturbance in the southern Russian steppe and in Iran. Others claim that the Dravidians, an already highly developed, non-totemic people, entered India around the middle of the second millennium B.C., either by sea or along the coastal land-route as far as Coorg, Mysore, Tamilnad, and Āndhra, as well as Bengal. The use of the Aryan–Dravidian ethnic dichotomy in the analysis of modern Indian ethnic composition has no scientific basis except in a linguistic sense. The Aryanization of the Dravidian peninsula was a very gradual process which did not get under way until the Mauryan period and was facilitated by the Sātavāhana colonization of the Deccan in the last century B.C. The Epics reflect the process of socio-cultural assimilation. The *Rāmāyana* deals with the conflict of the Aryans with the then natives of India and the latter's Aryanization. The *Mahābhārata* accommodated the beliefs and teachings of the various tribes, and was the first major literary creation to be attractive to all the peoples of India.

Despite the fact that the racist theory for the origin of the caste system has been disproved, there is no doubt that the white Aryan despised the black *dāsa*. There are contemptuous references to the black colour of the indigenes in many ancient and classical texts. At best these were of the 'black but comely' type, as in the *Song of Solomon*; at worst the natives were described as of repulsive appearance.[1] The connotation of black skin with menial status has never changed since ancient times. Indians are extremely conscious of the gradations in skin colour, from the so-called 'fair' and 'wheaten' to the dark, as may be seen from the matrimonial advertisements which are a common feature of Indian newspapers. For the frankest discussion by an Indian of Indian colour prejudice the reader is referred to the works of N. C. Chaudhuri. On numerous occasions I have been in receipt of confidences by Indians with regard to the embarrassment which they felt at having dark-skinned children, and more especially, dark-skinned daughters-in-law.

When dealing with the process of de-tribalization and assimilation, we have taken into account the fact that in the Vedic period *all* Indian peoples were tribally organized, regardless of their ethnic origin, and whether or not they acknowledged the sacred authority of the Vedas, and whether they were or were not *Āryā*. With the rise of kingdoms during and after the Epic period (*c.* 900 B.C.) and the development of urbanism, the process of de-tribalization began in earnest; King Bimbisāra of Magadha (in the second half of the sixth century B.C.) was probably the first man to initiate a consistent policy of de-tribalization. At this point the social order and the

---

[1] It has already been noted that the word *varṇa* means 'colour'; more specifically, white was associated with the Brahman, red with the Kshatrya, yellow with the Vaiśya, and black with the Śūdra. Such colour symbolism is very widely used for classifying the social order in tribal societies throughout the world. In Egyptian art it was customary to portray Egyptians as red, Asians as yellow, Northerners as white, and Africans as black. But Hocart discounts even this connotation for *varṇa*, says it has a ritual significance associated with the four points of the compass, and specifically refers to the four quarters of an enclosed town reserved for each of the four *varṇas*.

caste system were extremely fluid; Aryanization included the assimilation of peoples of diverse ethnic origin. The history of Hinduism and the caste system is one of a long and incomplete process of de-tribalization.

Between 500 B.C. and the beginning of the Christian era, Persians, Greeks, Scythians, and the nomadic Kushānas from Central Asia invaded northern India. In the fifth century A.D. another nomadic horde, the Ephthalite Huns of the upper Oxus, invaded the north, followed by the Gurjaras, whose tribal chiefs may have formed the original Rājput clans. Successive waves of Muslim invasions brought in a number of peoples—Arab, Persian, Turko-Afghan. The tribes of modern India represent the untransformed residue of the original primitive culture, probably because of their physical isolation in the rugged terrain of central and south India. The tribes of the north-western and north-eastern frontiers are a special case, by reason of their peripheral location. The non-Indian Rājput clans, and the aboriginal tribes who were incorporated into the Rājput clan system, represent perhaps the most important example of successful Indian relations with the social Antipodes, although in this case they were eventually assimilated into Hinduism. It is evident that this came about first through the sheer military prowess of the clans, secondly by reason of their readiness to accept, and to become valiant champions of, the Hindu belief pattern.

Tribal republicanism was evidently a widely favoured form of political organization, especially from about 600 B.C. in the less fertile sub-Himalayan Terai and foothills. Some of the great tribes associated with this form of government, such as the Śākyas and the Lichchhavi, although Aryanized by this time, were of non-Aryan origin, and had probably intermarried with Aryans. Buddhism and Jainism originated in the heterodox climate of the republican areas, and found considerable support there for many centuries. The Greeks, Scythians, Kushānas, and Huns were assimilated into these tribal societies, which continued to produce leaders after they had finally merged into the caste system as Kshatryas. Tribal republicanism had a great influence on the development of social and political ideas in the formative Indo-Aryan period when the society was in a state of institutional fluidity and ferment. The system lasted for about a thousand years with varying success, although its early importance as the rival of monarchical rule in shaping Indian ideas on government yielded, after about three centuries, to the superior concentration of power of the latter. It was an archaic, natural republicanism of peer groups of tribal leaders similar to that of many other societies elsewhere in the world; it has survived in a crude form in the Pathan *jirga* of the Northwest Frontier. In fact, its viability may have been due to the smallness of the tribal societies in those regions, where members could defend their territory without an elaborate standing army, such as there was on the plains. The principal characteristic of this archaic republicanism, as still of aboriginal tribal societies, was its emphasis on individualism, a trait which from time to time has affected the pattern of leadership within caste society from below. In institutional terms, the phase of its corporate vigour contributed to the stock of indigenous political ideas some elements from its form of government through assembly. This is a point we shall return to later.

Tribal culture

There are roughly thirty million people in India today whose culture is designated as tribal. They are divided into numerous different ethnic, linguistic, and cultural groups. Statistically they comprise a small minority of the population, but they are of great importance to our study since they, and a slightly smaller number of partially de-tribalized castes who fall within the larger official classification of Scheduled Castes (there are more than sixty million in the latter category), comprise what I have called the antipodal culture. The greatest emphasis should be given to Kosambi's remark: 'The entire course of Indian history shows tribal elements being fused into a general society.' This fusion should be viewed alongside the role which the Antipodes have played in the development of Indian culture by the very fact of their separateness and their difference from caste society. The Antipodes consist of two layers: pure tribal remnants who have not taken to regular food production, and little bands of tribal or partially de-tribalized people living on the fringes of society, even in the neighbourhood of well-developed modern cities. It is through the culture of this second layer that we can form a more accurate picture of the continued interaction and cultural exchange between caste and tribe, and the way the aboriginals acquired the status of castes (generally of the lowest ranks, but in some cases of Kshatrya class).

The refusal to produce anything useful for general society beyond the tribe entails rough treatment as potentially criminal elements. . . . The different methods whereby the tribal elements were formed into a society or absorbed into pre-existing society are prime ethnic material for any real historian.[1]

The most important difference between tribe and caste is the non-specialization of the former. In cases where a tribe has taken to one specialized occupation it has behaved as a caste. In another context Géza Róheim once described primitive man as 'free, untrammeled, and truly self-reliant' in comparison with the members of more organized society.

[1] D. D. Kosambi, *An Introduction to the Study of Indian History*, Popular Book Depot, Bombay, 1956, p. 25.

Plates 29. Goddess Chamunda. Vermilion cult image. Dewas. *Author*. 30. Ganesha. Vermilion cult image. Aurangabad. *Author*. 31 Fertility deity. Painted pottery. South India. *Author*. 32. Hanuman slaying demon. Film poster. Benares. *Author*. 33. Demon. Folk mural. Tanjore. *Author*.

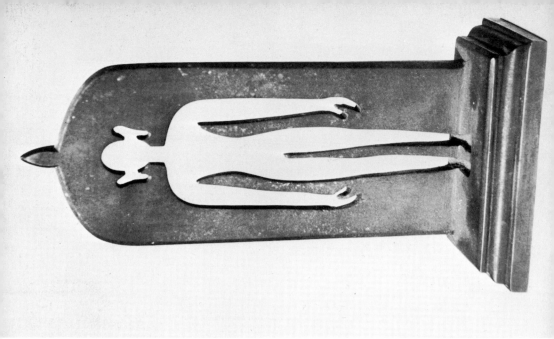

left 34. Vishnu as supreme
deity. Jaipur. *c.* A.D. 1810.
John R. Freeman.

right 35. Jain Tīrthankara.
Horniman Museum, London.

below left 36. Yogic system
of anatomy.

below right 37. Buddha as
ascetic. Gandhāra. Third to
fourth centuries A.D.
Giraudon, Paris.

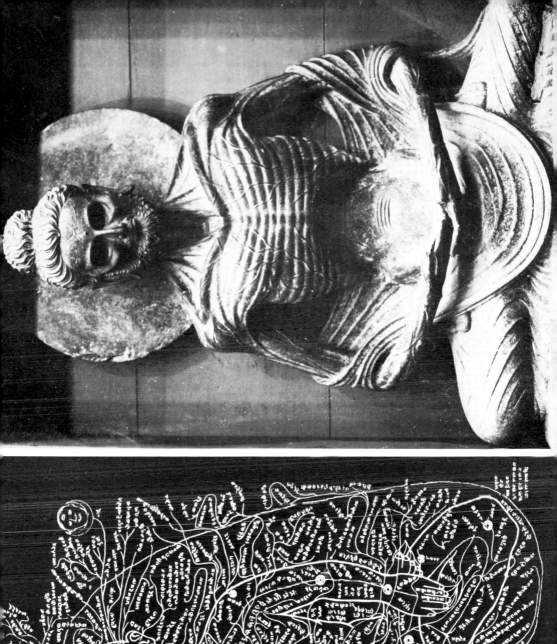
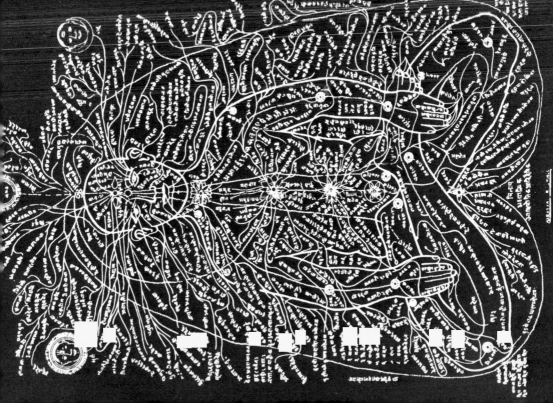

The outstanding characteristic of primitive economies is the absence of a true differentiation of labor. . . . This means that every individual is technically a master of the whole culture or, where certain modest qualifications are necessary, of almost the whole culture. In other words, each individual is really self-reliant and grown up.[1]

Verrier Elwin applied the same principle to the contrast in the outlook of the Indian caste and of the aboriginal tribe. Dr. Carstairs compares the 'controlled, inhibited Hindu model' to the 'spontaneous, violent ebullience' of a Bhīl tribe; my own knowledge of the same tribe accords with this view. Similarly, my observation in Bihār and Bengal prompts me to draw the conclusion that the aesthetic tribal way of life recalls the sensuous exuberance of Indian classical culture more than does the way of life of the rural Hindu castes.

Until very recently the tribes lived in those less accessible territories which preserve the ecology as it was in classical times. The forests and hills were not subjected to the intensive cultivation normal to the over-populated plains of the caste villages since the feudal period. Classical India had not yet forgotten—and in many regions was still in intimate relation with— untrammelled, tropical fecundity. Its culture, particularly the nostalgic ideal of the forest hermitage, was, as we have seen, directly modelled on the relatively carefree tribal life of food-gatherers. In fact, classical culture is shot through with a Rousseauesque primitivism. Admiration for tribal physical prowess and physical grace is combined in descriptive passages of Sanskrit literature with intense pollution-phobias. Survival in such close proximity to civilization may be accounted for by the unavowed Hindu tendency to exploit tribal culture to meet its own emotional needs—Dr. Carstairs calls the latter 'the reverse of the medal'; but some equally positive feeling must have been present among the tribes too if these external groups were to preserve their identity through such a long stretch of time. In his study, *The Religion of an Indian Tribe*,[2] Verrier Elwin describes how the Saoras of Orissā are 'married' to Hindu ghosts, an interesting variant of the King Lavana theme in the *Yoga Vāsishṭha*, suggesting a similar emotional need among tribes in the reverse direction, the satisfaction of which would at the same time safeguard their independence and separate identity.

There are grounds to believe that the Aryan class had a greater liking for the tribal hunter than for the caste peasant, in spite of the fact that the latter was theoretically of higher status and a member of the fourfold social order. Such powerful tribes as the Raj Gonds, who exercised considerable political power for many centuries over an area the size of the British Isles, no

---

[1] Géza Róheim, *Magic and Schizophrenia*, International Universities Press, New York, 1956.

[2] Bombay, 1955.

Plate 38. Head of deity in roots of temple tree. Terracotta. *Author.*

doubt commanded the respect of neighbouring Hindu rulers through their valour and resourcefulness. But caste society, with its insistence on endogamy, accepted the difference between itself and the tribes as natural and immutable. Nor was there an *organized* attempt to bring the tribes into the fold of the caste system as separate endogamous units. Tribes in close proximity to the main body of society, whose unity had been disrupted by economic factors and acculturation, were gradually absorbed without design into the castes. The vast size of India, the tenuous lines of communication in wild, forested country, left plenty of living-space for all. Moreover, the tribes have survived on a subsistence economy only in those areas where hunting and food-gathering have been comparatively easy. More than a hundred natural products could be gathered in a season, such was the natural fertility of some tribal regions. Until the population pressure in any given area became too acute, tribe and caste lived at peace.

This does not mean that the tribes led a completely separate existence; out of their interaction with the castes came the important developments we are concerned with here. The tribes have for long been involved in the economic network of weekly village markets, where they have had contact with Hindu or Hinduized artisan castes. On the cultural plane the artisan castes have been very active at village level; their economic ties with tribes are reflected in their religious cults, festivals, and arts. No sharp distinction can now be drawn between tribal religion and Hinduism, just as the gradations of social structure among those tribes in the process of absorption into the caste system cannot be classified as belonging either to one or the other, but rather as parts of a continuum.[1]

[1] Lévi-Strauss would define the structural differences along this continuum as the conceptual transformation marking the passage from totemic exogamy to caste endogamy. Social groups in tribal totemic systems are distinguished on the basis of natural differences, on the analogy of natural species, each group responsible for the control of a species of plant or animal, while those of the caste system derive from specialization of occupation, 'totemic groups conceived in terms of a cultural model'. (Lévi-Strauss (1966), p. 102.) The natural order or the cultural order provide the 'objective model on which they can draw for establishing relations of complementarity and co-operation among themselves'. (Ibid., pp. 123–4.) Among the Oraon of Chota Nagpur, 67 totems are recorded as derived from animals or plants; among the Munda, the majority of the 340 exogamous clans also have animal or plant totems, but different kinds of totem are already manifest: moonlight, rainbow, copper-bracelet, verandah, umbrella, basket-maker, and torch-bearer. The clans of the Devanga caste of weavers have few plant or animal names, but include many manufactured objects—products or symbols of functional activities—which can better serve to express distinction between social groups within the caste, and which receive special respect, like totemic plants and animals. Lévi-Strauss regards both totemic groups and occupational groups as 'exo-practising', the former in the exchange of women, the latter in the exchange of goods and services. Thus he sees totemic groups and occupational castes as contrary illustrations of social complementarity, the former being homogeneous in function and heterogeneous in structure, the latter exactly the converse. (Cf. ibid., pp. 116–33.)

In common with Hindu lower castes, the tribes emphasize equality in social behaviour within the ethnic group, greater equality of status for women, more liberal relations between the sexes (men and women work together), a more personal relationship between husband and wife, a more 'romantic' type of courtship, love adventures and love feuds, and, as would be expected, a greater emphasis on self-reliance in child care. Pollution rules are far more relaxed among the tribes than among castes. The absence of puritanism, frank indulgence in pleasure, and a strong sense of corporate identity all favour the tribal passion for music and dance, at which many tribes excel.

The absence from self-assured tribal life of the subservient mentality common in the larger system of castes is most striking. In fact, tribes who have not taken to settled agriculture or artisan specialization, but who have been industrialized—there are many such cases, since much of India's mineral wealth is located in tribal areas—tend to develop a greater sense of corporate independence. This is possible because a tribe is a complete, self-contained, integral society, but a caste is only a part of a society. Endogamy among members of industrial castes is as strict as among rural castes; therefore intermarriage between individual tribal members and individual caste members is exceedingly rare. In consequence, the identity of industrialized tribes in modern steel towns is likely to be preserved for some time to come, whatever changes may occur in their social structure.

The climate of psychological dependence in which a higher-caste child grows up is unknown in tribal life. The most characteristic tribal institution, common to many, but perfected by the Murias, is the village youth-dormitory (which has already been referred to in Chapter Three of this Part), a highly sophisticated organization which compares favourably with any similar adolescent institution. Known as the Ghotul among the Muria of Kondagaon, it is as complete a form of audio-tactile social education as man could devise. Aesthetically, the youth-dormitory served tribal India as Sanskrit drama and the cave sanctuary served classical India; socially, it was of fundamental importance, and caste society had no equivalent institution. It was in the youth-dormitory that the subtle aesthetic culture of tribal India was formed. It has had no direct influence (at least, none that has been recorded) on the development of Indian civilization, but in terms of resultant character and sensibility its role as the basic educational agent of the tribes (together with other adolescent customs of the tribes) has, in my view, imbued the flagging cultural vitality of India with a new sensuous exuberance at critical moments in history. When the Great Tradition was on the verge of sterility, when asceticism and dry scholasticism threatened the general health of Hindu society, waves of fresh energy seem to have coursed upward from the Antipodes, inspired by culture heroes nurtured among pastoral folk with wholly different ideas on the upbringing of the young. This is not a point that can easily be substantiated. Nevertheless the Krishna cults and even the imagery of the Ajantā frescoes were evolved in periods when tribalism was still a major cultural force, suggesting an affinity with the cultivation of balanced interplay among the senses, the total togetherness of the Ghotul.

The Ghotul is not only a club but a self-governing commune where the two sexes develop tribal solidarity, train for the adult duties of social and economic life independent of adult control, and give assistance to the tribe on payment of certain specified fees. The boys assemble at the dormitory in the evening for dancing, games, and social and sexual training unhampered by the interference of elders; they sleep there after the departure of the girls. Each girl is paired off with a boy, combs his hair, massages his limbs, dances and sings with him, and is initiated into sexual life with him. According to Elwin, sexual congress is regarded by the Murias as natural and healthy, and continence is not admired; while consummation is the goal of Ghotul attachments, pregnancy is the exception rather than the rule. He finds the divorce rate far lower than in tribes without youth-dormitories, and comes to the conclusion that the discipline and social sense taught in the Ghotul is responsible for creating a psychological attitude favourable to stability in marriage. Instruction is given in mimetic dances depicting the various adult skills in work and craft, love play, and sexual intercourse,

while ideas about the sanctity of tribal discipline, social approbation, social justice, reciprocity of obligations, law and order in society, as well as the relations between effort and reward, between crime and punishment, are inculcated through stories and anecdotes which graphically describe individual doings and their repercussions on the social life of the community.[1]

One can well imagine the annoyance of a Muria Ghotul when Majumdar flashed his torch through the small entrance one night at 1 a.m., picking out the intimate groups of boys and girls, like a guide directing his torch on the frozen details in the magical resonating dimness of an Ajantā cave. A youth lay on his back with six girls massaging him while he recounted recent exploits, and various other groups in the shadows covered themselves, affronted to be thus subjected to alien inspection.[2] In his sensitive studies of the Ghotul and translations of Muria poetry, Elwin gives the highest praise to this innocent and aesthetic institution where the play instinct reigns supreme.

The most comprehensive ethnographic survey of youth-dormitories in

[1] D. N. Majumdar, *Races and Cultures of India*, Bombay, 1961, pp. 278–9.
[2] Ibid., pp. 279–80.

India is to be found in Christoph von Fürer-Haimendorf's 'Youth Dormitories and Community Houses in India'.[1]

The evidence contained in this paper gives no conclusive proof of my speculative hypothesis, but it provides valuable material of a supportive nature. Fürer-Haimendorf suggests that the institution of youth-dormitories was diffused over the Indian sub-continent by a neolithic agricultural civilization spread over a very wide area including Assam, the Himalaya, Burma, Malaysia, and Indonesia. The migration into India of these tribes, who lived in more or less permanent agricultural settlements, originated, he believes, in the Nāga Hills of Assam. One movement followed a course westwards along the southern Himalayan slopes as far as Garhwal (in the Punjāb hills), the other south-westwards into the hills of Bihār and Orissā, probably penetrating to the Western Ghats, and (possibly independently, by the maritime route from Indonesia) as far south as the Malabar and Nilgiri hills. Youth-dormitories are to to be found among the Nāgas of Assam, a number of Munda and Dravidian-speaking tribes of Bihār, Orissā, and Bastar, semi-nomadic forest tribes of south-west India, the Kotas and other tribes of the Nilgiris, and the cattle-breeding, semi-nomadic Bhotias of Garhwal and Almora. Fürer-Haimendorf points out that while the distribution, in the twentieth century, is 'patchy', there is a likelihood that the institution was found among *populations* akin to the present-day Kotas, for instance. He also believes it highly likely that the numerical rarity of the institution is

... a result of social pressure and disapproval on the part of politically dominant populations. Throughout Peninsular India the youth-dormitories are faced with condemnation and criticism of Hindu populations who invariably object to the freedom of intercourse between unmarried boys and girls ... the uneven distribution of the institution today may partly be due to similar cases of outside pressure in previous times.[2]

While there are wide differences in the youth-dormitories, 'there is', says Fürer-Haimendorf, 'an imponderable likeness in general atmosphere' among the many widely scattered tribes who possess them.

The youth-dormitory itself must be regarded as the expression of a social tendency, an 'ethos', rather than an isolated 'element' of culture.[3]

What evidence, then, is there for any influence of the youth-dormitory 'ethos' on that of the cave sanctuaries? Fürer-Haimendorf includes a number of features common to all varieties of this tribal institution which the non-tribal society of the relevant period did not possess (save perhaps among those heterodox sects who, as has been shown already, had borrowed from the tribal republics certain ideas necessary to build an

[1] *American Anthropologist*, 45, 1950, pp. 119–44.   [2] Ibid., p. 142.   [3] Ibid., p. 136.

alternative community life): the youth-dormitory can evolve only in a tribal society tuned to communal living which is neolithic (the caves were excavated adjacent to neolithic cult-sites); it permits a *separation* and organization of the *unmarried* boys and girls; it is a men's club and a ritual centre associated with powerful magical forces; it is a self-administered institution which serves as a focus of communal solidarity; in some instances, it serves as a village hall and rest-house for visitors.[1]

From [one youth-dormitory of a particular type] it is probably only a small step to a village shrine and we cannot indeed exclude the possibility that the men's house in its role as the depository of sacred objects is one of the prototypes of the temple.[2]

In other words, if the heterodox sects *were* seeking for a model for a segregated institution to shelter the unmarried, the youth-dormitory was already a firmly established practice in the secluded regions frequented by anchorites. As Elwin points out, Ghotul education condemns possessiveness, is against the concept of private property and individual accumulation of wealth, prominent features of early Indian monastic sects and an essential feature of their 'renunciation'.

Another precedent is to be found in the aesthetic domain. Youth-dormitories are adorned with numerous carvings and wall-paintings, providing an important stimulus for artistic creation. The Juang dormitory contains 'beams and pillars elaborately carved with elephants, hunting and dancing scenes, female figures, and rows of women's breasts.[3] Among the Bondos, one type of girls' dormitory used to consist of underground shelters, dug some 10 feet deep into the ground and roofed over with branches, bamboo, and pounded earth. In all cases, it seems, the dormitories were the scene of festivities, music, singing, dancing, playing—'an expression of the communal art of the people' (Elwin).

The heterodox sects had strong tribal connections, both ethnic and cultural; their institutions of the *vihāra* (assembly hall, with a village-hall character) and *Saṇgha* were derived from the tribal council and men's club; the origins of much of their symbolism and their architectural prototypes must be sought in tribal culture; their segregation of the unmarried reveals a cultural nostalgia for the life of the food-gatherer, and a preference for choosing retreats near tribal cult-sites endorses this trend. It would also be scarcely surprising that the sensuous refinement and erotic overtones (but not the artistic *style*) of the cave ethos would share with the youth-dormitory 'an imponderable likeness in general atmosphere'. For the longing to restore an initiatory pattern and a rusticity of life-style were compellingly

---

[1] Fürer-Haimendorf (1950), p. 141.
[2] Ibid., p. 141.   [3] Elwin (1947), p. 302.

urgent, perhaps more so than was the need to impose ascetic *discipline*. To borrow a phrase from Erikson, this asceticism was never intended as a repudiation of the erotic facts of life, but to insist on a rigorous truthfulness towards them.

Tribal influence in caste society

There are a number of ways in which tribes have contributed to the institutional pattern of the majority society, and these will now be considered.

Strongly formed totemism, for example, is confined to a small tribal area in the north-east of central India from where it radiated out, long before the Aryan invasions, far into south India, westwards to the borders of Gujerāt, north as far as the Ganges, and eastwards down to its estuary. Strong traces of totemism are to be found today among the lower Telugu, Kanara, Marāthi, and central Indian *castes*.[1] The precise definition of totemism is much disputed, but it may be described as a system of classification or cosmology whereby a tribe orders the species of nature and sees itself in relation to that order.[2] According to Claude Lévi-Strauss totemism is 'a particular expression, by means of a special nomenclature formed of animal and plant names (in a certain code, as we should say today), which is its sole distinctive characteristic, of correlations and oppositions. . . .' It is, he concludes, a way 'to make opposition, instead of being an obstacle to integration, serve rather to produce it'.[3] Now this throws light on the process of opposition-integration between Indian society and the Antipodes. While Aryan society was evidently not totemic, there is evidence to suggest that before the commencement of detribalization around the sixth century B.C.—at a time when all Indian social organization was still completely tribal—the principle of totemic complementarities was borrowed by the Aryan tribes from non-Aryan societies, or at least influenced Vedic social theory. As Lévi-Strauss says: 'It is because man originally felt himself identical to all those like him (plants and animals) . . . that he came to acquire the capacity to distinguish *himself* as he distinguishes *them*, i.e. to use the diversity of species as conceptual support for social differentiation.'[4] It will be clear from this why caste and tribe are polarized social institutions, and why both are, in different ways, particular applications of

[1] Cf. J. V. Ferreira, *Totemism in India*, Bombay, 1965.

[2] Géza Róheim: 'By totemism I mean . . . an intimate relation supposed to exist between a group of kindred people on the one side and species of natural or artificial objects on the other side, or, expressed more psychologically, the self-projection of a social unit in a natural unit.'

[3] Lévi-Strauss (1963), p. 89.

[4] Ibid., p. 101.

thinking by pairs of contraries. There is no question of one having evolved from the other, an evolutionist idea which has been rejected. Totemic social organization was never completely abandoned by a very large number of castes in the vast central belt referred to above. Ferreira concludes that the less totemic the caste, the higher its status. An analogy would be the higher status of large scientifically oriented Western classes in relation to those which retain mythical thinking. The retention of tribal totemism by castes extends to totemic names and totemic descent, totemic tabus and exogamy, worship of the totem image at marriages, and mourning for the dead totem. Ferreira refers to a number of cases where totemism has only recently been assimilated by a caste.

The question of dual organization as a structural determinant of relations between two castes or exogamous tribal moieties, as distinct from a fundamental tendency to think in pairs of contraries (purity and pollution, natural and cultural, order and disorder, etc.) is a complex one. Classification systems of this kind were undoubtedly features of a high proportion of caste and tribal organizations, as the following list suggests: the former custom in South India of dividing castes into Right and Left Hand; patrilineal and matrilineal descent; dichotomous castes and exogamous-totemic sub-groups; colour dichotomies in Gujerāti castes. As with totemism and pollution tabus, the evidence is sufficient to indicate that Indian social organization in general, both caste and tribe, is rooted in a polar worldview which becomes less distinct the higher the caste, until it is overstepped in the pure monism of the Brahman philosophers. More important is the emotional need of lower castes for a supplementary belief system such as totemism, which would unite them in a sympathetic relation with nature in a more concrete way than the caste system.

Other significant instances where tribal society has had a direct influence on caste society include the derivation of the Aryan and Brahman exogamous clan, or *gotra*, from the virtually universal clan organization of the tribes. The endogamous caste is subdivided into exogamous *gotras*—the word is Sanskrit for cow-pen (each *gotra* had its own branding mark for cattle held in common). This idea may have been assimilated by peripatetic Brahmans who intermarried, as ancient texts record, with tribal women (the systematic application of the *gotra* is attributed to a South Indian Brahman); it was subsequently imitated by the Kshatryas and later by the lower castes who wished to raise their status. The idea has recently turned full circle: Hinduized tribes anxious to conceal their totemic names have borrowed the names of Brahmanic *gotras*.

The idea of animal 'vehicles' for Hindu deities (Plate 45) and animal incarnations (Plate 32) is probably totemic, as are tree and snake worship (Plates 7, 16, and 38), 'tree marriages' performed among both tribes and higher castes, and the numerous instances in Puranic myths of animals who give birth to human beings or vice versa. Ganesha, the elephant-headed deity (Plate 30), and Shiva's horrendous dance in the skin of a flayed elephant, both suggest tribal Shamanism. Hindu mythology, the Krishna cult, yoga, and Tantra are replete with magical lore and symbolism of tribal origin. Robert Redfield summed up the process: 'rural [i.e. caste] India is a primitive or a tribal society rearranged to fit a civilisation.'[1]

In the reverse direction, the main features of acculturation occur through ethnic or demographic intermixture: bilingualism, transformation of tribe into caste, adoption of caste religion more or less distantly related to the Hindu Great Tradition, change to settled means of production and specialization, acceptance of caste rules with regard to marriage, diet, pollution tabus, joining a Hindu sect and losing the tribal name in the process. Not a single tribe in the great central and southern belt has been unaffected by Hinduism. Christian missionaries have also been active in the tribal regions. With the advent of a uniform administrative system under the British, colonists from the lowlands encroached on tribal territory and denuded the hills of the dense forest on which the aboriginals depended for sustenance. Once the ecology had been upset, the tribes were forced to devise new modes of life, to specialize, and to enter the caste system in the lowest ranks. Recent changes will be reviewed later, along with those which have occurred in the Scheduled Castes.

[1] Redfield (1960), p. 34.

Chapter Five Fission and Fusion

In this chapter the institutionalized forms for checking the innate fissile tendencies of the social system will be examined. It will also be shown that the fusion of pluralistic elements in traditional Indian society ensures a certain degree of mobility and vitality. The system's stability is usually accounted for by the 'freezing' of caste barriers; but this does not take into account the fact that the so-called 'frozen' caste system sustained its creative energy over a very long period before stagnation set in. Our task here is to identify the means whereby society overcame excessive social division and ensured solidarity in the face of internal or external threats. The field of investigation will cover, in turn, the following institutionalized activities which have been instrumental in achieving social fission and fusion:

The cultural media.
Festivals, play, and conflict.
Religious rapture and possession.
Emotional religiosity of *bhakti* sects.
Mystical renunciation.

The cultural media

The role of the arts in the restoration of lost unity by a process of creative fusion has already been examined in Part One. The artist as culture-bearer operates on two levels: one pertains to the Great Tradition and concerns society as a whole, while the other functions at the local level in relation to the Little Tradition.

The culture-bearers were generally organized according to their different roles. All Indian cultural media ultimately derive from sacred culture, in which the Brahmans have enjoyed a monopoly, though not an exclusive one. Thus the diversity of media can all be traced to their origins in the root-pattern of ritual as evolved in temples and shrines, in domestic rites and collective rites (births, marriages, deaths), and in festivals. The media were either associated with the folk culture of the Little Tradition (*deśī*) or the classical culture of the Great Tradition (*mārga*). Brahmans generally acted as patrons, supervisors, teachers, choreographers, 'script writers', but were also performers, particularly in the Sanskrit media belonging to the Great Tradition. On the other hand, vernacular culture-bearers and cultural performers of the Little Tradition were generally representatives of a caste, such as potters, weavers, basket-makers.

Popular media emphasize total sensory awareness, a high level of audience participation, synaesthesia (a combination of several art forms: music, dance, poetry, costume, ritual, etc.), and emotional religiosity (*bhakti*, or devotion; *līlā*, ritual play); classical media, on the other hand, have a more exclusive appeal to a single sense, reduced (passive) audience participation, a mystical or yogic type of concentration both of audience and performers, and aesthetic purity (still within a sacred context, as in classical music, which seeks to utilize pure sound to achieve mystical union). Drama and the religious festivals at great temples were mixed media and drew from both streams of tradition, classical and popular. The Kathakali dance drama is the most notable example of this fusion. Rites performed on a colossal scale at famous temples of pilgrimage included cultural performances running the entire gamut of media, employing a complex hierarchy of specialists. An important element in culture diffusion was 'sacred geography': association of places, physical features of the landscape, temples, and shrines, with either the local mythology of the little traditions, or the universal mythology of the Great Tradition. Centres of pilgrimage (some dating back to neolithic times) have always been the principal points of cultural diffusion as well as for economic exchange on a large scale, a pretext for crowds to gather from all points of the compass, often from very great distances. A high proportion of all cultural performances, both classical and popular, were held under the auspices of feudal courts.

A brief examination of the traditional media will reveal the type of social organization in which they originate. Popular inter-caste media, with their emphasis on devotional religiosity, include rhythmic chanting of religious hymns (*Bhajans*) in honour of a local or a universal deity (the latter include famous deities such as Rāma and Krishna, Durgā and Kālī), carried to a pitch of emotion bordering on, and frequently entering, states of ecstasy, trance, or possession; recitals or dance dramas from the Epics and Purāṇas (Rām Līlā, Krishna Līlā); bardic recitals in celebration of a local or national hero, local dynasty, or caste dynasty; hymn-singing in honour of a local saint; poetry contests; folk dances on the occasion of a festival or life-cycle rites. Any of these performances may also be held exclusively for one caste. The local dialect or regional language is the medium of expression.

All these popular media come under the dominion of synaesthesia and oral tradition. They recall, on a cruder, less co-ordinated level, the magical echo-chamber of the cave sanctuaries. Although they depend on the spoken or chanted word, their effect demands empathy and participation of all the senses; performance is composition, extemporization—and the audience is drawn into a vortex of multi-levelled and multi-sensuous awareness. One could say that these collective, mixed media are the forms with which the organismic unity of society is repaired, each artistic specialist acting as a representative limb of the social body, identifiable by his caste and by his degree of 'purity' or sacredness. Lost unity through specialization results in a frenzy of sound to recover the over-all interplay of forces, and ensures a furious activation of all performers, all the social components. The myth- or story-teller 'speaks as many-to-many, not as person to person' (Harry Levin). But this is not the total togetherness of the tribe, with its relaxed and confident exuberance; it is the straining after balanced interplay of a pluralistic society through formalized role-playing. Nevertheless, the drummer and the trance dancer—those who evoke the magic power of the collective most assertively, one through overwhelming sound, the other through violent paroxysm—belong to low castes whose organization still retains traces of their tribal origin.

Classical cultural media, while basically under the dominion of oral tradition, still elicit relatively deep participation from the audience, and use a stream-of-consciousness technique. The purest example is the *Alap* of classical music, a wordless song, a caressing of the inner ear. Yogic concentration rather than emotional religiosity is the discipline of these media, which include, in addition, Vedic chanting—a meta-science of sound, mystical prayer; scriptural recitation in Sanskrit, which is restricted to high castes and performed in temples; *bhārata nātyam*, the temple dance; Sanskrit drama; Puranic recitation by literati. The dance and the drama, both derived from the village folk play and ritual, utilize the synaesthesia of the latter with the 'wrap-around' sound effects which are the essence of popular media. These classical arts, while directed and taught by Brahmans, are performed by grades of caste specialists. The dancers and actors in dance dramas are members of the *devadāsī* community, associated with temple prostitution, and many of the musicians are male members of this community.

On the other hand, the popular media transcend inequality; their relation with the irrational is revealed in the not infrequent use of psychedelic techniques, drugs, and alcoholic intoxication in keeping with their orgiastic character. Both classical and popular media share in common the all-inclusive medium of the Epic tradition, the greatest cultural integration between Little and Great Traditions, itself a living synthesis of universal culture constantly accommodating its narrative to suit parochial interests. The motley bands of professional artists, bards, wandering minstrels, and holy men who have been travelling the roads of India in unending procession since antiquity may be counted as an important element in this 'link language'. So too are the caste and sect *gurus* who have acquired their charisma through resolution of life's contradictions, the 'play of opposites', the multiplicity of cultural allegiances. The brotherhood of mystical devotees of the *bhakti* sects originated in popular movements which attempted to cut across caste lines and to bring people from all walks of life together.

In the final analysis it is a single unifying power which the Indian culture-bearer utilizes to draw together the diversity of peoples in this consistently oral society: the power of music. Social fusion is achieved through the universal appeal of melody, rhythm, and cadence; for, as Élie Faure writes, music comes into its own

when men are separated to such a point from one another that, even when they ignore—even when they deny the fact—they tend to draw nearer to one another. It no longer expresses man at the summit of himself, but man allowing that summit to be assailed by murmurs, cries, complaints of other men, and the forgotten universe. Social pantheism does not possess any means of action more powerful than music.[1]

Festivals, play, and conflict

Hindu society ascribes religious significance both to the separation of groups into castes and to the interdependence among those castes. This is a universal phenomenon of all religiously oriented societies. The seasonal festival dramatizes these two facts through religious rapture, ecstatic orgiasticism, trance dancing, and art. The festival restores the sense of unity which specialization endangers; this is generally accomplished by a reversal of the customary regulation of daily social interplay and work.

On the one hand, any tendency towards segmentation or loss of corporate solidarity within a caste is checked by the fervent ecstatic celebration of its communal identity at its own temple festivals. On the other hand, excessive *inter-caste* rivalry or sense of exclusivism is countered by festivals in which the entire community co-operates. Until recently, in most parts of India the castes combined at least once a year in rituals sponsored by the *jajmān* and conducted by both Brahman and non-Brahman temple priests.

For institutionalised ritual draws into cooperation, in common acts and a common belief system, the very categories of persons upon whose mutual ambivalence the rites are founded. More than this, by bringing home to the participants a sense

[1] Élie Faure, *The Spirit of the Forms*, Bodley Head, London, 1930, p. 51.

of their common helplessness in face of the dangers and mysteries which confront man both in his own nature and in his world, ritual appears to transmute their very hatred into sentiments of mutual dependence and love.[1]

In some regions of India, community festivals also involved the active participation of not only Hindus but members of other religions too. For example, Muslims and Hindus mutually co-operated in each other's rural ceremonial in Bengal and Uttar Pradesh, as do Christians and Hindus in Goa to this day.

Within the sacred continuum the Hindu passes from the ritualized *order* and *pattern* of daily life to regenerative *flux* and *transgression* in the festival—returning once more to the regular rhythm of daily life. Here we find a consistent series of rhythmical polarities. Thus: order—chaos; submission to rules and regulations—surrender to irrational impulses; emphasis on division and differentiation—emphasis on union and undifferentiation; obedience to tabus—transgression of tabus; discipline under the reality principle—indulgence of the pleasure principle; thrift—excess; caste rivalry—glorification of the collective. These rhythmic oscillations interact on each other and occasionally combine, as in the fast preceding orgiastic license during a festival. As with festivals throughout the world, seasonal rites in India are accompanied by accelerated circulation of wealth and the flaunting of prestige through the distribution of accumulated reserves by the members of the *jajmāni* collective. The universal fact of a seasonal cycle is reflected in the social calendar, so that the Hindu festivals involving the whole community link the renewal of nature with rejuvenation of social life. In the symbolism of the festive rites, the world is recreated out of chaos at the time of socially creative paroxysm when emotions reach their greatest intensity and man experiences a metamorphosis of his own being.

The festival is also the occasion when the play instinct has a free rein. Play activities have been instrumental in maintaining social fusion precisely in those aspects of Indian life where political institutions have failed to achieve unification. It is not surprising that an aesthetically oriented religious culture such as India's would reveal an exceptionally rich diversity of cultural activities permeated by the spirit of play.

We usually associate play with childhood, but a line of development can be traced from the infantile phase, through childhood and adolescence, to maturity. Play begins as a spontaneous pleasure-seeking activity of the infant. The root *lās* in Sanskrit would appear to refer to playing in its primal form; it combines the meaning of shining, sudden appearance, sudden noise, blazing up, moving to and fro, with irrepressible playfulness —Blake's *delight*. But trained observers of young children have noticed that

[1] E. Kathleen Gough in *Traditional India: Structure and Change*, ed. Milton Singer, Philadelphia, 1959, p. 268.

play is not all pure pleasure, not the equivalent of the adult's recreation, or recovery of the repressed unconscious.

As the child grows up, the spontaneous manifestations of play become increasingly structured. Roger Caillois, in his essay *Les Jeux et les hommes*, places all play activity within the polarity of turbulence and order, or spontaneity and contest. I would call the metamorphosis of impulsive play into an institution, with rules, conventions, and highly trained personnel, a *formative process*. In Sanskrit, the normal term for play among children, animals, and adults is *Krīḍa*. In a second meaning it is a term for excessive gaiety, hopping, skipping, or dancing, and it approximates to the root *nṛt*, which is applied to the whole field of dance and drama, as in *nātya, nātaka*. Philologically Indian play terms are linked since ancient times with cultural activity. Significantly, *Krīḍa* is also applied to erotic play of an illicit nature,[1] which indicates some conscious connotation of play as the polyvalent sexuality of infantile eroticism identified in neo-Freudian psychology. *Kiri* is *argot* for love-play by touch. *Krīḍa* therefore seems to be descriptive of the play instinct when it has become a movement towards rhythmical repetition, towards cultural form, and away from the primal epiphany of rapture. It is the formative process of the play instinct to *imprint* its inherently turbulent, yet structured, pattern on 'ordinary' life—the sphere of work, earnest, struggle, the reality principle—as well as on cultural and social institutions.

This formative process operates in two directions. It may be seen as a movement to and fro between play and its antithesis, work; or it may be seen as a mutual influence between child and adult. The child plays at being an adult, imitating adult work; this play is modelled on the adult life around him. But the child becomes an adult through the aptitudes inculcated through his play (even though play has no goal other than itself). Similarly adult recreation recovers the ideal state of play.

Games seem to display in a simple way the structure of real-life situations. They cut us off from serious life by immersing us in a demonstration of its possibilities. We return to the world as gamesmen, prepared to see what is structural about reality and ready to reduce life to its liveliest elements.[2]

The idea that play is a form of cyclical *movement* is implicit in all the Sanskrit terms connected with it; *Krīḍa*, for example, can mean the movement of wind and waves. The most striking aspect of play activity in India (and elsewhere) is its tendency to set in motion, to propel the society forwards by

---

[1] Cf. Caillois (1958), p. 53.

[2] Erving Goffman, *The Presentation of Self in Everyday Life*, Doubleday, New York, 1959, p. 34.

an incessant circulation, a playful merry-go-round which we nowadays might call the 'social round' or the 'social whirl'.

Through the festival, therefore, the formative play principle acts as an instrument of social fusion. At the same time the spirit of play is culture-enriching and operates on many levels—in riddle contests, in versifying contests, and above all in its purest, highest, most 'Mozartian' form in the 'rivalry' of soloist and accompanist in Indian classical music. Until the present century most, if not all, Indian life was regulated like a noble game. Besides the artistic expression of an ideal heroic life there was an attempt to produce by conduct, custom, manner, costume, deportment, the illusion of life as one prolonged drama, full of dignity and honour, of wisdom and courtesy—*Rāmarājya*. Warrior contests, trials of strength, archery contests, Dravidian bullfights, ceremonial hunts, love-play with elaborate rules, were essential and popular aspects of social life, decked out in the flattering colours of a past age. Life elevated itself towards the sublime through the festival. The actions of the raja all assumed a quasi-symbolic form, to be imitated by the lower castes. From the apex of the social hierarchy to the poorest of low castes etiquette was ritualistic and at the same time a game (Plates 53 and 54).

We have had occasion to refer to the role of festivals in ensuring solidarity, but the question of how a balance between solidarity and mutually polarized castes can be maintained in India remains to be answered.

The application of conflict theory to the Indian situation has been rather neglected. Georg Simmel points out that 'the Hindu social system rests not only on the hierarchy, but also directly on the *mutual repulsion*, of the castes'.[1] According to this classic exposition of conflict theory, reciprocal 'repulsions' maintain the total Indian social structure by creating a balance of claims by rival castes. Lewis Coser has shown that pluralistic societies which are built, like India's, on multiple-group affiliation, tend to cohere by multiple conflicts between groups, and that the interdependence of these conflicting groups prevents deep cleavages along a single axis. The antagonistic interests of a multiplicity of conflict groups tend to cancel each other out.[2] The absence of revolutionary movements and the rarity of overt class-struggle in India originate in this multiplicity of conflict groups. Rivalries between castes have not drawn the total energies and allegiance of the low caste or Untouchable into a single area of class conflict, except in those regions where a multiplicity of gradations between the dominant, or Brahman, and the low castes is absent.

Overt expression of hostility between castes is common enough, but the resolution of conflict arising from hierarchical inequality by arbitration could never remove the ultimate cause of conflict—the principle of

[1] Simmel (1955), p. 18.   [2] Coser (1956), pp. 79–80.

hierarchy itself. Such expression of protest as was permitted to those who remained dissatisfied with formal rearrangement within the hierarchy occurred on ritual occasions and was thought to have mystical benefit. The anthropologist, Professor Max Gluckman, is of the opinion 'that the licensed ritual of protest and rebellion is effective so long as there is no querying of the order within which the ritual of protest is set, and the group itself will endure'.[1] It is perhaps more appropriate if, in the Indian context, we drop the term 'rituals of rebellion' and refer, as Edward Norbeck (1953) does, to 'rituals of expressing and relieving, if not resolving, conflict'. Such conflict-management is to be found in many societies all over the world, and it is characterized by a great variety of institutionalized departures from everyday practice—role-reversal, utterance of protest by oracles in a state of possession, great annual festivals that provide the occasion for the airing of grievances. These do not permit rebellions against authority but they do serve as dramas of conflict. Commonly, such festivals in India reveal how society tolerates, indeed insists on, the temporary reversal of rules of sexual behaviour, sanctioned sexual play through promiscuity and adultery, reversal of women's everyday behaviour, transvestism, lifting of restraints on the eating of certain foods, and institutionalized outlets for hostilities against the village headman, the Brahman, or the landlord. All the above traits are to be found in Marriott's account of Holī, the spring festival, at Kishan Garhi. To begin with, he says, Holī provides outlets for repressed personal drives.

The idiom of Holī . . . differed from that of ordinary life both in giving explicit dramatization to specific sexual relationships that otherwise would not be expressed at all and in reversing the differences of power conventionally prevailing between husbands and wives. . . .

Aside from the Holī festival, each of the other thirteen major festivals of the year seemed to me to express and support the proper structure of patriarchy and gerontocracy in the family, of elaborately stratified relations among the castes, and of dominance by landowners in the village generally.[2]

Marriott goes on to list examples of role-reversal and rebellious acts (some of them violent) that occurred in the village during Holī. The men beaten by wives of low-caste labourers and menials were Brahmans and peasant proprietors; six Brahman elders were belaboured by a sweeper of their latrines; four specialists in purification—a barber's son, a water carrier, and two Brahman priests—heaped mud and filth on the heads of the leading citizens; the police headman poured diesel oil over the head of his arch-rival and cousin, the village landlord. Marriott concludes:

Under the tutelage of Krishna, each person plays and for the moment may experience the role of his opposite: the servile wife acts the domineering husband

[1] Gluckman (1955), p. 130. [2] Marriott, in Singer (1966), p. 206.

and vice versa; the ravisher acts the ravished; the menial acts the master; the enemy acts the friend; the strictured youths act the rulers of the republic. . . . Each actor playfully takes the role of others in relation to his own usual self. Each may thereby learn to play his own routine roles afresh, surely with renewed understanding, possibly with greater grace, perhaps with a reciprocating love.[1]

In similar spirit of catharsis, the village tribunal traditionally settled caste disputes by arbitration and customary law, though it was less concerned 'to find "truth" and give "justice" than to abate conflict and promote harmony'.[2] G. M. Carstairs cites the case-history of a Hindu whose dream revealed his unconscious attitudes towards aggression, and then, almost casually, Carstairs makes a point which I believe to be of profound importance to Indian studies—the key to the social dialectic (to which we will return when analysing the role of Gandhi):

> This dream showed (and later direct observation confirmed the point) that a Hindu pictures a quarrel as typically a drama with three actors, two contestants and a peacemaker; and *it is not the protagonists but the peacemaker who is seen as the victor in the dispute.*[3]

Caste disputes, then, may be described as ritualized realignments, not rebellion against the caste system itself. Their functions are not to be sought in their relation to emotional needs alone (which are probably best fulfilled in the kind of role-reversal described above), but in the need to dramatize and uphold the principle of inequality in social relationships. The very fact that they are *disputes* indicates that they are institutionalized deviations from everyday norms. Gluckman and others have shown how ritualized conflicts 'are built into social life by the nature of social rules themselves'.[4]

Religious rapture and possession

The commonest means to achieve religious rapture during the Indian seasonal festival, whether tribal or caste, is the trance. 'Possession' means a particularly violent form of unconscious incursion in an ego that is still relatively weak and not yet fixated in consciousness. Since the researches of Herskovits it has been known that possession is not a mere chaotic hysteria but a structured, and in some cases a highly formalized, pheno-

[1] Marriott, in Singer (1966), p. 212.
[2] Rudolph and Rudolph (1967), p. 258.
[3] G. M. Carstairs, 'Cross-Cultural Psychiatric Interviewing', in Kaplan (1961), p. 545. Italics mine.
[4] Gluckman (1962), p. 46.

menon, which can be culture-creating and enrich the consciousness of the individual and the group. It is true that the individual in a crowd easily becomes the victim of his own suggestibility and that such a collective must have continual recourse to mass intoxication in order to consolidate the transporting experience. The attendant dangers of degeneration into hysterical mob psychology and psychic epidemics of a fascist nature have already been mentioned (Part One). But the inevitable regression within the group is partially counteracted by the structure of the ritual within which possession occurs. This is evident in the widespread and diverse forms it takes in Indian regional and tribal cultures, certainly in those which I have personally witnessed; for example, the masked transvestite Kālī trance dance of Bengal, the paroxysm of the *bhopa* (oracle), the convulsive pitching of the Muslim during the Mohurram festival, the violent seizure of the Deccani hetaeri, and the fire dances of low castes in Uttar Pradesh villages. The symptoms at commencement and termination of trance are clearly psychopathological—apparent loss of motor control, spasmodic or frenziedly rapid convulsions, head-shaking, sudden stiffening, and eventual loss of consciousness. During these manifestations assistants protect the oracle from harm, providing an atmosphere of moral and physical security. But the stylized and controlled nature of seizure, rigorously laid down by tradition, reflects the cultural preoccupations of the group, the trance being a kind of ritualized reflex and a means to embody the mythological traits of a deity, rather than an outlet for repressed personal drives. The fact that someone violently possessed can express his most secret aggressive thoughts with impunity, but, as it were, 'in character' with the deity who has seized him, and articulate repressed social grudges of the collective while convulsed by histrionic exhibitionism, is indication enough of disordered unconsciousness subjected to relatively well co-ordinated cultural control. True, oracular possession is not accredited by the Great Tradition because it is an attention-getting device of the antipodal society. But it is precisely because it forms an essential part of cultural expression in India's numerous Little Traditions that it should be regarded as an extremely significant, if archaic and risky, means of social integration. It appears to have spontaneously flared up on a mass scale from time to time in response to a severe crisis in the collective destiny.

Paradoxically, every manifestation of ecstatic paroxysm induced to restore the sense of collective solidarity entails a plunge into the depths of self, shutting off reciprocal communication. The subject often has no memory of what he has said and done in trance. There is nothing as totally *private* as the trance, nothing more totally, even scandalously, *public* than the exteriorization of emotion induced by trance. Its efficacy depends on highly volatile collective contagion, its stylization is almost mechanical;

under exceptionally favourable circumstances oracular utterance transcends its limitations, breaks into prophecy, and thence into poetry;
secularized, it is the very essence of theatre. Traces of this stylization are
frequent in the Vedic dialogues; it left its imprint faintly visible in classical
Sanskrit drama and always seems on the point of erupting in the greatest
lyrical scene, Kālidāsa's frenzied soliloquy for Purūravas in the Fourth Act
of the *Vikramorvasiyam*, for which he went back to the oracular sources in
the Ṛg *Veda* and the *Śatapatha Brāhmaṇa*. The extremely frequent use of the
swoon in Sanskrit drama also suggests the influence on this highly refined
art-form of the primitive trance.[1]

The element of theatrical mimesis in possession was forcefully brought
home to me by a scene which I witnessed at a Deccan festival. The dancers
entered trance by intensification or exaggeration of formalized paroxysms
and accompanying rhythmical cries until they were really 'seized'; later
they performed intricate rites, gave utterance, and finally fell into unconsciousness in a crowd overtaken by contagious rapture. After the excitement of the festival had died down I watched children, while *playing* at
trance in imitation, mechanically fall into trance deep enough to need
revival by anxious parents. But the children could only attain trance if
they played *together*; solitary imitation in a backyard remained ordinary
play, with no climax through collective contagion. I believe the absorption
in religious frenzy, at the same time 'incommunicado' and collectively
united, may be said to typify the conditions under which Indian 'individualism' emerges; it is a product of *excess* and only rarely can it be rationally
inflected under the conditions of hierarchic interdependence. In ordinary
daily life, as distinct from the festival season, it emerges as *eccentricity*,
aberrant, unstructured. In exceptionally intense cases this emergent, explosive individuality possesses its subject and assumes the pattern, or is an
imitation or 'playing', of a culture-hero's role in revolt against a merciless
fate. The case of the individual as mystic or renouncer will be dealt with in
due course; the point to emphasize here being the discharge of intense
emotion which accompanies recognition of self, otherwise submerged in
the network of reciprocity and caste relations. Arthur Koestler has been

---

[1] A dramatic theme such as the swoon, like dislocations of the time sequence, the
seasonal cycle, or destiny, can be vested with any number of cultural connotations. The
swooning of Othello, Charlie Chaplin, and Purūravas are qualitatively different, as is
the cultural referent in each case. The association of the trance with swooning in the
Vikramorvasiyam is emphatic—e.g. the manic behaviour of Purūravas in his dialogue
with the gods. Henry Wells, who gives a whimsical explanation for the unsurpassed
frequency of these swoons in Sanskrit drama as deriving from the collapse of the puppet
on its strings, seems more justified in relating it 'to their mental occupation with the
soul and its adventures' (cf. H. W. Wells (1963), pp. 90–8), and suggests that the state
of mystical enstasis may be designated a 'religious swoon' (i.e. possession).

quoted as identifying the polarity between self-assertive and integrative tendencies in the concept of hierarchic order. Different types of hierarchical social order will foster different types of self-assertive and integrative tendencies; there is no reason to assume that individualism and self-assertion in India will be the same as in Euro-America. Individual leadership of all sorts in Indian history is accompanied by the aura of mythical heroism or charisma which we would expect of an aesthetic, hierarchical, oral society.

The festival rite utilizes the potency of disorder. It harnesses the disorder of the 'other mind', possession, trance, dreams, ecstasy, swoons, and frenzies for creative use in re-establishing order. In the context of the Hindu village festival the holy men whose job it is to focus the dispersed energies of the society in sacred rites may be divided into two classes of specialists: priests and oracles. The priest offers to the gods the gifts of the community as a whole; in turn, the gods enter the body of the oracle—take *possession* of him or her—and direct community affairs through their chosen mouthpiece. Priests, even if not invariably Brahmans, are always of a higher caste than oracles. The hierarchical distinction is no doubt partly due to the fact that the priest 'aspires' towards union with, or mastery of, the deity in an active sense, while the oracle lets himself be 'possessed' or 'occupied'. Far more important, however, is the fact that possession is associated with the animism and magic of the Antipodes—the outcaste, the tribe, the seemingly threatening character of drugs, dance, hypnosis, and paroxysm. In other words, the priestly office belongs to the explicit social order and is credited with consciously controlled powers; whereas the oracle, whose role is less explicit, is credited with unconscious, uncontrollable psychedelic powers which balance—in some cases menace—those in well-defined positions of hierarchic status; if these powers are harnessed properly, the society recovers a special potency from chaos beyond the limits of order. The oracle completes the full circle of reality by restoring the element of disorder which normal regulation has outlawed. Furthermore, as a low-caste specialist, the oracle is associated with pollution, which is precisely what disorder connotes.

In India, as elsewhere, the occult power of the oracle is a direct result of his vulnerable position in the hierarchic order. He is either a member of the underprivileged castes or tribes, or, as often happens, he is an aberrant personality who is innately disposed to venture into the disordered regions of the mind. Outcast through his personality defect, he has been thrust beyond the confines of society, but recovers a power out of reach of the conformist. Like Joan of Arc—a truly representative figure of the European Antipodes—who heard voices in the woods and was endowed by legend with ancient magical powers over animals, men, plants, and fruits, the Hindu oracle is spokesman for the submerged, inchoate, mute, and primitive forces in opposition to Brahman authority. But unlike medieval Europe, where direct confrontation ended in ruthless suppression of the Antipodes, village India fosters co-operation between the two domains. Besides violence, ritual possession is the Hindu's prime means for canalizing aggression and voicing of social protest. Through the oracle those who have suffered unjust treatment speak up and demand redress.

We will now consider two cases where danger of internal fission within the society is checked through institutionalized possession, and conflict is transmuted 'into sentiments of mutual dependence and love'.

Kathleen Gough's interesting paper, 'Cults of the Dead among the Nayars'[1] refers to a custom observed during the annual ancestor festival of the joint family. It used to be common among this wealthy military and land-owning caste in Kerala to permit members of the servant low castes to give formal voice to their complaints of maltreatment. In the extended kinship system of this region the Nayar family, or lineage segment (*tāravād*), was large enough to comprise a significant social unit on its own (though naturally a part of the caste system), consisting of anything up to two hundred members. Twice a year on new-moon days a ceremony was performed on behalf of lineage ghosts in a room reserved as their shrine. After becoming drunk, male lineage members propitiated the ghosts of ancestors—men and women who had been head of the lineage. A second ceremony was then performed by low-caste propitiants. Wearing a mask, the propitiant became possessed by the ancestral spirit. Blood sacrifices and self-inflicted punishment in honour of the familial ghosts were performed with due humility. But during the trance the man would adopt an authoritative or aggressive attitude to his Nayar hosts, demanding gifts and threatening the lineage with misfortune. At the conclusion of the rite he returned to normal consciousness, removed his mask, once again assumed his humble role of servant, and accepted his fee. Although today we would regard such formalized protest as no more than a gesture which could not threaten the social *status quo*, nevertheless the servant possessed a kind of ritual weapon of sufficient religious significance to act as a deterrent to the Nayar authority, should the latter feel tempted to abuse his privilege as patron and master.

A member of the lower castes who felt that he was exploited by his Nayar landlord could only express his hostility and give vent to his suppressed aggression as a dependent through the authority of a supernatural agent. The challenge which the masked man poses to the social *status quo* is, like the mask he wears, *put on*. Such change or modification in social relations which he may thereby set in motion must also abide by the 'rules of the game'; in other words change is permissible *within* the system, but the

[1] In Milton Singer (ed.) (1959).

system itself cannot be changed. Kathleen Gough rightly emphasizes the fact that this festival reinforced the need for interdependence between the castes, but also drew attention to the lower castes' permanent role as submissive servants.

The next example shows the use of possession as a more positive instrument of social mobility. While it concerns a tribe in the Nilgiri hills of South India, it is important as an example of the role which internal regulation of conflict and change in religious cults has always had in no matter what type of community organization.

In his essay on the Kotas, 'Social Trends and Personal Pressures',[1] David Mandelbaum gives a fascinating account of how possession may effect social integration and change. In 1924, after an epidemic had decimated the population of a Kota village, the traditional annual festival was celebrated as usual. For as long as was known the priest of the tribe had conducted these rites, and at the appointed moment he would stand aside while an oracle was possessed by the deity, who then made his desire known; after a period of paroxysm and violent oscillation of the head, the oracle's jerky, strangulated utterances had, until the disaster of 1924, provided the tribe with a divine mouthpiece with which to articulate its sense of collective identity and provide answers to its problems. But in December 1924 all the priests and oracles were dead; no officiants stepped forward, no one was seized by the divine paroxysm. Soon after, a formerly discredited oracle of little social prestige, shiftless and irresponsible, became possessed in the traditional manner. To the annoyance of traditionalists, this man — Kusvain—gave utterance to the desires of a Hindu god worshipped in a village at the foot of the hills. On his instructions a new cult was established, a new shrine built, and new deities modelled on Hindu caste gods installed. As the years passed, priests were initiated and more men were possessed and became regular oracles. At the same time, the old cult with its tribal deities continued, in the usual Indian manner, to be practised without any sense of contradiction.

This pattern of symbiosis and acculturation of a tribe with Hinduism is instructive. A few visits to the lowlands by Kusvain had enabled him to acquire enough knowledge to incorporate traits of Hindu religion in the tribal cult; but the superficiality of these borrowed traits reflected the existence of language and status barriers between the two neighbouring communities. As Mandelbaum observes, the tribe

is shut off from any glimpse of the attitudes which surround the use of these material traits. Here, as in much of the history of culture change, we find that material traits and formalised modes of action are more amenable to diffusion

[1] Mandelbaum, (1941).

than are the less readily apparent complexes of behaviour. The [Kotas], no less than other peoples, have integrated the borrowed bits of material culture and formal procedure into a pre-existing larger pattern which remains, in bold outline, but little altered.[1]

The same situation prevails throughout the greater field of social and cultural change to which India is now subject as a whole.

Mandelbaum, who intermittently followed the tribe's affairs from 1937 to 1958, identifies three individuals who played key roles in this change: Kusvain, who had never been a person of any consequence; Sulli, the schoolmaster—educated, conversant with Hindu ways, sole member of the tribe who spoke English, both respected and disliked for his reformist ideas; and Ka.kn, the defender of the old—Sulli's senior, a respected elder, reactionary, aggressive, physically vigorous, knowledgeable in ritual lore, but without priestly authority.

It is the personal traits in each man on which Mandelbaum's interest rightly centred. Kusvain's momentous oracular paroxysm was for him 'the prime means of self-assertion, of personal dominance'. An aberrant personality on the fringe of society, disordered in his behaviour, the only way he was able to distinguish himself, to win personal victories, was by being an oracle. Furthermore, it was Kusvain's leadership in a crucial, violent encounter with a neighbouring Nilgiri tribe over the legitimacy of the new cult, which restored the self-respect and solidarity of the Kotas after the epidemic. But without Sulli's personal ambition to see progressive reforms introduced into the tribe, backed by his high social status as a kind of emergent Brahman, Kusvain's paroxysm would have been laughed out of court. Again, without the religious authority of oracular utterance through Kusvain, Sulli could never have furthered his own controversial ambition to introduce reform. Finally, had it not been for Ka.kn's vigorous resistance to the new cult, the old cult and its deities would never have been preserved. Paradoxically, it was the continuity of the religious *system* which ensured the establishment of the innovation. We may also note the element of imitation in Kusvain's role. Mandelbaum's account makes it reasonable to suppose that Kusvain's unexpected seizure was initially simulated in the way that trance technique often is—prompted by hysterical intensity of emotion—through mechanical imitation of the frenzied movements. Kusvain's whole performance appears to originate in mimesis, including his imitation of Hindu cult symbolism. Briefly, he played the part of a supernatural being according to the explosive dictates of a scarcely conscious ego. The title of Mandelbaum's essay emphasizes this point: social trends and *personal pressures*. This follows the specifically Indian pattern of imitation of superiors in the desire for social advancement and amelioration of

[1] Mandelbaum (1941).

status or living standards. A movement was initiated here which lies at the very root of the caste system: acceptance of the system by the tribe. For on Mandelbaum's last visit he noted that the Kotas were indeed in the process of acquiring the traits of a caste, as have thousands of other tribes in the course of Indian history.

In sum, the symbiosis of tribe and caste, acculturation, itensified group solidarity and hierarchic outlook, reparation for internal divisiveness and social change—fission and fusion—while not wholly accounted for by the unifying mechanism of festival rites and possession, were authorized through their agency and from them received emotional impetus. Kusvain, Sulli, and Ka.kn typify the way individual leadership can emerge in the Indian collective through violent personal pressures and correspondingly intense discharge of emotion, but receives little social support for its consistent development and acceptance in a recognized structure.

This case reveals the balance between collective solidarity and individual initiative. The stability and energy which the Indian social system has displayed in the face of crisis, stress, and change, must not be ignored. This system, while founded on reciprocity and interdependence, incorporates aberrant, eccentric, and essentially anomalous individualistic tendencies of the Antipodes into socially useful channels. This is certainly not to be confused with the creative use of individuality in Western-type societies; it is circumscribed by the very factors which prevent the social ascendancy of Kusvain. For his is the story of an unfortunate man who, once his day of glory was over, returned to his shiftless ways, the butt of contempt and ridicule. Sulli's example did not immediately give rise to innovation; resisted at every turn by Ka.kn, the process was exceedingly slow and uncertain. The story, however, is an instructive one, a microcosm of social change as it is commonly effected under traditional Indian conditions.

Emotional religiosity of *bhakti* sects

While the examples of fusion so far cited are not of a high cultural order, it is in their inchoate nature that their peculiar potency resides. But the progressive refinement of irrational psychic intervention in the cult of *bhakti* led not only to cultural expression of a high order but also to social changes which profoundly affected the course of Indian history. In fact, *bhakti* is historically one of the main agencies of social fusion developed in India. In origin it is a non-Brahman movement of popular religiosity which emerged in South India among classes which were resistant to the pressures of caste hierarchization; it is still very much a living force. True, as soon as any *bhakti* sect gained social influence it was incorporated into the social body; inter-caste as each successive wave has been, and emotionally appealing among low castes for this very reason, the *bhakti* sect which does not find a very large number of adherents tends to become just another *caste*.

It is evident from the ecstatic, sometimes orgiastic, nature of *bhakti* religiosity, that the states of feverish emotion it encourages can be traced to the paroxysm of the social outcast; devotees tend to merge the practices of *bhakti* with the erotic ritualism of Tantra. The very word *bhakti*, it may be remembered, can mean 'sexual desire' as well as 'religious devotion'.

Several distinct phases in the development of *bhakti* theology can be discerned. Its earliest formulation is to be found in the *Bhagavad Gītā*, probably written in the wake of the Buddha's radical heterodoxy, around the third or fourth century B.C. Here for the first time we find a *personal* God who 'shares or participates in' (the first meaning of the word *bhakti*) the life of his devotees, and vice versa. This God of the Gītā is Vishnu, or his incarnation as Krishna; the development of *bhakti* sects devoted to Shiva emerged slightly later and subsequently the two movements, Vaishnavism and Shaivism, evolved concurrently, each influencing the other. From the earliest phase *bhakti* has always been regarded as a way to salvation open to all castes, including Śūdras and women. The two major departures of *bhakti* are the introduction of the ideas of spiritual grace and love, which are quite alien to Vedic culture in feeling. But another significant shift in accent from mystical Brahmanism (which placed a class with privileged status almost on the same plane as divinity) was the new stress on the personal inadequacy of the worshipper, his remoteness from God. A streak of morbid self-abasement entered Indian religion which has remained with it ever since.

In its earliest phase the *bhakti* movement was no more than a body of received ideas deriving from folk culture, but exploited to brilliant advantage by the author of the *Bhagavad Gītā*. The sentiment of love did not, however, accord with the exalted ideals of high Brahmanism, as is apparent when the greatest mythical representative of *bhakti*, Yudhishthira, is reproved by Indra in the *Mahābhārata* for harbouring the emotion of human love at the doors of paradise; 'for', as Zaehner comments on this scene, 'in *moksha* (liberation) there is no love'. It was many centuries later, and through the prestige of saintliness manifest by the Tamil devotional sages, that the second and greatest upsurge of *bhakti* religiosity forced the Brahman establishment to take cognizance of this powerful religious movement from below. Nevertheless, in spite of the respect accorded to *bhakti* in the *Bhagavad Gītā*, it has always remained associated in the Brahman mind with the servile morality of the lower castes, unseemly emotionalism and the lowest common denominator of spirituality. But the high castes have reluctantly had to concede the element of *bhakti* an essential place in the total Hindu system, as one of the prerequisites for the attainment of salvation. They could hardly do otherwise, for some of the greatest saints in later Indian history were, pre-eminently, the masters of *bhakti*. After Shaṅkara, rare is the case of a great religious figure of Hinduism who was not, fundamentally, a *bhakta*.

The peak of Tamil devotionalism was reached in the sixth and seventh centuries A.D. with the composition of Tamil hymns by the Shaiva and Vaishnava saints. The greater part of *bhakti* literature was written not by Brahmans but by members of the artisan and cultivator castes, including women. In the south, Brahmanism came to be associated with a remote esotericism expressed in Sanskrit, the high-caste language imported from the north; while Tamil, and, later, Telugu and the other Dravidian languages, became the vehicle of the *bhakti* movement.

The somewhat protestant flavour of individualism on which the personal relationship of love between the devotee and his Lord is based needs explanation. First, by individualism we mean a higher degree of self-reliance. The peninsula was the last region of the sub-continent to come under settled agriculture. Its geophysical character made the maintenance of large unified kingdoms very difficult, and Aryanization was less consistent than in northern India. To this day the social structure of South India is not graded into an infinite number of intermediate castes between Brahman and Śūdra. Small kingdoms, a higher degree of local autonomy, archaic village republicanism, and a much higher proportion of non-Aryans are to be found associated with an individualism already noted as more a tribal trait than a caste trait. It is these residual traces of the tribal phase which constituted South India's greatest asset; they evidently contributed to the very considerable commercial initiative displayed by its merchants. These castes developed a flourishing overseas trade with South-East Asia during many centuries when north India had lost its initiative and dynamism. During the period of religious vitality in the peninsula, Dravidian culture displayed a risk-taking verve and initiative much more than has been known at any other period in Indian history save the great ferment which convulsed the north from the sixth to the third centuries B.C. Even the divine madness cultivated in Shaiva devotionalism had a virility quite different from the ecstatic fervour normal to the *bhakti* movement when it entered its third phase with the spread of Vaishnavism to northern India.

The key figure in the expansion and ultimate triumph of *bhakti* is Rāmānuja (late eleventh century A.D.). Significantly, this great theistic Tamil teacher was a Brahman, and the third phase of *bhakti* marks its final incorporation into the canon of religious philosophy. Rāmānuja's God is the first unambiguously ethical divinity in Hinduism, no longer the abstract pure being of Brahmanism, but infinite goodness, mercy, and beauty. While Rāmānuja's loyalty to his own caste prevented him from taking the final step to abolish caste distinctions, his philosophy added weight to a movement which, in principle at least, cut across caste differences. By constructing a theological basis for spiritual love, Rāmānuja went far towards providing caste society with a universal ethic. Later Hinduism left the individual free to pursue his religious beliefs in accordance with his conscience, so long as he abided by the group ethic of his caste *dharma*. The followers of Rāmānuja, and numerous teachers who were the fruit of the movement, occasionally proclaimed their antagonism to caste differences in much more outspoken fashion, but in practice this did not lead to a consistent offensive against the institution. Madhva, Rāmānanda, Kabīr, Vallabh, Čaitanya, Tulsīdās, Tukaram, and Nānak developed various aspects of the *bhakti* movement, while minor saints and gurus proliferated in every region, inspiring a large body of devotional literature in the emergent local languages. There was a good deal of inter-sectarian rivalry; the most extravagant display of emotional adulation focused on the figures of the most prominent gurus.

The streak of anti-intellectualism in the *bhakti* movement was its greatest weakness, in spite of Rāmānuja's intellectual qualities. On the one hand, it led to the glorification of the gurus' charisma and thence to the cult of power by the more ambitious. On the other hand, the emotional climate of psychological dependence, even self-abasement, of the devotees, and their extreme other-worldliness prevented them from transforming the social order from within. Such educational institutions as were founded by the devotional sects (and by the entire spectrum of religious communities) were of a purely religious character. In the changing circumstances of a multi-religious society during the Muslim period, these schools failed to meet the challenge of the times and turn themselves into secular institutions. Though Čaitanya (1485–1533) promoted the ideal of a casteless society, the ecstatic self-surrender of his *bhaktas* could hardly be expected to sustain his ideal in practice. The theme of his teaching sums up the essence of the *bhakti* movement: 'the humbleness of the grasses, the fortitude of the trees, self-abasement for the sake of fellow men, and constant remembrance of God's name'.

The exception was Sikhism, an offshoot of the *bhakti* movement, originally a kind of Hindu Taoism, founded by Guru Nānak (1469–1538) under the influence of the mystical Hindu-Sufi poet, Kabīr, in response to the positive challenge of Islam. Under the tenth Guru Govind Singh this pacific community was transformed into a militant, passionately anti-Muslim, crusading brotherhood. The habit of wearing unshorn hair by

Govind Singh's followers, most celebrated of all Sikh customs, reveals the closeness of the heterodox community to the ideals of the Indian holy men, the sadhus and fakirs. The Sikhs were the first of several religious groups to be organized on military lines, for in the same period the Hindu Bairagis, or Nāga Babas, naked ascetics of wild appearance, organized themselves into warrior bands and hired themselves out as mercenaries to the highest bidder, Hindu or Muslim. It is clear that the degeneration of certain sects (but not all) into spiritual incoherence was due to their fanatical reactionary mentality. In the political tension of the Muslim period the very people who, by reason of their emphasis on love and the brotherhood of man, might have fused particularistic groups into a unified community, displayed not the slightest glimmer of historical or political consciousness. The vitality of *bhakti* was confined to the religious and literary planes; it was impotent in the face of the most serious challenge to social unity by reason of its chronic organizational weakness, and its caste-like tendency to segment indefinitely into innumerable small sectarian groups.

In conclusion we might summarize the significance of the *bhakti* movement as constituting a powerful source of appeal to the sentiment of inter-caste fraternization, which focused attention less on particularistic caste ethics than on the universal ethico-social ideal of harmonious equilibrium. Nevertheless, its roots were also deep in the dependence psychology under-lying caste society, and when its *raison d'être*, ecstatic fervour, led to the adulation of the guru as divinity incarnate (Plate 54), the cult of spiritual power and other-worldliness proved even stronger than its unifying capacity. It played a role of primary importance in the centuries of its greatest vitality by pointing the way to new forms of social cohesion. It survived as a movement of undoubted spiritual and literary significance right into the twentieth century. The modern equivalent of the *bhakti* saints were such men as Rāmakrishna Paramahamsa, Swāmi Vivekānanda, and Mahātma Gandhi. The shortcomings of the *bhakti* movement as a force for social cohesion became particularly apparent in the anti-intellectualism, other-worldliness, emotionalism, and lack of historical consciousness which beset the Gandhian phase of modern Indian nationalism. Throughout history the strength of the movement has lain in the exceptional calibre of its leaders; its weakness has been the total trust which its followers placed in these men, elevating them to the status of quasi-divine prophets who would answer their every need. *Bhakti* is an accurate reflection of the chronic helplessness of the Indian masses and their burning zeal to recognize in supreme authority a force transcending the strictures of the social system.

Mystical renunciation

It remains for us to scrutinize two major factors which stimulate fission and fusion within the overall framework of the caste system. These are the linked roles of the Renouncer and the concept of the Universal Soul. The caste system could not have survived so long without them.

It has frequently been claimed that the only true *individual* which the traditional society of India tolerates is the holy man—*sādhu, sannyāsin,* scholastic monk, or Renouncer—the man who renounces his role in caste society for the life of a holy wanderer *in* that society. The scriptures are replete with references to the unimaginable freedom which initiation into the orders of monks confers on a man. There is no doubt that the psychology of the highly educated and more intellectual Hindu monk reveals personal traits which are, in comparison with the group mentality of caste members, more individualized. But if the term 'individual' is to be applied both to them and the other 90 per cent of India's holy men—by the standards of genuine Hindu religious culture, the latter are often 'frauds'—it can only be in a special sense. For the vocation of the Renouncer not only implies renunciation of ordinary material possessions and the duties of caste, it also assumes the consistent effort to destroy the ego, or more familiarly, 'dying to self'. Whether this realization of selfhood is to be equated with the 'individual' it purports to destroy is debatable. Certainly concentration upon the 'island of self', which, roughly, is what the Renouncer seeks, has profoundly influenced Indian culture and its ideals of sociability.

The question is important, because it is precisely these men, liberated from the confinements of caste, no longer tied down to a constricted existence in one place, no longer burdened with economic and familial responsibility, learned in the heritage of literature and metaphysics, who have been the main culture-bearers in India since very ancient times (Plate 50). Further, it is the Renouncer, more than the Brahman, who has been the principal architect of Indian classical culture, and has imprinted on it his own special outlook, thereby transmitting his own bias to the Great Tradition. Thus he has had a direct, even an overwhelming, impact on the everyday attitudes and value systems of the Indian people—that very society from which he has opted out. True, he never, in a sense, abandoned all links with the social world of caste and hierarchy. But the prestige of the renunciation metaphysic, its higher status than Brahmanical ritualism, or, if one likes, its 'snob value', has been the cardinal factor in the development of Indian classicism, from the Upanishads to Śri Aurobindo and Dr. Radhakrishnan's *Vedāntin* apologetics. Why this is so is a question which the reader will find answered more fully in Parts Four and Five; for the moment we need to examine the dual role of the Renouncer in giving unity to the caste system and at the same time supplying the rationale to justify its segmentation.

The first point to note is the intimate link between renunciation of the social world and asceticism. The Renouncer ceases to have sexual relations (a condition insisted upon by most orders of *sannyāsi* is that the initiate should have no responsibilities or parental duties) and abandons the role of the householder. The origin of the personal sacrifice, or rather, the first recorded instance of incipient asceticism, is in fact the *dīkshā* rites already referred to (pp. 154–6) ,where the sacrifier retreats to a hut, fasts, and submits to a *rite de passage* involving imitation of the foetal posture and the complete dependence of the infant. The psychology of purification, narcissism, and withdrawal from the world to an introverted dependence-autonomy (psychological ambivalence) which constitute the hidden motivation of the Renouncer, also reside at the root of caste segregation, though different in intensity of motive. The Renouncer *does no work*; he depends on the society for gifts of food, clothing, and shelter, which he accepts as his right like the infant at his mother's breast. The society depends on him in so far as he alone is sufficiently detached from the web of Karma to transcend its contradictions. The Renouncer's status does, in a curious way, mirror the relations between one caste and another.

The role of the Renouncer will be clearer if we recall the creative harnessing of potent disorder in the Antipodes. The Renouncer wanders on the edge of life, subjecting the dark, irrational mental processes to a form of more structured discipline than is at the command of the oracle. The principal techniques he uses originated in the culture of the Antipodes and come under the heading of yoga, a body of ideas which is non-Brahmanical in origin: he becomes the instrument of unconscious forces and learns to control them. The goal of this plethora of physiological disciplines and mysticism is the slow purging away of all 'impurities'—false identification with body and ego—until the stainless essence of selfhood—*Puruśa* or Ātman—is attained. According to the central tradition of Hindu mysticism it is the very 'isolation', this coming into full realization of selfhood, which ends in identity of the Self with the Universal Soul: Ātman is Brahman ('Thou art That'), the Self is united with the All. For those who attain this state, all division, all differentiation, all opposites, simply dissolve, and the primordial mystical Oneness, the unity unattainable on the mundane, social level of the caste hierarchy, raises the Renouncer to the level of a veritable superman, the *jīvanmukta*.

The Brahman, who has always nursed his animosity against the Renouncer, is, to adapt a term used in the Indian revenue system, the Collector. He it is who has always preserved, synthesized, aggregated the social plurality in ritual. The Renouncer privately circumvents or transcends the network of social obligations which the Collector 'dissolves' in the calendary round of corporate ecstasy induced during festivals. But whereas the Renouncer's individual goal is, when attained, permanent, the most which Brahmanism can offer on a community level is a temporary effervescence. There is no kingdom of heaven on earth in Hinduism; unity is either atemporal, mystical, private—or temporal, cyclical, and collective. Overarching the entire system is the Cycle of Brahman, the inexorable law of eternal renewal within which the cosmos and man are successively born, degenerate, and die. At the most, a few rare souls dissolve into the inexhaustible plenitude of the divine substratum, while the collective fitfully attains partial enlightenment on the wheel of rebirth until another year of Brahmā ends, a cosmic holocaust ensues, and the whole process begins again.

At the level of the caste system, this cosmology is devastatingly consistent. From the angle of any one human being, the Hindu world offers him attractions, implants instinctual needs in him, while his family life leaves him unsatisfied. From birth he has been conditioned to accept his state of dependence, while joint-family life continues to foster this craving in adult life. He is surrounded by people older than himself who place supreme emphasis on the need to preserve or enhance, never to lose, social status. 'Any dependence of one human being upon another involves a degree of differences in strength, capability, wealth, maturity, wisdom, or other factors. To that extent dependence implies a high–low relationship.'[1] The merit of Hsu's study of caste is its stress on the perpetual uncertainty of inter-caste *status*, the tension resulting from this rivalry, and the absence of any deep or concerted motivation which would lead to its dissolution. He traces this unceasing restlessness within the body social to profound and early experience of 'the mutability of all things', which we have already noted to be a basic factor in the child's personality formation, response to parents, training, and environment:

. . . since the family, and its extension the clan, as the internal system cannot in the normal course of events satisfy the social needs of the individual, the Hindu seeks permanency in another grouping in the external system—the caste. Caste is thus a device to compensate for the diffusedness of the supernatural-centred way of life, for impermanency in the kinship situation, and for the lack of definable landmarks due to the mutability of all things.[2]

The caste system is a collective social expression of a people whose world view is suffused with an awareness of impermanence and mutability. While caste rules have led to greater rigidity imposed according to concepts of ritual purity and pollution, the boundaries of the castes have themselves been subject to the same centrifugal and fissiparous tendencies as char-

[1] Hsu (1963), p. 181.   [2] Ibid., pp. 179–80.

acterize the conflicts between the main kin groups within the joint family. If, to compensate for feelings of mutability and emotional insecurity, rigid caste walls had been virtually impregnable and static, then the system would have remained a simple matter—a small number of clearly and unmistakably defined exclusive categories with a vertical stratification more or less constant throughout history. But this, as we have seen, is not the case. Caste disputes are axiomatic to the caste system; subcastes proliferate, split, regroup, and again segment. A brief look at the history of the castes and their innumerable fissions is enough to indicate that, intrinsic to the system, is the necessity to '*break out of one set of walls into another*' (Hsu). Caste status is calibrated vertically; according to the laws of *karma*, inequality of status and privilege at birth are the consequences of ethical conduct in previous lives. If collectively an entire subcaste decides to discipline itself, adopt a stricter sexual code, refrain from eating meat, pay greater attention to ritual, and improve its ethico-religious conduct generally, it can qualify for superior caste status.

From time to time a religious leader offers a salvation ethic which cuts across caste lines, ignoring differences in caste cults, usually by a non-caste appeal to participate in collective emotional religiosity; it is a substitute *dharma*, an improvement on caste *dharmas*, drawing people with its promise of escape from existing restrictions and, through devotional ecstasy or paroxysm, from the round of rebirth and into the blessed freedom of union with the Universal Soul. There is always the risk, of course, that the other castes who dislike or envy the new creed will agitate in order to ensure that the newly fissioned group gets a *lower* status; such would be the case, for instance, if the new sect were to reject the authority of the Vedas, or to relax rules on commensality, marriage selection, and pollution. Sanskritization, with its progressively Brahmanical imitation, lays increasing emphasis on ascetic practices and *restricts* sociability. To move up in caste status a subcaste will have to sacrifice some of its freedom to mix, dine, and marry with others. Though the religious rewards—promise of salvation to all— are high, greater solidarity and improved status are the underlying social aims, and these are achieved at some cost.

In my opinion, Hsu is only partly justified in claiming that the Universal Soul (which he calls Atma) 'is the apex of all statuses toward which all must strive and toward which no living being is ever near. The Atma is the ultimate goal [the quest for the Great Ultimate—see p. 245] which sets the unknown ceiling of Hindu hierarchy and which, therefore, inspires unceasing efforts to reach it.'[1] If all did, in fact, strive towards this goal, the hierarchy would become top-heavy and unbalanced. For, in the final analysis, realization of Atma is a state achieved through renunciation. On the

[1] Hsu (1963), p. 180.

other hand, Hsu's theory may also be correct in the sense that, while the rules of the caste system slow down the chances of attaining renunciation as effectively as they do the attainment of higher status, the absence of any ultimate possibility of release from its strictures would have frozen the society into total immobility.

Caste society is indeed sustained by a belief in a spiritual goal, but the specific character of that goal could only be posited by the Renouncer. Similarly, the Renouncer could never have sustained his quest in a vacuum; the existence of both is interdependent, neither can do without the other. The Renouncer has had a decisive influence on the internal fission of caste society, for it is through his insistence on a rationale which imparts *spiritual* significance to the purification ritual that a caste strives to raise its status by ethical development. But at the same time the Renouncer has had a decisive influence on the fusion of society, formulating the ideology of the unitary, interdependent whole after systematically exploring the means to attain a state of blissful union and absolute oneness with the Universal Soul. An implicit assumption of the Hindu social system is that the state of absolute purity *is* attainable, not within the social world but in the isolated state of *Kaivalya*; while relative purity is the keystone of the caste hierarchy. Mobility and change depend on the potent disorder of the Antipodes— impurity, the non-structured elements of life beyond social control—either serving the ends of an inclusive ritual on behalf of society as a whole, or raising the individual to a supra-human status. Hierarchy, as we said earlier, is subject to infinite expansion. It can spread in every direction but it cannot change *structurally* unless the keystone is destroyed. The latter—a balance of purity and pollution—has remained in uneasy stability through-out history, the former element always accommodating itself to the latter according, one might say, to the imperfect laws of nature. If the caste system is ever destroyed it will only be through some unprecedented eruption of unstructured anarchic forces, the likely nature of which it is as terrible to contemplate as the prospect of *no* structural change at all.

The synchronic analysis of the social system has now been completed; in the remaining chapters of Part Three a diachronic scheme will be followed. We will trace the evolution of the socio-political system through history, and the kind of change which could be accomplished on the political plane prior to modern times. Now that we have observed the impetus for change from below it is time to consider the social process from the opposite direction. This dual dynamics should, as has been said, be viewed more as a cyclical interplay than as a dialectic. Thus the ground will be prepared for assessing the way in which the traditional socio-political system continues to exert its influence on current events.

Chapter Six The Social Order and the Idea of a State

The central feature of Indian political history is the Brahman-Kshatrya division of power into a sacred and a secular domain. Its legacy to the political ideology of modern India is still conspicuous. The historic period when society was in a state of ferment comparable with that of modern times will therefore be the starting-point of the present chapter.

The usual terminology of modern political science will be avoided, as it tends to project nuances of meaning on the Indian situation which are alien to it. Such terms as 'contractual theory of kingship', 'sovereignty', 'nation state', 'village democracy', and 'tribal republicanism' are of no more than limited use, and Western-type institutional terminology should not be applied to the political system of pre-British India. Its institutions resemble those of many phases of historical evolution elsewhere in the pre-industrial world; but comparative analysis will be confined to India and medieval Europe.

Political developments in the period beginning in the sixth century B.C. and continuing until the aftermath of Mauryan supremacy have left their stamp on much that followed in Indian history. It was a period of complex change, with institutions in a state of extreme fluidity; any number of conflicting opinions were held, especially on the question of kingship, and more than at any other period in Indian history there were the liveliest controversies on matters such as the king's role, the position of the priest-hood, the guilds, bureaucracy, and the concept of property. Virtually every development in these spheres was prefigured in this period. I believe that many parallels could be drawn between the Magadhan–Mauryan period and the turbulent events in India of our own day, even though they are separated so widely in time. Both eras face sudden population increase, expansion of trade, increased agricultural productivity, mushrooming urbanism, and the feelings of anxiety and guilt which these have precipitated. Furthermore, both eras demand organization of larger social units, political unification, heavy military expenditure, top-heavy bureaucracy, and liberalization of professed social attitudes towards the underprivileged (in the Magadhan period the status of the Sūdras is upgraded, in the modern period that of the Untouchables). In both, a debate between nostalgia for primitive, decentrlaized village democracy and glowing optimism for the benefits of sophisticated urbanism sways government policy this way or that and engages the minds of the intelligentsia. Finally, and most important, is the disagreement in both periods on republican democracy and centralized, semi-totalitarian, strong-arm government, on individualism versus collectivism, secularism, and religion.

The Brahman

It is reasonable to suppose that the prestige accruing to Brahman sacrificial priests whetted their appetite for power. It is a normal tendency for the priesthood in a highly integrated, ritualistic society to become more worldly, more ambitious; the sacred domain is secularized from within. In India it appears that this happened in the late Vedic age; as already mentioned, the priests and the tribal kings and chieftains reached a compromise in the differentiation of power: *brahman*, or holy power, and *kshatra*, secular power.[1]

The Brahmanical system left the king free to exercise his secular powers in his, and the society's interests, without interference from the priesthood in such matters as warfare, state industries, business, and tax levying. In India such distinct entities as Church and State have never developed in opposition to each other as they did in Europe. The disjunction between the role of the Brahman and the Kshatrya must be viewed within the enveloping system of social order, which prevented this differentiation into Church and State *ab initio*. The Brahmans were not and could not be ecclesiastically organized. Similarly, Indian monarchy could never establish what we mean in the West by a State. Nevertheless, a line must be drawn between

---

[1] The philological meaning of the word *brahman* can help answer the question: How was it that Brahmans came to be regarded as gods among men? In the texts known as the *Brāhmaṇas* and *Upanishads* the word *brahman*, from the root *bṛh* 'to make', 'to form', 'to grow', always has a sacred connotation. While *bráhman* means 'sacred utterance', as opposed to *kshatra*, secular power, on the other hand *brahmán* (the difference is in the accent) means 'one imbued with the power of the sacred utterance or word' (in the Vedas the word *Vāc* means the 'Word', first principle of the universe). *Brahmán* came to mean *both* the creator, or absolute, universal, divine substratum, and a man—a Brahman or, more correctly *Brāhmana*, commonly spelt Brahmin. The important point to remember is that the members of the Brahman *varṇa* claimed to be 'the possessors of an eternal and timeless dimension' (Zaehner) through mystical affinity with *bráhman*, the sacred power. 'Who knows the *bráhman* in man knows the highest Lord.' (*Atharva-Veda*.)

The brahman in man is, then, the same as the *bráhman* in God . . . it is implied that man, through his participation in Brahman, is coextensive with the universe; in Brahman macrocosm and microcosm meet, but this union is only fully achieved in the Brahman who is the depository of Brahman or in the Brahmaćārin, 'the man who follows the path or Brahman', that is, the young Brahman student.

Zaehner (1962), pp. 62–3.

the area of manoeuvrability in which status was supreme and another area where power was supreme.

'Priest' is not an adequate rendering of the term Brahman, for Brahmans could be ritualists, scholars, king's councillors and chief ministers, or even frontiersmen—pioneers who spurred on the process of 'Aryanization' or 'Sanskritization' for thousands of years, or who played a key role in the opening up of virgin land and established land settlements under royal protection—for kings, castes, cults, and tribes. They set the stamp of sacred approval on any unavoidable change, they guarded the entry to Hindu society. On the one hand they were the most rigid and authoritarian of dogmatists, on the other they were extremely flexible if it suited their interests. The Brahmans were strong because they had no organization with which to bolster their status except their relationship with the entire caste system. They renounced power not because they had no desire for it but because they thereby gained something greater: sacred authority. Their rigidity in matters of ritual and observance of caste rules could be unyielding; at the same time they themselves often followed professions forbidden to them in the law books or rewrote the latter when the occasion arose. During the centuries of monarchical consolidation, Brahmans occasionally reversed roles with Kshatryas.

The Brahmans began as agents for the expansion of a homogeneous social order and enlarged it until the entire sub-continent was included, leaving pockets of the unassimilated to their own devices. In the early centuries of their history they acted as ritual priests for the privileged and the wealthy; only under feudal conditions were they in a position to expand their activities and evolve a ritualism which pervaded every stratum of society. They ended by very nearly petrifying the later society in a welter of ritual and social observances, discouraging innovation, arbiters of the class structure and the *status quo*. At the same time they preserved a degree of cultural unity, which cut across the frontiers of rival dynasties, by integrating the innumerable Little Traditions and bringing some measure of unified coherence to the Great Tradition.

The Brahman's function as a unifying agent was particularly effective because he was the man who understood *dharma*—the totality of social, ethical, and spiritual harmony. *Dharma* consists of three categories: the eternal, or *sanātana dharma*, principle of harmony pervading the entire universe; the caste *dharma* (*varṇāshrama-dharma*), relativistic ethical systems varying from caste to caste; and *svadharma*, the personal moral conduct of the individual, close to our 'conscience'. It is not true, as some would claim, that there is no universal *Hindu* ethic, only relativistic morality. For the vast mass of Hindus, the most authoritative source of instruction on the universal *dharma* has always been the Epics (as distinct from that portion of the *Mahābhārata*, the *Bhagavad Gītā*, which was less well-known), and to a lesser extent the Purāṇas. But more accessible, because written in the regional languages spoken by people of all classes, are the simpler precepts of the popular *bhakti* texts, such as the *Tirukuṛaḷ*. True, the universal *dharma* is only vaguely outlined. This is not to say that its main doctrines are of no importance, for they have played a fundamental role in shaping, ordering, and regulating the society. Among the prime traditional virtues are: leading a generous and selfless life, truthfulness, restraint from greed, respect for one's elders—principles in accordance with a virtually global idea of 'righteousness', which, according to the *Mahābhārata*, 'is not easy to indicate. . . . That mode of living which is founded upon a total harmlessness towards all creatures or (in case of actual necessity) upon a minimum of such harm, is the highest morality.'

Since the Brahmans were invested with 'sacred power' their *knowledge* of *dharma* was not regarded as a mere intellectual accomplishment, for *dharma* is an essential quality of absolute sacred power, or Brahman. Nor did the Brahmans merely conceive of *dharma* as 'duty'. '*Dharma* is total cosmic responsibility, including God's, a universal justice far more inclusive, wider and profounder than any Western equivalent, such as "duty".' [1]

The claim of absolute spiritual power by the Brahmans was not invariably accepted, though their superior ritual status was axiomatic. In this latter respect the Kshatryas, especially kings, played a key role in upholding the status of the Brahman. They alone had the power to protect the Brahmans and this they did. Since the caste system is the product of a total outlook on life, kings were as much affected by it as were Brahmans. If they were to make the most of their situation within an apparently God-given system, both had need of each other. In the name of religion the Brahman endorsed the king's right to rule by fabricating sacred genealogies and legitimizing his exalted claims to divine kingship; in return the king lavished gifts on the Brahman. True, gift-giving was a formal obligation of *dharma*, particularly Kshatrya *dharma*; nevertheless, it cannot have been a purely cynical arrangement. An enormous number of land-grants to Brahmans are recorded on surviving inscriptions and frequent reference is made in literature to royal gifts bestowed with prodigal liberality on Brahmans. There are not a few cases of the recipients' names on inscriptions over a thousand years old remaining unchanged among those Brahmans living on the same land today. If we are to understand Indian history we have to take into account this enduring alliance between Brahman and Kshatrya (Plates 11 and 54), for it is their interdependence which prevented either from assuming unilateral control, denying the one an opportunity to organize a Church as rival to the other's State. Furthermore, there was no bourgeois or capitalist sponsor-

[1] Heimann (1937).

ship of royal sovereignty to resist the power of an aristocracy or Church. In actual practice it is best to imagine a sharing of power by a kind of *troika* of three specialist, 'twice-born' (i.e. initiated) classes: Brahman religious control, Kshatrya military control, and Vaishya economic control. Of this last category more will be said in a later chapter.

The king

In ancient times India evolved two different concepts of kingship, the mystical and the contractual. The earliest reference to the origin of kingship occurs in the *Aitareya Brāhmaṇa*, and it leans to the latter, more mundane way of thinking. This late Vedic text suggests that when the society was still at a comparatively simple level of development kingship was an institution based on a mundane human need and that the king's job was primarily warfare. But by the time the *Taittirīya Upanishad* was written the king was regarded as divine in origin, surrounded by magical power and invested with the sacred duty to govern the tribe on behalf of Indra. Thus in the *Mahābhārata* kingship was definitely sacred in character. In the *Laws of Manu* the king is described as 'a great deity in human form'; 'he must be beautiful in the sight of his subjects as is the moon in the eyes of mankind . . . he must draw revenues from his kingdom as the sun draws water from the earth'. It is probable that Persian ideas on divine kingship played a significant role in the evolution of Indian kingship. Both sources, Vedic and Persian, were drawn on from time to time (similar Chinese ideas were of less importance) throughout Indian history down to Moghul times, when Akbar and his descendants claimed quasi-divine status.

With the consolidation of the universal empire under the Mauryas, the idea of the *chakravartin*, or universal emperor, was introduced and became the commonest ideal of kingship for orthodox Hinduism. The *chakravartin* was a kind of temporal *avatār*, somewhat resembling the Mahāyānist Buddhas and the *avatārs* of Vishnu (viz. Krishna and Rāma), born at auspicious times to proclaim the universal empire and righteous government within the grand cosmic scheme. The idea appealed to many ambitious rulers of later date and provided the medieval Rājput kings with their mystique of descent from the sun (Plate 39).

In the early Buddhist period it appears that less ritualistically oriented kingdoms either continued to prefer the more secular type of kingship mentioned above, or revalorized it in the quasi-mythical ideal of the Mahāsammata, 'the Great Chosen One', which is recorded in the Pali canon of Buddhism, and is actually put into the mouth of the Buddha himself. The Mahāsammata derives from a form of primitive social contract and probably originated in the more secular, individualistic climate of tribal republicanism. It stresses the elected king's role (he was also called *rājā*, a word derived from *ranjayati*—'he who pleases') to establish order as servant of his people, on whose suffrage he is ultimately dependent. This striking contractual theory of the state evidently influenced monarchic institutions in the eastern Gangetic plain, including Magadha, in the centuries following the Buddha's death (fifth century B.C.)

When the Mauryans came to power (third century B.C.) the idea of the Mahāsammata was very much alive. But the *Arthashāstra*, traditionally believed to have been written by Kauṭilya, Chandragupta Maurya's minister, and certainly a Mauryan text in its original form, adopts in this instance an evasive position. It acknowledges the propaganda value of myths about the divine origins and divine rights of kings. But it tacitly endorses the contractual theory by instructing the king's agents to spread the old myth of the *Brāhmaṇas* that the first king in the world was elected by his subjects.

The magico-religious ideas of kingship were never developed to the point where the king assumed the supreme religious function of sovereign priest, as in Egypt, Sumer, and China. The logic of the Vedic sacrifice, probably the most developed and complete system of its kind ever devised, ensured that the king as sacrifier was always religiously subordinate to the Brahman *purohita*, the sacrificer. Nevertheless the king was the guardian— the 'sword-arm', so to speak—of the total, divine, social order. In the sacred texts and in the panegyrics composed by court bards, the king is described as 'father of his people' and 'husband of his realm'. Vedic sacrificial symbolism associates the king with the movement of the sun across the sky, linking the king's rule with the cycle of the seasons and his annual rebirth at the New Year rites.

The people

Three elements which figured in the formative period, tribal republicanism, village republics, and the cult of power, all of which are treated in the great classical text on statecraft, the *Arthashāstra*, have sometimes been dismissed (for example, by Professor Basham) as playing no more than a minor role, exerting only faint influence and that for only the briefest period, soon to be replaced by Indian feudalism, quasi-divine monarchy, and the caste system. In terms of subsequent institutional developments there is, no doubt, much to be said for this theory; primitive republicanism, tribal or rural, was soon outmoded, the ideals and even the socio-economic conditions in the third century B.C. to which the *Arthashāstra* refers were abandoned. However, we are here concerned with a pattern of attitudes that has, in fact, endured in one form or another throughout recorded Indian history. If the cult of power and the so-called 'Machiavellism' of the *Arthashāstra* is supposed to have been relegated to the lumber-room of history in favour of an obsession with the finer points of *dharma*, what of the chilling cynicism which so often motivates king and priest in later centuries, and what of the political chicanery and intrigue in our own day? True, none of the three elements I refer to were consciously avowed in later Indian periods. My point is that behind them lie attitudes which have remained more or less constant until the present day. By concentrating exclusively on the religious principles of the *dharma*, we tend to lose sight of secular ambitions which are as much a part of the Indian character as of all humanity (cf. Part Four).

For most of India's history the stability prevailing among the vast mass of the people was due to the comprehensiveness of the caste system and the holistic *dharma*. Nothing like the same degree of consistent control was achieved in the domain of government. Nor was this self-sustaining social system seriously dislocated by turbulent conflict and warfare conducted by Indian rulers. The characteristic suspended animation of caste interdependence is offset by the overweening political ambition and cult of power by those who, as is the way with ruthless ambition everywhere in the world, were misfits in the inclusive society. In fact, it is the thirst for power which alone provided the ambitious with the necessary drive to gain for themselves an area of greater personal manoeuvrability, whether they chose to seek adventure in mysticism as Renouncers, as usurpers in government, or as traders beyond the protective limits of society. There is enough evidence to suggest that it was frequently those individuals whose positions in caste society were either anomalous or uncertain who were motivated to seize power. In compensation for the dangers attendant on any such enterprise, which was bound to entail offence against the social tabus, the claims of such men were assured of legitimization on the sacred plane through the force of their exceptional charisma and by the force of arms. The release of antipodal energies in the society which accompanies sudden rise to power ends with equilibrium between the self-assertive and integrative tendencies, symbolized by legitimization.[1] Weber compares hereditary charisma with our more familiar 'divine right of kings' and 'blue-blooded nobility':

> But the strongest motive for the assimilation of Hinduism was undoubtedly the desire for legitimisation. . . . Hinduism could provide an incomparable religious support for the legitimisation interest of the ruling strata as determined by the social conditions of India.[2]

[1] According to Max Weber,
> Originally charisma was thought of as a magical quality . . . . The authority of the war leader, like that of the sorcerer, rested upon strictly personal charisma. The successor also originally claimed his rank by virtue of personal charisma. . . . In India . . . this led to the inheritance of charisma, which originally had nothing to do with heredity.' Weber (1958).   [2] Ibid.

The list of dynasties whose founders were of non-Kshatrya origin is impressive evidence of the effectiveness of this religious legitimization. Though many dynastic genealogies were either false or shrouded in obscurity, the following list indicates the prevalence of this significant psychological drive to compensate for precarious social status: the founder of the Nandas was the son of a Śūdra mother (another claim has it that he was born of a union between a barber and a courtesan); the Mauryas were probably Vaishyas; the Śuṅgas were Brahmans; Chandra Gupta married a princess from the great aboriginal tribe of the Lichchhavis; the Pallavas were probably of aboriginal origin; the Pratihāras were descendants of a Gurjara tribe from Central Asia; the Pāla King Gopāla (probably an aboriginal) was elected at a time of acute crisis; a Brahman usurped the Turkish Shaliya dynasty and established his rule over the Punjāb; Harihara, founder of the Vijayanagar kingdom in the south, had previously been a captive who was converted to Islam in Delhi, but before his coronation he was reconverted to Hinduism in the name of Virupaksha, a local deity; the Hoysaḷas were chieftains of a tenth-century tribal family from the Deccan. In addition we may mention the fact that whatever their origin, most Hindu dynasties from the fifth century A.D. onwards vied with one another for the most exalted and grandiose religious titles. Among the supposedly blue-blooded Rājput clans, some of whom claimed descent from the solar race (as did the southern Cholas), the Sisodias were probably chiefs of invading Hun tribes, while the Rathors and Bundelas were from aboriginal tribes.

Alien or underprivileged peoples and parvenu castes—usually those who were actively involved in dynastic conflicts—availed themselves of the socio-economic opportunities arising from such power realignments, thus revealing an element of mobility and social change, even though this was officially disavowed according to the normative ideals of Brahman sacred texts. The apparatus of legitimization utilized in such instances operated on lines similar to those of dynastic legitimization. It is reasonable to deduce that it was through this process that the significant majority of the present Kshatrya *varṇa* are the descendants of those so legitimized.

Feudalism

By the sixth century A.D. the Indian form of feudalism began to crystallize and gradually became the system of government throughout India. Its success depended on a number of factors, of which perhaps the most important was the absence of citizens' armies and of military or police protection which could have mitigated the helplessness of the villages. In comparison, medieval European feudalism, which was also accompanied by a retreat to the villages, did not preclude the development of a citizenry and of citizens' armies. Since kings were preoccupied with war they became remote from their subjects, who transferred their loyalties to local feudal lords. Feudal cash salaries became far rarer than land grants; cultivators handed over a fixed share of their produce to the landowner. Control over land tenure was maintained in two ways: levying of tribute by the king from local rulers and tribal chiefs without an intermediary class of landowners; or through small intermediaries who collected taxes locally, passing on a portion of this to the feudal hierarchy. In the course of time it was the intermediary stratum between king and society which came to constitute the basic rural ruling class, whose function it was to reduce the surplus of the peasantry by every unscrupulous means, leaving the majority of the population to survive on a subsistence economy. The *jajmānī* system, which was incorporated in the feudal system, was powerless to check this kind of exploitation in spite of its professed ideal of ritualized gift-exchange. The expropriated surplus wealth was not invested in craft production or trade but passed to the upper feudal strata who squandered it on extravagant urban living, sumptuous monuments, and temples, and in costly warfare, fortifications, and importation of Arab horses. The principal feudal obligation was to supply men and arms to the king for inter-state warfare. Armies campaigned along the tax route, extorting money as they went with which to pay the militia. Among the most important concentrations of feudal power was Rājasthān; here the main weakness of the system was the absence of any extensive labour force of cultivators. It became the custom, especially in Muslim regions, for the feudal élite to be dispossessed of all their property on decease. Thus the system endured through the easy exploitation of the peasantry, but it lacked a cohesive infrastructure to spur development. Nevertheless, such stability as Indian feudalism achieved within restricted areas was due to regional loyalties, each centred on a common culture.

The principal difference between Indian and other types of feudalism was the relation between lord and vassal, established in this case by conquest rather than by economic contract. Life was progressively confined to cultivation, to religious festivals, and, more and more, to martial exploits of the ruling class. The stimulus to cultivate a surplus was nullified by the certainty of its appropriation by landlords, a problem which continues to bedevil Indian productivity. The decline in incentive reflected the pluralistic socio-economic structure rather than any sense of religious fatalism. Such upsurge of popular feeling as occurred was sublimated in the *bhakti* cults, but the somewhat morbid surrender to the will of God originated in, but did not cause, the atmosphere of psychological dependence.

Brahmans played an important role as genealogists and Sanskrit panegyrists in return for the usual land gifts. The survival of Sanskrit is due to the fact that its mastery secured the Brahman highly lucrative employment. The fourteenth-century *Sahitya Darpana* flatly states that excellence in Sanskrit procures wealth, and with wealth sensual enjoyments can be bought. But the Brahmans also benefited in the general conversion from a mercantile cash economy to immovable land wealth. Temple property was often substantial; the organization of enormous staffs to run these complex corporate institutions and supervise cultivation of the estates by peasants may be compared with the management of the medieval European châteaux. The status of the Śūdras sank even lower after the Brahman consolidation, physical labour and technical activities were condemned as degrading and polluting. Brahmans had complete control over education, and in consequence the emphasis was on theology and scholasticism at the expense of science and vocational training (within the given terms of the period).

Feudalism was much concerned with the ideal form of manly perfection in military life. Its noblest human representative was the chivalrous Rājput warrior Prithviraj. As in feudal Europe, chivalry was both an honourable ideal and a cloak for violence and self-interest. The ascetic element, extreme fatalism, self-sacrifice, and the morbid craving of the male who suffers for the woman he loves, are present in the Rājput ideal of the warrior on horseback, spiritual heir of the Aryan charioteer and the war-lord of the Epic period. Confusion between the erotic and saintliness, as in the *Roman de la Rose*, is to be found in the literature inspired by this Indian form of chivalry.

The social order

If the pursuit of power among the ruling class was sterile and wasteful, it should not be thought that the cohesion of the social order had weakened. There certainly were periods when society displayed no more than the hardiness of the chronic invalid, but these alternated with phases of intense cultural activity. Mercantilism and Buddhism may have declined along with large unified states (except for the establishment of colonies *outside* India in South-East Asia, based on the more liberal, *bhakti*-oriented Tamilnad), but devotional religion spread northwards over the entire sub-continent, bringing in its wake the unification of caste ideology and the final triumph of *dharma* as the main organizing principle. The mysticism, gnosis, and ritualism associated with Brahmanism was practised by no more than a small proportion of the population; for the rest, *bhakti* religiosity became largely a matter of *svadharma*, of personal choice, although when any particular cult grew large enough it either evolved its own caste system or became an endogamous unit following its own caste *dharma*.

At this point it may be fruitful to clarify and sharpen the outline of the Hindu value system which has prevailed for at least a thousand years (and is still very much alive in rural India) by comparing it with that of medieval Christian Europe.

The central idea of both medieval Hinduism and Christianity was the concept of a divine saviour or saviours (e.g. Christ, Krishna, Rāma) who assumed human form in order to show mankind the way to blissful life. While Christianity increasingly tended to accept the idea of reason, which contains the comparatively aggressive features of the performance principle, the work ethic, progress, and increased productivity, none of which received strong emphasis in India, both cultures philosophically recognized a higher form of reason—namely, receptivity, contemplation, enjoyment. Behind the organized activity of the society engaged in productive pursuits—in Indian terms, the ego-activity of *kāma* (pleasure, love, affective impulses) and *artha* (power, wealth, calculating egotism)—lay the ideal of the redemption of the ego, 'the coming to rest of all transcendence in a mode of being that has absorbed all becoming'. India's feudal caste system and Europe's feudalism both reflect this ideal in terms of social structure, and vice versa; they were elements in an interlocking system.

Hinduism and Christianity propagated the ideal of renunciation as the base of all personal and social perfection. But both religions also endorsed their intrinsically repressive, often coercive juridical systems; and this had a dampening effect on material and political progress. The idea of a purposed and continual reform and improvement of society did not exist in India till its importation in the late nineteenth century; in Europe it emerged with the breakdown of feudalism during the Renaissance—the point of bifurcation in this comparison between the two cultures. Institutions, having been sanctioned by scripture, were regarded as inherently good in both feudal societies. What therefore was in need of remedy was the individual soul. Administration by the king never consciously and avowedly aimed at creating a new social organism, it only claimed to restore good old law (*dharma* in India) or mend special abuses. The king looked more towards an ideal past than towards an earthly future, a point we have already seen reflected in Indian art.

In both value systems the world, objectionable in itself, could only be acceptable by its symbolic purport. For every object, each common trade, had a mystical relation with the holy, which ennobled it. Sexuality was attached by a symbolic connection to divine love. Social life and work were imbued with ritualistic formality correlated with salvation.[1] This religiosity did not, however, mean that Indian society was universally preoccupied with spirituality any more than was European society. For the supposed transcendental feelings seldom came up to the expectations of religious teaching, and whenever this was the case, especially in India, all that was meant to stimulate spiritual consciousness was reduced to common-place profanity, to that startling Hindu worldliness in other-worldy guise which is so often the dismay of the modern Western observer. Had it not been otherwise we would be confronted with the most improbable situation: a society entirely composed of saints. The mass of Indians have always been conformist and acquiescent in their religious convictions. But the endless growth of observances, images, religious interpretations, in the late medieval period of both cultures, led to a constant blending of sacred and of profane thought, and sacred things became too common to be deeply felt. The same people who in their daily life mechanically followed the routine of worship were in a state of mind more prone than ever to respond with fervent emotional religiosity (in India to reach almost unparalleled degrees of excess) to the preaching of the saints and *bhakti* reformers, or to focus their loyalty on the figure of some charismatic aspirant to power. The pheno-menon of mass Indian loyalty to a warlord or to a guru springs from a common source: the dependence psychology rooted in the hierarchical caste system. There is no precise equivalent in Christianity for this kind of loyalty, unless we include phenomena such as the cult of Joan of Arc. Catharism and the cult of Russian priest-saints, such as Dostoievsky describes in *The Brothers Karamazov*, can both be traced to Asian influence.

These similarities make it imperative to outline the most striking dif-ferences between the two cultures. The symbiotic growth of various institutions in India, from a mixture of classical, folk-archaic, tribal, Hindu, Buddhist, and Jain elements, occurred without the imperial dominance of a hereditary nobility over an organized Church, as in medieval Europe. Nor

---

[1] The concept of social order in India resembles that of medieval Christianity. Professor Heer characterized the latter as follows:

Men, animals and things were entirely interdependent. Since everything was in a state of constant danger, from war, famine, pestilence and civil influences of all kinds, it was up to each member of the community—man, animal or thing—to play his part within the right order of things, in his own proper field of service toward all others. . . . *Ordo* is the name which the middle ages, from Sedeline Scotus to the nineteenth century, gave to this interplay of all things. The *ordo* of the scholastics, Leibniz's 'pre-established' harmony, the 'magical idealism' of German romanticism, are all only attenuated reflections of this sacred order in which every member, in work and leisure, in technology and in cult, was responsible for every other member of his sacral group.

F. Heer, *The Intellectual History of Europe*, Weidenfeld and Nicolson, London, 1966, p. 55.

was there a totalitarian monism of imperial state theology to weld the elements together, as in Byzantium.

Another crucial difference between Europe and India was the doctrine of transmigration, a basic Hindu article of faith which Christianity regarded as a dangerous heresy. This is another manifestation of the Indian idea of oneness of all life. It leads to an open-ended sense of perfectibility, less anguish in the face of time, a less fanatical will to achieve everything in a single lifetime. Moreover, for the Hindu, the world is subject to infinite cyclic repetition and the cosmos is immense in size. Till the scientific revolution Europe's Ptolemaic cosmology projected the image of a comfortably small mechanical world in comparison. The sense of finality was absent from the Hindu world-view; in such a scheme the drive of the performance principle tends to be viewed as no more than absurd vanity.

Indian inclusiveness operates at a level deeper than the polarities of good and evil. It has never shown comparable insistence on the need for a choice between opposites of right and wrong, as did the Zoroastrians, the Jews, the Christians. Aristotle's law of the excluded middle—if a proposition is not true, it is false—does not strike a responsive chord in the Indian mind. Similarly, 'Thou shalt have none other Gods but me', the polarities of believer and infidel or saved and damned, and fanatical proselytism, are all alien to the Indian spirit. In sum, we may say that the fundamental Indian tradition of inclusiveness, of striving to assimilate apparently opposing elements, has, in what may superficially seem a paradoxical manner, been the main obstruction to social and institutional development, accompanied by social upheaval, such as occurred in Europe.

The Muslim invasion

The greatest challenge to Indian inclusiveness was the Muslim invasion. Nothing of comparable gravity had faced India since the arrival of the Aryans. It has often been said that the incompatibility of Islam and Hinduism is based on the clash between monotheism and polytheism. This is not true, for India had believed in a universal principle, *brahman*, since the late Vedic age; even if polytheism was an enormously exuberant appendage, its underlying monism was not at loggerheads with Islamic monotheism. In fact, looking outwards from the Indian point of view, its monism was sufficiently flexible and accommodating to leave a wide area in which monotheism had freedom of movement. Such had evidently been the case with Indian Christianity since its introduction in the early centuries of our era. True, the exclusivist claims of both alien religious systems, and their aggressive proselytizing stance on Indian soil, have proved intractable in the prevailing, if negative, climate of Hindu tolerance. No, the essence of the undoubted conflict must be looked for in the Muslim world-view. The Muslim invaders were part of a larger world, with extensive, virtually global interests spread through a vast area of the Eurasian *oikoumene*. They erupted into the closed Hindu world with, for that period, an almost unequalled military strength based on mobility and discipline. Here was a 'People of the Book' inspired by the ideal of a universal state, a sense of history, supreme self-confidence, pride, and optimism. In a word, the Muslims were expansionists with a tenacity of purpose in total contrast with the already shrinking, nostalgic, Indian world; this confidence invested even their most ruthless and underhand exploits with an aura of exhilaration rare among Hindus of those days. The success of the early European colonizers in the eighteenth century was due to a similar mobility and dynamism.

On every previous occasion when India had failed to repulse and turn away invading hordes, society had succeeded in accommodating the new-comers within the ever-elastic caste system. This it did to some extent with the Muslims, in spite of the latter's proselytizing zeal. Nowhere else in the Islamic territories did Muslims become stratified into hierarchic, more or less self-contained social groups. This hierarchy, which still exists, is a shadowy version of the Hindu caste system; it is a sociological factor of some importance in understanding the extent, depth, and limit of the Hindu–Muslim synthesis. Stratification falls into two categories: on the one hand were the *Ashraf* or nobles, supposedly the descendants of Turco-Afghan immigrants, divided into four grades (Saizid and Shaikh, 'Men of the Pen'—roughly the equivalents of the Brahmans—Pathan and Moghul, 'Men of the Sword'—roughly the equivalents of the Kshatryas, to whose ranks small numbers of converted Rājput nobility were admitted); on the other hand were Indian converts to Islam, divided into numerous groups on caste lines. In the eyes of Brahmanism, the beef-eating Muslims were technically untouchables. But in conformity with the principle of legitimized *power*, Muslims, whether immigrants or converts, were accorded a position in the caste society which contradicted pollution rules. A great many of the Muslim leaders who made their mark on Indian history were upstarts and misfits obsessed with power; this struck a familiar note among Hindus who remembered the deeds of their own war-lords and rajas. Similarly, these Muslim generals were inspired by the dream of a universal *imperium* such as had goaded numerous Hindu kings to conquer their neighbours.

The Muslims were domiciled in the village *pattis* of the higher castes and enjoyed the natural privileges accruing to those who belong to, or have sided with, the ruling power. The greater proportion of converts were from artisan castes in the towns, employed by the Muslim rulers in their extensive architectural and craft activities, who, outwardly at least, adopted the Muslim style of living through close proximity to the courts. Among the peasantry, assimilation proceeded with greater ease. It could be said that 'Persianization' was no more than an extension of 'Kshatrya-ization', for it took as its standard of values the culture pattern of a class whose status derived from military power.

However, this typically Indian arrangement has not led to cultural assimilation and Hinduization comparable with earlier ethnic infusion, firstly because the Hindu social system had become more rigid towards minorities, more closely tied to religion than it had been in earlier phases of immigration; secondly, the Muslim conquest of India was essentially a *colonial* enterprise, tied, moreover, to the principle of conversion by the sword—a new feature in the pattern of foreign invasion. The sheer numbers and military might of the Muslims who settled in India, and the fact that, even in the Moghul period, they still regarded themselves as *foreigners*, members of a sovereign state (an idea implicit, if rudimentary, in Islām from the days of the Prophet, and particularly of the Caliphate), made them adopt the stance of conquerors. In the early centuries (the period of the Delhi Sultanate), they were strong enough militarily, and arrogant enough as citizens of the larger Islamic world, to impose the hated *jizya* tax on Hindus just for being Hindus, and to forbid them the wearing of expensive clothes.

Hindu India had met its match on another, equally important plane besides that of military might. Islam, like the Hindu universal order of *dharma*, conceived of a unitary society in which the spiritual and temporal were merged under unifying religious doctrine. The main difference was that this doctrine was revealed by a Prophet. On Indian soil the sovereignty of Muslim religious doctrine was actually accorded wider respect by its adherents. Its in-built receptivity to the integration of secular and religious power was well suited to the climate of Indian opinion. Under the Caliphate tension had developed between the secular and religious institutions of the Muslim community, and the *ulema*, doctors of the Islamic law, had been wary of conceding any spiritual authority to the caliphs. When the Turco-Afghans arrived in India and established the Delhi Sultanate they discovered the Hindu association of divinity with kingship favourable for the introduction of a similar idea. They were already familiar with divine kingship through acquaintance with the Sassanian political system of Persia. A compromise was reached with the *ulema*, whereby the Sultan became identified with the existence and protection of the state. The prevailing climate of religiosity in India, and the preference for equilibrium in the social order rather than political stability, left the Brahmans wholly indifferent to alien political institutions. The Muslims had little difficulty, therefore, in establishing a ruling militaristic order through their own immigrant officials, thereby introducing a comparatively stable, unifying political element into the country. On the other hand, in this religious atmosphere of India the clerical class was presented with a providential opening to power. The *Sadr-us-sadur*, chief theologian of the state, acquired immense authority and power in the application of Islamic law to government. Muslim saints and mystics, to whom were popularly ascribed similar religious powers as those of the Hindu gurus, also played a significant role in securing popular loyalty to the Sultan. As with the Brahmans and Kshatryas, this mutual interdependence assured the Muslim mystics comfortable endowments, land, and hermitages from the Sultan.

Similarly Sufi mysticism—cultivating the rapture of personal absorption in God—which had long existed as a more popular vehicle for religious feeling than the colder, formal discipline of the *ulema*, found India peculiarly fertile soil. The Sufi movement was close in spirit to *bhakti*. Sufi *pirs* and *shaikhs* tended to retreat from the world like their Hindu counterparts, the guru and the *santa*. Both forms of religiosity could muster popular support against rationalistic free-thinking among the secular rulers. Similarly, the two movements acquired an element of fervent anti-intellectualism, as if in compensation for the failure of their respective God-directed universal states. A number of important Hindu saints were profoundly influenced by this almost heretical branch of Islam. The Sufis and the *bhaktas* often joined common cause; differences of Muslim and Hindu doctrine were so blurred in some cases as to result in the formation of sects and mendicant bands whose denominational identity had almost completely dissolved (Plate 50). Among the most notable examples of the new syncretists were the *bhakti* saint, Rāmānanda, and the Muslim weaver-poet, Kabīr.

By mollifying discordant elements within the new Muslim *imperium* of the Moghuls, the 'Men of the Pen' accomplished at the grass-roots of the social order the kind of preparatory groundwork essential for the ultimate success of Akbar's (1556–1605) innovations about three centuries later. There was no conscious political objective in what they did; but we can see from the perspective of history that Islam accidentally brought to fruition a trend which had been developing since the great upsurge of *bhakti* religiosity had raised the *dharma* to its ascendant position. The real weakness of these religious institutions was the absence of anything more stable than an extremely volatile organizational framework. It was the genius of Akbar which provided virtually the solution to the situation. The challenge presented to him was the creation of the first viable pan-Indian state since the time of Ashoka (273–232 B.C.), though his empire was confined to north India and parts of the Deccan. Inheritor of an impressive, but dangerously fickle state machinery controlled by a military élite, Akbar's problem was to neutralize the emotional strength of two religious systems lacking intellectual venturesomeness and organizational cohesion. What he did was to reverse the process initiated in the compromise between Sultan and *ulema*: he restored the concept of quasi-divine imperial sanctity and introduced a Persian type of imperial government apparatus. Now it was a *religious* duty to obey the emperor. Akbar abolished the *jizya* in 1564, curtailed the powers of the *ulema*, and permitted all citizens to worship as they pleased in the private domain, while insisting on their allegiance to the authority vested by divine right in himself. The policy worked because the Indian masses were already emotionally conditioned to the idea of a charismatic religious ruler. In one sense this was a step backwards, perhaps even a conscious archaism, echoing the ancient Indian and Persian concepts of sacred kingship. On the other hand, Akbar went far towards creating the basis for common citizenship with equal rights for all regardless of religious differences. It is perhaps typical of the Indian situation that in daring to establish something approaching a secular state Akbar still had to appeal to his subjects through the elaborate apparatus of a state religion, with himself at its apex (Plate 49). In their very different ways, Ashoka before him and Gandhi after could only establish a unified value-system through religion.

Akbar's most solid achievement, the great administrative system of the Moghul empire, might have met with sullen obstruction at every level without religious symbolism to give it authority. Yet the imperial religion which he devised, the Din-i-Illahi, dissolved (for reasons already examined in Part One); first the British and later independent India built the secular state, which had eluded every previous ruler, on the remaining Moghul administrative substructure. However, this legacy contained one fatal flaw, directly arising from Akbar's inability (and he could not have conceived of any alternative) to separate religion from government: the unresolved conflict between Hindu and Muslim. Not even Gandhi could avoid the association of his nationalist religious syncretism with only one of the two communal entities. Nehru, whose policies had shallower roots in popular sentiment by comparison, could never have been a national figurehead of secularism without the neutralization of the Muslim minority by Partition, with the remaining Muslim minority on Indian territory relegated, in effect, to the status of an 'external' caste.

Chapter Seven Economic Change and the Middle Classes

The third *varṇa*, the Vaishyas, or traders, played a significant role in affecting the gradual, but uneven transition from a 'pre-economic' to a fully monetized market economy. The latter phase of this development was accompanied by the emergence of the middle classes.

Historical background

The prosperity and business acumen of the great industrial and commercial houses in modern Bombay and Calcutta indicate that in the commercial sector India has a considerable potential for modernization. The Indian millionaire industrialist, as much as the petty trader, is a familiar figure on the international scene today, whether in New York and London, or in innumerable African and South-East Asian towns. In fact, the Indian merchant has enjoyed a reputation for shrewdness *outside* India since antiquity, when Indian goods and luxuries were prized on the Mediterranean, in the Arab world, in China and Indonesia. In early times, the development of this cosmopolitan business community, with its fleets of three-masted sailing ships, could only have been accomplished by its maintaining active contact outside the framework of the ritualistic system of reciprocal exchange. Trade centred on the towns and seaports, and the business community was organized into a strong system of guilds (*sreṇi*) designed to regulate prices and protect trading rights against envious royal interference. Every ruler subsequent to the Magadhan-Mauryan era strove to emulate the kings and emperors of that thriving period by establishing state trading monopolies, though few succeeded on anything like the same scale. In consequence, the business community, which never enjoyed more than a low social status, tended to develop a defensive minority outlook, and when times were bad it was forced into a subservient position under the close supervision of the palace, distrusted by the Brahmans, and deprived of initiative. In the *Arthashāstra*, the merchant is listed among the 'thieves that are not called by the name of thief'. The feudal pattern of the economy was self-defeating in terms of market expansion. It was in overseas trade that the Indian merchant found scope for expansion; although internal trade was certainly extensive, the real drive and initiative originated in the outward-looking seaports.

The fluctuating fortunes of the business community reflected the freedom and mobility of society; when the latter was fettered to Brahmanic ritualism, trade was subject to every form of taxation and regulation, while the concept of private property, and therefore of profit, was deeply suspect. When secularism was on the up-grade, stimulated by a collective need to open up new territory for land settlement, trade boomed; these periods of prosperity, however, were rarely sustained beyond the early years of a newly established dynasty or political hegemony. At other times, society succumbed to an inward-looking, village-oriented, rustic outlook, its indifference to commerce amounting almost to active distaste. The making of money and the desire to do so were not lacking; but the pursuit of *artha* (wealth) was subordinate to the emotional compulsion to sustain the magico-religious cycle of the *dharma*—what might be called the conspicuous consumption of the potlatch mentality. 'Potlatch' is a Chinook Amerindian word, literally 'place of getting satiated', which used to be a favourite term of anthropologists to describe tribal festivals of conspicuous consumption and gift-exchange.[1]

Foreign traders had no such reservations, and their Indian counterparts felt less inhibited in dealing with them, as the latter had no stake in the ritualistic reciprocity of the Indian social order (*jajmānī* system, gift-exchange). We may compare the Vaishya with the Kshatrya in so far as both felt secure in their adventurist policies when unhampered by ethical and ritual strictures at home. The temptation to 'wheel and deal' may be compared with the adventurer's ambition to seize political power; the Vaishya tended to indulge in profiteering by circumvention of moral restraints. The alternative was conversion to one of the heterodox religions, notably Buddhism or Jainism, within which a business ethic evolved in harmony with religious principles. Once again, the stimulus to enterprise, risk-taking, and an outward-looking alertness accompany the same centrifugal movement away from the closed society of Brahmanism and caste. As we have seen earlier in Part Three, there was an individualistic, anti-caste, not to say Protestant, element in these apparently other-worldly salvation religions which outweighed their contrary tendency towards mysticism. Buddhism and Jainism began as anti-ritualistic, intellectually oriented movements of self-inquiry which appealed precisely to those urban classes who were affluent, educated, and emancipated from magico-religious superstition. In response to the secular mentality and liberal predilections of their followers, both religions encouraged a form of parish organization

[1] As defined by Franz Boas in *Kwakiutl Texts*.

among the laity with a lively, generous sense of solidarity cutting across caste barriers; this lay ethic was republican, democratic, and conducive to free discussion in assembly. The guilds were probably modelled likewise, free of priestly domination; they stressed the inalienable right of the individual to private property, individual effort and responsibility (echoing the heterodox techniques of self-knowledge), truthfulness, and frugality (echoing the heterodox monastic rules of conduct). The combination, in this case, of business expertise and ethical systems rooted *in* the society, gave the Buddhist and Jain traders a solid basis for free action. Consequently there was less danger, in this relaxed atmosphere, of over-reaching the social code, less need to circumvent restrictions through unethical practices. (It is worth pointing out that it was through a second, but basically similar, Protestant stimulus and endorsement of individual rights cutting across caste divisions, that—its ethic rooted in the traditions of the merchant castes—was fostered under British rule in the nineteenth century.) After the decline of Buddhism in South India it was the liberal, anti-caste, anti-Brahman popular religious movement of the *bhakti* cults which stimulated a fresh wave of maritime commercial contact with South-East Asia, East Africa, and the Persian Gulf. The Jain religion also went into decline in the Gangetic valley, but survived in the region most favourably situated for trade with the West—Gujerat and Rājasthān.

Once Indian society had crystallized round the nucleus of the *jajmānī* system, the inland cities suffered a marked decline. But the seaports continued to thrive, to expand, and to proliferate. The Gujerāti, or Gulf of Cambay area, which had long been a trading region (the Harappans constructed a remarkable brick dockyard at their port of Lothal), arose to fresh prominence around the eleventh century A.D.; it included the extensive territory comprising Kutch, Kāthiāwār, Saurashtra, Marwar, and Gujerāt. It was located at the centre of important land and maritime trade-routes, with several good ports, the rich and celebrated temple of Somnāth, and the city of Ahmedabad (the Hindu city of Asaval in pre-Muslim times), which remains the centre of the Indian textile industry. The principal religious allegiances of this trading community were Jainism and Vaishnava devotionalism, the latter a local offshoot of the *bhakti* movement, with its own gods of non-Brahmanical origin. In addition, the region became the home of exiled Zoroastrians from Persia—the Parsis. In this heterodox climate a separate community was formed which, like its forebears elsewhere in India, cut across caste and religious barriers. It produced most of India's biggest bankers and their modern descendants, the founders of the great industrial corporations. But the majority of these highly centralized family empires belonged to the more austere Jain community, with its ancient traditions of thrift and parsimony.

There were two classes of merchants originally. One consisted of a few highly placed families of merchant bankers who financed large-scale business, generally occupying an uneasy position at court, but occasionally powerful enough to function independently. While India had no joint-stock companies prior to British rule, in the late feudal period there emerged a hereditary class of enterprising merchant-manufacturers who advanced capital and monopolized the import–export business. The other class were the numerous retail traders and money-lenders, who also acted as middle-men between the towns and the village artisans; some of these were also local representatives of the loosely organized 'managing agencies' of the big mercantile houses. While the petty money-lender, stock figure of avarice in Indian tradition, limited himself to small-scale transactions at the usurious rate of 25 per cent, sometimes even twice that, the city banker went for much larger business at lower interest rates, and also accepted deposits.

It may be asked why, if the Indian merchant succeeded in emancipating himself from the closed, xenophobic national outlook, he failed, on return from abroad, to exert pressure on society to overcome the stultifying effects of ritualism. Such pressure would undoubtedly have led to the emergence of an organized bourgeoisie, in active opposition to the monarchy. Some of the interrelated factors which operated to check the emergence of a bourgeois class have been noted earlier in Part Three; but it may be worthwhile to recall, in this context, that the pre-economic system was basically a *circulation* of gifts; this dovetails with the whole deeply rooted orientation to cyclical causation, arising from the feeling of helplessness in the face of nature. During its formation Indian civilization was based on an economy of abundance rather than of subsistence. In spite of the ravages of a destructive climate, nature was immensely, almost overpoweringly fertile. The lesson of the first millennium and a half of settled agriculture was that, however freely one took from nature, the cyclical equilibrium of the ecology was not upset; that lesson was never forgotten and, in consequence, the concept of productive *increment* was never consciously formulated when exhaustion of the soil did later upset the ecology. Nature and society were both seen as systems of equilibrium, of balance in the distribution of resources, not of unilinear increase. The gods of fertility were both creators *and* destroyers, perpetually engaged in maintaining a balance between opposed forces.

While this outlook certainly affected attitudes towards material gain, the more concrete arrangements of the social order were even more inhibiting. The gradation of castes prevented the formation of a middle class with its own solidarity. In a country endowed with exceptionally skilful artisan castes, whose manual dexterity is possibly unrivalled, there are nevertheless no known cases of enterprising master-craftsmen who emerged from the workshop to found businesses based on practical knowledge. A member of the artisan castes could not become a merchant. It has also been pointed out that the motive for making money is individualist, the opposite of collective reciprocity. Now it is obvious that neither the individual nor the group within the caste system has the kind of freedom of movement in social space indispensable to commercial risk-taking. Further, the caste system was based on a land economy of quasi-feudal character and laws of hereditary succession through adequate performance of obligations. The domestic system of production in the joint family was, similarly, an inseparable part of the social order, and this prevented even an ambitious family from undertaking a multiplicity of economic functions in a joint-stock business or in large-scale manufacture. The laws of inheritance in the joint-family system also led to the fragmentation of property, denying a son the chance either to conserve or increase inherited capital. Under Muslim rule even the wealthiest in the nobility were dispossessed of their property and movable wealth by the king on their decease. Thus immense fortunes were rapidly depleted through fragmentation, and the insecurity of undivided property rights. As Dr. B. B. Misra points out in *The Indian Middle Classes*, 'Indian society was, in fact, not a money-dominated society with freedom for individuals to move up or down the social scale according to economic circumstances.'[1]

The political factors in retardation were never so strong (until the Moghul period) as to prevent either individual merchants or the guilds from obtaining greater power. Nor did the power structure actively prevent the merchant community from organizing itself through control of municipal governments, citizens' armies, and the police, as in the West. But the motivation was lacking. The guilds served their purpose adequately so long as the main body of society was not yet wholly dominated by the caste mentality. But once the guilds recruited members from the castes (in the south, for example, the Brahmans became active members and engaged in commerce), their inter-caste solidarity broke down, undermining the initiative on which their early success was based.

To conclude, vigorous entrepreneurial enterprise was socially frowned on, if not actively distrusted. One consequence of prolonged conditioning by the pre-monetary *jajmāni* system is the continuing unpopularity of the business community in modern times. This was a far more potent factor in the sympathetic public reaction to the nationalization of the banks in 1969 than any conscious mass avowal of specifically socialist ideology. In fact, this was a significant instance of deep-seated traditional sentiment coinciding with a politically motivated effort towards modernization.

[1] Misra (1961).

Formation of new classes during British rule

The first signs of modern economic and social change appeared soon after the commercial penetration of India by Western traders, when contact was established between the East India Company and the commercially more advanced west coast. The merchant bankers benefited from this early phase of trade, but except in the cotton textile industry, the British soon circumvented the monopolists to establish their own managing agencies, with Europeans occupying all the chief posts. With the establishment of British state banking the old family empires lost their pre-eminent position at the apex of the trading community in the seaports. Most had to be content with small-scale traditional business and moneylending in the hinterland. They did not regain their dominating position until the last decade of British rule.

Writing in 1853, Karl Marx summed up the objectives of British rule: 'England has to fulfil a double mission in India: one destructive and the other regenerating—the annihilation of old Asian society and the laying of the material foundations of Western society in Asia.' So far as the regenerating aspect of this mission was concerned, there was a historical link with the Moghul empire, from which the British inherited the centralized revenue and administrative apparatus. The two most vital innovations of the period were the introduction of Western knowledge and techniques and a desire to create a democratic way of life. The key areas in this early modernization after the British assumed power were: land reform, legal reform, and a new educational system. The most important consequence of legislation was the emergence of a new concept: individual rights; and instrumental in bringing this about were the new class of Indian public servants and the monetization of the rural economy. The creation of a modern bureaucracy involves, as Max Weber pointed out, a hierarchy of functions, jurisdiction fixed by law, operation by way of written orders, and a professional class of full-time officers working according to certain legal principles to eliminate arbitrary authority. While there is no doubt that the introduction of these methods resulted in a more efficient, stable, impersonal, and unified system of government, protected from the whims of any one man, it did, nevertheless, weigh heavily on the subject people. Implicit in the new value system was a wholly fresh challenge to self-reliance and initiative; since this value system was legally imposed by foreigners, it generally had precisely the opposite effect on the Indian psychology, the unfortunate effects of which are only now becoming apparent. Active steps to overcome the resulting servility were initiated over a century ago by Indian leaders, and the process continues to the present day.

The first step of the British administration was taken in land reform, enabling individuals to transfer their interest in land, thus reducing the power of the landholders and ensuring security of private property. New revenue laws and tenancy reforms led to the very gradual redefinition of the rights of the agricultural classes, a process which also still continues in independent India. Enormous errors were made, resulting in the emergence of absentee landlords, chronic indebtedness, and dispossession of the peasantry, rather than the emancipation of the most enterprising and vigorous sections of the community. There was a considerable increase in litigation and a demand for a quite different kind of legal system employing a new class of professional lawyers, which struck at the traditional priestly monopoly in this sphere.

The secularization of Indian law has been a very long process since there was no code of law generally recognized, nor were there any regular courts in existence before the British arrived. Lord Macaulay, describing the situation in 1833, wrote of 'the Hindu law, Mohammedan law, Parsi law, and English law perpetually mingling with each other and disturbing each other, varying with the person, varying with the place'. Even now, Mohammedan law has not been consistently modified in accordance with the otherwise uniform legal system applicable to all communities, irrespective of caste or creed. Legislation was designed to abolish inequality before the law and discrimination according to caste. The new Penal Codes strove to uphold the rights of the individual. In principle, the effect of legal reform was to free the individual from his attachment to family, caste, kin, and community, by recognizing his personal right rather than the collective right of caste, association, or institution. In reality, the individual was often hesitant to seek justice in a court of law independently of his kin; in the villages, for example, legal equality was the antithesis of communal justice and a threat to hierarchical caste privileges. Thus any individual legal action was fraught with the risk of total alienation from the traditional society and the web of kinship security.

The original intention of the education system introduced by the British was to create through English-style schooling a middle class of professionals to administer the imperialist economy and administration. In 1835 Macaulay wrote: 'We must at present do our best to form a class who may be interpreters between us and the millions whom we govern—a class of persons Indian in blood and colour, but English in tastes, in opinions, in morals and in intellect.' For all its faults, not the least of which were the fulsome Victorian sentiments in which declarations of policy were wrapped, this imposition of a foreign secular education was of incalculable and timely significance. It was a major step towards the creation of a new professional expertise and sense of citizenship 'based', as Dr. Misra puts it, 'not on religion or caste but on the discharge of certain common civil obligations to the state'. While the unification of the political system made a deep impression on those classes who benefited from education, the idea of nationhood has been slow to take root among the masses. The British never succeeded in destroying the collectivist structure of the society, either through legal or educational reform; in both instances it was a new élite who attained dominant status—the collectivist mentality of the hierarchy merely readjusted itself to accommodate the bureaucracy at its apex. Implicit in the education system was the transformation of society from a basis of status to one of contract, whereas the products of that system, middle-class candidates for posts in the judicial and revenue branches of public service, continued after their appointment to be motivated by ambition for higher status within the traditional hierarchy. In the long term, however, the British ensured limited freedom of movement in social space for the individual. The new middle classes imbibed the principles of English liberalism and took the lead in movements for social and political reform; it is from their ranks that the modern leadership emerged which initiated the nationalist movement.

The main weakness of an education system geared to the needs of the bureaucracy was its excessively literary content. Vocational training was ignored because the economic policy of imperialism excluded development of indigenous industries in competition with the home market. It was not in the interests of the British to promote technical knowledge or technical change, and posts in the managing agencies demanding practical expertise were exclusively reserved for the British themselves. In effect, therefore, the system favoured the Brahmans and other literary castes. This had two serious consequences: the persistence of a bureaucratic mentality unsuited to the kind of practical initiative and risk-taking needed in the running of a modern industrial economy, and inadvertent support for the persistence of caste exclusivism.

From the circumstances of their growth the members of the educated professions, such as government servants and lawyers, college teachers and doctors, constitute the bulk of the Indian middle classes. The mercantile and industrial elements which dominate the composition of the Western middle classes are still in a minority, limited for the most part to cities like Calcutta, Bombay, Madras and Kanpur, Ahmedabad and Jamshedpur.[1]

It was not until a need arose for accelerated technological and industrial development in the Second World War that the professional classes moved into fields beyond educational, judicial, and administrative posts. Nevertheless the bureaucracy and literary professions continue to be dominated by the Brahmans and higher castes.

[1] B. B. Misra, *The Indian Middle Classes*, Oxford University Press, London, 1961.

This is the exact opposite of the situation in Japan, a nation which was not colonized by the West and which was free to learn Western techniques and know-how from the very beginning of its modernization. It has been said that when the British were no more than traders in India, various rulers had adopted the same attitude towards Western technical innovation, especially in the field of warfare, as had the Japanese; but imperial conquest reduced India to a state of passive acquiescence and brooding introspection. There is no doubt that during the period of British rule India showed greater interest in the theoretical knowledge and philosophical ideas of the West, while the post-Independence period reversed this trend; it is technical know-how with which India is now more concerned, while recent Western literary and intellectual movements are no longer followed with the same alert curiosity as previously.

At the same time as the literary classes were reaping the benefits of education, the long-suppressed trading castes seized on legislative reform, such as the enforcement of the debtor's obligation by law, to enlarge their activities as moneylenders. The freedom with which property could be alienated and the disposal of land in exchange for cash, both dealt a blow to the *jajmānī* system. Now that the individual profit motive and a cash economy had reached the agricultural classes, the moneylender and the middleman found themselves in a particularly favourable position at the expense of the less prosperous. 'In brief, British rule brought the expansion of that type of business activity which has the lowest possible prestige rating in India or elsewhere.' [1] The expected transformation into a vigorous, competitive agrarian society did not, for this reason, come about. It was against the interests of the new rural propertied class to assist in an agrotechnical revolution; on the other hand, the application of Western *laissez-faire* economics suited this dominant class and they were able to entrench themselves at the head of the rural hierarchy, thus effectively blocking the release of individualistic forces from below.

The spread of the Marwari moneylenders throughout the country in the early nineteenth century is a typical example. There are nearly five million people who speak the Marwari dialect of Rājasthān, but it is the trading castes, under the generic title of *baniyā*, a title which is now derogatory through its association with sharp business practices, who succeeded in penetrating the entire business structure of the nation. 'So entrenched is this mercantile and industrial elite today that eight Marwari families, some of them related by marriage, hold 565 directorships in Indian industry, banking and insurance.' [2] Now that legal restrictions have been placed on managing agencies, nepotism on such a scale is on the decline.

[1] Helen B. Lamb, 'The Indian Merchant', in Singer (ed.) (1959), p. 31.
[2] Harrison (1960), p. 115.

The Marwaris are not alone: there are numerous instances, perhaps on a smaller scale, of the ability of enterprising castes and linguistic communities to expand and consolidate their interests through institutions spread over a very wide area of the country and abroad. Notable examples are the Punjabi and Sindhi small traders, Chettiar moneylenders and Naidu landowners in the southern textile industry, Parsis in industry, Saraswati Brahmans in the literary professions, Kerala high castes in the northern administrative services, certain Gujerati and Sindhi castes in East African trade. The very fact that the Chettiars and Naidus, for example, cannot compete with the aggressive non-indigenous Marwari moneylenders and entrepreneurs reveals the continued existence of checks on the businessman who remains within the social network of his local community. Mobility through vertical change in status and geographical migration makes the Marwari, or similar entrepreneur, an outsider 'absolved from the restraints of customary regional business behaviour'.[1] This recalls the situation of the Indian trader in antiquity. Whereas the usurper could always have his claim to kingship legitimized through Kshatrya-ization, legitimization of the Vaishya was more ambiguous. The Marwaris, and similar-minded outsiders, are always careful to perform their religious duties as members of their respective castes in as ostentatious a manner as their extensive financial resources permit (their richest members are lavish in temple-building, endowments to religious and charitable institutions, and financing of caste associations, medical care, property co-operatives, and the like). Thus they can, when they so choose, perform any status-enhancing action, or transact power-enhancing 'wheel-and-deal' business in the name of their caste *dharma*. This business élite, many of them Jains, are 'like the elect of early Calvinism who substantiated their claim to election by a strenuous dedication to acts and articles of faith'.[2]

The peculiarly cosmopolitan position of the migrant businessman, while it may assist in the erosion of chronic parochialism, is also one of the principal sources for financing rival inter-state political movements. The Marwaris, and similar businessmen with regional vested interests, have played an important role in the formation of the various political parties, and assist in the organization of the Congress Party. But since their prosperity is in no small part based on their power as outsiders in local society, they have not contributed to political stability; on the contrary, factionalism is axiomatic to the migrant.

Today, the Indian economy is divided into public and private sectors; both, however, are controlled by élites numerically thin in composition and remote from the life of the masses. The institutional checks against their

[1] Harrison (1960), p. 117.
[2] Helen Lamb, in Singer (ed.) (1959), p. 32.

arbitrary use of power are complex and diverse, but uneven in their effectiveness since they are of recent origin. Nationalized industries are directed by government servants who belong to, or socialize with, the élite of the private sector. The British managing-agency system had the effect of concentrating business into very few hands; even after 'Indianization' this system survived intact until 1967, ensuring a small circle of financiers an unduly high proportion of reward.

Only in recent years has India begun to shake itself free from its centuries-old bias in favour of Brahman-dominated literary education; and since the nationalized industries are likely to be run for some time to come by men who received such an education, the urgent task of accelerated production is administered with extreme bureaucratic diffidence.

Chapter Eight Recent Changes in Society

Reformism and nationalism

While the history of modern Indian nationalism is beyond the scope of the present study, it is necessary to understand the social and cultural ideas which inspired this movement and have been instrumental in achieving social reform.

The introspection resulting from the impact of Western values, knowledge, and institutions was to some extent the continuation, though in a subtly altered key, of a mood which came naturally to Indian thinking during the many centuries when Hindu culture had been on the defensive. But the Western method of detached and objective research, of historical and scientific thinking, was something entirely new to the Indian outlook in virtually every domain, especially in attitudes towards national and cultural identity. India rediscovered herself. Re-orientation consists of two strands, Westernization and Indianization; their synthesis results in a modernized Great Tradition, usually called Universalization.

Perhaps the deepest, and therefore the slowest, change has occurred on the philosophical and religious planes, notably in the movement called neo-Hinduism, which is basically of a universalistic character, in spite of the fact that the pluralistic society includes other very large religious communities. In actual fact, it was not Western ideas which initiated this movement; the ground had long been prepared by the presence on Indian soil of Islamic monotheism and Sufism. With the establishment of *unified* Western rule, and the presence of Christian missionaries who, similarly, worshipped *one* God, the pluralistic, polytheistic culture of India was subjected to a process which intensified a single, but extremely important strand in its total pattern, the quest of the Great Ultimate. By now the reader will be familiar with the diversity of principles and factors associated with this quest: the concept of *Brahman*, holy power, the role of the Renouncer, the holistic *dharma*, the universalizing tendency of *bhakti*, and the unifying agency of the Great Tradition. The greatest figure in the movement was the reformist, Rājā Rām Mohun Roy, who launched an attack on the multiplicity of creeds, replacing superstition and polytheism by an intellectualized principle of cosmic causality. More daring still, he expounded his ideas in accordance with the principles of Western logical argument, not by the aphoristic and symbolic language of the traditional poetic *sūtra*.

The mystical monism of the Upanishadic and Vedānta schools, as reinterpreted by Vivekānanda, Aurobindo, and Tagore, has played a significant role in advancing a form of neo-Hinduism based on a modified concept of the Ātman. On the other hand, the Theosophists revived the confidence of the anglicized middle class in the traditional cultural and religious heritage—long a source of scorn and contempt among Christian missionaries and British officialdom. Annie Besant (Irish ex-socialist and Fabian, friend of Charles Bradlaugh and Bernard Shaw), for many years president of the Theosophical Society, added enormous prestige to this movement, mainly because she herself was also one of the greatest political reformers on the Indian scene during the first two decades of this century, and was president of the Indian National Congress in 1917.

While the historical movement of universalization has included attempts to transform Hinduism into a unified monotheistic religion, the facts of the pluralistic social organization have precluded its success. But many Hindu sects have emerged with something approaching ecclesiastical organization, as for example, the Rāmakrishna Mission. Although these sects have been influenced by Christianity, no unified Church has been formed, nor is it likely to be formed in the foreseeable future, for the alternative to a ritual-oriented hierarchy under Indian conditions can only be secular in character. Universalization, then, began as a basically Westernizing movement and rapidly assumed a predominantly Indianizing function. It is this movement which has proved both more attractive and more effective as a culturally unifying force than Sanskritization, and has a far wider basis of appeal than Westernization.

None of these developments could have occurred without the introduction of the printing press. For the first time Indian religious texts and commentaries circulated freely, newspapers became the forum of public opinion, and the educated classes were brought into close contact. The beginnings of nationalism should be viewed against this cultural background of intellectual ferment, with the Westernized élite turning towards liberalism and the conservatives to Hinduism. The liberal advocates of social and political reform were uncompromising in their disapproval of traditional culture, which they considered a retrogressive force that submerged the masses in superstition. From its earliest days, therefore, Indian nationalism was confronted with the problem of an intellectual élite divorced from the majority of Indians. In 1885 Allan Hume founded the Indian National Congress as a tribune for this élite in the hope that it would provide a link between the British imperial system and the Indian masses. But the conservatives had no faith in alien ideas and an alien language as means to activate the masses out of intellectual apathy and servitude. They were less concerned with social reform (which conflicted with their affirmation of resurgent Hinduism) than with throwing off the yoke of foreign rule. They repudiated the intellectualism of the liberals in favour of traditional ideals and symbols closer to the hearts of the people. Indian nationalism became increasingly oriented towards the traditionalist outlook, as represented by the reactionary political philosophy of Tilak, and the Hindu reform movement of Vivekānanda and Aurobindo. In the first two decades of this century the Congress gradually moved away from the British intellectual tradition, and the Westernized élite were effectively isolated, deprived of their political voice by the same class which they had previously inspired. Thus the dynamic activism of the nationalist leadership in the struggle for independence developed hand in hand with an emotional ideology, its roots deep in the traditional religious culture. Ultimately, it was more the humanity of Gandhi than any intellectually progressive movement which rescued the nationalist movement from the conservative, not to say fanatically reactionary, principles which often motivated the older generation.

The political history of the Indian nationalist movement has, therefore, always been associated with religion. Reduced to its simplest terms, the legacy of the Muslim period was the division of India into two antagonistic religious communities, Hindu and Muslim, their symbiosis incomplete, their fusion cut short by the exigencies of power politics. The imposition of foreign rule on these peoples who had never resolved their differences could lead to but one outcome: since neither had fused with the other, each would have to assert its identity first in the fight against foreign domination. A prior condition to the attainment of corporate identity was separate reaffirmation of religious unity, since neither community was yet organized politically. The outcome of this internal confrontation was that the minority religious community of the Muslims, which also had the disadvantage of not being considered indigenously rooted, was faced with the risk of being submerged by the pluralistic Hindu community.

The first phase of nationalism was therefore the affirmation of the religious community as a political group, the Hindus preceding the Muslims in this process by half a century, led by Rām Mohun Roy. Politicization proceeded hand in hand with a campaign to build a monist superstructure on a polytheistic foundation, with a reaffirmation of the holistic *dharma* whereby caste differences were explained away as relativistic categories subsumed by the Great Ultimate. From the viewpoint of the Hindu masses this universalism was no more than a dimly comprehensible gloss on the vast and complex body of tradition, which bore no relation to the social realities of the caste system and to their uneasy day-to-day co-existence with Muslim neighbours. Not until Gandhi concretized the new nationalist mystique did the masses feel any sense of involvement. Nevertheless, Hindu revivalism and reformism within the inclusive evolution of universalism was not long in spurring the Muslims into adopting a similar but rival stance, thereby introducing a separative effect, namely, communalism. Like Rām Mohun before him, Sir Syed Ahmed Khan initiated a reformist movement, its immediate goals identical with those of Hindu nationalism: education, professional diversification, and posts in the British administration. While Islam was not confronted with the pluralistic problems inherent in the transformation of the Hindu religious community into a political group, the revivalist rationale in the Muslim movement underwent a not dissimilar process of universalization: a reassertion of doctrinal purity and communal solidarity in keeping with the Pan-Islamic movement popular at the turn of the century.

Referring to these religious features of Indian nationalism, Dumont identifies 'a change in the nature or place of religion in communalism; religion becomes here a mere appearance: people are not really concerned with the substance of religion, religion having become the sign of their being distinct.'[1] It would be well to point out that, bedevilled as the evolution of the Indian nation-society has been by communalistic bifurcation, the religious trappings concealed the political goal in the struggle against foreign imperialism. Dumont describes this underlying political movement as:

a synthesis in response to a Western challenge which is still more political and social than religious; an integration of the new social and political values within a reformed traditional, and at least outwardly, religious view; a reaffirmation of supposed Hindu values on a new level. The major fact for us here is that this integration and internalisation of modern Western views, which was conscious of being a victorious reaffirmation of traditional Hindu values, was a preliminary condition of an active political struggle against foreign domination on the part of Hindus. One is led to speak of 'Hindu Nationalism', an expression which, were it not self-contradictory, would well describe the common ground between tendencies as different as those of Tilak and Gandhi. This was obviously not destined to make for the union between Hindus and Muslims.[2]

The division into India and Pakistan, the precarious minority position of the Muslims who remained in India (10 per cent of the total population), and recurrent communalist disturbances, are the most significant and well-known features which have resulted from this sad and bitter separative legacy. In accordance with the same tendency for religion to become a sign of a community's corporate existence, other religious communities in India have felt a similar compulsion to assert their political strength, namely Sikhs, Jains, and Christians. There is, in this context, but a hair's breadth to

[1] Dumont and Pocock (eds.) (1957–66), VII, p. 45.   [2] Ibid., p. 55.

distinguish between communalism, sectarianism, and casteism, since all three, though different in composition, assert their identity through the mere appearance of religious ideology.

Change in the caste system

With the promulgation of the Constitution on 26 January 1950, the caste system lost its quasi-legal basis. The individual citizen and not caste was declared the basic unit of Indian society, with equality of all citizens before the law. The socio-economic structure was based in principle on agreement between free and equal individuals, not between one caste or sect and another. Legislation alone has not, however, wrought structural changes in the caste system, and the Constitution should only be viewed as a definition of objectives.

Legislative reform was the fruit of a long campaign which had been spurred by the liberal and Gandhian leadership during the period of nationalist struggle. As Professor M. N. Srinivas has pointed out, success in legal reform of the caste system should, however, be viewed against a contrary current of public opinion:

It must be clear that in this country only a small minority which is numerically insignificant but which may be—and probably is—powerful, really desires that the caste system ought to go. The vast majority of the population, especially Hindus, not only do not want caste to disappear, but they would probably find it impossible to envisage a social system without caste. . . .

But it is still true to say that the vast majority of people do not consider caste as evil. It is essential to remember this fact, for nothing effective can be done unless the people themselves are made to realise that caste necessarily means casteism [political representation on a caste basis], and that the benefits it offers are bought at a heavy price for the country as a whole. It is not at all an easy task to put across this point to the people, and so far neither the politicians nor the social workers have displayed any awareness of the existence of this difficult problem of communication.[1]

The principal changes in the society as a whole since the establishment of British rule, and later of Indian rule, can be summarized as follows: security of private property and the consequent alteration in the position of property-holding classes; increase in the population and reversal of the ratio of manual labour to cultivated land from one of labour scarcity to one of land scarcity; the introduction of a comprehensive land revenue system; development of the market economy; acceleration in productivity to feed the growing population and create a viable national economy; increase in

[1] M. N. Srinivas, *Caste in Modern India*, Bombay, 1962, p. 70.

the circulation of money in the rural areas; improvement in transportation and communication; gradual replacement of subsistence farming by cash crops; the advance of technology; increased power for the moneylender at the expense of the peasant; development of modern professions religiously neutral in character, with consequent scope for increased social mobility; accelerated urban development, with a mass exodus from the rural areas; territorial unification and spatial mobility; and, finally, the introduction of universal adult franchise.

These gradual improvements have had a greater cumulative effect on the structure of the caste system than the various legislative reforms specifically designed to abolish social inequality. Despite these changes, caste distinctions still exist, though they are of greater structural importance in the rural than in the urban areas. Caste continues to determine the function, the status, the job opportunities, as well as the social handicaps of a very large majority of the population. Caste differences also influence the modes of domestic and social life and the types of houses and cultural patterns of the peasantry. Administrative functions are also often divided according to castes.

It should be evident from the changes listed above, notably in the economic sphere, that the modern occupational pattern has disrupted the vertical structure of hierarchy and status. Similarly, there has been a decrease in the prominence of pollution rules, and greater permissiveness in dietary tabus. These innovations have not, however, neutralized the caste mentality; in consequence, the division into endogamous groups remains substantially unaffected. The question is whether, once the principles of hierarchy, relative degrees of impurity, and ritual status have been eroded, there remains anything which may legitimately be called a caste system.

Professor G. S. Ghurye was the first to identify the key to the structural changes in the caste system: the development of caste associations. It might be assumed that accelerated urban development would necessitate caste mixture; this has not been the case. The castes tend to group themselves in districts and housing estates owned by caste associations and reserved for their members. These caste associations, the revivified *sabhās*, comprising all the members of the caste who speak the same language, or an affiliation of related sub-castes, have enhanced their solidarity by property investment, banking, financing of schools, provision of scholarships, hospitals, and co-operatives. Caste associations are occasionally organized on an all-India or regional basis, publish their own caste newspapers and journals, protect the status of the caste, and control such matters as the marriage age and retention of certain customs. Whether urban or rural, the caste association acts as an employment agency and a pressure group which seeks to maintain its influence at all levels of government. For it is through universal suffrage that the caste associations have also become aware of their political strength. While the traditional system permitted only the dominant caste to achieve a corporate political existence, now all large caste associations are corporate political bodies within their linguistic region. On caste in politics we will have more to say later; suffice it to quote here a remark by the second President of the Republic, Dr. Radhakrishnan:

> Though caste is today ceasing to be a social evil, it has become a political evil; it has become an administrative evil. We are utilising these caste loyalties for the purpose of winning our elections or getting people into jobs, exercising some kind of favouritism or nepotism.

Casteism is an inclusive term to describe any form of political loyalty on the basis of caste, the use of caste influence, nepotism, pressure, or bribery to further the ends of a caste body. It may be considered as an innovation *within* the caste system, a form of pressure group, usually arising from an alliance between castes whose interests happen to coincide—a response to the normal procedure of democracy to develop organized demands and community associations.

Furthermore, an important structural change arises from the combination of factors in the transitional society outlined above: as Ghurye pointed out, caste has moved away from a holistic, hierarchical system of *interdependence* with a high degree of restlessness and ambiguity of status, to a system of massive, impenetrable, self-sufficient caste blocs, virtually identical in their internal character, and in *competition* with one another for greater *power*. Professor Srinivas is more cautious; he proposes the thesis that the last hundred years have actually seen a great increase in caste solidarity, though there has been a proportional decrease of interdependence between different castes living in the same region. This latter formulation is preferable, as the former suggests the transformation of a caste bloc into a virtually self-sufficient society, a kind of re-tribalization through improved communications somewhat on the lines of Professor McLuhan's 'electronic tribal village'. No doubt McLuhan's general theory on the universal influence of the printed word can be applied here, in the sense that print is an indispensable medium in the organization of a caste scattered throughout a large, linguistically homogeneous region. This is even more marked in the case of migrant castes, such as Marwaris and Chettiars. Solidarity was impossible on this scale when the members of a caste were tenuously linked by oral communication alone. The relatively impenetrable exclusivism of the new, competing caste blocs, arising from modernization (economic prosperity, the printed word, and political organization) is an alarming prospect— indeed it has already changed the social climate—but the likelihood that the electronic media will carry it one step further into some mysterious form of neo-tribalism is, in fact, remote. The most significant innovation is overt competition, as distinct from the traditional competitive *play*; whether this will result in the transformation of the caste associations into modern, mobile classes is a question that cannot be answered with any certainty at this stage. When Gandhi expressed the hope that India would return to the 'purity' of the *varṇa* 'class system', he should not be taken too literally, since these categories have not the remotest affinity with the socio-economic realities of the modern world. True, there is an increasing tendency to use the terminology of the *varṇa* model in preference to that of the *jāti* system, since the latter has derogatory connotations associated in the public's mind with backwardness. But it is hard to see where the professions or the skilled technicians, for example, fit into the categories of priests, warriors, traders, and cultivators.

Yet Gandhi was pointing to what appears to be the obvious evolutionary pattern of the caste system in a modern economic framework. For, in the long run, the consolidation of caste associations may bring about a modification in the *varṇa* system, based on a modern occupational stratification, more or less on the lines of the Euro-American class system. With each caste or subcaste group confident of its own position in the national context, the spirit of economic competition could be directed inwards and result in different occupational groups within the same caste competing among themselves; this in-fighting could result in occupational groups cutting across caste divisions to make common cause against other occupational groups. But the evolution of the caste system into a class system depends on the further consolidation of caste associations. Such a development would be possible only during a long period of national stability and prosperity. This would give the occupational groups the confidence to break free from the protection of caste associations.

Several observations should be made with regard to the political role of caste blocs and caste associations. Not even the most rigorous Communist dialectician has, in practice, found it feasible to ignore them in his efforts to establish a workable party organization. Communist successes have invariably been accompanied by the same shrewd manipulation of conflicting caste interests as in the case of every Indian political party, from the extreme left to the extreme right. Similarly, the principle of universal suffrage has been adapted with particular success to the machinery of caste associations by underprivileged castes. Almost for the first time in history it is the *dominated* castes, not the *dominant* castes, who are benefiting from superior organization. This helps to explain why the process of popular representation on democratic lines has been utilized so successfully in accordance with caste interests (as distinct from the interests of the individual voter). By and large, India is deeply conservative in its political orientation; hence the 'shadow' system of caste has served as a convenient means to accommodate rival interest-groups without actually subverting the social order through revolution and overt fomenting of class struggle. The early success of the Kerala Communist Party, for example, was based on the support of a powerful, ambitious, well-organized caste, low in status, the Ezhavas.

It is the considered opinion of Professor Adrian Mayer that caste is rarely the decisive factor in politics, that it exerts the strongest pressure in local rural politics and diminishes in strength as political activity broadens in regional and national scope. There is some danger here of confusing the ephemeral ebb and flow of political power with stable or enduring factors. If we project on Indian politics the Western model of a strong, unified, central government and the linked assumption that increase in industrialization will reinforce power at the centre but diminish that of rural interest-groups, Mayer's conclusions will no doubt be fully substantiated in the future. At the time of writing, however, I find two related factors which exert a contrary movement. First, increased rural prosperity through improved agricultural techniques, co-operatives, and marketing facilities (notably among the peasant proprietors, a class which produces a very high percentage of the country's food, out of all proportion to its numbers)[1] goes with the formation of caste associations and powerful alliances between sub-castes. These caste associations are beginning to exert considerable political weight through the capacity of the proprietor to enhance his own status as 'patron in control of a "vote bank" which he can place at the disposal of a provincial or national party' (M. N. Srinivas). Second, despite increasing urbanization, the locus of political strength seems to be moving from urban to rural areas. We have already observed that the ruralization of the *economy* had the gravest political consequences in ancient India. Under modern conditions of industrialization a similar economic regression is exceedingly unlikely. Nevertheless, taken in conjunction with the fact that most Indian voters live in the rural areas, it seems reasonable to expect that during the next few decades the ruralization of *politics* will remain a fairly constant, if fluctuating, feature of the Indian institutional system. The following figures support this conclusion: roughly 80 per cent of the population lives in 557,000 villages, the remaining 20 per cent in 3,000 towns; slightly over 70 per cent of the population are illiterate; agriculture accounts for 48 per cent of the national revenue but supports 70 per cent of the population, with the agricultural labour force representing 40 per cent of the population, whereas in developed countries it is between 8 and 12 per cent. The overwhelming majority of this agricultural population is still either firmly organized in the traditional caste system or in the new caste

[1] Three per cent of the rural population provides 30 per cent of the total agricultural production.

associations; the rule of caste endogamy remains substantially, if not totally, unchanged (save for liberalization of inter-subcaste marriage). Thus the ruralization of politics and the continued activity of caste organizations on the social plane are bound to interact and mutually influence each other. While the politicization of caste is a foregone conclusion, and has indeed already made an appreciable effect, the 'casteization' of politics in this larger perspective is an ever-present danger. This is a point to which we will return later.

The ruralization of the political locus is reflected in the reaction against intellectualism and in the calibre of party leadership, which is now more plebeian and is recruited from lower rungs of the society than the generations of nationalist leadership immediately before and after Independence. Rural group and sectional interests have had the consequence, particularly in South India, of leadership promotion on caste lines; in several cases, caste was the only factor behind the rise to power of men who now figure prominently in peninsular politics. No State cabinet is without its ministers who represent the main castes in the region. A concomitant of this trend is the disjunction of talent from politics; professional vote-collecting élites are formed through the maintenance of power by mutually adjusting positions and privileges rather than through recruitment on the principles of achievement, personal competence, and integrity. In many regions of India, whatever a man's organizing and administrative talents may be, if he belongs to a caste without power, or fails to obtain the support of numerically dominant castes, he cannot hope to get elected to office. It is in political representation at district level that the realities of this situation become apparent. According to Professor V. M. Sirsikar, in 1962, of 418 elected office-bearers in the Zila Parishads, 71 per cent were members of the dominant, peasant-proprietor, Marāthā caste, though they constituted only 40 per cent of the total population of Mahārāshtra.

Whatever structural changes have occurred in caste organization, one point stands out clearly: it is *power* which is now in ascendance over *status*. The general trend of secularization would point in this direction, and the facts certainly bear it out. In the past, changes in the balance of power were accompanied by readjustments in the hierarchical status of castes. In modern times, change in status through dislocation in the equilibrium of power has been stepped up by a more comprehensive system of political representation. Dr. André Béteille has recently shown that the gaps between traditional caste, class, and power have widened and no longer correspond to the traditional hierarchical scheme.[1] In the first place, this arose when ownership of land ceased to correspond to caste status and occupation. In the second place, the formerly dominant castes were the

[1] Cf. Béteille (1965).

pupil's development is largely steered by endogenous process. A satisfactory outcome is, of course, by no means assured; the number of failures among those who embark on this psychic excursion is fairly high.

While much depends on the guru's competence, an almost equal degree of tolerance is expected of society too, whose members were, in former times, socially conditioned to regard total immersion in inner space as neither anti-social withdrawal nor in any sense discreditable. The lavish financial endowments to *ashrāms* in modern times are no doubt often motivated by desire to gain merit; nevertheless, implicit in the fact is recognition of the need for protection of the inmates. That secularized India now tends to regard the inmates of *ashrāms* as social parasites and their patrons as motivated by outmoded values is justified. Famine, poverty, and epidemics are ignored by almost all *ashrāms*; nothing in the external world is allowed to disturb the inmates' spiritual exercises.

No doubt there still exist a number of mystics whose integrity is not in question. An institution which contributed greatly to the cultural life and psychic health of India in the past has, nevertheless, been marred by political corruption. The spiritually perfected individual, however, is probably as widely idealized in India today as he ever was, even if few live up to the model. Nothing of comparable mass-appeal has replaced him at the symbolic hub of the social wheel.

This being so, the question arises whether the guru cannot himself change. Perhaps this question could never have been posed before Gandhi appeared. That he inverted the role of the Indian holy man and gave it a socially constructive goal is a point which will be amplified in Part Five, Chapter Two. The large following which a number of gurus continue to enjoy, the relatively limited but by no means inconspicuous response to Āchārya Vinoba Bhave, and the resurgence of militant religiosity, are features of the post-Independence period. These facts alone justify analysis of the guru-cult, so as to obtain from it fresh insight into the social and psychological mores of the transitional society. Widespread interest in the psychology of perception, the Gestalt psychologist's concern with unified awareness, the search for the origins of schizophrenia in the psychic excursion, and experimentation with paranormal or enhanced mental states have greatly enlarged the avenues of approach. These branches of knowledge have engaged the attention of scholars because they point to the possible solution of urgent problems. These problems are shared by India, and in India it is the guru-cult which has been the focus of comparable psychic experiment. However, it is a sociological fact that the individuals who most assiduously pursue the guru-cult and are its main financial supporters belong to the privileged élite of the old order—the aristocrats, the rajas and their dependants, the landlords, the businessmen from the 'managing

percentage of administrative posts and legislative seats reserved for them by law. In such cases it pays to be officially classified as 'backward', an attitude common to similarly placed classes in all welfare-state systems.

The Harijans have developed a keen awareness that Sanskritization is less effective than acquisition of power. They increasingly realize that they are in a position to overcome their civic disabilities and assert their democratic rights as equal citizens through organized political activity. Though they are still segregated from the higher castes, often in their own settlements, and are debarred from many areas of social and ritual life, they remain in close interdependence with them. They are courted by all the political parties as valuable mascots, as vote-banks, and as proof that welfare ideology is more than mere propaganda. Successful as the Harijans have been, however, in making their voice heard, they remain economically dependent on the higher castes and are therefore not in a strong position to press far with their demands for legal equality. Disputes easily lead to violence, in which the Harijans are almost invariably the losers. The greatest source of hope to the Harijans is modern education which acts as a solvent of caste barriers.

The question of change among the Scheduled Tribes is complicated by detribalization. Throughout the developing world, socio-economically backward or underprivileged tribes are caught up in the process of unified nation-building. Change in the economic pattern of a tribe invariably threatens its integral culture with total destruction. This is certainly the case in India where, as we have seen, the unique and admirable qualities of the tribes survive under considerable duress. This tribal culture has been in a precarious state for at least a century. Unequal regional development, dispossession of tribal land, disruption of the forest ecology, acculturation through contact with the castes and urban industrialization, have all rendered the preservation of integral tribal *culture* unfeasible (though not tribal *identity*, as we shall soon see). The progressive élite took its lead from Nehru in seeking ways to rescue the tribes from their economic plight, while salvaging the very qualities which their integrated way of life had fostered. This protectionist policy led to tribal isolation, which has been dubbed the 'anthropological zoo' by its critics. Whatever measures were taken to protect the tribes from exploitation were in one sense bound to be of no more than short-term value, for the pressures inherent in their position made the tribes aware of the need for some form of change. Many, in fact, have been progressively integrated into the caste system through sheer economic necessity. The very fact that a significant number of tribes have been Sanskritized, while others have been converted to Christianity during the last hundred years, is indication of their dissatisfaction with their status within the encircling social system.

With the introduction of adult franchise, interest in Sanskritization has declined for the same reasons as in the case of the Scheduled Castes. Even when tribal society breaks down, industrialization does not lead to loss of tribal identity or loyalty. It is likely, therefore, that industrialized tribes (as distinct from agricultural tribes) will not become castes, and will preserve some of their durable individual values, if not their crafts, poetry, and dancing. The political leadership of the tribes is now more concerned with improvement in living conditions than with questions of ritual and social status. The tribal languages are already giving way to those spoken by the dominant communities. The policy of isolation and cultural conservation is steadily on the wane wherever politicization has been strong. But in areas newly opened up by development of heavy industry, mining, and mechanized agriculture, such as the Dandakaranya project, where 30,000 square miles of tribal forest land are being intensively developed, there are signs that the influx of outsiders into the forest seclusion of the tribes may still result in the slow and regrettable process of alienation, exploitation, and displacement which marred the previous century with confusion between unplanned detribalization and uneven (though frequently enlightened) government welfare programmes. The social attitude towards the tribes continues, in these areas, to be one of paternalism, condescension, and contempt. In spite of the fact that these are intensive development areas, the gap between the economic standards of the tribals and the rest is unfortunately increasing.

On the positive side, however, there is the undeniably hopeful and interesting prospect of large numbers of tribal workers bringing to the new industrial settlements an attitude of robust self-confidence and exuberance, perhaps an aesthetic sensibility too, which had long been ground out of their counterparts in the lower castes. These thirty million members of the Scheduled Tribes could well play a role of incalculable importance in the future development of the nation. It is the opinion of Professor von Fürer-Haimendorf that they will for a long time to come form a separate and unassimilated element within the Indian nation. But if they can display the same verve, solidarity, and endurance in securing a position in the expanding world of individual enterprise as they did in preserving their integrity for so many centuries, they will no doubt contribute to the cultural enrichment of India.

Co-existence of two institutional systems

To understand the process of Westernization in India it is important to distinguish two phases in its evolution: the colonial and the nationalist, the latter having continued in the post-Independence period. Custom accorded the European colonial invaders a status in keeping with their superior military power. In the days of the 'nabobs', soldiers, merchant adventurers, and administrators showed a willingness to acquiesce in the familiar process of acculturation and assimilation, as had every invader before them; but for a variety of reasons, one of them undoubtedly white racism, this was not to be so with the European colonizers. The British remained foreigners, completely detached from the holistic social order, and, in turn, excluded from the Hindu socio-religious hierarchy. But the British policy of recruitment to the administrative system, and the instinct to adopt the ways of those who are vested with power, resulted in the Westernization of the Indian middle and upper classes. This involved the adoption of Western elements in dress, manners, habits, customs, education, and the use of the English language at work and on social occasions. Westernization soon led to the adoption of Western values and was not limited to mere imitation. Since it involves changes in customs of a fairly radical nature from the viewpoint of the caste, including the breaching of pollution, dietary, and ritual rules, effective Westernization would place the individual or family outside the caste; but open rupture and formal out-casting, once common, are now on the decline. While British rule lasted, Westernization was confined to a comparatively restricted group; among the classes who were not Westernized were nationalists and intellectuals who resisted it out of pride and patriotism.

After India gained its independence, economic development, education, and democratization were accelerated. At the same time, the process of Westernization has also accelerated, as indeed it has done almost every-where in the non-Western world. This phenomenon is primarily the result of technological innovation—is actually determined by it, for technology is 'Western'. A comparable interaction of technology on rural societies has occurred in the West itself, where the industrial revolution has invariably imposed a higher degree of uniformity in the way of life of those affected by it. It follows that Westernization, sooner or later, of course, encounters resistance from traditional elements.

From the viewpoint of the traditional society, Westernization is an extension of Kshatrya-ization, following the same pattern as the assimilation of the Muslim convert—theoretically low on the scale of ritual status, due to customs regarded as pollution-prone, empirically high due to association with political power. Indeed, it is not difficult to see that Kshatrya-ization often proved more popular than Sanskritization, since the ascetic ideals of the Brahman are less attractive to the popular imagination than the econ-omic privileges and hedonistic-sensual enjoyment of the former. The status of the Westernized Indian has occasionally been compared with that of the Renouncer, in so far as the Renouncer himself partly owes his status to his individuality, and renunciation of caste ties; there the comparison ends, for while both enjoy a special status by reason of *power*, one is religious power and the other secular.

There is a marked difference in the life-styles of the pre-Independence and post-Independence Westernized classes. The former, who are sometimes known as the 'Anglicized' or, more condescendingly, 'Indo-Anglian', modelled themselves on the British Establishment and public-school type. The latter have been called the 'modernizing élite', while a useful distinction can be made between the 'modernizing élite' and a 'modernistic élite':

> To the extent that an elite has acquired merely the symbols and styles of life, or even the skills of high status groups in more advanced societies, it is modernistic. It becomes modernising only when it succeeds in utilising these skills in a socially significant way, without attaching too much importance to styles of life which may have been historically associated with groups in which such skills originated.[1]

Of special significance in this context has been the creation of a sovereign, independent Indian State on a secular basis, where modern institutions and office-holders are Indian, no matter what their cultural style of life may be, and no matter what the historical origin of those institutions may be. This is where the second phase of Westernization begins to operate; it is more accurate to refer to this later phase as modernization.

How effective is the modernizing élite in transforming the traditional society? The status and office of the newly elected representatives, legitimized by the constitution, can only be exercised through a mandate from society, namely adult franchise. While society as a whole has sanctioned the new institutional framework irrespective of caste and creed, the new institutions take no account of caste. Nor is this merely a legal question; the traditional hierarchy has lost all empirical and theoretical support within the new political system. What remains of the old holistic moral order (*dharma*) has lost its institutional anchorage in the two hereditary offices of Brahman and Kshatrya. Blackstone's maxim that 'the King never dies' cannot apply, for neither the secular state nor the modernizing élite can arrogate to themselves the power of the king or the dyarchy of King and Priest. Yet the old caste system continues to operate and, as we have seen, to influence political life. Examination of this striking anomaly is rarely carried further than to speculate on the improbability of the caste system's survival. The fact that caste divisions *have* survived and will probably continue to exist for a long time to come through the institutionalized

---

[1] André Béteille, 'Elites, Status Groups, and Castes in Modern India', in *India and Ceylon: Unity and Diversity*, ed. P. Mason, London, 1967, p. 242.

solidarity of prosperous caste associations, makes it imperative to assess the significance of two incompatible, but co-existing institutional systems.

As in religious allegiance, loyalty to one's caste is morally binding, but has no legal substance. There is no longer any power on earth with the authority to ensure adherence to the castes; there is only the voluntary desire of the castes to do so, sustained by the practical advantages gained from belonging to a caste association. This is the reason why interdependence has largely been replaced by competition, and therefore, while the castes may each be internally regulated by voluntarist rules, the caste system as a whole has lost its *moral* cohesion. This follows from the political situation; the caste system is 'unadministered'. Viewed in the perspective of the newly established nation-society, the caste system survives outside the jural framework of the social order; it has been relegated to a quasi-anarchical plane and, I would suggest, in the course of time it will sink into the irrational substratum, the Social Antipodes. Like tribal organization, caste institutions are obsolete from the point of view of the modern political entity of the Indian State. This does not mean that they will dissolve in the space of a few decades; on the contrary, they are likely to endure in the same way as the tribes have.

There are a number of reasons for drawing this conclusion. As has already been shown, traditional Indian culture reveals a need for co-existence between a social order subject to repressive regulation and an antipodal society, the unstructured and potent disorder of which is harnessed to positive ends within the structured order. This arises from a fundamental human instinct, the regressive but creative reparation of libidinal freedom— a safety mechanism of a society organized through its division into constituent elements (earlier references to conflict theory apply here). Now that India has established a form of democratic political institutions which accords equal status before the law to every ethnic, religious, or cultural group, the irrational substratum might be expected to have lost its *raison d'être*. However, the ascendancy of the new political system over the social order has not taken place solely through its imposition from above. As we have seen earlier, a universalistic movement from below interacted with an imposed system, and the emergent synthesis is the sovereign secular state; secularization, therefore, is not wholly divorced from the socio-religious framework, and, conversely, these links with the old order are not in opposition to the universalistic-secularist society. The survival of a fragmented caste institutionalization merely indicates a practical need of the reorganized secular society for voluntarist grouping in caste associations founded on strict endogamous rules, and with the power to protect the interests of its members against the much harsher competitive climate of a modern national economy. One may see this movement either as the transitional stage in the emergence of effective secularization, or as a reflection of the weakness of the secular aspects of the political system. In the course of time, with the spread of secularization either as a result of more effective secular–political action or of the intrinsically secular demands of a modern economy, the potent sentiments of caste solidarity will assume an irrational, antipodal character in relation to the political institutions. Indeed this has already happened in certain spheres of political life. It seems reasonable to deduce (by way of paraphrasing a remark of Kosambi's already quoted with regard to the continued existence of tribes) that the future course of Indian history will show caste elements being fused into a general society. This is not to say that the castes will disappear, any more than have the tribes, but that castes are likely to remain an empirical part of the total pluralistic society. There is more than a mere technical curiosity in the deduction, for it indicates continuity of pluralism even within the framework of the unified nation-state, not the establishment of a monolithic state, a common assumption rooted in nineteenth-century romantic nationalism. It also suggests that India is likely to remain subject to the threat of constant political instability.

In an important study, *The Modernity of Tradition*, Professors L. I. and S. H. Rudolph advance the following thesis on caste associations:

> In its transformed state, caste has helped India's peasant society make a success of representative democracy and fostered the growth of equality by making Indians less separate and more alike.[1]

They present an impressive array of data to indicate how extensive is the proliferation of district and regional caste associations. They then go on to claim that these pressure groups are active and highly successful instruments for achieving egalitarian change; but their data do not support any such contention. Caste associations may secure rearrangements in the ascriptive hierarchy, and they may eventually contribute to the growth of equality, but they have never yet challenged the basic premises on which hierarchical caste status and caste endogamy are founded. The Rudolphs characterize these quasi-legalistic natural associations and parochial structures as already integrated into the nation's political system, and as promoting the latter's stability and legitimacy, thereby permitting the States and Centre to mobilize mass support for *national* integration and socio-economic development. It is possible that the integration of traditional structures into the nation's political system will, by preserving a degree of organic continuity, eventually reinforce the democratic process, and will, as the Rudolphs anticipate, emerge as the Indian counterpart of the ethnic, racial, and religious organizations that survive in modern Western democracies.

[1] Rudolph and Rudolph (1967), p. 11.

However, at the time of writing, the most successful caste associations are those which represent the vested interests of the propertied castes, but still within a *local* or *regional*, rather than a national, context. Their success is limited to obtaining preferential treatment in the award of licences, contracts, and loans, or in advancing the claims to patronage of innumerable factions. In the immediate future it is unlikely that hierarchical mobilization will achieve anything more positive than the exacerbation of local rivalries and the undermining of national integration by forcing from the Government concession after concession to parochial pressures. If and when the politicization of low-caste associations leads to the mobilization of the rural and urban masses, only then is there a likelihood of true participatory democracy being achieved through the modernization (as distinct from the destruction) of traditional caste institutions. One doubts, however, whether such mobilization would proceed on similar lines to that already achieved by the caste associations of the middle and higher castes. It appears more likely that the modernization of the political system itself will, by then, have accelerated, relegating both the caste and the caste association to the undemarcated region of the social Antipodes. If the society's repressive attitude towards the Antipodes were, in effect, extended so as to exclude even caste associations from participation in the democratic process, the eventual opposition of the Antipodes would assume the character of an elementary force ready to violate every rule of the society's game.

Problems of the economy are beyond the scope of this study, but the broader trends in economic development are relevant in so far as they reveal structural changes in the society. It would be natural to expect that enhanced economic activity would work towards the formation of a unified secular institutional system. But actually, the pattern of India's economic development has accentuated this co-existence of two institutional systems; in the Westernized sector of the urban areas, for instance, it is industry, the market economy, and the work patterns which these impose, that have determined the changes in the value systems, family organization, and style of life of the affected urban classes. But as far as the traditional sector in the cities is concerned, the modern world (or such of it as they see) does not present an attractive model, nor is it of obvious superiority to the traditional purposes of life and society. The traditional sector is frequently sickened by the crass materialism and imposition of changes in the means of production. Thus the pace of development in the Westernized fringe economy has been retarded by its apparent incompatibility with the age-old value systems and work patterns. However, this is mainly due to the failure of the planners to take into consideration the needs and the customs of the traditional society. While the Sanskritic culture and value systems of the higher castes are resistant, the type of innovation which is relevant to the everyday needs of the peasants is readily accepted. Indeed the farmers have proved themselves not only receptive to improved techniques, but have also adopted them much faster than the bureaucracy had anticipated. But as new ideas for development projects spread from the Westernized urban sector to the traditional rural sector, much more attention is paid to the anticipated resistance or lack of skills of the rural labour force than to their anxiety to increase production through improved methods. What has so far largely been ignored is the need to apply the most highly sophisticated and inventive of engineering skills to devising an 'intermediate technology', which would be more within the reach and work patterns of the rural labour force, and which would ameliorate the lot of the lower caste groups through increased agricultural productivity. Of special significance in this context is the fact that since technological innovation and change in the means of agricultural production, particularly when backed by agrarian reform, lead to change in the social hierarchy of the village community, there is active resistance on the part of peasant proprietors as soon as their ascendancy over the agricultural labourer is threatened. Unless greater attention is paid to the landless agricultural labour force, enhanced economic activity in the agricultural sector cannot be effective in bringing about a unified institutional system in the rural areas. As we have seen, it is the proprietors who have generally been favoured by government development programmes, while the economic status of the lower and Scheduled Castes have not improved.

On the other hand, the mass migration from the rural areas to the cities of the unemployed, mostly unskilled, has led to the appalling and all too familiar problem of alienated workers living in a state of destitution and degradation in the swarming 'bastis' on the outskirts of urban industrial belts. These shanty towns often grow at a rate ten times that of the cities themselves. The rate of urbanization does not correspond to the rate of industrialization, as the exodus from rural areas is not prompted by job opportunities so much as by the deceptive promise of a more attractive way of life. This situation has resulted in a genuine crisis of identity among the disaffected. The questions for such unfortunates who, due to their lack of skills and as a result of the still limited pace of industrialization, cannot be absorbed by the modern economy (they number many millions), is to whom or to what are they to offer their loyalty, on whom to model the self, which pattern of behaviour to adopt or adjust to. It is feared by some economists that the rush for modernization financed through foreign aid has actually intensified the exodus from the country to the urban centres, and that increases in national income are eaten up by the crushing burdens produced by this cancerous form of suburban growth, the consequences of which are pockets of affluence surrounded by much larger slum areas of human misery. This is a relatively recent phenomenon in Indian history.

India was without unified, popularly elected municipal governments, charters of liberty, or the concept of a 'citizenry' until a hundred and fifty years ago. Nevertheless, it is well known that the largest towns and cities (Calcutta is a notorious example) have developed at a frightening pace, acquiring all the universal features and institutions of modern urbanism, while the majority of the population continue to live under archaic conditions. The city of Bombay, for example, has a raw, relentless pace and competitiveness which makes life in most Western European cities, with their long history, seem mellow and tranquil by comparison. The Friday rush-hour traffic carrying middle-class Bombay families out to the suburbs and the country, serves to remind one that the weekend jaunt, symbol of the ex-urbanite commuter, has reached India, when the mass of the population still live in Neolithic huts.

In an underdeveloped country like India, fighting for economic survival against the threat of chronic insolvency and intolerable population pressure, there is the ever-present danger of disrupting national stability through unequal rates of economic development in the different areas of the country and possibly within the same area; even within the framework of a planned economy there is the temptation to favour those sectors likely to produce the quickest results to the neglect of the fundamental problems which affect the whole society. It was Gandhi who first identified the inherent dangers in such a process of unequal development pockets; but his solution—cottage industries and handicraft-oriented 'basic education'—are no longer economically feasible in the worsening situation of the population explosion. The solutions which have been proposed, and partly implemented, are well known. They fall under three headings: a concerted drive for education; the introduction of intermediate technology; and the gradual industrialization of the 'mixed economy'. These would help towards the voluntary transformation of a village society into a modern economic structure. It is the pace of this transformation which is now in question—whether these measures will lead to the accelerated economic development India must sustain if it is to keep one step ahead of population increase.

Changes in the social order linked with economic development may be considered from two different angles: the capacity of the society to adopt improved methods of production and the effects on the dual institutional system of a modernized economy. It is clearly proved by the considerable density of industrial expansion in the urban areas and regions selected for intensive industrial development (the latter sector includes mines, fertilizer factories, hydro-electric projects, and steel plants) that the caste system does not act as a deterrent to economic activity of the kind which India has so far developed. Whether an integral, all-India, indigenously generated, and self-sustaining industrial economy would be adversely affected by the caste mentality is a question we are not yet in a position to answer, as such complete industrialization is still a remote goal.

As for the impact of enhanced economic activity on the caste system, the prospect is not as encouraging. The type of economic activity, improved methods of production, and industrialization in urban areas do to some extent allow for social mobility, and the exodus from the rural areas to the cities may give the impression that enhanced economic activity undermines the cohesion of the caste system; nevertheless, the historical development of India has shown that geographical mobility has not dissolved the divisions between castes. Therefore, in the economic sector, just as in the political sector, caste factors continue to play a decisive role in allocation of jobs, promotion, and rewards. On the other hand, enhanced economic opportunities in both the industrial and services sectors offer better outlets to enterprising and educated individuals than in any previous age. While these individuals are accepted in society as a result of their accumulated wealth and have played an important role in civic life, they do not yet form *classes*, as their equivalents do in the West.

One point remains to be examined: the motivational drive for social reform which is essential for sustaining economic development on a nation-wide basis; in other words, the capacity of the society to re-examine and transform its values, attitudes, and emotive idealism to allow for greater social mobility and equity. So far, the pattern of economic development in India has shown that, when divorced from corresponding social reforms, economic prosperity benefits the already favoured sectors of the population. The gap between the affluent minority and the disadvantaged masses, as well as between the traditional and modern sectors, is widened. To describe this situation as a common occurrence in developing countries is to evade the main issue of a national imperative to work towards social and economic development of the country as a whole. Efforts in this direction can, in the main, come from two sources: a popular movement of reform, or a dynamic centrally-oriented programme of social action.

With regard to the first of these possibilities, the nature of a social reform movement in the Indian context poses serious problems. In quite a few developing nations, the society practises a single religion with a unified ethic, and this acts as a co-ordinating framework for evolving values, subject to the normal interaction between it and the socio-economic situation. Even in the absence of strongly developed secular ideologies, social and religious reformers have a comparatively straightforward problem if they seek to activate and mobilize from inside those elements of the traditional religious ethic that could sustain the modernizing process. But the pluralistic Indian religious structure and absence of a universal ethic greatly intensify the problem of mobilizing the motivational forces embedded in the cultural religious matrix. True, the presence of conflicting religious systems, philosophies, and world-views has facilitated the emergence of secularism in the absence of a unified religious system cohesive enough to have offered resistance; but beyond a certain point, the malleability of the value-complex constitutes an obstacle to further unification and prevents emotional commitment to a secular ideology. Secularism as a national policy is too remote from the religious world-views of the majority in every Indian community to constitute an urgent and meaningful appeal. The sole workable universal social ethic in India under modern conditions is an emergent phenomenon of very recent origin, subscribed to by no more than a small minority. Admirable as are the motives and ideals which inspire the secular institutional system—the vast majority of the population approves of them *in principle*—to engage the nation in any deep involvement with such ideals is an exceedingly slow process. In the first place, it can only be done in the vaguest ideological terms which command no more than lukewarm interest; in the second, it is but a poor rival to the only alternative source of appeal, one which is made every day by countless demagogues in every corner of the land: blatant self-interest of the group for immediate material gains, regardless of whether or not this is in the interests of the nation as a whole.

Certainly there exists a universal code of ethics within the Hindu *dharma* scheme, or its equivalent in every other Indian religion, which is in no way inimical to the abolition of poverty, ignorance, and indignity. But in the foreseeable future, appeals to even the worthiest humanitarian causes in the name of a major Indian religion will be fraught with danger, as can be seen from the virulence of communalism. So long as there are at least five major religious communities in India, to mobilize religious energies is to court disaster. Such an appeal can only be accomplished at the expense of alienating the sensibilities of enormous numbers of the population; it also constitutes a violation of civil rights, may court open secession, and, invariably, provokes bloodshed. There is a very acute dilemma here, one which the greatest religious reformer of the twentieth century, Gandhi himself, was unable to solve.

However, the hold that religion has over the people, and the suppression of class-conflict by the organization of society into castes, do not inevitably rule out the emergence of a secular ideology. There is undoubtedly a recognition of the need for change, and people expect the nation's leaders to give direction to, and facilitate, change. When they do not get it, those groups which are sufficiently organized express their frustration through agitation and pressure, often based on communalistic associations, but not through the classic pattern of class struggle. Aspiration to a better way of life in itself constitutes a cardinal factor of change and this hopeful sign should not be ignored.

Of special significance in this regard is the role of education as an agent for promoting attitudes favourable to the acceptance of a secular ideology. This calls for a drastic revision of the educational system, which, on the one hand, would correspond more closely than hitherto to the national cultural context, and on the other, would supply the directive towards a unifying national ethos in which the needs of social and economic development would be reflected. Such a new educational approach, whether in school or for orienting the adult population, can only emerge from a true understanding of the interaction between traditional attitudes and the needs of a modern society. For this reason an examination of the attitudes and value systems of the traditional society, and the possibility of constructive opposition between them and the transitional, modernizing society of today, will be undertaken in the closing parts of this study. The focus will first be directed on basic modes of traditional thinking, later on ethics and the influence of ethical systems on political affairs, and finally on those figures whom society has vested with sacred authority. While many of the ideas and values to be analysed reflect the archaic character of the society at the time when they were first formulated, it will be shown that they have continued to exert a lively influence on attitudes even in modern times. It will also be shown that the specific nature of these ideas, when pitted against a more contemporary way of thinking, can lead to unpredictable results—the more so when the unforeseeable human element, the exceptional personality, takes a hand. Who, for example could ever have foreseen the emergence of so unique and curious a man, in the context of the twentieth century, as Gandhi? Unexpected results can only be accounted for after they have resulted. Indian thought in its full vigour is full of instances where someone recognized that unpredictable events disprove the inevitability of gradualism. This was the first secret of Indian thought to be lost. It is also the first in most urgent need of rediscovery.

Part Four Value Systems and
Attitudes

Introduction

Part Four is not an academic survey of Indian thought; its purpose is to conduct a strictly functional analysis of value systems and attitudes. An explanation of basic concepts will also be included. These concepts, though abstract, are relevant to everyday life, both religious and secular—and are of considerable importance in the elucidation of unconscious attitudes. In order to understand them, however, one has to trace their origins in the past. Although our sources will be the chief schools of classical thought and the most important ancient texts, it should be pointed out that the traditional ideas which enjoy the widest currency, though formulated with the greatest subtlety in literary form, normally reach a vast audience in more popular form. From childhood the Indian absorbs, both aurally and through reading, movies, or other media, a diversity of sayings, proverbs, tales, verses, and songs which distil the principal ideas of the greatest Indian thinkers.

In so vast a field compression is essential; this, however, is not easy, as Indian systems of thought—of which there are many—do not usually lend themselves to Western-type logical analysis, and there is no reason why we should expect them to do so. On the other hand, an aesthetically orientated civilization such as India's has evolved a highly sophisticated logic of symbols, a language of metaphor with its own form of inner consistency. The great French authority on Indo-European culture, Georges Dumézil, characterizes the specific qualities which may be identified in the archaic type of thought with which we will be dealing:

However primitive he may be, man from the moment he thinks at all thinks in systems; certainly he contradicts himself . . . but still it is systems which are contradictory. . . . The religious system of a group expresses itself at the same time on several levels; first of all in a conceptual structure more or less explicit, sometimes almost unconscious but always present, which is, as it were, the field within which all else is disposed and oriented; next in myths which figure forth and enact these fundamental conceptual relations; next in rites which actualise, mobilise and use these same relations; finally often in a social organisation, a distribution of occupations, or in a sacerdotal body which administers these concepts, myths and rites.[1]

[1] G. Dumézil, *Trial of Mitra-Varuna*, Paris, 1948, p. 38. Translated and quoted in *Contributions to Indian Sociology*, II, p. 63.

This Part will begin with an analysis of Indian modalities of thought which form the basis of enduring attitudes. The second chapter explores those ethical and political ideas which continue to influence the method of approach to current problems. Although for the purposes of analysis the themes of the two chapters must be kept distinct from each other, they are integrally related. The common conceptual basis of thought and ethics may be described as aesthetic in orientation, with a deep retrospective faith in the undifferentiated unity of Origins. While there are grandeur and profundity in this unified sensibility, it will become apparent that it does not sufficiently take into account the complexity of empirical reality. It should be pointed out that the first chapter of Part Four marks the axis round which the general argument of the latter half of this study revolves. In it will be found the germs of several ideas which will be successively examined from a number of different angles until, in the Conclusion, their prospect for survival in the future, and the possible role which they may play in shaping it, will be the final theme of this book.

Chapter One Indian Thought

Three elements of continuity

In this chapter several important features of Indian thought will be analysed which have demonstrated their 'survival value' over a very long stretch of time. The fact that they originate in remote antiquity, when the society was still organized on a relatively primitive basis, is often, and mistakenly, regarded by progressive Indians as a cause for shame. Today, there are no grounds to give rise to such reservations because, as any scientist or physicist knows, the most advanced and sophisticated ideas of the twentieth century are often analogous to those which are the product of non-literate unified sensibility. This does not mean that the concepts to be analysed here are of the same order as those to be found in Heisenberg, for example. They *are* archaic, but we have come to respect them as the products of an impressively penetrating insight. Among the most important to be examined will be Sanskrit phonology, non-sequential logic, the theory of constant change and perpetual motion, and the cyclical time concept. Without prior knowledge of these traditional thought-patterns the attitudes of the modern Indian would be almost impossible to understand.

The outstanding characteristic of primitive society is its sense of the unity of all life, the sense of solidarity and emotional sympathy with the various levels of nature. For this reason primitive man conceived the idea of *co-operation* with nature and its sacred powers by means of propitiatory sacrifice. The Vedic Aryans organized such a society, and evolved a sacrificial religion at the level of magic. At this early stage of Indian culture the relation between sacrificial lore, myth, and language was so close that it is now almost impossible to separate one from the other. It was so totally an *oral* culture that the Vedic Aryans believed that a deity could be compelled by utterance of the correct verbal formula to do exactly what the worshipper desired. Here we have our first example of a primitive trait—the magical power of the word—which has at no stage in the cultural evolution of India been wholly abandoned. Many such examples will be cited. From this belief in the magical efficacy of a formula is derived an extremely widespread and persistent Indian conviction in the mechanical *efficiency* of spirituality, rites, or mystical exercises: providing the right formula is applied at the right time and with the right pronunciation, it is bound to succeed. The first and most basic trait in the continuity of Indian thought may therefore be summarized as the absolute authority of the Word as a universal metaphysical principle.

The next element of continuity is to be located in the concept of the 'flux of all things', an idea which India shares with Heraclitus, but which, unlike the subsequent evolution of Western thought, has maintained its position among the fundamental concepts of Indian thought. To cite Jane Harrison writing on Greek religion (the word 'Hindu' will be inserted twice for our purposes to replace 'Olympian'):

> our minds are imbued with classical [Hindu] mythology, our imagination peopled with the vivid personalities, the clear-cut outlines of [Hindu] gods; it is only by a severe mental effort that we realise that *there were no gods at all*, but only conceptions of the human mind, shifting and changing colour with every human mind that conceived them. Art which makes the image, literature which crystallises attributes and functions, arrest and fix this shifting kaleidoscope; but until the coming of art and literature and to some extent after, the formulary of theology is 'all things are in flux'.[1]

There is one crucial difference between the evolution of Hindu and Greek religions: the idea of flux never disappears in Hindu mythology, even when literary art is interposed between the reader (or listener) and the apprehension of continuous transience. The goal of knowledge is to pierce the veil of appearances and perceive the flux of *continuous creation* and dissolution wherein the plurality of gods, all variety of name and form participate. We have here a second example of a primitive trait preserved. Even after the introduction of a phonetic alphabet and the consolidation of literate castes at the apex of the social order, oral culture maintained its prestige. It is virtually an axiom of Indian culture that the oldest is best, on the analogy of Heidegger's maxim: great things begin great. The magic power of the Word and the idea of flux, as we shall see, conform to the archaic pattern of retrospective faith in the potency of things as they were 'in the beginning'.

The third basic and continuous element may be described as *hylozoistic*: the primitive tendency to draw no clear distinction between matter, life, and mind. This monistic conception is a common feature of thought at the tribal stage of social organization. We have already encountered this idea in the theory of the three *gunas* (*rajas*, *sattva*, and *tamas*), the common stuff of which both mind and matter are composed, which originated in one of the most characteristic of Indian philosophical systems—Sāṃkhya. Both pre-Socratic Greek thought and Indian thought started from the assumption that without an identity between the knowing subject and the reality

---

[1] Jane Harrison, *Prolegomena to the Study of Greek Religion*, Cambridge, 1922, p. 164.

known, the fact of knowledge would be unaccountable. According to Parmenides, being and thought are one and the same. According to Indian thought, subject and object, thesis and antithesis, are not opposed to one another, but constitute two aspects of the same thing. All differentiation springs from the *coincidentia oppositorum* of a unitary Absolute. It is Heraclitus who provides us with a clue to the origin of this identity of opposites: 'Don't listen to me, but to the Word, and confess that all things are one.' Aristotle considered Heraclitus to have belonged to the 'ancient physiologists', for whom the faculty of speech still occupied a central position between physical phenomena invested with the power of magic and pure semantic function. In India the Word was never valorized in the same way as the *Logos* of Heraclitus. It preserved its magic power even after the analysis of the structural problems of Sanskrit phonology were brought to an almost unparalleled degree of perfection by the scientific grammarian Pāṇini (*c.* 350–250 B.C.). Thus we find an Indian philosophy of language co-existing side by side with a more archaic philosophy of nature.

But one should be wary of ascribing hylozoistic thought to some form of 'pre-logical irrationalism', as do the evolutionists. Under primitive, pre-technological conditions man is in an especially favourable position in relation to nature; as a microcosmic organism he sees himself as an exact counterpart of the macrocosm—Nature. For this reason he obtains knowledge of the latter in a direct way: by immediate sensory awareness. The authenticity of intuitive knowledge of this sort is less under question today than it was for several centuries immediately after Galileo banished colour and sound, heat, odour, and taste from the realm of physics to that of subjective illusion. But to assume a 'non-rational' source for certain kinds of knowledge is to imply that this kind of thinking is somehow inferior to 'rationality' itself. A logic of symbols such as India's proceeds not only on assumptions but on modes of perception which happen to have been suppressed in Western thinking for many centuries through specialization in a certain kind of consciousness. There is nothing 'mystical' or 'uncanny' in this kind of thought if one uses the word 'mystical' in the sense which Santayana gives it: the most *natural* mode of thinking. The nature philosophers of ancient Greece and India understood and interpreted the identity of being and thought in a strictly material sense. The Hindu was not content to leave it at that; each successive school of philosophy, each mystic, sage, or saint, sought by one means or another to appropriate the external world to the mind-brain. He enhanced, expanded, intensified, and deepened his sensory awareness of colours, sounds, and textures until they were transformed into vibrations continuous with his own consciousness. In this state of enhanced consciousness induced by special techniques of concentration, the inside and the outside, the subject and the object, the self and the world, did not remain separate entities but fused in a single process. Alan Watts has analysed descriptions of perceptual modification and alteration of the nervous system by yoga (fasting, sense deprivation, hyper-oxygenation) and concludes that the closest analogy to hylozoistic thought would be the scientist's description of ecological relationship. The scientist sees the behaviour of the environment and the behaviour of the organism as a single *unified* field.

Very early in Indian history the Brahmans developed a form of purely connotational semantic adapted to the explication of this logical 'beyond' —the ineffable domain which, in a modern context, Wittgenstein was content to call the 'unspeakable'. In fact, man frequently seeks the aid of music to express the 'unspeakable'. The Brahmans, as we will soon see, devised a system of musical incantation uniting the laws of phonetics and the physiology of sound waves. The oral culture of the Vedic period was uniquely suited to the expression of inspired knowledge which accorded with the three basic concepts identified above: magic power of the Word; the flux of all things; identity between the knowing subject and the reality known.

The Word

The resilience of oral Brahman culture may be judged from the fact that the four Vedas took roughly a thousand years to compose and *were not written down* until centuries after their composition. The White Yajur Veda alone consists of 3,000 quarto pages of printed Sanskrit text. Until the invention of the phonetic Sanskrit alphabet, memorization of the Vedas by Brahmans was the sole means to ensure their transmission. The Brahman names Trivedi and Chaturvedi signify that some ancestor of the family once memorized three or four Vedas respectively. The Brahmans, who ascribed their own origin to the mouth of the Primordial Man (Puruśa), are the custodians of the sacred Sound—personified as the all-powerful goddess Vāc—through the magical potency of the holy language of Sanskrit and the holy scriptures of the Veda. The distinguished Sanskrit scholar, W. Norman Brown, explains why the mouth, as the organ of speech, endowed the Brahman with special power:

For sound has in itself a metaphysical power. The hymns of the R̥g *Veda* as recited by the trained priest have such power because they consist of the right sounds in the right combinations (words—and, of course, these are Sanskrit words) uttered in the right sequence and with the right intonation; and when they are so recited and accompanied by the right manual acts, they are irresistible. They are sure to accomplish the reciter's purpose. Demons and gods are subject to their power.[1]

We live in a world from which the magic power of the word has been abstracted, and therefore we experience some difficulty in understanding how potent words and sounds are for so deeply and subtly oral a culture as that of Vedic India. The Brahmans succeeded in impressing upon the minds of every subsequent generation a need to study the influence of sound phenomena on human consciousness and physiology by orientating the perceptual centres towards the inner acoustic space of the unseen. The musicologist Alain Daniélou demonstrates the high degree of perfection obtained in the control of the human voice by Indian musicians when he states that they have the ability to produce and differentiate between minute intervals (exact to a *hundredth of a comma*, according to identical measurements recorded by Daniélou at monthly recording sessions). This Indian sensitivity to microtones is well known, though from a purely musicological point of view it is of no particular significance. Nevertheless, it is an indication of the care with which the 'culture of sound' is developed, for Hindus still believe that such precision in the *repetition* of exact intervals, over and over again, permits sounds to act upon the internal personality, transform sensibility, way of thinking, state of soul, and even moral character. In other words, the Hindu has never divorced the physical from the spiritual; these 'ancient physiologists' ascribed an ethical significance to physiological sensitivity. The aristocratic cult of *kalokagathia*, 'beautiful goodness', has never been abandoned in India, even if its metaphysic bears little resemblance to the *kalokagathia* of the ancient Greeks.

An integral aspect of this Vedic 'culture of sound' is the so-called 'science' *mantrashāstra*—systematic application of magic incantation in ritual. The Word is Brahman; the Word is Revelation, an icon of the Absolute, *mūrti* —a 'momentary deity'. Words, magical formulae, sacred verses—*mantra*— exist in relation to the divine as the *yantra* to the god; words are machines. The following lines by Śrī Aurobindo Ghosh summarize the significance of the Word to Hinduism. When the *mantra* falls on receptive ears, he says:

> Its message enters stirring the blind brain
> And keeps in the dim ignorant cells its sound;
> The hearer understands a form of words
> And, musing on the index thought it holds,
> He strives to read it with the labouring mind,
> But finds bright hints, not the embodied truth:

[1] W. Norman Brown, 'Class and Cultural Traditions in India', in Singer (ed.) (1959), p. 36.

Then, falling silent in himself to know
He meets the deeper listening of his soul:
The Word repeats itself in rhythmic strains:
Thought, vision, feeling, sense, the body's self
Are seized unalterably and he endures
An ecstasy and an immortal change;
He feels a Wideness and becomes a Power,
All knowledge rushes on him like a sea:
Transmuted by the white spiritual ray
He walks in naked heavens of joy and calm,
Sees the God-face and hears transcendent speech. . . .[1]

It is worth pointing out in passing that these lines, apart from explaining the concept of *mantrashāstra*, also encapsulate the Indian theory of poetics. Most, but by no means all, Indian poetry is sacred verse for incantation, repetition, 'circulation' in the mind, with or without the aid of music, until it produces the appropriate aesthetic *rasa*, or emotive resonance. While the poetry of the saints is not regarded as *śruti*, or revealed truth, as are Vedic verses, they aspire to a level of meaning-sound which is not far short of *mantra*, the word as 'momentary deity'.

The marriage of words to music, as of music to numbers by the Pythagoreans, constitutes one of the great philosophical preoccupations of ancient India. Words are the Vedic *yoga*: they unite mind and matter. Pure, ecstatic contemplation of phonetic sound reverberating on the ether in the sacred chant may be compared to the contemplation of geometrical forms and mathematical laws by the Pythagoreans. The Word is God, Number is God—both concepts result in a kind of intoxication. Only the Pythagorean Master can hear the music of the spheres: only the perfected Hindu sage can hear the primordial sound—*Nāda*. One system exalted numbers, and the other words; the vital difference is that since words are less pure and abstract than the content-free language of mathematics, they tend to confine the exercise of the mental faculties within subjective processes. Whereas, once numbers acquire a separate life and intensity, the reasoning faculty tends to develop along a different line, reducing all objects to numerical quantities.

True, Indians became great mathematicians, inventing the zero, the decimal system, and the sine function, but it was not numbers which became the key to both power and wisdom, as in Europe, but the Word. One consequence is the widespread tendency of Indians to use language as a form of incantation and exuberant rhetorical flourish on public occasions. Orators rend the air with verbose declamations more for the pleasure of the sound than for the ideas and facts they may more vaguely desire to express. The audience is swayed by the cadence of sound as by the music

[1] Śrī Aurobindo, *Savitri*, Pondicherry, 1954, p. 426.

of the classical singer, when the latter uses only phonetic syllables with no significance other than their intrinsic physiological capacity to soothe or exalt the listener.

According to Tobias Dantzig, the kinaesthetic sense of non-literate peoples is more developed than their number sense. One sees this in the Indian system of *tālas*, the rhythmical time-scale of classical music, which modern methods of analysis reveal to be of extreme mathematical complexity; in conception, however, the basis of the system is not conventional arithmetic but *pattern-recognition*. In the hands of a virtuoso the *tālas* are played at a speed so fast that the audience cannot possibly have time to *count* the intervals; due to the speed at which they are played, the *tālas* are registered in the brain as a cluster configuration, a complex Gestalt involving all the senses at once. While the structure of the *tālas* can be laboriously reduced to a mathematical sequence, the effect is subjective and emotional. This may be compared with the modern Gestalt approach to the teaching of mathematics by pattern-recognition, which is closely linked with the need for high-speed calculation. The audience at a recital of Indian classical music becomes physically engrossed by the agile patterns and counter-patterns, responding with unfailing and instinctive kinaesthetic accuracy to the terminal beat in each *tāla*. One is reminded of the Indian faculty to figure difficult compound interest calculations without the aid of pen, paper, or abacus. This kinaesthetic pattern-recognition is not unique to India; the children of East African herdsmen, for example, are taught to 'count' the herd at a glance rather than one by one. Similarly, Vedic hymns are recited by men who are often ignorant of their meaning; the sounds are themselves physiologically emotive, hallowed by usage. This kinaesthetic response is linked to another characteristic trait of the Indian mind which has already been mentioned: indifference to the logical procedure defined in Aristotle's law of the excluded middle. This is not to suggest that India is unconcerned with logic, but that it employs a different system of logic from that of the West. More precise analysis of this system need not concern us here, but Professor A. L. Basham summarizes one important feature as follows:

A correct inference was established by syllogism, of which the Indian form was somewhat more cumbrous than the Aristotelian. Its five members were known as proposition, reason, example, application, and conclusion. The classical Indian example may be paraphrased as follows:

1. There is fire on the mountain,
2. because there is smoke above it,
3. and where there is smoke there is fire, as, for instance, in a kitchen,
4. such is the case with the mountain,
5. and therefore there is fire on it.

The third term of the Indian syllogism corresponds to the major premiss of that of Aristotle, the second to Aristotle's minor premiss, and the first to his conclusion. Thus the Indian syllogism reversed the order of that of classical logic, the argument being stated in the first and second clauses, established by the general rule and example in the third, and finally clinched by the virtual repetition of the first two clauses.[1]

Basham also lists the chief fallacies recognized by the Indian logician: *reductio ad absurdum*, circular argument, infinite regression, dilemma, and *ignoratio elenchi*.

The Indian 'thinks', as Betty Heimann vividly describes, 'in a circle or a spiral of continuously developing potentialities, and not on the straight line of progressive stages. . . . Indian terms can overlap or mutually cover each other like the overgrowth of plants in the jungle . . . the Indian term grows, as it were, from inside, and expands in layers of petals.'[2] The most concrete evidence of this radial mode of thinking is to be found in linguistic structure.

Speech gives utterance to messages received from all our senses simultaneously. The highly sophisticated science of Sanskrit phonetics (on which nineteenth-century Western scholars modelled the modern science of language) permits the meaning of a sentence to be grasped immediately after the physiological reaction to its sound, but before sequential word-correct traduction. According to Daniel Ingalls, Brahman children learning Sanskrit 'will be given a Sanskrit inflectional form, say the form *vijigisavah* and told to construct it from the beginning. They then take the simple root, reduplicate for the desiderative, add the sigmatic suffix, retroflex it after the high vowel, append the participal suffix and so forth and so on. Often there are ten or twelve steps.'[3] The word-games of the Brahman grammar school are spiral in form, not linear; their consequence is the preservation of a 'unified field' awareness. While these prodigious mnemonic word-games are a normal part of the training of a specialist caste, it should be remembered that before the introduction of Western education *every* Indian child was born into the resonant world of sound. He learnt by looking and listening, and developed a hyper-receptivity to the dynamism of the auditory world.

Unified-field awareness, basic to Indian thinking, may be more clearly understood from Professor McLuhan's reference to that 'magical resonating world of simultaneous relations that is the oral and acoustic space'. 'There is nothing lineal or sequential', he writes, 'about the total field awareness that exists in any moment of consciousness. Consciousness is not a verbal

[1] A. L. Basham, *The Wonder that was India*, London, 1954, pp. 501–2.
[2] Heimann (1964).
[3] *The Brahman Tradition*, p. 4.

process. Yet during all our centuries of phonetic literacy we have favoured the chain of inference as the mark of logic and reason.'[1] Implicit in this statement is what Lévi-Strauss calls a 'science of the concrete', distinct from modern science articulated in abstract concepts and usually compartmentalized into specialist branches. This is applicable not only to archaic, tribal, and primitive non-literate societies (such as the nomadic Vedic Aryans) but also to those cultures whose thought-processes are not structured on a chain of reference. These types of speculative organization should not be considered as 'different stages of development of the human mind but rather . . . two strategic levels at which nature is accessible to scientific enquiry. . . .'[2] It is to the credit of McLuhan that he has drawn a connection between the 'strategy' of a certain kind of speculative organization and exploitation of the sensible world through auditory media. Given the physiology of the sensory apparatus, oral transmission of knowledge and of intuitions of the nature of reality will impose a non-linear structure on thought itself.

Perhaps the full implications of the preference for non-sequential logic to the development of Indian culture will become clearer if some of its cardinal traits, which have already been identified earlier in this study, are briefly reviewed. It has been shown in Part One, devoted to the aesthetic domain, how the cave sanctuaries and Sanskrit drama projected a resonating sensuous immediacy by a 'wrap-around' effect. In the next two Parts we saw how the pattern of child care, the joint-family system, and the multi-dimensional hierarchy (also in a sense wrap-around effects) preserve and dramatize the body's own awareness of itself, and the individual's unified awareness of himself as inextricably linked to a system (Plate 34). Now, common to all these facets is a visceral apprehension of reality as a non-sequential total field of awareness, of simultaneous relations. Time and change follow a cyclical, non-linear, eternally recurring pattern (Plate 48); it should be pointed out here that all Sanskrit terms for Time are primarily *spatial* concepts. The visualization of chronological sequences, McLuhan claims, is unknown to oral societies. But other factors contributed to the formulation of the cyclical concept, and these will be considered shortly. I would not go so far as McLuhan in claiming that the origin of these related phenomena is the ascendance of the spoken word; what I do suggest is that the mentality of Indian society was profoundly conditioned by the spoken word as the means of communication among a predominantly non-literate population. McLuhan has, in fact, assembled a wealth of data to support his important thesis that pre-print cultures do not *visualize* in the same way as literate societies with phonetic alphabets. While he may exaggerate the

[1] McLuhan, *Understanding Media: The Extensions of Man*, London, 1964, p. 95.
[2] Lévi-Strauss (1966), p.15.

effects of media on cultural content, he is surely justified in asserting that the change from multi-sensuous, simultaneous, and non-sequential awareness to linear, sequential awareness and logical inference, is one of the most momentous in the history of man.

In India, only the Brahmans and other high castes were literate, and their manuscript culture differs, again, in important respects from, say, those of Byzantine and Medieval Europe. All books were written on uniform strips of palm leaves, the limited space imposing its own form of literary style. Each strip contained a brief portion of the whole, a *sūtra* or a *śloka* for example, which could be read over and over again, memorized, and scanned rather as the Brahman child learnt the word-structure of Sanskrit—cyclically. This meditative form of learning was further emphasized by the habit of composing commentaries on each verse, word by word, so that each fragment of a text was encircled by speculation before proceeding to the next. A second commentator would comment on the first commentator, later a third, and so on; thus the reader arrived at the full meaning of a verse by a spiral course. To summarize: we have here a synchronic, rather than a diachronic attitude, a multi-dimensional way of thinking, of organizing, of experiencing. Indians were structuralists several thousand years before the boy Claude Lévi-Strauss lost all sense of time and became totally absorbed in tracing the labyrinthine geological strata of the Cévennes—before structuralist physics was developed with the aid of non-numerical, computerized pattern-recognition.

Unitary thought

The question of what is and what is not *Indian* philosophy, long a matter of controversy, becomes to some extent irrelevant in the light of the foregoing remarks. The important point is that India has used a logic of aesthetic forms and *thought* about the great problems of life for thousands of years. It is not surprising, therefore, that there exist innumerable 'contradictions' between one school of thought and another when these are judged by the standards of 'Western logic'. The religion of the Indian people is a composite of many sects and cults, which, unlike all the other major religions, is confined within the geographical limits of the Indian subcontinent and its emigrant communities. The Persian word 'Hindu', for instance, means 'Indian'. But Hinduism is not, strictly speaking, a national religion; it is a religious *system*, a way of life, and the basis of a social system. Neither the sects nor the schools of philosophy can be very precisely differentiated one from another, due to close mutual influence. Not even the famous Six Schools of philosophy are *schools* in the usual sense of the word; they are more like *styles* of thought expressed in the language of metaphor. Moreover a large proportion of the ancient texts were in the poetic form of the *sūtra*, a kind of aphorism. I am not concerned here to show the imagined superiority or inferiority of Indian thought—an approach which has bedevilled objective research for generations—but to identify its intrinsic function, which is aesthetic and symbolical.

Professor F. S. C. Northrop, who gives first place to the aesthetic in his analysis of Eastern thought, has said that India concentrated, 'as the West has not, upon a portion of the nature of things which can only be experienced. . . . Asia in general and India in particular have formulated a philosophy in terms of the *aesthetic component* of things, and the development of religions and other cultural forms in terms of such a philosophy. Western science has been concerned with the indirectly verified, unseen, theoretic component in things upon which the philosophy and culture of the West are based', distinct from the 'Oriental conception of the nature of things and of the nature of the divine as essentially immediate, passionate and aesthetic in character. . . . [in the East] they insist that no reality exists except that which is immediately apprehended.'[1] The aesthetic orientation of Indian thought is summed up in a Hindu saying which recognizes that 'aesthetic sentiment indeed is He, the Universal'. It is also implicit in the fact that the various philosophical systems are known as *darshanas*, revelation, from the root *dṛs*, 'to see',[2] and are traditionally taught by a method of patient inward meditation, verse by verse orally memorized. The Sanskrit term for philosophy is *anu-īkṣikī*, the 'survey of all things' or contemplation of reality by pattern-recognition.

According to the gradation into which the Indian classifies phenomena, the One is at the apex of the pyramid, the many are its base (Plate 41); union is hierarchically superior to division, the undifferentiated to the differentiated. *Avidyā*, ignorance, sees everything as separate, differentiated: *vidyā*, true knowledge, unitary knowledge, is 'the synoptic vision of the whole' (Heimann). Here we touch on the theme of inclusiveness and holism which has already been mentioned in this study a number of times. It must still be contrasted with a contrary trend towards a dualistic, rigorous, ascetic outlook as thorough in its application as any in the history of thought (compare Plates 34 and 36 with 35 and 37). If, for the sake of clarity, a comparison may be made with Western concepts, this refers to the relation of Matter and Mind; that is, man and Brahman, or empirical reality and transcendental reality. However, the major element in Indian thought may be characterized as a unitary, inclusive, concrete, and

[1] Northrop (1946).
[2] The word Veda is derived from the root *vid*, 'seeing', or vision—compare Plato's description of philosophers as Lovers of Spectacles.

affirmative outlook, intimately linked with the sense of magic power in the Word.

If the Word is one small fraction of Brahman, what is Brahman? Certainly it is not God, not Pure Spirit. What inchoate and molten *magma* is to our planet, so is Brahman the Great Inchoate to the phenomenal universe. Brahman is inexhaustible plenitude, the measureless reservoir, both emptiness and fullness (Plates 35 and 34 respectively), and more important still, both primeval Matter *and* Spirit, which in India are *external* principles. If God is the human father exalted to inconceivable magnitude, Brahman is Nature exalted to an immensity which is indescribable, because only a small fraction of Brahman is manifest, on the analogy of the tip of the iceberg or the lava from the volcano. The rest is silence—*Nāda Brahman*. To call Brahman the 'Ground of Being' or the undifferentiated 'aesthetic continuum' is scarcely adequate to the poetic grandeur of the concept; Western terminology is notoriously unsuited to the interpretation of Indian concepts. According to the Sāṃkhya system, which may be regarded as particularly representative of Indian modes of thinking, man's intellect, *buddhi*, is an emanation of primeval Matter—a good example of the peculiar concreteness and physicality which pervades even apparently abstract Hindu speculation. There is no absolute distinction in India between Matter and Spirit; both are *equal* aspects of one single principle—the two sides of the same coin. Where the different schools of thought diverge from this inclusiveness is in the valorization of empirical reality and transcendental reality. For the Buddhists and Vedantists the sole reality is that which we normally regard as ineffable unreality. For the mainstream of the Great Tradition, empirical reality is a transient derivation; form and change, becoming, the world, are an overspill from the eternal plenitude of transcendental Reality or Being. The sole means of grasping this greater immensity of Being is by establishing a correct relation with the transience of Becoming.

Indians have devised various methods of bringing themselves into harmonious and integral relation with the larger Reality. For some, the starting-point is the mystery of deep, dreamless sleep—the point in time where the individual dissolves into Great Time. For others there are three planes of reality, the Divine, the profane, and the sacrificial mean—on the Vedic altar the substance of the profane mingles with the Divine and is fused in the sacred fire and feast. For the *yogin* and the various schools of mystical gnosis, the body is the sacrifice (Plate 37); through acrobatic physical conditioning and heightened perception of the body, the doors of perception are cleansed, making it possible to break down the culture-conditioned fiction of separateness. Again, the different schools diverge in the degree of isolation which mystical and immediate apprehension of

Reality imposes. For the matter-hating dualistic systems, the realization of Infinite Oneness is the state of *kaivalya*, which means isolation. For others, realization also comes through absolute withdrawal, but the antinomian transcendence of subject–object relationships, the reconciliation of opposites, finally brings immediate experience of solidarity with all things and a stance of benign tranquillity is attained amidst the contradictions of everyday life. Whatever the course, spiritual realization is invariably believed to permit the emergence of other than normal forms of consciousness, aesthetic, visionary, or mystical.

Communication in the state of enhanced consciousness comes through the revelation of the Word. The utterances of the *jivanmukta*, or completely realized man, the guru, the sage, are revelations of That—absolute truth—proclamations, so to speak, *ex cathedra*. The famous Upanishadic formula—Ātman is Brahman, Thou art That—is not universally accepted, but it summarizes much that is essential and characteristic of Indian thought: ideas based on the intuition that the essence of Self is identical with the Ground of Being.

Ātman is *not* an exclusive trait of the human individual (indeed the individual in the Western sense is specifically denied by this very fact); Ātman is a vital force present in *all* things, creatures, and persons. The techniques devised to grasp the identity of Ātman with Brahman may, but do not invariably, necessitate ascesis and withdrawal; nevertheless, implicit in the identity, in the last analysis, is a total, unified awareness. Clichés about Indian pessimism and fatalism notwithstanding, even the most rigorous matter-hating systems are sustained by an 'innate optimism which postulates a perfect state of happiness beyond human understanding.' (Heimann.)

Rebirth and causality

The personal God—the God of the *bhakta*—the Supreme Deity (Shiva or Vishnu), and the host of mythological deities, are purely accidental and transitory, mere ripples on the surface of manifoldness in the immense, protracted drama of cyclical change. God is therefore *subject* to the inexorable laws of *saṃsāra* and *karma*, rebirth (reincarnation, or transmigration) and causality. Certainly God is in everything, but the idea of an Almighty responsible for good and evil is alien to Indian thinking. True, the deities of the little traditions may not appear subordinate to the greater scheme of Brahman from the point of view of their devotees, while the theistic sects certainly recognize Bhagavān, the Lord, as supreme. Nevertheless, in so far as we are attempting to analyse the principles on which the thought of the

Great Tradition operates (rather than its content) we must agree with Heimann that the Indian God is subject to impersonal laws:

It might however be supposed that, in place of one God or a plurality of gods, the laws of *karma* etc., to which even the gods themselves are subject, would be regarded as the supreme principles of all Being. But all these regulative laws are impersonal; they do not rule the world from without according to their own imposed schemes, but are immanent in all cosmic phenomena and processes. In other words, they are not external entities existing anterior to world events, but unities which can be grasped only when they become disintegrated and manifested throughout the infinite diversity of cosmic phenomena. The eternal principles of *karma*, and Reincarnation, that is to say, are not pre-existent to cosmic happenings, but come into existence together with these. Neither they, nor the gods, then, can be regarded as the origin of all things.[1]

Max Muller described all Indian religion as a kind of 'kathenotheism', one god selected for a certain occasion by a certain sect to play the supreme role. But the plurality of gods participate in the field of constant change, of permanent crisis, to which the entire cosmos and natural processes on earth are subject. They intercede on behalf of men, a kind of vast peonage in constant mobility, with access to the hidden vital force. The only constant phenomenon of empirical reality is the fact of dynamic change. The corollary of this idea is that an unchanging reality subsists beneath all apparent change, and therefore that change itself is without ultimate significance. There is nothing comparable in Indian thought to the Western idea of unrepeatable events, unique historical avatars or messiahs, an exclusive God, an exclusively true religion, or a standard of constant value. And since empirical reality is subject to the laws of *karma* and rebirth, there is no eternal individual soul.

In its original sense *karma* had no ethical connotation, it was simply a biological law of causality linked with that of *saṃsāra*, rebirth. Both concepts are the product of the synchronic and fundamental sense of tribal solidarity. In spite of his evolutionist ideas, Cassirer justifiably ascribed to primitive societies a

feeling of the indestructible unity of life . . . so strong and unshakeable as to defy the fact of death. . . . In a certain sense the whole of mythical thought may be interpreted as a constant and obstinate negation of the phenomenon of death. By virtue of this conviction of the unbroken unity and continuity of life myth has to clear away this phenomenon. . . . What [primitive man] opposed to the fact of death was his confidence in the solidarity, the unbroken and indestructible unity of life. Even totemism expresses this deep conviction of a community of all living beings—a community that must be preserved and reinforced by the constant efforts of man, by the strict performance of magical rites and religious observances.[2]

[1] Betty Heimann, *Indian and Western Philosophy*, London, 1937, p. 48.
[2] Ernst Cassirer, *An Essay on Man*, Yale University Press, reprinted 1962, pp. 83–6.

Even when it reached a much more advanced stage of religious development, ancient India persisted in this refusal to accept the finality of death, as can be seen from the emphasis it gave to the doctrine of the transmigration of souls, *saṃsāra*. The unity of life is here prolonged beyond the limits of a single human life, and linked by the doctrine of *karma* to the attainment of *moksha*, or the escape from Time. 'Present, past, and future blend into each other without any sharp line of demarcation; the limits between the generations of man become uncertain.'¹ The death of the body becomes insignificant in relation to the soul's pilgrimage to eternity through a sequence of incarnations within the social body, which, in turn, is structured (so it is believed by the caste Hindu) to ensure that the reborn soul acquires a body appropriate to that particular stage on its way back to primal unity.

Karma and *saṃsāra* are the bonds which ideologically weld the social system and the Hindu religion together. *Karma*: compensation for good and evil (literally 'deed' and the 'result of deed'); *saṃsāra*: the doctrine of rebirth in a caste appropriate to the karmic legacy. Good and evil deeds will be rewarded either in this life or in the next—the application of the law of causality to human destiny. Nobody can escape from *karma*; it is inexorable and unfailing. 'What a man thinks that he becomes.' This is why one of the techniques of meditation in the *Yoga Aphorisms* of Patañjali is to suppress what we call 'normal thinking'.

The consequences of one's deeds in this life are not inherited by one's own children; *karma* is not hereditary. The karmic residue is only exhausted by being born again and again, in different castes, or even in animals. It is not clear how the deeds which determine rebirth affect or are attached to the soul. Here lies the curious inconsistency of *karma*; it can earn a man a better social position in his next life, but this contradicts the principle of hereditary transmission of caste and ritual duties from father to son. This is probably due to the juxtaposition of two contradictory beliefs. The departure of the 'spirit' to the heavenly world of the family ancestors was of non-Aryan origin, a belief which has never been reconciled to the Brahmanic idea of *saṃsāra*. Ancestor-worship plays a very small role in Hinduism.

Taken in isolation from the system of which it is a part, the doctrine of *karma* is rigidly determinist (see p. 294). It was one of the cardinal graces of Buddhism to postulate a salvation ethic whereby a man could indeed escape from the net of *karma*. Nevertheless, *karma* should be viewed in its proper context, that is to say in the perspective of life seen as one vast drama, in which the actors assume a succession of masks in accordance with the laws of their *karma* without the essence of self being affected by

¹ Ibid., p. 83.

the taint of each impersonation. According to one interpretation, *Bhārata Varsha*, the ancient name of India, literally means 'land of the actors'. There is no freedom in the individualist sense, but the very word 'freedom' begs the question. The idea of life as a masquerade may to some extent mitigate the feeling of hopelessness in the face of inexorable destiny; it equally reduces the significance of any effort to escape from the grip of fate in the worldly sense, but not in the ultimate sense of liberation into 'a perfect state of happiness beyond human understanding'.

The terror of Time

The mysterious process that creates and sustains the great game of life is called *māyā*, a term pregnant with multiple meanings and itself the primordial matrix, the womb of time. It variously means: illusion, cosmic illusion, creative illusion, becoming, magic, art. The flux of *māyā*, recreating the 'many' and dissolving itself back into the primordial unity, or unmanifest condition of Brahman, constitutes the cosmic cycle. The phenomenal world is made of the same stuff as dreams; both are *māyā*. Creation is conditioned by time; everything is born only to die, for the life-urge not only contains the seeds of its own decay but also is magnetically attracted to the primal source. Man can reverse the outstreaming course of Creation rather as a space satellite which has escaped the earth's field of gravity can re-enter it and burn up in the atmosphere from whence it emerged. The Vedic sacrifices re-enact Creation in reverse, fusing multiplicity back into the primordial unity which centrifugal Creation had burst asunder.

'Life is sorrow,' as the Hindu says, but man must escape from the anguish of time. Suffering is a fact which must be dissociated from its connotation of *pain*; it arises from the instinctual libido, or 'desire'; it is but one part of a larger reality, the 'playfulness' of the divine itself. From the point of view of one who has freed himself from phenomenal existence (*māyā*), the whole of creation is seen as a paradisal vision, a state of divine play, in which he recaptures the innocent vision of the child. This does not mean that he is in a state of infantile regression, but that he recovers and has complete control over the child's spontaneity in a state of solidarity with the collective; he brings to an unformed, undifferentiated state a superior, agile awareness. In a normal state of mind the phenomenal world appears concrete, real, profane; only in an exalted state is it no longer what it had seemed to be—it is something *more* not less than real—it is magical, it is *sacred*. At such moments (in the rapture of the festival, for instance) the sense of time is annulled, the flux of life is no longer experienced as pain but as ecstasy.

It should now be possible to view the usual definition of *māyā* as 'illusion' in its proper perspective. It does not mean that most Indians 'see life as unreal'. Only in the metaphysical system of Advaita Vedānta is the world consistently viewed as completely *unreal*. For Sāṃkhya and yoga, the Upanishads, Jainism, Tantrism, Shaivism, and the southern schools of *bhakti*, *māyā* is *not* unreal but a cosmic *play*; the word 'illusion' is derived from the Latin *ludere*, to play. There is no need here to recapitulate the ideas and cultural manifestations implicit in the association of Indian religious thought with play, as they have been described in Part Three, but we can now see more clearly that it is the concept of *māyā* which integrates the *līlā*, in which men and gods participate, with the overall philosophical outlook. Finally, it should be pointed out that *māyā* should not be mistaken as an absurd and gratuitous illusion comparable with the existentialist view that all is Nothingness. Only when it is seen as divine play is the world of contingencies finally revealed as *sacred*. This discovery leads to feelings of bliss, not of anguish.

Obviously the term *māyā*, which covers the whole of phenomenal existence, has been interpreted in many different ways. Since it is temporality it must be sacramentalized, or melt into Great Time, the cyclical cosmic rhythm. Since *māyā* is a collective hallucination veiling transcendental Reality, Absolute Truth can be grasped by various spiritual exercises (*sādhana*) through which one wakes to full consciousness. This does not mean that *māyā* is the unconscious; it is much more than is usually meant by this term, although in one sense it does mean the dark, feminine, instinctive side of human nature, neither good nor evil. Its most ancient meaning of magic and deceit relates it to the primitive concept of the sacred as something so potent that it must be appeased by abject self-abasement. In fact Tantric Hinduism revalorized the archetypal figures of Shiva and Kālī to preside over the world of *māyā*. This mysteriously potent force also represents nature, matter, the primordial matrix, tricking man into maintaining false solidarity with the profane—a fatal and unholy liaison. But Hinduism never made the same mistake as the Manichee by identifying matter with evil or concupiscence. *Māyā* is not to be equated with *original sin*. Eyes that hitherto saw the profane world as a meaningless cycle of sorrow, once opened to a direct apprehension of reality, perceive that *māyā* belongs to the realm of awe, rapture, and the supernatural.

The influence of this concept of *māyā* is of incalculable importance to patterns of thinking today. It is positive in the sense that it expresses India's sense of the transience of life, of mutability, and that this provides solace to those who can look forward to nothing but suffering. It is negative in the sense that the brute facts of life are, in the final analysis, either illusory or of secondary importance and that nothing one does can alter them for the better. While *māyā* is therefore a consolation in the face of sorrow because it implies that life need never be taken too seriously, it also serves as a rationale for apathy.

The concept of *māyā* is integrally related to the concept of Time—*Kāla*. Among the principal constituents of the mythic time concept, Éliade includes the return to origins, the prestige of beginnings, and the conquest of time. It is the first manifestation of a thing that is significant and valid. The Time of Origin, Sacred Time, or Great Time, is the 'receptacle' for a new creation. 'It is not enough to *know* the 'origin', it is necessary to re-establish the moment when such-and-such a thing was created. This finds expression in "going back" until the original, strong, sacred Time is recovered.'[1] According to the Indian temporal scheme, the 'prestige of beginnings' is most clearly asserted in the cyclical theory of creation of the World, its differentiation through the four successive *yugas*, till its destruction and re-emanation. In the First Age, or Krta Yuga, a classless, unified state of paradisal grace prevails, after which there is steady social degeneration until, at the end of the Kāli Yuga—the Age in which, it is believed, we are now—Kāli, goddess of destruction, dispeller of the fear of *Kāla*, brings the World to an end in a cosmic holocaust, after which the process begins all over again. Change is therefore a process of Perishing, not of Becoming.[2]

It is not unlikely that the ideal of the Krta Yuga, like the paradisal myth of Uttarakuru, originated from memories of tribal collectivist societies; moreover, a similar classless state figures in the legendary Śākadvīpa of the *Mahābhārata*, where the inhabitants are described as black. Hindu society was probably aware that the time sense of surrounding tribal societies was even more consistently non-linear than their own.

Ritual re-enactment of the cosmogonic myth, mysticism, yoga, art, and thought are the means of escaping from the outstreaming flow of Time and recovering initial plenitude.

The method is to cast off from a precise instant of Time, the nearest to the present moment, and to retrace the Time backward (*pratiloman* or 'against the stream') in order to arrive *ad originem*, the point where existence first 'burst' into the world and unleashed Time. Then one rejoins that paradoxical instant before which Time was not, because nothing had been manifested. We can grasp the meaning and the aim of this technique: to re-ascend the stream of Time would necessarily bring one back ultimately to the point of departure, which coincides with that of the cosmogony. To re-live one's past lives would also be to understand them and, to a certain degree, 'burn up' one's 'sins'; that is, the sum of the deeds done in the state of ignorance and capitalised from one life to the next by

[1] M. Éliade, *Myth and Reality*, London, 1964, p. 37.

[2] The Four Ages last 4,320,000 years, or *mahāyuga*; one thousand *mahāyugas* constitute a single day of Brahma, or *kalpa*, which is again multiplied in *mahākalpa* units.

the law of *karma*. But there is something of even greater importance: one attains to the beginning of Time and enters the Timeless—the eternal present which preceded the temporal experience inaugurated by the 'fall' into human existence.[1]

This retrospective modality is as fundamental as the non-sequential thought-process of which it is a part. It will be recalled that the Indian syllogism is the reverse of the Western: the notion of effect is formed first, and that of the cause is retrospectively inferred and stated afterward. *Phalahetu* means 'effect and cause'—in that order, not the other way round.[2] This does not imply that the effect is regarded as more important than the cause—on the contrary, the sentiment of impermanence, of uncertainty, of the transience of life as opposed to the 'prestige of beginnings' rules this out. The thought-process itself is retrospective, cyclical. When Indian Buddhist texts were translated into Chinese and Japanese, this retrospective structure of syllogism dismayed the scholars and was invariably reversed. The grammatical structure of Sanskrit is one example of a persistent tendency to assert the 'prestige of beginnings'; but Sanskrit semantics also reveal the same non-sequential bias and indifference to temporality of a linear order (but not, as many imagine, indifference to Time itself). For example, *parson* can mean either 'day after tomorrow' or 'day before yesterday', while *atarson* can equally mean 'three days ago' or 'three days from now'.[3] Temporal connectives and the dynamic relation of acts are seldom lineally articulated in Sanskrit grammar. A sequence of connected events, while it may be perceived lineally, is not valued in the same way as a *non-lineal pattern* outside history. *Karma* is lineal, a cumulative process which is a hindrance to the attainment of a goal of higher value—transcendence of 'effect and cause', transcendence of opposites. To escape from *karma* is to escape from Time.

Change does not increase the good; there is no such thing here as *progress*; value lies in sameness, in the repeated pattern of the known, not in novelty. What is good in life is exact identity with all past experience, and all mythical experience. Karma Yoga, the spiritual path of action, as distinct from the spiritual path of contemplation (Jñāna Yoga), is the antithesis of the Protestant work-ethic: no job, no labour, no drudgery should be performed for a reward outside the act. All work contains its own satisfaction. The present should not be regarded as a means to future satisfaction; the present is not evaluated in terms of its place within a course of action leading upward to a worthy end. In the West we see our history climactically; we plan our future experiences climactically, leading

[1] M. Éliade, *Myths, Dreams and Mysteries*, New York, 1960, p. 50.
[2] Cf. Hajime Nakamura, 'Time in Indian and Japanese Thought', in J. T. Fraser (ed.), *The Voices of Time*, Allen Lane, London, 1966, p. 84.
[3] Ibid., p. 81.

up to future satisfaction or meaning, and to fulfilment through pursuing a *career*. In India, action is a series of anti-climactic masquerades. This particular time-sense is nowhere more clearly demonstrated than in the ideal of anti-climactic sexual pleasure, attained through prolonged temporal diffusion of sensation, which does not end in orgasm (and from which the technique known as *carezza* derives). It was shown in Part One that the plot of Sanskrit drama is anti-climactic, while the presentation of narrative in the art of fresco painting is based on accentless simultaneity.

The ethical implications of non-sequential logic are of considerable importance. In a brilliant analysis of the contrast between the non-lineal Trobriand concept of reality and Western linearity, Dorothy Lee writes:

> Our conception of personality formation, our stress on the significance of success and failure and of frustration in general, is based on the axiomatically postulated line. How can there be blocking without pre-supposed lineal motion or effort? . . . If the undertaking is of value in itself, a point good in itself and not because it leads to something, then failure has no symbolic meaning; it merely results in no cake for supper, or less money in the family budget; it is not personally destructive. But failure is devastating in our culture, because it is not failure of the undertaking alone; it is the moving, becoming, lineally conceived self that has failed.[1]

This does not mean that a society with a similar non-lineal value system, such as India's, is wholly free from frustration and alienation—a matter which will be examined at the end of Part Five, Chapter One—but Dorothy Lee's contrast between the two systems goes a long way towards explaining in human terms the implications of India's ahistorical outlook and non-developmental time-sense.

The Indian cyclical concept of continuous change is associated with the wheel, or *chakra*—the perfect shape with the focal point of the universe situated at its centre in mysterious stillness. A classical metaphor for defining *māyā* is the Wheel of Fire—an apparently continuous circle of fire made by a whirling torch, representing also the continuity of time and moving events by the whirring succession of *kṣaṇa*, or atomic instants. The weapon of Vishnu is a whirling fire wheel (upper right hand in Plate 34), Shiva in his destructive aspect is ringed with a fire wheel, and the solar wheel figures prominently in Vedic, Brahman, and Vaishnava symbolism (Plate 39). Even more important are the Buddhist Wheel of the Law and the Wheel of *Saṃsāra*, or wheel of existence. In the *Bhagavad Gītā* the Lord 'causes all beings to revolve by His divine deluding power [*māyā*] as if they were mounted on a wheel' (18.61). The word for wheel here is *yantrarudha*, an implicit reference to the *noria*, a wheel provided

[1] Dorothy Lee, 'Lineal and Nonlineal Codifications of Reality', *Psychosomatic Medicine*, 12 May 1950.

with buckets for the irrigation of fields, one of the most important inventions which India gave to the world.[1] This direct association of cyclical time with man's efforts to preserve the ecology in a state of balanced equilibrium is most significant. For it is in this conjunction of proto-scientific knowledge of irrigation and the philosophical idea of continuous change, of the *noria* and the ethics of the *Gītā*, that the idea of perpetual motion acquired heuristic value. Lynn White, an authority on medieval technology, is of the opinion that in India, 'the idea of perpetual motion was entirely consistent with, and was perhaps rooted in, the Hindu concept of the cyclical and self-perpetuating nature of all things'.[2] The *Āryabhaṭīya* of the great mathematician Āryabhaṭa (written in A.D. 499) is the first text which refers to an invention peculiarly characteristic of the Indian mind—the perpetual-motion machine: 'One should cause a sphere of light wood, equally rounded and of weight on all sides, to move in regular time by means of quicksilver, oil, and water.' The next reference appears in the *Sūrya Siddhānta*, which claims that by the application of water (presumably with the aid of a wheel) 'a knowledge of time will be gained by the diligent'. The philosophical context here is important when we turn to the last reference, the *Siddhānta Śiromaṇi*, written by the extraordinary mathematical genius Bhāskara in A.D. 1150. Bhāskara (who was the first Indian scientist to prove that zero was infinity) describes in some detail how to construct a perpetual-motion machine by secretly filling the rim of a wheel with quicksilver. It is evident that Bhāskara's quicksilver wheel was meant as a device for displaying the magical power of the scientist working in harmonious unity with the energies of nature, and to provide a graphic demonstration of life as a process of continuous change. 'It may very well not be fanciful', Joseph Needham comments on the Indian fascination with perpetual motion, 'to seek the ultimate origin or predisposition of the Indian conviction in the profoundly Hindu world view of endless cyclical change, *kalpas* and *mahākalpas* succeeding one another in self-sufficient and unwearying round. For Hindus as well as Taoists, the universe itself was a perpetual-motion machine.'[3]

Bhāskara's quicksilver wheel is a uniquely Indian product of the aesthetically oriented creative imagination which seeks to harness and to balance

---

[1] In their translations of the *Bhagavad Gītā*, both Hill and Zaehner follow Shaṇkara's suggestion that a comparison with wooden puppets whirling on a machine may be meant; Indian puppets, however, are not mounted on wheels. Zimmer's translation of the passage (Zimmer, 1951) includes the gloss: '*yantrarudha*: e.g. on a wheel provided with buckets for the irrigation of a rice-field', i.e. what is technically called a *noria*, formerly 'Persian wheel'. Lynn White, Joseph Needham, and others no longer believe that the *noria* was invented, as was thought earlier, in ancient Egypt, but almost certainly in India.

[2] L. White Jr., *Mediaeval Technology and Social Change*, Oxford, 1962, p. 130.

[3] J. Needham, *Science and Civilisation in China*, Vol. 4.2, Cambridge, 1965, p. 540.

the forces of nature. But it is of larger historical consequence, as White and Needham show. For the *Siddhānta Śiromaṇi* was translated into Arabic a few decades after it was written and found its way to Europe by A.D. 1200, where the quicksilver wheel appeared soon after, in almost identical detail, in the sketchbook of Villard de Honnecourt, setting in train a spate of research into perpetual motion which 'deeply influenced modern scientific thought at one of its most crucial early stages'.[1] We may conclude by saying that the aesthetic concept of cyclical time, which in India assumes a highly playful, paradoxical character, need not necessarily end in sterile circular argument but, under certain conditions, can spark off a dynamic creative movement.

This is why the concepts of *māyā* and cyclical time are so important in understanding the Indian attitude towards history and the problem of social responsibility. Contrary to the Islamic and Judaeo-Christian traditions, history has no metaphysical significance for either Hinduism or Buddhism. Professor Éliade states the archaic principle very clearly: 'Profane time must be abolished, at least symbolically, so that man forgets his "historical situation".' The highest human ideal is the *jivanmukta*—one who is liberated from Time. Man, according to the Indian view, 'must, at all costs, find *in this world* a road that issues upon a trans-historical and atemporal plane'.[2] The whole purpose of life is to pierce the veil of ignorance (*avidyā*) blinding him to the nature of ultimate reality. The quest for immortality and the overcoming of death involves the seeker in active flight from climactic history and the developmental flow of time. A majority of Hindu ceremonies and rites are primarily concerned with the initiatory pattern of 'death and rebirth' into another mode of being. Various kinds of irrational or emotional states, trances, ecstatic or orgiastic rites, all transport the seeker into the realm of the timeless. On the social plane, as we have seen, *karma* and *saṃsāra* are an essential element in the ideology of the caste system and reflect the same basic desire for release from the anguish of history, the terror of irreversible time.

The prolonged period during which India's economy was linked with the system of non-commodity-producing village communities, low productivity, restrictive social organization, conformist religious thought, and immediate sensory experience of simultaneous, non-sequential relations, certainly contributed to the endurance of this concept of cyclical time even in modern times. This very marked (and deeply felt) indifference to the Western concept of history and of man's incapacity to change it is far more consistent than in most other civilizations, including the Chinese and the Islamic. The durability of the cyclical-time concept at the most advanced

---

[1] J. Needham, *Science and Civilisation in China*, Vol. 4.2, Cambridge, 1965, p. 542.
[2] M. Éliade, *Yoga, Immortality, and Freedom*, London, 1958.

levels of Hindu metaphysical thought makes this indifference to what we would call history one of the distinguishing traits of the Indian cultural tradition. In merging with the collective lies the hope of magical transformation, the ecstasy of Oneness, or absorption of all in the All. There is no room in this scheme for the modern idea that man is the subject and agent of *history*; there is no admission of the possibility of ameliorating the human condition, nor confidence in the ability to master a hostile environment. On the other hand, the cyclical-time concept, 'return to Origins', and mythical ideal of the Kṛta Yuga, Uttarakuru, and Śākadvīpa do not altogether rule out the millennialist concept of history, which is to be found in different form at the root of Judaeo-Christian messianic ideology and even of Marx's classless society.

Widespread nostalgia for the past, and dreams of India returning to a mythical golden age, are not just signs of Indian complacency at the fact that it has a great past, or simple manifestations of national pride; they are built into the very fabric of religious belief, as they once were in Christian Europe. Even today, when India has become familiar with the idea of historical studies and produces able historians, the underlying desire to study India's history and culture is often unconsciously motivated by the longing to be restored to paradisal innocence in some supposedly Golden Age. As can be seen from the collectivist movements of the twentieth century, millennialist mythology can be used as a potent source of appeal with which to arouse the masses.

Creative intellects were plainly not interested in the kind of historical concerns familiar to the West since Herodotus. But the idea that 'Indian society has no history at all', as Marx asserted, is a gross over-simplification. The rarity of accurate records merely makes it more difficult to reconstruct history. We can at least be sure of one point—the ascendancy of the social order over the political system; there is no doubt that, since the individual cannot essentially alter the course of history, acquiescence in the hierarchy of power and wealth, and legitimization of ambitious war-lords as quasi-divine protectors of the millennialist *dharma*, form an integral part of this attitude towards and desire to escape from the terror of time, to preserve the immediacy of a non-sequential unified-field awareness. The next chapter is devoted to the consequences of this attitude on ethical and political ideas.

Chapter Two The Ethical Dilemma

In the Hindu scriptures history is represented as a ceaseless conflict between the Dharma and Adharma—between the moral, idealistic, spiritual forces and the unregenerate forces of darkness, lust, and evil—in which the Dharma always wins. History, ethics, politics, and social speculation are blended together in a cosmic ritual scheme, with gods and culture-heroes acting as conciliatory mediators between the sacred world and the profane world. The battle between good and evil is conceived as a cosmic sacrifice for the common good, ultimately uniting gods and men in the rule of *Rājadharma*. This conception is extremely archaic but astonishingly durable; at heart the Hindu still sees history, even in modern times, in terms of the archetypal tension between Dharma and Adharma. It is a favourite theme of the rural political orator and it represents a constant substratum of thought which permeates the Hindu outlook on political affairs and moral problems. This is what the Hindu means by the *permanent* history of India.

It has often been said that India has no developed indigenous ethical system, that it has concentrated more on the mystical apprehension of an ultimate reality which transcends good and evil than on differentiating between good and evil acts. At best, so this theory runs, the pluralistic society of India has evolved a pluralistic religious system in which the sole ethical feature shared in common by all its elements is that of moral relativism. It is the experience of the anthropological field-worker that the popular ideology of practising Hindus in any given region is confined to the moral relativism of the caste. Nevertheless, abstract Hindu philosophy and the ethical teaching of the Epics does, as has already been mentioned, adumbrate a universal moral code for all Hindus. To understand the central evaluative and moral concepts of the Hindu Great Tradition is to recognize that there are certain criteria. As has been pointed out by Professor F. G. Bailey, Hindu ethics has its public face—Dharma, or normative rules —and its private wisdom, or pragmatic rules, to distinguish between the principles men espouse and the tactics they adopt. For example, Bailey has shown that the normative Hindu concept of cyclical time is rigidly deterministic, whereas the more pragmatic *bhakti* sects concede that the individual can perform spontaneous actions by means of grace and devotion, hence ignoring or reversing the normative, preordained karmic time-cycle.

Hindu moral relativism, *as we now know it*, is partly a response to the fact that India is not exclusively a nation of Hindus (a problem which has never been fully faced even by the universalists). India finds itself in the same ethical dilemma as any Euro-American nation of modern times. The effective and honest use of moral predicates does presuppose a shared moral vocabulary, but neither India as a whole community nor the Western nations share a single such vocabulary. The extent to which different moral criteria are established in common among the Indian peoples is extremely uncertain, and therefore the kind of appeal their leaders are able to make when they use moral predicates is also uncertain. That I have, in these last two sentences, adapted to the Indian situation the remarks of Professor Alasdair McIntyre[1] on the ethical dilemma of the modern West indicates how close the ethical predicament in which India finds itself is to that of Western nations. It is occasionally claimed that while India's is a society more dominated by religion than most, it is also one of the most immoral. Perhaps it would be more constructive to investigate the possible origins of this assertion. Our task is to distinguish between diagnosis and valuation.

The basic postulate of *śīla*, character or behaviour, as an ethically neutral and productive centre, stems from the experience of singleness in the deeps of the mind rather than in the heat of action. *Śīla* can assume the traits of either 'good' or 'bad' character. Since all empirical phenomena are transient they can have no decisive significance or axiomatic moral value. There is no such thing as *sin* in Indian ethics, only errors of cognition—*avidyā*, or ignorance. In other words, action is wrongful to the degree that it is motivated by the sense of separateness or alienation from the cosmic plenitude. Action is 'good' to the extent that it is committed to reinforcing the interconnectedness of all empirical phenomena, the common ground in all of them. Ethical tension, therefore, is the conflict between solidarity and separateness: 'only connect'—*sam-vid*, the science of contact, literally *con*science. Supra-personal cosmic responsibility, to us a seemingly remote and vague principle, is at once concrete and of greater moral significance to the Indian (or at least to the Hindu) than social conduct, which has no permanent value. This is, in origin, a tribal attitude rationalized by a caste society, but reduced to romantic aestheticism when social organization is no longer geared to the enactment of the cosmic rite. There are only three essential moral predicates (derived from the nouns for 'gift', 'sympathy', and 'restraint' respectively): *dāna*, 'to give others their due'; *daya*, 'to sympathize with one's fellow creatures'; *dama*, 'to restrain one's passion'. The three *d*s comprise a model conservation policy, an intense desire to preserve the equilibrium, a subsistence ethic which is never permitted, so to speak,

[1] *Secularization and Moral Change*, Oxford, 1967.

to upset the social ecology. In sum, the cardinal virtue is *ahiṃsā*, non-violence.

The institutional framework in which Indian ethics previously functioned included the exchange of services in the *jajmānī* system, personal devotion to a protector in the feudal court, and participation in the ritualized seasonal round of production and feasting. The model of the hero was projected on the master, lord, or leader, with the entire social body co ordinated in a collective enterprise subject to the biological ethics of cause and effect. *Karma* is the ethical correlative of social reciprocity, an endless gyration or *rebondissement*, like billiard balls rebounding one against the other with every strike of the cue, each strike being ethically neutral in relation to the whole but not in relation to each individual element. Thus a network of reciprocal activity is established with varying degrees of intensity among the individual elements.

In this chapter, the various strands of the ethical value system will be identified. At the same time, the specifically Hindu relation between politics and morals will be described; for one of the outstanding characteristics of twentieth-century Indian history is the fact that no distinction is drawn between them. This theme will also be examined from a different angle in Part Five.

Dharma in the Epics

The oldest major Indian sources of ethical ideas are the two Epics, which continue to be the inspiration for all teaching on morality. Thus the main outlines of Indian ethics were established at least two thousand five hundred years ago. The *Mahābhārata*, or Great Epic, is eight times the length of the *Iliad* and the *Odyssey* put together. The richest part, from the point of view of its ethical content, consists of the *Shāntiparva* (1,400 verses) and the *Anuśānaparva* (8,000 verses), both of which are devoted to the exposition of the Dharma. The *Bhagavad Gītā*, one of the earliest interpolations (in Book VI), is in a class by itself and will be described later. The *Mahābhārata* took at least a thousand years to compose and was subjected to countless interpolations. The earliest version, a heroic saga in praise of warrior nobles organized in a clan-system, was probably completed between the seventh and sixth centuries B.C. Subsequent editions reflect the slow transition from a tribal to a caste system, the eventual ascendancy of the Brahmans as the guardians of all knowledge, and the establishment of their authority in all matters pertaining to the Dharma. Nevertheless, the aristocratic assumptions of the heroic tradition on which both Epics were originally based do not disappear in later redactions.

The Epics are a repository of beliefs including orthodox Brahmanism, heterodox doctrines, tribal custom, Upanishadic mysticism, theism, *bhakti*. They reveal the influence of many philosophical schools, they contain frequent allusions to the systems of Sāṃkhya and yoga, and they were subjected to the indirect influence of Jainism and Buddhism. The *Bhagavad Gītā*, which bears signs of having been influenced by both theism and Buddhism, was probably composed around the period of Ashoka, when Buddhism thrived on the munificent patronage of the Mauryan empire and the Brahmans were in retreat. The Epics represent a synthesis (however inconsistent) of beliefs based on a single assumption: ascendancy of the Dharma in the affairs of society. Philosophically, Buddhism, Jainism, and Hinduism differ but little in this particular aspect.

A certain kind of moral action—the heroic (and what Brahman editors thought heroic action ought to be)—gave a slant to the ethics of all sub-servient castes and classes, although a distinction was drawn between the universal and the caste Dharma—*sanatana dharma* and *varṇashrāma dharma*. Since the Epics, and later the mythological Pūraṇas and the *sūtra* form of the Law Books, were the media in which Indian ethics crystallized, aesthetic ambiguity in the formulation of values is added to the relativism of morality itself. Yet this subtle and elusive moral reasoning has been so integrated with the dramatic narrative of the Epic tales as to appeal to vast audiences. The *Mahābhārata* and *Rāmāyana* have been a constant source of comfort, guidance, and entertainment to millions down the ages. Whereas the Homeric Epics have never been sacred books and have long since ceased to occupy a central position in Greek culture, the Indian Epics are the most widely read and respected religious books of the Hindus today, even if their public recitation no longer commands quite the same widespread interest.

As G. J. Held puts it, the conflict which provides the central drama of the Great Epic 'concerns two parties representing the two halves of the cosmos, which means that we have here to do with a cosmic ritual, i.e. an event in which the entire cosmos is understood to participate'.[1] Held took as his point of departure a remark of Marcel Mauss on the tribal character of the *Mahābhārata* story. In advance of his time, Held applied the insight of an anthropologist to an analysis of the symbolism of the epic battle in terms of a tribal phratry-relationship. Devas and Asuras (already mentioned as an example of dual organization, cf. p. 174), and their human delegates, the Kaurava and Pāṇḍava clans, reflect the two moieties of a tribe. The Devas and Asuras are rivals who also co-operate, on the analogy of contrasted pairs which make a tribal whole. But the Vedic brotherhood of Devas and Asuras is in the process of being eclipsed, during the composition of the

[1] G. J. Held, *The Mahābhārata: An Ethnological Study*, London, 1935, p. 332.

Great Epic, by a new pair of deities, the black Krishna and his white brother Balarāma, trickster and benefactor who live together and complement each other. Krishna eventually emerges fully from his tribal origins as the terrifying genius of *initiation* into the caste society. The complexities and inconsistencies of the Epic arise from the fact that underlying its plot is the hidden drama of a social transformation from the heroic ideals of the tribe to a more religious and Brahman-directed caste society.

The central position occupied by play in the dramatic scheme of the *Mahābhārata* takes us right to the heart of the matter. The world itself is conceived as a game of dice which Shiva plays with his queen. The whole story hinges on the fateful *dyūta*, or gambling tournament, in which Yudhishṭhira plays dice with the Pāṇḍava tribe and loses all his property, his kingdom, and his wife, Draupadī. The place where the tournament was played, the consecrated playground, was the *dyūtamaṇḍalam*, a gaming circle. It was drawn with the greatest care according to geomantic rites of orientation. A special hall was erected for the game and consecrated as holy ground (a whole chapter is devoted to the erection of this assembly hall). The players were not allowed to leave the ring until they had discharged all their obligations. The fateful game of dice was the climax to a feast which included a diversity of agonistic contests and exchange of gifts. But to understand the larger significance of the *dyūta* we should first recall the fact that the earliest literary reference to gambling is the celebrated 'Gamester's Lament' in the Ṛg *Veda*. Here too the gambler loses his wife, with 'a throw too high by one'. There is more than mere coincidence in the similarity of theme, and it is Marcel Mauss who provides a clue to the connection. 'The Mahābhārata', he writes, 'is the story of a tremendous potlatch.' In this sense, the gift-giving of the modern Christmas is nothing but a 'tremendous potlatch'. Mauss saw the exchange of goods in archaic societies not as a mechanical but as a moral transaction, maintaining relationships between groups. Yudhishṭhira accepted the challenge of the *Mahābhārata dyūta* not as a personal whim (he was notorious for his gambling addiction), but because he was 'King of Dharma', personification of the moral order; it is clear, therefore, that the gambling tournament was a sacred obligation. This is because the *dyūta* was the traditional means to ensure the constant circulation of tribal wealth.

For it is groups, and not individuals, which carry on exchange, make contracts, and are bound by obligations; the persons represented in the contracts are moral persons—clans, tribes, and families; the groups, or the chiefs as intermediaries for the groups, confront and oppose each other. Further, what they exchange is not exclusively goods and wealth, real and personal property, and things of economic value. They exchange rather courtesies, entertainments, ritual, military assistance, women, children, dances and feasts; and fairs in which the market is but one element and the circulation of wealth but one part of a wide and enduring contract.[1]

Held, in his study of the *Mahābhārata dyūta*, shows how the reckless consumption and destruction of wealth characteristic of the potlatch was also a feature of Vedic tribal life in the Epic period. The conflict resulting from the dice game concerned two parties representing the two halves of the cosmos; in the seasonal enactment of the great cosmogonic myth the king 'played' the sun. We might call it 'total theatre', with the play principle again the imprinting element (Plate 39).

The symbolic import of the *dyūta* is typically Indian: a ritual contest in which the final decision is left in the hands of the gods. Though the *dyūta* scheme consists of the two most basic play elements—*competition* and *chance*, much the greater emphasis is on the latter. In games of chance the player has an entirely passive role, while in games of contest the player is active. Destiny is the architect of victory or defeat in games of chance. Here all effort, work, skill, training, and strength are at a minimum. The player's success depends on a mystical apprehension of interconnectedness, on the essential equality of the antagonists which is denied to them outside the play circle, and on submission to collective fate; the slightest inattention to rules and procedure may bring total disaster. The gambler in the game of chance is frozen into immobility, given over to the mysterious regimen of the great chain of being.

Games of competition are the exact opposite. They depend on individual skill, the maximum of effort, speed, strength, and assiduous training. The player wins by personal merit against an adversary, not against destiny. Triumph comes through a demonstration of individual superiority, vindication of personal responsibility.

We may say that the Epic marked a change in the structure of play activities, with chance still at the forefront, as in the *dyūta*, but agonistic, individual contest transferred from tribal to caste (or team) rivalry. It is my thesis that the endless contest and concern for social status among the castes is itself a covert expression of the play instinct, and that far from leading to sterile and endless dispute, the play instinct has channelized group conflict into an extraordinary diversity of caste-oriented cultural expression. Later redactions of the *Mahabharata* place greater emphasis on the deity Krishna than on the human king, Yudhishthira. As Held explains, when Krishna initiates Arjuna into the new, religiously oriented ethical system of the caste society, with the latter's presupposition of mutual interdependence, Arjuna 'imagines that his attitude towards the opposing group (ranged in battle formation on the plain of Kurukshetra) is to be

---

[1] M. Mauss, *The Gift*, Cohen & West, London, 1966, p. 3.

determined by his own individual feelings; he cannot yet understand that it is not for the individual alone to determine the place he shall occupy in the cosmic order and the function he shall exercise in the religious rites by which that order is influenced.'[1] Arjuna's role is to maintain the social equilibrium at all costs. He must fight because contest between groups is a *ritualized game*; there are no real victors outside the play enclosure, the staked-out field of battle, the demarcated area in which the rules of the agonistic contest must be observed. Whether it is a game of chance or a game of competition, the play principle in the caste society does not cater for individual merit or vindicate personal responsibility.

Traditional Indian society as we now know it obviously favours the game of chance over the game of competition. Life itself is one vast lottery in which the individual is subordinate to the collective, in which the chance circumstances of birth in a certain social niche predetermine the stakes in the game of life, which has to be played according to the inexorable laws of *dharma*. Implicit in the social order is submission to destiny. At the same time, and again strictly according to the rules, the society is divided into groups which incessantly contest their status. This will take the form of caste disputes, pure and simple, or it will be manifest in the game of position jockeying—who eats with whom, who smokes with whom. The moments of dramatization of status are the caste feast, the marriage feast, and the collective festival. In these institutions the spirit of the tribal potlatch survives. The big cities in the wedding season, with their multi-coloured wedding tents, or *shamianas*, present a scene of staggering waste and conspicuous consumption. The wedding feast, like the *dyūta* in the *Mahābhārata*, and the great village fairs, during which livestock, and in some rare cases even today women, are exchanged, remain the chief social pretext for gift-exchange and play-contests of extraordinary diversity. A man's honour is at stake in the provision of a dowry, or in his capacity to give and to return gifts; his inability to do so will bring him and his family dishonour, if not ruin.

Concerning intercaste rivalry, Huizinga noted that the play instinct would promote 'the formation of social groupings that tend to surround themselves with secrecy'. This is one trait of the closed outlook of a caste (and in a parallel process, that of a sect or esoteric circle of initiates). Another aspect endorses one of Caillois' most important points: *play creates no new element*; it is free, isolated, uncertain, unproductive; the situation at the end of play is identical to that at the start. In economic behaviour, play creates no wealth, no work, no capital increment; in the potlatch, gifts, property, and cash *circulate* from hand to hand, or they are consumed, destroyed. Exchange in the *jajmānī* system is an essentially moral activity

[1] Held (1935), p. 336.

under the patronage of the Brahman: its rewards are tokens—prizes, we might say, for the players in a game, awarded by the 'king' in playful imitation of the courtly style. Such creation of new balances in power and prestige occur through winning the game of dominance among castes. In view of the prevailing role of chance in most Indian play activities, the natural superiority of the individual or group which is proved in play lasts as long as play lasts. It does not alter the pre-existing hierarchical inequality. This is the moral of the whole epic war in the *Mahābhārata*, its carnage, fratricide, and waste: *nobody* is the real victor.

It has already been seen that *māyā* and *līlā* provide a philosophical rationale for the sublimation of the play instinct. According to this scheme, the epic war is the play of *māyā*. Ultimately, the actors strip off their masks and return to a state of paradisal equilibrium and peace. *Shāntiparva*, the title of the long book in which the ethics of the *Mahābhārata* are expounded, means the 'book of peace'; its implicit assumption is that, in the course of cyclical time, all returns to a quintessential peace.

The two philosophical problems with which the authors of the Epics are confronted is how the relation with a supra-ethical divine ground can be combined with an ethic of action in the world, and how this ethic could accommodate the rival interests between different castes. How can thinking, suffering, active men become one with an infinite, supra-ethical, inactive, infinite Being? In part, the problem originates in the fact that the Brahman literati held quite different views from those of the tribal warlords. It is unlikely that in their original form the Epics revealed the same concern as the Brahman's with meditation on the transience of life, or placed so little importance on purely human achievement. The consequent blending of the heroic tradition—interest in the mysterious forces of destiny and death, of passion and cruelty, of freedom and responsibility—with the metaphysical quest, is a distinctive trait of Indian epic literature. True, a universal trait of epic literature is the intermingling of the human and divine worlds in a third dimension of heroic tragedy. But the hero of the *Rāmāyana* is elevated to the status of a divine incarnation and the typical hero's fascination with the more human issues of reality has been subordinated in both epics to the cosmic symbolism and initiatory mysticism. No Greek or Nordic hero is prompted to seek retirement in the peace of the forest after a life of passionate activity as do the heroes of the Indian Epics. For the Greek hero human existence is something to be enjoyed for its own sake, and the highest good is the enjoyment of *tīmē*, public esteem. 'And the strongest moral force,' writes Professor E. R. Dodds, 'which Homeric man knows is not the fear of god, but respect for public opinion, *aidōs*.'[1]
The Indian hero is exhorted to fight and his heroic deeds are extolled in

[1] *The Greeks and the Irrational*, Cambridge University Press, reprinted 1966, p. 18.

similar fashion to those of Homer's heroes. But the decisive struggle is not, in the final analysis, fought on the battlefield, but within: liberation from bondage to the fleeting world of appearances (*māyā*). The survivors of the epic wars discover that public esteem and power are no more than hollow victories in an illusory struggle. It is not bravery but wisdom which is the key to the mystery of life.

In his brilliant and deservedly well-known analysis of the *Mahābhārata*, Professor R. C. Zaehner sees Yudhishthira, 'King of Righteousness', as the focal point in the ethical struggle. The story of the *Mahābhārata* concerns the great war between the Pāṇḍavas and the Kauravas. Of the five Pāṇḍava brothers who represent the cause of righteousness in the struggle, the most important are Yudhishthira and Arjuna. Yudhishthira's *karma* and unswerving virtue make it impossible for him to break a vow under any circumstances, which include the abandonment of his kingdom to the Kauravas when he loses the game of dice. For fourteen years he and his brothers are banished to the forest in fulfilment of their *dharma*, and at the end of this period can reclaim their share of the kingdom. Duryodhana, the eldest Kaurava, a glutton for power who has meanwhile ruled the kingdom, will not relinquish his throne. Yudhishthira, in whom all the ideals of a quasi-divine king are embodied, knows that he is expected to declare war, recoils at the thought of bloodshed, and asks Krishna to plead with Duryodhana on behalf of the Pāṇḍavas. But Duryodhana, like all the protagonists, is a Kshatrya warrior, and he does not baulk at fighting, for to fight is in accordance with his *varṇashrāma dharma*. Yudhishthira, the morally upright man, knows that the highest ethic of all is to refrain from violence. However, war is eventually declared, even though Yudhishthira realizes that it will mean the virtual extinction of the warrior *varṇa*.

The battle is joined on the field of Kurukshetra, and it is at the moment when the ranks of the army are assembling that Krishna appears to the faltering Arjuna and tells him (in the section which forms the *Bhagavad Gītā*) that it is his *dharma* as a Kshatrya to fight. The war ends not only with the destruction of the Kauravas but also with the slaughter of the victorious Pāṇḍava hosts through the vengeance of the gods. There now begins a long discussion among the five Pāṇḍava brothers on which of the three pursuits, *dharma*, *artha*, and *kāma*, is the highest. First it is *dharma* which is held to be man's highest goal on earth, because it is the moral foundation of the entire ethos in revealed truth. With a trace of Kautilyan shrewdness Arjuna disputes this, claiming the supremacy of economic motives, of which pleasure and righteousness are the two faces. The two youngest brothers prefer compromise. First, they say, should come the pursuit of *dharma*, after which wealth and power should be acquired in accordance with *dharma*, and only then should men turn to the fruits of pleasure. Bhīma, the ferocious warrior, a Gargantua among the Pāṇḍavas, violently disagrees. Desire, he says, is the supreme motive of all action; he quotes the Vedic creation-myth to support his claim, for it is through desire that the Primordial Man (Puruśa archetype), Golden Seed, creates the world. Liberation, too, is the fruit of desire. Therefore a balance should be maintained and all three aims pursued with equal vigour. The man who is strong enough to undertake the 'triple pursuit', *Trivarga*, is superior to those who can only master one. Hence, Zaehner suggests, this could be described as a debate in which the Marxist, the Freudian, and the Gandhian viewpoints are each represented.

The bitter and disillusioned Yudhishṭhira rejects them all. A righteous king steeped in the aristocratic ideal of remaining impassive in the face of *daivam*, regal destiny, he declares that Fate alone controls all men, and Fate is stronger than all three motives combined. Not by any action of his own can a man attain a goal that is intrinsically beyond his reach. Thus the one man who is the very embodiment of truth submits to his fate. But Yudhishṭhira is a man in conflict with himself. He is appalled by the discrepancy between traditional *dharma* and his own conscience, reluctant to do anything contrary to his sense of compassion; his own *dharma* (*svadharma*) had actually made him sin against truth. He had always unswervingly upheld his vow of truth, but once in an unguarded moment during the turmoil of the battle his brothers made him party to a deceitful stratagem which necessitated his telling a lie. It was Krishna as trickster who initiated the action; the Beloved Lord himself egged Yudhishṭhira on, offering the lame excuse that to tell a lie in a just cause was both expedient and justified—particularly since in this instance only a lie could trick the foe. Yudhishṭhira reluctantly obeyed this casuistical command from God (his beloved Krishna), mumbling his lines when he told the fatal lie. And though the lie led to swift retribution for the barbarous cruelty of the enemy, Yudhishṭhira was tormented by a gnawing sense of guilt at disobeying his own conscience. In fact, at the very instant when he mumbled his lie, his chariot which had hitherto run a few inches above the ground, came down to earth and thereafter moved like every other mortal's chariot. Nobody, not even Krishna, could relieve Yudhishṭhira of his self-hatred for telling that lie.

Yudhishṭhira is a crypto-Brahman, secretly holding to the high moral code of a superior caste—a predicament in which not a few Hindus have been caught in the centuries since the days of the Epics. He is often rebuked for this by his friends, including Krishna; he is the dove with the hawk's aggressive plumage who instinctively strives for all the Brahman virtues: detachment, non-violence, temperance, asceticism. He is further confused because he has also been told by the elders of the kingdom that the true *varṇa* distinctions are not hereditary but those of actual conduct—as a man acts, so is he, in truth, a member of the *varṇa* whose *dharma* it is to behave in that fashion.

Yudhishṭhira was especially bitter because he had also been told that the highest *dharma* was non-violence; but since his own warrior duties included the slaughter of his foes he had, nevertheless, engaged in battle. Every time he hears that war itself is a sacrifice pleasing to the gods he protests with great vehemence. He tries to abdicate the throne and retire to the forest in search of spiritual liberation from the contradictions of life. The story might have ended here in the conventional way, with Yudhishṭhira bidding farewell to his family, donning the garb of an ascetic, and setting off to wander homeless to perform penance, until many years later his devotion to God earns him his release. But the Great Epic is not written with the same exclusive bias towards Brahmanical asceticism as are the majority of the Puranic myths. And this is where our Hindu Job gains special interest.

Persistent pressure is brought to bear on Yudhishṭhira to dissuade him from renouncing the throne. However, Bhīṣma, his dying grandfather, feels it is his duty to warn him that kingship involves deceitful manoeuvring. Eventually it is Krishna, mouthpiece of the newly emergent *bhakti* cult, to whom Yudhishṭhira listens; Krishna tells him he cannot retire to the forest, but must renounce renunciation itself if he is ever to win his final battle with himself. Krishna had previously counselled Arjuna to fight, but now it is Yudhishṭhira he tells to fight his own *inner* battle. Arjuna had not suffered from similar agonizing remorse once the battle was over. He even had the gall to ask Krishna to repeat the Gītā to him all over again, because he had forgotten every word of it! Arjuna is the stock Hindu figure who is baffled by the abstractions of his religion. But Yudhishṭhira, the Hamlet of the kingdom, is torn with anguish for having been the ultimate cause of a catastrophic and useless war, as Gandhi was to feel tormented when he realized that he had unwittingly instigated acts of violence in the Satyāgraha campaign he himself had launched. Gandhi was a member of the most despised of twice-born castes, the *banīya*, and he too must sometimes have felt he was a crypto-Brahman.

Once Krishna had persuaded Yudhishṭhira to stay on his throne, he ruled his kingdom for fifteen bitter years, beset by what could be compared today with post-Independence disillusionment. But as soon as he hears that his beloved Krishna, incarnate *avatār*, has departed this world, he renounces his throne and retires to the forest with Draupadī and his brothers, still cursing his fate to have been born a Kshatrya. His wife and brothers all die in turn leaving him alone, save for the companionship of a little dog, most despised of all domestic animals. Indra descends in his chariot to carry him to heaven; but Yudhishṭhira demurs until assured that his wife and brothers are already there. He also insists that he take his faithful dog with him. Indra is irritated; paradise is no place for dogs. But Yudhishthira thinks this is wrong, for he has been told that to renounce any creature who has shown loyalty is evil. The dog turns out to be King Dharma (his own father) in disguise, and so Yudhishthira is led into paradise by his heavenly father.

As soon as he is seated in paradise, whom should he see but Duryodhana, the villainous Kaurava king, seated in great pomp and majesty with the hosts of the righteous—Duryodhana, the warrior, had fulfilled his *dharma* by fighting. Yudhishthira is indignant and descends to the frightful pit of hell, and there watches while his wife Draupadī and his brothers are tortured prior to their entry to paradise. At last Yudhishthira's monumental patience snaps. Once again faced with the persistent conflict between his own personal conviction and traditional ethics, he now irrevocably decides in favour of his conscience, his personal knowledge of truth. He explodes in a towering rage, demanding that he be sent to hell himself, calling down curses on the heads of the gods and the hypocrisy of their *dharma*. For thus venting his rage and disobeying the *dharma* he would have to be punished. Yudhishthira had allowed himself to be swayed by his passions, displaying affection for his family when they were no longer in the world of the living. This was the sole flaw in his perfect detachment, disqualifying him from his final release and liberation. He would have to return to the world of sorrow. The stark moral of this extraordinary tale is that even the attachment of love must eventually be dissolved.

Was it the *dharma* preached by the Brahmans that was the 'eternal' *dharma*, or was it the *dharma* that was the well-spring of Yudhishthira's being, the *dharma* by virtue of which he was the 'King of *dharma*'—'King of Righteousness' because the conscience of a truthful man cannot lead astray? He hesitated because God himself had driven him into violence and war, and had made him lie, but he nevertheless knew that his conscience transcended the 'righteousness' of the Brahmans and of Krishna himself.[1]

It is extremely rare in Hinduism for such a high value to be placed on individual conscience. In fact it is very often forgotten in the accounts of scholars whose motive (often unconscious, perhaps) is to reveal the weak points of Indian ethics. This is especially important in the modern context, since Hinduism is faced with a crisis of conscience in its treatment of low castes and Untouchables.

This will not mean that the *sanātana dharma*, the eternal *dharma* that is the especial property of the Indian people, will disappear; for this *dharma*, though it may be 'subtle' and 'difficult to know', is what gives Hinduism in all its phases

[1] R. C. Zaehner, *Hinduism*, Oxford University Press, London, 1962, p. 225.

its peculiar bitter-sweet flavour—the flavour of self-forgetfulness and renunciation certainly, but the flavour too of a thirst for righteousness in an unrighteous world and a constant yearning for truth wherever it may be found. This flavour is embodied as nowhere else in the legendary figure of Yudhishthira, the gentle and compassionate 'King of Righteousness', and in the historical figure of Mahātma Gandhi who declared that Truth was God.[1]

The *Bhagavad Gītā*

Besides being the most widely known of all the sacred books of India, the *Bhagavad Gītā* is the most important. It marks a turning-point both historically and philosophically, for it is the first time that the love of God for man finds expression in the Hindu scriptures. This luminous poem is an audacious attempt to fuse together the divergent traditions of the past and express their synthesis in universal human terms. It is also the ethical basis of modern Hinduism. No attempt will be made to describe the full range of ideas this remarkable poem covers, but rather to single out those aspects of its teaching which are of particular importance in the value system of the Great Tradition in modern times.

The *Bhagavad Gītā* is a poem of seven hundred stanzas in eighteen short sections, inserted in Book VI of the *Mahābhārata*. Krishna has consented to act as Arjuna's charioteer for the battle about to commence on the plain of Kurukshetra. Arjuna is distressed by the thought of killing his own kin who are ranged against him among the enemy. 'I will not fight!' he declares, and awaits Krishna's reply. Thus begins the debate around which revolves every ethical issue which has exercised the Indian mind for more than two millennia: its two main aspects the problems of action versus non-action, and of violence versus non-violence. All converges on the dialogue between initiator and initiate: Krishna—the trickster and genius of initiation—and Arjuna—the archetypal disciple, an Indian Everyman caught on the horns of an ethical dilemma. Krishna's advice has been used by contemplatives and activists, by Gandhian apostles of non-violence as well as by their opponents, to support their arguments for and against war.

Krishna answers Arjuna thus:

Thou dost feel pity where pity has no place. Wise men feel no pity either for what dies or for what lives. There never was a time when I and thou were not in existence, and all these princes too. Nor will the day ever come, hereafter, when all of us shall cease to be. . . .

In other words, the soul, or Ātman, is eternal and therefore cannot be slain, whatever form it may take in its pilgrimage from birth to rebirth.

[1] R. C. Zaehner, *Hinduism*, Oxford University Press, London, 1962, p. 17.

Krishna employs the same argument with which we are familiar from the story of Yudhishthira: 'Again, seeing thine own duty thou should'st not shrink from it: for there is no higher good for a Kshatrya than a righteous war.' This is followed by the famous injunction which has inspired so much controversy: 'If you are killed in action, heaven will be your lot; if you survive, you will rule the World. Hence fight!'

Many have found this argument immoral; the glorification of worldly power as a just reward for violence has often been cited as an example of Hindu hypocrisy, even by those who admire the essential teaching of the Gītā. The answer to this charge is implicit in the text: acts must be performed without attachment to their fruits. The Gītā formulates this most important ethical doctrine as follows:

He who resigns his activities to the Universal Self by forsaking attachment to them and their results, remains unstained by evil—just as the lotus leaf remains unstained by water.

The manner in which Krishna expresses his injunction to fight seems to come dangerously near to moral equivocation, for it appears to be no more than a specious declaration that a violent action cannot be wrong as long as the doer is detached from what he is doing. To say that it is impossible to kill an opponent's *soul* because one only kills his *body* might conceivably be right in Arjuna's case, but the Gītā is couched in terms which clearly imply universal applicability. One school of thought advances the idea that the Gītā resorts to paradox in order to shock the reader into an awareness of its deeper meaning. This is to turn the Gītā into a kind of Kshatryan mysticism, not unlike that of Japanese Zen Buddhism (which originally appealed to the Samurai class). This idea of 'Zen Hinduism' has some historical justification, as can be seen from the inconsistencies of the Gītā. For example, if, as it says in one section, one must act according to the *dharma* of one's *varṇa*, in this case the Kshatrya's, the exhortation to act according to one's *conscience* (*svadharma*, or personal morality) in other verses contradicts Krishna's instructions to Yudhishthira, whose conscience rebels against his Kshatrya *dharma*. This question is not answered by the Gītā.

Gandhi offered a slightly different interpretation: the Gītā is an allegory, 'not a historical work'; Kurukshetra is within, a battlefield of the soul. 'Krishna is the dweller within, ever whispering to a pure heart . . . under the guise of physical warfare'. For Gandhi, the Gītā 'described the duel that perpetually went on in the hearts of mankind. . . . Physical warfare was brought in merely to make the description of the internal duel more alluring.' But this does not square with the integral scheme of the epic, the central episode of which had always been a war. The whole epic, of which the Gītā is a small part, started as a bardic tale of Kshatrya valour, extolling the Kshatrya *dharma*. In the course of time, it became permeated with the initiatory symbolism of *rites de passage*, and a more universally acceptable ethic was introduced in order to take into account the needs of a more complex, caste-graded society. True, the author of the Gītā may have decided to utilize this popular text as a means to express his personal views on moral conduct. This, however, cannot be proved; we can only go by the text in its present form, and this cannot be divorced from the context, namely, the plot of the *Mahābhārata*. If the Gītā is to be read as it was intended, as an incident in a Kshatrya war, its moral teaching explicitly refers to conduct when *fighting*. The *Mahābhārata* war must be viewed for what it is—a cosmic rite—of which killing the foe is an integral part. It seems more likely that it was the epic which found a home for the Gītā, not the Gītā which found a home for the epic. Gandhi shows signs of finding his own theory a little hard to swallow, for he knows perfectly well that the Gītā contradicts his own unswerving faith in non-violence. He adopts the more charitable view that a poet cannot always anticipate the full implications of his own words. 'A poet's meaning is limitless', he says. This is true, for the meaning of the Gītā, as of all great works of art, has been something slightly different for each reader. In the course of two thousand years signs of strain in its philosophical structure have become increasingly apparent; the various elements which it attempts to synthesize do not completely accord with each other. The ethical core of the Gītā, the essential part which has survived the test of time, undoubtedly appears in the following verse, which Gandhi was fond of quoting: 'The sages say that renunciation means foregoing action which springs from desire, and relinquishing means the surrender of its fruit.' But Arjuna could renounce the fruit of his actions and still obey Krishna's command to fight. Gandhi was not happy with this. 'Let it be granted', he wrote in 1929 in an introduction to his Gujerāti translation of the Gītā, 'that according to the letter of the Gītā it is possible to say that warfare is consistent with renunciation of fruit. But after forty years' unremitting endeavour fully to enforce the teaching of the Gītā in my own life, I have, in all humility, felt that perfect renunciation is impossible without perfect observance of *ahiṃsā* [non-violence] in every shape and form.'

Arjuna is not entirely satisfied either, but not so much with the question of non-violence as with Krishna's promise that he will 'rule the World'. So he asks Krishna to explain the highest reward, which is liberation, *moksha*—here called *nirvāṇa*. First Krishna describes the conventional figure of the ideal man as *yogin*, whose mind is stilled and to whom 'supreme bliss draws nigh, his passions stilled, for he has become Brahman and is free from stain. . . . Seeing himself in all things and all things in himself, he sees the same thing everywhere.' At this point Krishna takes on a new tone, and

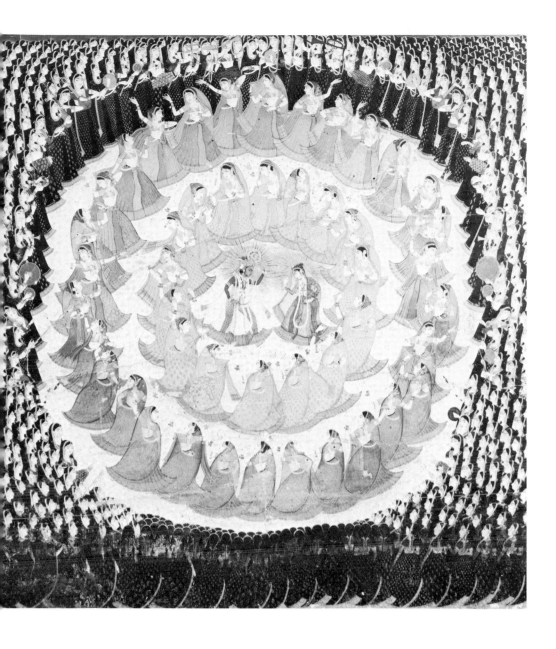

39. Ring Dance of Krishna and Gōpis. Rājasthān. *c.* 1790 A.D. *Jaipur Museum.*

40. Sri Chakra. Tantric *yantra*. *Author*.

41. Sri Chakra. Metal tantric *mūrti*. *Author*.

42. Benares as sacred enclosure. *Author*.

43. Hindu paradise garden. Temple fresco. Benares. *Author*.

44. Yoni-liṅgā. Dance *mudrā*. *Author*.

45. Yoni-liṅgā *mūrti*. Stone. Benares. *Author*.

46. Yoni-liṅgā *puja*. Punjab Hills. Nineteenth century A.D. *John R. Freeman*.

47. Chakras of Kuṇḍalinī Yoga. Nineteenth century A.D. *John R. Freeman*.

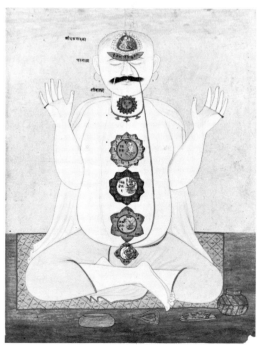

48. Wheel of the Law. Sānchī gateway. First century B.C. *Robert Skelton.*

49. Akbar's pillared throne. Fatehpur Sikri. A.D. 1575. *Martin Hürlimann.*

speaks of himself: 'For him who sees all things in me and me in all things, I am not lost nor is he lost to me.' The way of knowledge (*jñana yoga*) and the way of devotion (*bhakti yoga*) lead to the *nirvāṇa* of Brahman—but devotion is the easier way, open to all men including Śūdras and women.

This first reference to *bhakti*, like numerous examples from later periods, implies the inferiority of *bhakti* as a means to achieve union with God, even though at this point the *personal* God (Krishna himself) is elevated above the *impersonal* Absolute, or Brahman. By grace alone can bondage to *karma* be severed and the soul 'become Brahman'; here the Gītā affirms that only *after* becoming Brahman is the soul ready to draw near to God. Experience of the grace of a personal God figures in the tenth and thirteenth chapters, but it is not until right at the end of the Gītā that the climax is reached in this new revelation of God's love for man. During most of the discourse Krishna preserves the complete detachment of divinity: 'I am indifferent to all born things; there is none whom I hate, none whom I love.' The same detachment is enjoined on Krishna's worshippers: 'He who is without affection on any side, who does not rejoice or loathe as he obtains good or evil, his intelligence is firmly set [in wisdom].' Of this imperturbable indifference to the human craving for warmth Arnold Toynbee writes: 'As an intellectual achievement it is imposing; as a moral achievement it is overwhelming; but it has a disconcerting moral corollary; for perfect Detachment casts out Pity, and therefore also Love, as inexorably as it purges away all the evil passions.'[1]

The final revelation of Krishna's true identity as Vishnu the Supreme Lord in the great theophany of Chapter 11 (Plate 34)—with its echoing reverberations of a *rite de passage*—contains no hint of Krishna's ultimate message of love in the last chapter. The Hindu concept of God, unlike that of Christianity, includes the idea that He is author not only of all the good in the world but all the evil as well.

> I am come as Time, the waster of the peoples,
> Ready for the hour that ripens to their ruin.

The shattering revelation of Krishna's identity, which he has concealed from everyone by his earthly incarnation, prompts the terrified human being who has witnessed it—Arjuna—to exclaim: 'In a vision I have seen what no man has seen before: I rejoice in exultation, and yet my heart trembles with fear. . . . Show me again thine own human form. . . . When I see thy gentle human face, Krishna, I return to my own nature, and my heart is at peace.' Faced with Krishna as the Terror of Time, Arjuna surrenders, becomes the agent of the divine will.

[1] Arnold J. Toynbee, *A Study of History*, Oxford University Press, London, 1939, VI, p. 144.

The last verses of the Gītā are introduced with the same air of drama as were the secret revelations concerning the real meaning of *ātman* and *karma* introduced in the Upanishads. One has the impression that the author of the Gītā devoted very little space to so important a doctrine, and surrounded it with an air of mystery, lest he endanger his position with more orthodox Brahman monists:

Listen again to My final word, the most mysterious of all. With strong desire have I desired thee; therefore shall I tell thee thy salvation. Think on Me, sacrifice to Me, pay to Me homage; so shalt thou come to Me. I promise thee truly, for I love thee well. Give up all things of the law, turn to Me only as thy refuge. I shall deliver thee from all evil; have no care.

For most of the text the Gītā has maintained the traditional view that all activity is dictated by the *dharma* of *varṇa*, the *varṇas* being divinely ordained ('the fourfold order was created by Me'). Now Krishna gives precedence to action prompted by the heart (thinking, sacrifice, and homage include acts performed as a service to Krishna), a change in the Hindu outlook of considerable importance to the subsequent development of religious thought. Yet at public recitation and commentary on the Gītā nowadays it is not usually this last verse which receives the greatest emphasis, but one which, important as it is, keeps to the familiar ground of the Hindus' essential relativism for the means of attaining salvation. On several occasions I have seen non-Brahman *gurus* deliver this verse, with its invitation to all men, no matter what their caste, the tears rolling down their cheeks, unable to proceed further:

When any devotee seeks to worship any aspect of faith, it is none other than Myself that bestows that steadfast faith, and when by worshipping any aspect he wins what he desires, it is none other than Myself that grants his prayers. Howsoever men approach Me, so do I welcome them, for the path men take from every side is Mine.

The Gītā is loaded with emotional significance, especially for the lower castes. It offers the Hindu an ethic of action which is not explicitly tied to the ritual of the Brahmans. The idea of ritual sacrifice is transformed into one of self-sacrifice, the dedication of *all* one's acts to God as a form of penance. Nevertheless, Arjuna still wants to know which is the higher of the two paths, the classical renunciation of the sage or the life of un-self-seeking action. Krishna's answer is that 'both renunciation and holy work are a path to the Supreme; but better than the surrender of work is the Yoga of holy work. . . . No work stains a man who is pure, who is in harmony, who is master of his life, whose soul is one with the soul of the all.' Had the Gītā, at the same time, not emphasized the divine origins of the social hierarchy, it might have undermined concepts of purity and pollution.

For those who must earn a living and make their way in the world its ethic of action is somewhat remote. In today's world the Gītā is in many respects a discouraging text. To the modern eye it has one vitally important limitation—it ignores the essential creativity of man. True, it reveals a sensitive awareness of human responsibility, and enjoins people in all walks of life to act from the highest ethical standards. But the Gītā's emphasis throughout is on action without attachment to the fruits of one's labour. This is hardly an encouragement for a positive attitude to work, or the mobilization of religious energies for an inner drive towards work. Like the Buddha, Krishna is silent on the transformation of the world. 'Giving up or carrying on one's work,' he says, 'both lead to salvation; but of the two, carrying on one's work is the more excellent.' Unless the individual is a man of almost superhuman self-restraint and disinterestedness, the fruits of that work are themselves the greatest snare of all, entangling him in the causal network of *karma*. Moreover, since most commentators on the Gītā are ascetic Renouncers, *karma yoga* is generally presented as a dangerous compromise, an unfortunate necessity for the average man, to whom the path of pure contemplation (*jñana yoga*) is even more difficult.

The strength of this austere ethic is also its own weakness, for while it can summon a man to the peaks of spiritual achievement, it fails in any concrete sense to give guidance at a more humble level of human behaviour. One is struck by the fact that Indian thought seldom, if ever, shows any trace of the realism arising from personal commitment to workaday tasks. Not until the fifteenth century do we find a Hindu sage who had the down-to-earth realism of the practical man. For the work of the weaver Kabīr (later of Gandhi, who, besides being proficient at spinning and weaving was for many years a successful lawyer), gave him an understanding of the matter-of-fact realities of life which we miss in the princely personality of the Buddha and in the unknown author of the Gītā. Acquaintance with Indian thought, from monism to the pantheists, from the epics to the medieval literary masters, forces the student to conclude that one must work not because there is fulfilment to be gained thereby, or, negatively, because life has nothing better to offer, but only because otherwise one would starve. 'Nowhere does Krishna show even a faint appreciation of the usefulness of pain, of frustration, of sorrow . . . because Krishna cannot have his individuals tolerate pain, he cannot have them enjoy pleasure.'[1] There is no trace of the flute-playing trickster and lover of the cow girls (Plates 55 and 56) in the Gītā, as there is in the major text of the Krishna cult—the *Bhāgavata Purāṇa*.

This has undoubtedly been India's loss, and to some extent it has militated against the possibility of achieving the deepest fulfilment promised

[1] Narain (1957).

by Krishna in the last few words of the Gītā. For he who renounces the
fruits of his actions 'does not through his action burden himself with *guilt*,
for he acts only for the sake of the body and is content with what offers
itself'.[1] That word 'guilt' has dampened the spirits of many who would
otherwise have been willing to embrace the contradictions and stresses of
purposeful activity. Although the Gītā does not say it in so many words,
it nevertheless implies that the quietist, contemplative life is safer in the
long run, more likely to help a man achieve salvation than action—if for
no other reason than that he avoids unnecessary suffering.

This should not blind us to the merits of the Gītā, and to the fact that it
has given great consolation to millions.

When doubts haunt me, when disappointments stare me in the face, and I see not
one ray of light on the horizon, I turn to the Bhagavad Gītā, and find a verse to
comfort me; and I immediately begin to smile in the midst of overwhelming
sorrow. My life has been full of external tragedies and if they have not left any
visible or invisible effect on me, I owe it to the teaching of the Bhagavad Gītā.[2]

Certain Indian thinkers of today claim that the Gītā is of *universal* validity
for India. It is true that it contains a message that transcends, but does not
offend, caste distinctions; this has made it, on the ethical level, a unifying
factor in the pluralistic Hindu society. But India's cultural unity, if it is to
become a firm and durable reality, must inevitably be based on secular
principles, if for no other reason than the fact that approximately one-fourth
of the population is not Hindu. It should be clear from what has been said
in Part Three that, in the communalistic atmosphere of India, the ethical
principles of the Gītā cannot be distilled from it and rendered secular. In
the foreseeable future, inter-religious rivalry is unlikely to be resolved by
well-meaning, eclectic ecumenism.

A former President of India, Dr. Radhakrishnan, has played a conspicuous role in defining the relations between the Hindu religion and the secular
state. 'It may appear somewhat strange that our government should be a
secular one while our culture is rooted in spiritual values. Secularism here
does not mean irreligion or atheism or even stress on material comforts. It
proclaims that it lays stress on the universality of spiritual values which
may be attained by a variety of ways.'[3] Many Indians would sharply disagree
with this statement, for elsewhere Radhakrishnan has made it clear that he
regards differences of doctrine, dogma, and ritual, which for him are mere
symbols, as contradicting the essential unity of all religions, and that in
India this religious unity is a political reality: 'This is the meaning of a
secular conception of the state though it is not generally understood.'[4]

---

[1] Italics mine.   [2] M. K. Gandhi, *Young India*, 6 August 1925.
[3] S. Radhakrishnan, in Foreword to S. Abid Hussain, *The National Culture of India*,
Bombay, 1956, p. vii.   [4] Ibid., p. viii.

Radhakrishnan's critics infer from this line of reasoning that he is saying all religions are equal and Hinduism is the only true religion. Certainly it is an argument which is much resented by Indian Christians and Muslims.

K. M. Panikkar, whose views on the ethics of the Gītā contain a number of contradictions, states that the basis of the secular state 'is not built upon the foundation of ancient India, or of Hindu thought'.[1] But he goes on to explain how the modern Hindu reformers endowed 'the Hindu people as a whole with a new ethic and a message for social action', and that they found this 'dynamic doctrine for action' in the Gītā. Panikkar made it clear that this doctrine was offered to 'the Hindu people'. But then, in one leap, he extends his claim to include the entire Indian population: 'The Gītā has thus become the scripture of the new age. The main foundation on which its social doctrines, and even its political action depends. . . . No one can understand the developments which are taking place in India who has no appreciation of this fundamental fact.'[2] That the Gītā played a major role in the ethical reform of modern India is no doubt true, but to *secularize* the Gītā, as Panikkar seems to propose, and to make the unity of all religions the basis of Indian secularism, as Radhakrishnan suggests, are likely to result in the undermining of secular unity by partisans of religious creeds. It is stretching the limits of the Gītā's secular message too far to say, as Panikkar does of the ethical struggle in India today, that '—the battle is enjoined as at Kurukshetra'.

Had the roots of secularism been more solidly based in India's indigenous culture, and not in European liberalism of the last century and a half, there might have been greater internal checks against religious fanaticism. As it turned out, the traditions of the dominant community of the Hindus have not been of any positive help in the creation of a strong secular ethic during the crucial years of the independence struggle. That morality has never been separated from religion in the Hindu value system is something to do with the intrinsic nature of the Hindu religion itself; many respected Hindus believe this to be its source of greatest strength. Recent events in India suggest the contrary.

Before proceeding farther, we need to correct the impression of an exclusively religious bias in India's ethical teaching by examining it in relation to the concrete issues of daily life, politics, economics, and history. In the following section, therefore, another key text, the *Arthashāstra*, will help us to pursue the argument at a more secular level.

[1] K. M. Panikkar, *The State and the Citizen*, Bombay, 1956.
[2] K. M. Panikkar, *The Foundations of New India*, London, 1961.

The *Arthashāstra* and the cult of power

The *Arthashāstra* is one of the world's earliest books devoted to statecraft, written in terse, unadorned Sanskrit prose. Its chief concern was the establishment of a monolithic totalitarian state. Kauṭilya, to whom the authorship of the *Arthashāstra* is ascribed, is identified with the Kauṭilya who was chancellor to the grandfather of Ashoka, Chandragupta, in the late fourth century B.C. Whoever its author was, he possessed an intimate knowledge of state affairs and administrative policy during the Mauryan period. 'It went far beyond what was familiar and average practice for the *signores* of the early Italian Renaissance in these respects and was completely devoid of all "ideology" in our sense of the word.' (Max Weber.)

Almost certainly a Brahman, the *Arthashāstra*'s Kauṭilya was something of an aristocratic rebel: he cannot be said to have followed the orthodox teaching of the Brahmans. The *Arthashāstra* shows still more clearly than books in a similar vein how firm principle can be combined with total unscrupulousness and Realpolitik. For example, Book II is concerned with techniques for breaking up tribes in the interests of political unification:

Agents provocateurs should gain access to all these tribes, discover the possible sources of jealousy, hatred, contention among them, should disseminate the seeds of progressive dissension. . . . Let those of higher rank [within the tribe] be discouraged from eating at a common table with, and marriage with those of lower standing. Tribesmen of lower rank should, on the other hand, be instigated to [insist upon] commensality and intermarriage with the higher. The lesser should be provoked to claim equality of status in family, prowess, and change of place. Public decisions and tribal custom should be brought to dissolution by insistence upon the contrary. Litigation should be turned into a fight by the [king's paid] bravi who, at night, injure property, beasts, or men [of one party, to throw the blame upon the other, thereby fomenting the quarrel]. On all occasions of [such intra-tribal] conflict, the king should support the weaker party with funds and army, should instigate them to annihilate their opponents; or he [the king] might deport the splinter groups. Otherwise, he might settle the whole lot upon the land in one region, in detached farming units of five to ten families each. If they all remained together in one place, they might be capable of taking up arms. [Therefore] Let [the king] set a fine against their reunion. . . . Thus might he proceed against the tribes [to become] the sole absolute ruler [over them, as over the rest of the land]; so, on the other hand, might the tribes protect themselves against being thus overcome by the [external] absolute monarch.[1]

For replenishing the state treasury in times of emergency Kauṭilya proposes extraordinary measures; 'such demands', however, 'are to be made only *once*, never a second time.' These include the confiscation of

[1] *Arthashāstra*, 2.1.

property, robbery, murder, false accusations—'only against the seditious and the wicked, never against others'. Temple and monastic property could be confiscated by the proper minister on the pretext that it would be held in safe keeping. Disguised spies of the State were to set up cult images for the sake of cash gain, or to invent miracles for mulcting the credulous. Spies disguised as ascetic monks would thus gain access to all classes as agent of law and order. Revenue collectors were to solicit voluntary contributions by hiring spies disguised as private persons who, in turn, publicized their own pseudo-contributions. Spies were to trade with merchants, but to arrange to be robbed later by colleagues of the cash already collected in part payment. The extensive system of espionage proposed by the *Arthashāstra* was probably never fully adopted, but there seems little doubt that spies did, in fact, foment quarrels between two parties suspected of harbouring ideas subversive to the State in ways which Kauṭilya suggests. By poisoning one party and accusing the other, secret agents had a pretext to confiscate the property of both. Citizens who became too powerful could be sent off, inadequately armed, on some minor expedition, only to run into a staged ambush. An over-ambitious district official could be killed by his own son or brother at the instigation of the king's agents with the promise of the inheritance.

The author is realistic enough to admit that in such a climate of mutual suspicion and greed:

> The chief collector of revenue looks first to his own profit, and then to the king's, or destroys the king's gain altogether. In taking the property of others [as taxes] he diverts it according to his own sweet will.[1]

It is hardly surprising that Kauṭilya is reduced to comparing the detection of embezzlement with the difficulty of knowing when a fish drinks water. True, the *Arthashāstra* proposes more reasonable measures, such as pensions for disabled soldiers, and the employment of registrars in both cities and villages to keep a check on all material and human resources, births and deaths, immigration and emigration.

The ideal *janapada* (basic Mauryan administrative unit) is described thus:

> Free from swamps, rocks, salt-impregnated land, uneven land, thorn thickets, savage beasts, and savage tribesmen. Lovely, furnished with crown-lands, mineral wealth, elephant forests. Fit for cattle, human beings, with well-guarded herds, rich in herd-beasts, not watered by the rainfall alone. Well furnished with waterways and roads, and with trade goods of great value and variety, able to bear the army and taxes. With peasants who are dutiful, lords that are childish, a population mostly of the lower castes, and with men who are loyal and clean-lived. Such is the perfection of the *janapada*.[2]

[1] *Arthashāstra*, 8.4.   [2] Ibid., 6.1.

The implications of this deceptively idyllic scene become clear if the passage is compared with two others:

As for settling a land with the four *varṇa*, the one where the lowest *varṇa* predominates is better because it will permit all sorts of exploitation.[1]

From the helplessness of the villages there comes concentration of the men upon their fields, hence increase of taxes, labour supply, wealth, and grain.[2]

One phrase—'the helplessness of the villages'—reveals the true temper of the *Arthashāstra*. Since the only thing that matters is power, and since the only person with the character and intelligence to secure power is the king, any tactical move is justified if it serves the ultimate purpose of preserving his power. Therefore, he will flatter or mislead, bully or cajole, as circumstances demand, and much more freely than his ministers, who have to pretend to respect moral values and may even believe in them.

The daring originality of this difficult, complex work is unquestioned; the nature of its novel thinking is less well understood, largely because its problematic, amoral aspect is nevertheless firmly set within the larger scheme of *dharma*. Kauṭilya has been compared with Machiavelli in this respect; from their similarities and their differences much useful clarification can be obtained. The *Arthashāstra* was written approximately eighteen hundred years before the publication of *The Prince* (its final recension was probably written in the Gupta period).

It is the amoral elements of both *The Prince* and the *Arthashāstra* which provide our starting-point. The originality of Kauṭilya and Machiavelli, which makes them stand out in sharp relief against the diffuse body of received ideas on polity current in their respective periods, is of an aesthetic nature. In their methodology both men were *artists*, in so far as they had the artist's ability to project an ideal whole, then *theoreticians*. Their works are imaginative constructions of an extremely high aesthetic order, and if their viewpoints on religion, politics, and morals appear at times profoundly equivocal this is because works of art do not usually give prime importance to moral issues. True, Kauṭilya's objective was a shrewd exposition of the uses of power, and Machiavelli's the application of political science to government, but that they were fundamentally artists is revealed by, among other things, the degree to which they played with irrational, prophetic, and supernatural ideas. It is interesting that both their works are rooted in the archaic tradition of common-sense associated with the beast fable. As the inheritor of traditional science of royal pólity from the Parivrajakas— the Wanderers—who collated tribal lore (like surviving tribal ideas, these were couched in the terms of animal fables), Kauṭilya was familiar with such

[1] *Arthashāstra*, 7.12.   [2] Ibid., 2.1.

Orwellian themes as the Law of the Fishes (Matsyanyāya), or 'Big Fish eat Little Fish'. Machiavelli's symbols of the fox and the lion are borrowed from popular political sermonizing. In turn this tradition drew on the *Fables of Pilpay* and other famous beast fables whose origins have been incontestably traced to India. 'Pilpay' was probably a corruption of 'Bidyapat' or 'Vidyapati'. Indeed, it could be said that the sophistication and canny political realism we have come to associate with Indian officialdom are the products of an unbroken tradition reaching back to the early literature of the *Arthashāstra* period, when jungle lore, like the Pastoral in Europe, still served as a model for propounding ideas on statecraft. The Indian beast fable similarly travelled to Persia and China. This detail from the history of world literature serves to remind us of the common foundations of the Eurasian *oikumene*. 'Kautilyanism' is not exclusively oriental, nor is it a thing of the past.

There are many instances in world history when a period marked by political expansion or innovation such as that of the Mauryan Empire, encouraged vigorous political elites to aggrandize their power at the expense of the traditional restraints placed upon it, and to ignore the religious sanctions supporting those restraints. Cynical manipulation of religion in support of naked power is to be found in the political thought of the Legalists in ancient China, roughly contemporary with the *Arthashāstra*, in the Greek sophists and Melian debates, and in the medieval Islamic author Nizam-al-Mulk. The example of Machiavelli similarly prompted many latter-day, often lesser, political theorists to exceed even his excesses in this genre. Some of these thinkers directly influenced the actual policies of regimes, as did the Legalists in the Ch'in dynasty. In other cases, notably that of the *Arthashāstra*, we find that, non-conformist as its author was in many respects, he had the genius to articulate the unvoiced thoughts of numberless generations—thoughts too dangerous to avow, even if they frequently goaded men into following a particular line of action. This we may deduce from a comparison of Kauṭilya's *ideas* with a multitude of otherwise unreasoned or anarchic actions. As we shall see, the real power behind Kauṭilya's corrosive intelligence is that the extreme policies which he advocated (and not only he, for we find passages with the same devastating realism in the more conventional, wholly orthodox *Shāntiparva* and *Laws of Manu*) are related to the holism of *dharma*.

It is an error to believe that the abundant detail on government policy in the *Arthashāstra* has anything more than a *theoretical* bearing on actual conditions prevailing in Mauryan times. It opens by stating its main purpose thus:

Having gathered together all the diverse *arthashāstras* composed by former magistri, for the purpose of gaining [rule over] the whole earth and maintaining it, this single *arthashāstra* has been composed. . . . Material gain alone is the principal aim, for morality and pleasures are both rooted in material gain.

Kauṭilya definitely broke with Brahman tradition when he went so far as to state that the Vedas, philosophy, agriculture, and trade, are dependent *for their well-being* on the science of government, but he did not go so far as to take an anti-religious stand. He dared describe his work as nothing less than a *Veda*, a claim that could only be justifiable from the viewpoint of relative *dharma*—in this case monarchical *dharma*. This is not hypocrisy if we adjust ourselves to the fundamental and thoroughgoing moral relativism which Kauṭilya takes for granted. He is also precise in his priorities:

> Whenever there is disagreement between history and sacred law or between evidence and sacred law, then the matter shall be settled in accordance with sacred law.
> But whenever sacred law is in conflict with rational law, then reason shall be held authoritative. . . .

Is this, as is frequently claimed, 'a daring attempt at divesting politics of religion'? It is not easy to decide, because the author often fails to make it clear when he is advocating the manipulation of religious ideals as an expedient, such as propagandizing on behalf of kingship by invoking the name of the Vedic deity Indra as the kingly model, and when he is sincerely upholding the *dharma*. Viewed in the context of his period, Kauṭilya reflects the ferment of ideas which then prevailed concerning the sacred and the secular, which, as we have seen, were never clearly differentiated. The secularist and individualist element in his thought reveals the influence of tribal republicanism. The sense of expediency which informs much of the text, prompted him to take into account the most urgent need of his time— a strong centralized government. He was too much of a realist to imagine that tribal republicanism was equipped to achieve this aim. For Machiavelli a republic was also 'out of season'. Kauṭilya's innovation, therefore, was to apply his secular temperament to advocacy of monarchical government, of neither the sacred nor the contractual kind, but rule in the name of *dharma* in keeping with Mauryan pretensions. He could do this since the holistic *dharma*, of which divine right is an intrinsic part, was then elastic enough to permit his ideal king to manoeuvre without violating either his caste *dharma* as Kshatrya or his conscience (*svadharma*, his *personal* morality). Thus Kauṭilya's enumeration of qualities desirable in a ruler conforms to the highest ideals one could wish, but only those which should be applied to society as a whole. In his role as protector of his people, which Kauṭilya views within the perspective of social interdependence, the ruler must act in accord with the *dharma*—preserve *social* harmony. As a Kshatrya ruler among other rulers of adjacent territories, his moral obligation is that of a soldier who must achieve victory at any price.

Kauṭilya's intricate manipulation of religious *mores* favours the conclusion that his commitment to *dharma* is purely formal, whereas his philosophy of kingship is based on certain received ideas as to the relation between the human microcosm and the cosmic macrocosm. His king is instructed to gain mastery over himself through intellectual self-discipline and physical self-restraint, not so much as a religious duty in the conventional sense of the word, but because yoga of this sort is precisely that aspect of the Indian cult of power which unites the human to the cosmic power of Brahman. The *Arthashāstra* demonstrates, among other things, how pervasive is the yogic model in India's mental outlook. It is a textbook which extends to the sphere of politics that mental detachment which the most advanced Indian thinkers have cultivated. Kauṭilya not only scrutinizes the body politic with the same ruthless detachment as the yogin scrutinizes the functions of his own body and mind; he also proceeds from the assumption that a king can only obtain mastery over others by the kind of mastery over himself which harnesses to his own ends the infinitely more awesome, quasi-magical cosmic power. It may be recalled that this cosmic power is itself utterly impartial concerning good and evil. The king, as Heimann points out, is the 'no-person or all-person . . . an instrument of the community', an archetypal figurehead who oversteps the human sphere. The king is the Zero, an idea which originates in the magico-religious substratum of thought, an analogy of the generating and destroying capacities inherent in cosmic power. The cult of political power and the cult of mystical power were rooted in a single tradition: yoga. Kauṭilya's idea of disciplined manipulation of kingly authority is indeed chilling:

> It is power and power alone which, only when exercised by the king with impartiality and in proportion to guilt, either over his son or his enemy, maintains both this world and the next.

Kauṭilya is not alone in propounding this kind of doctrine. To take only two examples, both of them from texts of impeccable orthodoxy (the first, since it is from the *Mahābhārata*, is regarded as revealed truth):

> When wishing to smite [the king] should speak gently; after smiting he should speak gentler still; after striking off the head with his sword, he should grieve and shed tears. (*Shāntiparva.*)
>
> Punishment alone governs all created beings, punishment alone protects them, punishment watches over them while they sleep; the wise declare punishment to be identical with the law. If punishment is properly inflicted after due consideration, it makes all people happy; but inflicted without consideration, it destroys everything. . . . The whole world is kept in order by punishment, for a guiltless

man is hard to find; through fear of punishment the whole world yields the enjoyment which it owes. (*Laws of Manu.*)

Manu is dealing here with an important concept in traditional Indian social theory: *daṇḍaniti*, the science of punishment, which, if practised consistently, ends in the cult of power for its own sake. The word *daṇḍa* literally means a staff or rod; it can equally mean power and authority which the staff of the holy man or of the king implies, and also 'punishment'. The Daṇḍins, a celebrated order of ochre-robed renouncers who are a common feature of life in India today, with their rods of office wrapped in ochre ('wands' might be a more appropriate word) which must never touch the ground, are a reminder that behind the Reichsmarschall-Goering overtones of Daṇḍa symbolism lies the idea of moral restraint, the acquisition of knowledge, and spiritual discipline through yoga, rather than ruthless material aggrandisement. Kauṭilya was more aware (notice the persistently shrewd realism) than Manu that the unrestricted use of punishment could easily recoil upon its author. When we say that Kauṭilya shared in common with the *Shāntiparva* and *Manusmṛti* the common notion of government by coercion, we mean that he reflects the juridical ideas of the time; criminal law preceded civil law, and the primary function of the king was coercive. The functions assigned to the Indian deities and their earthly representatives of the Mauryan period were predominantly penal. The same could be said for most, if not all, archaic civilizations; the difference is that in India the emphasis on coercion has never altered, as may be judged from the fact that in the ordinary daily evaluation of conduct in interpersonal relations there is a strong legalistic stress on caste-rules. Kauṭilya, and a modern village or caste council, both speak the same language of power and conformist morality, Daṇḍa and Dharma, with the strong authoritarian note characteristic of Hindu ethics. The cult of power —*daṇḍaniti*—as first expounded in the great texts on polity, has the same familiar ring to it as the following passage from the much older *Chāndogya Upanishad*, which is entirely religious in inspiration:

Power is superior to knowledge. One powerful man can defeat a hundred men of knowledge. If a man is powerful, he triumphs. By power the world stands firm. Meditate on power. He who meditates on power as Brahman is, as it were, lord over all.

I would suggest that Kauṭilya was not so much challenging the holistic *dharma* as attempting a new synthesis between its two basic components— the power of *brahman* and the power of *kshatra*—in the interests of political realism. He was, as far as we know, the first total political specialist; he created a political monism by applying his all-embracing intelligence to the politicization of Brahmanism. We have to set the *Arthashāstra* within its political context. As has been suggested by P. C. Chakravarti:

In the congeries of small states into which India was habitually divided, often without natural frontiers marking them off into separate geographical units, military strength was the only guarantee not merely against strong rivals in the neighbourhood but against the subtler forces of internal disintegration. But there was perhaps a deeper reason behind this ceaseless advocacy of war. The Hindus, it is well known, had evolved a synthesis out of the heterogeneous mass of customs, traditions, values, tastes, and beliefs, held by the various tribes and races inhabiting this vast continent. This synthesis was already a well established fact before the rise of the Mauryan empire, and was never seriously disturbed till the advent of Islam. But there was nothing corresponding to this cultural unity in the political sphere. From early times, therefore, men longed to set up a common political organisation for the whole country. This longing gave birth to the concept of Chakravartin. . . . The motive force behind the endless campaigns and expeditions of the Mauryas and the Guptas, of the Gurjara-Pratihāras, the Pālas and the Rāṣhtrakuṭas does not seem to have been mere ambition, a passion for conquering for the sake of conquering, but a conscious or unconscious urge to bring the whole country under one single hegemony.[1]

We might add that Kautilya himself was among the most zealous advocates of this programme. Against this tendency to subdue by force and to rule absolutely may be placed the ideal 'conquest of the universe' as treated in the *Rāmāyana*: *Digvijaya*. Implicit in the latter is a form of decentralized political structure. According to the *Digvijaya* theory, vanquished kings were reinstated in their kingdoms as a matter of principle. They had to pay allegiance to the paramount king in the form of either tribute or personal service. The practice was common, particularly in the treatment of the most powerful tribal dynasties. The disadvantage of such a policy was the inherently fissile structure of its various political units. It was certainly the cause of loose national cohesion, contributing to the failure of universal empires, and it discouraged the evolution of a unified nation-state theory.

Kautilya advocated an extremely dangerous policy of secret diplomacy between neighbouring states which is a reflection of chronic rivalry. He called it the theory of the Maṇḍala, or Circle of States, a political application of the Indian concern with perpetual motion. If it is remembered that India invented the game of chess, which originally had four opposing sides (it seems always to have been played by two opponents), based on the traditional four wings of Indian armies, and the four provinces of Mauryan political administration, Kautilya's pedantic, but shrewd Maṇḍala system (a maṇḍala presupposes a quadripartite division) may be seen for what it really was: a game in the balance of power, but a game played in deadly earnest. Kautilya preferred to change his territorial chequerboard from a square to a circle.

The game was designed to maintain power alliances with neighbouring

[1] P. C. Chakravarti, *The Art of War in Ancient India*, Dacca, 1941, p. 192.

states. The king on whose territory the Maṇḍala is centred is called 'he who desires conquest'. The kings in the various sectors of the encircling ring are *Para*, 'the other', or 'the enemy'. When one of these kings gets himself into trouble he must be attacked. The circle outside this neighbouring ring —and one must imagine a centrifugal pull away from the centre in ever-expanding circles—are 'friends', and beyond the 'friends' are the 'enemy's friends' and the 'friends' friends' in alternating circles of alliance and hostility, ring around ring outwards from the original territory *ad infinitum*. How often does one not hear reiterated today all over Asia the ancient jingle: 'The enemy of my enemy is my friend!' The purpose of the *Artha-shāstra* Maṇḍala is to show that neighbours are natural enemies, while neighbours beyond the neighbours are natural allies. Indian history is full of cases of canny alliances between alternate states who joined campaigns of encirclement to harass the State caught between them. It could also be said that Kauṭilya, in the interests of politics, applied his systematic mind to the normally unconscious programme of harnessing the dangerous power of the Antipodes. The disintegration of warring states can be correlated to the corrosion of group solidarity, which Kauṭilya regards as no more than one among many rules of the game. 'The same style of Indian thought,' says Zimmer admiringly of Kauṭilya, 'that invented the game of chess grasped with profound insight the rules of this larger game of power.'[1] Maybe, but it can be proved fallible.[2] Within the state, such a policy tends to follow a common pattern—the growth of personal (or palace) rule, the seclusion of the ruler, the proliferation of the bureaucracy and its alienation from the groups on whose support the dynasty originally depended, the formalization of ideology, the increase of luxury spending on the part of the élite, the growing burden of taxation, the decline of economic activity with the growth of village settlements and ruralization in fear of urban innovation and change. In economic terms, Kauṭilyan greed for taxes, vast armies, and bureaucracies could only lead to helotry and exploitation of the peasantry after an early, short-lived urban expansion.

In my view it is this aspect of Kauṭilyan ambition which should be regarded as a characteristic feature of Indian history. It may not appear so very different from despotism anywhere else in the world, yet it arises less from economic factors than from ethical assumptions: moral relativism, the conception of *dharma* as immanent in the social structure, and the alienation of the king through his subordinate role in its encircling framework. Kauṭilyan psychology is the result of historic pressures: a pluralistic society and the vastness of a tropical environment which, even with the

[1] Zimmer (1951) reprinted 1956, p. 139.

[2] In a hypothetical instance, A may rely on D and E against B and C, but B is a friend of E against C and D, and E passes intelligence secrets to B against C and D. . . .

application of modern technology, is exceptionally resistant to control and the establishment of efficient means of communication.

Kauṭilya advocated a policy for a rising dynasty who governed an expanding urban society, promoted an aggressive programme of land settlement, and pursued its military ambitions with utter ruthlessness, but there is a total absence from his work of any understanding of the need for a sense of solidarity among his ideal ruling class. Kauṭilya's king is at all times appallingly *alone*. Zimmer compares the Hindu king to a lonely beast of prey doomed to die alone in the jungle. The king 'stands merely for himself—himself and those he can pay or bribe, gain with favour, or threaten and bully into his service. And when he falls, it is simply he who falls—together with those who depended on his rule or misrule.' Continuity of power on earth, says Zimmer, is in the hands of those at the summit of the Hindu social pyramid who act as repositories of the holy power. 'But as for kings: their valour, their fate [*daivam*], their agony is their own.'[1] It was with the aid of Kauṭilyan methods that the Mauryan empire accomplished prodigious feats of state industry, road construction, and public works; similarly, it is by Kauṭilyan methods that comparable labours have been undertaken in modern times. Is there not a profound affinity between the picture which the *Arthashāstra* evokes of a giant, top-heavy bureaucracy, and the obsession with the intricacies of power, conspiracy, and intrigue which pervades the neo-Mauryan bureaucracy housed in Delhi's stone and concrete palaces today? True, a solitary ruler has been replaced by the machinery of parliamentary institutions; nevertheless, it is the absolute remoteness of the seat of power from the ferment in society as a whole which rings like an echoing note across the intervening millennia. The institutions of government have changed beyond recognition, the psychology of the bureaucracy but little. With rare exceptions, government has come to be regarded as marginal to an Indian's daily life and a thing apart— an attitude which has been widely prevalent for well over a thousand years, a continuous demonstration of the alienating mentality which was first reflected by Kauṭilya. Turkish, Afghan, Moghul, and British rule have accentuated this apathy. Faced with an attitude of antipathy to, and deep suspicion of, all government as something alien, even the most well-meaning modern official tends to retreat behind bureaucratic privilege to manipulate people on the assumption that they are as passive as pawns on a chessboard. This antipathy is mutual and has a long history, while its sublimation in organized opposition and constitutional co-operation is a recent innovation, slow to put down roots.

[1] H. Zimmer, *Philosophies of India*, New York, reprinted 1956, pp. 103–4.

The Dharma of Crisis

It is not only in the *Arthashāstra* that we find in Indian thinkers the advocacy of political cunning. But before an analysis of a Kauṭilyan type of political theory in the staid, respectable *Shāntiparva*, the word 'cunning' should be explained. Archaic societies, especially those organized on a tribal basis, often ascribe virtue to what we would today describe as 'cunning'; the trickster figure is but one example of this tendency.

The original and natural idea of knowledge is that of 'cunning', or the possession of wits. Odysseus is the original type of thinker, a man of many ideas who could overcome the Cyclops and achieve a significant triumph of mind over matter. Knowledge is thus a capacity for overcoming the difficulties of life and achieving success in the world.[1]

In India, the Odysseus type is represented by the Vidyādhara, culture hero of popular literature, whom Hans van Buitenen describes as follows:

Although his actions are primarily self-centred, this very constancy in the pursuit of his purposes renders him dependable for others when his self-interest happens to coincide with theirs. If he is in a subordinate position, which of course does not happen often, this makes for an unstraying loyalty. . . .[2]

Perseverance and constancy have as their function dependability. The word is *dhira*, describing poise and mental equilibrium which is the condition of constancy and reliability, frequently likened to the repose of the ocean deeps which, in spite of minor disturbances at the surface, remain largely unperturbed. This is synonymous with wisdom as expressed in action, and the qualification of *gambhira*, 'deep', denotes less the penetration of a man's intelligence than the profundity of his imperturbability.[3]

This is the best description known to me of the secular Indian heroic ideal. Although van Buitenen does not say so, the character of the Vidyādhara is virtually universal in all heroic traditions of pre-literate culture. Presence of mind, pinpointed concentration of purpose, ruthlessness in the pursuit of knowledge—these are typical heroic features of the resourceful man prior to the advent of book-learning.

If the folklore associated with 'cunning' is taken into account, we are in a better position to assess an example in its proper perspective, as expounded by the author of the *Shāntiparva*. The dying King Bhīṣma, lying on a bed of arrows after the decimation of his people in the Mahābhārata war, expounds the orthodox theory of non-violent political rule. In the course of this long discourse he concedes, and indeed upholds, the right

[1] G. S. Brett, *Psychology Ancient and Modern*, London, 1928, p. 37.
[2] H. van Buitenen, 'The Indian Hero as Vidyādhara', in Singer (ed.) (1959), p. 100.
[3] Ibid., p. 101.

of a king to resort, in cases of dire necessity, to the Dharma of Crisis or Apaddharma.[1] He does this in response to the persistent questioning of Yudhishthira on the correctness of political ethics at a time when the moral values of the society have degenerated, the financial resources of the government are depleted, and the army is harried by its enemies, to whose side former allies have deserted. An atmosphere of extreme tension is created by Yudhishthira's importunate inquiry, with its implicit criticism. Yet he alone of the characters in the epic, since he had displayed a strength made perfect in weakness, had earned the right to raise the problem of means.

In reply, Bhīsma grants any man the right to transgress the injunctions of the Dharma at a time of crisis, but that at all other times in the course of normal life the Dharma of Righteousness must be observed. This is a point of extreme importance, for it raises the whole problem of the extent to which Indian tradition sanctions immoral actions in wartime, and the degree of guilt to be imputed to those who have recourse to such actions in their effort to defeat an implacable foe. Bhīsma quotes the sage Bhārad-vāja (whose remark on striking off the head of an enemy appears earlier):

A person [or king] should never act in accordance with these rules [of Apad-dharma]. These measures laid down by me should be taken recourse to only in times of extremes of distress. Inspired by the motive of doing good to you, I have said this for instructing you in counteracting the use of these measures by the enemy.[2]

Bhīsma is careful to qualify his answer by asserting that the Dharma of Crisis is only to be resorted to in time of war, but that the canons of the Dharma of Righteousness cannot be transgressed at any other time. D. Mackenzie Brown puts forward a view which goes a long way to excuse this policy:

The section [of the *Shāntiparva*] dealing with periods of disaster contains some of the most cold-blooded realism in the history of political theory. Unless the modern reader fully appreciates the tenacity and restraining power of Dharma in traditional Indian government, he may easily conclude that cynicism is the guiding tenet of the author of the Shāntiparva. But behind all the brutal expedien-cies there remains an ultimate accountability to the rule of Dharma.[3]

India, of course, is not alone in being subject to the dangers of Machi-avellian politics. However, the poetic form of the *Mahābhārata* does not

[1] *Shāntiparva*, lxxx, 5.
[2] *Shāntiparva*, cxl, 70, translated by V. P. Varma, *Studies in Hindu Political Thought and its Metaphysical Foundations*, Delhi, 1959, p. 151.
[3] D. Mackenzie Brown, *The White Umbrella*, University of California Press, Berkeley, 1953, p. 37.

make it particularly easy for the modern mind to assess the moral implications behind the Dharma of Crisis. Let us, therefore, compare the latter with a modern treatment of a similar dilemma—Rolf Hochhuth's play, *The Soldiers*—in which he touches on this issue when referring to the moral attitudes of those who were responsible for the Dresden fire raid. He has Churchill declare: 'Two wars have taught me a lesson: the man with the will to conquer must be as evil as the man who seeks to destroy.' In effect, Hochhuth was firmly in accord with the outlook of Bhīṣma when he personally stated that 'whoever has Hitler for an enemy cannot rely on the Christian code of morals alone'. Unless one adopts a consistently Gandhian approach, this point is probably unanswerable. Indeed Hochhuth gives George Bell, Bishop of Chichester, the opportunity to advance a Christian equivalent of the Gandhian point of view. Gandhi himself would not endorse the Dharma of Crisis under any circumstances, and on this point he is perhaps unique in Indian history. In practice, he admitted that he fell far below his ideal on a number of crucial occasions, but not, I believe, because he did not sincerely hold a totally consistent policy of non-violence and an undeviating adherence to the Dharma. The deeper reason for his occasional failing lies, I would suggest, not in moral weakness but in the more general Indian failure to have a firm sense of developmental history. Gandhi was a man who lived in the moment—and with prodigious courage —translating his immediate response to a moral challenge into extempore political policy. In the expediency of the moment no more than the finest moral distinction can be drawn between the sudden reversal of his policy in accordance with his 'inner voice'—the Dharma of Righteousness—and the human proclivity to follow the Dharma of Crisis.

To the Hindu *every* moment is a crisis and yet no moment in historic time can ever have decisive significance in the scheme of Great Time. Hindu thought 'disregards the standard of constant value', writes Betty Heimann, and she compares the Greek concept of *kairos*, 'fertile moment of decision', with the Sanskrit *kṣaṇa*, an especially accidental aggregation of moments. 'Each event is but a temporary coagulation of circumstances which the next moment again dissolve.'[1] It is the attitude revealed in this idea, more than any moral deficiency or cynicism, which, it would seem to me, makes the sincere adherent of righteous Dharma prone to resolve ethical antinomies according to the Dharma of Crisis.

I referred above to the Hindu idea that, in one sense, every moment is a crisis; in the context, the negative aspect of this theory was implied. But this idea need not be applied in a negative fashion. Indian thought also reveals one impressive consequence of its unflinching realism in the face of unceasing change from moment to moment. For the corollary of permanent

[1] B. Heimann (1964), p. 64.

crisis is imperturbability before the catastrophe of the unforeseen. Zimmer had a profound understanding of this attitude; his brilliant analysis warrants quotation *in extenso*. In his interpretation of a Puranic myth, he explains how 'the unexpected constitutes the form-building principle of the plot'; the divine comedy 'proceeds . . . by surprises, involuntary acts, and abrupt reversals'. Zimmer compares the Hindu view of creation to the metabolism of the human body:

> Like the human body, the cosmos is in part built up anew, every night, every day; by a process of unending regeneration it remains alive. But the manner of its growth is by abrupt occurrence, crises, surprising events and even mortifying accidents. Everything is forever going wrong; and yet, that is precisely the circumstance by which the miraculous development comes to pass. The great entirety jolts from crisis to crisis: that is the precarious, hair-raising manner of self-transport by which it moves. The interpretation of the world process as a continual crisis would have been rejected by the last generation as an unwarranted and pessimistic view of life; the state of world affairs, however, almost forces such a conception on our minds today. . . .

Zimmer goes on to explain the consequences of the consistent application of such an attitude:

> . . . there is some secret safety even in the disorderliness of natural occurrences, some hidden power that creates surprising balances which keep the car of destiny from being finally overturned or smashed. Throughout all the pommeling that they suffer while creating the world and sustaining it through its ever self-renewed re creation, the divine forces remain always true to their essential nature. That is why they are never ultimately frustrated by the startling, puzzling, and breath-taking violence of events. . . The course of the world runs awry, but therewith it goes directly to its goal. The catastrophe of the previously unforeseen is what breaks the world progression forward, and the moment the catastrophe has come to pass it appears to be what was intended all the while. For it is creative in a deeper way than the planning creative spirit supposes. It transforms the situation, forces an alteration on the creative spirit, and throws it into a play that carries it beyond itself, carries it, that is to say, really and properly into play, and into a play that entrains the entirety of creation. The planner, the watcher, is compelled to become the endurer, the sufferer. Such a metamorphosis into the opposite, into the absolutely alien, is what throws the knots that reticulate the net of the living whole and mesh the individual alive into the fabric.[1]

Two ethical experiments

Since the disappearance of Buddhism from Indian soil (with the exception of the Himalayan border states) its influence has been only slight. Its

[1] Heinrich Zimmer, *The King and the Corpse*, New York, reprinted 1960, pp. 251–9.

significance for the present study lies in the mode whereby such a strong protestant ethic rose to great prominence in India, but was then absorbed back into the orthodox faith. Its historical evolution, its relation to social and political institutions supply us with comparative material which is relevant to the study of modern forms of Hindu protestantism, particularly Gandhism, and of the difficulties which any Indian ideological movement has in an attempt to break with established order—a constant factor since the Buddhist period, placing identical forms of constraint on heterodox movements.

The origin and development of Buddhism should be viewed in its historical context. Three phases can be distinguished: the first begins with the organization of monasteries during the Buddha's own lifetime, and the establishment of the Saṅgha, the Buddhist monastic order, which has been preserved elsewhere in Asia in unbroken continuity for twenty-five centuries. The second phase begins with the conversion of the Mauryan emperor Ashoka to Buddhism, and the transformation of pure Buddhist self-analysis into a salvation religion. The third phase may be described as the Hinduization of Buddhism.

As we have already seen, just before the birth of the Buddha, in the sixth and fifth centuries B.C., the first large state in India since the conquest of the Harappans, the north-eastern kingdom of Magadha, rose to power. Its colossal capital city of Pāṭaliputra was probably larger than Imperial Rome. This state and its rival neighbour, Kosala, provided the scene against which the activities of Gautama, the Buddha, and of another great reformer, Mahāvīra, founder of the Jains, were set. Magadha is important in Buddhist history because it gave the heretical new movement patrons who were powerful enough to bolster its institutions against the hostility of Brahman orthodoxy. The same protection was also afforded to the Jains. The cultivated language of Brahmanism was Sanskrit (spoken only by priests and the intelligentsia),[1] but in the days of the Buddha the masses spoke in the vernacular languages, or Prakrits. The Buddha himself probably taught in the Magadhi Prakrit. His doctrine was first written down two centuries after his death in Pāli, the most important of all the Prakrits. The Buddha could therefore offer the urban middle-class laity (hitherto ignored by the Brahmans) a more attractive alternative to Brahmanical ritualism—liberation from the eternal wheel of rebirth, and from social and productive obligations—which he taught in a language all could understand. His ethical experiment was conducted with relative indifference to political

[1] 'Sanskrit'—'sam-skṛta—used in the sense of "ritually pure" in the etymological (true) sense of the word; "put (—skṛta—) together (sam—)".' Paul Thieme in *India, Pakistan, Ceylon*, ed. W. Norman Brown, University of Pennsylvania Press, Philadelphia, rev. edn., 1960, p. 72.

institutions. But the emperor Ashoka, whose ethical experiment will form the second theme of this section, welded the teachings of the Buddha to his system of government.

It will be seen at once that there are several historical parallels here between the rise of Buddhism and the rise of Gandhism: middle-class patronage; an emotionally attractive challenge to the sacred authority of the Brahmans by a charismatic, saintly leader of non-Brahman origin; a disciplined, puritan ethic; the nation-wide attempt to propagate this ethic in a single language; a mobile merchant caste, the Hindi-speaking *baniyas*, to finance the organization throughout India; and finally, at the head of the movement an ascetic of uncompromising truthfulness who based his doctrine on the thirst for individual salvation, with 'liberation' and 'freedom' the primary goals.

Prince Gautama was born in 545 B.C., son of a Kshatrya clan-king of the non-Aryan Śākyas who ruled in the city of Kapilavastu. The Jain, Mahāvīra, came from a neighbouring district, close enough for his ideas to have left a profound influence on the aristocratic society in which the younger man was brought up. At the age of twenty-nine Gautama left his wife and child, and became a wandering ascetic.

Gautama's teaching after he became the Buddha (all the evidence is limited to texts written after his death) was concerned with a radical diagnosis and cure for the sufferings of life and existence in Time. He was far more interested in human psychology than in religion. He was not an atheist, but neither was he a theist; he discouraged excessive and, as he thought, fruitless preoccupation with the nature of Ultimate Reality. What it was and how it originated were entirely irrelevant to Gautama, who urged his followers to attend to what he regarded as the more urgent problem of individual salvation. He ignored the questions of the Ātman's identity with Brahman, of the existence of a Godhead, world-soul, or first cause.

Thus the Buddha gained his reputation, and his earliest followers, as a spiritual physician more than as a religious reformer. He had no creed, he ignored polytheism, cosmology, the Brahmanic worship of temple deities. 'Birth is suffering, old age is suffering, death is suffering, to be united with what one loves not is suffering, to be separated from what one loves is suffering, not to attain one's desires is suffering.' It is desire that leads from birth to rebirth. We are already familiar with this vein of thought from the Hindu tradition; the Buddha's philosophy, however, places greater emphasis on suffering.

But the originality of his teaching was to give world-negation an ethical alternative. First, he adapted the idea of *ahiṃsā*, non-violence, turning it into the first ethic of compassion in religious history. The Buddha objected to violence, not because it was polluting, as in Jainism, but because it was cruel—the active agent of suffering. Secondly, the Buddha made his ethical disposition the means to achieve salvation, *nirvāṇa*, or liberation. Classical Hinduism, on the other hand, made virtuous conduct the means to achieve status in the sequence of rebirths of the individual soul. To obtain *moksha* in this life, the Brahmans had invented their system of contemplative analysis aiming at realization of the soul's identity with Brahman; in this teaching ethical conduct plays a negligible part, for the *latent* identity of Ātman with Brahman is beyond good and evil. For the Buddha, a pure mind and a compassionate heart lead to release from suffering. Inward detachment from the world should be outwardly expressed in ethical conduct.

Thirdly, it was the Buddha's originality to regard the possession of ethical feeling as the only real charisma—the 'radiation of kindliness'. This was why he rejected hereditary priesthood. One is not born holy, one can only become holy by ethical conduct. 'The righteous monk is sympathetic and merciful, and strives with friendly feeling for the good of all living things.' But by this he does not imply active love, for active love feeds attachment to earthly cares, and though Buddhism is an ethic of inner perfection like the teaching of Christ, it does not promote *active* compassion. The Christian idea that evil in the world can be transformed into good is not to be found in the teachings of the Buddha, who is silent on the question of redemption of the world. 'The perfect man' is he 'who cares not for others, who has no relations, who controls himself, who is firmly fixed in the hearth of truth, in whom the fundamental evils are extinguished, who has thrown hatred from him: him I call a Brahman.' 'Those who love nothing in the world are rich in joy and free from pain.' To a father who has lost his son he says: 'What one loves brings woe and lamentation.'

Like the teaching of the *Bhagavad Gītā*, the doctrine of Buddhism enlarged on the original Hindu orthodoxy. The All-Compassionate One, the concepts of *karuṇā* (compassion) and *metteya* (the sentiment of friendliness), or as Oldenberg puts it, 'the tranquil feeling of friendly concord', are not the same thing as Christian *charitas*. True, it is said that 'like a mighty wind the blessed one blows over the world with the wind of his love, so cool and sweet, quiet and delicate'. But although the Buddhist is taught not to *hate* his enemies, he is given no encouragement to love them.

The principal innovations of Buddhism are ethical; for our purposes its differences with the ascetic tradition of the post-Vedic period are of minor importance. The most distinctive metaphysical doctrine of Buddhism is the non-existence of the self, and the concept of ultimate reality as Nothingness, the Void, or *Śūnyatā*, but this doctrine is thought to post-date the

Buddha's lifetime. These ideas were even more austere than those of Vedānta since Buddhism considered the identity of Ātman and Brahman unreal, a vital shift in viewpoint, for it reduces everything until nothing is left.

The Buddha's ethic of compassion was soon recognized by those classes excluded from Brahman ritual to be superior to the traditional *dharma*, especially in its relation to the eternal *dharma*, or eternal moral law. Compassionate love breaks down caste barriers; it bases social obligation on the moral ideal of purity of heart. The Buddha's fame was soon to spread 'like the sound of a great bell hung in the canopy of the skies', but his doctrine was not regarded as absolute truth; the searcher was invited to put it to the test of personal experiment.

Buddhism was anti-political—it was not concerned with changing the social order. By emphasizing a moral principle of conduct for the individual rather than ritual duties it disengaged itself from the hierarchical interdependence of the caste system. This worked to its disadvantage in India but greatly facilitated its diffusion throughout the non-caste societies of East Asia. The Buddha's own teaching was too pessimistic and austere to be widely acceptable without some special leaven. Without Ashoka's organizing genius it is doubtful whether Buddhism would have been one of the world's great religions.

The Mauryan empire was carved out of northern India by the ruthless and brilliant statesmanship of Ashoka's grandfather, Chandragupta, absorbing the kingdom of Magadha in the process. Only one other powerful state, Kalinga, remained independent when Ashoka became emperor in 260 B.C. It was remorse at the bloodshed which Ashoka inflicted on this kingdom when he crushed it in battle that moved him to become a Buddhist. But he had first extended his domain as far as the deep south, Tamilnad, and thus he had become the ruler of a vast territory extending across virtually the entire sub-continent.

Ashoka was a sincere Buddhist, and a few years after his conversion became a full member of the Saṇgha. He was a benevolent despot who revived the figure of the Chakravartin, the ruler of the Dharma, in his own person. He engaged in vigorous public construction work and social welfare schemes, and also encouraged an extensive missionary programme for the propagation of the faith, both in India and Ceylon. His humane and carefully worded edicts, which he probably composed himself, are justly celebrated; they also provide one of the chief means for documenting this period in Indian history. But behind the benign, somewhat Confucian exterior of the imperial lawgiver was a will strong enough to maintain power; the author of the elegantly chiselled edicts also established institutes of espionage in the established style of the *Arthashāstra*, and an all-powerful bureaucracy for the supervision of trade and administration. Here is Ashoka writing at his most genial:

> His Sacred Majesty desires that all animate beings should have security, self-control, peace of mind and joyousness. . . . And for this purpose has this pious edict been written in order that my sons and grandsons, who, maybe, should not regard it as their duty to conquer a new conquest. If, perchance, they become engaged in a conquest of arms, they should take pleasure in patience and gentleness and regard as the only true conquest the conquest won by piety. That avails for both this world and the next. Let all joy be in effort, because that avails for both this world and the next.

It is a question whether Ashoka's advocacy of Buddhism was a matter of personal conviction or a shrewd expedient. In Ashoka's commitment to Buddhism as a challenging alternative to the Brahmanic *dharma* the strength of Buddhism to provide a united India with a universal ethic was subjected to its severest test. Ashoka did not, as used to be claimed, make Buddhism a state religion, but used it as an institutional check against the future abuse of power, the effectiveness of which was probably severely in doubt in the lifetime of Ashoka himself. India already had a plurality of long-established religious beliefs when Ashoka made common cause with the relatively small, though prosperous, Buddhist sect. To make Buddhism the *state religion* would have been fraught with risk, which, as we have seen in our examination of the modern pluralistic society, is liable to end in violent communal resistance. That Ashoka was cautious in religious matters is evident from Rock Edict XII:

> On each occasion one should honour another man's sect, for by doing so one increases the influence of one's own sect and benefits that of the other man, while, by doing otherwise, one diminishes the influence of one's own sect and harms the other man's . . . therefore concord is to be commended so that men may hear one another's principles. . . .[1]

Ashoka had an undoubtedly genuine belief in non-violence, as reformulated in his 'conquest by *Dhamma*' (the Prakrit form of the Sanskrit word *dharma*): 'Love is won in conquests by *Dhamma*. That love may be indeed slight, but his Sacred Majesty considers it productive of great fruit. . . .' Now *Dhamma* is not, strictly speaking, a Buddhist doctrine, but, as Dr. Thapar ably claims, an attitude of social responsibility.

It would seem that the people of the Mauryan empire required a focus or common perspective to face all these divergent forces [sects and dissidents], something that would draw them together and give them a feeling of unity.

[1] Tr. in Romila Thapar, *Aśoka and the Decline of the Mauryas*, Oxford University Press, London, 1961, p. 255.

Owing to the structure of Mauryan India, such a focus, in order to be successful, had to derive from the king. In seeking a group of unifying principles Ashoka concentrated on the fundamental aspects of each issue, and the result was his policy of *Dhamma*. The principles of *Dhamma* were acceptable to people belonging to any religious sect.[1]

There is no doubt, however, that without Buddhism Ashoka could not have formulated a universal ethic cutting across caste and sect beliefs. He went one step farther than the Buddha when he extended the latter's doctrine of non-violence to the level of governmental or kingly ethics—a point on which the Buddha had remained silent. It is here that Ashoka's ideas constitute a repudiation of Kauṭilyan imperialism by violence, but not a repudiation of Kauṭilya's system of government by surveillance. For he created a special class of functionaries, the officers of *Dhamma*, who were granted extensive powers to supervise mass indoctrination. These officers acted as the emperor's spies, somewhat on the lines advocated in the *Arthashāstra*. On the other hand, imperial patronage and an internal, popularist movement within Buddhist religious circles—the latter a consequence of prevailing social conditions in the Mauryan period—saw the radical transformation of a minority heterodoxy into a mass movement. The new script—*Brāhmī*—from which the *Devanāgarī* of Sanskrit derives, the emergence of the Prakrit languages as the vehicle of a powerful vernacular culture, and the impressive communications system established by the imperial government, combined to create conditions favourable to the advancement of a Buddhist-oriented universal *dharma*. At the same time the devotional deities, such as Krishna, Rāma, Shiva, and Vishnu, seized the popular imagination and infused even the Buddhist movement with a religious emotionalism closer to the hearts of the people.

Why then did Ashoka's *Dhamma* fade into oblivion with his death, and why did the Mauryan empire collapse? The economic causes for the empire's decline have already been analysed. On the ethical and ideological plane, non-violence and tolerance of heterodoxy did not succeed in containing social tensions. On the administrative plane, Kauṭilyan methods undermined the solidarity of the ruling class, espionage sowed discontent, and the isolation of the king and bureaucracy rendered them impotent to combat dissension and intrigue.

It is the problem of a loose, vaguely defined, unitary principle which failed to take into account the complexities of empirical reality. There is a persistent tendency for the eternal, a-temporal, holistic *dharma*, whether Buddhist or Hindu, to be replaced in the expediency of the moment by the *dharma* of crisis. Our analogy from modern times—Gandhism—is again relevant. For this too was a political movement with a strong sense of

[1] R. Thapar, *A History of India*, London, 1966, I, p. 86.

moral responsibility, which, due to the persistent lack of a sense of history (amounting almost to active distaste), translated the response of an intuitive leader to the situation at any particular moment into an extemporized policy. In both cases this, and the lack of a stable institutional framework, led to the corrosion of a noble ideal from within after the death of the leader.

The Mauryan empire collapsed eighty-three years after Ashoka's death with the murder of the last emperor by his commander-in-chief. Buddhism was never again so closely linked on the institutional level with the political destiny of India, although a number of dynasties subsequently afforded it their protection and lavish patronage. The internal affairs of the Buddhist religion during the process of Hinduization remain to be considered.

Unlike the parish organization of Jainism and Brahmanical caste ritualism, the Buddha himself had no methodical ethic to offer the laity. The layman was simply instructed to follow a moral code of Five Precepts: refrain from killing, stealing, unlawful sexual indulgence, wrong speech, and drinking liquor. In practice Buddhist families employed priests to perform religious functions, and since there were no Buddhist priests but only monks, they had to call in the Brahmans. The Buddha himself was ·against the establishment of an order of monks; however, subsequent to his death, the monks were ecclesiastically organized. The monasticism originated from a combination of the usual Indian preference for secret doctrine and the particularly austere discipline which the Buddha taught. Weber calls it a 'religious technology', and 'the most radical form of salvation-striving conceivable—but solely a personal act of the single individual'. Buddha said the individual must 'wander lonely as the rhinoceros'. The role of the Renouncer is here carried to its extreme. It is significant that the one example of a well-organized ecclesiastical hierarchy in the history of Indian religion failed to endure.

As we have seen in Part One, Buddhist monasticism was not as rigid as might appear from the above remarks. It was nevertheless as an organized religion that Buddhism maintained its hold; with the Indian penchant for synthesis it accommodated its doctrine, symbolism, ritual, and pantheon to the popular needs of the society.

Within a hundred and fifty years of the Buddha's death, at the second great council of the Saṇgha, the first great schism of the order developed. The eventual result was that the majority adhered to the more orthodox view and were called Hīnayāna (or Theravādā), the Lesser Vehicle, and the minority regrouped gradually to form the Mahāyāna, or Large Vehicle. For the Hinayanists the Buddha is a historical figure; but for the Mahayanists he is eternal and absolute. The evolution of the latter into a great religious movement with a complex pantheon of gods and goddesses, a hierarchy of saviour-figures, and an impressive philosophical literature, was to have far-reaching significance in Asia. Mahāyāna might well be called '*bhakti* Buddhism'; it was a redemption religion which incorporated substantial portions of Hindu metaphysics and polytheism. It also borrowed virtually the entire theistic creed of the *Bhagavad Gītā* (the latter had probably been influenced in the first place by the ethical teaching of the Buddha). The Buddhist saviours were almost exact replicas of the Hindu *avatārs*. Similarly both Hinduism and Buddhism incorporated unorthodox Tantric magico-orgiasticism. The gradual Hinduization of the Mahāyāna school on Indian soil resulted in its being reabsorbed entirely, leaving scarcely a trace of its former existence. Buddhist influence on Hinduism also paved the way for its gradual assimilation, notably through the immense prestige which the ideas of Shankara (a 'crypto-Buddhist', as he was accused of being) enjoyed around the eighth and ninth centuries. This evolution of Buddhism took many hundreds of years to accomplish. Meanwhile a parallel movement in the field of recondite philosophy thrived during the first seven centuries of our era. The great Mahāyāna Buddhist logicians—Nāgārjuna, Asanga, Vasubandhu, Dignāga, and Dharmakīrti—were among the first philosophers in the world to employ dialectical logic.

Mahāyāna Buddhism assumed its full stature in Gandhāra, the north-west region of India, where a school of Buddhist art flourished for a period of five hundred years (Plate 37). Kanishka's famous council altered the whole Buddhist organization. As a result many new ideas from outside India were blended into Buddhism, including the concept of a messianic saviour, or *Soshvan*, a prophetic figure who appears in several Middle Eastern creeds. As Maitreya Buddha this mythical figure was to spread far and wide. In addition, Nāgārjuna (second century A.D.) was among those who were responsible for the introduction of the Hindu deities into the new Buddhist pantheon. The most important addition to Buddhism was the merciful Bodhisattva, the ideal man who must renounce renunciation (in this case the renunciation leading to *nirvāṇa*) to achieve the higher truth.

In the Bodhisattva the Buddha's ethic of compassion comes to full flower. The supreme spiritual poise of the Bodhisattva leads him to see all opposites as 'emptiness', the Void itself, *Śūnyatā*. Thus Mahāyāna was prone to the ethical limitations which mysticism rarely avoids, and while Buddhist ethics gains from the conception of the Bodhisattva, something is also lost—the hard edge of historical actuality which gave Gautama's message its strength.

More etheric than a human being (and not very different in conception from the Jain Tīrthankara—see Plate 35), the Bodhisattva becomes self-radiant in the clear light of the Void until the essence, 'suchness' (Self), shines out, like the sun breaking through cloud. In the transparency of the Void the

Bodhisattva sees ignorance and bliss as meaningless opposites. From this lofty vista pain and joy are no longer seen as polarity of tension but an ecstasy, the *Mahā Sukha*, 'trance of delight', the boundless, unhampered freedom of enlightenment. This is the Buddhist equivalent of the divine *līlā* of the Hindus.

The 'trance of delight' is different from the blissful identity of Ātman and Brahman only in respect to the subtle conceptualization of Brahman and Śūnyatā; the former is directly apprehended by the solitary process of introverted concentration, the latter by merciful acts. The *Mahā Sukha* is virtually identical with the self-radiant bliss of the great Hindu deities, Shiva and Krishna. The Void is not so far removed in conception from the zero dot, the *bindu* (literally, 'semen'[1]), in Hindu mystical terminology the source of Love, conjunction of Shiva and Shakti (Plates 40 and 41), an inexhaustible potentiality beyond the pain and pleasure which generate it. This is the flash-point where Buddhism dissolves into Hinduism. Through the influence of *bhakti* and the revalorization of folk magic by Tantrism the 'trance of delight' acquires erotic undertones foreign to early Buddhism.

Buddhism was smothered in the embrace of Hindu inclusiveness long before the Muslims destroyed the monasteries. But when the end came Buddhism vanished so completely from India's religious life that even the location of some holy places of Buddhism associated with Gautama's life were forgotten. It was not until European archaeologists arrived in India that these sites were excavated.

The fate of Buddhism affords us a highly instructive instance of India's efforts to assimilate its own rebellious and intractable elements. Movements of various kinds, political, social, religious, arose either in conscious protest against the prevailing system, or from an instinctive need for emancipation from the uniform, and often stagnant, social environment. In each case the pattern of assimilation is similar in most respects. Some were cases of positive synthesis, others were more like wars of attrition in which the protest movement was bled white. We can observe the way Hinduism all but swallowed the movements of Kabir and the Sikhs; and in our own time Gandhism, anti-casteism, and egalitarianism have all been subjected to the same embrace until their edges have begun to blur.

Aesthetic pessimism

It would be impossible to include here more than a few of the problems with which the traditional Indian value-systems are confronted in the

[1] This meaning is given in the *Dhyānabindu Upanishad*. Also used in Tantric texts to mean 'semen'.

modern world. Of greater importance is to identify a fairly consistent bias in classical ethics towards detachment in response to the 'terror of Time'.

Indifference to developmental history is part and parcel of the feeling of helplessness in the face of inexorable destiny. To illustrate this point, let us briefly consider a celebrated Puranic tale which used to be a favourite theme of popular oleographs, and which has long been regarded in India as a perfect paradigm of the human condition: A man being chased by a tiger climbs out on the branch of a tree. The branch bends dangerously over a dried-up well. A pair of mice gnaw the branch on which he hangs. Below he sees a mass of writhing snakes at the bottom of the well. Growing on the wall of the well is a blade of grass, on its tip a drop of honey—and he *licks up the honey*. It should be emphasized that this Puranic fable is very widely known and bears the characteristic traits of 'Indian wisdom': an image of aesthetic immediacy, a wry comment on the transience of life, a sense of predicament without conviction of the ability to do anything about it—except perform an act of conscious aestheticism in a spirit of fatalistic detachment.

The vein of aesthetic pessimism in this fable is not entirely alien to the Western mind. Schopenhauer, whose pessimistic ideas have coloured so much Western thought of the last century, and who was deeply influenced by Indian thought, stated that 'what is real, is worthless; what is valuable lacks reality. And where reality and value are thus seen and felt to be mutually exclusive, there *all* values, indeed truth itself, must in the end lose any *real* significance.'[1]

It is interesting to see how an Indian traditionalist interprets this Puranic fable. According to S. H. Vatsyayan, editor of the Hindu journal *Dinaman*, the story is an illustration of what he calls the unique Indian sense of predicament (Zimmer's 'permanent crisis'):

As I see it, this sense of predicament is more than sufficient compensation for what is frequently criticized as a lack of a sense of history. The predicament is immediate, pervasive, and so far as courses of action go, imperative. As for the sense of history, well, one can live in history without ever being part of it, far less influencing its course. . . . The changes that even rural India has taken in its stride are an example of this sense of predicament. . . .

I am in fact an observer of the pain that I am undergoing. . . .

What is important . . . is this assumption of the status of observer. An awareness of predicament changes the predicament by itself becoming a factor in the predicament; a separation of pain, from the suffering which it might (or might not) bring, changes the nature of the pain. In both cases one has extricated oneself from the situation; one has become an outsider, as it were.

Revolutions are not made by outsiders. In this sense, the awareness of predicament I refer to is not a revolutionary force. But revolutions are not *necessary*.

[1] Tr. in Heller (1958).

Change is necessary; growth is necessary. And the status of the outsider makes change both easier and more acceptable. A transformation can come without a destruction. . . .

We are being trained more and more in the sense of history; we are losing this engrained sense of predicament. We are learning to *suffer* pain. . . . We are thus moving towards a situation in which change, though no less necessary, is less easily acceptable. We are replacing situations for transformation by situations for revolution. We are making revolutions 'necessary'.

But the pity is that we are not becoming revolutionary ourselves; we are creating situations for revolutions to be brought about by the managers of revolutions—the elite which combines a sense of history with a sense of predicament—*his* predicament.

Can we as a whole, as a people, move and change fast enough to catch up with him, rediscover our predicament, make it our own?[1]

The attitudes which are neatly summarized by these remarks are particularly representative of the Indian traditionalist view. The Indian traditionalist speaks from the position of unconquerable isolation and the fundamental self-centredness of what Thomas Mann called the aesthetic man. It is not surprising that the Puranic fable is cherished by the traditionalist bourgeois artist. This class shares certain attitudes in common with those of its German counterpart of which Mann wrote in the early years of this century. As Professor Heller points out,

if the aesthetic man is isolated, if he refuses to play the game of people who all 'know what they want' and unproblematically 'take sides', this is not a matter of choice. He is under compulsion. What compels him is the aesthetic vision of that which necessarily is, of a wholeness of being in which all moral clashes and contradictions of individual men are both contained and surpassed. His ethics, therefore, are the ethics of 'being', not the morals of 'doing'. He may appear—to others as well as to himself—as one concerned with himself alone. But this is an illusion caused by the fact that he cannot have any seriously felt concern for the arbitrary fluctuations of the social dispute. Instead his isolation has an opening into religion.[2]

One might add, an opening into acquiescence in total ideological order, in line with the process of legitimization of power.

Vatsyayan's remarks show him cloaking the evasion of a painful political choice with ancient wisdom. It is interesting to note that he sees how, as time goes by, the position of the traditionalist hardens and that change is actually *less* acceptable, not more. An *awareness* of predicament, as Gandhi well knew, only changes the predicament in the mind of the man who suffers it with detachment. Objectively, however, the pain remains. There

[1] S. H. Vatsyayan, in a speech given at a seminar on the 'Quality of Life in India' held by the Indian Committee for Cultural Freedom, New Delhi, 1966.
[2] Erich Heller, *The Ironic German*, Secker & Warburg, London, 1958, p. 138.

is no sign in the traditional Indian outlook of any confidence in the capacity to ameliorate human conditions, or even to feel that such efforts should be undertaken. By extricating himself from the situation, or imagining that he has done so, the traditionalist renders himself impotent. In *kaivalya* he is reduced to the state of the monad, of imagined purity. Change *is* necessary, growth *is* necessary; but the man in the ivory tower cannot make the need for change more acceptable, because he passively, masochistically, refuses to participate in it. Furthermore, it is significant that the aesthetic man sees that his own role will necessarily be *overtaken* by revolution; he recoils from the pain of creative social action. This is the fate of the Indian traditionalist —he has no faith in his power to change history because for him there is no history.

Part Five Sacred Authority and
the Secular State

Introduction

There is every reason to believe that there exists a certain point in the mind at which life and death, real and imaginary, past and future, communicable and incommunicable, high and low, cease to be perceived in terms of contradiction.

André Breton, *The Surrealist Manifesto*, 1929

THIS quotation places the Indian principle of the conjunction and reconciliation of opposites in a larger, more modern context. The imagination of twentieth-century man is much attracted by such a possibility, as can be seen from the thematic material of much literature and certain schools of philosophy and popular culture (including popularized mysticism and science fiction). To overcome the basic antinomies of existence is associated with the attainment of godlike or supernormal powers, and with the exploration of the most elusive phenomena of the space–time continuum. According to the Indian religious systems, the transcendence of opposites is a state which can be attained by a human being and is indeed the goal of human life. The unique social status of absolute oracular authority is ascribed to the individual who attains this liberation. The consequences of positing a hypothetical transcendence of opposites are important in the domains of thought, ethics, and social organization.

Since the individual who is believed to have penetrated to the roots of causality is vested with the highest status recognized by society, Part Five will be devoted to an analysis of the effects which this has had on the pattern of leadership in general. There is much more involved here than a craze for gurus, visionary states of mind, and investigation of paranormal modalities of consciousness. To derive any useful benefit from the study of the over-publicized figure of the Indian sage we will have to ignore Western nostalgia for the guru and the desire to escape into that uncertain terrain where the Ganges flows into the Californian desert. The field for research is extensive but it will be restricted here to two aspects only: the phenomenology of sacred authority, and the significance of Mahātma Gandhi's leadership during the period when that authority was challenged by the establishment of a secular basis of social organization. The first chapter will be an analysis of the old and closed world-view as affirmed by the traditional guru, and the second will trace the opening phase of a change which challenges that view.

The most important Indian symbol of the *coincidentia oppositorum* is the Zero. While in mathematics zero means 'nought', for the Indian thinker the Zero or *bindu*—'dot', 'seed', 'semen'—is an unlimited entity, the *productive* point of potentiality (Plate 41). Zero and Nirvāṇam are both called Śūnyam, the Void, which means 'excessive', 'swollen' (*śūnya* and *śūna*, the swollen and the void are from the same root, *śūn*). Heimann calls Zero the *No- or All-figure*, 'the only mathematical symbol which extends beyond every temporary value'. In other words, by reason of its *coincidentia*, the Zero refers to a plane higher than that of empirical reality, of the flux of things, while signifying the point where empirical reality dissolves into transcendental reality. Both void and *plenum*, it subsumes the plus and the minus signs. Similarly, Nirvāṇa is called 'the Whole'. Any attempt, therefore, to equate Nirvāṇa with negation, or to take the fat off the Zero idea, is unwarranted. Rather, the Zero should be regarded as the matrix of negative and positive, the fulcrum, the hub of the wheel.

A numerical system must precede the idea of zero. We know that before the fourth century A.D. the Arabs, the Indians, and the Chinese left a blank space in their numerical systems where the zero should have been. But the question of who invented the place system and the decimal point is still a matter of learned debate among scholars. That the Indians, with their algebraic gifts, invented the zero is little in doubt; Arab texts of around the fourth century A.D. describe it as an Indian invention. This momentous innovation was preceded by centuries of speculation on the idea that nothing was a kind of thing. *Śūnya*, the earlier term for Zero, connotes the point at the outer reaches of what either language or art can state (Plate 35). The *bindu* is a something which mysteriously embodies mathematical truths. The quicksilver wheel of Bhāskara, paradigm of the unchanging state beyond all temporal appearances, is the most vivid example we have of the application of the self-perpetuating Zero principle, Eternal Present, still point in the eye of life's cyclone. The Indian Zero idea ever veers away from the science of mathematics towards speculation into the enigma of life itself.

Philosophically, the Zero idea is a meditation on the paradox of the maximum potential contained within an irreducible minimum—what Mies van der Rohe expresses in the technological domain by the maxim 'less is more'. From the cultural and social points of view, this is by far the most significant and productive aspect of an almost obsessive concern with 'undifferentiatedness'. The concept of the Ātman, or essence of Self, is the correlative of the Zero in the various mystical systems. In Tantrism, the *bindu* is equated with semen, not in a reductive, 'nothing but' sense, but as the empirical substance which can transform a man into a godlike being. But common to all the philosophical and mystical applications of the Zero idea is the tendency, exemplified by the Tantric attempt to 'store' semen, to associate the latent power of the irreducible minimum with self-containment, completeness, consistently perfect continence (*brahmāchārya*). The man who fully comprehends the mystery of the Zero is the man who has reduced himself to Zero—the ego-less monad suspended in the stratosphere of the Void which, under normal conditions, would asphyxiate ordinary mortals. In other words—weakness is power. A poetic expression of this self-containment would be Rilke's image of the angel as a mirror reflecting his 'outstreamed beauty'.

Chapter One Sacred Authority

The *guru-shishya* relationship

During the extraverted Vedic period of tribalism when the symbolism first appears of the sacrifier ritualistically reborn, the Zero idea is an integral part of the cosmic scheme. The perfected sage endures a period of regression, of initiatory latency separate from the tribe, but returns to play a role in the collective; in a sense he is more indissolubly a part of it, since he has been in a state of unified awareness. His role is within the society, as the seer who *sees* the interconnectedness of all things. Vedic sacrificial rites are a dramatization of integral oneness; there is no question of the sage *renouncing* society. This ideal of cosmic interconnectedness is never abandoned in Indian history, but with the disintegration of the sacrificial, tribal, potlatch-type society and its replacement by the caste society, an entirely new emphasis is given to the Zero idea and the Zero ideal. The state of spiritual revelation when the opposites are transcended, variously called *nirvāṇa*, *moksha*, *mukti*, or *samādhi*, can equally be conceived as absolute plenitude or absolute negation. The non-Vedic, probably non-Aryan, ideal of *moksha* as a distinctive, separate goal was only differentiated much later from the triple scheme of the Brahmanical Aims of Life (*Trivarga*), fulfilment through *dharma*, *kāma*, and *artha*, and elevated to the status of a fourth and final end of human seeking. Similarly, the elevation of the sage to the status of guru (literally, 'teacher', 'master') at the head of a religious community represents a comparatively late stage in the development of an Indian religious sect from its origins in magic and sorcery. At an intermediate point between the stage of sorcery and the institutionalization of the sage as sect guru, the sage evolves a special form of esoteric instruction for initiates, the *guru-shishya* relationship. The word *Upanishad*—associated with the teachings of the forest hermits long before the guru-cult reached its extravagant pitch of emotional adulation—literally means 'sitting down opposite somebody'. The role of the tribal magician is inverted: *moksha* can be attained only by a *denial* of the *Trivarga*. The Renouncer must be 'naughted of all things', which is to say that his course is a systematic denial of his rights as a personality; but his aim is utterly concentrated on the single irreducible remnant of his personality, the Ātman. As we have seen, attainment of this state makes the Renouncer, in the eyes of society, a mirror in which to glimpse its own concealed and lost sense of unity. The bond of interconnectedness remains, in so far as the Renouncer attains *jīvanmukti*, or individual liberation, thereby becoming the symbolic apex of the society (Plate 54). Nevertheless, in so highly structured a society, the *jīvanmukta*'s role was eventually institutionalized, especially by the *bhakti* movement. Worshipped as a quasi-divine figure and without economic function, the guru, and the *ashrām* where he lives and teaches, are financially dependent on voluntary donations. The leitmotif running throughout the manifold ramifications of the Zero idea can therefore be said to be a play on the paradox of perfect self-containment and total dependence. The realized man becomes a sacred authority who radiates a beneficent numen; he is worshipped as an embodiment of Truth, the man who has resolved the contradictions of life. Whether he teaches or not is immaterial, for his charisma itself is his sermon. His potency resides in the fact that he does nothing; he inhabits the zone of no-thing, the deeps of silence. If he chooses to talk, the essence of his message is that he can only indicate by language why language cannot say what it cannot say.

Strictly speaking, a guru is a man or woman who gives *dīkshā*, initiation into a sect of renouncers.[1] The guru, or guru-figure in general, should not be regarded as a kind of inert and passive social mascot. In one sense, he plays a highly positive and active social role. This is his readiness to act as master to his disciple—the *guru-shishya* (or *guru-chela*) relationship. Under the conditions of a caste society, hierarchical interdependence and ritualistic interpersonal relations introduce into every relationship an element of formal and emotional constraint. The only authentic meeting that can still occur between two human beings stripped of their masks, is within the initiatory magic circle of the *guru-shishya* relationship. Apart from the obvious link between master and pupil, the essential element of the relationship is the disciple's attempt to recover the sense of wholeness through undertaking a psychic excursion into inner space. Adaptation to the outer world, or rebirth to a state of enhanced being, follows complete psychic reorientation. Implicit in the inequality of the relationship is the complete surrender of the disciple's will; in this sense, submission is axiomatic to the relationship. There are, it is true, a variety of relationships to which various local or sectarian traditions ascribe similar ultimate value, e.g. *sahaja*, or the perfect union of flesh and spirit in ecstatic love. Underlying the free interaction of two individuals (or between the members of an initiated

[1] At least in the context of an actual, consistent, master–disciple relationship. To say of a man, 'He is my guru,' can either mean, 'I respect him as a teacher,' in a vague general sense, with which we are not concerned here; or it can mean, 'I have been *initiated* by my teacher, whom I obey implicitly, and with whom I have a relationship of a specific spiritual and psychological nature.'

circle) there is a more subtle form of interdependence: the guru-ideal is considered an imperfect projection on to another person of the 'inner master', the 'guru within'. In the final analysis there can be no 'other', neither master nor pupil, only the One. The *guru-shishya* relationship is, however, a perfectly genuine psychic reality which satisfies, though not invariably, the Indian (gurus of one sort or another are to be found in every Indian community, including Christians, Muslims, and Parsis). While it would not be described in these terms by individuals who have experienced it, the *guru-shishya* relationship expresses the product of shared conditions.

The mass need for the guru may have waned in the twentieth century, but the continued success of a host of *swamis*, *sādhus*, *mahātmas*, and *sants* in securing a means of livelihood, by 'teaching', by acting as gurus, whether based on quackery or genuine human insight, indicates that it is not a negligible feature of modern times. At least as long as India continues to be in transition from a sacred to a secular society, the guru-figure will remain the model for the Indian charismatic leader, not because India is more or less religious than the supposedly advanced cultures, but because the guru-figure answers a cluster of psychological needs. It has been claimed, and with justification, that the relations between India's political leaders and their immediate circle of supporters is a modification of the relationship between the guru and his disciples. There is a similar polarization of personalities which is of psychological origin; but in every other sense the two kinds of circle differ. The fact that both are based on a common psychological need (distinctively Indian in pattern) is of considerable significance, as we shall see when the case of Gandhi is examined.

The *guru-shishya* relationship incarnates a specific form of psychological bond; with the disintegration of traditional social roles and institutions it tends to be diffused or imprinted on relationships in no way connected with, let alone confined to, the religious domain with which it was originally associated. Specific examples of this are the popular cult of Nehru as Panditji and of the poet Rabindranath Tagore as Gurudev. Renowned artists in every medium, once they attain a certain age, attract a cluster of pupils who are something more than 'students', as the master is something more than their 'teacher'. The emotional link is similar to that of the *guru-shishya* relationship, and is recognized as such, often to the extent of ritualized worship, or *guru-pūjā* on the master's birthday. There is a convergence here of the master–apprentice bond and the mystical ideal of 'sitting down opposite somebody'.

The virtually total isolation of some renouncers in the state of *kaivalya* will not concern us here. The more active ideal of the spiritual 'teacher' is associated with the Indian concept of compassion, or *karuṇā*. The specifically spiritual guru is self-perfect, but he chooses, like the mythical figure of the Bodhisattva, to help his fellow-men to attain liberation. He is not a philosopher, nor is he a priest who leads the people in supplication and represents them before their gods. He may work on their behalf, but he does not represent them; he may relieve certain kinds of tensions in individuals and he does it dramatically, which means artistically. This specialized human type is prepared for high office by a yogic discipline designed to modify the whole psychic structure. He must submit to a dedication that largely cuts him off from normal satisfactions. Whatever value may be ascribed to his spiritual stature and to that of his disciples, he is supposed, first of all, to be a competent therapist, and second, capable of supplying correct answers to the riddles of life because he has transcended the law of opposites. Since the training of a guru follows, more often than not, such a yogic pattern, most gurus also employ teaching methods which endorse the somewhat harsh mechanistic world-view of yoga. Life in an Indian *ashram* is not all sweetness, dreams, and garland-giving; on the contrary, it is more like the clamour of a railway station, the lesson of which is that inner concentration can be achieved in the midst of hectic activity by the consistent practice of certain techniques, all of which have a physical basis.

Yoga is the name for the pan-Indian corpus of techniques for achieving enhanced states of consciousness. Max Weber has described it as 'a rationally systematized form of emotional asceticism and therein somewhat comparable to the exercises of Ignatius'. The drastic nature of this mental control, or witnessing consciousness, may be appreciated if it is realized that according to the classic teaching of Patañjali, the final goal of yoga is literally the total suppression of consciousness. 'Pure consciousness', absolutely free and unconditioned, ultimately replaces psychological self-analysis. *Samādhi*, the perfect state of realization in which the soul rests in itself, could be interpreted either as re-integrated consciousness or a living suicide. The yogin does not see man as split in two, a dual creature at odds with himself, but as capable of achieving once more the complete unity which ignorance has divided. He does not neglect his body, he perfects it. He makes it the effective instrument for obtaining complete concentration (Plates 9, 36, 37, and 47).

In his sceptical and salutary critique of yoga, Mr. Arthur Koestler failed to notice works of impressive scholarship by such men as Hauer and Éliade. Both have assembled a mass of material which reveals that yoga, despite its archaism (Éliade describes it as a uniquely durable *fossil* system), contains many insights into the psychology of perception. It is a *method*, not a philosophy, and should be judged as such. Nowadays, scientists are attempting to check on the yogin's ability to achieve prodigious feats of control over mental and physical processes. No more than a few physiologists have succeeded in using the electroencephalograph (EEG)

to any effect in scientific investigation of yogic concentration under laboratory conditions. The most interesting results, from sophisticated methods
and standard modern instruments, were obtained in a Calcutta *ashrām* by
H. Gastaut and N. N. Das, extracts from whose report in a scientific
journal follow:

No muscular electrical activity whatsoever appears during the hours of perfect
immobility which the subject maintains.

The electroencephalography shows progressive and very spectacular modifications during the deepest meditations in those subjects who have the best
training.

The evidence enables us to conclude that yogic meditation, and the ecstasy to
which it leads, represent a state of intense concentration of attention. One can
even suppose that the electroencephalographic modifications found at the
beginning of meditation or in poorly trained subjects may correspond to those
described in Europe and America during the deepest states of attention. On the
other hand, the modifications recorded during very deep meditation and *samādhi*
are much more dramatic than those known up till now (from scientific observation), which leads us to suppose that western subjects are far from being able to
attain the yogic state of mental concentration.

The modifications of the cardiac rhythm are clear and almost perfectly parallel
to those of the EEG: definite acceleration during profound meditation and
especially during ecstasy; a clearer slowing down after the end of the ecstatic
period.

It is probable that this supreme concentration of attention on the sole subject
of meditation is responsible for the perfect insensibility accompanied by immobility and pallor, which often led people to describe this state as sleep, lethargy, anesthesia or coma. The electroencephalographic evidence here described
contradicts such opinions and suggests that a state of intense generalised cortical
stimulation is sufficient to explain such states without having to invoke associated
processes of diffuse or local inhibition.[1]

The yogin is delighted to obtain such corroboration of his working
methods; but it is one thing to obtain scientific proof of their efficacy and
another to advance the claim, made by many adepts, that the method itself
is scientific. Much of the conceptual theory on which yogic thought is
based derives from the Sāṃkhya system, and central to the latter is the
theory of the three *guṇas*, which gives an explanation of physical and mental
phenomena. The theory of the *guṇas* is not a scientific theory; it functions at
quite a different level. The yogin ignores all scientific caution in making his
claims.

Religion is a most practical thing. It doesn't matter whether one believes or
not. It is like science. If one performs spiritual disciplines, the result is bound to

[1] *International Journal of Electroencephalography and Clinical Neurophysiology*, Supplement
No. 6 Masson & Cie., Paris, 1957.

come. Although one may be practising mechanically—if one persists one will get everything in time.[1]

This peculiarly mechanistic attitude captures the authentic accent of blithe shrewdness which is often detectable in the utterances of Indian gurus. It is also responsible for considerable confusion over the psychedelic techniques of yoga. To storm the Kingdom of Heaven by an act of yogic violence is one thing; to extend the procedure to the taking of drugs is often regarded as the next logical step. But to assert, as N. C. Chaudhuri does in *The Continent of Circe*, that every Indian guru prescribes cannabis to his disciples is untrue. From Patañjali's yogic aphorisms to Rāmakrishna, the taking of drugs as an aid to mystical concentration is regarded as a step back into the cult of magic. That the ineffable state of ultimate revelation can only be attained in a semi-doped condition has never been seriously advocated. Drugs are regarded as a crude and uncertain aid; they are referred to in texts as dangerous because the yogin cannot, under artificial stimulus, obtain complete control over the body. Further, it is said that drugs contain Karmic toxins which, if assimilated, bind the taker to the Karmic chain from which he is seeking complete release (see footnote on p. 50).

The oracular authority of the guru partly rests on the mysterious ability which is recognized by most civilizations as the mark of saintly wisdom: an almost uncannily penetrating insight into human nature. His gift is not arrived at with artificial stimulants but through disinterestedness. He is not caught in the net of contradictory pressures, selfishness, irrationality, and contesting emotions. But it takes also a devoted disciple to elicit a valid response from a guru. As one modern guru defined this symbiosis: 'I need you more than you need me.' The guru can easily become the prisoner of society; he is not a prophet or a social reformer, he cannot change society, only mirror its needs back on to itself. 'I am only a mirror.' 'I am the drum: you play the tune.' In reply to the question, 'Who are you?', back came the reply, 'I am whatever you take me to be.' This same guru, when asked to sign autograph books, makes no more than a dot in the centre of the page with the remark: 'In the *bindu* all is contained.'

The behaviour of the guru and the *shishya* frequently assumes a seemingly pathological character. In this respect the guru-cult reveals its remote but common origin with the Shamanism of tribal society. But what is madness, what is pathological? The Vaishnavas compare the estrangement of the *bhakta* from God to the emotional derangement of Rādhā separated from Krishna. Tension, anxiety, insomnia, emaciation, pallor, incoherence of speech, sickness, mental imbalance, trance—are all ascribed both to the divine couple in the frenzy of separation, and to the devotee in quest of his

[1] Swami Brahmananda, quoted in Christopher Isherwood, *Rāmakrishna and his Disciples*, Methuen, London, 1965.

God. The emotional disturbance of the disciple who has surrendered his will to his guru, but is separated from him, follows the same pattern.

The psychic disorder of the Indian mystic at certain stages in his development is called *deevyon mada*, 'divine madness'. It is regarded as a temporary or recurring phenomenon, but not as a goal. Socrates is made to say in the *Phaedrus*: 'Our greatest blessings come to us by way of madness—provided the madness is given by divine gift.' Plato, like Indian thinkers, draws a distinction between 'divine madness' or 'prophetic madness' and the ordinary kind which is caused by disease. Thus he departs from the primitive belief that *all* types of mental disturbance are caused by supernatural interference, without disclaiming the idea that mental aberration is one of the conditions which favour the emergence of supernatural powers. Many Indian gurus deliberately encourage their disciples to attain a cathartic state of *deevyon mada* as a form of homeopathic remedy to ward off more serious psychic epidemics. The ultimate aim of the guru who employs such techniques is not to hypnotize his followers but to bring about a profound alteration of personality.

Without the prior existence of alienation the guru would have no social role. In fact most disciples seek the aid of a guru only when their own personal predicament seems to have become untenable. Whatever a man in such a position does, he feels that he is the subject of unbearable, irresolvably contradictory and paradoxical pressures, both psychic and social. Like the schizophrenic, his submission to the will of a man whom he believes to be infallible is a special but dangerous strategy to which he will resort only when caught in an unlivable situation. There appears to be little doubt that the *guru-shishya* relationship was institutionalized because it was found effective as a means of warding off psychoses among the alienated.

A distinction should be drawn between the exhibitionism of freakish *sādhus* and the conduct of the authentic mystical virtuoso. The virtuoso courts danger by inducing in himself, or others, various states of dissociation as a means to develop enhanced consciousness and coherent spiritual goals. Pathological states, if left alone, generally lead to the progressive *disintegration* of the personality and can only operate negatively towards disorder, breakdown, and insanity. Mystical states, on the other hand, are, as Éliade points out, 'of an initiatory pattern and meaning'. Once the *guru-shishya* relationship is established, the master precipitates a destructuring of the ego, the symptom of which is a helpless sense of ego-loss. It would appear that this process must first run its course through the gamut of transference and dependence until the initiated pupil returns to the normal world equipped with new insights. The ultimate stage is the pupil's discovery of the 'guru within'; the effectiveness of the guru depends on the skill with which he exercises his authority, while recognizing that the pupil's development is largely steered by endogenous process. A satisfactory outcome is, of course, by no means assured; the number of failures among those who embark on this psychic excursion is fairly high.

While much depends on the guru's competence, an almost equal degree of tolerance is expected of society too, whose members were, in former times, socially conditioned to regard total immersion in inner space as neither anti-social withdrawal nor in any sense discreditable. The lavish financial endowments to *ashrāms* in modern times are no doubt often motivated by desire to gain merit; nevertheless, implicit in the fact is recognition of the need for protection of the inmates. That secularized India now tends to regard the inmates of *ashrāms* as social parasites and their patrons as motivated by outmoded values is justified. Famine, poverty, and epidemics are ignored by almost all *ashrāms*; nothing in the external world is allowed to disturb the inmates' spiritual exercises.

No doubt there still exist a number of mystics whose integrity is not in question. An institution which contributed greatly to the cultural life and psychic health of India in the past has, nevertheless, been marred by political corruption. The spiritually perfected individual, however, is probably as widely idealized in India today as he ever was, even if few live up to the model. Nothing of comparable mass-appeal has replaced him at the symbolic hub of the social wheel.

This being so, the question arises whether the guru cannot himself change. Perhaps this question could never have been posed before Gandhi appeared. That he inverted the role of the Indian holy man and gave it a socially constructive goal is a point which will be amplified in Part Five, Chapter Two. The large following which a number of gurus continue to enjoy, the relatively limited but by no means inconspicuous response to Āchārya Vinoba Bhave, and the resurgence of militant religiosity, are features of the post-Independence period. These facts alone justify analysis of the guru-cult, so as to obtain from it fresh insight into the social and psychological mores of the transitional society. Widespread interest in the psychology of perception, the Gestalt psychologist's concern with unified awareness, the search for the origins of schizophrenia in the psychic excursion, and experimentation with paranormal or enhanced mental states have greatly enlarged the avenues of approach. These branches of knowledge have engaged the attention of scholars because they point to the possible solution of urgent problems. These problems are shared by India, and in India it is the guru-cult which has been the focus of comparable psychic experiment. However, it is a sociological fact that the individuals who most assiduously pursue the guru-cult and are its main financial supporters belong to the privileged élite of the old order—the aristocrats, the rajas and their dependants, the landlords, the businessmen from the 'managing agencies', and the old industrial dynasties. It is ironical that while the exploration of the perimeter of man's mind is now conducted by some of the most politically and socially advanced minds in the world, one field of their research—the *guru-shishya* relationship—is associated with a reactionary class whose slogan is: *Dharma desh ka nata hai*, 'religion and nation are one'.

Narcissus and the Nirvana Principle

The psychological formation of the guru, and subsequently of his relationship with his disciple, centres on the dialectical unity between union and separateness, between interdependence and independence, between a passive, dependent need to be loved and the narcissistic dream of omnipotence. Before describing the life of one guru for whom narcissistic traits play a key role, a brief explanation should be given of what is meant here by 'narcissism'. As was suggested earlier, the narcissistic element is of some importance in the psychology of the Renouncer: the Indian mystic *retreats into a narcissistic position*. No value-judgement is implied by this remark; narcissistic traits can be found in most cultural modalities. In fact, the solipsism which is so much a feature of modern Western life reveals a narcissistic element, and this may, in part, explain the affinity which is now felt by some Western intellectuals between their own world-view and that of Indian mysticism. We should, however, be on our guard against the tendency to project on either the Renouncer or the guru-figure the reification of individuality familiar to us in the West. Narcissism is an important, culturally enriching strategy which features in the cultivation of mystical autonomy and qualified passivity by the guru.

When Freud, in mid-career, identified the infantile situation of narcissistic omnipotence, he named it the Nirvana Principle, characterized by the 'oceanic feeling' of union of the self with the All. Later, he called this 'limitless extension and oneness with the universe' *primary narcissism*, to describe an early developmental stage of unified libido prior to the division into ego and external objects. This would imply a certain kind of existential relation to, rather than egotistical withdrawal from, reality—'a feeling which embraced the universe and expressed an inseparable connection of the ego with the external world'.[1]

This, perhaps, is the origin of that sensibility which pervades the legends of Krishna—most loved of all India's culture-heroes—who is prince of moonlight, the dancer whose body moves in its own fullness, the sound of whose flute is a call to a life of enchantment and beauty. Images of Krishna show trees leaning towards him, fronds swaying over him, rivers eddying

[1] S. Freud, *Civilisation and Its Discontents*, Hogarth Press, London, 1949, p. 13.

round his limbs, cattle bounding to his side, cow-girls encircling him like the petals of an aquatic flower—all in response to his desire. He is shown wading, plunging, merging together with death-dealing protagonists until they yield, not to force, but to an inner strength concealed in his boyish form (Plates 39, 55, and 56). Primary narcissism seeks not mastery and dominance, but liberation and peace, not exploitation of the earth by man, but ecological harmony, uniting man and nature, subject and object.

The quietism which is a characteristic feature of the narcissistic personality helps to explain why the *guru-shishya* relationship remains ringed by the social and ideological integument, cannot break free of it. Narcissus seeks his own identity in a reflected image of himself; but, of course, there is no life in a mirror. There is a tendency on the part of the average, less integrated, egoistic narcissist to allow the world to 'die' and to concentrate on the island of self (ego-fixation) in a state of homeostasis. While the mirror of Krishna is Woman, and Krishna is associated with devotional sects, a few quotations from Hindu texts will serve as examples of the purely mystical retreat into a narcissistic position:

On the vast canvas of the Self, the picture of the manifold worlds is painted by the Self itself, and that Supreme Self itself seeing but itself, enjoys great delight.

Svatmanipūraṇa, attributed to Shaṅkara.

Just as in a mirror, the observer can see his own reflection, so the man possessed of spiritual knowledge, in trying to seize the object of knowledge, sees in everything his own form.

Dhyāneśwar.

The yogin who is identified with the all-pervading consciousness and looks on all equally, sees the self in all beings and all beings in the self.

Bhagavad Gītā.

Becoming one with the Absolute through inner vision, the soul becomes one with the seamless sphere of the universe.

Maṇḍalabrāhmaṇa Upanishad.

The identification of the ego with the universe is an idea central to Indian thought; the above quotations could all be condensed into the Upanishadic dictum: 'Thou art That.' Two popular themes of Indian mythology may be cited as particularly vivid illustrations of this idea. One of the most striking icons to bring together the related themes of the identity of opposites and the union of the Self with the Divine is that of Shiva as Prakasha, the 'first radiance', holding his spouse Vimarsha, reflection of his radiance, on his knee. She holds a mirror to him at an angle where both Shiva and a hypothetical worshipper contemplating the icon would each see the reflection of the other. Like Narcissus, the Hindu worshipper seeks, with the aid of the icon, to inhabit his own solitude and perceive in the reflection the continuous vision of himself.

Joachim Gasquet once said: '*Le monde est un immense Narcisse en train de se penser.*' This is the theme of Vishnu asleep on the shoreless sea of the cosmic ocean. It might seem justifiable to link this celebrated myth, not with primary narcissism, but with narcissistic fixation on the ego, when all other objects lose reality except the ego, on the analogy of the sleeping colossus. But, absorbed as Vishnu is in his dream of the universe, he has 'embraced the universe' by absorbing it within his own dormant body.

The most concrete example of Hindu mystical narcissism which I have personally witnessed (no Westerner had previously been permitted to observe this) is the Attāḷa Pūjā, or Night Watch, performed every evening at Śuchīndram temple near Cape Comorin. A procession filed through the cavernous halls illuminated by a myriad oil lamps to pay obeisance to the deity in each of some thirty shrines. The high-priest then entered an undecorated sanctum containing nothing but a mirror symbolizing the unmanifest aspect of Shiva. Standing before the mirror the priest worshipped his own reflection. It is believed that he who sees his own reflection in that mirror attains union with the Universal Soul.

Egoistic narcissism, at least, ends in homeostasis. Narcissus, after all, became so addicted to the impossibility of enjoying himself that he committed suicide. The society has endowed the retreat of the Renouncer with the highest prestige, not because of superstition, but because it sees in the quietness of his primary narcissism an unlimited potential for good, the potential of the Zero. He is *aware*—he has arrived at the still point of the turning world and penetrated, thereby, the mystery of constant flux. But the mere awareness of the natural dialectic, while it is effective in accomplishing change in man's relation to himself, is not a strong determinant of fundamental change or control over continuous change. The man who has reduced himself to zero, but retains the Bodhisattva's ability to accept the nature of continuous change, to give, and to succour with compassion, is as rare as tradition claims, according him the highest veneration.

Heraclitus declared: 'You cannot step into the same river twice.' Vyasa, who also employed the Heraclitan river metaphor, took a fresh look at the tradition of eternal flux as a continuous perishing and restated it as a process which moves towards a goal through change, without disrupting the overall cyclical recoil. The Copernican revolution produced a profound metaphysical change, a new outlook on the universe, not only on the solar cycle, while twentieth-century India is in the process of evolving its own new metaphysic with which to understand the physical environment, and to emancipate itself from the negative aspects of its traditional ideology. In an age when, intellectually at least, we have accepted an open-ended, scientific system, it has become very difficult for us to imagine how consistent was the old closed system. For this reason the present chapter will include the case of a traditional Indian guru whose story presents an extremely vivid picture of the closed system—in contrast to the inner transformation of India initiated by Gandhi, whose role is a modification of the guru's.

The guru's magic circle

Of the gurus I have observed, the most representative of the traditional ideal is a Bengali Brahman woman known as Śrī Ānandamayi, currently regarded as the most distinguished living exemplar of Hindu mysticism. Śrī Ānandamayi was born in 1896 of a poor Brahman family in East Bengal (now East Pakistan) and given the name Nirmala. She appears to have behaved, as a child, with the obedience and passivity of a simpleton. She behaved like an ecstatic at an early age and frequently fell into trance, burning herself at the kitchen stove. Her father left home to become a holy man when she was still a young girl. Her marriage at the age of thirteen, after almost no schooling, to a man many years older than herself, was never consummated. After several years her husband took vows of asceticism and became a *sannyāsi*, regarding his wife as his guru even while she was still in her teens.

Her ecstatic behaviour became more pronounced as she grew up; in a less religious environment such a child would have had little chance to play up to its elders and attract the attention of respected citizens by her strange behaviour, but there already existed a tradition of ecstatic conduct. These seizures did not scandalize others, who let her behave as she wished; nor did they prevent her from dancing before the gods with Corybantic frenzy during festivals. Until well into her fifties she continued to behave in this fashion during the annual celebrations of the Holī festival of Spring.

People came from miles around to gaze at the beautiful young Nirmala during her states of trance—which now took on the characteristics of deep *samādhi*. Sometimes she stood for hours like a frozen Bacchante in acrobatic postures, on the tips of her bare toes, for instance, her back arched over, her head hanging down, and her hair reaching to the floor behind her, completely motionless. To watch her was considered an act of devotion, the contemplation of the Devi in the form of a young girl. At other times she would break into peals of laughter for no apparent reason; these fits lasted for quite some time. To the band of people who began to visit her home regularly, the states of *samādhi* and fits of laughing were uplifting experiences and they dared not intervene, even though they sometimes lasted all night. This adoration of virgin beauty followed the lines of mystical tradition and worship of the universal goddess, which is widely practised in Bengal.

One interesting feature of her life is the fact that it outwardly appears to have followed a completely unstructured, aimless pattern. As she repeatedly claims, 'I am always the same'—no crises or changes, she says, have ever occurred in her life. Nevertheless, in spite of her seemingly chaotic and irrational behaviour, the familiar initiatory pattern is there, leading from undisciplined pathological behaviour (*deevyon mada*) to a gradual ritualization of everything she does, until her conduct assumes the highly formal outline of a respected guru's. This metamorphosis from unstructured spontaneity into a deeply conservative way of life could be described as a typical progression from the antipodal oracle, who overturns every convention, into the Sanskritized teacher.

In 1922 Nirmala's *sādhanā* (structured spiritual discipline) began, but without instruction. Finally, she went through the complete ceremony of initiation, or *dikshā*, playing the role of the guru herself and giving herself her own initiatory *mantra*. After this event she observed silence for three years. She gave up feeding herself altogether and never brought food to her mouth with her own hand again. She is still fed by an attendant, even in public. She travelled incessantly according to no predictable pattern, acting on a sudden whim at any hour of day or night. One such journey took her to the sacred Lake Mansarowar across the Himalayan frontier in Tibet. She would think nothing of suddenly getting up in the middle of the night to catch a train and head for a destination a thousand miles distant, nor of the vagaries of the weather, the fatigue of her followers, nor the folly of her actions. She slept no more than two hours at a stretch and was up most of the night talking and laughing. She behaved like a wanton child, the first guru to make trains and motor-cars the toys of her *līlā*, turning her incessant wandering into an apparently absurd and meaningless flight from nowhere to nowhere. It is said that under all conditions, even of distraction and turmoil, the sage maintains the inner poise of cool detachment, a witnessing consciousness which scans every passing event with unflagging wakefulness. There must be no strain nor effort in the performance of a purely disinterested act; it should spring from the spontaneous centre of the personality; Śrī Ānandamayi calls this 'effortless being'.

For her disciples, the absence of rules, the spontaneity, are proof of her unique qualities. Only after diligent search in the emotional literature recording her life can one identify its central initiatory event. It seems that, in her early twenties, after a violent storm, Nirmala fell into a state of ecstasy on a walk through the woods of her forest retreat with her husband. Suddenly she stopped, walked three times round a certain spot, drew a circle on the ground in a rite of orientation, and sat down. She pronounced mantras and placed her hand on the earth. 'It mysteriously felt as if layer after layer of the solid ground was slipping away beneath me,' she relates, 'like the removing of curtains, and my hand and arm went into the soil unimpeded right up to the shoulder.' With the help of her husband she withdrew her arm from the hole and warm red water oozed from it. As the liquid welled up out of the soil she stood and marvelled at this mysterious and sudden 'eruption of the sacred'. Subsequently, she had a brick *vēdi*, the sacrificial altar, built round the hole and *axis mundi* construction rites performed in it. This *vēdi* was surrounded by a platform, so that it formed an egg-shaped hollow at its centre, around which the main room of her first *ashrām* was built. Occasionally she would curl herself into a foetal posture within the *vēdi* (cf. pp. 154–5), overcome by a state of rapture. On one such occasion her favourite disciple was so astonished at the radiant expression on her face that he turned to the other devotees and declared that henceforward she would be called Ānandamayi—'steeped in bliss'. The association with *māyā* carries a suggestion of the 'magic enchantress' or 'mistress of illusion'. Thus the *vēdi* became the locus of her 'naming' within the magic circle of initiates, the moment when society invested her with sacred authority.

The event is symbolically associated with the return to the womb, identity with the unveiled, soft, moist mother earth and rebirth to a new mode of being. Śrī Ānandamayi's body is claimed by the earth and merges with it. In the state of rapture no distinction is drawn between symbol and import. She sees only the physical liquid in the hole, not a symbol made by human art, but one chosen among natural objects. 'There is no explicit reason,' Suzanne Langer writes of such eruptions of the sacred, 'why sacredness belongs to such an object, only a strong feeling that in it the luck and hope and power of man is vested. The practical efficacy attributed to Sacra is a dream-metaphor for the might of human ideation. Their 'mightiness' is thought of as specific efficacy; whatever expresses Life is regarded as a source of life.[1]

This small incident, which led to the establishment of an *ashrām* and an extensive network of subsidiary institutions in various parts of India, is a revealing instance of how the guru is reintegrated into society after a period of isolation. It begins with a mystical experience of identity with the earth and a state of ecstasy. The guru-figure becomes a child once more in the hallowed spot where the absolute and relative coincide; Stefan Andres calls this conjunction the 'abyss of the nucleus'. Its discovery and detachment from the surrounding chaos of the forest by means of the circle and its consecration as sacred space are familiar stages in the establishment of a

[1] Suzanne K. Langer, *Philosophy in a New Key*, New York, reprinted 1948, p. 123.

symbolic, axial *centre* which, as we have seen, is called the 'naval of the earth'. A portion of life is brought under control. Following on this immersion in and identity with nature, the guru repeatedly returns to that state by ritualistic re-enactment of the original event in the hollow of the *vēdi*. The two phases of the story involve two quite different types of experience. She does not immerse herself in the same hole in the earth itself, but goes to a symbolic artefact—the altar—constructed over it. From the 'chaos' of the primary experience order crystallizes and a rite is born.

Through the irrational, discordant element in her make-up, this evidently disturbed and what we would call 'mentally unbalanced' young woman was laid open to the influence of life, acted upon, and through the contact with an alien, mysterious, unknown element, transformed. But transformed into what? She once said: 'If there were *aham-jñāna* in me, I-consciousness, I could express who I am. As it is not there, I am what you choose to say about me.' To another disciple who wanted her to declare her identity she replied: 'I am conditioned as well as unconditioned. I am neither infinite nor confined within limits; I am both at the same time. I am with everybody, whatever their age; I exist before there is any creation, duration, or dissolution of the world.' It was she who was quoted earlier in this chapter as saying, 'I am the drum: you play the tune.' In other words, she is a kind of mirror for Narcissus.

Her spiritual element is the *līlā*, the eternal sacred play in which divinity manifests itself in the physical world like the play of a child. We have already seen that Hindu tradition recognizes a state of absent-mindedness, when the cares of the world are temporarily put aside, called in Sanskrit *anya-manas*: the 'other mind', a state of *possession*. In her earlier years the atmosphere in Śrī Ānandamayi's *ashrām* used to be one of almost continuous *līlā*. Like numerous saints and sages she behaved as a holy fool, making her daily acts a kind of playing at belief, playing at religion, a divine comedy in which all solemnity is seen to be no more than a stratagem of the mind. Against the tyranny of the heart she led a conspiracy of folly. On festivals and holidays—holy days—the mood of the *ashrām* was like a carnival; everyone dressed up, the rooms were decorated, and all soon abandoned themselves to the mood of the occasion, spun into a maelstrom of dissociation. The focus was Śrī Ānandamayi herself; she *played* at being God, *became* God, to the entranced eyes of her devotees.

She spoke of herself as 'this little girl' or 'this wanton child', addressing men as 'Pitaji', father, occasionally playing the role of Bal Gopāl, Krishna as Divine Child. Her re-enactment of childhood states revives a universal desire to restore the image of childhood and represent to the conscious mind the link with the original condition of innocence. For a guru to do so suggests that consciousness limits spirituality; thus he checks any one-sided mental development by emphasizing an unchanging state throughout all stages of growth. Childhood is a state of *dependence*, a unity with origins and a process of evolution towards independence. The wantonness of the child exposes the sterility of moral conflict. It is a personification of wholeness inaccessible to ordinary consciousness, a state of unity with the impenetrable depths of Nature. Mystical initiation and baptismal rites are devices for the re-experience of that unified state, attainable after symbolic death and rebirth. 'The "eternal child" in man,' says Jung, 'is an indescribable experience, an incongruity, a handicap, and a divine prerogative; an imponderable that determines the ultimate worth or worthlessness of a personality.'[1]

In all initiatory symbolism regression plays some part, but with Śrī Ānandamayi it has been the *raison d'être* of her mystique from the very start and the potent source of her appeal—an invitation to the instinct of protectiveness and parental solicitude as well as providing others with an object of transference. Her personal infantilism did not continue much beyond her middle years, although, as we have seen, she is still literally hand-fed. In response to the emotional needs of the devotee she also inspires identification with the fantasy hero-figure. 'The epiphany of the hero shows itself in a corresponding inflation: the colossal pretension grows into a conviction that one is something extraordinary. . . .'[2] This identification with the hero, says Jung, can lead to a synthesis of the conscious and unconscious, which leads in turn to a shifting of the centre of personality from the ego to the self. However, the psychoanalytic encounter with instinct does not accord exactly with spiritual therapy such as we are dealing with here. By initiating a psychic transformation in the disciple a guru does not, for example, insist on his subjecting himself to the same close *intellectual* scrutiny as does the analyst. The guru's control over his disciple is intuitive. Both *sādhanā* (spiritual exercises) and therapy instigate this self-encounter, but in quite different ways. A patient's sources of erotic feeling are held up to an intellectual light by his analyst and his every motive put in question. To a guru, such an approach intellectualizes an essentially mysterious process; instead he prescribes the consistent practice of meditation. His own persuasive personality is believed sufficient to ensure the disciple's safe passage through the psychic labyrinth.

The first thing that strikes the visitor to one of Śrī Ānandamayi's *ashrāms* is the concern to preserve the entire gamut of pollution rules—which almost everywhere else in India have been liberalized. The intricacy of these rules, the thoroughness with which they are carried out, the inconvenience they cause, the time and energy consumed in executing them or thinking about them, surpass description. Again, a fiercely exclusive, Brahmanical atmosphere attends every ritual performance in the *ashrām* temples; a

[1] Jung and Kerenyi (1949).   [2] Ibid.

formidable hierarchy of aristocratic high-caste Brahman women attendants guard the guru. When asked why she tolerates such a tyrannous regime, she replies: 'It is not I who am concerned with such things; I accept the rules because the people who live here prefer it that way.' While she tolerates every whim of her followers, they tolerate hers. The assertion of her absolute authority as guru is interpreted by the disciple according to the traditional theory of *kheyal*—volition free of *karma*, or 'disinterestedness', 'impartiality'. The acts of the one mirror the acts of the other, *regressus in infinitum*.

The concept of *jivanmukti* is monist and the tradition of the guru, though it has been associated for so long with the *bhakti* cults, has inevitably been deeply influenced by monist thought, with its idea of absorption into a non-dual absolute. According to the *bhakti* mystics, perfect identity of Ātman with Brahman in a state of pure isolation precludes the further possibility of a relation of love to God, and can only lead to a condition of spiritual sterility. Professor Zaehner, in his brilliant critique of Indian monism, quotes (in his *Mysticism, Sacred and Profane*) a remarkable passage by one of the greatest mystics in history, Ruysbroek; Ruysbroek employs the words 'emptiness' and 'unity' in a description of a state of spiritual homeostasis which, as Zaehner suggests, is a perceptive and compassionate diagnosis of the predicament in which the guru-figure is likely to be ensnared. It could well be an explanation of the rapture which seems to hold Śrī Ānandamayi and her devotees in the motionless suspension of *Ānanda*.

In this emptiness rest is sufficient and great, and it is itself no sin, for it is in all men by nature, if they know how to make themselves empty . . . when men wish to exercise and possess this rest without the works of virtue, then they fall into spiritual pride, and into a self-complacency from which they seldom recover. And at such times they believe themselves to have and to be that which they never achieve. . . .

For according to their way of thinking, they possess everything that they might pray or yearn for. And thus they are poor in spirit, for they are without desire, and they have forsaken everything, and live without any choice of their own, for it seems to them that they have passed beyond everything into an emptiness where they possess that for the sake of which all the exercises of Holy Church are ordained and set. And thus, according to them, no one is able to give to them or to take from them, not even God Himself; for it appears to them that they have advanced beyond all exercises and all virtues. And they have attained, they think, to a perfect passivity in which they are finished with all virtues. And they say that greater labour is needed to be finished with virtue in passivity than to attain to virtue.[1]

The rapture of Śrī Ānandamayi within a circle inscribed on the earth may be understood even more clearly by contrasting it with the 'horrible ecstasy' of Roquentin in *La Nausée*, the novel by Jean-Paul Sartre.

[1] Blessed Jan van Ruysbroek, *The Spiritual Espousals*, tr. Eric College, London, 1952.

Roquentin is the first of this author's anguished men for whom the fact that God does not exist is a source of profound anxiety. He sees the physical world as a sticky, unformed, half-solid, half-liquid mass which nauseates him. One day in a public park he gazes at the black root of a chestnut tree, and its blackness, as he perceives it, is not a colour but 'like a bruise or a secretion, like an oozing—and something else, an odour, for example of wet earth'. As he gazes fixedly at the root, Roquentin feels himself 'plunged into a horrible ecstasy'. He suddenly realizes what his nausea signifies, and hence what existence is: contingency. 'I mean that one cannot define existence as necessary. To exist is simply to be there.' He realizes that in a universe whose laws are contingent he is insecure. He experiences, like Kierkegaard, the lonely anguish of the sinner separated from God.

But this 'horrible ecstasy' teaches him a single comforting lesson. If the universe is contingent, it is also *free*. 'All is free,' he tells himself, 'this park, this city, and myself.' To the Hindu mystic, on the other hand, the most intense contemplation of an object in a conflation of seeing and knowing is not experienced as contingent but as *māyā*: 'All is *māyā*,' all is illusion. To be aware of this is to experience, not, as Roquentin does, a 'horrible ecstasy', but the ineffable bliss: Ānanda Māyī. To perceive the world as illusion is to participate in the divine comedy; the only consistent response is laughter. After his experience Roquentin concludes that no 'reason for living' is given by God or Nature, and hence life is an absurdity. Since this would be unbearable anguish every man must invent his own 'reason for living'. Roquentin's response to the same existential situation as confronts the Hindu is in the tradition of modern Occidental man: he will become an artist, he will *create* literature, a novel. Roquentin suddenly feels the faint cold dawn of a new hope when he resolves to find a kind of salvation from anguish through art. He reflects: 'A time would come when it would be written, when it would be behind me, and I think that a little of its clarity might fall over my own past. Then because of it, I could remember my life without repugnance.'

Roquentin's resolve to create works of art brings him to a conscious awareness of the importance of memory. His novel will give clarity to his *past*, he will *remember*, he will have a sense of participation in history. Śrī Ānandamayi's moment of revelation, when her body sinks precariously into the earth, obliterates memory and she lives in the Eternal Present. Gandhi experienced quite another, but equally intense moment of truth—in his case a sense of guilt which he remembered throughout his life. Gandhi's is the guru-figure inverted. He tentatively recognizes the reality of history, he has a sense of participation in it, of being capable of effecting change; in this he attempts what no guru has done before. A guru is as much *aware* as any sensitive Indian of the degradation and misery which surround him; but

Gandhi also *understands*. In fact, the guru concentrates exclusively on aware-ness; Krishnamurti, for example, talks of 'choiceless awareness'. 'To understand the misery and confusion that exist within ourselves, and so in the world, we must first find clarity within ourselves, and that clarity comes about through right thinking. . . . Clarity is not the result of verbal assertion, but of intense self-awareness and right thinking.' This is the 'alert passivity' which endlessly recoils upon itself in a sterile circle; for intense awareness is a condition either of anxiety or of ecstasy. The difference be-tween awareness and understanding is the difference between detachment and co-operation, between indifference and concern.

A strategy of desperation

Western society, we are so often told, is not only suffering from a general *malaise*, it has also infected the developing world with its own sickness. Westernization is but one aspect of this mass epidemic which the Occident has inflicted on the Orient, and, according to the same line of thought, Indian society is the chief sufferer in this respect. I will pursue a slightly different course in this section in order to determine more precisely how two forms of alienation have interacted, one Indian in origin, which will engage our attention more closely than the other, Western in origin, which merely exacerbates the first. I would suggest that the therapeutic *guru-shishya* relationship is the most typical form of cure for a certain pattern of alienation which is the consequence of the Indian social system. Further, the *guru-shishya* therapy was specifically devised to cure precisely this kind of alienation.

It should be pointed out immediately that, for want of a better term, the over-used word 'alienation' will be employed here only in the most general sense. A variety of specific individual motivations impel those who submit themselves to the tutelage of a guru, and they cannot be given any more than the most generalized characterization here.

All forms of Indian therapy are homeopathic in character, operating on the principle of *similia similibus curantur*—likes are cured by likes. There is a Tantric saying which condenses with the utmost brevity the principle on which it is believed to operate: 'Shiva administers poison in order to neutralize the poison.' The *guru-shishya* therapy is no exception; to overcome alienation, alienation is *accentuated*. However, the chief distinction between homeopathic medicine and this form of psychotherapy is that whereas the doctor restores the patient to health, the guru aims higher; not only does he attempt to cure the state of alienation, but to initiate his disciple into an enhanced mode of being superior to that of 'normal health'.

According to homeopathic procedure, while the state of alienation is accentuated by the guru, the consequence is a condition which, from the Western point of view, is commonly diagnosed as a psychic illness. In India, since it is redirected into an exemplary and valued pattern, it cannot be so regarded.

This state of alienation initially impels the victim to adopt what will be called here a strategy of desperation: total surrender of the will to that of the guru. The acute form of the condition is evidently rare, but since it is a response of the individual to certain pressures inherent in the caste society, a mild form is very frequently found. Accentuated by the homeopathic therapy (which is not always successful), accorded a high religious value, and infiltrated back into the society from the precincts of the *ashrām* by the drop-outs, the alienating condition spreads. As we have seen, the initiated Renouncer who has successfully passed through the guru's tutelage acts as a culture-bearer, influencing and modifying the norms of the majority. In the course of time, what has begun as a strategy of desperation can result in its idealization by the society; it is then built into the religious system, assimilated, and normalized as model conduct. Because such normalization is now widespread within the very castes from which the alienated have originally opted out, the procedure begins again, creating stress in those individuals whose genetic formation makes them peculiarly vulnerable. Thus we are viewing the fluctuating fortunes of the society from a different angle from that in Part Three. Whereas, previously, we examined the paradox of fission and fusion, now we are observing the paradox of sickness and health. In both cases there is a cyclical dynamic—the restoration of lost unity. We thus approach the kernel of this book's theme, which is to identify the sources of the difficulties which India is currently experiencing.

In his humanist approach to alienation and psychic illness, Dr. R. D. Laing utilizes the Eastern psychic excursion into inner space to explain the phenomenon of the 'divided self'. We will reverse the procedure and utilize knowledge of behaviour on the borderline between mental health and illness as a means to find out how the strategy of the psychic excursion works in the context of both traditional and transitional Indian social conditions.

In *The Divided Self*, Laing defines the conduct of his patients as an attempt to preserve a being that is precariously structured. His starting-point is the problem of 'ontological insecurity'. Such individuals in Western society feel that the self is threatened. I believe that it is an analogous (but not identical) feeling of insecurity which motivates the *shishya* who retreats to an *ashrām*. We must try to imagine what it feels like to be such a threatened individual within the interdependent Indian social system where the sense of self is less. In the Indian family and social systems the web of kinship is insufficient to protect the individual who, because of his genetic develop-ment, has a low threshold of security. The plurality of parent surrogates, the highly structured, formalized role-playing demanded by the joint-family and hereditary caste system, exert particularly acute pressures on any individual whose formation deviates from the norm. It is a vicious circle in so far as this system does not permit more than a precarious differentiation of the individual from the rest of the world, so that his identity and auton-omy are always in question. The physical environment and the value system provide no more than a frail sense of temporal continuity. The individual who, for one reason or another, does not feel himself to be autonomous, is likely to depend unilaterally on others in relations of merged identity rather than to develop attachments of genuine mutuality. In acute cases of insecurity there exist only two alternatives: the utter detachment of *kaivalya*, isolation, or the utter attachment of the *guru-shishya* relationship.

The need to be seen is one of the key traits in an individual who suffers from an acute sense of insecurity:

> The need to be perceived is not, of course, purely a visual affair. It extends to the general need to have one's presence endorsed or confirmed by the other, the need for one's total existence to be recognised; the need, in fact, to be loved.[1]

One of the commonest features in a Hindu *ashrām* is the compulsive need of the disciples and suppliants not merely to have *darshan*—the 'blessing' of the guru's presence—but also to ensure that they are each, personally, *seen* by the guru. Considerable amounts of time and energy are spent in devising ways to achieve this end. 'Did he *look* at you?' is the question asked among themselves. Retreat into the protection of the *ashrām* magic circle is in part motivated by a desire to preserve the self's identity, to go into hiding. In actual fact, like Laing's patients, the inmates of an *ashrām* dread the look of another person because this implies relationship, to be bound up with the existence of another, and therefore to be ensnared in the net of *karma*. In an *ashrām* personal attachments are rigorously discouraged. But rapport with the guru is another matter, and here we have the first example of homeopathic therapy. The depersonalized gaze of the guru directed upon the disciple is unattached, disinterested; it is therapeutic if the disciple can respond in similar fashion, without hunger for recognition and attachment. In one sense this means that he is more terribly alone than in the outside world. In another, the unflinching mutual 'plumbing of the depths' of the depersonalized gaze is an exchange of disinterested love. If the disciple is 'not ready' it is said that the guru cannot really look at him; hence the dual anxiety—fear at being seen, fear at not being seen.

[1] R. D. Laing, *The Divided Self*, London, 1965 edn., p. 119.

The next trait in the behaviour of Laing's patients with which to seek analogies in an Indian stress situation concerns a basic symptom of the 'divided self'—dualistic body perception:

In this position the individual experiences his self as being more or less divorced or detached from his body. *The body is felt as more one object among other objects in the world than as the core of the individual's own being.* Instead of being the core of his true self, the body is felt as the core of a *false self*, which a detached, disembodied, 'inner', 'true', self looks at with tenderness, amusement, or hatred as the case may be.[1]

I think it would be correct to say that the majority of novices who submit themselves to the tutelage of a guru feel this divorce of mind and body. They are taught various physical exercises and follow certain dietary rules which intensify this mode of body perception. The consequence is a sensation which they find agreeable and call 'transparency'; under Western conditions this effect, which Laing calls 'discarnate spirituality', is negative. The *shishya*, on the other hand, is taught, for example, to regard physical illness and pain as if they were happening somewhere beyond the fringe of the true self, and that any damage to the body could not *really* hurt the self. This way to perceive the true nature of the body is to plumb the mystery of *karma* (to which mind and body, but not the true self, are subject) by right recollection, to perceive that which remains constant before, during, and after illness, sleep, and meditation. Another discipline enjoined on the disciple is correct perception of the body during sexual intercourse. The spouse is to be regarded as a manifestation of the divine, a god or a goddess; both man and wife are to recite *mantras* as an aid to this end. It could be said of this practice that it is a strategy of the self to enjoy a sense of freedom which it fears it will lose if it abandons itself to the real. To regard one's spouse as a *person* is to increase attachment, to be further ensnared in the karmic net, just as it is blasphemy to regard the guru as a *person*. That is why a Hindu *swami*, Yatiswarananda, has stated that 'all human relationships are unsatisfactory'.

The majority of Indian schools of thought are monist, in the sense that their ultimate goal is to overcome all division, all duality, to dissolve the split between false self and true self, mind and body. The false self, or 'ego' must be burnt up, leaving the imperishable true self, the Ātman. Dualism is a strategy arising from *avidyā*, or ignorance. The starting-point is for the disciple to ask himself the question: Who am I?—*Sva haṃ*? The answer is: I am That—*Haṃ sa*. The guru may teach the *shishya* various techniques of dissociation—intermediate, homeopathic means to achieve psychical withdrawal into the true self and out of the body, so that the world and the body are actually *seen* to be what they are—*māyā*—the

---

[1] Ibid., p. 69.

conjuring trick of the divine enchantress.[1] Those systems of thought which
do not subscribe to this idea of the phenomenal world as illusion do,
nevertheless, dissociate Matter from Spirit. The valorization differs, not the
basic dissociation.

Laing's description of the individual under immediate physical threat, or
imprisonment in a concentration camp, as a mental observer who looks on
detached and impassive at what his body is doing or what is being done to
his body, closely resembles accounts of the sensation induced by the willed
technique of the yogin. Ideally, this acrobatic technique of subjecting the
body to acute stress is a homeopathic cure for the pain of existence in time,
achieving a state of dissociation in which the yogin would like to remain for
as long as possible. Laing suggests that a patient who always experiences his
body in this fashion will be of a split nature.

This kind of dissociation is experienced at one time or another by every
human being. But in India it is not only commonly experienced in a mild
form, it is actively sought, and is one of the ethical foundations of Hinduism
and a major feature of the *Bhagavad Gītā*.

The act is always the product of a false self. The act or the deed is never [the
individual's] true reality. He wishes to remain perpetually uncommitted 'to the
objective element'—hence the deed is always (or at least he believes it to be) a
pretended, a supposed performance, and he may actively cultivate as far as he
can that 'inner' negation of all that he does in an effort to declare everything
that he does 'null and void', so that in the world, in reality, in 'the objective
element', nothing of 'him' shall exist, and no footprints or fingerprints of the
'self' shall have been left. Thus the self withholds itself from 'the objective
element' both in respect of perception and of action. There can be no spontaneous
action as there can be no spontaneous perception. And just as commitment in
action is avoided, so perception is felt as an act of commitment that endangers
the freedom to be nothing that the self possesses.[2]

This, I believe, could be considered a valid interpretation of the ethical
detachment enjoined by the Gītā. However, it happens to be Laing's
description of schizoid attitudes in the alienated Western individual.

[1] Alan Watts, while conceding that *māyā* is not merely 'illusion', but 'the entire world-
conception of a culture', says that its unreality 'lies in the concepts or thought forms by
which it is described'. His hypothesis 'that liberation is from the *māyā* of social institutions and not of the physical world', is a fruitful one in the context of traditional Hindu
psychotherapy, which, he rightly claims, primarily seeks to cure those who are 'suffering
from a social institution'. Nevertheless, he takes too limited a view when he reduces
traditional therapy to liberation from what he calls 'social *māyā*'. Liberation from false
apprehension of *māyā* involves more than disinterested *playing* at 'the social game instead
of taking it seriously', although this is, indeed, an essential feature of every guru's
teaching. For the classical view (including Śrī Ānandamayi's paradoxical 'This body is
THAT') is that false apprehension of the physical world is also an error, and one even
more fundamental. See Alan Watts, *Psychotherapy East and West*, Pantheon Books, New
York, 1961, Ch. 3.   [2] Laing (1960), 1965 edn., pp. 88–9.

Whereas, under Western conditions, the state of mind described here manifests non-pathological schizoid tendencies, Indian society sustains it as one aspect of an inclusive, ethically valued ideal; it therefore has no negative connotations as long as it is an integral part of the overall value system. To accentuate incipient dissociation is the Indian homeopathic therapy, the goal being reunion of the divided self.

Laing's case studies suggest that this dissociation is often linked with a tendency to regard everyone as an actor playing a role. To some extent this too is a universal experience; but it is in the degree of consistency to which the attitude is carried that the individual will be regarded as healthy or morbid. Caste society demands that every member play a number of very highly formalized *roles, without the true self beneath the mask being affected*. For the social misfit, such consistent playing of 'someone else's part' (hereditarily designated) rather than following one's own inclinations, is likely to make experience of the true self more difficult. All social activity involves role-playing; only when it ends in completely stereotyped behaviour can it be said to have overreached its functional purpose. The caste society is certainly prone to this danger; hence the compensatory ethic of detachment —although both are connected in a spiral of reciprocating influence.

A schizoid case recorded by Laing coincides with the character of the idealistic Hindu *shishya*. This is not paradoxical if it is remembered that the traditional caste society normalizes what in the West is an anomaly. The *shishya* differentiates between his own true self, 'inner self', or Ātman, which is free, unembodied, transcendent, and his 'personality'. The self is divorced from all activity that is observable by another, which is the domain of the personality, false self, persona, mask, 'front', or 'ego'. Of the plurality of masks assumed, none is so fully developed as to have a 'personality' of its own. Observable behaviour may comprise quite deliberate impersonations along with compulsive actions. To this person the real self is experienced as a mental entity. The individual's actions are not felt as expressions of his self; the self is not felt to participate in the doings of the false self, which it tends to regard in a highly critical light. Such a person is trying to be omnipotent by retreating within his own being, abstaining from a dialectical relationship with others since, in a sense, there is no 'other'—other people, the outer world, and his own false self being ultimately 'unreal'.

Laing points out that in the West such a strategy is accompanied by a sense of haunting futility with regard to the outside world, which the individual 'affects to despise as petty and commonplace compared to the richness he has *here*'. Anyone who has some acquaintance with the attitudes of the inmates of an *ashrām* will know how closely this description accords with their outlook. Here the comparison ends, for Laing's patients experience, as a result, a feeling of inner deadness. It is the possibility of overcoming deadness which forces the Hindu individual to retreat from the two-dimensional world of the caste masquerade to the one-dimensional, or 'one-pointed' (*ekāgratā*), discipline of the *ashrām*. Viewed from inside the *ashrām*, the ordinary world is indeed a place of futility.

We can also compare Laing's description of interpersonal schizoid relations with certain prevailing conditions in ordinary life, outside *ashrām* walls, where these traits are milder and more diffuse. Here the habit of *depersonalization* is also the ideal. In the West we usually adopt such a technique of dealing with the other only when he becomes too tiresome or disturbing. The Indian habit of depersonalization can best be observed at the opposite extremes of the caste hierarchy, where the stress to conform to stylized behaviour is at its maximum. The rigidly orthodox, religious Brahman is a man who shrinks from the public gaze. This is carried to such extremes that in Benares the hyperorthodox only bathe in the Ganges at the dead of night. The corollary of this anxiety is the Brahman's habit of regarding a member of the inferior castes (whose pollution he dreads as a threat to his true self) as if he were an object, or as though he or it did not exist. 'The essential feature of a thing', says Laing, 'as opposed to a *person* is that a thing has no subjectivity of its own, and hence can have no reciprocal intentions.'[1] The Untouchable also shrinks from the public gaze, but for the opposite reason; he feels he is nobody (has no body), he instinctively moves about, enters a room, steps away from the higher castes as though he were trying to plead in his own defence, 'I do not exist.' One of Laing's patients felt guilty, as he put it, 'simply at being in the world in the first place'; he felt he had no right to occupy space and that the stuff he was made of was rotten. As in every other instance, the therapy which the guru administers to a disciple who suffers from this sense of self-loathing is homeopathic: he is sent out to wander from place to place, protected by his socially valorized status as an anonymous holy mendicant, thereby he is freed of his dread of commitment and disengaged from the feared reciprocity of false relations between masked workmates (or 'caste-mates') in one permanent place of residence.

Laing considers that in the precariously structured character of his patients there is an insecurity in the laying down of the foundations, but a compensatory rigidity in the superstructure. The situations of the Brahman and the Untouchable are analogous; they are extreme cases of the depersonalization and alienation from which no actor in the caste masquerade is entirely free. Those who suffer most will be 'afraid of letting anything "go", of coming out of himself, of losing himself in any experience'.[2]

Once commit itself to any real project and [the self] suffers agonies of humiliation—not necessarily for any failure, but simply because it has to subject itself to

[1] Laing (1960), 1965 edn., p. 76.   [2] Ibid., p. 84.

necessity and contingency. It is omnipotent and free only in fantasy. The more this fantastic omnipotence and freedom are indulged, the more weak, helpless and fettered it becomes in actuality The illusion of omnipotence and freedom can be sustained only within the magic circle of its own shut-up-ness in fantasy. And in order that this attitude be not dissipated by the slightest intrusion of reality, fantasy and reality have to be kept apart.[1]

This description of psychic illness by a trained clinician bears a striking resemblance to the account of normal attitudes in a Rajasthan town by another clinician, Dr. G. M. Carstairs. The latter has been criticized for his *pathological* characterization of Indian behaviour patterns; it seems to me that this criticism is justified. The guru's homeopathic therapy is to orientate negative autism round the concept of the still point, Ātman, or Zero. In this he is no more than advocating a consistent and thorough application of basic ethical teaching. It will be recalled that, according to Patañjali, yoga aims at the abolition of *all* consciousness, including fantasy and object-perception. This frightening consistency of the mystical acrobat includes (or tends to include) body-denigration; the self-scrutiny of the ascetic is basically punitive (Plate 37). The yogin, for example, should never look at himself in a mirror. In fact, the therapy divides on the question of body-perception. The narcissistic aspect is epitomized by Śri Ānandamayi's assertion, 'This body is THAT'; the anti-narcissistic by the assertion of another well-known modern guru, Ramana Maharshi, 'This body is nothing but a lump of clay.' The Western therapist, to whom such statements are familiar, would probably regard both as distress signals; the psychologist would define both as narcissistic traits; I would describe them as the two sides of one coin.

Laing is careful to concede that while the extreme, tortuous strategy of the schizophrenic (and milder anxieties of the schizoid) have a disintegrating effect, or at least a negative one, this is not invariably so in Western society; he cites one type of creative artist as an example of a successfully harnessed schizoid nature. A negative feature of the traditional Indian social system— precariously structured individual autonomy—is compensated by the advocacy of ethical conduct; this is often inadequate, but more drastic homeopathic methods are only resorted to in emergency. This can be dangerous, as it tends to increase the symptoms of alienation before eradicating them. While the homeopathic therapy may be regarded as a bold attempt to overcome insecurity, should it not follow its course to a logical conclusion, disaster could easily occur. Once the cohesive social system began to disintegrate, the homeopathic remedy lost much of its efficacy. The consequences are there for all to see: the heartbreaking desolation which blights so much of modern Indian life is not solely caused by poverty, but also by the attitude of dissociation, which attaches little

[1] Ibid., p. 84.

importance to physical suffering or poor living conditions. Much of India today is a terrifyingly accurate physical reflection of alienated psychology.

The material condition of modern India, particularly the squalor of the urban areas, is an indictment of Westernization. However, it is not only Westernization which is on trial but the traditional system. The alienating situation implicit in the caste society is exacerbated by the pressure to perform a whole new series of Western impersonations. Under the traditional social system, the false self was the prey of innumerable transitory identifications. Mannerisms, turns of speech, gestures, modes of address that were not expressions of the self, but belonged to someone else, had a negative effect on the sense of identity. With the addition of Western roles the sense of identity is under even greater threat. When, in former times, institutional safeguards effectively channelled these feelings into a personal quest rated high by the value system, psychic danger was mitigated. Once those break down, there is every likelihood that individual stress will become pathological. A situation has arisen for which the guru has no homeopathic cure.

On the one hand, Westernization is an urgent economic necessity; on the other, it is the cause of an increased feeling of alienation. This in itself is sufficient to foster a profoundly ambivalent attitude towards innovation (because innovation is associated in the minds of Indians with something foreign, something vaguely, if not specifically, 'Western'); but there is a psychological dimension to the feelings of ambivalence. When Indians look around at their own world and contrast it with the immense affluence enjoyed by the societies of the Western world, they may not necessarily conclude that the latter is preferable. But their reaction may be better understood if we view it as a desperate manoeuvre by a sick person. One last quotation from Laing provides us with a compassionate description of how the human being responds to the *malaise*.

If the patient contrasts his own inner emptiness, worthlessness, coldness, desolation, dryness, with the abundance, worth, warmth, companionship that he may yet believe to be elsewhere (a belief which often grows to fantastically idealised proportions, uncorrected as it is by any direct experience), there is evoked a welter of conflicting emotions, from a desperate *longing* and yearning for what others have and he lacks, to frantic *envy* and hatred of all that is theirs and not his, or a desire to destroy all the goodness, freshness, richness in the world. These feelings may, in turn, be offset by counter-attitudes of disdain, contempt, disgust, or indifference.[1]

Against this setting of ambivalence and desperation, we will now turn to the curious mixture of traditional and novel means with which Gandhi tackled India's predicament.

[1] Laing (1960), 1965 edn., p. 91.

Plate 50. Hindu and Sufi mystics. Moghul. A.D. 1630. *British Museum.*

left 51. Muslim domestic scene. Moghul. A.D. 1603. *British Museum.*

above 52. Hindu domestic scene. Punjab Hills. Late eighteenth century A.D. *Alpa Studio, Venice.*

below left 53. King with outcastes. Moghul. *c.* A.D. 1600. *Chester Beatty Library, Dublin.*

below 54. King with guru. Moghul. *c.* A.D. 1600. *Chester Beatty Library, Dublin.*

Individuation

Like the child who adapts to the secular world, we have 'abdicated from ecstasy' (Mallarmé). But the process took many centuries to accomplish; in India it began more recently. One man, Mohandas Karamchand Gandhi, in the course of a lifetime lived through the experience which elsewhere has usually lasted for many generations. There have been many Indian reformers who have consciously grappled with the issues of secularism, from Rām Mohun to Jawarharlal Nehru; but no man has endured the stress of transition from the depths of sacred solidarity to the alienation of the modern world more acutely than Gandhi. He refracts the scattered beams of the archaic sacred world through the prism of his magnificently flawed, unique person, and projects them on the dark, unpredictable future. There is something terrifying about the dimensionless *now* which he inhabits. There is no resonance of the past, or, if one likes, no Proustian dimension, to Gandhi's outlook. He is neither an Arcadian nor a Utopian, but a relentless explorer of immediacy—immediate needs, immediate means, immediate ends.

It is hard to imagine how, at that time, he could have done other than extemporize, modifying his means to meet a situation without precedent. He was born at a moment in Indian history (1869, eleven years after the Mutiny, seven years before Queen Victoria was proclaimed Empress of India) when the social institutions of the old world had not yet entirely disintegrated. The myriad groups into which society was divided were still living units in which all members were connected with one another in tribe, caste, sect, clan, family. They were emotionally bound to one another through common experience and initiations. Gandhi died when those groups had lost much of their emotional significance and institutional integrity; by then India had already entered the phase of mass associations. It was pragmatism not nostalgic primitivism which unconsciously led him to project on the movement he initiated the assumption that society could still be institutionally linked through the system of *jajmān, panchāyats,* and village republics which belonged to the old unitary social order.

Plates 55 *above*. Water sports of Krishna and Gōpis. Kāngrā. Eighteenth century A.D. *Bharat Kala Bhavan, Benares.* 56 *below*. Serpent king submits to Krishna. Guler. *C.* A.D. 1760. *Metropolitan Museum, New York.*

It should be pointed out that besides non-violence, non-co-operation, and non-possession, Gandhi also practised what could be called non-renunciation. Early in his life he learnt that men cannot be good, because they cannot be themselves, outside society. There was every temptation for him to follow the classic path of the Renouncer, to opt out of the apparent hopelessness of the struggle for political liberation, and withdraw into quietism. In India, where protest had hitherto involved renunciation, Gandhi deflected this strategy on a different course; but renunciation is once more the motivation of some who would now follow him.

The cool, humane disposition which scarcely, if ever, failed him throughout a period of exceptional turbulence in Indian history, was the outcome of an unlikely medley of influences. Gandhi never really got to know India at first hand until he was well into his middle years, and then it was after immersion for a long period in the Western ambience as a pro-British Westernized Indian. Moreover, he had first come to conscious grips with his Indian heritage through Western eyes: like many educated men of his and later generations, he first read the most important classical texts of the Great Tradition (such as the *Bhagavad Gītā*) in English translation (not the most accurate available). In the formative years, 1915–19, after his return to India, his Western-influenced outlook was modified by an uprush of childhood memories; he developed a new viewpoint on the Indian situation of some complexity, but one at the same time deeply in tune with that of the Indian masses. The leaven to the curious mixture had been quietly at work in Gandhi's mind for nearly thirty years. While still a law student in London (1888–91) he had the good fortune to stumble almost somnambulistically on a forward-looking, somewhat bizarre group of English liberal humanists who belonged to a tributary of the Protestant nonconformist tradition of radical dissent. At the same time and later in South Africa, through his personal contact with British nonconformism and his fitful sallies into Western thought through reading Ruskin, Thoreau, Tolstoy, Carlyle, Chesterton, and others, he was influenced by the broader tradition of European dissent as a whole.

But he was not imitative; he applied his aesthetically orientated Indian mind to assimilating what Northrop would, rather bloodlessly, term the theoretically designated and inferred factor in Western thought. The result was something entirely different again, wholly dissimilar from either Western or Indian ideas. That it was not consistently worked out, that it bore the stamp of his self-tutored mind, is obvious, but the fact is that the urgency of India's plight did not permit him to refine it.

He was affected in his twenties, perhaps unconsciously, by a conflict which had preoccupied European thought since the eighteenth century. That conflict is contained in a dual opposition, on the one hand between the idea of the sacred individual judgement and the idea of necessary social harmony, and on the other, between the evangelical mood in religion and morals and the prevailing humanitarian attitudes of the Enlightenment. The leading English dissenters, for example, had been non-conformist preachers who were at the same time radicals with passionate sympathy for revolutionary effort. William Godwin, the first anarchist, whose thought Gandhi's resembles in certain respects, was at one time a preacher. William Blake—friend of Thomas Paine—was a visionary. In the crucible of Blake's imagination the underlying conflict developed into a dialectic of contraries and progression which, in its ethical aspect, is not unlike the Gandhian dialectic of Satyāgraha. The sacred integrity of individual energy affirmed by Blake and Godwin was to have a profound influence on the course of nineteenth-century English radical thought. Gandhi was a distant heir to that tradition, built, as it and later his ideas were, on the belief that the function which individuates is also the basis of human equality, and that a full recognition of the function is the sole possible basis of human liberty. Gandhi never ceased to insist, even in the conformist, non-individualist social climate of India, that to recognize individuality is to establish the bond of brotherhood. We cannot read Gandhi without finding echoes of eighteenth-century Western European thinkers who first gave articulate expression to horror, pity, anger, and grief for a society in which men who work go poor.

He never wholly lost touch with English liberal-humanist circles; by the time he returned to London for the Round Table Conference in 1932 and stayed in the East End, such fringe groups were merging into the broader stream of the Labour movement. But while Gandhi's early London contacts had links with inner parliamentary circles, Gandhi did not. The Gandhian movement in India developed independently of the liberal-humanist, anti-imperialist dissenters within Britain itself; in India, moreover, after the early years there was seldom a time when the objectives of Gandhi and the Congress nationalists were identical. The ascendancy of anti-imperialism within the British power structure at the time of the post-war Labour Government coincided with Gandhi's relative isolation from Indian constitutional procedure within the Congress. He was never one of the elected representatives of the Indian people, as was Nehru. India gained independence in 1947 not as a direct result of Gandhi's non-violent resistance but, among other significant historical reasons, from a delayed response in Britain itself to the dissenting attitudes of Englishmen who had laboured so long to transform the British power structure from within. Gandhi was but one contributor to a diversity of factors. The English friends of his student years had accidentally set him on his course of extreme non-conformity with every kind of official institutionalism. The position of odd man out which he thereby came to hold in India was his greatest limitation in the political field (while still permitting him greater freedom), once the stage of dramatic agitation had been passed. Unlike Britain, where dissent had a diversity of institutional channels through which to operate, India had scarcely any; those that existed were almost moribund. Gandhi had to create his own single-handed as he went along; they have proved less durable than the inherited infrastructure of British rule because they were devised to meet his own immediate needs. His enduring legacy to India is of another order, more difficult to assess, and this will be the subject of the ensuing sections.

The Gandhian dialectic

With the publication in 1958 of *Conquest of Violence: the Gandhian Philosophy of Conflict* by Joan V. Bondurant, the study of Gandhism entered a new phase. Coming ten years after Gandhi's assassination and ten years before Martin Luther King's, it played no small part in moulding the minds of the generation of students who initiated 'campus revolts', participated in civil rights campaigns, or became involved in the nationalist struggle of the non-Western world. What Bondurant did was to analyse the philosophical implications not of Gandhism as a whole but of Satyāgraha—literally 'firm grasp of the truth'. She therefore helped to pave the way for the re-assessment of Satyāgraha as a dialectical tool for political advancement. In recent years, Satyāgraha has been shown to possess limited but effective potential for initiating significant social change in conditions very different from those prevailing in South Africa and India when Gandhi first invented it.

However, in the emotional atmosphere of the nationalist struggle for independence and its aftermath, the significance of Gandhi's contribution to Indian life was too deeply associated with religious issues and the Hindu–Muslim conflict for objective assessment of Satyāgraha techniques. Almost every topic associated with Gandhi is still loaded with emotional overtones, but it is to the credit of Bondurant that the core of Gandhi's thought was subjected to close analysis at an opportune moment. In this chapter her thesis will serve as the point of departure in an attempt to identify the moment of historic transition from one value-system to another. Gandhi played a key role in this process, quite apart from his significance in the context of Indian political history. He dramatizes a transition of deep, fundamental, and far-reaching importance in a campaign that outwardly assumes a political character.

According to Bondurant, the foundation of Gandhian thought is a dialectic of creative conflict, a conclusion with which I agree. My aim, on the other hand, is to show how the Gandhian dialectic acts as the catalyst in the transformation of a closed system to one which is open. Historically, Gandhi's is the first successful indigenous attempt by an Indian to solve the dichotomy between tradition and modernity, as distinct from partial, short-lived movements initiated by such men as Rām Mohun Roy and Vive-kānanda. It is a transitional modality capable of development; indeed it *has* to develop, irrespective of its earlier association with Hinduism, if Indian society is to accomplish its own secularization. In order to understand how the Gandhian dialectic transforms the traditional value-system and ulti-mately surpasses it, we will have to trace the origin of its separate com-ponent elements, which have been at all times present in the body of Indian tradition, but which fuse to form a wholly new agent for change.

All these elements derive from the Hindu value-system, while Gandhi himself, according to Nehru, was 'a Hindu to the depths of his innermost being'. It is therefore important to make a distinction here between, on the one hand, the integral function of the ethico-religious Hindu value system in the Gandhian way of life, and the crowning achievement of Gandhi's career—the formulation of a new dialectic potentially broad enough to transcend the immediate cultural matrix. But before identifying the tradi-tional modalities from which the Gandhian dialectic ultimately derives, Bondurant's thesis will be briefly summarized. In discussing the criteria of dialectical thinking, she quotes Sidney Hook:

> Only when that whole or unit or continuity which has been destroyed by the presence of conflicting factors has been restored in *another* whole can we claim validity for our procedure.[1]

For Marx any material which is the subject of man's activity generates its own normative ideals in relation to the way it succeeds in fulfilling human needs. From the reciprocal influence and interaction between the ideal and the actual *a new subject matter* is produced out of which in turn are born the means by which *it will be changed*.[2]

There is little point in applying rigorous standards of logical *thinking* to Gandhi's programme of *action*. On the other hand, Gandhi was a reasoning and intelligent man who gave a great deal of thought to devising Satyāgra-ha. That he never used the word 'dialectic' to define it does not mean that his method was undialectical.

But as a man of action, he was acutely aware that reflection was essential not only to the strategic decision as precursor to act, but also to the more subjective understanding of what he, his followers, and his opponents were, and what they could become . . . he fashioned a method of conflict in the exercise of which a man could come to know what he is and what it means to evolve. In Satyāgraha dogma gives way to an open exploration of context. The objective is not to

[1] Sidney Hook, *From Hegel to Marx*, London, 1936, p. 72.
[2] Loc. cit.; italics mine.

assert propositions, but to create possibilities. In opening up new choices and in confronting an opponent with the demand that he make a choice, the Satyāgrahi involves himself in acts of 'ethical existence'. The process forces a continuing examination of one's motives, an examination undertaken within the context of relationships as they are changed towards a new, restructured and reintegrated pattern.[1]

Satyāgraha refers, not to an end-product, but to a means for achieving agreement.[2]

The Satyāgrahi must recognise that elementary to his technique is the first step of full realisation that his immediate goal is not the triumph of his substantial side in the struggle—but rather, the synthesis of the two opposing claims.[3]

The implicit assumption of all Satyāgraha may be said to be convertibility of the oppressor. In its simplest terms this means the resolution of conflict arising out of differences of opinion. To claim that Gandhi proposed the universal applicability of non-violence to every situation is not substantiated by his own statements:

Where there is a choice only between cowardice and violence, I would advise violence.[4]

I would risk violence a thousand times rather than the emasculation of a whole race.[5]

It is often forgotten by those critics who believe that non-violence is to be equated with weakness that Gandhi was advocating a policy which demanded exceptional courage. Should there be any doubt about this, I quote some relevant remarks which he made on this point:

Never has anything been done on this earth without direct action. I reject the word 'passive resistance' because of its insufficiency and its being interpreted as a weapon of the weak.[6]

Non-violence presupposes ability to strike. It is a conscious, deliberate restraint put upon one's desire for vengeance. But vengeance is any day superior to passive, effeminate and helpless submission. Forgiveness is higher still.[7]

In life, it is impossible to eschew violence completely. Now the question arises, where is one to draw the line? The line cannot be the same for every one. . . . Evil and good are relative terms. What is good under certain conditions can become an evil or a sin, under a different set of conditions. . . . At every step, [Man] has to use his discrimination, as to what is *ahiṃsā* and what is *hiṃsā*. In this, there is no room for shame or cowardice.[8]

[1] Joan Bondurant, *Conquest of Violence: the Gandhian Philosophy of Conflict*, University of California Press, Berkeley, 1958, pp. vi–vii.

[2] Ibid., p. 90.   [3] Ibid., p. 196.   [4] *Young India*, 11 August 1920.

[5] Quoted in N. K. Bose (ed.), *Selections from Gandhi*, Ahmedabad, 1948, pp. 195–6.

[6] Ibid., p. 153.   [7] Loc. cit.

[8] Quoted in D. G. Tendulkar, *Mahatma: Life of Mohandas Karamchand Gandhi*, VII, Delhi, 1953, pp. 152–3.

The Rudolphs relate Gandhi's quest for a 'sense of personal competence' during the early years of marriage to the national quest for self-esteem in reaction to the negative judgements of Englishmen on Indian courage. The Rudolphs stress the difference between martial and non-martial caste traditions concerning courage:

Occupying inferior bureaucratic positions in the context of their conquest, Indians were obliged to nurse compliance, with its female implications, as a condition of success.[1]

The authors believe that this compliance led to a sense of impotence combined with the fear of moral unworthiness arising from impotence. Militant communities responded by launching fundamentalist cults of muscle-building and aggressive spirit-building in Bengal, Punjāb, and Maharashtra. But the core of the nationalist leadership (including Gandhi) were Brahmans, Vaishyas, and Kayasths, who adopted the opposite cultural attitude:

. . . cultivated by sections of the explicitly and self-consciously non-martial castes and communities of Indian society, [it] draws on self-control rather than self-expression, on self-suffering, and calls for restraint of the impulse to retaliate. It is misleading to see this willingness to suffer as a failure of will or surrender to fatalism, although it may have that meaning as well. Self-restraint may be and has been another way of mastering the environment, including the human environment. . . . Gandhi turned the moral tables on the English definition of courage by suggesting that aggression was the path to mastery of those without self-control, non-violent resistance the path of those with control.[2]

Gandhi rejected the aggressive self-assertion with which he had attempted to dominate his wife, but adapted the asceticism, vegetarianism, and non-violence of his traditional upbringing to a dynamic nationalist struggle— 'the means to affect and master the environment . . . not in order to yield to it'.[3] Taken in its widest sense, this also implies a conscious extension of the traditional (though often ineffectual) Indian respect for the ecology.

One of the difficulties in analysing the Gandhian dialectic may be due to the translation of the word *ahiṃsā* as 'non-violence'. The basic antitheses could more correctly be called 'aggression' and 'non-aggression', or 'violence' and 'not-violence'. Non-violence is a *synthesis* arrived at by resolving an inner conflict between aggressive and non-aggressive *instincts*. Non-violence is not an instinct but an ethical stance which demands long training and self-discipline.

The most characteristically Gandhian traits can already be discerned in the foregoing quotations: a realistic acceptance of permanent crisis and conflict in the arena of human affairs and an idealistic conviction that opponents (or

[1] Rudolph and Rudolph (1967), p.164.   [2] Ibid., pp. 184–5.
[3] Ibid., pp. 207 and 215.

opposites) must be reconciled. We have already examined sufficient material to know that both originate within the body of Indian tradition. Their combination provides the basis for a dialectic, and while Indian thought, particularly in Puranic myths and certain Buddhist logicians (Dignāga), may legitimately be described as dialectical (as can much mystical thought), nevertheless, as Bondurant points out, 'Satyāgraha as a social instrument has projected the traditional ethical laws into the realm of social action'.[1] This is the crucial transformation, and its source is not be be found in Hinduism, nor in any other Indian value system, but in the unique psychological make-up of Gandhi himself. It is the chemistry of this vital reorientation which will be the focus of the ensuing analysis.

Creative disequilibrium

In 1915 the poet Rabindranath Tagore set the fashion by calling Gandhi, then forty-seven, *Mahātma*—Great Soul—thereby elevating him in the public eye to the status of a sage. A Mahātma is a man who is believed to possess a form of consciousness different from the average; it is an in-clusive term which may or may not imply that he is also a guru (which Gandhi, technically, was not). Tagore was thinking of Gandhi's spiritual and moral stature when he conferred the title; it is interesting, however, to note how Satyāgraha is a modification of the *guru-shishya* relationship. Gandhi sees the reconciliation of conflict as a co-operative inquiry into the truth of a given relationship. It is, in a sense, a 'de-hierarchization', a demo-cratic master–disciple relationship. The I–Thou polarization is exteriorized on the social arena and assimilated to modern socio-political ideals of egalitarianism. Gandhi's role as Mahātma echoes the archaic ideal of the magician and healer who restores the lost social unity by identifying the hidden cause of division. While he possesses many of the traits of the Renouncer—asceticism, and sexual continence (*brahmāchārya*)—he revives the more ancient ideal of the sage who remains within the society. 'The quest for Truth', he once said, 'cannot be prosecuted in a cave.'

There is another crucial difference between the Gandhian confrontation, in which conflict is implicit, and that between the disciple and his guru. Since the latter is the embodiment of Absolute Truth, there can be no ques-tion of conflict; on the contrary, the pupil surrenders his will to his master and obeys him to the letter. 'Despite the tremendous faith that Gandhi had in divine power, the technique of Satyāgraha is based upon the admission of relative truths and the rejection of absolutes which are not knowable for mortal man.'[2] This is Buddhistic, but Gandhi arrived at it intuitively,

[1] Op. cit., p. 110.   [2] Bondurant (1958), p. 179.

probably before he absorbed the teachings of the Buddha, more through an innate and deep-seated affinity with the Buddhistic emphasis on the *individual* quest for truth.

Satyāgraha proceeds on the same principle as psychoanalysis. The Satyāgrahi and the analyst uncover a repressed truth, deeply hidden beneath the stratagems of weakness, acquiescence, submission, and complicity. While Bondurant was the first to make this comparison, Erikson devotes several pages to it, emphasizing the need for the Satyāgrahi to probe his own motivations constantly, as Freud subjected his own dreams to the same scrutiny as he gave those of his patients. The analyst

would have to include self-analysis, that is, the acceptance of himself as a person who shared his patients' inner mechanisms: the truth could cure the patient only in so far as the doctor had faced the corresponding truth in himself. . . . Freud thus called for a strict equality between patient and doctor, with the dictum that only as long as this non-violent equality is maintained can the truth emerge.[1]

I would suggest that Gandhi's own role as *therapist* in Satyāgraha, while partly derived from the tradition of the *guru–shishya* relationship of inter-dependence, evolved in a different direction by his striving to reduce himself to zero through self-suffering—a phase which a guru is supposed to have accomplished *before* he accepts disciples. Gandhi's rejection of the inequality of the master–disciple relationship in favour of a dialectic between equals is decisive. But the guru is a therapist who heals the alienated soul, and Gandhi sees his own role as nurse to an alienated society. Accentuated alienation is the homeopathic cure in both cases; Satyāgraha opens with a formal declaration of weakness, a deliberate dramatization of one's vulnerability to the 'opponent'—or 'patient'—and 'passive resistance' when threatened with violent assault by the 'patient' (ego-resistance of the disciple is often deliberately induced by the guru). As with the guru's therapy, part of Satyāgraha's psychological efficacy is its educative value: the disciple and *both* parties in Satyāgraha learn by a process of self-discovery. Ideally, Satyāgraha ends with mutual liberation by a 'firm grasp of the truth'. It has been shown how retrospective analysis from effect to cause is employed in Indian logic—what mathematicians call 'inverting the problem' which is refractory to ordinary approaches—taking as one's point of departure that which one seeks to prove and then working back from that point to the premises. This technique is common to the therapy of the guru, psycho-analysis, and Satyāgraha. Gandhi's innovation was to subject the whole master–disciple dialectic to retrospective analysis (during his experimental years with *ashrām*-type communes in South Africa), to lay bare the repressed truth—the autocratic element in the *guru–shishya* relationship—and

[1] Erikson (1970), pp. 245–6.

to devise a dialectic which could eliminate hierarchical dependence. However, the dialectic of Satyāgraha ultimately rests on the mystical premise that realization of truth mutually liberates both parties and establishes them in love for all.

The helpless dependence of the pure monad through asceticism—*tapasya*—which has been shown earlier in this study to be linked with sacrificial initiation, has not altogether disappeared from the Satyāgrahi's ideal of self-suffering, also called *tapasya*. The ancient discipline is disinterested and undertaken for its own sake. In Satyāgraha it is fused with elements of coercion, or *daṇḍa*, a modification of the ancient concept of punishment which, as we have seen, is associated with the yogically conceived role of Kauṭilya's king. There, disciplined mental concentration is emphasized as a means to *power*, whereas Gandhian coercion is tempered by the 'willingness to suffer in oneself to win the respect of an opponent' (Bondurant). Thus Gandhian *tapasya* results in *equality*. As Erikson has pointed out in one of his characteristic *aperçus*, Gandhi's greatest innovation is his method of *building up* the opponent. However, there is a limitation to Gandhian *tapasya*: the fast of the Satyāgrahi does make him *dependent* on his opponent, and while the Indian character is normally responsive to such appeals this is not invariably so. Gandhi earned himself the lasting resentment of Ambedkar, leader of the Untouchables, when the focus of a celebrated fast (as Gandhi believed, in the cause of social uplift for this community) subjected the latter to intolerable moral pressure.

Another aspect of Gandhi's revalorization of archaic modalities is to be found in his concept of *sarvodaya*—'the welfare of all'—or economic reconstruction, with the self-sufficient village as the basic unit of society. There is no doubt that one of Gandhi's major contributions to the political leadership of India during the nationalist struggle was his correct diagnosis of India's economic ills as arising from socio-economic dualism. He saw the poverty of India as having been exacerbated by the rural-urban conflict of interests. To an economist like Gunnar Myrdal it is a question of the 'backwash' effects of urban economic growth nullifying the 'spread effects'.[1] In more emotionally vivid terms, the humanitarian finds it sickening 'to human feeling to witness these myriads of industrious, patriarchal, and inoffensive social organisations disorganised and dissolved into their units, thrown into a sea of woes, and their individual members losing at the same time their ancient form of civilisation, and their hereditary means of subsistence'. It was not Gandhi who wrote that, but Karl Marx.[2] 'Strange as it may appear,' wrote Gandhi in similar vein, 'every mill

[1] Cf. Myrdal (1957).
[2] *The British Rule in India*, London, 1853. Reprinted in Karl Marx and F. Engels, *On Britain*, Moscow, 1962, p. 397.

generally is a menace to the villagers. . . . Bit by bit, the villagers are being confined only to the hand-to-mouth business of scratching the earth. Few know today [1934] that agriculture in the small and irregular holdings of India is not a paying proposition. . . . The extinction of village industries will complete the ruin of . . . the villages of India.'[1] We are not concerned here with the apparent failure of Gandhi, and of the post-Gandhian Sarvodaya movement under the leadership of Āchārya Vinoba Bhave and Jayaprakash Narayan, to devise an effective economic policy for rural reconstruction; but what is interesting in the present context is to trace the process whereby Gandhi came to identify himself with the Indian peasant.

In the context of the historical period when Gandhi lived, his culture and his values are coloured by a streak of strong anti-intellectualism, curious anachronisms, and homespun naïvety. In comparison with Vivekānanda, Aurobindo, Tilak, Tagore, and Nehru, the autodidact Gandhi is an untutored man of the people. When the nationalist movement was thinking in terms of representative democratic institutions and wrestling with the intricacies of the Morley-Minto reforms or provincial legislative councils, Gandhi was talking of spinning wheels, cow protection, village *panchāyats*, and 'bread labour'. He comes closer to the archetype of the medieval leader of a peasant revolt than he does to the twentieth-century leader, either reactionary or revolutionary. His Hindu piety is that of the *bhakta*; but even then, there is an almost uncouth bluntness about his religious beliefs which is wholly devoid of the flowery and effusive religiosity of the *bhakti* sects. In this respect Gandhi is a leader who rises from the submerged culture of the Antipodes; as an educated (and at one time very prosperous) lawyer, son of the chief minister in one of India's small princely states, he makes a *conscious effort* to merge himself with the excluded and underprivileged classes. From whichever angle the man is viewed the upsurge of sentiment which he inspired is, at its base, what has been called *antipodal* in this study. It is characterized by the alarming (but none the less potent) frequency with which the charismatic leader obeys the dictates of the 'inner voice', the inner utterance of the self, which, in its fearful immediacy, literally 'possesses' him. Whether or not Gandhi was in the grip of this, or had an active and conscious control over it as a creative human being, the masses who came in direct contact with him invested his person with the quasi-sacred character of an Unveiled Prophet; his every act was seen to be infused with the primordial fire of revelation. He could say, with Yeats, that he made his song a coat out of old mythologies.

The mark of the leader who identifies with the Antipodes is in the emphasis Gandhi placed on work with one's hands—in which he reveals a deep affinity with those nineteenth-century European leaders of the masses

[1] *The Economic Thought of Mahatma Gandhi*, J. S. Mathur (ed.), pp. 296–7.

who tried to counteract the alienation of man from the culture of the Antipodes by an increasing emphasis on work. Work was the one remaining way of establishing contact with things. Magic and sacramental contact with them was no longer possible after the disruption of the archaic society by industrial production. The spinning wheel, the hand loom, the handicrafts and cottage industries which Gandhi sought to revive originated in a Ruskin–William Morris ethos which was both pragmatic and symbolic.

In an earlier period, the classes which rose under Gandhi's leadership would not have been antipodal; but in the twentieth century, under British rule, the rural caste society was in effect, the victim of relentless, socially sanctioned exploitation, reduced to sub-human status by a class of predatory landlords, merchants, and money-lenders. The true revolutionary power, at that point in history, lay in Gandhi's harnessing the energies not of the Western-oriented middle classes nor of the urban or industrial proletariat, but of those who had been disinherited, the mute, the powerless. The influence of Gandhi's own bourgeois social origins did not nullify the antipodal character of his insurrection; the point to be stressed is the archaic value-system on which Gandhi leaned heavily for ideas. 'The key to Gandhi's leadership lay in his utilization of tradition, but utilization only to transform and to invite a mass following to partake of a philosophy and programme of action.'[1]

The sequence of achievements whereby Gandhi attained his unique status of Mahātma in the garb of humble peasant is well known and amply documented. While the psychological factors, also amply documented and frequently commented on, cannot account for the moral temper and stature of the man, they are of as decisive importance in determining the outward form of the Gandhian method as were those (of a very different character) which influenced the course of Martin Luther's life—a man whose career in many respects resembles that of Gandhi (Erikson calls them *religious actualists*). The psychological traits in the make-up of a single, unique individual interlock sufficiently closely with a constellation of responsive attitudes, more or less constant in Indian society, to generate a new, purposive, and dynamic ethic of change. The catalytic element—that no-thing which is moral strength made perfect in weakness—has been generated from *within* the society (as distinct from being imported, like some tool in the kit of a foreign aid expert), releasing hidden reserves of creativity.

The story follows the mythical 'wound-and-the-bow' pattern. We have already noted that in a hierarchically interdependent society individuality

[1] Bondurant (1958), p. 122. If the reader is in any doubt as to the high-caste Hindu's instinctive identification of Gandhi's ideology with the low castes and his consequent revulsion from Gandhi's mass movement, he is referred to the relevant chapters in Chaudhuri (1951).

tends to manifest itself in a sudden uprush of unconscious contents and that those of its members who become specialists in this form of possession are often gifted but unstable personages who become a mouthpiece voicing collective needs. Something of a similar nature is manifest in Gandhi and put to exceptionally creative use in socially meaningful ways.

Born at Porbandar, a Forsterian coastal town on the Kāthiawār peninsula, Gandhi was the youngest son of well-to-do Vaishnava gentlefolk, and belonged to the Modh Banīya sub-caste. His father married four times; from him Mohandas apparently inherited a powerful sexual impulse with which he was to wrestle constantly throughout his life in ways that are characteristically Indian. There is evidence to suggest that he was the recipient of a somewhat higher degree of maternal indulgence than was the local norm.[1] During boyhood and adolescence he was surrounded by an atmosphere of calculating rectitude and rigid religious conformism associated with the tradition-directed Gujerāti business community. Culturally, the Vaishnava Gandhis were also conditioned by the dominant Jain community, with its extreme, morally antiseptic pollution phobias, close communal solidarity, and total ban on all acts of violence—not out of compassion but as a studied precaution against physical and oral pollution. The ascetic and the emotionally effusive were to be the systole and diastole of the Gandhian life-style.

As a boy, Mohandas (*das* is a typical Vaishnava suffix and means 'servant') identified with two Hindu mythological son-figures of unswerving filial obedience and truthfulness—Harishchandra and Prahlād. Nevertheless, the Oedipal conflict is apparent in his negative reaction to the sternly paternalistic *Laws of Manu*, which he borrowed from his father, and his instinctive preference for the pious emotionalism of the *Rāmāyana* in the popular Tulsīdās version, associated in his mind with his mother's more congenial *bhakti* devotion. As has been pointed out by his biographers, the greatest emotional crisis of his early life was the mode by which he, aged sixteen and already married, was prevented from being present at the death of his father, thereby associating disobedience with sexual guilt throughout his life. This is no exaggeration, for Gandhi himself wrote of his father's last moments with complete frankness in his autobiography:

Every night I massaged his legs and retired only when he asked me to do so or after he had fallen asleep. I loved to do this service. I do not remember ever having neglected it. . . . This was also the time when my wife was expecting a baby—a circumstance which, as I can see today, meant a double shame for me. . . .

[1] Erikson discerns, in Gandhi's childhood propensity to tease and behave mischievously, unconscious compensation for his moral precocity, and even a desire to play parent to his parents. The deep compassion of Erikson's analysis is clearly evident when he says of Gandhi, 'he knew that one must build on the values of one's childhood as long as they are revalidated by experience, until one perceives a wider truth which may make them relative or obsolete'. Erikson (1970), p. 398.

Every night whilst my hands were busy massaging my father's legs, my mind was hovering about the bedroom—and that too at a time when religion, medical science and commonsense alike forbade sexual intercourse. I was always glad to be relieved from my duty, and went straight to the bedroom after doing obeisance to my father. . . . It was 10.30 or 11 p.m. I was giving the massage. My uncle offered to relieve me. I was glad and went straight to the bedroom. My wife, poor thing, was fast asleep. But how could she sleep when I was there? I woke her up. In five or six minutes, however, the servant knocked at the door. I started up with alarm. 'Get up,' he said, 'Father is very ill.' . . . I ran to my father's room. I saw that, if animal passion had not blinded me, I should have been spared the torture of separation from my father during his last moments. . . . It is a blot I have never been able to efface or forget.[1]

Gandhi's relationship with his wife, Kasturba, is also exhaustively described in his books, articles, and public speeches. It is also clear from numerous statements he made that the basis of his whole technique of Satyāgraha resides in his decision, taken in South Africa at the age of thirty-eight, to observe total sexual abstinence. The only way he could conceive of total dedication to the communal cause was to apply a form of absolute ascetic monism, or *brahmāchārya*, to every aspect of his personal life.[2]

Gandhi's views on sexual continence are clear from the following statement by him:

A man whose activities are wholly consecrated to the realisation of Truth which requires utter selflessness, can have no time for the selfish purpose of begetting children and running a household. . . . If a man gives his love to one woman, or a woman to one man, what is there left for all the world besides?

[1] M. K. Gandhi, *An Autobiography, or The Story of My Experiments with Truth*, Navajivan, Ahmedabad, 1927, pp. 21–2.

[2] For confirmation that Gandhi's vow of chastity shares several features in common with widely prevalent traditional Hindu ideas on sexuality the reader is referred to G. M. Carstairs, *The Twice Born*, and an interesting case history in Gitel P. Steed, 'Personality Formation in a Hindu Village in Gujerāt', in *Village India: Studies in the Little Community*, ed. M. Marriott, Chicago, 1955. Miss Steed records a case of a Rājput landlord who, like Gandhi, was subject to a conflict between his role as leader, due to hereditary caste rank, and a religious inclination to withdraw into private retreat. He described his self-punitive ascesis as 'attacks against himself'.

One alternative role which Indrasingh did not attempt, but which he extolled in conversation . . . and dreamed about, was the practice of religious bachelorhood (*brahmāchārya*). Because first it permitted withdrawal from domestic affairs; second, it offered access to powers which Indrasingh found himself incapable of acquiring through following Rājput norms. Indrasingh believed that sexual continence practised as a technique of religious bachelorhood gives inordinate strength and success. According to Indrasingh, the monkey deity Hanuman, by containing his semen, gained the strength to overcome otherwise insuperable obstacles. Rāma's brother, Lakshman, he also believed, practised religious bachelorhood for twelve years and was therefore able to kill the demon Ravanna (pp. 134–5).

... What about people who are already married? Will they never be able to realise Truth? Can they never offer up their all at the altar of humanity? There is a way out for them. They can behave as if they were not married. . . . If the married couple can think of each other as brother and sister, they are freed for universal service.[1]

Until he was over thirty, Gandhi had treated his wife, of whom he was 'passionately fond' but regarded as his inferior in education and culture, as an object of sexual gratification, over whom he exercised what he called the 'masterful authority of a husband'. The tragedy of this vow is that Gandhi projected his own guilt-feelings on the entire domain of sexuality and identified the sexual impulse with violence. He frequently reduced the issue to a grossly over-simplified matter of the superiority of 'Truth force' or 'Soul force' over 'Body force'. Reinhold Niebuhr observes that:

Gandhi's identification of 'Soul force' with non-egoistic motives and 'Body force' with egoistic ones, is almost completely mistaken. The type of power used by the will to affect its purposes does not determine the quality of the purpose of motive.[2]

Perhaps the most remarkable aspect of this flawed understanding of human nature is the almost total exposure of his and his wife's privacy. True, there is a psychological link between sexual guilt-feelings and an unconscious desire to be caught *in flagrante delicto*. But it is one thing to desire it *secretly* and another to perform a moral equivalent *voluntarily* before the eyes of the whole world. With this pattern of persistent exposure we draw near to the kernel from which the paradox of Satyāgraha mysteriously germinates:

I learned the lesson of non-violence from my wife. . . . Her determined resistance to my will on the one hand, and her quiet submission to the suffering my stupidity involved on the other hand, ultimately made me ashamed of myself and cured me of my stupidity in thinking I was born to rule over her; and in the end she became my teacher in non-violence. And what I did in South Africa[3] was but an extension of the rule of Satyagraha which she unwittingly practised in her own person.[4]

Through Gandhi's vilified sexual relationship with his wife he learnt how to use the most potent technique which he ever devised—Satyāgraha. But his biographer, Geoffrey Ashe, in making this point, fails to draw the essential connection. For it is precisely in the *failure to resolve the conflict of*

[1] Quoted in Geoffrey Ashe, *Gandhi: A Study in Revolution*, Heinemann, London, 1968, pp. 180-1.

[2] Reinhold Niebuhr, *The Nature and Destiny of Man: Human Nature*, New York, 1943, p. 261 n.

[3] Gandhi formulated the technique of Satyāgraha one month after taking his vow of continence, while engaged in promoting better conditions for Indian immigrants to South Africa.

[4] Quoted in John S. Hoyland, *Indian Crisis*, 1943.

the sexual libido that the secret element of unrest, of disequilibrium in himself, lies. It is this disequilibrium which made him ever alert to the challenge of conflict in the social arena, forbidding him to rest until reconciliation be achieved.

Three times in his life Gandhi volunteered for service in wartime as a stretcher-bearer. Countless times in his life he actively sought the opportunity to act as a male nurse to friends and acquaintances, mostly women, who fell sick. Satyāgraha itself became, for him if not for others, a means of *nursing society*. In one of his most famous remarks he expressed the desire 'to wipe every tear from every eye'. But just as nursing is his consciously avowed act of self-suffering, of service to others, so also are his fasts 'unto death' the opposite side of the same coin—forms of unilateral dependence, of subtle coercion, learnt, as he expressly states, from his mother in early childhood. We have this on the authority of a trained anthropologist and distinguished scholar, Professor Nirmal Kumar Bose, who knew Gandhi in the last years of his life (here talking about Gandhi's *brahmāchārya* to Francis Watson in a recorded interview):

> . . . it is quite true that in his writing he again and again refers to his mother and to the tremendous influence which his mother exercised over him. For him it was necessary to control some of the ordinary passions to which mankind is subject—hunger, for instance, or sex: these have to be controlled in our traditional religion, as well as in other religions, when a man seeks companionship with God. Now, in this context I do believe that his ideas—which he derived from his mother—and also the austerity which he saw in his mother was very much reflected in his own character. It was not inborn, but it was something which he gathered from the behaviour of his mother in his early childhood. But later on I do believe that when sex became an obstruction in his way as he has described in his own autobiography, I do believe he tried to conquer sex by identifying himself in a very distant way with his mother; he tried to play the part of a mother to all individuals who came in contact with him. And I do believe that the tenderness which I very often noticed in him in relation to every human being who came sorrowing for consolation to him or for courage to him, was an aspect of that motherhood which he had gradually developed inside himself by constant effort. Among our religious seekers we do come across such endeavours.[1]

Stranger quirks of individual psychology than this have inspired similarly successful mass-movements. The degree of deviance from the norm can never, even so, account for the immediacy of its appeal and the depth of the response. Outwardly, Gandhi's non-violence and disciplined dialectic were informed by reason and an unshakable conviction in the power of individual self-reliance to effect fundamental social change. Sexual continence was

[1] Francis Watson and Maurice Brown (eds.), *Talking of Gandhiji*, Longmans, Green, London, 1957, pp. 27–8.

adopted as a purely pragmatic means to accomplish certain short-term aims. By examining the link between his attitude towards sex and his religious views, we can understand how he made positive use of his disequilibrium.

Gandhi was a Vaishnava; he was religious, but he certainly was no mystic; he showed not the least tendency or desire for that dissolution of the personality or yearning for absorption in the All which pervades the Indian aesthetic outlook. His intuitions do not have a religious so much as an ethical content; they deal less with man's relationship to God than with man's relationship to his total being and to other men. True, there is an oscillating rhythm to his life, an essential part of which is occasional withdrawal (either enforced, as in his jail sentences, or voluntary) into a solitude which, relative to his periods of intense activity, is pervaded by an introspective mood. But his emergence from these phases—what Geoffrey Ashe describes as a series of 'transfiguring upsurges'—shows him transforming self-knowledge into something moral, political, and dialectical. His starting-point could have been the watchword of the Vaishnava-Sahajiyās: 'Listen, O brother man: there is no truth higher than Man!'

The peculiar flavour of ethical religiosity which pervades Gandhi's life is not wholly without precedent in Indian tradition, even if the political and social uses to which it was put definitely are. This may be seen in the two domains—caste and sex—where Vaishnavas hold heterodox views. The Vaishnava movement may be said to relate to the Great Tradition of India as Franciscanism to that of Medieval Europe. Gandhi's dislike of caste distinctions, Untouchability, and the legalistic tyrannies associated with organized religion, were a part of his Vaishnava background. In turn he was heartily disliked by orthodox, Brahman-oriented Hindus for this very reason. A leading authority on Vaishnavism, Professor Dimock, to whose books on this subject I am much indebted, points out that 'the Vaishnavas were not always accepted by the society in which they lived, and they did not always accept it. Vaishnavism itself was slightly socially deviant.'[1] The most recent and in many ways the most typical, the one with the most lasting impact, of the many dramatic Vaishnava waves of emotional fervour, is that of Caitanya (A.D. 1486–1533), which affected the course of the entire movement far beyond its place of origin, Bengal. The reason for its social importance was the threat which Caitanya's qualified disapproval of caste distinctions posed to orthodoxy. His disregard for pollution rules had an explosive effect on the Brahman establishment, partly because it came to be associated in the popular imagination with a monist conception of love as an equilibrium between flesh and spirit, no distinction being drawn between castes in the ecstatic rapture of *sahaja* (literally, 'easy', 'natural'), a state of blissful unity. Gandhi was to take a stand with regard to caste close

[1] Dimock (1966), pp. 111–12.

390 The Speaking Tree

to those of Ćaitanya, the Sahajiyās, and the *Bhāgavata Purāṇa* (the principal Vaishnava text): 'Social superiority was not a matter of birth but a matter of right-mindedness' (Dimock). Gandhi made many statements on caste and frequently contradicted himself. The following, in his own newspaper, *Young India*, is about the furthest he ever went in condemning it:

Nor do I believe in inequalities between human beings. We are all absolutely equal. But equality is of souls and not bodies. Hence, it is a mental state. We need to think of, and to assert, equality because we see great inequalities in the physical world. We have to realise equality in the midst of this apparent external inequality. Assumption of superiority by any person over any other is a sin against God and man. Thus caste, in so far as it connotes distinctions in status, is an evil.

We may conclude from this that Gandhi found the accepted ways of society were not wrong, but merely external and therefore incomplete. He inverted the Vaishnava attitude, however, by affirming equality not because it was a religious value but a social one. That it received minority religious sanction was merely incidental. His ethic of humility also resembles that of the Vaishnava-Sahajiyās.[1]

At the outset, Gandhi's vow of chastity meant abstinence, no more and no less. Subsequently he made it clear that, in his view, to repress the sexual impulse in the manner of the orthodox Hindu ascetic was to court disaster; sublimation through association with women in social work was his solution. Despite his rigid attitude towards chastity, his identification with women and the role of motherhood permitted him to develop keen insight into certain aspects of their psychology and to win their confidence. In the puritanical climate of India his open use of this gift could have been regarded with deep suspicion. Gandhi not only accepted the risk but on numerous occasions he delegated great responsibilities in public affairs to women drawn from every social rank. It was this mutual confidence which Gandhi's psychological make-up inspired in women which is to a very large extent responsible for the unusually high proportion of important posts in India today being held by women. This had not been common in India since classical times. For his championing of women's rights Gandhi deserves full credit; they repaid his loyalty with feats of remarkable courage.

Centroversion

The Indian nationalist movement in the 1920s was imprinted with the quirks of Gandhi's own forceful personality; the latter rested, as we have seen, on

[1] It should be pointed out that Gandhi's grandfather was a follower of the Vallabhāchārya Vaishnava sect, whose doctrine of love and surrender to Krishna is among the most intensely emotional of all the *bhakti* cults; the devotee identifies with the role of the *gopis*, cow-girls, in the Krishna-līlā.

a substratum of near-neurotic emotional impulses. One is reminded of a similar situation—that of Akbar. The strange, synthetic, universalistic religion with which Akbar sought to infuse life into an unpopular administrative system, was a consequence of his series of acute emotional crises. Out of introverted, unbalanced experience of the self he fashioned a syncretist religion, with the aim of rallying the pluralistic society round himself as quasi-papal figurehead. Himself the symbolic religious head of a new *imperium*, he sat in the eye of the cyclone atop his pillared throne in Fatehpur Sikri (Plate 49). In Gandhi's case a similar axial modality can be traced, but divested of every last residual element of cosmic (*axis mundi*) symbolism. There are two crucial points of difference between the two modalities. First, Gandhi was not the head of a government. In fact, like the Tantric and *bhakti* movements of old, Gandhi sought to establish a parallel system. During the first decade of his leadership in India he and the Congress machine were so closely identified as to present a virtually united front against British rule. As time went on the Gandhian organization became increasingly differentiated from that of Congress, and in a sense a parallel system to a parallel system. 'Wherever Gandhi moved,' says Krishnalal Shridharani, 'whether it was in a remote village, or outside in the jungle, it became a sort of hub of the country.' Congress never was a hub, but *coalesced* into a political and legally constituted entity. Gandhi's own parallel organization had no constitutional substance. Rather it remained what it had essentially been from the beginning—a rallying-point at the Antipodes of politically constituted organization. Second, Gandhi's sublimation of his inner conflict differs from that of Akbar in so far as he made a point of publicizing the source of his private dilemma. He is probably unique in history for the mode in which he utilized this self-exposure as a prime instrument in the clarification of larger, indeed momentous, national issues, even helping thereby to resolve them. At the height of his power, there is an almost total congruence between Gandhi's subjective processes of arriving at the truth within himself and his objective assessment of the external situation.

Not for nothing had his supporters in South Africa been dubbed 'Proper-Gandhists', for he was the first Indian leader of modern times to master the art of applying public relations to affairs of state. He relayed to his vast audience every new development in his struggle to control his egoistic impulses with the same attention to detail as he applied in his weekly, often daily reports on the progress of intricate political negotiation. The two were often inseparable. Self-suffering, self-purification, fasting, and crises in health were the substance of his moral endeavour, his 'quest for Truth', and success or failure in these personal struggles was dialectically fused with creative social conflict. Gandhi's dietary fads and obsession with hygiene are deviant versions of archaic Indian ideas on the body's metabolism and projection of the body's wholeness on the holistic social order. Erich Neumann coined the word 'centroversion' to describe this process: 'The unity of the psyche . . . functions immediately and without reflection in the totality of a self-regulating and self-balancing psycho-physical system. In other words, the tendency we call centroversion has a biological and organic prototype.'[1] Morally and physically, the destiny of India centred on the minuscule dramas of Gandhi's life. The self-adminis-tered searchlight of publicity, focused by its inventor on himself with all the technical resources of the modern media of communication at his command, did occasionally reveal grotesque and unattractive details, and this is the source of the pronounced aesthetic dysphoria felt by many of Gandhi's critics.

The weakness of centroversion is the tendency to relapse into quietist immobility; Gandhi's imperfect self-balance gave him no rest and saved his movement from grinding to a halt. Yet, for all his unflagging energy, tireless hard work, and attention to detail, there was a good deal of 'slack' in his life. 'Tremendous power was at his command but it often remained unused,' writes Louis Fischer; 'in very crucial issues he bowed to the wishes of opponents whom he could have broken with a crook of a finger. He had the might of a dictator and the mind of a democrat. Power gave him no pleasure. . . . The result was a relaxed man. The problem of maintaining an impression of omniscience, infallibility, omnipotence and dignity never occupied him.'[2] He could not only afford the luxury of thinking aloud, and thinking, moreover, on his feet, inventing and perfecting his technique as he went along—it was the form of Satyāgraha to turn the cross-examination of the lawyer into self-examination, and turn the latter into a continuous animated debate with society. Gandhi's method was as 'peripatetic' (in the sense applied to Aristotle's teaching) as his ceaseless journeys through India. 'I must reduce myself to zero,'[3] Gandhi declares on a number of occasions, seated on the mud floor of his hut in remote Sevagram *ashrām*, absorbed in turning his spinning wheel at the geographical centre of the peninsula. Among other things, this implies that there is a point at the hub of human knowledge where the rational and the irrational go hand in hand. One doubts if Gandhi's choice of the spinning *charkha* as the instrument with which India was to weave her destiny is wholly devoid of conscious symbolic associations—for example, with Kabīr, poet and weaver who worked for Hindu–Muslim unity, and with the *chakravartin* (literally,

---

[1] Neumann (1954), 1962 edn., p. 286.   [2] Fischer (1951), p. 364.
[3] 'In being zero, you aspire to be everything for everybody.' Erikson (1970), p. 253. 'Nothing is more powerful in the world than conscious nothingness if it is paired with the gift of giving and accepting actuality.' Ibid., p. 397.

'abiding in the wheel', sometimes rendered as 'wheel-king' or 'wheel turner'—Plate 48). In 1921 he personally designed the flag of the Congress Party, placing the *charkha* on a white ground between bands of green and orange. Characteristic of the man, however, is that his wheel *processes humble cotton*. The reference to productivity and the work ethic under the aura of a symbol was not lost on the masses; while the material benefits of the homespun *khadi* programme were marginal and the economic theory used to rationalize it was absurd, the change in attitude it initiated cannot be lightly dismissed. The aesthete Tagore missed the propaganda value when he argued that trying to liberate three hundred million people by making them all spinners was like urging them to drown the English by all spitting together. Gandhi's spinning-wheel has nothing to do with the perfect purposelessness of Bhāskara's self-rolling wheel.

As Yeats wrote in *Discoveries*: 'There is an old saying that God is a circle whose centre is everywhere. If that is true, the saint goes to the centre, the poet and artist to the ring where everything comes round again.' Gandhi was probably the first Indian wonder-worker to whom Yeats's highly personal conception of a 'saint' could apply; the Gandhian schema is the antithesis of the 'teleological suspension of ethics' within the guru's closed circle. He could remain at the centre of the circle and yet be ethically and socially active, thus refuting the challenge which William Blake amusingly poses 'To God':

> If you have form'd a Circle to go into,
> Go into it yourself & see how you would do.

This insistence on placing himself within a circle might appear to have nullified the self-assumed catalytic role of ethical agent. But the zero of consistent non-violence was, according to Pyarelal Nayar (his secretary for twenty-seven years), neither in conflict with Gandhi's immediate political objectives nor impotent to solve them:

> He said that the least, the weakest in the country, even the halt and the lame, must be able to enjoy the full measure of independence and the fruits of independence with the tallest. So it had got to be a battle which the weakest and the least could wage with equal success, and that was the moral battle, and therefore non-violence.[1]

To equip himself as leader of the disinherited, Gandhi knew, in the deeps of his mind, that there must be perfect identity between his and their interests, not a mere 'policy' of uplift. His soul must be 'naughted of all things', but his aim was concentrated on the single remnant of his personality that he spared—the irreducible zero, the no-thing made perfect in weakness. One is reminded of the Taoist metaphor of the water's superior strength over the rock. When a friend asked him how he had succeeded in

[1] Quoted in Watson and Brown (1957), p. 51.

arousing the masses from the torpor of their despair, he replied: 'It's the man of our country who realizes when he sees me that I am living as he does, and I am part of his own self.' In other words, all political, social, and ethical conflicts are intimately and organically related to the charismatic leader by a vitalistic sympathy, not by a ritualistic contract. 'I must undergo personal cleansing,' he explained in *Young India*. 'I must become a fitter instrument able to register the slightest variation in the moral atmosphere about me.' Given the impotence of a people deprived of arms, demoralized to an almost unimaginable degree, the zero of the leader in conjunction with the static charge of the people generates a massive voltage. In a letter to Lord Lothian, Nehru described what Gandhi accomplished with the masses:

> Non-cooperation dragged them out of the mire and gave them self-respect and self-reliance . . . they acted courageously and did not submit so easily to unjust oppression; their outlook widened and they began to think a little in terms of India as a whole; they discussed political and economic questions (crudely no doubt) in their bazaars and meeting places. . . . It was a remarkable transformation and the Congress, under Gandhi's leadership, must have the credit for it. It was something far more important than constitutions and the structure of government. It was the foundation on which a stable structure or constitution could be built up.[1]

The qualification is implicit in Nehru's view: Gandhi laid the foundation, but whatever actual improvement was subsequently effected in the material conditions of the millions was the result of constitutional procedure outside the preferred range of the Gandhian movement. There were numerous instances when Gandhi's conscious control over the course of his Satyā-graha campaign came to an abrupt and startling halt through the mysterious promptings of his own 'inner voice'. At such moments the dialectical momentum relapsed into something very close to mysticism. Such an occasion was the Gandhi–Irwin pact of 1931, the result of direct negotiations with the Viceroy, Lord Irwin (later Viscount Halifax). Congress leaders were aghast at the concessions which Gandhi made. Nehru wept and told him: 'What frightens me is your way of springing surprises on us. . . . Although I have known you for fourteen years, there is something unknown about you which I cannot understand. It fills me with apprehension.' To which Gandhi replied: 'Yes, I admit the presence of this unknown element and I confess that I myself cannot answer for it nor foretell where it might lead to.'

Nehru had the edge over Gandhi in this vivid exchange; the Satyāgrahi must have a rational grasp of the situation. The dialectic collapses if its initiator neglects to give adequate reasons for his political decision, especially when its essence is indefinite extension, continuous development, and modification of its ends by a mass of participants. Despite his attentiveness

[1] Jawarharlal Nehru, *A Bunch of Old Letters*, Bombay, 1960.

to immediate needs and the exploration of context, Gandhi's 'willed poverty' concedes too much to the narrow mentality of a 'sunset economy'. He showed little inclination for long-term planning or to explore deep-rooted historical, political, economic, and social factors indispensable to the successful implementation of Satyāgraha. There is nothing in the theory of Satyāgraha which imposes this limitation; in practice, however, Gandhi narrowed his quest for truth unnecessarily. I believe that this limitation arose from the deeper incompatibility between his methods and those of Congress. His was a unified sensibility based on an intuitive sense of timing. Satyāgraha works to the clock, not, as has been claimed, in a discontinuous series of unrelated presents; nor does it operate in the non-sequential time of traditional India, but in a dialectical continuum—timed almost to a split-second. Congress, on the other hand, worked in the constitutional manner of the period, in orderly sequence (or attempted orderly sequence), geared to the modality of British legalistic procedure. As Satyāgrahis have subsequently discovered, this seemingly archaic method needs the instantaneous means of communication now at man's disposal in order to obtain the necessary degree of co-ordination. The shortcomings of Gandhi's campaigns were essentially a breakdown in communication. The paradox is that his dialectical method was in advance of its time and lacked the media resources to be sustained over a long period.

Stable socio-economic equilibrium

Gandhi was a Banīya; he was conditioned by birth to follow the ethic of the Porbandar bazaar-entrepreneur. As we have seen, there was also a Jain influence in the family background. Max Weber notes that Jainism affirms the 'positive relationship of a confession to economic motivation which is otherwise quite foreign to Hinduism'. The value-system of Gandhi's caste was a blend of unsystematic but calculated rationality and an aesthetic orientation which was directly empirical. Nevertheless, in the highly structured society of India, it is the aesthetic faculty which operates at a deeper level; the instinctive aesthetic desire to preserve the stable equilibrium and *status quo* of society is more developed than the rational desire to change the forces and relations of production. As practised by Gandhi, the dialectic of Satyāgraha stops short of *class* conflict while nevertheless refusing to balk at creative *social* conflict. It does not ignore economic motivation—indeed it is frequently focused on immediate economic objectives. The two greatest Satyāgraha campaigns—Champaran and the Salt March—are examples of this. But while the *motivation* contains a strong economic element, the initial *appeal* to the opponent is ethical, not economic—evidence of

Gandhi's shrewd concession to the religious temperament of the individuals with whom he is dealing, which points, in my view, to his conditioning as a Banīya.

Throughout his twenty-five years in South Africa, when he evolved every major technique he was to utilize in India, he fused his brilliantly successful and prosperous legal practice (earning as much as £5,000 a year) with a concern to champion the rights of the Indian minority. Without the one the other would have been impossible. On his return to India at the age of forty-seven all the essentials of Satyāgraha were already formulated, and while he may have renounced the earning of money, he did not renounce his methods, which were an organic consequence of his original role as a lawyer in a bourgeois capitalist society. This society, says Weber, 'forces the individual, in so far as he is involved in the systems of market relationships, to conform to capitalistic rules of action'. The organizational nucleus of Gandhi's nation-wide movement, based on his *ashrāms*, was not economically self-sufficient; it depended on financial contributions large and small, from industrialists, businessmen, professionals, and people of more modest means, all of whom were economic participants on the fringe, if not at the heart, of a capitalist system. Further, those wealthy industrialists who subsidized the conservative Gandhian egalitarianism no doubt recognized in it a safeguard against the development of a class struggle initiated by the low castes and industrial employees. Sarojini Naidu once remarked of the protected existence which Bapu—as Gandhi was called—then led, 'It takes a great deal of money to keep Bapu living in poverty.'

The formative influences to which he was subject at the level of practical expertise were even more complex than his spiritual formation. As a Westernized pro-British student of law in London, he had picked up ideas which, as we have seen, were derivations of the Protestant ethic. While Gandhi was still preoccupied with his legal studies he came, by a series of intellectual adjustments in his Vaishnava-Jain value-system, very close to its consistent practice. To the short-term acquisitive drive of a shrewd bazaar-entrepreneur, Gandhi added a substantial ingredient of theoretical Western reasoning, socially rational values, and an economic 'attitude which seeks profit rationally and systematically' (Weber). Since Gandhi's time such a contribution has become increasingly common for the educated classes of the non-Western world. The form which this conjunction assumes is by no means uniform; Gandhi's is perhaps the most unlikely and eccentric because it is the result of a peculiarly intense insistence on identity of value- and thought-systems. The ethical strategies of Gandhism in the face of legalistic tyrannies do not, at any point, depart from the premises which are also at the root of Gandhian economic policies. Both are accurately reflected in the organizational structure and the objectives of

Gandhi's Satyāgraha campaigns. The recruitment of supporters, lieuten-
ants, and workers in the Gandhian programme from the ranks of the
Indian capitalist class is consistent on two counts: first, Gandhi himself
shared with these influential supporters the rational modalities and calculated prudence associated with their common background in the business
and professional classes. Secondly, Gandhi's refusal to countenance the
application of Satyāgraha to class conflict was based on his concept of
capitalist 'trusteeship'. Again, the origin of these ideas is part-Western,
part-Indian. On the one hand, Gandhi's views resemble Paine's: 'Though I
care as little about riches as any man, I am a friend of riches because they
are capable of good' (*The Rights of Man*). On the other hand, they preserve
the essentials of the *jajmānī* system:

> My ideal is equal distribution, but so far as I can see, it is not to be realised.
> I therefore work for equitable distribution.[1]
> Indeed at the root of this doctrine of equal distribution must lie that of the
> trusteeship of the wealthy for superfluous wealth possessed by them. . . . The
> rich man will be left in possession of his wealth, of which he will use what he
> reasonably requires for his personal needs and will act as a trustee for the re-
> mainder to be used for the society.[2]
> Economic equality is the master key to non-violent independence. Working
> for economic equality means abolishing the eternal conflict between capital and
> labour. . . . A violent and bloody revolution is a certainty one day unless there
> is a voluntary abdication of riches and the power that riches give and sharing
> that for the common good.[3]
> I shall be no party to dispossessing the propertied classes of their property
> without just cause. My objective is to reach your hearts and convert you so that
> you may hold all your private property in trust for your tenants and use it pri-
> marily for their welfare. . . . You may be sure that I shall throw the whole
> weight of my influence in preventing a class war. . . . Our Socialism or Commun-
> ism should be based on non-violence, and on the harmonious co-operation of
> labour and capital, the landlord and tenant.[4]

The anachronistic Gandhian ideology of class harmony was a shrewd
compromise with the pluralistic realities of the caste society. While it was
conservative, inadequate, and a product of that caste society, it avoided the
dogmatic and frequently disastrous assertion of Indian Marxists that the
solution to India's social ills is dialectical class conflict, based on the false
assumption that a class *system* (as distinct from loose coalescence of class
strata) already exists in India (a point examined earlier in the present study).
The orthodox Marxist division of society into bourgeoisie and proletariat

---

[1] M. K. Gandhi, *All Men are Brothers: life and thoughts of Mahatma Gandhi as told in his
own words*, UNESCO, Paris, 1958, p. 77.
[2] Ibid., pp. 78–9.   [3] Ibid., pp. 77–8.
[4] Statement to the landlords of Uttar Pradesh, *Maratha*, 1934.

was no more based on reality then than it is now. Dr. A. R. Desai advances a Marxist appraisal of the facts when he claims for Gandhi no more than limited success within his preferred range: 'He was the first national leader who recognised the role of the masses and mass action in the struggle for national liberation in contrast to earlier leaders, who did not comprehend their decisive significance for making that struggle more effective.'[1]

To observe Gandhi's method of combining ethical and economic motivation in a unified act of mass resistance, thereby bringing into effective use what Nehru described as the 'unknown element', we will now turn to the historic moment when Gandhi reached the pinnacle of his success—the Salt March. This display of non-violent technique was a supreme achievement because the several impulses of his talent were congruent, his acts neither those of the mystagogue nor the reactionary.

The weapons of stupefaction

Satyāgraha depends on the accuracy with which the leader identifies the flaw in a massive power structure. If he can then 'zero in' on this one weak spot at exactly the right moment, with the right congruence of public interest and the right co-ordination of his resistance groups, the edifice topples. While Satyāgraha proceeds on the same principle as psychoanalysis, there is another comparison which is helpful for our purposes: the structure of Sanskrit drama—though its validity is confined to the specific mode in which Gandhi himself applied the techniques of Satyāgraha in India. It is also useful as it supplies us with a measure of the degree to which Satyāgraha departs from the traditional Indian attitude towards social change. The limitations of Satyāgraha must be ascribed not only to its experimental nature; Gandhi's reluctance to pursue the dialectic of social conflict to a logical conclusion arises from a deeply characteristic Indian trait. This may be defined as the conviction that there is a point in time when life ceases to be perceived in terms of contradiction, and that it is the primary objective of society to attain this ideal state of equilibrium in every aspect of social relations. In India, this idealism is projected with aesthetic subtlety in the Sanskrit poetical drama.

Gandhi conceived the moral drama of Satyāgraha aesthetically, not theoretically, nor even politically. Every Satyāgraha campaign was a 'happening', based on a scenario, either worked out in detail beforehand or as the action proceeded. The drama and Satyāgraha equally depend on the sense of showmanship; both are *staged* in highly formal and unmistakably

[1] Desai (1966), p. 347.

aesthetic terms—demonstrations of life idealistically conceived. By comparing the conception of the Salt March with Sanskrit dramatic structure we pick up an earlier thread of ideas—the role of the culture-bearer in the restoration of lost unity. The same intuitive, patterned sensibility informs these two outwardly dissimilar media of communication. Such resemblances as may exist between their thematic contents refer back to the common source—an attitude towards life; in every other respect they are not connected.

In India various words for 'drama', applied to conflict in everyday life, implicitly connote the *a priori* assumption of ultimate reconciliation, or the 'happy ending'. A typical village *tamāsha*, for example—what we would call 'a fine old row'— sees the opponents unleashing vituperation at each other in a *cadenced* singsong, as if it were really a play for the benefit of the spectators, with each participant fulfilling a set role in a patterned dispute, the ultimate reconciliation of which is virtually a foregone conclusion. That this does not invariably occur is beside the point: under normal conditions conflict tends to become a *tamāsha—a play*.

In Part Three it was shown that traditional conflict management in the pluralistic society is linked with the play instinct: combined, they tend to restore the *status quo* by arbitration and compromise; overt class-conflict is, for example, avoided. Further, Carstairs shows (see p. 198) how a quarrel is typically seen as a *drama* with three actors—two contestants and a mediator. Traditionally, the mediator was the priest, the king, or the guru, whose role to restore peace through the exercise of self-restraint originated in the sacrificial structure of the Vedic religion; this was eventually delegated in the majority of cases to the *panchāyat*, which has, ever since, settled disputes by the consensual process as distinct from the adversary process.

Similarly, a literary play—in Sanskrit or in any other Indian language— aims at restoration of the spectator's harmony, not so much with himself but with the universe, based on a deeper conception of life than can ever be included in the sentimental notion of the 'happy ending'. As Henry Wells puts it, this harmony is conceived without 'the falsification of a morally invalid optimistic illusionism'. We have seen how the Sanskrit drama is a 'tying together of diverse threads', with equilibrium restored in the poise between opposites. It is no accident that this art-form usually conforms to a tragi-comic mould in keeping with the ironic Hindu conception of the universe as a conjunction of complementary forces morally opposed to each other, as in a tournament or game. 'This is at once the form of art and the formula of life.' According to Wells, the aesthetician Sāgaranandin 'declares the highest type of play to be that employing the maximum number of dialects and styles practically available, that is, the play containing the largest number of conflicting elements to be reconciled, for Sāgaranandin himself uses the mage of the whole work as developed from a single seed [i.e. the *bindu*]'.[1]

If we now turn to the Satyāgraha scenario it will be noted that it is also based on the assumption of an ultimately attainable reconciliation; its very 'staginess' reveals the play instinct. The agonistic component of consistent Satyāgraha resistance literally *dramatizes* in the starkest outline the urgent need to seek a truthful resolution of conflicting views. The Salt March makes its point through richly tragi-comic incident, sustained by the belief that it is enacted in conformity with the principle of ultimate convergence between morally opposed forces. It is important to draw a distinction between the Western conception of morality and that of the Satyāgrahi. The definition proposed by the Farmington Trust may represent the Western conception of morality: 'The extent to which people feel a concern for the interests of others, commit themselves to a general principle of respecting them, and so act.' This open-ended conception does not coincide with the Satyāgrahi's:

Despite the protestations of a few followers of Gandhi that Satyāgraha is always persuasive and never coercive, the method does contain a positive element of coercion. Non-cooperation, boycott, strike—all of these tools which may be used in Satyāgraha involve an element of compulsion which may effect a change on the part of the opponent which initially was contrary to his will— and he may suffer from the indirect results of these actions.[2]

This element of coercion has the dual effect of asserting from the outset that the ultimate objective is fixed: namely, reconciliation; and, paradoxically, introducing an element of purposeful momentum of a dialectic subject to indefinite extension: namely, change of heart. Social change will be initiated by a chain-reaction in attitudes. This is an important point of divergence from the cyclical schema of the traditional value-system, as exemplified, among other modalities, by the drama. The reader may recall a point made by Roger Caillois, cited earlier: *play creates no new element*; the situation at the end of play is identical to that at the start. In economic behaviour, play is unproductive, it creates no wealth, no work, no capital increment. Satyāgraha, on the other hand, breaks through these limitations in so far as it introduces a new element: change of heart—and it creates *work*.

The sequence of events in the Salt March is plateresque, magnetic; like the drama, 'in its structure all lines lead inward as if to the centre of the circle' (Wells). Gandhi marches for twenty-four days from his *ashrām* in Ahmedabad to Dandi, 241 miles distant on the seashore, there to pick up salt in defiance of the Salt Laws imposed with crushing effect on the Indian

---

[1] Henry W. Wells, *The Classical Drama of India*, Asia Publishing House, Bombay, 1963, p. 51.
[2] Bondurant (1958), p. 9.

peasant by the British Rāj. After defying the laws *he withdraws from the action* to the still turning-point of the circle. The Salt March never develops on the analogy of the Long March; something else happens. The extent to which this comparatively brief upsurge falls short of a concerted and pro-longed mass action, consolidated by a diverse programme of social recon-struction and institutional change, is partly compensated by the intensity with which an unexpected element comes into operation.

Behind the Salt March lie years of patient preparation and months of intensive training for resistance workers in the discipline of non-violence. The Satyāgrahis are taught how to obtain strength through perfect weak-ness, or, if one likes, *how to do nothing.*[1] Gandhi identifies the weakest point in the power structure, where he can exert the maximum pressure with the minimum of resources. He summons Indians to stoop and pick up their inalienable birthright, a portion of the earth on which they tread. This is the small seed from which the drama develops. He asks them to do this because it is absurd—to do something *in defiance* of an absurd law forbidding every-one to engage in an activity which they have as much right to do as breathe. In a tropical climate salt is a staple food; Gandhi had already renounced the eating of salt for six years. In advance, he announces his intention to break the law himself by writing to his 'Dear friend' the Viceroy of India, Lord Irwin, that British rule is 'a ruinous expensive military and civil administration . . . [which] has reduced us politically to serfdom. It has sapped the foundations of our culture. And by the policy of cruel dis-armament, it has degraded us spiritually.' The Indian individual feels less free than ever to make ethical choices, and has lost all conviction of the ethical importance of his choices when made. By the shrewd fusion of a minimum gesture of protest, a maximum appeal to the self-reliance of the individual faced with violent opposition, and a substantial economic motivation, Gandhi will coerce his fellow-countrymen into shaming their opponent; united, the nation will then coerce the opponent into a reversal of policy.

The image of Gandhi marching in a loin-cloth to the seashore with a motley band of seventy-eight workers set on picking up a pinch of salt is deceptively anachronistic, even in 1930. The march was to last sufficient time for the eyes of India and the world to be riveted on the frail old man of sixty-one plodding on under a merciless March sun, tightening the dis-cipline as the journey progressed. All the resources of the mass media

---

[1] Perhaps the secret of Gandhi's success on the Salt March is, in part, derived from what Erikson calls the 'seasoned playfulness' which he ultimately owed to his childhood need to alleviate his moral precocity: Erikson (1970), p. 133. He appears to have acted consciously on the play principle that all effort is mysteriously satisfying if disproportion-ately large results are obtained from the expenditure of comparatively little energy.

were brought to bear on publicizing the march. 'On the Salt March he fully entered the world of the newsreel and documentary. Henceforth we have many glimpses of him flickering in black and white, a brisk, mobile figure, with odd but illuminating moments of likeness to Charlie Chaplin.'[1] When men in their millions pick up salt the gesture will be *timed* in accordance with a co-ordinated plan. As Gandhi marched, behind him 'the administration was silently crumbling as three hundred and ninety village headmen resigned their posts'.[2] For twenty-four days a masterly programme of slowly mounting propaganda sustained international interest. There was an air of something great about to happen in the emotional and spiritual life of mankind. The British Government was frozen into immobility by its own cynicism, unable to decide if it was more dangerous to arrest Gandhi and thereby unleash a wave of violence, or let him stay free, thereby ensuring his control over his non-violent demonstrators. By the time the column reached Dandi it had swollen to a throng.

And there was Gandhi, walking along, with his friends round him, it was a sort of terrific anti-climax. There was no cheering, no great shouts of delight, and no sort of stately procession at all, it was all rather, in a sense rather farcical . . . there I was, seeing history happen in a strange anti-climax way: something completely un-European and yet very, very moving.[3]

When they reached Dandi they camped for seven days, eating parched grain, half an ounce of fat, and two ounces of sugar daily. On 6 April Gandhi rose at dawn, took his bath in the sea, and then walked over to the natural salt deposits. Photographers at the ready, he picked up a treasonable pinch of salt and handed it to a person standing at his side. Sarojini Naidu cried out, 'Hail deliverer!' and then he went back to his work.

The news flashed round the world and within days India was in turmoil; millions were preparing salt in every corner of the land. Vast demonstrations were held in every large city in the country, from Karachi to Madras. Women in purdah mounted demonstrations in the streets. Like automata, the British administration responded with blind and incoherent action of extreme violence. The army and police moved as if hypnotized into a response from which all meaning had vanished. Indians were beaten, kicked in the groin, bitten in the fingers, and fired on by vindictive constables. They were charged by cavalry until they lay on the ground at the horses' feet. At Peshawar, 'an armoured car, in which the Deputy Police Commissioner was seated, first ran full tilt into a crowd and then machine-gunned it, killing seventy and wounding about one hundred'.[4] Between 60,000 and 100,000 non-violent resisters went to jail. Save for one small incident at Chittagong, Bengal, no Indian struck a violent blow. Gandhi

[1] Ashe (1968), p. 286. [2] Ibid.
[3] Glorney Bolton in Watson and Brown (1957), pp. 58–9. [4] Fischer (1951).

was arrested after midnight sleeping under a tree in camp near Dandi and sent to jail. On his release eight months later he concluded the Gandhi–Irwin pact, after which the government abandoned its repressive measures and released political prisoners. This was the occasion when, as we have seen, Nehru wept.

In response to Gandhi's arrest, and while the country was in turmoil, the same ambivalent 'unknown element' which had urged Gandhi to undertake the march, and which was subsequently to have disastrous consequences on the national morale at the conclusion of his parley with Lord Irwin, suddenly took possession of 2,500 Satyāgrahis. A protest march was organized with the objective of trespassing on the grounds of the Dharasana Salt Depot in the centre of a vast brown expanse of flat, sun-scorched terrain. The salt-pans were surrounded by ditches and barbed wire, guarded by four hundred Surat policemen under the command of six British officers. Sarojini Naidu addressed the *khadi*-clad Satyāgrahis: 'You will be beaten, but you must not resist. You must not even raise a hand to ward off blows.' Webb Miller, correspondent of United Press, filed a despatch giving an eye-witness account of what ensued—syndicated to over a thousand newspapers throughout the world:

> In complete silence the Gandhi men drew up and halted a hundred yards from the stockade. A picked column advanced from the crowd, waded the ditches, and approached the barbed-wire stockade. . . . Suddenly, at a word of command, scores of native policemen rushed upon the advancing marchers and rained blows on their heads with their steel shod lathis. Not one of the marchers even raised an arm to fend off the blows. They went down like nine-pins. From where I stood I heard the sickening whack of the clubs on unprotected skulls. The waiting crowd of marchers groaned and sucked in their breath in sympathetic pain at every blow. Those struck down fell sprawling, unconscious or writhing with fractured skulls or broken shoulders. . . . The survivors, without breaking ranks, silently and doggedly march on until struck down. . . . Although everyone knew that within a few minutes he would be beaten down, perhaps killed, I could detect no signs of wavering or fear. They marched steadily, with heads up, without the encouragement of music or cheering or any possibility that they might escape serious injury or death. The police rushed out and methodically and mechanically beat down the second column. There was no fight, no struggle; the marchers simply walked forward till struck down. . . . The police commenced savagely kicking the seated men in the abdomen and testicles. . . . Hour after hour stretcher-bearers carried back a stream of inert, bleeding bodies. . . . By eleven the heat reached 116 and the activities of the Gandhi volunteers subsided.[1]

The same scenes were repeated for several days—a silent response to those who, both Indian and British, had dismissed non-violence as a 'weapon of the weak'.

[1] Quoted in L. Fisher (1951), pp. 298–9.

Louis Fischer concludes his account of the Salt March with a crisp comment: 'India was now free. Technically, legally, nothing had changed.' Lord Irwin wrote to George V: 'Your Majesty can hardly fail to have read with amusement the accounts of the several battles for the Salt Depot.' According to the Viceroy's biographer, 'his religious convictions seemed to reinforce the very ruthlessness of his policy of suppression'. On the other hand, the wonder-worker who inspired the action had released an invincible force which left his opponent morally paralysed. The nationalist movement proceeded, after the Salt March, along a halting, stop–go course, but the forces which had been released were not easily kept under control. Nehru's alarm at the 'unknown element' was compounded of respect for its occasional efficacy and dejection at its blind irrational impulses. This same force which could be non-violent and transform the whole temper of the country, could equally inspire violence of the most fanatical character.

The great battle which takes place towards the conclusion of Bhavabhūti's play, *Rāma's Later History*, is won by the spontaneous manifestation of a magical force, conjured from the deeps of the hero's mind. The theme of entrancement which runs like a leitmotif throughout the play, mounts through successive climaxes till an entire army is completely demoralized— 'fixed motionless on every side'—by the 'weapons of stupefaction'. This is an old feature of Indian epic literature; indeed it is explained in the play that these 'weapons of stupefaction' which take the army by surprise, are handed down by tradition from the primeval seers of the Vedas. Just as Gandhi disclaims conscious control when possessed by his 'inner voice', so also those to whom the 'weapons of stupefaction' are manifest can only explain the eruption as an entirely spontaneous phenomenon. But whereas possession by psychic powers leads, in Bhavabhūti's play, to the suspension of all movement, the perfect weakness of the Satyāgrahi's weapons leads to one mind-blowing surprise after another. The dialectic cannot *secure* a better life, however, unless it is followed by organized social reconstruction, the establishment of new institutions which are ultimately written into the constitution. The parallel, anarchist organization of insurrection then merges back into the body politic. There is a concise maxim of William Blake: 'Unorganised Innocence: An Impossibility.'

Zimmer's ideas on the Indian tendency to view life as a continuous crisis may be recalled. Everything is for ever going wrong, in Satyāgraha as in the myths. Yet, while no mass insurrection anywhere in the world is likely to pursue an even course, one cannot help drawing the conclusion that Gandhian Satyāgraha is peculiarly well suited to permit the transformation of setbacks into what Zimmer describes as 'miraculous development', jolting the movement from crisis to crisis. Zimmer ascribes this familiar 'muddling through' in the Puranic myths to insight into the essential nature of the contending forces, as if the balance between them had been left to find its own level without external pressure. Ultimately, this rests on acquiescence in 'the catastrophe of the previously unforeseen' by acceptance of suffering—a more organic attitude than conscious, willed planning. Under certain Indian conditions this 'passivity' is probably more effective than an aggressive approach; it can result in chaos, indifference, or sheer apathy, but it is equally capable of inspiring concerted, effective, dynamic action. Those who feel nauseated by this 'passivity' should remember that when India confronts its problems in its own way, it almost invariably does so according to the principle which Gandhi made peculiarly his own: through strength made perfect in weakness.

He never again attained the same mastery of a situation after the Salt March, nor applied his methods with the degree of consistency needed for them to triumph. It had been his character to use every non-violent weapon at his command and exploit to the full every conceivable opportunity; the reason why he subsequently did not, I would suggest, resides in the gradual lessening of the disequilibrium which had originally goaded him into activity. The moral balance which Gandhi preserved in his last years gave his every act a kind of near-perfect self-containment. Finally he appears to have been caught within the Circle, reduced, as he had wanted, to zero; in consequence he became the object of worship as a saint. He now wore the only mask of his life, the mask of the Mahātma—thrust upon him with what he called 'the tyranny of love'.

If this interpretation is correct, it would imply that the 'dynamic passivity' of India only works so long as it is goaded into operation rather in the same way as the pearl-oyster by a grain of sand. This is the exact opposite of the sentimental notion that India is true to itself only when it acts in perfect harmony. At least it offers hope for the future, since modern conditions are hardly conducive to the re-establishment of so ideal, not to say unreal, a state. Besides, young Indians today are bored to distraction by the repeated assertion, on the part of their elders, of the need for perfect equilibrium. Gandhi was anything but perfect, and when the particularity of his imperfections became blurred, orthodoxy was ready to step in and blunt the hard cutting edge of his ideas and smother 'Gandhism' with the odour of sanctity.

It remains for us to look briefly at the final transformation of his character and to identify the cause for his later quietism. Faced with bloodshed between Hindus and Muslims, Gandhi did not fail, he was defeated. 'Humble and colossal'—his last years recall a remark of Rilke's about Tolstoy, Gandhi's idol—devoted to his unrealizable dream, he let his life grow around him like a wilderness. The lonely march through Noakhali was a magnificent moral gesture of encouragement to the victims of communal bloodshed. Momentarily it halted the flow of blood, but it redounded to the credit of the man more than it saved the mutual respect of the two communities. Strange too was the mode whereby he then resolved, in the Noakhali wilderness, the conflict in his personal life on which so much restless activity had fed. With advancing years, Gandhi's sexual abstinence began to show signs of its original neurotic inspiration. He recognized this imbalance and made great efforts to resolve it. These took an increasingly religious tinge; in a man of lesser stature, the direction in which the sublimation of his never wholly extinguished sexual impulse was leading him might well have ended in the cult of Sahajiyā chastity, where temptation is actively sought in order to transform desire into *prema*, spiritual love.

At the age of 77 and 78 years old, Gandhi occasionally suffered from severe attacks of shivering at night. He asked several middle-aged women to 'cradle' him between them for bodily warmth, and claimed publicly that he had them naked beside him to test his *brahmāchārya*. Pyarelal and Nirmal Bose have both described this incident in some detail. As Gandhi told the latter, 'He was thinking of a bold and original experiment whose "heat will be very great" '—as if he conceived this as an experiment in *tapasya*. The orphaned Manu Gandhi, his nineteen-year-old grandniece who wrote a book entitled *Bapu—My Mother*, was also asked to share his bed, as Gandhi wrote in a letter to Āchārya Kripalani: 'my grandniece shares the bed with me, strictly as my very blood . . . as part of what might be my last *Yajna* [sacrifice].'

Erikson proposes that we 'be sparing with our interpretations':

> But I wonder whether there has ever been another political leader who has almost prided himself on being half man and half woman, and who so blatantly aspired to be more motherly than women born to the job, as Gandhi did. This, too, resulted from a confluence of a deeply personal need and a national trend, for a primitive mother religion is probably the deepest, the most pervasive, and the most unifying stratum of Indian religiosity.[1]

There is a consistent psychological pattern in the Hindu emphasis on the worship of mother-goddesses, the bisexuality of the son-figure—Shiva Ardhanārīśvara (Plate 18)—and the Shaiva *yoni-lingā* (which may unconsciously refer to the Oedipal fantasy of the phallic mother—Plates 44–6).[2] Erikson believes that Gandhi 'tried to make himself the representative of that bisexuality in a combination of autocratic malehood and enveloping maternalism'.[3]

Gandhi's last, chaste, and highly idealized relationship with a woman on

[1] Erikson (1970), p. 402.   [2] Cf. Haldar (1938).   [3] Erikson (1970), p. 44.

the Noakhali trek also suggests a distant resemblance to the story of a Sahajiyā saint:

Rāmānanda Rāya had two temple girls of surpassing beauty, youthful, skilled in music and the dance. Rāya used to take them both into a lonely garden, where they would sing to him. With his hands he would rub their bodies with oil and bathe their bodies and limbs and clothe and decorate them; but still the mind of Rāmānanda remained unaffected. His passion was the same at the touch of a piece of wood or a stone as it was at the touch of a young woman: such was the nature of Rāmānanda Rāya.[1]

Here was a modality with a long and honoured tradition. The constellation of psychological traits which may lead a man on such a course also fosters, if it does not wholly determine, the emotional character of the Vaishnava, *bhakti*, and Tantric movements, which now comprise the principal elements in modern Hinduism. It is this which places Gandhi's ideas on religious sublimation of sex in the broad stream of the Great Tradition. But by the time Gandhi resolved his problem he was concerned with bigger things. What for others might be the ultimate goal Gandhi had already surpassed. The searchlight of publicity was switched off: such things no longer mattered and were wholly private. Even his visit to Noakhali was essentially the gesture of a private individual. He had undertaken his agonizing walking tour through the desolation of Noakhali following some of the bloodiest Hindu–Muslim mass killings; the resolution of his personal conflict pales into insignificance beside it.

For some years he had watched helpless from the sidelines while India headed towards Partition.

Gandhi's tragedy probably was that he appeared, the pupils were ready, but the world with its needs and its lessons had already advanced, for better or worse, beyond them. The cool, collected, performance of Mountbatten, cutting through the thicket of Indian rivalries, fears and prejudices with the confidence of a man who knew they were largely irrelevant, showed how far beyond.[2]

Seventy-eight years old, Gandhi trekked for four months through forty-nine villages, walking barefoot for several miles every day to reach the peasants in a remote, nearly inaccessible region. 'I have come to Bengal,' he said, 'not to give consolation, I have come to bring courage here.' He taught himself how to cross swaying bamboo bridges by walking on poles, but fanatics also strewed his path with brambles and broken glass. Professor Bose more than once heard him muttering to himself as he surveyed the charred ruins of pillaged huts, '*Kya karun? Kya karun?*' ('What

---

[1] Quoted in Dimock (1966), pp. 53–4.
[2] *Times Literary Supplement*, 11 April 1968, p. 368.

should I do?') 'Now this was the man whom we saw,' says Bose, 'not merely great but immensely great.' Pasternak would have called this greatness 'the ultimate heresy of an unheard of simplicity'.

Anarchist political philosophy

A common argument of Gandhi's critics is that his brand of non-violence reflects an arrogant and moralistic personality. Erikson draws a distinction between the universal potential of Satyāgraha and such personal limitations as its inventor may have had, and concludes with his own declaration of faith:

> Non-violence, inward and outward, can become a true force only where ethics replaces moralism. And ethics, to me, is marked by an insightful assent to human values, whereas moralism is blind obedience; and ethics is transmitted with informed persuasion, rather than enforced with absolute interdicts. Whether the increasing multitudes of men can ever develop and transmit such an ethical attitude I do not know; but I do know that we are committed to it, and that the young are waiting for our support in attempting it.[1]

Nevertheless, young Indians tend to reject Gandhi as an old-fashioned paternalist; the important question of the link between Satyāgraha and anarchism as a practical political philosophy seems to have been largely ignored by them, although the Indian student is quick to seize on ideas current in student circles internationally. In almost every country students seem to be groping towards a new form of anarchism and Satyāgraha is one of the main features of its composite philosophical basis. The craze for things Indian among the Euro-American young is a manifestation at a superficial level of a deeper and growing sense of affinity, vague and ill-defined as it may be, between two philosophically similar world views.

In the long term, Gandhi's contribution was twofold: he convinced the Indian masses that they must change their socio-economic system themselves; and he brought together those traditional Indian concepts which could fuse into a metaphysic of change. This metaphysic assumes the perfectibility of man and society; it also implies a self-sustaining process of continuous innovation, change, and development. Some of the means which he advocated have an affinity with anarcho-syndicalism.

Thus Gandhi confronted India with an urgent choice, the radical nature of which was rarely faced during nearly two decades of the Nehru era. It is common to find critics of Nehru pointing out—rightly in my view— that while he was relatively successful in the field of international affairs,

[1] Erikson (1970), p. 251.

he was far from successful in his handling of India's internal affairs, particularly its social problems. This latter failure, and the reluctance of the national leadership as well as the public to face the issue raised by Gandhi, are of a piece. What Gandhi did accomplish in concrete terms of action was to organize *a series of rehearsals for fundamental social change*. Gandhism carried to its logical conclusion would result, under present conditions in India, in a revolution. However, the ruling party in the two post-Independence decades was unalterably opposed to revolution, not because it was against the violence which would inevitably accompany it, but because such changes would pose a direct threat to the ruling class.

The style of Congress nationalism may be described as an idealist campaign first against imperialism and then against neo-colonialism. It was an attempt to change bourgeois values by bourgeois means, made by members of that very class, who never in any decisive way separated themselves from it. They were attempting to modify it by appealing to what they saw as the best elements within it.

To have a clearer idea of what a 'series of rehearsals' means, we will compare Satyāgraha with the typical mass street demonstration by unarmed assemblies of people who deliberately offer themselves as a target to the forces of repression. Such demonstrations are not necessarily non-violent in method; however, the objectives which they share with Satyāgraha are the following: first, a symbolic show of strength of popular feeling; second, an appeal to the democratic conscience of the oppressor; third, a procedure which imparts a sense of corporate identity and strength to the participants; fourth, control over a given terrain (the Spanish term, *querencia*, comes to mind)—e.g. a street, a public square, a university, a theatre; fifth, a demonstration of the weakness of the opponent's authority, or of his overweening authoritarianism, cruelty, injustice, and irrationality.

The differences between Satyāgraha and the mass street demonstration are crucial to the argument: consistency of non-violence, and locations which work most efficiently if in a large number of both rural and urban areas. On the one hand, Satyāgraha proposes the *consistent* application of democratic principles—and in India that can only mean social revolution; on the other, it proposes no strategy with which to maintain the democratization at the point when it encounters violent opposition from caste or class. Nobody, and certainly not Gandhi, has yet devised a successful strategy for breaking down the divisions within Indian society, whether of caste or class. Moreover, if by a 'series of rehearsals' we mean an incomplete sequence of actions prior to a full-scale 'performance', then the defects of Satyāgraha in the face of violent conflict between the Hindu and Muslim communities, and their continuing friction after Partition, is substantial evidence in support of such a description.

There is a possibility, however, that the cellular organization of Satyā-graha could be fruitfully applied to the unique situation of India's caste system. Attempts to legislate caste out of existence, to 'eradicate' the traditional system because it is 'wrong', have proved totally ineffective. As we have seen, the majority of Indians do not regard the caste system as 'wrong'. If modified to meet the different needs of the post-Independence society, Satyāgraha seems to be uniquely qualified to transform the caste system from a negative, outmoded, pluralistic system into an as yet undefinable egalitarian structure. The ground for such action is already being prepared by the simultaneity of the modern communications network, which secures a sophisticated form of social interdependence. For a caste system originates under conditions where everything affects everything all the time, and Satyāgraha infuses the simultaneity of this social interdependence with new moral content.

Satyāgraha is anarchist (in the philosophical sense of the word, which has nothing to do with the popular misconception of 'anarchy' as nihilism and destruction) in so far as Gandhi linked it with classless, stateless, decentralized democracy based on local and individual initiative.

Gandhi's series of rehearsals conforms to the phase of mass demonstration which precedes long-term, comprehensive revolutionary action. But the aims of Satyāgraha and revolution are not the same; revolution culminates in the taking over of state power, whereas neither power nor control of the state form part of the Satyāgrahi's aims. Gandhi repeatedly made it plain that the aim of his movement was a complete moral and social change of heart, both of the Indian people and of its foreign rulers. Satyā-graha was not to end with political independence but involved the entire society, including the disinherited poor, in the continuous process of self-rule. Gandhi himself could not have elaborated with any precision what form of action the latter phase of Satyāgraha was to take following Independence, since its ambitions were those of a movement initiated before the political means to realize them had been created. If the Satyāgrahi were in earnest about *sarvodaya*, or 'building from below'—a programme which involves the complete inversion of the bourgeois capitalist system of India—it could only be accomplished by the tactics and strategy of the performance, not of the rehearsal. Gandhi himself stated that 'a society organised on the basis of complete non-violence would be the purest anarchy'. We could apply to him the comment of Keir Hardie on Kropotkin: if we were all like him, 'anarchism would be the only possible system, since government and restraint would be unnecessary'.

Is Satyāgraha of no further use as a political philosophy in India? The successful challenge of established authoritarian rule by organized student agitation all over the world in recent years suggests that a modified form of

Satyāgraha could well emerge on the Indian campus sooner or later. Widespread student agitation in India has been a cause for serious concern; it has a long history and originated in the early years of Gandhi's influence. As Professor Edward Shils points out, the motivation for student agitation is not difficult to trace:

The college and the university are the first way-stations on the road to this modern world, so uninviting, so unrewarding, so unprotecting. They are encountered when the aspirations towards individual existence are in most tender embryo, when the fears of harshness and coldness are most timorous, and when resistance to the impositions of authority is most strenuous. A mind which cannot attach itself to intellectual objects, a libido which is prevented from attaching itself to sexual objects, a spirit which resents the burden of familiar discipline and resists incorporation into modern impersonal adult institutions—what direction can it take except rebellion, blind, causeless rebellion?[1]

I disagree with the view that this student unrest is 'blind' and 'causeless'. In terms of the new realities, India's students have every cause to be distressed by the incompetence and complacency of the traditional political parties, and by the unimaginative administration of educational institutions. In a society like India's, where the channels of democratic communication are choked by oligarchy, students have learnt that they can be a very effective opposition through their nuisance value. Since they also know that they cannot take power themselves, their natural inclination is to follow an anarchist course and combine debate with action and action with moral legitimation, in the belief that reform of the education system itself entails the eventual transformation of society. Like Satyagraha in Gandhi's time, the new anarchism expresses ambitions before the political means necessary to realize them have been created. We have no idea what form this anarchism will take under changing technological conditions. But Satyāgraha is likely to be an agent in its crystallization. Underlying the variety of ideological allegiances held by the new international student movement, and despite its frequent recourse to violence, there is a unifying *style* which, after generations of utilitarian politics, is approaching very close to the modality which India has always made its special province— the aesthetic. Perhaps it is this more than anything else which lies also at the very root of the movement which Gandhi initiated.

[1] Edward Shils, ' Indian Students', *Encounter*, 1960, p. 20.

Conclusion

In the last third of the twentieth century, no aspect of the Indian situation is simple or self-evident. This book has attempted to uncover the web of complexity and to show that India's need is not for simplicity, clarity, or certainty here and now; that is too much to ask.

Things are complex, and what the mind needs to find is *some order* in the complexity, the mind itself being an ordering organ which even imposes a spurious order when necessary as a short cut or a first step. Instead of immediate clarity and certainty we need something both less and more: a provisional working hypothesis concerning the kind of order in each complexity. Less, because tentative; more because admitting complexity at the start.[1]

This passage was written by a historian of ideas trained in the exact sciences who has in mind not the Indian situation, but a much more general one; it emphasizes the necessity to view the Indian predicament as closely linked with much larger problems, and to view it, moreover, in the context of scientific and technological change.

The methodology of this book is based on the assumption of the total interconnectedness of things: social institutions, religion, values, ethics, thought, art, politics, are all closely interconnected. If we could imagine life in India several centuries ago, this interconnectedness would have been all the more striking. Today the situation is more complicated because the Indian is now living simultaneously in two contrasted forms of society and experience. The connections remain, but in the course of transition from one perceptual framework to the other, with numerous gradations visible in the mixture of old and new, the components pass through a highly fissile phase, so that the inclusive awareness which was a product of interconnection itself breaks down and the society presents a picture of disintegration and turmoil. This complexity makes it all the more important to find one's bearings within the traditional social matrix, and from there to work outwards from elements which have remained more or less constant for many centuries to elements which are subject to change.

If all things are interconnected then change in any one part of this system necessarily entails changes in every other part. We know, for example, that technology predetermines social structure, that tools prefigure the psychology of their users, and that technological innovation reshapes the way

[1] L. L. Whyte, *The Unconscious before Freud*, New York, 1962 edn., p. 175.

people see the world around them, the way they behave, and the way they think. The last century and a half have given dramatic proof of this fact. New tools, new technology, alter, enlarge, and at the same time debase sensibility and imagination. Development of technical resources has accelerated with such bewildering rapidity that the repercussions of a single extension of man's perceptual framework scarcely have time to register before the next development alters the whole situation. The lessons of the railway, the cable, and the internal combustion engine have still not been fully assimilated, while we are hardly beginning to study the effects of atomic energy and electronic technology, and although they have literally transformed consciousness. In India, where the earlier of these two series of inventions already plays a significant role in changing attitudes and behaviour, the pattern of transformation wrought by them is not at all similar to that created with the same technological means by Western nations. It is not true that technology alters the perceptual framework according to a uniform mechanistic pattern. In India there is an alarming disjunction between the material changes wrought on the life-style by technology and the attitudes of those whose lives are thereby externally modified.

The decisive factor in the perpetuation of the cultural dichotomy between tradition and modernity is the exclusion of the traditional culture from formal education. In other words, the relationship between tradition and modernity is allowed to remain in a state of perpetual dichotomous tension; no encouragement is given to conceiving this relationship as dialectical, creative, rejuvenating. While it is true that a certain amount of *information* about their own cultural background is imparted to students— though it is often poorly conveyed—the value-system of modern Indian education radically diverges from the traditional. The teacher feels compelled either to disparage traditional culture or to extol its 'spirituality' with fulsome platitudes. It is a striking fact that the by no means rare (even fashionable) enthusiasm of African students for rescuing their surviving oral literature and folklore from oblivion is absent from the Indian student scene, where Brahman bias has long discouraged interest in the robust, vigorous, and living heritage of folk culture. But it is this heritage which, with the right encouragement, is likely to command more immediate respect from youth than the metaphysical abstractions of high culture. The latter is assimilated, much of it subconsciously, through socialization, which usually takes place in the home, and is strongly associated with deeply religious and tradition-directed women. Socialization and personal relationships in the home are determined by an authoritarian, group-oriented, caste-dominated pattern which discounts individuality, initiative, and free inquiry. The ethical values of this system are clearly incompatible with those of conventional modern education. Formal schooling nevertheless, remains predominantly authoritarian in character, though it cuts across caste distinctions. In the imported education system is the inculcation, hesitant and uncertain as it may be, of the concepts of 'rationality', and what A. B. Shah calls 'the liberal spirit in its broadest sense, plurality of opinion and centres of decision-making, autonomy of the various fields of experience, secular ethics, and respect for the private world of the individual'. [1] Those who have spent many years in schools, and subsequently continued their studies abroad, are likely to experience a very acute conflict of values.

Milton Singer calls this uneasy, dichotomous co-existence of 'traditional' Indian and 'modern' Western, 'compartmentalization'. I disagree with the Rudolphs that compartmentalization 'is a way for those who refuse both outright assimilation and cultural reaction to "Indianize" modernity'. [2] Such dualism is not dialectical symbiosis; it is more like the double alienation, or 'double-bind', referred to in connection with schizoid tendencies.

It was something of a landmark in India's intellectual life when Professor Edward Shils published his survey, *The Intellectual between Tradition and Modernity: The Indian Situation*. [3] This pioneering study focused public attention in India on the fact that while the intellectual, political, and economic élites have accepted Western thought-processes and life-styles, they have not adopted the socially relevant values which this system entails. In other words, the Westernized Indian still clings to traditional habits in his *private* life. Furthermore, since the traditional value-system is emotionally far more significant to him than the professional domain, his traditionalism will also unconsciously influence his overall decision-making whatever the latter may concern. Shils, however, does not see any particularly alarming signs in this inner contradiction. He quotes 'one sweetly smiling socialist editor, dressed in a dhoti, his bare feet drawn out of his sandals', as saying that he was not unduly disturbed by this contradiction between tradition and modernity in his own life: '"Why should I be *alienated, uprooted*, or *ambivalent*? I live in two spheres and there is no conflict between them. Why should everything be logically consistent?"' [4] Shils considers this to be a dispassionate and 'very reasonable judgement'. But persons who are so relaxed in the two worlds are unlikely to be in a position which makes them effective agents of the dialectical process which alone can give their fusion a purposeful dynamism. India already suffers enough from a loose pluralism.

A. B. Shah had the following to say of the belief which 'presupposes that there already is a body of men who share modern values and are determined to spread them in society'.

[1] *Quest*, 46, 1965, p. 16.   [2] Rudolph and Rudolph (1967), p. 122.
[3] Shils (1961).   [4] Shils (1961), p. 68.

Except for a handful, Indian intellectuals do not yet seem ready for the task. Many of them give the impression of wishing for the impossible, for their approach to the past is characterised more by intellectual and emotional inertia than by critical selectivity. Their modernism does not extend beyond the narrow sphere of their own professional work. . . . This would not have mattered much if their traditionalism were confined to the strictly private sphere of life. In point of fact, it is not so; nor would it be possible to keep traditionalism so confined unless it were to be reduced to mere form as in the West. . . . What seems to have happened with most of us is that we have accepted modernity in our professional work alone. In all other spheres of life, not necessarily personal, we continue to be traditional in our values and attitudes unless personal gain is involved. Consequently, even the Western liberal institutions—universities, for example, or the press—introduced in India, still function largely in an authoritarian way.[1]

On the other hand, Dr. M. K. Haldar, Head of the Department of Philosophy at Delhi University, does not seem to be disturbed by the existence of the contradiction:

My problem is: Is there a real contradiction between the two habit-patterns? I think from a strictly logical point of view, there is a contradiction. But life is not governed by formal logic alone. We actually keep two opposing sets of habit-patterns in two watertight compartments and keep flitting from one to the other. In this matter, possibly there is no other mind which can surpass the Hindu mind. If there is a contradiction in the Western mind or society, they try to resolve it. They feel and suffer the stress of the contradiction. . . . We may talk about the contradictions between the habits of a tradition-bound society. But is the stress felt in our society? I believe not. And I do not see any special reason why it should be felt at all when, as a matter of fact, we do not feel it. Our excessive preoccupation with doom . . . gives us the feeling of being detached from the major issues of life; we remain content with our seriousness about the immediate, special, and narrow issues. For solving the compulsive problems of life we would not hesitate to take the help of modern science; but we stop at that and keep other problems of life detached from our knowledge of modern science. And everything, all problems, all our achievements are proved to be meaningless in our excessive preoccupation with doom.[2]

The danger of such views is that, if the individual, or the whole society, feels that contradiction between two habit-patterns as fundamental as this really is irreconcilable, then the will to be modern, the ability to innovate, will be seriously affected—and with it economic performance as well. Take the hypothetical case of a man prominent in the field of education who is prepared 'to take the help of modern science' in a restricted field of 'immediate, special and narrow issues': how is it possible for him to function effectively and to the full extent of his knowledge when there is no unity

[1] A. B. Shah, 'Tradition and Modernity in India', *Quest*, 46, 1965, p. 15.
[2] In *Tradition and Modernity in India*, ed. Shah and Rao, Bombay, 1965, pp. 144–5.

between his way of life and his professional expertise, between the fundamental values he has unconsciously acquired from his background and those he has consciously acquired in his formal education? This is not so much a question of the different effect of upbringing on his personality from what we in the West are used to, but of the dissociation of his deepest motivations from his professional work. The dissociated man is all too familiar in the West, particularly in the sciences; like yoga, science gives scope and power to the man who can readily divorce himself from his birthplace, his community, his family ties. The depersonalized scientist and his yogic counterpart are at their best in a world from which the personality itself has been removed. Both disciplines demand self-restraint and self-abnegation, and there is no doubt that the state of dissociation can prove fruitful in terms of results. This is not to suggest that all scientists, of course, manifest a split nature; it is the *dissociation* of the cold, impersonal scientist of which we in the West are rightly terrified, since it is this, more than *science*, which has contributed to the atrocious inhumanity of our time.

The requirements of social and economic development in a tradition-directed society demand an overall policy rather than expertise in isolated problematic situations; for the latter results in a piecemeal solution severed from human needs. This is not a matter of conflict between religion and science. Most of the great scientific innovators of the West, from Kepler and Newton to Einstein, were men of deep religious faith. Aesthetic orientation is no hindrance to scientific inquiry.

Contradictions there may be in every human being, and inconsistencies too. But this deeper contradiction is not restricted to a few individuals. The incidence of this fundamental contradiction in India's top leadership may very well be an important factor in numerous failures of implementation in the country's development programme. There is almost certainly a causal link between ambivalent attitudes towards modernity and an unconscious reservation as to the ultimate value of modernization.

Shils considers the Indian intellectual to be no more uprooted nor alienated than intellectuals anywhere else in the world. He emphatically disagrees with the common assertion that Indian intellectuals belong neither to India nor to the West.

They would not be intellectuals if their culture were the autochthonous culture in which they grew up. By becoming intellectuals, they participate in a tradition which transcends their local culture, and therewith, to some extent, they renounce that local culture. They do not renounce it entirely in France, Germany or any other modern country. In this respect, the Indian intellectual is not in a fundamentally different position from the intellectuals of modern Western countries.[1]

[1] Shils (1961), p. 61.

On this point a number of Indians disagree with Professor Shils. At a seminar held in Calcutta to review Shils's study, Professor A. S. Ayyub, editor of *Quest*, strongly refuted that assertion:

The Indian intellectual is placed in a unique situation which his Western counterpart has not to face. The Western intellectual finds himself in the midst of currents and crosscurrents of ideas, attitudes, norms and institutions which have grown out of a long historical past, a past to which he 'belongs'. Whatever he chooses, he does not have to wrench himself out of anything, to cut his umbilical cord, so to say. This is precisely what the Indian intellectual has to make up his mind about. He was born to a culture which he values and feels as his own. Yet he also feels that this culture is no more fully living; it has been stagnant for many centuries. On the other hand, the Indian intellectual feels himself powerfully drawn to a great and virile culture which appears to be more than only the culture of the modern West; it challenges his as the future culture of the world. He feels the pull of both— one to which he 'belongs' but whose life blood seems to him to be running its course out, the other very much alive and growing but alien to him. Basically, the culture of ancient India and the culture of the modern West stand opposed to each other. The Indian intellectual is torn between them. He realises that he cannot resist long the charm and the power of the West; and yet this is felt as an act of disloyalty, almost a form of spiritual matricide.[1]

I agree with most of this but not with the claim that the dilemma is unique; in many other parts of the non-Western world, in Asia and Africa, the predicament of the intellectual is basically the same. Indian tradition does, however, exert a more tenacious hold than that of some other cultures similarly placed. But the relation between the individual intellectual and a transitional society such as may be found in all developing nations is fundamentally different from that enjoyed by the intellectuals of the modern Western countries to which Shils refers. The role of the modernizing élite in developing nations cannot be so compared, simply because of the urgency of the basic human needs in these countries and the precarious instability of the socio-cultural environment. More important still is the fact that the Western intellectual minority shares the reification of the individual with the social majority, whereas in India, outside a numerically small class, individualism in the Western sense does not exist. Hence the psychological gulf between the intellectual minority and the rest of Indian society is infinitely more acute.

I believe, however, that the dichotomy between tradition and modernity can be solved if their deeper affinities are recognized. The whole question of India's future devolves upon the problem of how an internal motivation to change can be generated when change itself is regarded as possessing no

[1] *Quest*, 34, 1962, p. 62.

ultimate value. The question is complicated by the fact that the solution to each problem of modernization appears to have already been arrived at elsewhere in the world, usually in the West. If someone else has stumbled on the answer, the excitement of discovery is correspondingly diminished and the enthusiasm to proceed independently soon wanes. It would be more satisfactory to identify a pattern of problem-solving within the traditional system vigorous enough to generate and sustain an indigenous process of modernization which does not need ready-made external solutions and is in accord with indigenous needs and attitudes. This is the hidden dialectical factor within the process of modernization which has been responsible for every positive interrelation between indigenous and alien value-systems already achieved.

The first aspect of this procedure has already been demonstrated as feasible, if only partially and inadequately, by the Gandhian dialectic of creative social conflict. This particular feature of the dialectical process, with its deeply rooted foundation in the popular ideology of the masses, has been shown capable of development; if it is to be effective in future it will have to be radically modified in accordance with more complex political, social, and economic conditions.

The latter aspect of dialectical modernization centres on the primacy of scientific knowledge as an agent of change. The scientific spirit is commonly regarded as the antithesis of India's traditional modality. This is based on outdated notions of science and of 'rationalism' as unalterably opposed to the 'irrationality' of 'mysticism' and 'intuition', a misconception which is fostered by the hybrid Indian educational system. Only when it is realized that science and intuition are both rooted in the irrational can the real issue of creating a comprehensive order proceed, so that pathological disorder of a primitivist, reactionary nature can be averted.

'Scientific reason', in the sense of a reliable intellectual instrument as the servant of deeper impulses, flourished in India during periods of creative vitality in the distant past. As in ancient China, it was the artisanate which contributed most to the fund of practical knowledge and technological skills, inventing for example the *noria*, or irrigation water-wheel, and a highly sophisticated craft of metallurgy. The problem of creative renewal could be condensed into the question: how can the quicksilver wheel be turned into a dynamo? Joseph Needham has defined the preconditions for a transformation of archaic, practical knowledge into a modern science as follows: removal of class barriers between the technicians, or 'higher artisanate', and the theoreticians, in order to promote a marriage of craft practice with scholarly theory; a basic curiosity about Nature, leading to the isolation from the flux of things of specific phenomena for the purposes of systematic study; and finally, the 'reduction of all quality to quantities, the affirmation of a mathematical reality behind all appearances, the proclaiming of a space and time uniform throughout all the universe'.[1]

The most interesting aspect of Needham's analysis from our point of view is the connection he draws between proto-scientific Chinese thought, mystical Taoism, and shamanist magician-technicians, one of the most striking indications that mysticism need not necessarily be associated with reaction; on the contrary, mysticism has proceeded hand in hand with revolutionary social movements on a number of occasions—the Levellers and the Diggers, for example. Taoism combined a retrospective faith in primitive collectivism, resembling that of the Indian mystics (according to the mythic pattern of the prestige of beginnings), with political anti-feudalism and the beginnings of a scientific movement. The Taoists, like their Indian counterparts, evidently had direct contact with tribal collectivist societies and their texts refer to a classless ideal not unlike Uttarakuru, Śākadvīpa, and the mythical ideal of classlessness in the myth of the Kṛta Yuga. Unlike their Indian counterparts, however, the Taoists were prepared to relate the lessons they had learnt through their observation of Nature to a democratic social theory. Nature is no respecter of persons, so their argument ran—you cannot force people to do things against their inclinations; just as there is no real greatness and smallness in Nature, so there should be none in human society. Needham asserts that the birth of science requires the bridging of the gap between the scholar and the artisan, contrasting Taoist acceptance of this principle and the lack of sympathy shown by the Confucian literati for artisans and manual workers. In India it was the caste system which virtually prevented mutual service between scholar and artisan, while the *Laws of Manu* and the Brahman literati ensured that any such free exchange was severely curtailed. It was also the caste system which hindered the emergence of a bourgeois mercantile class, a uniform currency (and therefore of computing), and a universal standard of value. As in Taoism, it was the Indian of relatively humble origins who was less hampered by the value-system in the free, extraverted, systematic study of Nature, while the scholar tended to develop an introverted outlook, concentrating more on the systematic study of his own inner nature. In consequence, the Indian's retrospective faith in primitive collectivism remained fixated at the level of vague nostalgia. It failed to develop an analogous dynamism or critical attitude towards rigid feudal institutions, as did Taoism. We may conclude, therefore, that in the past the development of Indian science was retarded by three factors: inter-caste jealousy, high-caste introversion, and authoritarianism. The strength of all three has already been reduced, but not to the degree likely to generate a current of real enthusiasm and concerted will to explore the frontiers of

[1] Needham (1954–), Vol. 3 (1956), p. 166.

knowledge. Meanwhile internal structural changes and improved means of communication have permitted, in the field of knowledge, a uniform standard of value, quantification, and measurement; external influences have led to the introduction of a mathematics, and a metaphysic, of change. A deep-rooted, internal, organic scientific revolution, however, is not likely to occur until more positive concepts, long cherished by Indians, are actually *seen* to be of value in even the most sophisticated scientific context.

Needham points out that one of the greatest strengths of the ancient Chinese was their brilliant employment of Gestalt-like thought-processes— visualization of patterns 'all falling into place'—or *sudden* insight into the nature and relations of things. This is very similar to the unified-field awareness of traditional Indian thought-processes and the idea of 'revelation', which originated thousands of years ago in initiatory experience. As has been shown, Indian thought is permeated by the assumption that right perception can only be achieved through synaesthesia, cultivation of simultaneous awareness by all the senses, and that, in consequence, truth is best attained by sudden 'revelation'. It is commonly believed that scientific discovery proceeds by a series of reasoned and orderly steps, by the sequential linearity of logic; this is not always the case, as the discovery, for example, of the DNA double helix clearly shows. Often the scientist 'does not advance toward knowledge but is advanced on, grasped and overwhelmed' (Gerald Leach). He shares this kind of 'possession' with the artist; the psychological mechanism resembles that of the oracle's possession, since all three are rooted in unconscious mental processes.

There is general agreement that the Indian education system has failed to achieve the radical and profound transformation of attitudes expected of it. The fundamental reason for that failure (and one that underlies the economic difficulties of launching a modern educational programme, shortage of trained teachers, and even its outmoded non-vocational, literary bias, inherited from the days of British rule) is the profound and devastating effect of the attempt to suppress an instinctual mode of perception and replace it by one which is not only artificial but counter to the unified sensibility which is India's greatest asset. I am *not* advocating a return to the traditional, religious-oriented pattern of instruction. On the contrary, a way must be found to reorientate the intuition of order as a unified field towards a system of knowledge which is open and constantly invites and welcomes correction by being put to the test of more and more precise facts.

The education system has failed to 'catch on' as a primary agent in social change; so too has repression failed to destroy the traditional perceptual mode. Relegated as the latter is to the shadowy value-system of the submerged Antipodes, it still exerts a compelling unconscious appeal in all domains of Indian culture. The low status of the teacher in India, and more particularly the widely held view that formal education is merely a *quantitative* accumulation of superficial facts and therefore inferior to the nobler and more enduring acquisition of *values*, are due to a largely unexpressed conviction that they violate the basic Indian goal of all learning. Whereas, in the traditional scheme, knowledge is a means to acquire 'direct apprehension of reality' and this 'reality' is 'transcendent', the modern idea of learning is firmly based on knowledge of empirical reality. The former is the domain of the *guru*, the latter of the *schoolmaster*, and one gets the impression that when an Indian has to make a choice he will not rate the latter higher than the former. The two domains have been designated superior and inferior because one is 'spiritual', the other 'material'. But the very latest of modern teaching methods are gradually reducing this outmoded distinction. The 'new mathematics', the 'direct method' of language instruction, and the latest techniques of teaching the child how to read, for example, are based on pattern-recognition, simultaneity, and multi-sensory perception—a radical departure from the old linear method of factual accumulation. Once more they approach the language of algebraic metaphor which is the very basis of all Indian learning, whether of the *gurukul*, the *gharana*, the *ashrām*, the forest hermitage, or the Buddhist university. There are vital differences, certainly, but the conceptual framework of these new teaching methods is infinitely less alien to the Indian way of doing things. If there *is* a stigma attached to religion, whether because it is associated with 'superstition' and 'backwardness', or because it obstructs secularization, here is surely one prime means of removing it—by identifying the common basis of two perceptual systems, which is deeper and more basic than the differentiation into 'spirituality' and 'materialism'.

Looking ahead to the future from the perspective of a moment when the scientific mind seems poised on the threshold of a mysterious, startling domain which is neither religious nor mythic, something like them but again something new, one thinks of how a great genius, Kepler, faced a similar situation of transition. His example can spell hope for India too, even more than for the West. L. L. Whyte, who has done much to promote study of Kepler with finesse and subtlety over several decades, best explains in what way this seventeenth-century astronomer and physicist lets in a chink of light on the creative possibilities of those caught between two seemingly antithetic worlds. Whyte defines Kepler's genius as *'the power of aesthetic enthusiasm to disclose universal objective truths'*.

... only the emotional non-rational belief in the existence of more general forms of order as yet undiscovered, which is the product of the aesthetic propensity of the mind, brings to our attention the gaps and disorders which we call 'ignorances'. The aesthetic sense calls attention to these discontinuities and misfits.

... Kepler's passion is single. To the Western mind it may appear as a fusion of religious enthusiasm and the exact scientist's passion for numerical discovery. But it was something simpler. Kepler lived at the one moment in history when the religious and scientific passions could be identical. This is not hyperbole. At its root religion is an expression of man's search for unity; so also is science. Before Kepler the subjective element was predominant and there was no science. In Kepler the two were balanced; the subjective did not confuse the objective; religious enthusiasm assisted the scientific aim, and the aim of the discovery was a religious offering. But this dual language obscures the true situation; Kepler's passionate belief in a harmony unifying diversity flowed at once into religious emotion and into the organisation of fact. After Kepler the objective quantitative element predominated, and the subjective religious passion, divorced from the real world of exact science, faded into the background. Objective number is essentially alien to the human spirit and its gods; only at Kepler's time was the state of knowledge such as to bring the two into balance and to conceal their antithesis.

... Kepler's life symbolises the process of discovery; a process of long preparation and swift fulfilment; expressing unconscious tendencies, yet subject to the critique of consciousness; using capacities which are neither consciously rational nor irrational, but formative and organic.[1]

As this remarkable passage suggests, the tendency to condemn intuitive pattern-recognitions and synaesthesia as 'unscientific irrationalism' is a tragic misconception, particularly in a society like India's, which consistently displays a talent which, though long repressed and vilified as archaic, has recently begun to regain ascendancy over the step-by-step, unilinear progression of sequential logic. This repressive aspect may once have served a limited but useful function as long as the Newtonian conception of the universe prevailed. But now it is crippling to every form of endeavour, not merely the domain of learning.

As the Italian sculptor, Boccioni, presciently declared half a century ago, 'We are primitives of an unknown culture.' With the development of electronic technology, we are witnessing a revolution in modes of perception of far-reaching consequences. This may be described as an extension of consciousness which resembles, but is not identical with, the collective, simultaneous awareness of the pre-technological organic group. Wherever this technology has transformed the environment in the advanced nations, people already dimly feel that they are living in a changed, new, multi-sensible world of simultaneous interconnectedness and all-at-oneness quite unlike the old mechanized, industrialized world. India, along with vast areas of the underdeveloped world, is in the strange position of being in contact with this perceptibly altered way of life and intellectual climate which is a direct result of the new technology in the affluent nations, of

[1] L. L. Whyte, *The Next Development in Man*, London, 1944; reprinted in his *Focus and Diversions*, Cresset Press, London, 1963, pp. 88–9.

being physically as yet little affected by the environmental changes consequent upon its application in such fields as automation, computers, and
television, while still unconsciously conditioned to perceive the objective
world in a mode analogous to this scientifically induced unified awareness,
despite the contrary emphasis of the Indian education system. It is this
unconscious habit of mind more than any other element in Indian tradition
which seems to me likely to prove of incalculable importance in the future.

All the more urgent therefore is the need for a drastic reappraisal and
overhauling of the education system, so that it can meet the immensely
constructive possibilities deriving from the fact that, in one aspect of its
intellectual formation, India is probably better fitted to meet, and more
predisposed to face, the challenge of a future change of attitudes than almost
any other country in the world. However, at the present moment there is
no sign that Indian educationists are aware that they are sitting, so to
speak, on a goldmine of promising aptitudes. On the contrary, according
to the present line of thought the more that scientific instruction is completely dissociated from what are regarded as hopelessly outmoded and
archaic attitudes bound up with religion and mysticism, the more likely is
India to produce students who can effectively function in the exact sciences.
Dispirited boredom, in the face of problems which were long ago solved
elsewhere, will only be removed if and when it is realized that India has an
unrivalled opportunity to overcome some of the most intractable difficulties
of underdevelopment in an entirely new yet readily accessible way, peculiar
to itself (such as sophisticated Indian intermediate technology co-ordinated
with decentralized, small-scale community living—in other words, *modernization* of the 'self-sufficient' village community). Cultural changes of this
order, remote as they may seem from the practical concerns of a country
preoccupied with economic and political crises, are the decisive levers of
historical progress.

The non-linear, cluster configuration of Indian thought does not proceed
along a developmental line progressing to a climax, but is a spiral from a
germinating point and swelling in value by return and repetition. The
Western concept of history, and of all activity, is a climactic arrangement
which the Indian accepts with the greatest reluctance. But the world is
probably reformulating its most basic concepts with regard to time and
volition, spurred by a wholly new concept of productivity: 'maximum
gain of advantage from the minimal energy input' (Buckminster Fuller);
'less is more' (Mies van der Rohe). The minimal point of maximum
potential, the Indian Zero, receives support in an area whence, not so very
long ago, it would have incited derision—modern technology. Conventional
segmented linear thought and modes of visualization are quite inadequate
to meet the intellectual challenges of the non-Euclidean world of advanced

mathematics and quantum physics. But the Indian mind is at home among the non-visual velocities and relations of the subatomic and astronomical worlds. It is not surprising that it is in these fields rather than in more humdrum applied science that Indian scientists have attained the greatest distinction. For example, Professor E. C. Sudarshan has investigated the properties of *tachyons*, theoretical particles that move faster than light, on the supposition that, if they exist, they could lead to communication with the remote corners of the universe. This is a clear demonstration from the field of exact science of the conscious Indian mind working as the servant of deeper unconscious modes of perception.

On the other hand, the work of a distinguished library scientist, Dr. S. R. Ranganathan, reveals the strain to which the mind is subject if its natural bent for pattern-recognition is forced into the segmented, old-fashioned mould. Had Ranganathan been a young man today, equipped with all the resources of electronic circuitry, servomechanisms, and feedback which, however crudely, are structured like the central nervous system, his feat of devising a modern system of classification would probably have been more effectively formulated. I base this conclusion on his own admission to me that he arrived at his system 'in a flash of revelation', as an 'instantaneous pattern', and that this had to be laboriously broken down into the artificial linear abstraction of segmented thought.

Two more examples come to mind of this affinity between ways of thought on the frontiers of modern knowledge and the traditional Indian modality. On the one hand, we have the way the Indian perceives life as flux, as constant change, constant crisis, and the source of energy as stemming from a single point; on the other, we have Buckminster Fuller contrasting Relativity with Newton's first law of motion, where 'a body persists in a state of rest except as it is affected by other bodies. Normal was "at rest". Einstein turned it the other way: 186,000 miles a second is normal. We are living in a world where change is normal.' 'My ideas', Fuller says on another occasion, 'have undergone a process of emergence by emergency;' he finds himself in a vortex of unpredictable and startling metamorphoses from 'the wire to the wireless, the track to the trackless, the visible to the invisible, where more and more could be done with less and less'. This is not only the metaphysic of strength made perfect in weakness, couched in scientific metaphor; it is also an example of that flexibly tenacious state of mind which, up till now, only the aesthetically oriented artist and philosopher were trained to cultivate, on the frontiers of experience. Without a firm basis in the natural sciences the Indian mind turned in upon itself in an attempt to achieve the psychedelic transformation of the environment. The possibility of bringing this intuitive aesthetic faculty into a dialectical relationship with the exact sciences will demand conscious inspection and replacement of the old-fashioned, rationalist perceptual framework. This is now demanded not only of the Indian but of Western man too.

Far from being a hindrance to modernization, the aesthetic orientation of Indian society is the source of its inner strength and of its co-ordination in the face of an immeasurably complex predicament. If it persists, however, in associating its unified sensibility with but one small fraction of its possibilities—namely, religion—its thought-system will be grievously restricted to the magic circle it has drawn round the people. The dangers of aesthetic orientation (which, along with its positive features, we have seen operating in Gandhism) only become serious when it degenerates into emotional religiosity or aestheticism. India has fallen into both traps and, like the West, has also turned to two false strategies of escape, one after the other, either by proclaiming the false dawn of rationalism or toying with fascistic unreason.

We encounter the most advanced and sophisticated ideas of twentieth-century art and science at the deepest layers of the mind—a Keplerian kind of dredging process. This fact was brought home to me most forcibly by an encounter with the physicist, C. V. Raman. This eminent investigator of light waves and crystals revealed, in the course of some of the most dramatic hours I have spent in a laboratory, a unified aesthetic sensibility of piercing insight, in which the scientific spirit was perfectly contained. But his intuition was more what one would expect from the mystical virtuoso than from the exact scientist. A second display of his creative insight, at the Ajantā caves, made me revise my preconception that there is a necessary antithesis between the two ordering faculties of the mind. By their fusion Raman gained himself the Nobel Prize for physics. I believe that this points to something extremely significant: Raman's unified sensibility had not withered, as it usually does in the repressive educational climate, which suggested that if the Indian mind is consciously trained in a way which takes into account its deepest inclinations, its creative potential in a scientific world will be incalculable.

Despite the acute stress to which India is now subject, and despite many centuries of willed dissociation, introversion, and ecstatic enervation, the unified awareness of the Indian mind has not been irrevocably split. There is little doubt that an almost obsessive concern with the unitary and undifferentiated has precipitated India into a vortex of complexity; this same unified sensibility has been responsible for everything great it has ever achieved. It is also reasonable to expect, therefore, that it is by bringing this quality of mind to bear on contemporary problems that India will extricate itself from its predicament. There is something of Kepler already present in the Indian genius (as there is something of his master, Tycho, in that most Indian of astronomer-kings, Jai Singh). Koestler includes Kepler among his 'sleep-walkers' and describes him as 'too sane to ignore reality, but too mad to value it'. Tycho, Kepler, Jai Singh, Raman, Akbar of Fatehpur Sikri, Kauṭilya, Pāṇini, Bhāskara of the quicksilver wheel, the anonymous man who first used the *bindu* in mathematics—all display in varying degrees a quality which L. L. Whyte refers to in an imaginary letter addressed to Kepler: 'For you, Kepler, the aesthetic ordering passion was single; we have since damaged ourselves by a process of fission. Perhaps the only thing that can save us is neither a new science nor a new religion, but the rediscovery of that aesthetic sense of harmony which was so powerful in you. What a hope! It's a task for a century!'[1] In the Indian context this idea would be less Utopian than it might seem, if it could be extended to the political domain as well as to the rarefied air of exact science.

In the diaries of the octogenarian Igor Stravinsky we can glimpse how the creative mind derives fresh impetus from retrospection without ever losing its dynamism:

> Four cerebral thromboses seem to have unshuttered the remotest reaches of memory or spilled a restorative chemical over the palimpsest of my baby book. I have been able to roam in the park of my childhood as I could not a decade ago, but I tug at my memory only as a mountain climber tugs at his rope: to see how and where it is tied; I do not go back, in the threat of time, because of a wish to return. And even though my subconscious may be trying to close the circle, I want to go on rectilinearly as always.[2]

There are, of course, immense difficulties in achieving the kind of creative fusion envisaged here. Electronic technology, the tool which is modifying our modes of perception in ways we know very little about, has barely begun to affect India yet. We have little or no idea how a society which still has not fully accepted the implications of the old assembly-line means of production can leap straight from pre-literate unified thought-processes to the attitude of mind needed to ensure a continual movement of augmented production and accelerated change and exchange of goods and services.

The social regroupment of people who have undergone psychic transformation from individualism and nationalism to the close interinvolvement of the electronic age is not the same process as the transformation from archaic to modern interinvolvement without passing through individualism and nationalism. There is an urgent need in the emergent nations to overcome a tendency of individualism to degenerate into the Western pattern of a pathological obsession with one's frustrated emotions. Gandhi's

[1] Whyte (1963), p. 84.
[2] Igor Stravinsky and Robert Craft, *Dialogues and a Diary*, London, 1968.

'self-reliance' avoided all such and proved highly effective in the context of his day; if it is dissociated from the primitivism into which the Gandhian movement degenerated, it will be a pointer in the right direction.

It is widely assumed that individualism is a precondition of industrialization and that without it there can be no 'economic take-off'. The irony is that in the West electronic technology and complexity of organization no longer permit the survival of individualism, but encourage unified-field awareness and interdependence. Western youth has already rejected the extreme individualist position as a moral mistake and an intellectual error. The catalyst of individualism is claimed to be a necessity by those who have observed work-attitudes in countries like India where economic growth is proceeding too slowly. It is also based on the unfounded assumption that the pattern of technology in the poorer nations will have to go through the painful mechanistic phase of old-style industrial revolution, the tackling of all things and operations one bit at a time.

It does not seem beyond the bounds of human inventiveness to devise a technology appropriate to developing nations, which avoids the segmentation of thought and the alienation of the individual. Once again it is the artist who is far in advance of society; the kinetic artists, the design engineers of 'fun palaces', world fairs, and the electric gadgetry of the latest children's playgrounds, are producing sophisticated and inexpensive machinery aesthetically conceived in a spirit of play, the antithesis of everything hitherto associated with the word 'machine' and closer to the quicksilver wheels and hydraulic marvels of the ancient world. Already these ideas are being applied to industry. This new breed of 'super-artisans' owes its existence to a marriage of the primitive and the modern. The man who gave his name to the neo-Gandhian Ambacharkha (a four-wheel spinning machine)—a brilliant near miss in this domain of refreshingly gay technology—would be more at home among kinetic artists in Paris than he would with the dam-builders of Bhakra Nangal.

We have to imagine a line of historical development in India which would proceed from a position roughly analogous to that of Jakob Boehme, explorer, 'by introspection, of a unity hidden in his own nature beneath all conflict', as L. L. Whyte puts it, to

the confident spirit of enquiry, the combination of reverent inquisitiveness and scientific concentration, that marks a later period. In the ultimate analysis science is born of myth and religion, all three being expressions of the ordering spirit of the human mind. But it is only when the individual mind accepts its own authority as superior to the inherited tradition that this spirit becomes aware of itself and confident of its powers.[1]

[1] L. L. Whyte, *The Unconscious before Freud*, 1962 edn., New York, p. 76.

This, it would seem to me, is the extent to which the reification of the individual need be carried in the Indian context, and it avoids the blind alley of individualism.

In view of its importance in Indian culture, Whyte's passing reference to the origin of science in myth should be taken up and developed here. An analogy can be drawn between the instantaneity of mythic thought-patterns and the simultaneous presentation of cause and effect through electronic circuitry. 'We *live* mythically but continue to think fragmentarily and on single planes.' McLuhan and Éliade, each in his different way, have forcefully brought home to us how universal is the urge to preserve the retrospective 'nowness' of mythic thinking in the modern world and how modernized societies reassert ever more insistently the time-bond with the most ancient past. History, archaeology, psychology, all modify but never wholly destroy the pattern of mythical solidarity with origins, while in both Marxism and hip culture we have potent ideologies founded, like Taoist mysticism and the Kŕta Yuga, on eschatological and millennialist myth—'the redeeming role of the Just Man' (Éliade); 'the community of brethren . . . are no longer estranged from their labour and all share in the holy communion of free work' (Heer). In India the myth of the Golden Age has been employed to disastrous political effect, whereas the more positive case of Gandhi has already been put forward. It is important to point out how conscious utilization of retrospective mythic thinking can be harnessed and applied as an extremely effective modern intellectual tool. For example, one of McLuhan's least modish insights, and for which he has deservedly gained credit, concerns Edgar Allan Poe's method of working back from a desired effect (a technique which is also applied in Satyāgraha):

... the technique of beginning at the end of any operation whatever, and of working backwards from that point to the beginning. . . . Planned production means that the total process must be worked out in exact stages, backwards, like a detective story. In the first great age of mass production of commodities, and of literature as a commodity for the market, it became necessary to study the consumer's experience. In a word it became necessary to examine the effect of art and literature before producing anything at all. This is the *literal* entrance to the world of myth.

It was Edgar Allan Poe who first worked out the rationale of this ultimate awareness of the poetic process and who saw that instead of directing the work to the reader, it was necessary to incorporate the reader in the work.[1]

McLuhan compares Poe's method with the rigorous, impersonal rationale of the industrial process, and cites Whitehead's opinion that the greatest discovery of the nineteenth century was the invention of the method of

[1] Marshall McLuhan, *The Gutenberg Galaxy*, Routledge & Kegan Paul, London, 1962, p. 276.

invention. There are several points of comparison between this cluster of ideas and certain domains of Indian thought. First, Indian logic also works backwards from effect to cause, just as Indian myth retraces Time to the causal point, *ad originem*. Secondly, the creation of a work of art according to the Indian theory of aesthetic *rasa*, emotional mood, demands prior examination of the *effect*. Thirdly, as we have seen when discussing Sanskrit drama and even Satyāgraha, completion of dramatic effect requires the total participation from moment to moment of the spectator. Fourthly, in straining after absolute precision, the most advanced system of Indian thought, Navya-Nyāya, was preoccupied above all with the analysis of concepts on which the system of thought itself was based—the self perceiving the thought. The unconscious preference for this modality has survived the test of usefulness in a scientific age. For the one intellectual skill which has gained its Indian exponents virtually universal admiration among development economists is that which is based on the method of working back from a desired effect—*planning*!

Heisenberg recounts an ancient Chinese tale of an old man who declines expert advice to use a draw-well in his garden:

> I have heard my teacher say that whoever uses machines does all his work like a machine. He who does his work like a machine grows a heart like a machine, and he who carries the heart of a machine in his breast loses his simplicity. He who has lost his simplicity becomes unsure in the strivings of his soul. Uncertainty in the strivings of the soul is something which does not agree with honest sense. It is not that I do not know of such things; I am ashamed to use them.[1]

Despite the failure of the non-repressive, aesthetically oriented Gandhian approach to machinery, there are grounds to believe that the most sophisticated forms of intermediate technology are already eroding this 2,000-year-old peasant prejudice. The very fact that Gandhi *did* evolve a new Indian metaphysic of change is proof, that, in the less mechanistic climate of avant-garde scientific thinking today, its realistic and organic development to meet new conditions is also feasible. The self-perpetuating conditions which feed distrust of innovation and change will no doubt be loosened even more. Uncertainty itself is the foundation of the new system—its only absolute—just as certainty was the basis of the old order. But no amount of juggling with intellectual concepts among the educated élite, or of brilliant technological solutions based on *participation* in natural processes or eco-systems rather than their *conquest* by mechanized armaments, will have the slightest effect on the general outlook unless they are co-ordinated with vigorous socio-political action.

Immediate obstacles to development appear insoluble only because some

[1] Werner Heisenberg, *The Physicist's Conception of Nature*, London, 1958, p. 20.

of the hitherto non-existent factors are not taken into account. Among these I would place the potential strength of the student population (two million in higher education) combining forces with the vast population of the Scheduled Castes and Tribes to forge a co-ordinated programme of radical dissent. The latter are beginning to have a sense of identity, to participate in democratic processes, to be aware that they too have powers, to exert pressure, and to claim their rights. This immense sector of the Indian people has an incalculable potential, particularly since it is the least affected by introversion, other-worldliness, and the world-as-illusion syndrome of the upper castes. It is these people who have the flinty realism of the worker confronted with the 'brute particular'. All the various concrete measures which can be taken will end in one more turn of the circle unless an alternative system is created, detached from the old ideological integument of the majority. The society will remain suspended in a state of polarized tension until there are a sufficient number who dissent, even though at first united solely by their common 'No'. The more science there is in India, for example, the less absolute do all absolutes become. The last barrier which falls to science is the absolute that change has no ultimate value but inevitably coils back upon itself. Open-ended multi-dimensional change then gives the old concept of permanent crisis a new, urgent significance.

In the final analysis we come back to creative potential; where and when it exists it becomes part of the whole situation, and therefore modifies it. The best kind of creativity can only be accounted for afterwards, because the results are always unexpected. The unpredictable element not only creates, but alters the pattern in such a way that creation again becomes possible. It is sometimes imagined that if only India were to calculate things correctly, if it were to do the right thing, then the future must yield the desired results. But we cannot *secure* tomorrow in this way. Similarly, however much the observer would like to bring a little order and clarity to his interpretation of the complex web of Indian life, he cannot *know* the future; others are already *making* it as he writes.

We have become prisoners of our intellectual freedom, an amorphous mass of victims to our sense of rational order. We are the chaos inhabiting the tidiest of all worlds. We calculate splendidly, but our calculations show that we have not enough to live by; we predict infallibly—even unpredictability is merely a factor within high statistical probability—but what we predict is not worth living for. More often than not it is an eclipse of the sun. What do I mean by true order? An order that embodies the incalculable and unpredictable, transcending our rational grasp precisely where it meets the reasons of the heart. The symbol is the body of that which transcends, the measure of the immeasurable, and the visible logic of the heart's reasoning.[1]

[1] Erich Heller, *The Disinherited Mind*, Bowes & Bowes, London, 1952.

One feature of universal significance is the importance which Indian civilization has attached to the simplification and reduction of needs through self-scrutiny. At its most positive a means to reduce social conflict and the dehumanization inherent in the pursuit of material gain, this kind of humility is rare in Western science and technology. It is also the touchstone of our success or failure to reduce tension even within the domain of our personal lives. In an overpopulated world with severely limited resources the current Western method—expansion and cultivation of needs—is plainly unrealistic. The wisdom of smallness and the Zero principle, encouragement of small-scale pluralistic activity in community living, a non-violent ecological perspective, all of which originate in self-scrutiny, are age-old Indian responses to life's dilemmas—the fine flower of crisis. It is hoped that the impersonal character of this book's analytical structure has not concealed my desire to share with the reader a sense of urgent human involvement in these issues raised, perhaps to the benefit of us all, by India's struggle for survival.

Bibliography

All book publication dates given in the footnotes refer to the editions published in Britain, unless otherwise indicated.

Abul Fazl, *Ain-i-Akbari*, tr. Blochmann and Jarrett, Calcutta, 1875–91.

B. Allchin and F. R. Allchin, *Birth of Indian Civilisation: India and Pakistan before 500 B.C.*, Penguin Books, Harmondsworth, 1968.

A. S. Altekar, *The Position of Women in Hindu Civilisation*, Culture Publication House, Benares Hindu University, Benares, 1938.

Mulk Raj Anand, *Kama Kala*, Nagel, Geneva, 1958.

W. G. Archer, *Indian Painting in the Punjab Hills*, Victoria and Albert Museum, London, 1952.

—— *The Loves of Krishna in Indian Painting and Poetry*, George Allen and Unwin, London, 1957; Grove Press, New York, 1958.

— *Vertical Man: a study in primitive Indian sculpture*, George Allen and Unwin, London, 1947.

Arthashastra, T. Ganapati Sastri (ed.) and R. Shamasastry (tr.), 5th edn., Sri Raghuveer Printing Press, Mysore, 1956.

Geoffrey Ashe, *Gandhi: a study in revolution*, William Heinemann, London, 1968.

Sir Leigh Ashton (ed.), *The Art of India and Pakistan*, Faber and Faber, London, 1950.

Atharva-Veda Samhita, W. D. Whitney and C. R. Lanman (trs.), Harvard Oriental Series, Vols. VI and VIII, Harvard University Press, Cambridge, Mass., 1905.

Atmananda (ed. and tr.), *Words of Sri Anandamayi Ma*, Shree Shree Anandamayi Sangha, Benares, 1961.

F. G. Bailey, *Politics and Social Change: Orissa in 1959*, University of California Press, Berkeley, 1963.

A. L. Basham, *Aspects of Ancient Indian Culture*, Heras Institute of Indian History and Culture, Asia Publishing House, Bombay, 1966.

—— *The Wonder That Was India*, Sidgwick and Jackson, London, 1954; 3rd edn., Taplinger, New York, 1968.

André Béteille, *Caste, Class and Power: Changing Patterns of Stratification in a Tanjore Village*, Cambridge University Press, Cambridge, 1966; University of California Press, Berkeley, 1965.

Bhagavad Gita, (trs.) Annie Besant and Bhagavan Das, 3rd edn., Theosophical Publishing House, Adyar, 1940.

—— —— W. D. P. Hill, Oxford University Press, London, 1928.

Bhagavad Gita, (trs.) Juan Mascaro, Penguin Books, Harmondsworth, 1962.
—— —— S. Radhakrishnan, George Allen and Unwin, London, 1948.
—— —— R. C. Zaehner, Oxford University Press, London, 1969.
Bhaiji, *Mother as Revealed to Me*, G. Das Gupta (tr.), Shree Shree Anandamayi Sangha, Benares, 1954.
Agehananda Bharati (Leopold Fischer), *Esthetical Norm and Value Judgement in Modern Hinduism*, Renaissance Publishers, Calcutta, 1962.
—— *The Ochre Robe*, George Allen and Unwin, London, 1961.
—— *Tantric Tradition*, Rider, London, 1967; Hillary, New York, 1965.
Deben Bhattacharya, *The Mirror of the Sky: songs of the Bauls from Bengal*, George Allen and Unwin, London, 1969.
Joan Bondurant, *Conquest of Violence: the Gandhian Philosophy of Conflict*, University of California Press, Berkeley, 1958.
Nirmal Kumar Bose, *My Days with Gandhi*, Nishana, Calcutta, 1953.
Medard Boss, *A Psychiatrist Discovers India*, Oscar Wolff, London, 1965; Dufour, Chester Springs, Pa., 1965.
Paul R. Brass, *Factional politics in an Indian state: the Congress party in Uttar Pradesh*, Cambridge University Press, Cambridge, 1966; University of California Press, Berkeley, 1965.
D. Mackenzie Brown, *The White Umbrella: Indian Political Thought from Manu to Gandhi*, University of California Press, Berkeley, 1953.
Norman O. Brown, *Life Against Death: the psychological meaning of history*, Wesleyan University Press, Middletown, Conn., 1959.
Percy Brown, *Indian Architecture, Buddhist and Hindu*, Taraporevala, Bombay, 2nd edn., 1949.
G. Buhler, (tr.), *The Laws of Manu*, Sacred Books of the East, Vol. XXV, Clarendon Press, Oxford, 1886.
Roger Caillois, *Les Jeux et les Hommes*, Gallimard, Paris, 1958.
—— *Man and the Sacred*, Meyer Barash (tr.), Collier–Macmillan, London, 1959; Free Press, Glencoe, Illinois, 1959.
Cambridge History of India, Vols. I, III–VI, Cambridge University Press, Cambridge, 1922–.
Joseph Campbell, *The Hero with a Thousand Faces*, George Allen and Unwin, London, 1951; Bollingen Series XVII, Pantheon Books, New York, 1949.
—— *The Masks of God: Oriental Mythology*, Martin Secker and Warburg, London, 1962; Viking Press, New York, 1962.
G. Morris Carstairs, *The Twice-Born: a study of a community of High-Caste Hindus*, Hogarth Press, London, 1957; Peter Smith, New York, 1968.
Ernst Cassirer, *An Essay on Man*, Yale University Press, 1944.
Nirad C. Chaudhuri, *The Autobiography of an Unknown Indian*, Macmillan, London, 1951; University of California Press, Berkeley, 1968.
—— *The Continent of Circe: an essay on the peoples of India*, Chatto and Windus, London, 1965; Oxford University Press, New York, 1966.

Kenneth Clark, *Leonardo da Vinci*, (rev. edn.), Penguin Books, Harmondsworth, 1959.

Alex Comfort, *Darwin and the Naked Lady*, Routledge and Kegan Paul, London, 1961; George Braziller, New York, 1962.

E. Conze, *Buddhism, its Essence and Development*, Cassirer, Oxford, 1953; Harper-Row, New York, 1953.

—— *Buddhist Thought in India*, George Allen and Unwin, London, 1962; University of Michigan Press, 1967.

—— L. B. Horner, D. Snellgrove, and A. Waley (eds.), *Buddhist Texts through the Ages*, Faber and Faber, London, 1954.

Ananda K. Coomaraswamy, *The Dance of Shiva*, Simpkin Marshall, London, 1924; Noonday, New York, 1957.

—— *History of Indian and Indonesian Art*, Edwin Goldston, London, 1927; (reprinted), Dover, New York.

—— *Rajput Painting*, Oxford University Press, London, 1916.

—— *The Transformation of Nature in Art*, Constable, London, 1934; Harvard University Press, Cambridge, Mass., 1934.

Margaret Cormack, *The Hindu Woman*, Asia Publishing House, Bombay, 1961.

—— *She Who Rides a Peacock: Indian students and social change*, Asia Publishing House, Bombay, 1961.

L. A. Coser, *Functions of Social Conflict*, Routledge and Kegan Paul, London, 1956.

Alain Daniélou, *L'Érotisme divinisé*, Buchet/Chastel, Paris, 1962.

—— *Hindu Polytheism*, Routledge and Kegan Paul, London, 1964; Bollingen Series LXXIII, Pantheon Books, New York, 1964.

D. Dalton, *The Indian Idea of Anarchism*, Oxford University Press, London, 1966.

Frieda H. Das (Frieda Hauswirth), *Purdah: the status of Indian women*, Kegan Paul, Trench, Trubner, London, 1932; Vanguard Press, New York, 1932.

N. N. Das, *see* H. Gastant.

Shashibhusan Dasgupta, *Obscure Religious Cults as Background of Bengali Literature*, University of Calcutta Press, Calcutta, 1946.

Surendra Nath Dasgupta, *A History of Indian Philosophy*, 5 Vols., Cambridge University Press, Cambridge, 1922–52.

Amlan Datta (ed.), *Paths to Economic Growth*, Allied Publishers, New Delhi, 1962.

W. Theodore de Bary (ed.), *Sources of Indian Tradition*, Columbia University Press, New York, 1958.

A. R. Desai, *Social Background of Indian Nationalism*, (4th edn.) Popular Prakashan, Bombay, 1966.

Beryl de Zoete, *The Other Mind: a study of Dance in South India*, Victor Gollancz, London, 1953.

Edward C. Dimock, Jr., *The Place of the Hidden Moon: erotic mysticism in the Vaisnava-Sahajiya Cult of Bengal*, University of Chicago Press, Chicago, 1966.

E. R. Dodds, *The Greeks and the Irrational*, Cambridge University Press, Cambridge, 1951; University of California Press, Berkeley, 1951.

Mary Douglas, *Natural Symbols: explorations in cosmology*, Barrie and Rockliff, London, 1970.

—— *Purity and Danger*, Routledge and Kegan Paul, London, 1966; Frederic Praeger, New York, 1966.

Norman Douglas, *An Almanac*, Chatto and Windus, London, 1945.

S. C. Dube, *Indian Village*, Routledge and Kegan Paul, London, 1955; Humanities, New York.

Louis Dumont, *Homo Hierarchicus: essai sur le système des castes*, Gallimard, Paris, 1966.

—— and D. Pocock (eds.), *Contributions to Indian Sociology*, I–IX, Mouton, Paris—The Hague, 1957–69.

Émile Durkheim, *The Elementary Forms of the Religious Life*, J. W. Swain (tr.), George Allen and Unwin, London, 1961; Humanities, New York, 1964.

Mircea Éliade, *Birth and Rebirth*, W. R. Trask (tr.), Harvill Press, London, 1961; also titled *Rites and Symbols of Initiation*, Harper Row, New York, 1965.

—— *Images and Symbols: studies in religious symbolism*, P. Mairet (tr.), Harvill Press, London, 1961; Sheed and Ward, New York, 1969.

—— *Myths, Dreams and Mysteries: the encounter between contemporary faiths and archaic realities*, P. Mairet (tr.), Harvill Press, London, 1960; Harper Row, New York.

—— *Myth and Reality*, George Allen and Unwin, London, 1964; Harper Row, New York, 1964.

—— *The Myth of the Eternal Return*, W. R. Trask (tr.), Routledge and Kegan Paul, London, 1954; Bollingen Series XLVI, Pantheon Books, New York, 1954.

—— *Patanjali and Yoga*, C. L. Markman (tr.), Funk and Wagnall, New York, 1969.

—— *Patterns in Comparative Religion*, R. Sheed (tr.), Sheed and Ward, London, 1958; Meridian World Publishing, New York, 1958.

—— *The Sacred and the Profane: the nature of religion*, W. R. Trask (tr.), Harcourt Brace, New York, 1959.

—— *Shamanism: archaic techniques of ecstasy*, W. R. Trask (tr.), Routledge and Kegan Paul, London, 1964; Bollingen Series LXXVI, Pantheon Books, New York, 1964.

—— *Yoga: Immortality and Freedom*, W. R. Trask (tr.), Routledge and Kegan Paul, London, 1958; Bollingen Series LVI, Pantheon Books, New York, 1958.

Verrier Elwin, *The Muria and their Ghotul*, Oxford University Press, Bombay, 1947.

—— *Tribal Art of Middle India*, Oxford University Press, London, 1951.

Erik H. Erikson, *Childhood and Society*, (rev. edn.), Hogarth Press, London, 1964; W. W. Norton, New York, 1964.

—— *Gandhi's Truth: on the origins of militant nonviolence*, Faber and Faber, London, 1970; W. W. Norton, New York, 1969.

A.-M. Esnoul, *Ramanuja et la Mystique Vishnouite*, du Seuil, Paris, 1964.

J. N. Farquhar, *Modern Religious Movements in India*, Macmillan, London, 1929; Macmillan, New York, 1915.

Élie Faure, *History of Art*, Vol. V: *The Spirit of the Forms*, W. Pach (tr.), John Lane, The Bodley Head, London, 1930.

Ernst Fischer, *The Necessity of Art*, A. Bostock (tr.), Penguin Books, Harmondsworth, 1963.

Louis Fischer, *The Life of Mahatma Gandhi*, Jonathan Cape, London, 1951; Harper Row, New York, 1950.

E. M. Forster, *Abinger Harvest*, Edward Arnold, London, 1936.

—— *The Hill of Devi*, Edward Arnold, London, 1953.

—— *A Passage to India*, Edward Arnold, London, 1924.

A. Foucher, *see* Sir J. Marshall.

Max-Pol Fouchet, *The Erotic Sculpture of India*, George Allen and Unwin, London, 1959; S. G. Phillips, New York, 1959.

J. T. Fraser (ed.), *The Voices of Time*, Allen Lane, London, 1966; George Braziller, New York, 1966.

Louis Frédéric, *Indian Temples and Sculpture*, E. M. Hooykaas and A. H. Christie (trs.), Thames and Hudson, London, 1959.

Christoph von Fürer-Haimendorf, *Morals and Merit*, Weidenfeld and Nicolson, London, 1967.

—— 'Youth-Dormitories and Community Houses in India', in *American Anthropologist*, Vol. 45, 1950.

M. K. Gandhi, *All Men are Brothers: life and thoughts of Mahatma Gandhi as told in his own words*, UNESCO, Paris, 1958.

—— *An Autobiography, or The Story of My Experiments with Truth*, Mahadev Desai (tr.), Navajivan Publishing House, Ahmedabad, 1917; Beacon Press, New York, 1957.

G. T. Garratt (ed.), *The Legacy of India*, Oxford University Press, London, 1937.

H. Gastaut and N. N. Das, Report on Colloque de Marseille, November 1955, in *International Journal of Electroencephalography and Clinical Neurophysiology*, Supplément No. 6, Masson, Paris, 1957.

H. H. Gerth and C. W. Mills (eds.), *From Max Weber: essays in sociology*, Routledge and Kegan Paul, London, 1948; Peter Smith, New York, 1948.

U. N. Ghoshal, *A History of Indian Political Ideas*, (rev. edn.) Oxford University Press, Bombay, 1959.

G. S. Ghurye, *Caste and Class in India*, (3rd edn.) Popular Book Depot, Bombay, 1957.

—— *Gods and Men*, Popular Book Depot, Bombay, 1962.

—— (with the collaboration of L. N. Chapekar), *Indian Sadhus*, Popular Book Depot, Bombay, 1953.

Siegfried Gideon, *The Beginnings of Art*, Vol. I: *The Eternal Present*, Oxford University Press, London, 1962; Bollingen Series, Pantheon Books, New York, 1957.

Max Gluckman, *Custom and Conflict in Africa*, Basil Blackwell, Oxford, 1955.

—— (ed.), *Essays on the Ritual of Social Relations*, Manchester University Press, Manchester, 1962; Humanities, New York, 1962.

—— *Order and Rebellion in Tribal Africa*, Cohen and West, London, 1963.

Hermann Goetz, *India: Five Thousand Years of Indian Art*, Methuen, London, 1959; Crown, New York, 1959.

Erving Goffman, *The Presentation of Self in Everyday Life*, Allen Lane, London, 1969; Doubleday Anchor, New York, 1959.

Geoffrey Gorer, *The American People: a study in national character*, (rev. edn.) W. W. Norton, New York, 1964.

Percival Griffiths, *The British Impact on India*, Cresset Press, London, 1948.

R. Haldar, 'The Oedipus Wish in Iconography', in *Indian Journal of Psychology*, Vol. XIII, No. 1, Calcutta, 1938.

Selig S. Harrison, *India: The Most Dangerous Decades*, Oxford University Press, London, 1960; Princeton University Press, Princeton, N.J., 1960.

Arnold Hauser, *The Social History of Art*, 2 vols., Stanley Godman (tr.), Routledge and Kegan Paul, London, 1951; Random House, New York, 1951.

E. B. Havell, *Ideals of Indian Art*, John Murray, London, 1911.

—— *Indian Sculpture and Painting*, John Murray, London, 1908.

Friedrich Heer, *The Intellectual History of Europe*, J. Steinberg (tr.), Weidenfeld and Nicolson, London, 1966; World Publishing, New York, 1966.

Betty Heimann, *Facets of Indian Thought*, George Allen and Unwin, London, 1964; Schocken, New York, 1964.

—— *Indian and Western Philosophy: a study in contrasts*, George Allen and Unwin, London, 1937.

G. J. Held, *The Mahabharata: an ethnological study*, Kegan Paul, Trench, Truber, London, 1935.

Erich Heller, *The Disinherited Mind*, Bowes and Bowes, Cambridge, 1952.

—— *Thomas Mann: The Ironic German*, Martin Secker and Warburg, London, 1958.

J. T. Hitchcock, *see* L. Minturn.

A. M. Hocart, *Caste: a comparative study*, Methuen, London, 1950; Russell, New York, 1950.

H. J. N. Horsburgh, *Non-Violence and Aggression: a study of Gandhi's moral equivalent of war*, Oxford University Press, London, 1968.

Francis L. K. Hsu, *Clan, Caste and Club*, Van Nostrand, Princeton, N.J., 1963.

H. Hubert and Marcel Mauss, *Essay on the Nature and Function of Sacrifice*, Cohen and West, London, 1965; University of Chicago Press, Chicago, 1964.

Johan Huizinga, *Homo Ludens: a study of the play-element in culture*, R. F. C. Hull (tr.), Routledge and Kegan Paul, London, 1949; Beacon Press, New York, 1955.

R. E. Hume (tr.), *The Thirteen Principal Upanishads*, Oxford University Press, Madras, 1949.

J. H. Hutton, *Caste in India*, (4th edn.) Oxford University Press, Bombay, 1963.

Aldous Huxley, *The Doors of Perception*, Chatto and Windus, London, 1954; Harper Row, New York, 1954.

—— *Heaven and Hell*, Chatto and Windus, London, 1956; Harper Row, New York, 1956.

—— *The Perennial Philosophy*, Chatto and Windus, London, 1946; World Publishing, Cleveland, Ohio, 1946.

Christopher Isherwood, *Ramakrishna and his Disciples*, Methuen, London, 1965; Simon & Schuster, New York, 1965.

—— (ed.), *Vedanta for the Western World*, George Allen and Unwin, London, 1952; Marcell Rodd, Hollywood, 1945.

K. R. Srinivasa Iyengar, *Indian Writing in English*, Asia Publishing House, London, 1962.

R. N. Iyer (ed.), *The Glass Curtain*, Oxford University Press, London, 1965.

Jayadeva, *Gitagovinda*, George Keyt (tr.), Kutub Publishers, Bombay, 1947.

Carl G. Jung, *Civilisation in Transition*, R. F. C. Hull (tr.), *Collected Works*, Vol. X, Routledge and Kegan Paul, London, 1965; Bollingen Series, Vol. XX, Princeton University Press, Princeton, N.J., 1964.

—— *Contributions to Analytical Psychology*, H. G. and C. F. Baynes (trs.), Kegan Paul, Trench, Trubner, London, 1928.

—— *Psychology and Religion: East and West*, R. F. C. Hull (tr.), *Collected Works*, Vol. XI, Routledge and Kegan Paul, London, 1958; Bollingen Series, Vol. XX, Princeton University Press, Princeton, N.J., (2nd edn.) 1969.

—— *Psychology of the Unconscious*, B. M. Hinkle (tr.), Kegan Paul, Trench, Trubner, London, 1944.

—— *Two Essays on Analytical Psychology*, R. F. C. Hull (tr.), *Collected Works*, Vol. VII, Routledge and Kegan Paul, London, 1953; Bollingen Series, Vol. XX, Princeton University Press, Princeton, N.J., 1966.

—— and C. Kerenyi, *Essays on a Science of Mythology*, R. F. C. Hull (tr.), Bollingen Series XXII, Pantheon Books, New York, 1949.

—— *See also* R. Wilhelm.

Kabir, *One Hundred Poems of Kabir*, Rabindranath Tagore (tr.), Macmillan, Calcutta, 1954.

K. M. Kapadia, *Marriage and Family in India*, Oxford University Press, Bombay, 1963.

K. William Kapp, *Hindu Culture, Economic Development and Economic Planning in India*, Asia Publishing House, Bombay, 1963.

Iravati Karve, *Hindu Society: an interpretation*, Deccan College, Poona, 1961.

A. B. Keith, *The Religion and Philosophy of the Veda and Upanishads*, 2 vols., Harvard Oriental Series, Harvard University Press, Cambridge, Mass., 1925.

C. Kerenyi, *see* Carl G. Jung.

Arthur Koestler, *The Ghost and the Machine*, Hutchinson, London, 1967; Macmillan, New York, 1967.

—— *The Lotus and the Robot*, Hutchinson, London, 1960; Macmillan, New York, 1967.

Arthur Koestler, *The Sleepwalkers*, Hutchinson, London, 1959; Macmillan, New York, 1967.

Koka Shastra, Alex Comfort (tr.), Preface by W. G. Archer, George Allen and Unwin, London, 1964.

D. D. Kosambi, *An Introduction to the Study of Indian History*, Popular Book Depot, Bombay, 1956.

—— *The Culture and Civilisation of Ancient India in Historical Outline*, Routledge and Kegan Paul, London 1964; Pantheon Books, New York, 1966.

—— 'Living Prehistory in India', *Scientific American Monthly*, New York, February 1967.

—— *Myth and Reality*, Popular Prakashan, Bombay, 1962; Humanities, New York.

Stella Kramrisch, *The Art of India*, Phaidon Press, London, 1954.

—— *The Hindu Temple*, photographs by Raymond Burnier, 2 vols., University of Calcutta Press, Calcutta, 1946.

—— *Indian Sculpture*, Oxford University Press, London, 1933.

—— *A Survey of Painting in the Deccan*, The India Society, London, 1937.

R. D. Laing, *The Divided Self*, Tavistock Publications, London, 1960.

—— *The Politics of Experience and The Bird of Paradise*, Penguin Books, Harmondsworth, 1967.

H. T. Lambrick, *Sind*, Sindhi Adabi Board, Hyderabad, 1964.

Suzanne K. Langer, *Philosophy in a New Key*, Oxford University Press, London, 1957; Harvard University Press, Cambridge, Mass., 1942.

Richard Lannoy, *India*, Photographs, Thames and Hudson, London, 1955; Vanguard, New York, 1955.

Edmund R. Leach (ed.), *Aspects of Caste in South India, Ceylon and North-West Pakistan*, Cambridge University Press, Cambridge, 1960.

—— *Rethinking Anthropology*, Athlone Press, London, 1961; Humanities, New York, 1963.

Dorothy Lee, 'Lineal and Nonlineal Codifications of Reality', *Psychosomatic Medicine*, No. 12., Washington, Philadelphia, May 1950.

Claude Lévi-Strauss, *The Savage Mind*, Weidenfeld and Nicolson, London, 1966; University of Chicago Press, Chicago, 1966.

—— *Totemism*, R. Needham (tr.), Merlin Press, London, 1964; Beacon Press, Boston, 1963.

—— *Tristes Tropiques*, Plon, Paris, 1955.

W. Arthur Lewis, *Theory of Economic Growth*, George Allen and Unwin, London, 1955.

Jean Lyon, *Just Half a World Away*, Hutchinson, London, 1955.

Marshall McLuhan, *The Gutenberg Galaxy : the making of typographic man*, Routledge and Kegan Paul, London, 1964; University of Toronto Press, Toronto, 1962.

—— *Understanding Media: the extensions of man*, Routledge and Kegan Paul, London, 1964; McGraw-Hill, New York, 1964.

—— and Edmund Carpenter (eds.), *Explorations in Communication*, Beacon Press, Boston, 1960.

William H. McNeill, *The Rise of the West*, University of Chicago Press, Chicago, 1963.

Mahabharata, Pratap Chandra Ray (tr.), 11 vols., Bharata Press, Calcutta, 1884–94.

D. N. Majumdar, *Caste and Communication in an Indian Village*, Asia Publishing House, London, 1958.

—— *Races and Cultures of India*, Asia Publishing House, Bombay, 1958.

R. C. Majumdar, H. C. Raychaudhuri, and K. Datta, *An Advanced History of India*, Macmillan, London, 1950.

André Malraux, *Des Bas-Reliefs aux Grottes Sacrées*, La Galerie de la Pléiade, Paris, 1954.

—— *The Temptation of the West*, R. Hollander (tr.), Vintage Books, New York, 1961.

—— *Voices of Silence*, S. Gilbert (tr.), Martin Secker and Warburg, London, 1956.

David G. Mandelbaum, 'Social Trends and Personal Pressures', in *Language, Culture, and Personality: essays in memory of Edward Sapir*, Spier, Hallowell, and Newman (eds.), Sapir Memorial Publication Fund, Menasha, Wisconsin, 1941.

Thomas Mann, *Stories of a Lifetime*, 2 vols., Martin Secker and Warburg, London, 1961.

O. Mannoni, *Prospero and Caliban: a study in the pyschology of colonisation*, P. Powesland (tr.), Methuen, London, 1956.

Herbert Marcuse, *Eros and Civilisation*, Sphere, London, 1968; Beacon Press, Boston, 1955.

McKim Marriott (ed.), *Village India: studies in the Little Community*, Chicago University Press, Chicago, 1955.

Anne Marshall, *Hunting the Guru in India*, Victor Gollancz, London, 1963.

Sir John Marshall and A. Foucher, *Monuments of Sanchi*, 3 vols., Calcutta, 1940.

Philip Mason (ed.), *India and Ceylon: unity and diversity*, Oxford University Press, London, 1967.

P. Masson-Oursel and others, *Ancient India and Indian Civilisation*, reprinted, Routledge and Kegan Paul, London, 1967.

E. Powys Mathers (tr.), *The Garden of Bright Waters: one hundred and twenty Asiatic love poems*, Basil Blackwell, Oxford, 1920.

—— *Love Songs of Asia*, Pushkin Press, London, 1944.

Marcel Mauss, *The Gift: forms and functions of exchange in archaic societies*, I. Cunnison (tr.), Cohen and West, London, 1966.

—— *See also* H. Hubert.

A. C. Mayer, *Caste and Kinship in Central India*, Routledge and Kegan Paul, London, 1960; University of California Press, Berkeley, 1960.

J. T. Meyer, *Sexual Life in Ancient India*, 2nd edn., Routledge and Kegan Paul, London, 1952.

Henri Michaux, *Un Barbare en Asie*, Gallimard, Paris, 1961.

Leigh Minturn and John T. Hitchcock, *The Rajputs of Khalapur, India*, Six Cultures Series, Vol. III, John Wiley, New York, 1966.

Mirabehn (Madeleine Slade), *The Spirit's Pilgrimage*, Longmans, Green, London, 1960.

B. B. Misra, *The Indian Middle Classes*, Oxford University Press, London, 1961.

Ajit Mookerjee, *Tantra Art: its philosophy and physics*, Ravi Kumar, New Delhi, 1967.

C. A. Moore, *see* S. Radhakrishnan.

W. H. Moreland, *India at the Death of Akbar*, Macmillan, London, 1920.

Kenneth W. Morgan (ed.), *The Religion of the Hindus*, Ronald Press, New York, 1953.

Warner Muensterberger, 'Orality and Dependence, Characteristics of Southern Chinese', *Psychoanalysis and the Social Sciences*, Vol. 3, London.

Gardner Murphy and Lois B. Murphy, *In the Minds of Men: the study of human behaviour and social tensions in India*, Basic Books, New York, 1953.

Murray's Handbook for Travellers in India and Pakistan, Burma and Ceylon, 16th edn., John Murray, London, 1949.

Henry A. Murray (ed.), *Myth and Mythmaking*, Bailey, London, 1960; George Braziller, New York, 1960.

Gunnar Myrdal, *Asian Drama*, 3 vols., Penguin Books, Harmondsworth, 1968.

—— *Economic Theory and Under-developed Regions*, Gerald Duckworth, London, 1957.

Jan Myrdal, *Report from a Chinese Village*, M. Michael (tr.), Penguin Books, Harmondsworth, 1967.

V. S. Naipaul, *An Area of Darkness*, André Deutsch, London, 1964; Macmillan, New York, 1965.

Kusum Nair, *Blossoms in the Dust*, Gerald Duckworth, London, 1961; Frederic Praeger, New York, 1962.

Dhirendra Narain, *Hindu Character*, Bombay University Press, Bombay, 1957.

Joseph Needham, *The Grand Titration: science and society in East and West*, George Allen and Unwin, London, 1969.

—— with the collaboration of Wang Ling, Lu Gwei-Djen, Ho Ping-Yü, Kenneth Robinson, Tshao Thien-Chhin, and others, *Science and Civilisation in China*, 6 vols., Cambridge University Press, Cambridge, 1954–.

Jawarharlal Nehru, *A Bunch of Old Letters*, Asia Publishing House, Bombay, 1960.

—— *The Discovery of India*, 4th edn., Meridian Books, London, 1960.

Erich Neumann, *The Great Mother*, R. Mannheim (tr.), Routledge and Kegan Paul, London, 1955; Bollingen Series, Vol. XLVII, Princeton University Press, 2nd edn., Princeton, N.J., 1963.

—— *The Origins and History of Consciousness*, Routledge and Kegan Paul, London, 1954; Bollingen Series XLII, Pantheon Books, New York, 1954.

Edward Norbeck, 'African Rituals of Conflict', *American Anthropologist*, Vol. 65, No. 6, 1963.

F. S. C. Northrop, *The Meeting of East and West: an inquiry concerning world understanding*, Collier–Macmillan, London, 1960; Macmillan, New York, 1946.

George Orwell, *Shooting an Elephant and Other Essays*, Martin Secker and Warburg, London, 1950; Harcourt Brace and World, New York.

F. Osborn, *Population: an International Dilemma*, Princeton University Press, Princeton, N.J., 1962.

Rudolph Otto, *Christianity and the Indian Religion of Grace*, Christian Literary Society, Madras, 1929.

—— *The Idea of the Holy*, J. W. Harvey (tr.), Oxford University Press, London, 1925.

K. M. Panikkar, *Asia and Western Dominance*, George Allen and Unwin, London, 1953; Hillary, New York, 1959.

—— *Hindu Society at Cross Roads*, Asia Publishing House, Bombay, 1955.

Patanjali, *The Yoga-System of Patanjali*, J. H. Woods (tr.), Harvard Oriental Series, XVII, Harvard University Press, Cambridge, Mass., 1914.

Stuart Piggott, *Prehistoric India*, Penguin Books, Harmondsworth, 1950.

D. Pocock, *see* L. Dumont.

Sri Prakasa, *Annie Besant*, Bharata Vidya Bhavan, Bombay, 1954.

Sarvepalli Radhakrishnan and Charles A. Moore, *A Sourcebook in Indian Philosophy*, Oxford University Press, London, 1957; Princeton University Press, Princeton, N.J., 1957.

C. R. M. Rao, *see* A. B. Shah.

T. A. Gopinath Rao, *Elements of Indian Iconography*, 2 vols., Law Printing House, Madras, 1914–16.

H. G. Rawlinson, *India, a Short Cultural History*, Cresset Press, London, 1937.

—— *Intercourse between India and the Western World*, Cambridge University Press, Cambridge, 1916.

Philip S. Rawson, *Indian Sculpture*, Studio Vista, London, 1966.

—— *Music and Dance in Indian Art*, Edinburgh Festival Committee, Edinburgh, 1963.

Robert Redfield, *The Little Community*, University of Chicago Press, Chicago, 1956.

—— *Peasant Society and Culture*, University of Chicago Press, Chicago, 1960.

Louis Renou, *Religions of Ancient India*, Athlone Press, London, 1953.

—— and Jean Filliozat, *L'Inde classique*, Vol. I, Payot, Paris, 1947; Vol. II, Imprimerie Nationale, Paris, 1953.

Rigveda, R. T. H. Griffith (tr.), 3rd edn., 2 vols., E. J. Lazarus, Benares, 1920–6.

Rigveda Brahmanas, A. B. Keith (tr.), Harvard Oriental Series, Vol. 25, Harvard University Press, Cambridge, Mass., 1920.

Aileen D. Ross, *The Hindu Family in its Urban Setting*, Toronto University Press, Toronto, 1961.

Benjamin Rowland, *The Art and Architecture of India*, Penguin Books, Harmondsworth, 1953.

L. I. Rudolph and S. H. Rudolph, *The Modernity of Tradition: political development in India*, University of Chicago Press, Chicago, 1967.

Jean-Paul Sartre, *Nausea*, L. Alexander (tr.), Hamish Hamilton, London, 1962; New Directions, New York, 1959.

Albert Schweitzer, *Indian Thought and Its Development*, Adam and Charles Black, London, 1956.

Ronald Segal, *The Crisis of India*, Jonathan Cape, London, 1965.

K. M. Sen, *Hinduism*, Penguin Books, Harmondsworth, 1961.

A. B. Shah and C. R. M. Rao (eds.), *Tradition and Modernity in India*, Indian Committee for Cultural Freedom, Manaktalas, Bombay, 1965.

I. C. Sharma, *Ethical Philosophies of India*, rev. and ed. S. M. Daugert, George Allen and Unwin, London, 1965.

Edward Shils, *The Intellectual between Tradition and Modernity: the Indian situation*, Mouton, The Hague, 1960.

—— *Political Development in the New States*, reprinted, Mouton, The Hague, 1960.

Georg Simmel, *Conflict*, K. H. Wolff (tr.), Free Press, Glencoe, Ill., 1955.

I. R. Sinai, *The Challenge of Modernisation: the West's impact on the non-Western world*, Chatto and Windus, London, 1964.

Milton B. Singer (ed.), *Krishna: Myths, Rites and Attitudes*, East-West Center Press, Honolulu, 1965.

—— —— *Traditional India: structure and change*, American Folklore Society, Bibliographical and Special Series, Vol X, American Folklore Society, Philadelphia, 1959.

Madanjeet Singh, *Ajanta: painting of the sacred and the secular*, Thames and Hudson, London, 1965.

—— *India, Paintings from the Ajanta Caves*, UNESCO, Paris, 1954.

D. E. Smith, *India as a Secular State*, Oxford University Press, London, 1967; Princeton University Press, Princeton, N.J., 1963.

Vincent A. Smith, *A History of Fine Art in India and Ceylon*, rev. K. de B. Codrington, Oxford University Press, Oxford, 1967.

Percival Spear, *A History of India*, Vol. 2, Penguin Books, Harmondsworth, 1965.

Philip Spratt, *Hindu Culture and Personality*, Manaktalas, Bombay, 1966.

M. N. Srinivas, *Caste in Modern India*, Asia Publishing House, Bombay, 1962.

—— *India's Villages*, Asia Publishing House, London, 1960.

—— *Religion and Society among the Coorgs of South India*, Oxford University Press, London, 1952.

—— *Social Change in Modern India*, University of California Press, Berkeley, 1967.

Adrian Stokes, *Three Essays on the Painting of our Time*, Tavistock, London, 1961.

W. S. Taylor, 'Basic Personality in Orthodox Hindu Culture Patterns', *Journal of Abnormal and Social Psychology*, Boston, Vol. 43, No. 1, January 1948.

D. G. Tendulkar, *Mahatma: Life of Mohandas Karamchand Gandhi*, 8 vols., V. K. Jhaveri and D. G. Tendulkar, Bombay, 1952–.

Romila Thapar, *Ashoka and the Decline of the Mauryas*, Oxford University Press, London, 1961.

—— *A History of India*, Vol. I, Penguin Books, Harmondsworth, 1966.

E. Thompson and G. T. Garratt, *Rise and Fulfilment of British Rule in India*, Macmillan, London, 1934.

M. T. Titus, *Indian Islam*, Oxford University Press, London, 1930.

James Tod, *Annals and Antiquities of Rajast'han* (1829), rev. edn., Routledge and Kegan Paul, London, 1950.

J. R. R. Tolkien, *Tree and Leaf: on fairy stories*, George Allen and Unwin, London, 1964.

Giuseppe Tucci, *The Theory and Practice of the Mandala*, Rider, London, 1961.

Roy Turner (ed.), *India's Urban Future*, Oxford University Press, 1962.

V. P. Varma, *Studies in Hindu Political Thought and its Metaphysical Foundations*, 2nd edn., Motilal Banarsidass, Benares, 1959.

Vatsyayana, *The Kama Sutra*, Sir Richard Burton and F. F. Arbuthnot (trs.), W. G. Archer (ed.), George Allen and Unwin, London, 1963.

————— S. C. Upadhyaya (tr.), Introduction by K. M. Panikkar, Charles Skilton, Bombay, 1963.

Francis Watson and Maurice Brown (eds.), *Talking of Gandhiji*, Longmans, Green, London, 1957.

Alan W. Watts, *Nature, Man and Woman: a new approach to sexual experience*, Thames and Hudson, London, 1958.

—— *Psychotherapy East and West*, Pantheon Books, New York, 1961.

Max Weber, *The Religion of India: the sociology of Hinduism and Buddhism*, H. H. Gerth and Don Martindale (trs.), Collier–Macmillan, London, 1967; Free Press, Glencoe, Ill., 1958.

—— *See also* H. H. Gerth and C. W. Mills.

Myron Weiner, *The Politics of Scarcity*, Asia Publishing House, Bombay, 1963.

Henry W. Wells, *The Classical Drama of India*, Asia Publishing House, Bombay, 1963.

—— (ed.), *Six Sanskrit Plays*, Asia Publishing House, Bombay, 1964.

Sir Mortimer Wheeler, *Civilisation of the Indus Valley and Beyond*, Thames and Hudson, London, 1966.

—— *Early India and Pakistan*, Thames and Hudson, London, 1959.

—— *The Indus Civilisation*, Cambridge University Press, Cambridge, 1953.

Lynn White Jr., *Mediaeval Technology and Social Change*, Oxford University Press, London, 1962.

Lancelot Law Whyte, *Focus and Diversions*, Cresset Press, London, 1963.

—— *The Next Development in Man*, Cresset Press, London, 1944.

—— *The Unconscious before Freud*, Tavistock Publications, London, 1962.

Richard Wilhelm and C. G. Jung, *The Secret of the Golden Flower*, Routledge and Kegan Paul, London, 1931.

W. and C. V. Wiser, *Behind Mud Walls*, Agricultural Missions, New York, 1951.

Sir John Woodroffe (Arthur Avalon), *The Garland of Letters*, Ganesh, Madras, 1955.

—— *The Serpent Power*, Ganesh, Madras, 1953.

—— *Introduction to Tantra Shastra*, Ganesh, Madras, 1957.

—— *Shakti and Shakta*, Ganesh, Madras, 1951.

G. Yazdani and others, *Ajanta*, 4 vols., Oxford University Press, London, 1930–55.

—— *History of the Deccan*, Vol. I, part VIII: *Fine Arts*, Oxford University Press, Bombay, 1953.

R. C. Zaehner, *Hinduism*, Oxford University Press, London, 1962.

—— *Mysticism, Sacred and Profane*, Oxford University Press, London, 1957.

Heinrich Zimmer, *The Art of Indian Asia*, Joseph Campbell (ed.), 2 vols, Oxford University Press, London, 1968; Bollingen Series XXXIX, Pantheon Books, New York, 1948.

—— *The King and the Corpse*, Joseph Campbell (ed.), Oxford University Press, 1968; Bollingen Series XI, Pantheon Books, New York, 1948.

—— *Myths and Symbols in Indian Art and Civilisation*, Joseph Campbell (ed.), Kegan Paul, London, 1946; Bollingen Series VI, Pantheon Books, New York, 1946.

—— *Philosophies of India*, Joseph Campbell (ed.), Routledge and Kegan Paul, London, 1951; Bollingen Series XXVI, Pantheon Books, New York, 1951.

George K. Zollschan and Walter Hirsch (eds.), *Explorations in Social Change*, Routledge and Kegan Paul, London, 1964.

Index

Figures in bold type show the pages on which a word or name is principally defined or explained.

Dumont, Louis, 99–100, 136, 140, 142, 143, 144, 145, 154, 246
Durkheim, E., 141
Duryodhana, 302, 305
dvarpalas, 40; Plate 18
dyūtamaṇḍalam (*see also* dice), **298**

ecclesiastical organization, 216, 244, 334
Eckhart, Meister, 27
ecology (*see also* nature, relationship with), 181, 182, 189, 235, 254, 274, 291, 355, 379, 429, 431
economic conditions, 75 & n., 124–5, 223, 233, 238, 240, 316, 382–3
economy, market, 247, 260
— pre-monetary, 160–62, 163, 223, 235
— subsistence, 157–62, 223, 235, 248
— traditional, 260–61, 395–8
— village, 15–16, 33, 111, 157–62, 163, 164, 223, 251, 316
ecstasy, artificial inducement of (*see also* drugs), 62, 76, 79; portrayal in art, 61, 62, 64; religious cult of (see also *ekstasis*; rapture; *sahaja*; Vaishnava-Sahajiyā), 209, 336, 357–363, 389
education: Brahman, 35–6, 58, 224, 239, 242, 278, 280, 413; and castes, 248, 253; co-education, 123, 128, 129; élite, 166–7, 238–9; Gandhian: *see* Gandhi; modern, 256, 262, 265, 410–11, 413–14, 418, 420–21, 423, 425, 430; sexual, 120, 184; traditional, 85, 96–8, 103, 119, 208, 413–14, 420–21; tribal, 183–7; Westernized, 125, 237, 238, 256, 257
egalitarian measures, 247, 259
egalitarianism, Western, 135, 139, 140, 336, 375
ego (*see also* self), 112, 198, 211, 225, 352, 354–5, 361, 367, 369
ekāgratā, **370**
Ekavīrā (*see also* Yamāī), 32
ekstasis (*see also* ecstasy, spiritual; rapture), 19–20, **25**, 50, 64, 170
electroencephalography, 349–50
Éliade, Mircéa, 50 n.–51 n., 171 n., 288–9, 292, 349, 352, 428
élites, modern, 239, 240, 241, 244–5, 252; modernizing, 257, 416–17
Elwin, Verrier, 181, 184, 186
emotional constraint, 88–9, 93, 110, 347; effusiveness, 110, 112, 206, 209, 385

Engels, F., 382
Epics (see also *Mahābhārata*; *Rāmāyana*), 10, 59, 65, 117, 191, 192, 217–18, 294, 296–306, 324–6
— Homeric, 296, 297, 301, 324
equilibrium, social, 209, 217, 221, 229, 235, 252, 295–6, 405
Erikson, Erik H., 98–9, 108–9, 187, 381, 382, 384, 385 n., 392 n., 532 n., 406, 408
eroticism: in art: *see* art; Buddhist, 336; and play, 195, 196; in religion, 28–30, 95–6, 224
esotericism (*see also* circle, magic), 300, 346
Eternal Present, 49, 288–9, 344, 363
Eternal Return, myth of (*see also* time, cyclical concept of), 39, 212
ethic, universal, 207–8, 209, 217–18, 230–31, 263–4, 312–13, 332–3
— work: see work
ethics (see also *dharma*; morality), 85, 87, 96, 98, 111–12, 119, 207–8, 290, 291, 294–339; of action, 300–1, 306–7, 310–11; Buddhist, 329–34, 335–6; business (*see also* work), 232–4; Gandhian: *see* Gandhi; martial (*see also* Kshatrya *varṇa*), 379; political (see also *Arthashāstra*), 324–6; salvation, 213
ethnic structure, 6, 12, 177–8, 179, 185, 228
exchange of goods and services (*see also* gifts), 141, 143, 157–62, 163, 182 n., 223, 232

family system, extended, 85 ff., 100–1, 102, 103–6, 122, 124–6, 212–13, 236, 279, 365–6
— nuclear, 106, 123, 124–8, 129, 130
family disputes, 87, 88–9, 92, 100–1
— value system of, 85, 300, 413–14
fasting (*see also* Gandhi), 194, 211
fatalism, 223, 224, 286, 303, 323, 337–9, 415
Fatehpur Sikri, 72–3, 391; Plates 28, 49
father, 86–8, 99–101, 103, 110; and child, 94, 96; in nuclear family, 126–8; and son, 97, 99–101, 102, 106, 115, 129, 285, 385–6
Faure, Élie, 56, 193
Ferreira, J. V., 187, 188
fertility rites, 22, 63, 235
— symbols, 9, 39–40, 41, 42; Plates 9, 13, 29, 31, 45